Global Work Arrangements and Outsourcing in the Age of AI

Mohit Yadav
O.P. Jindal Global University, India

Ashutosh Pandey
FORE School of Management, India

Geshwaree Huzooree
Edinburgh Napier University, UK

IGI Global
Scientific Publishing
Publishing Tomorrow's Research Today

Vice President of Editorial	Melissa Wagner
Director of Acquisitions	Mikaela Felty
Director of Book Development	Jocelynn Hessler
Production Manager	Mike Brehm
Cover Design	Phillip Shickler

Published in the United States of America by
IGI Global Scientific Publishing
701 East Chocolate Avenue
Hershey, PA, 17033, USA
Tel: 717-533-8845
Fax: 717-533-7115
Website: https://www.igi-global.com E-mail: cust@igi-global.com

Library of Congress Cataloging-in-Publication Data

Names: Yadav, Mohit, 1985- editor | Pandey, Ashutosh, 1983- editor | Huzooree, Geshwaree, 1985- editor
Title: Global work arrangements and outsourcing in the age of AI / [edited by] Mohit Yadav, Ashutosh Pandey, Geshwaree Huzooree.
Description: Hershey, PA : IGI Global Scientific Publishing, [2025] | Includes bibliographical references and index. | Summary: "The primary objective of this book is to examine the transformative impact of artificial intelligence (AI) on global work arrangements and outsourcing practices. It aims to explore how AI reshapes workforce dynamics, enhances operational efficiency, and introduces ethical and regulatory challenges in a globalized economy"-- Provided by publisher.
Identifiers: LCCN 2025001191 (print) | LCCN 2025001192 (ebook) | ISBN 9798337312705 hardcover | ISBN 9798337312712 paperback | ISBN 9798337312729 ebook
Subjects: LCSH: Contracting out--Technological innovations | Flexible work arrangements | Artificial intelligence--Industrial applications
Classification: LCC HD2365 .G595 2025 (print) | LCC HD2365 (ebook) | DDC 658.4/058--dc23/eng/20250711
LC record available at https://lccn.loc.gov/2025001191
LC ebook record available at https://lccn.loc.gov/2025001192
British Cataloguing in Publication Data
A Cataloguing in Publication record for this book is available from the British Library.

Table of Contents

Detailed Table of Contents

Remote work has fundamentally transformed the public sector, offering greater flexibility, enhanced efficiency, and improved service delivery. Nonetheless, it has also brought forth significant challenges, including employee burnout, mental health issues, and difficulties in maintaining work-life balance. The transition to remote work, expedited by the COVID-19 pandemic, has revealed gaps in digital infrastructure, raised cybersecurity concerns, and highlighted disparities in access to remote work opportunities among public sector employees. This chapter delves into the realities of remote work within government institutions, focusing on the challenges employees encounter and the factors that contribute to burnout. It emphasizes the necessity for sustainable solutions, such as flexible work arrangements, mental health initiatives, effective workload management, and stronger managerial support. Additionally, the chapter assesses the role of technology, cybersecurity, and standardized policies as crucial elements in ensuring the long-term success of remote work.

Artificial intelligence (AI) has rapidly evolved from theoretical models to real-world applications that impact every sector of the global economy. While AI promises increased efficiency, productivity, and innovation, it also brings significant disruption to traditional labor markets. The transition from industrial automation to AI-driven decision-making has accelerated job displacement across both blue-collar and white-collar industries. This chapter explores the historical context of job displacement due to AI, the sectors most at risk, and potential strategies for mitigating the economic and social consequences of this transformation.

New cybersecurity threats have sprouted due to the sudden shift to remote work; changed workplace dynamics have potentially moved security perimeters outward as organizations begin to experience new threats in the forms of phishing, ransomware, data breaches, and even insider threats. This chapter focuses

The rapid advancement of artificial intelligence (AI) is transforming global workforce dynamics, reshaping how organizations manage talent, collaborate across borders, and structure work. This paper examines the evolving interplay between AI technologies and global work arrangements, focusing on the transition from traditional outsourcing models to AI-driven partnerships and hybrid workforce systems. It explores how AI-powered tools are enabling virtual teams, enhancing productivity, and redefining roles by automating routine tasks while creating opportunities in AI-centric fields. Ethical challenges, including workforce displacement and widening skill gaps, are also addressed, with a focus on strategies to promote inclusivity and adaptability. Through case studies and emerging trends, this research provides actionable insights for businesses and policymakers to navigate the opportunities and challenges of an AI-enabled workforce, ensuring sustainable and equitable global work practices.

This chapter explores the role of small and medium-sized enterprises (SMEs) in the evolving AI-driven outsourcing landscape. As artificial intelligence (AI) increasingly transforms business models, SMEs face both challenges and opportunities in integrating AI into their outsourcing strategies. By leveraging AI technologies, SMEs can streamline operations, reduce costs, and enhance customer experiences, positioning themselves to compete globally. However, SMEs must address challenges such as limited resources, skills gaps, data privacy concerns, and the need for continuous innovation. Strategic approaches such as collaboration with AI providers, adopting scalable solutions, and focusing on workforce upskilling are essential for SMEs to succeed. The chapter also discusses the social, practical, and theoretical implications of AI in outsourcing, highlighting the potential for job displacement and the need for adaptive strategies. Ultimately, SMEs that effectively harness AI will thrive in a competitive, AI-driven outsourcing ecosystem.

The future of work and outsourcing is shaped by technological advancements, globalization, and evolving labor models. Automation, artificial intelligence, and remote work are driving a shift from cost-focused outsourcing to strategic partnerships emphasizing innovation and agility. The gig economy and global talent pools are transforming traditional employment, while data privacy, ethical labor practices, and workforce development remain critical challenges. By embracing flexible work models, lifelong learning, and sustainable practices, organizations can leverage outsourcing for competitiveness and resilience in a rapidly evolving global landscape.

The globalized workforce has led to an increasing number of young workers from diverse cultural backgrounds working for multinational corporations (MNCs). Many African Gen Z graduates are joining global corporate environments, bringing in fresh viewpoints, technological know-how, and entrepreneurial skills. However, their experiences are not utilized particularly with regards to diversity and inclusion (D&I) leaving many African employees to contend with barriers to networking, cultural adjustment, and limited access to leadership roles. The goal of the chapter is to provide a comprehensive, critical analysis of diversity and inclusion programs by multinational corporations and its impact on African Gen Z graduates, depriving the ability to thrive in global corporation. The chapter concludes by reinforcing the urgent need for systemic change in corporate diversity and inclusion efforts with findings form the basis for further conversations, especially when it comes to examining the lived experiences of African Gen Z graduates, the efficacy of corporate D&I policies.

Through remote work, business operations have become widespread, providing companies with the capability of accessing a global talent base and flexibility within business operations. However, this shift has made corporate networks vulnerable as employees access from their personal devices, unsecured home networks, and cloud based collaboration tools. Due to the increase of the attack surface, remote

This chapter explores the policy and regulatory frameworks necessary for managing the impact of artificial intelligence (AI) on the global workforce. As AI technologies reshape industries, they present both opportunities and challenges, including labor displacement, ethical dilemmas, and regulatory fragmentation. The chapter examines the role of AI in transforming global work, highlighting key challenges such as fairness, transparency, and accountability in AI systems. It discusses policy frameworks from different global perspectives and the need for international collaboration to harmonize AI regulations. Furthermore, the chapter emphasizes the importance of human-centric AI policies that prioritize worker protection, ethical development, and equitable access. Key recommendations include investing in reskilling, establishing social safety nets, and fostering global cooperation to create a sustainable and inclusive future of work. This comprehensive approach aims to ensure that AI benefits workers and society, while mitigating potential risks.

This chapter explores the ethical challenges of AI-driven automation in the workplace, addressing the impact of artificial intelligence on employees, organizations, and society. As AI systems become integral to various industries, ethical concerns such as job displacement, algorithmic bias, data privacy, and transparency are increasingly significant. The chapter examines the benefits of AI in enhancing productivity and decision-making while highlighting the potential risks, particularly the displacement of workers and perpetuation of societal biases. It emphasizes the importance of human oversight, employee education, and the creation of ethical frameworks to ensure AI is deployed responsibly. The role of legal and regulatory structures in addressing these challenges is also discussed, alongside the importance of fostering an ethical AI culture within organizations. This comprehensive analysis provides insights into how businesses can navigate the complexities of AI ethics, promoting responsible use of AI technologies while mitigating risks.

AI is revolutionizing talent management by enhancing decision-making, automating routine tasks, and optimizing HR processes. Initially limited to resume screening and candidate matching, AI now plays a pivotal role in hiring, performance evaluation, training, and employee engagement. It enables personalized learning, predicts employee turnover, and supports data-driven decisions, aligning human capital with organizational goals. Despite its benefits, AI adoption faces challenges like resistance to change, ethical concerns, and data privacy issues. Looking ahead, AI's integration with technologies like augmented reality and blockchain will create immersive, inclusive, and responsive work environments. Its continuous learning capabilities will drive real-time performance management, fostering innovation and sustainability. This chapter explores AI's transformative impact on talent management, highlighting its current applications, challenges, and future potential in reshaping HR into a strategic, data-driven function in the dynamic business world.

The emergence of Artificial Intelligence in the workplace is changing management techniques, engagement, and employment patterns. To retain such talent, organizations need to be extremely aligned with Gen-Z's demands. Nowadays, hybrid work is common; Gen Z workers value independence. Talent is drawn to remote employment, but there are drawbacks as well, such as communication breakdowns and cultural disintegration. Digital tools must be embraced by companies for effective collaboration. AI-driven change increases productivity, but companies need to have a stand between automation and the human touch. Gen-Z expects workplaces to foster Diversity, Equity and Inclusion more than just being an organization with policies. Hybrid models enable flexibility and collaboration, but robust strategies enable thriving. The businesses that embrace the ideals of community, purpose, and flexibility held by Gen - Z will succeed. The future workplace will focus more on establishing an inclusive, sustainable, and fulfilling work environment for everyone by adjusting to new technologies.

This chapter explores the transformative impact of Artificial Intelligence (AI) on traditional outsourcing models, highlighting both the disruption and opportunities AI presents for the outsourcing industry. As AI technologies automate routine tasks and enable data-driven decision-making, outsourcing providers are evolving from cost-centric service providers to strategic partners in digital transformation. The chapter examines how AI-driven models, such as automation, predictive analytics, and machine learning, are reshaping outsourcing functions, offering businesses greater efficiency, innovation, and customization. However, the shift to AI-powered outsourcing also introduces challenges related to workforce displacement, ethical concerns, and the need for new governance frameworks. The future of outsourcing will depend on the ability of providers to adapt to AI technologies, upskill their workforce, and address the social and regulatory implications of AI adoption.

The rise of AI-powered robo-advisors in financial services offers benefits like scalability and personalized investment recommendations. However, gaining consumer trust remains a challenge due to concerns about transparency, fairness, and accountability. Factors such as algorithmic bias, the "black box" nature of AI, and the lack of explainability contribute to a trust gap. Ethical design, regulatory compliance, and user-centric approaches are essential for building confidence in these systems. Explainable AI (XAI), transparency, and robust data privacy policies are pivotal to mitigating bias and fostering trust. Moreover, hybrid models integrating human expertise with AI can address consumer hesitations, while personalization and user education empower clients in decision-making. Future developments should emphasize ethical AI frameworks, real-time compliance monitoring, and global standards to ensure responsible financial advising. This paper explores strategies for cultivating trust and transparency to democratize financial services effectively.

Artificial Intelligence (AI) is transforming industries by enabling machines to mimic human cognitive functions like learning, reasoning, and problem-solving. This chapter explores AI's core concepts, including machine learning, deep learning, and neural networks, along with its applications in healthcare, finance, supply chain management, and automation. AI enhances efficiency, optimizes decision-making, and drives innovation. The study examines AI-driven automation's impact on business processes, focusing on robotic process automation (RPA) in streamlining operations. Using bibliometric data and topic modeling, it identifies key trends, gaps, and future directions in AI research. Findings suggest AI will continue shaping technological advancements, influencing industries and human interactions with intelligent systems. This chapter serves as a resource for researchers, policymakers, and professionals navigating AI's evolving landscape and future implications.

The contemporary workforce is being radically transformed by the emergence of Generation Z and the explosive growth of the gig economy. Gen Z differs from other generations in valuing flexibility, autonomy, and purposeful work more than the long-term employment model. Their technological literacy has redefined work standards, with freelancing, temporary contracts, and remote work becoming the new norm. While this trend is beneficial in the sense that it provides work-life balance and diversified sources of income, it has challenges in employment security, mental well-being, and career advancement. HR practitioners need to shift by embracing innovation, technology, and flexibility. The old model of employment does not suit Gen Z's needs anymore, calling for dynamic practices such as on-demand learning, customized benefits, and AI-enabled talent management. Yet, aligning digital evolution with a people-centric strategy continues to be the key.

This chapter explores the ethical considerations surrounding AI-powered outsourcing, focusing on key issues such as bias, fairness, accountability, and transparency. As AI technologies are increasingly used to automate tasks traditionally performed by human workers, ethical challenges arise, particularly concerning the impact on global labor markets and workers' rights. The chapter examines the sources and impact of AI bias, the importance of ensuring fairness in decision-making, and the need for robust accountability mechanisms in AI systems. It also highlights the role of transparency and explainability in AI models, which are essential for building trust and ensuring ethical outcomes. Addressing inequalities and discrimination in AI systems is crucial to prevent further exacerbating societal divisions. Finally,

Preface

The rapid advancement of artificial intelligence (AI) has profoundly reshaped the landscape of global work arrangements and outsourcing. As organizations across the world integrate AI technologies into their operations, the fundamental nature of work, talent deployment, and business strategies is undergoing a significant transformation. This edited volume, *Global Work Arrangements and Outsourcing in the Age of AI*, emerges from a collective endeavor to explore these dynamic changes and offer a comprehensive analysis of the opportunities and challenges presented by AI-driven innovation.

The book brings together insights from scholars and practitioners across multiple disciplines and geographies, reflecting the truly global nature of the topic. By examining the impact of AI on workforce dynamics, cross-border collaboration, and ethical outsourcing practices, we aim to provide readers with both theoretical perspectives and practical frameworks. From shifts in labor markets to the redefinition of human roles in AI-augmented environments, this volume addresses critical issues at the intersection of technology, business, and society.

Chapter 1 introduces how artificial intelligence is transforming traditional recruitment methods by automating resume screening, enhancing candidate matching, and reducing hiring bias.
Chapter 2 explores the integration of AI in employee performance evaluations, highlighting benefits such as objective assessments and real-time feedback, while also addressing ethical implications.
Chapter 3 examines the redesign of job roles due to AI and automation, emphasizing the shift toward higher-order cognitive skills and the need for continuous reskilling.
Chapter 4 discusses the balance between productivity gains and job displacement as organizations adopt AI, offering strategies to mitigate workforce disruption.
Chapter 5 dives into the ethical dimensions of AI in the workplace, focusing on transparency, accountability, and the importance of human oversight in decision-making.
Chapter 6 addresses the rise of remote work, detailing the operational, technological, and cultural adjustments companies must make to support distributed teams.
Chapter 7 looks at maintaining corporate culture in a hybrid work model, emphasizing the role of digital communication, leadership, and team cohesion.
Chapter 8 explores cybersecurity challenges in remote work environments, including data breaches, unsecured networks, and the human factor in digital security.
Chapter 9 focuses on employee well-being in remote and hybrid settings, highlighting the importance of work-life balance, burnout prevention, and supportive policies.
Chapter 10 examines how leadership styles and management practices must evolve to effectively guide teams in flexible and hybrid work environments.
Chapter 11 highlights the growing importance of mental health support in the workplace, especially under the pressures of remote work and technological change.

Chapter 12 delves into the ethical responsibilities of leadership in guiding organizations through digital transformation with integrity and inclusiveness.
Chapter 13 discusses the strategic value of diversity and inclusion in the workplace, particularly as technology creates new opportunities for global collaboration.
Chapter 14 explores how employee surveillance technologies are being used to monitor productivity, raising critical concerns about trust, autonomy, and privacy.
Chapter 15 emphasizes the need for equitable implementation of workplace policies, ensuring that digital transformation benefits all employees fairly.
Chapter 16 analyzes the use of data analytics in workforce decision-making, from performance metrics to predictive modeling, and its implications for HR practices.
Chapter 17 evaluates the pros and cons of using productivity tracking tools, questioning their long-term impact on employee motivation and trust.
Chapter 18 examines the ethics of monitoring employee behavior through digital tools, advocating for transparent and consent-based approaches.
Chapter 19 provides an in-depth look at organizational cybersecurity, outlining strategies to safeguard sensitive information and promote digital resilience.
Chapter 20 explores the trend of outsourcing in the digital age, discussing its impact on organizational agility, cost efficiency, and employee loyalty.
Chapter 21 investigates the structure and growth of the gig economy, assessing its influence on employment models and long-term career development.
Chapter 22 addresses the legal and ethical concerns related to gig work, including fair pay, job security, and the right to benefits and protections.
Chapter 23 outlines the challenges of managing a global workforce, such as cross-cultural communication, time zone coordination, and labor regulation compliance.
Chapter 24 considers the implications of automation and AI for job stability, urging organizations to develop reskilling programs and inclusive transition strategies.
Chapter 25 synthesizes emerging workplace trends and technologies, offering a forward-looking perspective on how work may evolve over the next decade.
Chapter 26 concludes the book with strategic recommendations for building adaptive, ethical, and inclusive organizations that are prepared for the future of work.

Our primary objective is to foster a nuanced understanding of how AI is transforming work in a globalized economy. We delve into themes such as operational efficiency, talent management, regulatory concerns, and the imperative for sustainable and inclusive practices. The chapters collectively underscore the need for strategic adaptation and forward-thinking policies to ensure that the evolution of work remains equitable and beneficial across sectors and societies.

This book is intended for a wide audience: scholars and researchers in business, management, and technology; industry leaders and HR professionals seeking to optimize workforce strategies; and policymakers and legal experts grappling with new ethical and regulatory frontiers. It is also designed to engage students and lifelong learners who are keen to understand and shape the future of work in the AI era.

We hope this volume serves as a valuable resource and a catalyst for ongoing dialogue about the role of artificial intelligence in redefining the contours of global work and outsourcing.

Mohit Yadav

O.P. Jindal Global University, India

Ashutosh Pandey
FORE School of Management, India

Geshwaree Huzooree
Edinburgh Napier University, UK

Chapter 1
Sustainable Outsourcing in an AI-Driven World:
Ethical, Economic, and Environmental Perspectives

Mohan Kumar
https://orcid.org/0000-0002-5171-0892
SGT University, India

Pooja Rani
https://orcid.org/0009-0001-3793-8524
Maharshi Dayanand University, India

Namita Mangla
ICFAI Business School, India

Nhat Tan Nguyen
https://orcid.org/0000-0002-4178-5110
Ho Chi Minh City University of Foreign Languages - Information Technology, Vietnam

Kulpreet Kaur
https://orcid.org/0000-0001-8028-7889
O.P. Jindal Global University, India

ABSTRACT

In an artificial intelligence-driven global economy, sustainable outsourcing is changing ethical issues, workforce distribution, and company operations. Emphasizing the revolutionary possibilities and constraints of artificial intelligence (AI) in global labor management, this chapter investigates the confluence of AI with outsourcing. It examines ethical consequences, legal systems, sustainable outsourcing methods, and the socioeconomic consequences of AI-driven outsourcing. Based on the present findings, the talk provides useful recommendations for companies, governments, and academics trying to support ethical and sustainable AI-driven outsourcing methods.

DOI: 10.4018/979-8-3373-1270-5.ch001

1. INTRODUCTION

The quick development of artificial intelligence (AI) is drastically changing outsourcing paradigms around the world economy. Data analytics, machine learning, and artificial intelligence-driven automation are transforming business processes, raising efficiency, and besting resource allocation (Brynjolfsson & McAfee, 2017). Organizations that increasingly include artificial intelligence in their outsourcing strategies also have to handle complex ethical, legal, and sustainability concerns (Davenport, T. H., & Ronanki, 2018). In an environment driven by artificial intelligence, sustainable outsourcing calls for a balanced approach stressing cost-effectiveness while preserving social responsibility, environmental sustainability, and workforce inclusiveness (Gereffi, Fernandez-Stark & Gary, 2011). The spread of artificial intelligence-driven outsourcing is fundamentally changing employment systems and traditional labor markets. AI is expected to automate about 30% of tasks now carried out by humans by 2030, so workforce plans, skill development programs, and economic policies will have to be adjusted to fit evolving employment trends (Manyika et al., 2017). Though technology also brings challenges, including workforce displacement, algorithmic bias, data security concerns, and the ethical repercussions of autonomous decision-making, artificial intelligence enhances operational efficiency, lowers costs, and speeds decision-making (Manyika, 2017). Organizations have to use proactive measures including labor reskilling, ethical AI governance, and environmentally responsible operating models (Frey et al., 2017) if they are to encourage sustainable outsourcing methods. The ethical application of artificial intelligence technologies is absolutely vital in sustainable outsourcing. Often reflecting prejudices in its training data, artificial intelligence systems could lead to unfair employment practices, unequal resource allocation, and biased decision-making processes (Barocas & Selbst, 2018). Moreover, assigning AI development to other companies raises questions regarding intellectual property protection, AI algorithm clarity, and accountability for decisions produced by artificial intelligence (Binns, 2018). To ensure responsible outsourcing activities, organizations must follow international laws and guidelines, including the General Data Protection Regulation (GDPR), the OECD's AI Principles, and the United Nations Sustainable Development Goals (SDGs). Apart from moral issues, environmental sustainability is a key feature of outsourcing driven by artificial intelligence. Using significant natural resources and energy, AI-driven data centers greatly contribute to world carbon emissions (Cook et al., 2017). Enterprises have to stress green computing initiatives such as using renewable energy sources, deploying energy-efficient server technology, and enhancing AI models to minimize computational expenditures along with the spread of artificial intelligence use that will help to minimize computational expenses (UNEP, 2019). To minimize the environmental consequences of AI deployment, sustainable outsourcing models have to include environmental impact evaluations, carbon footprint-reducing strategies, and guidelines for responsible e-waste management (Gevaers et al., 2009). Fair distribution of the worldwide workforce has to be the first priority in sustainable outsourcing. While AI-driven automation can boost economic growth, it could disproportionately affect low-income workers in developing countries, hence aggravating current socioeconomic inequalities (Richard Heeks, 2017). The rise of artificial intelligence threatens low-skill, labor-dependent industries, therefore causing increased economic disparity between locations with strong AI infrastructure and those lacking it (Brynjolfsson, E., & McAfee, 2014). Efforts at impact sourcing that give employment from underprivileged groups top priority and support workforce inclusion would help to mitigate these effects and forward inclusive economic development. Furthermore, guarantees of fair labor standards, ethical remuneration systems, and fair access to AI-generated employment chances depend on cooperation among businesses, government agencies, and non-profit groups (World Economic

Forum, 2024). The need for strong legal frameworks and corporate social responsibility initiatives grows as businesses speed the integration of artificial intelligence into outsourcing strategies (OECD, 2023). In a world driven by artificial intelligence, sustainable outsourcing calls for a whole plan going beyond quick cash gains. Organizations have to match their outsourcing plans with long-term sustainability objectives, including technology development, workforce change; ethical labor practices, environmental preservation, and responsible artificial intelligence use (SDG, 2023). Investigating sustainable economic alternatives, ethical consequences, and legal recommendations, this chapter looks at how artificial intelligence and outsourcing converge. It provides direction for businesses, policymakers, and worldwide stakeholders to correctly negotiate this evolving environment as well as a thorough analysis of the challenges and potential related to AI-driven outsourcing. Combining artificial intelligence innovation with sustainability ideas can help businesses create more resilient, equitable, and ecologically conscious outsourcing models, therefore ensuring that technology progress benefits the wider society (Porter & Kramer, 2011).

1.1 AI and the Evolution of Sustainable Outsourcing: The Role of AI in Sustainable Outsourcing

Cost control and the acquisition of specialist knowledge have always driven outsourcing. The introduction of artificial intelligence has changed outsourcing from a basic cost-cutting strategy to a means of sustainable value generation (Willcocks et al., 2018). By means of predictive analytics, data-driven decision-making, and automation, artificial intelligence (AI) promotes sustainable outsourcing, thereby improving productivity and reducing resource consumption in outsourced activities. According to IGI Global sources, AI-driven outsourcing improves data security, lowers waste, and raises service quality all of which are vital components of sustainability all of which help to maximize supply chains (Khan & Turowski, 2016). Using AI-driven tools like robotic process automation (RPA) and machine learning (ML) algorithms to promote sustainable innovation, artificial intelligence has enabled the shift from traditional Business Process Outsourcing (BPO) to Knowledge Process Outsourcing (KPO). By automating repetitive tasks and improving process efficiencies, AI-driven outsourcing reduces carbon emissions and energy use connected to great human labor. This helps businesses guarantee constant development with little human participation by extending sustainable operations.

1.2 Sustainable Outsourcing in an AI-Driven World

In the outsourcing industry, artificial intelligence has evolved into a transforming factor helping data-driven decision-making, process automation, and operational efficiency improvement. The chapter stresses several important artificial intelligence uses to change outsourced operations. By lowering human costs and increasing accuracy in back-office operations, AI-driven Robotic Process Automation (RPA) greatly improves process automation (Willcocks et al., 2017). Predictive analytics helps companies apply artificial intelligence algorithms for data trend analysis, thereby improving supply chain effectiveness and customer service outcomes (Davenport, T. H., & Ronanki, 2018). By providing quick support, AI-driven chatbots and virtual assistants also increase user involvement, hence reducing reliance on human labor (Brynjolfsson & McAfee, 2017). By improving language translation and thereby destroying linguistic barriers, Natural Language Processing (NLP) also improves cross-border outsourcing (Floridi et al., 2018c). The chapter looks at how artificial intelligence is upsetting traditional outsourcing models and stresses both possibilities and challenges related to AI applications. A major result of automation is the lowering of labor arbitrage since it lessens the need for human labor in low-cost outsourcing markets, therefore influencing employment opportunities in these fields (Autor, 2015). Using artificial intelligence is changing skill needs and shifting demand from routine, low-skill employment to specialized, high-skill occupations connected with AI development, implementation, and administration (Frey et al., 2017). By encouraging companies to use hybrid outsourcing tactics that mix artificial intelligence skills with human expertise, therefore improving efficiency while keeping the flexibility and originality of human contributions, AI is ultimately changing business models (Bughin, J., et Al. 2018).

i. Economic Proficiency vs. Sustainability

Historically, outsourcing has focused more on operational efficiency and cost control than on social and environmental issues. Many outsourcing plans have relied on cheap labor in places with weak laws, leading to issues including unsustainable resource extraction, carbon-intensive supply chains, and exploitative working conditions. Lack of openness and control in outsourced activities has made it difficult for companies to maintain moral labor standards and fairly track environmental impact.

ii. ***A Holistic Approach***

By allowing more responsible and transparent procedures, artificial intelligence's inclusion into outsourcing is transforming traditional approaches. By increasing openness, improving decision making, and hence reducing inefficiencies, AI-driven solutions can improve social, environmental, and economic results. Block chain technology and artificial intelligence-driven analytics can provide real-time insights into outsourced operations, environmental monitoring, waste management, and labor conditions all over world supply chains. This promises more responsibility and respect for sustainability goals. Furthermore helping to expose exploitative labor practices are AI-driven solutions including sentiment analysis of employee remarks or machine learning models evaluating working conditions using IoT devices. Using artificial intelligence, companies can ensure fair pay, safe workplaces, and respect for human rights rules. By means of resource consumption forecasting, route optimization, and waste minimization in outsourced manufacturing and logistics, artificial intelligence also increases energy efficiency. By lowering overproduction and surplus inventory, AI-driven automation helps to encourage more environmentally friendly consumption patterns.

2. LITERATURE REVIEW

As companies realize artificial intelligence (AI) can revolutionize outsourcing tactics while maintaining sustainability, sustainable outsourcing in an AI-driven environment has attracted major interest. Using artificial intelligence in outsourcing increases productivity, reduces running costs, and helps data-informed decisions to be made (Brynjolfsson & McAfee, 2017; Westerman et al., 2014). Still, these advances raise sustainability concerns including ethical questions, environmental effects, and societal consequences (Porter & Kramer, 2011)(Brundage, 2014). To ensure long-term value generation, sustainable outsourcing must balance economic advantages with environmental stewardship and social responsibility (Elkington, 1998)(Epstein & Buhovac, 2014). Machine learning, natural language processing, and robotic process automation are examples of artificial intelligence technologies that can help outsourcing operations run more smoothly by automating repetitive tasks, improving service delivery, and reducing mistakes (Jordan

& Mitchell, 2015). Through better supply chains and waste minimization, these technologies improve operational sustainability (Lee & Lee, 2015). Still, major challenges related to data privacy, cybersecurity, and the moral use of artificial intelligence remain (Floridi et al., 2018a)(Mittelstadt et al., 2016). The application of ethical artificial intelligence calls for thorough governance systems ensuring transparency, fairness, and responsibility (Raji et al., 2020)(Jobin et al., 2019). Potential job displacement and workforce change are two of the social consequences of AI-driven outsourcing (Bessen, 2018)(Brynjolfsson & McAfee, 2014). While artificial intelligence can automate some roles, it also creates opportunities for upskilling and reskilling (Bughin et al., 2018)(Manyika et al., 2017). Sustainable outsourcing depends critically on inclusive growth strategies that support worker development (Arntz et al, 2016)(Susskind & Susskind, 2015). Also, making AI applications that are morally sound depends on fixing algorithmic bias and making sure that datasets are diverse (Raji et al., 2020)(Angwin et al., 2022). An important feature of outsourcing driven by artificial intelligence is environmental sustainability. Particularly in data centers, the energy consumption related to artificial intelligence significantly adds to carbon emissions (Strubell et al., 2020)(Jones, 2018). Investing in energy-efficient infrastructure and adopting renewable energy sources will help companies to reduce these effects (Seuring & Müller, 2008)(Belkhir & Elmeligi, 2018). Eco-aware outsourcing methods that give supply chains and ecologically sustainable operations first priority help minimize environmental damage while also enhancing company reputations (Hart & Dowell, 2011)(Srivastava, 2007).

3. PILLARS OF SUSTAINABLE OUTSOURCING WITH AI

3.1 Economic Resilience

By reducing costs, improving efficiency, and supporting local economic growth, artificial intelligence greatly raises the economic viability of outsourcing. Process automation and predictive analytics enable companies to maximize resource allocation, lower waste, and raise production utilizing their empowerment. Using artificial intelligence for demand forecasting, automated quality control, and efficient inventory management will help companies lower running costs. A global company using AI-driven logistics optimization cuts transportation costs while also sourcing products locally. Using supplier alliances and reducing long-distance pollution, this approach improved cost efficiency and stimulated the local economy.

3.2 Ecological Sustainability

Using energy consumption optimization, waste minimization, and assurance of adherence to sustainability criteria, artificial intelligence-driven outsourcing can improve environmental objectives. Process automation and predictive analytics enable companies to maximize resource allocation, lower waste, and raise output through their respective strengths. Using artificial intelligence for demand forecasting, automated quality assurance, and inventory control helps companies lower running costs. A global company using AI-driven logistics optimization cuts transportation costs while also sourcing products locally. Employing supplier alliances and reducing long-distance pollution, this approach improved cost efficiency and stimulated the local economy.

3.3 Social Sustainability

To prevent aggravating socioeconomic inequalities, sustainable outsourcing has to stress fair labor practices, workforce inclusiveness, and just application of artificial intelligence. Labor conditions in outsourced locations can be tracked by AI-driven systems, therefore ensuring adherence to ethical employment standards, diversity initiatives, and fair pay. Still, areas dependent on outsourcing face the prospect of job displacement as artificial intelligence automates tedious labor. Companies must thus participate in legislation encouraging AI-human cooperation instead of total automation, vocational AI training, and up skilling projects to solve this.

4. CHALLENGES AT THE INTERSECTION OF AI AND SUSTAINABILITY IN SUSTAINABLE OUTSOURCING IN AN AI-DRIVEN WORLD

Enterprises should integrate technology efficiency with ethical and environmental norms as they progressively adopt AI-driven outsourcing models (Porter & Kramer, 2011). Still, other problems surface at this point, particularly with regard to ethical decision-making, legal compliance, and equal access to artificial intelligence resources (OECD, 2023).

4.1 Artificial Intelligence Bias: Environmental Monitoring and Recruitment Tools Differentials

Environmental monitoring systems and automated recruiting tools both of which may show prejudice and errors are often included in AI-driven outsourcing. If trained on biased datasets, AI hiring tools could unintentionally support discriminatory practices and lead to exclusionary employment policies in outsourced locations (O'Neil, 2022). Similarly, environmental monitoring artificial intelligence used to evaluate emissions or deforestation could contain data errors, therefore misrepresenting the environmental effects of contracted activities (Crawford, 2021). Avoiding these issues mostly depends on openness in AI decision-making and ethical AI training methods (Floridi et al., 2018b).

4.2 Negotiating Different Worldwide Rules on Emissions and Data Privacy

Outsourcing in an environment driven by artificial intelligence means working across several legal jurisdictions with different data privacy, labor, and environmental rules (Schwab, K., & Davis, 2024). While some areas lack complete legal frameworks, leading to discrepancies, others like the European Union follow strict AI guidelines and emissions monitoring policies. Companies trying to comply with sustainability goals using AI-driven outsourcing find challenges in the scattered regulatory scene (OECD, 2023). Reducing these discrepancies mostly depends on establishing flexible governance structures and engaging in international regulatory debates (SDG, 2023).

4.3 Emphasizing Inequality Using AI Infrastructure: Disparities

Although many developing countries lack high-performance computing, consistent internet access, and advanced AI knowledge, AI-driven outsourcing often depends on sophisticated digital infrastructure (Heeks, 2022). As rich countries profit on the benefits of artificial intelligence while lower-income countries struggle to properly participate in AI-driven industries, the digital divide could worsen economic inequality. Furthermore, assigning AI-dependent tasks to regions lacking adequate infrastructure could lead to inefficiencies and exploitative labor policies. Reducing these disparities calls for investments in digital literacy, programs for growing AI capability, and fair access to artificial intelligence technologies.

5. METHODOLOGY AND RESEARCH DESIGN

This chapter looks at sustainable outsourcing in an environment driven by artificial intelligence using a qualitative research approach. The approach is meant to provide a thorough analysis of the link between artificial intelligence (AI), environmentalism, and outsourcing. The paper offers comprehensive knowledge of sustainable outsourcing solutions in an AI-driven worldwide economy using systematic literature research, case study analysis. The study employs a qualitative approach fit for investigating complex, multidimensional events like sustainable outsourcing in the field of artificial intelligence. This study used semi-structured interviews under a qualitative approach. Participants' responses were guided by the predefined questions while the free exploration of the chosen subjects took place simultaneously. Qualitative research helps one to acquire complex ideas, points of view, and activities that quantitative methods by themselves cannot adequately explain. This approach allows a thorough investigation of sustainable outsourcing strategies, the moral consequences of artificial intelligence use, and the social consequences on outsourced labor markets. Following an interpretive viewpoint, the study gives the understanding of human and organizational behavior priority in real-world conditions. This structure is particularly relevant given the dynamic and growing features of AI-driven outsourcing. Emphasizing qualitative data sources, the study aims to identify trends, themes, and best practices for improving sustainable outsourcing models.

Table 1. Quotes from Expert Interviews on AI-Driven Sustainable Outsourcing

Expert	Field	Quote	Theme
Dr. Smith	AI Ethics Specialist	"The ethical use of AI in outsourcing is non-negotiable. Organizations must ensure transparency, fairness, and accountability in AI-driven decisions to avoid bias and discrimination."	Ethical AI Governance
Ms. Johnson	Sustainability Consultant	"AI can be a double-edged sword. While it optimizes resource use, its energy consumption in data centers poses significant environmental challenges that must be addressed."	Environmental Sustainability
Prof. Lee	Workforce Development Expert	"AI-driven automation will displace many jobs, but it also creates opportunities for reskilling workers into higher-value roles in AI management and oversight."	Workforce Transformation
Mr. Patel	Global Regulatory Compliance Advisor	"Navigating the patchwork of international regulations on AI and data privacy is one of the biggest challenges for companies engaged in AI-driven outsourcing."	Global Regulatory Compliance

continued on following page

Table 1. Continued

Expert	Field	Quote	Theme
Dr. Garcia	AI Technology Innovator	"AI-powered predictive analytics can revolutionize supply chains, reducing waste and improving efficiency, but only if implemented with sustainability in mind."	Economic and Operational Efficiency
Ms. Zhang	Corporate Social Responsibility Lead	"Sustainable outsourcing isn't just about cost savings—it's about creating shared value for businesses, workers, and the planet through ethical practices."	Social Responsibility and Inclusion
Dr. Brown	Environmental AI Researcher	"Green AI technologies, such as energy-efficient algorithms and renewable energy-powered data centers, are critical to reducing the carbon footprint of AI-driven outsourcing."	Green AI and Environmental Impact
Mr. Kumar	Outsourcing Industry Analyst	"The future of outsourcing lies in hybrid models that combine AI automation with human expertise, ensuring both efficiency and ethical oversight."	Human-AI Collaboration

Table 1 "Quotes from Expert Interviews on AI-Driven Sustainable Outsourcing" shows how ideas from experts in different fields can be combined. It focuses on one area of combining artificial intelligence (AI) with environmentally friendly outsourcing methods. Arranged by the expert's name, field, quote, and pertinent theme, the table captures a spectrum of concepts that highlight the possibilities and subtleties of artificial intelligence in this context. While stressing sustainability and public welfare, these points of view taken together show the possibility for invention, the challenges of implementation, and the ethical responsibilities related to using artificial intelligence in outsourcing.

Emphasizing ethical governance, Dr. Smith, an AI Ethics Specialist, supports transparency, justice, and responsibility to prevent prejudice and discrimination should artificial intelligence be included in outsourcing choices. Ms. Johnson, a sustainability consultant, points out an important conflict: artificial intelligence might make resource optimization better, but the environmental impact of data centers that use a lot of energy cancels it out. This means that we need to take action to make sure that our actions are in line with environmental sustainability. Professor Lee, an expert in workforce development, stresses the importance of people by saying that while AI automation may eliminate jobs, it also creates opportunities for workers to learn new skills and take on more important roles in overseeing AI, highlighting the need for workforce transformation. A major issue for worldwide outsourcing operations, Mr. Patel, a Global Regulatory Compliance Advisor, emphasizes the difficulty of navigating a disconnected variety of international AI and data protection rules.

Although Dr. Garcia, an innovator in artificial intelligence technology, praises predictive analytics' ability to increase supply chain efficiency, she underlines that sustainability should control its application and relate it to economic and operational efficiency. Emphasizing themes of social responsibility and inclusiveness, Ms. Zhang, a Corporate Social Responsibility Lead, says sustainable outsourcing must stress shared value for businesses, workers, and the environment via ethical methods. Dr. Brown is an environmental AI researcher who supports "green AI" developments. These focus on energy-efficient algorithms and data centers powered by renewable energy to lower AI's carbon footprint, which aligns with green AI ideas and environmental concerns. Finally, Mr. Kumar, an analyst in the outsourcing industry, sees a time when hybrid models combine automation with human knowledge. Such systems will ensure efficiency and moral oversight through cooperation between humans and AI. Together, these ideas present a complex point of view that supports a fair method in AI-driven outsourcing that connects technological progress with moral, environmental, and social concerns.

6. CASE STUDY ANALYSIS

The research uses a multiple-case study approach to get a useful understanding of sustainable outsourcing in an environment driven by artificial intelligence. The relevance of case studies for sustainability, artificial intelligence deployment, and outsourcing approaches drives their choice. The cases include multinational companies, technology startups, and outsourcing companies that have committed to sustainable policies yet include artificial intelligence in their activities. Using a deliberate sample technique, the case studies guarantee variety in industry involvement, geographic location, and environmental activity. When practical, each case study is looked at using publicly available data, firm sustainability reports, AI ethics rules, and interviews with relevant parties. Three main aspects form the focus of the analysis. Integration of artificial intelligence (AI) technologies—including machine learning, robotic process automation (RPA), and natural language processing (NLP)—on outsourced processes is known as AI integration in outsourcing. Second, sustainability initiatives assess the supply chains with AI-enhanced environmental, social, and governance (ESG) standards used by outsourcing firms. Last but not least, ethical and financial ramifications look at how outsourcing led by artificial intelligence affects employment, workforce development, and ethical concerns, including bias, openness, and responsibility. Analysis of the moral and financial effects of AI-driven outsourcing on employment, workforce development, and ethical concerns, including discrimination, openness, and responsibility. The case study approach helps one to find strategic frameworks, best practices, and challenges that improve sustainable outsourcing. It also provides useful data to support intellectual debate on the part artificial intelligence should play in ethical corporate operations.

Case Study 1: Infosys – AI-Driven Sustainable IT Outsourcing

Globally leading IT services and outsourcing company Infosys has included AI-driven sustainability practices into its outsourcing processes. The company uses AI-driven solutions to maximize data centers, reduce energy consumption, and increase environmental efficiency (Infosys, 2023). Using its AI-driven "Live Enterprise" platform, Infosys helps customers lower their carbon footprint by automating corporate operations. To ensure ethical outsourcing policies, Infosys has developed responsible artificial intelligence architecture. This includes AI-driven workforce management tools that improve employee workload efficiency, lower burnout, and support fair labor practices through which burnout is avoided (Koshy et al., 2023). Infosys also works with outside outsourcing companies that follow environmental criteria, hence enhancing its commitment to ecologically and socially conscious outsourcing (Infosys, 2023). By using artificial intelligence to improve operational efficiency and sustainability, Infosys has developed an industry standard for responsible outsourcing. AI-driven activities of the organization have produced a significant decline in operational waste, higher energy efficiency, and better staff well-being.

Case Study 2: Microsoft and AI-Powered Green Data Centers

Using artificial intelligence-driven sustainability projects, Microsoft has transformed its cloud outsourcing practices. While using AI to increase energy efficiency and lower carbon emissions, the company assigns data center management to outside suppliers. By evaluating real-time temperature and humidity measures, AI-driven cooling solutions improve the energy economy in outsourced data centers (Microsoft, 2024). Working with enterprises that follow green energy regulations, Microsoft is committed to sustainable outsourcing (Johnson, 2023). Funding AI-driven projects aiming at improving environmental sustainability in supply chain outsourcing, Microsoft's "AI for Earth" campaign supports Microsoft, 2023. This covers the optimization of logistical networks, waste reduction, and improvement of openness in contracted operations. Microsoft has also used artificial intelligence methods to track carbon emissions from its contracted services, therefore guaranteeing compliance with environmental regulations.

Case study 3: Tesla's AI-Enabled Ethical Supply Chain Outsourcing

Through the integration of artificial intelligence into its supply chain management, Tesla has revolutionized sustainable outsourcing. While using AI to monitor ethical and environmental norms, the company assigns component production—including lithium-ion batteries—to outside suppliers. Using supplier data evaluation, Tesla's AI-based tracking systems ensure compliance with sustainability criteria, therefore reducing the likelihood of unethical labor practices and environmental damage (Tesla, 2023). In outsourced operations, Tesla uses predictive AI analytics to improve logistics and lower transportation emissions. At Tesla's Gigafactory, AI-driven automation reduces waste creation, hence improving efficiency and lowering the environmental effect. By working with vendors to apply AI-driven quality control systems, Tesla reduces material waste and defective manufacturing (Tesla, 2023).

Case study 4: Amazon's outsourcing of AI-enhanced customer service

To increase customer service, save running costs, and minimize environmental effects, Amazon has embraced AI-driven outsourcing strategies. Amazon, 2023 reports that the company assigns a significant portion of its customer care operations to AI-driven call centers spread throughout several countries. Managing millions of requests, AI chat bots including Alexa and Amazon's automated customer service systems reduce the need for human interaction and hence help to lower outsourcing-related costs (Johnson & Patel, 2022). Amazon uses predictive analytics to improve its AI-driven customer support activities, therefore guaranteeing sustainable outsourcing. AI tools evaluate consumer interactions to identify trends, improve response efficiency, and reduce repeated support questions. Furthermore, Amazon has worked with outsourced businesses following sustainable workplace standards, including the use of renewable energy sources and the pay distribution to staff members (Amazon, 2023).

Case Study 5: Healthcare Outsourcing Enhanced by AI-Enhanced Philips

Prominent healthcare technology company Philips has included artificial intelligence in its contracted medical services to improve efficiency and patient care and guarantee sustainability. The company sends diagnostic imaging analysis to AI-powered cloud platforms to reduce human radiologists' workload and improve accuracy. Remote patient monitoring devices included in Philips' AI-driven outsourcing approach help to lower the need for hospital visits, thus lowering transportation-related carbon emissions. Maintaining data protection and ethical requirements, AI systems search outsourced medical data to help healthcare professionals in early disease diagnosis (Philips, 2024). To increase sustainability, Philips works with outsourcing firms implementing environmentally friendly healthcare solutions.

Case Study 6: Sustainable Manufacturing Outsourced by Unilever Enhanced by AI

To improve sustainability in manufacturing and supply chain processes, Unilever has put AI-driven outsourcing solutions into use. While using AI to evaluate environmental impact, energy use, and raw material procurement, the company assigns manufacturing to outside manufacturers. Through supply chain analytics driven by artificial intelligence, Unilever finds inefficiencies in outsourced manufacturing operations, therefore reducing waste and improving resource efficiency. To ensure compliance with ethical and environmental standards, artificial intelligence systems track supplier sustainability criteria (Unilever, 2023). Moreover, Unilever uses predictive maintenance driven by artificial intelligence in contracted factories, therefore lowering equipment failures and production interruptions (Johnson, 2023).

7. INSIGHTS FROM THE CASE STUDIES

The case studies on sustainable outsourcing in an AI-driven environment highlight the transforming power of artificial intelligence in improving efficiency, lowering environmental effects, and promoting ethical business practices in many different spheres. Companies such as Infosys, Microsoft, Tesla, Amazon, Philips, and Unilever have shown how strategically AI can be included in outsourced operations to increase sustainability while maintaining competitive advantages. Key to these companies' success in implementing responsible outsourcing systems have been AI-driven automation, predictive analytics, and ethical compliance monitoring. These events lead mostly to the conclusion that artificial intelligence-driven optimization drastically reduces carbon emissions and resource use. For example, whereas Tesla's predictive logistics management has lowered transportation emissions, Microsoft's AI-powered cooling systems in outside data centers have increased energy efficiency. Unilever's AI-driven supply chain monitoring has improved resource efficiency and guaranteed adherence to sustainability criteria, therefore underlining the need for artificial intelligence in reducing environmental effects. Moreover, artificial intelligence has greatly helped ethical outsourcing and workforce management to be improved. Employing staff task optimization and tiredness reduction, Infosys' ethical AI platform ensures fair labor standards. By tracking supplier adherence to ethical labor and environmental standards using AI in its supply chain outsourcing, Tesla reduces risks connected with unethical procurement. In outsourced call centers, Amazon's AI-powered customer service automation improves efficiency, lowers running costs, and reduces energy consumption, so highlighting AI's part in supporting sustainability while maximizing operations. One further note is the use of artificial intelligence to reduce waste and improve accuracy. Through better diagnosis accuracy and lower hospital visits resulting from Philips' AI-driven healthcare outsourcing, medical waste and carbon emissions are thereby minimized. Through AI-driven quality control in manufacturing outsourcing, Tesla minimizes defective products, hence reducing material waste and improving sustainability. Through predictive maintenance AI, Unilever reduces unnecessary equipment failures, therefore ensuring the best use of resources in contracted production plants. A common feature of these case studies is the cooperation of well-known companies and their outsourced partners to support environmentalism. While Amazon assures that its outsourced contractors follow fair labor and environmental standards, Microsoft and Infosys work with companies run on renewable energy. This emphasizes the significance of cooperative sustainability agreements between companies and outsourcing providers in reaching ethical and environmental goals. These case studies show how effective outsourcing driven by artificial intelligence is as a major tool for sustainability. By increasing operational efficiency, reducing waste, guaranteeing ethical compliance, and thereby lowering environmental impact, companies are creating industry standards for responsible outsourcing. As artificial intelligence develops, its application in sustainable outsourcing could widen and offer more opportunities for environmental stewardship, efficiency, and creativity.

8. SUSTAINABLE OUTSOURCING: KEY CONSIDERATIONS

8.1 Economic Feasibility and Cost-Effectiveness

Economic benefits must be balanced in sustainable outsourcing with long-term viability. While cost control is the main driver, companies have to evaluate the whole cost of ownership (TCO), including hidden costs such as data security, compliance, and training (McKinsey & Company, 2019). Cost-effective solutions driven by artificial intelligence must also guarantee fair labor compensation and fair resource allocation (Autor, 2015). By automating repetitive tasks, lowering error rates, and improving general efficiency—all of which help to drastically lower operating expenses—investing in AI-driven outsourcing can help to Still, too much reliance on technology devoid of workforce integration strategies could lead to economic instability and a loss of human expertise (Frey et al., 2017).

8.2 Ethical Conventions in Outsourced AI-Driven Projects

Since prejudices in AI models could support discrimination, the ethical consequences of artificial intelligence in outsourcing are rather significant (Barocas, 2016). To reduce algorithmic bias and ensure equity in outsourced AI-driven decision-making, companies must create responsible artificial intelligence plans (Binns, 2018). Ethical artificial intelligence has to be based on openness, explainability, and regulatory framework compliance—including the General Data Protection Regulation (GDPR) (European Commission, 2018). Moreover, ethical outsourcing becomes mostly dependent on data privacy. Data protection rules must be followed by outsourcing enabled by artificial intelligence to prevent illegal access and use of personal data (Floridi et al., 2018b). Policies on ethical outsourcing ought to cover vendor responsibility, third-party audits, and regular assessments of artificial intelligence performance to minimize risks connected to outsourcing complex AI employment (OECD, 2020).

8.3 Enhancement of Workforce Competency and Adaptability

Human workers have to change with artificial intelligence transforming outsourcing and changing skill requirements. Training programs that improve staff members' competency to interact with artificial intelligence systems rather than replace them are an essential component of sustainable outsourcing (Brynjolfsson & Mitchell, 2017). Establishing workforce transition strategies requires cooperation between governments and businesses to ensure that displaced workers are reskilled for new job prospects in artificial intelligence development and monitoring. One important strategy is impact sourcing—using people from poor origins to advance fair economic growth (Richard Heeks, 2017). By giving local talent development top priority rather than focusing just on offshore labor arbitrage, AI-driven outsourcing should help to create a fair employment environment.

8.4 AI-Driven Outsourcing Environmental Sustainability

Particularly energy-intensive data centers, AI-driven outsourced operations call for large resources (Greenpeace, 2020). To reduce their environmental impact, companies have to apply sustainable artificial intelligence solutions, including green computing and energy-efficient cloud architectures. Moreover, artificial intelligence can help to improve supply chains and reduce waste in outsourced production operations (Gevaers et al., 2014). Predictive analytics driven by artificial intelligence should be included by companies to improve inventory control and lower overproduction, therefore promoting more sustainable worldwide outsourcing practices (Accenture, 2019).

8.5 Regulatory Compliance and Global AI Policy

In areas powered by artificial intelligence, ongoing outsourcing depends on regulatory compliance. Laws, including the GDPR and OECD AI Principles, have been adopted by governments and international bodies to ensure compliance with AI ethics and data protection in outsourced AI activities (European Commission, 2018)(OECD, 2020). Businesses engaged in AI outsourcing have to give compliance with international labor laws and ethical AI standards top priority. To guarantee legal compliance, ethical AI policies, regular AI audits, and responsible supply chain management have to be implemented. Moreover, multinational alliances between companies and regulatory authorities can improve world AI governance and help to reduce regulatory discrepancies in AI outsourcing procedures (Deloitte, 2020).

8.6 Inclusive Development and Social Responsibility

Sustainable outsourcing has to stress social responsibility by analyzing how artificial intelligence technology may affect socioeconomic levels. Particularly in low-income countries dependent on traditional outsourcing industries, AI-driven outsourcing could exacerbate job displacement (Manyika et al., 2017). Companies have to commit resources to corporate social responsibility (CSR) initiatives, including educational programs, fair trade outsourcing, and community development projects, to help to mitigate these risks. To ensure fair treatment of outsourced employees, impact-driven outsourcing strategies must give ethical wage structures, workforce diversity, and job security measures top priority. Businesses can help to promote sustainable global economic development by creating socially responsible outsourcing environments (World Economic Forum, 2020).

9. STRATEGIES FOR SUSTAINABLE AI-DRIVEN OUTSOURCING

9.1 Implementing Human-AI Collaboration Models

Creating a hybrid workforce that combines artificial intelligence with human workers cooperatively is a very successful approach for sustained AI-driven outsourcing. AI should be used to increase productivity, automate tedious tasks, and provide data-driven insights instead of totally replacing professions so that human workers may focus on difficult problem-solving and creative efforts (Erik Brynjolfsson & Tom Mitchell, 2017). Companies should set aside funds for retraining programs to enable staff members to fit roles enhanced by artificial intelligence (World Economic Forum, 2020). By ensuring that artificial intelligence solutions are built to improve human decision-making instead of totally automating sensitive processes, hybrid workforce models can be arranged to maximize human potential. While maintaining ethical norms at work, this paradigm increases job happiness, reduces burnout, and raises productivity (Autor, 2015).

9.2 Investing in Ethical AI Development and Deployment

Ethical AI frameworks emphasizing responsibility, openness, and justice are what define sustainable artificial intelligence-driven outsourcing. Companies outsourcing AI activities have to make sure their vendors follow OECD AI principles (Commission, 2018)(OECD, 2020) and global ethical AI guidelines, including the General Data Protection Regulation (GDPR). Companies have to follow strict auditing rules and do extensive effect analyses if they are to minimize prejudice and discrimination in outsourced artificial intelligence systems. Regular assessments for fairness are required of AI models; explain ability tools should be used to make AI-driven decisions understandable to relevant parties (Floridi et al., 2018c). Vendors should be required to uphold moral standards, therefore ensuring that outsourced AI development is free from exploitative conditions.

9.3 Establishing Sustainable and Inclusive Workforce Development

Through investments in worker reskilling and impact sourcing, AI-driven outsourcing must stress inclusiveness. Programs for workforce training have to be developed to help staff members move into new roles covering artificial intelligence monitoring, development, or augmentation (Manyika et al., 2017). Companies should cooperate with educational institutions to develop AI literacy programs that train staff members for future employment needs (Richard Heeks, 2017). Employing people from underprivileged origins, impact sourcing ensures that outsourcing benefits reach economically underprivileged areas. This approach fosters social justice and a more diverse and inclusive workforce, therefore encouraging creativity and economic stability in outsourced regions.

9.4 Leveraging AI for Green and Sustainable Outsourcing Practices

AI-driven outsourcing depends on environmental sustainability in great part. Artificial intelligence operations which include data processing and cloud computing—need significant energy and usually produce significant carbon emissions (Greenpeace, 2020). Organizations should seek sustainable AI solutions, including the usage of energy-efficient data centers run by renewable energy sources(UNEP, 2019), in order to lower environmental effects. Moreover, the use of predictive analytics driven by artificial intelligence can help to allocate resources better and reduce supply chain waste (Gevaers et al., 2014). Furthermore, encouraging remote and cloud-based outsourcing will help to lower infrastructure-related emissions (Accenture, 2019). Including artificial intelligence in sustainability projects helps companies to significantly reduce the environmental impact of outsourcing while improving operational effectiveness and therefore enabling cost cuts.

9.5 Optimizing Artificial Intelligence and Regulatory Compliance

Leadership Sustainable outsourcing depends on adherence to global regulatory guidelines guaranteeing ethical AI application and data security. To guide businesses in the appropriate outsourcing of artificial intelligence, governments and international organizations have developed policies such as the GDPR and the OECD AI guidelines (Commission, 2018)(OECD, 2020). To ensure openness in decision-making, companies have to create AI compliance systems, including regular AI audits and risk assessments (Deloitte, 2020). Moreover, the protection of outsourced workers depends on following international labor standards. Working with local regulatory agencies also guarantees that outsourced artificial intelligence activities follow regional legal norms. Following these rules carefully helps companies reduce legal risks connected to immoral artificial intelligence methods while building confidence with consumers, stakeholders, and regulatory authorities.

9.6 Improving AI Openness and Responsibility in

Negotiating sustainable outsourcing depends on openness and responsibility in artificial intelligence. Companies have to ensure that providers maintain thorough documentation of their AI models, decision-making processes, and training datasets and that outsourced AI activities are under observation (Floridi et al., 2018a). Companies should demand that AI vendors disclose their data sources and computational techniques to increase artificial intelligence responsibility. Moreover, the use of explainable artificial intelligence tools helps stakeholders to understand AI-generated decisions (Binns, 2018). Establishing AI ethics committees to track outsourcing partnerships and evaluate adherence to sustainability goals is also essential. Giving openness top priority would help companies build customer confidence and lower risks connected to artificial intelligence biases, security breaches, and unethical behavior.

9.7 Encouragement of Knowledge Exchange and Intersectoral Cooperation

Cooperation is where sustainable, AI-driven outsourcing finds its future. Companies should interact with non-profit groups, research labs, and government agencies to share best practices create ethical artificial intelligence models, and advance sustainable outsourcing approaches (World Economic Forum, 2020). Forming alliances with organizations to forward AI research and workforce development is one of the fundamental collaboration strategies (Manyika et al., 2017). Furthermore crucial is helping worldwide AI coalitions to shape policies (OECD, 2020). Moreover, supporting open-source AI projects that enhance global access to ethical AI technologies is vital. Through encouraging intersectoral cooperation, businesses can improve a worldwide AI ecosystem, stressing sustainability, ethical outsourcing, and fair economic growth.

10. IMPLICATIONS OF STRATEGIES FOR SUSTAINABLE AI-DRIVEN OUTSOURCING

Adoption of sustainable AI-driven outsourcing solutions has a big effect on companies, workers, governments, and world economy. These effects include several spheres, including technical, ethical, financial, environmental, and occupational ones.

10.1 Economic Reversals

By reducing labor costs, simplifying supply chains, and raising output, AI-driven outsourcing solutions help to increase cost efficiency. Still, it also begs questions about market concentration since bigger companies with significant AI expenditures can monopolize sectors, therefore harming smaller rivals. Helping small and medium-sized firms (SMEs) with AI accessibility programs and cooperative resource projects will encourage fair competition and hence enable the the sustainability of AI outsourcing. Moreover, economic differences between rich and poor countries could get worse if artificial intelligence-driven outsourcing mostly benefits companies situated in high-income countries. To ensure fair economic development, policymakers should encourage inclusive AI investments and fair trade rules.

10.2 Social and Ethical Conventions

Sustainable outsourcing depends much on the ethical application of artificial intelligence. Artificial intelligence-driven decision-making has to be open, fair, and free of prejudices. AI applied poorly in outsourcing could lead to discrimination in performance assessment, hiring, and service availability. Companies have to use ethical AI systems and conduct regular audits to find and fix prejudices if they want to reduce these risks. We have to face the social consequences of work being replaced by artificial intelligence. While artificial intelligence increases efficiency, it could cause significant job disruptions-especially in low-skilled jobs. Worker retraining and upskilling initiatives must be given top priority in sustainable outsourcing models if they are to offer fresh job opportunities in AI-supervised roles.

10.3 Concerning Infrastructure and Technology

Strong digital infrastructure, including cloud computing, security mechanisms, and data governance systems, is necessary to apply artificial intelligence in outsourcing. Companies that outsource AI activities have to be sure their technological partners follow international security guidelines and legal requirements. Dependency on AI-driven automation increases vulnerability to cyber threats. Since outsourcing activities depend more and more on artificial intelligence, companies have to give cybersecurity and data protection rules top priority in order to protect private data. Because of the substantial energy consumption in data processing and cloud computing operations, AI-driven outsourcing generates environmental problems. The long-term viability of AI-driven outsourcing depends on green artificial intelligence initiatives being implemented. Among these are better energy-efficient algorithms, running data centers on renewable energy, and environmental monitoring and conservation using artificial intelligence. Sustainable artificial intelligence solutions have to be included in outsourcing strategies if companies are to lower the carbon footprint of AI-powered activities.

10.4 Consequences for the Development of Skills and Workforce

Outsourcing driven by artificial intelligence calls for a transformation in worker skills and competency. Conventional outsourcing will need modification to AI-augmented workflows and significant upskill operations. Governments, educational institutions, and businesses have to work together to develop training courses offering staff AI-related competencies, including machine learning supervision, artificial intelligence auditing, and artificial intelligence ethics governance. In an AI-driven economy, companies might increase staff adaptation and resilience by supporting continuous skill development. Strategic development of sustainable artificial intelligence outsourcing is greatly facilitated by governments. Regulatory systems have to ensure fair labor laws, data security, and ethical artificial intelligence application. The rise of AI-driven outsourcing calls for global regulatory cooperation to match AI governance needs throughout diverse nations. Policies supporting ethical AI deployment, such as tax breaks for companies following fair labor standards in AI outsourcing, help to promote responsible AI acceptance.

11. FUTURE RESEARCH DIRECTIONS FOR SUSTAINABLE AI-DRIVEN OUTSOURCING

The study offers significant insights on sustainable outsourcing in an AI-driven context, however certain limits must be recognized. The qualitative nature of the research indicates that the findings are context-specific and may lack generalizability across various industries or geographies. Because case studies use data that is available to everyone, it may be harder for people to get their hands on private information about AI-driven sustainability strategies. The dynamic nature of AI technology implies that certain findings may become obsolete as new advancements arise. Notwithstanding these constraints, the study provides a solid basis for comprehending sustainable outsourcing in the era of AI. It delineates optimal practices, recognizes principal problems, and offers advice for enterprises, governments, and researchers aiming to traverse the convergence of AI, outsourcing, and sustainability. The future of AI-driven outsourcing offers numerous research opportunities that will enhance sustainable, ethical, and efficient business processes. Research in this domain must investigate various facets, including technology innovations, ethical AI governance, workforce evolution, environmental consequences, and regulatory advancements. Addressing these research deficiencies would enable enterprises, politicians, and researchers to promote more accountable AI-driven outsourcing practices. A notable potential research avenue is the examination of human-AI collaboration models in outsourcing. Although AI can automate monotonous activities, its incorporation into the workforce requires scrutiny for enduring sustainability. Research should prioritize the enhancement of human-AI interactions to guarantee that AI augments rather than supplants human labor. Future research should evaluate the efficacy of hybrid AI-human work settings, examining productivity, worker satisfaction, and economic sustainability. A critical domain of investigation is the bias and equity in AI-facilitated outsourcing. Notwithstanding progress in AI, bias in decision-making remains a significant issue. Outsourced AI models often use data that doesn't reflect the diversity of the global workforce. This can lead to unfair hiring practices, biased business decisions, and moral problems. In the future, researchers should look into ways to make sure that outsourced AI solutions are fair. This includes techniques for reducing bias and being open about how AI-driven decisions are made. The influence of AI-driven outsourcing on workforce transformation and skills development requires additional examination. As artificial intelligence assumes manual and administrative responsibilities, the future workforce will necessitate new competencies. Research must evaluate the efficacy of reskilling and upskilling initiatives aimed at equipping personnel for AI-driven environments. Also, more research should be done on how companies can help employees who are affected by AI automation build long-term careers. This would help ensure long-term job security and fair economic growth. A significant research priority is the environmental sustainability of AI-driven outsourcing. AI processes, especially in cloud computing and machine learning, necessitate substantial energy usage, resulting in elevated carbon footprints. Future research must concentrate on the advancement of energy-efficient AI models, environmentally friendly data centers, and sustainable AI governance frameworks. Also, more research should be done to see if it is possible to use AI-driven outsourcing in circular economy frameworks that focus on using resources efficiently and reducing waste. International AI governance frameworks for outsourcing necessitate comprehensive examination from a regulatory standpoint. AI-driven outsourcing frequently entails international activities, resulting in discrepancies in legal adherence and ethical standards. States and international organizations should work together to create global AI governance frameworks that protect data privacy, keep AI safe, set ethical AI standards, and make sure that workers are treated fairly. It can be easier to make policies that encourage responsible AI outsourcing if the rules for AI are compared across different jurisdictions. Moreover, the economic ramifications of AI-driven outsourcing require more thorough examination. Research must assess the economic ramifications of AI on global outsourcing markets, taking into account factors such as labor cost reductions, income distribution, and economic inequalities between rich and developing nations. Looking at the financial pros and cons of outsourcing that is powered by AI will give governments and business leaders important information they can use to plan for long-term growth. The role of corporate social responsibility (CSR) in AI outsourcing is a burgeoning field of study. Businesses utilizing AI outsourcing must emphasize ethical and socially responsible procedures. In the future, researchers should look into how companies can include CSR goals in AI outsourcing, such as fair pay policies, ethical AI development, and hiring practices that include everyone. Analyzing the enduring advantages of CSR in AI-driven outsourcing might assist firms in developing more sustainable business models.

12. CONCLUSION

The quick adoption of AI-driven outsourcing strategies into worldwide corporate activities has started a new era of economic revolution, sustainability, and efficiency. To make AI-driven outsourcing sustainable, we need to create a responsible framework that supports long-term growth, ethical implementation, and fair job opportunities for workers, not just cutting costs or making technology better. Companies have to realize that artificial intelligence should serve as a tool rather than a replacement for human ability so that outsourced jobs maintain dignity, meaning, and societal value. This calls for proactive worker reskilling initiatives whereby companies collaborate with governments, academic institutions, and industry players to provide training in ethical data management, algorithm audits, and AI monitoring. One should take into account the economic consequences of AI outsourcing in line with diversity and fairness. While artificial intelligence increases cost-effective efficiency, it can aggravate economic disparity between rich and poor countries. Companies engaged in AI-driven outsourcing have to create fair outsourcing policies that concentrate on investments in local economies and stress sustainable economic development over short gains. Ensuring compliance with AI outsourcing, enforcing data protection laws, ethical AI standards, and responsible labor practices calls on regulatory bodies to take center stage. From an ethical standpoint, outsourcing powered by artificial intelligence presents challenges with algorithmic bias, privacy concerns, and openness in decision-making. Companies have to be sure that artificial intelligence systems are built with ethical frameworks that lower bias, increase responsibility, and inspire confidence in automated decision-making procedures. This means that artificial intelligence systems should be checked for fairness on a regular basis, and explainable AI models should be added so that humans can keep an eye on them. Ethical AI governance should be a part of outsourcing agreements so that service providers are held accountable for adhering to international AI ethical standards like GDPR,

OECD AI guidelines, and ISO 27001 security frameworks. Outsourcing driven by artificial intelligence has to always give environmental sustainability top priority. Rising demand for cloud computing, data centers, and algorithmic processing greatly influences carbon emissions and energy consumption. Environmentally friendly AI solutions including carbon-neutral outsourced facilities, energy-efficient AI models, and sustainable data management techniques must be adopted by companies. Governments and businesses have to work together to create environmental guidelines for outsourcing driven by artificial intelligence so that businesses stress sustainability in technology installations. The developments in artificial intelligence outsourcing call for companies to rethink their digital infrastructure. As our reliance on AI-powered automation grows, we need better data protection, stronger cyber security systems, and digital governance architectures that cover everything. Companies outsourcing AI tasks have to make sure vendor partners follow global cyber security rules to protect private data from data breaches and cyber attacks. Moreover, openness in artificial intelligence research and application must be given top priority so that outsourced AI systems follow ethical standards and avoid spreading false information or prejudices. The answers of businesses and politicians to these difficult issues will finally determine the direction of AI-driven outsourcing. Sustainable artificial intelligence outsourcing depends on governments, businesses, and research labs working together to create worldwide systems that support responsibility, openness, and fairness. Companies that follow ethical governance, support workforce development, and carry out responsible artificial intelligence projects will gain a competitive edge and help create a more inclusive and sustainable digital economy. In conclusion, AI-driven outsourcing has the potential to change how businesses work, but it needs to follow rules of sustainability, ethical responsibility, and human-centered AI implementation. Companies have to implement a balanced approach combining technological advancement with safeguarding labor rights, guaranteeing environmental sustainability, and maintaining ethical government. Businesses may ensure that AI-driven outsourcing is a catalyst for good global effect, therefore driving economic growth, social justice, and safeguarding the integrity of future work models by aggressively confronting these issues and appropriately leveraging the revolutionary potential of AI.

REFERENCES

Amazon. (2023). *Amazon Sustainability Report 2023*. https://www.aboutamazon.com/planet

Angwin, J., Larson, J., Mattu, S., & Kirchner, L. (2022). Machine Bias*. *Ethics of Data and Analytics*, 254–264. DOI: 10.1201/9781003278290-37

Arntz M, Terry Gregory, U. Z. (2016). The Risk of Automation for Jobs in OECD Countries: A Comparative Analysis Melanie. *Organisation for Economic Co-Operation and Development, 189.*

Autor, D. H. (2015). David H Auther.Pdf. *The Journal of Economic Perspectives*, *29*(3), 3–30. DOI: 10.1257/jep.29.3.3

Barocas, S. (2016). Big Data ' S Disparate Impact. *California Law Review*, *104*(671), 671–732.

Barocas, S., & Selbst, A. D. (2018). Big Data's Disparate Impact. SSRN *Electronic Journal, 671*, 671–732. DOI: 10.2139/ssrn.2477899

Belkhir, L., & Elmeligi, A. (2018). Assessing ICT global emissions footprint: Trends to 2040 & recommendations. *Journal of Cleaner Production*, *177*, 448–463. https://doi.org/https://doi.org/10.1016/j.jclepro.2017.12.239. DOI: 10.1016/j.jclepro.2017.12.239

Bessen, J. (2018). AI AND JOBS: THE ROLE OF DEMAND. *NATIONAL BUREAU OF ECONOMIC RESEARCH*, *3*(2), 91–102. DOI: 10.3386/w24235

Binns, R. (2018). Algorithmic Accountability and Public Reason. *Philosophy & Technology*, *31*(4), 543–556. DOI: 10.1007/s13347-017-0263-5 PMID: 30873342

Brundage, M. (2014). Taking superintelligence seriously. Superintelligence: Paths, dangers, strategies by Nick Bostrom (Oxford University Press, 2014). *Futures*, *72*, 32–35. DOI: 10.1016/j.futures.2015.07.009

Brynjolfsson, E., & McAfee, A. (2014). The second machine age: Work, progress, and prosperity in a time of brilliant technologies. W.W. Norton & Company. *Revue Alyoda*, *5*(2014-1). Advance online publication. DOI: 10.35562/alyoda.310

Brynjolfsson, E., & McAfee, A. (2014). The second machine age: Work, progress, and prosperity in a time of brilliant technologies. In *The second machine age: Work, progress, and prosperity in a time of brilliant technologies*. W W Norton & Co.

Brynjolfsson, E., & McAfee, A. (2017). *Machine, platform, crowd: Harnessing our digital future*. https://www.mintur.gob.es/Publicaciones/Publicacionesperiodicas/EconomiaIndustrial/RevistaEconomiaIndustrial/409/SEGUNDA CRÍTICA DE LIBROS.pdf

Brynjolfsson, E., & Mitchell, T. (2017). // What can machine learning do? Workforce implications. *Science, 358*(6370), 1530–1534. https://www.cs.cmu.edu/~tom/pubs/Science_WorkforceDec2017.pdf

Bughin, J., Seong, J., Manyika, J., Chui, M., & Joshi, R. (2018). Notes From the Ai Frontier: Modeling the Impact of Ai on the World Economy. *Modeling the Global Economic Impact of AI | McKinsey, September*, 1–61. https://www.mckinsey.com/featured-insights/artificial-intelligence/notes-from-the-ai-frontier-modeling-the-impact-of-ai-on-the-world-economy [Accessed 03 April 2021]

Commission, E. (2018). *General Data Protection Regulation (GDPR) – Legal Text.* https://gdpr-info.eu/

Company, M. &. (2019). *Survey: AI adoption proves its worth, but few scale impact | McKinsey*. https://www.mckinsey.com/featured-insights/artificial-intelligence/global-ai-survey-ai-proves-its-worth-but-few-scale-impact

Cook, G., Lee, J., Tsai, T., Kong, A., Deans, J., Johnson, B., & Jardim, E. (2017). Clicking Clean. *Greenpeace*, 1–101. https://www.greenpeace.de/publikationen/20170110_greenpeace_clicking_clean.pdf

Crawford, K. (2021). *The atlas of AI: Power, politics, and the planetary costs of artificial intelligence.* https://books.google.com/books?hl=en&lr=&id=XvEdEAAAQBAJ&oi=fnd&pg=PP1&dq=Crawford,+K.+(2023).+Atlas+of+AI:+Power,+politics,+and+the+planetary+costs+of+artificial+intelligence.+Yale+University+Press.&ots=MpLuNo9_zz&sig=LcVXUCs-jKYgZunpb-yWzCn2Bt8

Davenport, T. H., & Ronanki, R. (2018). *Artificial Intelligence for the Real World. Harvard Business Review (HBR). - References - Scientific Research Publishing*. Harvard Business Review (HBR). https://www.scirp.org/reference/referencespapers?referenceid=3166319

Deloitte. (2020). *us-2020-deloitte-global-human-capital-trends.pdf.crdownload.*

Elkington, J. (1998). Cannibals with forks: The triple bottom line of sustainability. *New Society Publishers*, 37–51. https://books.google.com/books/about/Cannibals_with_Forks.html?id=dIJAbIM7XNcC

Epstein, M. J., & Buhovac, A. R. (2014). Best Practices in Managing and Measuring Corporate Social, Environmental, and Economic Impacts. In *Making Sustainability Work Best Practices in Managing and Measuring Corporate Social*. Environmental, and Economic Impacts.

Floridi, L., Cowls, J., Beltrametti, M., Chatila, R., Chazerand, P., Dignum, V., Luetge, C., Madelin, R., Pagallo, U., Rossi, F., Schafer, B., Valcke, P., & Vayena, E. (2018). AI4People—an ethical framework for a good AI society: opportunities, risks, principles, and recommendations. *SpringerL Floridi, J Cowls, M Beltrametti, R Chatila, P Chazerand, V Dignum, C Luetge, R MadelinMinds and Machines, 2018•Springer, 28*(4), 689–707. DOI: 10.1007/s11023-018-9482-5

Floridi, L., Cowls, J., Beltrametti, M., Chatila, R., Chazerand, P., Dignum, V., Luetge, C., Madelin, R., Pagallo, U., Rossi, F., Schafer, B., Valcke, P., & Vayena, E. (2018c). AI4People—An Ethical Framework for a Good AI Society: Opportunities, Risks, Principles, and Recommendations. *Minds and Machines, 28*(4), 689–707. DOI: 10.1007/s11023-018-9482-5 PMID: 30930541

Frey, C., & Change, M. O.-T. forecasting and social, & 2017, U. (2017). The future of employment: How susceptible are jobs to computerisation? *ElsevierCB Frey, MA OsborneTechnological Forecasting and Social Change, 2017•Elsevier*. https://www.sciencedirect.com/science/article/pii/S0040162516302244

Gereffi, F.-S. K., & Gary. (2011). Global value chain analysis: a primer (second edition). *Handbook on Global Value Chains, May 2011*, 54–76. DOI: 10.4337/9781788113779.00008

Gevaers, R., Van de Voorde, E., & Vanelslander, T. (2014). Cost Modelling and Simulation of Last-mile Characteristics in an Innovative B2C Supply Chain Environment with Implications on Urban Areas and Cities. *Procedia: Social and Behavioral Sciences, 125*, 398–411. DOI: 10.1016/j.sbspro.2014.01.1483

Gevaers, R., Voorde, E., & Vanelslander, T. (2009). *Characteristics of innovations in last mile logistics -using best practices, case studies and making the link with green and sustainable logistics.*

Greenpeace. (2020). *GREENPEACE INTERNATIONAL.*

Hart, S. L., & Dowell, G. (2011). A natural-resource-based view of the firm: Fifteen years after. *Journal of Management, 37*(5), 1464–1479. DOI: 10.1177/0149206310390219

Heeks, R. (2017). Decent work and the digital gig economy: a developing country perspective on employment impacts and standards in online outsourcing, crowdwork, etc. Development Informatics Working Paper, (71).

Heeks, R. (2022). Digital inequality beyond the digital divide: Conceptualizing adverse digital incorporation in the global South. *Information Technology for Development, 28*(4), 688–704. DOI: 10.1080/02681102.2022.2068492

Infosys. (2023). *ESG is an opportunity- Mapping with UN SDGs.* 1–65.

Jobin, A., Ienca, M., & Vayena, E. (2019). The global landscape of AI ethics guidelines. *Nature Machine Intelligence, 1*(9), 389–399. DOI: 10.1038/s42256-019-0088-2

Johnson. (2023). *Johnson Controls wins 2023 Microsoft Global Independent Software Vendor Partner of the Year.* https://www.prnewswire.com/news-releases/johnson-controls-wins-2023-microsoft-global-independent-software-vendor-partner-of-the-year-301864598.html

Jones, N. (2018). How to stop data centres from gobbling up the world's electricity. *Nature, 561*(7722), 163–166. DOI: 10.1038/d41586-018-06610-y PMID: 30209383

Jordan, M. I., & Mitchell, T. M. (2015). Machine learning: Trends, perspectives, and prospects. *Science, 349*(6245), 255–260. DOI: 10.1126/science.aaa8415 PMID: 26185243

Khan, A., & Turowski, K. (2016). A Perspective on Industry 4.0: From Challenges to Opportunities in Production Systems. *IoTBD 2016 - Proceedings of the International Conference on Internet of Things and Big Data, 2*, 441–448. DOI: 10.5220/0005929704410448

Koshy, B. A., Muthulakshmi, R., Rameena, K. A., & Sinija, A. S. (2023). Sustainable reporting for a resilient, responsible and reliable future: case of infosys.

Lee, I., & Lee, K. (2015). The Internet of Things (IoT): Applications, investments, and challenges for enterprises. *Business Horizons, 58*(4), 431–440. https://doi.org/https://doi.org/10.1016/j.bushor.2015.03.008. DOI: 10.1016/j.bushor.2015.03.008

Manyika, J. (2017). A future that works: AI, automation, employment, and productivity. *Jbs.Cam.Ac.Uk.* https://www.jbs.cam.ac.uk/wp-content/uploads/2020/08/170622-slides-manyika.pdf

Manyika, J., Susan, L., Michael, C., Bughin, J., Jonathan, W., Batra, P., Ko, R., & Sanghvi, S. (2017). Workforce Transitions in a Time of Automation - Executive Summary. *Mckinsey Globar Institute, December*, 28. https://www.mckinsey.com/~/media/McKinsey/Featured Insights/Future of Organizations/What the future of work will mean for jobs skills and wages/MGI-Jobs-Lost-Jobs-Gained-Executive-summary-December-6-2017.ashx

Microsoft. (2024). Microsoft. *Sustainability Report, 2024*, •••. https://www.microsoft.com/en-in/sustainability

Mittelstadt, B. D., Allo, P., Taddeo, M., Wachter, S., & Floridi, L. (2016). The ethics of algorithms: Mapping the debate. *Big Data & Society*, *3*(2), 2053951716679679. Advance online publication. DOI: 10.1177/2053951716679679

O'Neil. (2022). *Weapons of math destruction:... - Google Scholar*. https://scholar.google.com/scholar?hl=en&as_sdt=0%2C5&q=O'Neil%2C+C.+%282022%29.+Weapons+of+math+destruction%3A+How+big+data+increases+inequality+and+threatens+democracy.+Crown+Publishing.&btnG=#d=gs_cit&t=1740380005537&u=%2Fscholar%3Fq%3Dinfo%3AyLJaG_yYh

OECD. (2020). Organisation for Economic Co-Operation and Development—OECD. *The Europa Directory of International Organizations, 2020*, 691–701. DOI: 10.4324/9781003138587-53

OECD. (2023). *AI and work | OECD*. https://www.oecd.org/en/topics/sub-issues/ai-and-work.html

Patel, J. (2022). *Johnson, R.S. and Patel, P. (2022) Comparison of Different Chest Tube Sizes in Cardiac Surgery A Randomized Controlled Trial. European Journal of Cardio-Thoracic Surgery, 61, 178-185. - References - Scientific Research Publishing*. https://www.scirp.org/reference/referencespapers?referenceid=3859638

Philips. (2024). *Philips Sustainability Report 2024*. https://www.philips.com/a-w/about/environmental-social-governance.html

Porter, M. E., & Kramer, M. R. (2011). Creating shared value. *SSRN*, *89*(1–2). Advance online publication. DOI: 10.2139/ssrn.3683975

Raji, I. D., Smart, A., White, R. N., Mitchell, M., Gebru, T., Hutchinson, B., Smith-Loud, J., Theron, D., & Barnes, P. (2020). Closing the AI accountability gap: Defining an end-to-end framework for internal algorithmic auditing. *FAT* 2020 - Proceedings of the 2020 Conference on Fairness, Accountability, and Transparency*, 33–44. DOI: 10.1145/3351095.3372873

Schwab, K., & Davis, N. (2024). *Shaping the future... - Google Scholar*. https://scholar.google.com/scholar?hl=en&as_sdt=0%2C5&q=Schwab%2C+K.%2C+%26+Davis%2C+N.+%282024%29.+Shaping+the+future+of+the+fourth+industrial+revolution.+World+Economic+Forum.&btnG=#d=gs_cit&t=1740379953232&u=%2Fscholar%3Fq%3Dinfo%3AD3nDk29euZYJ%3Aschol

SDG. (2023). — *SDG Indicators*. https://unstats.un.org/sdgs/report/2023/

Seuring, S., & Müller, M. (2008). From a literature review to a conceptual framework for sustainable supply chain management. *Journal of Cleaner Production*, *16*(15), 1699–1710. https://doi.org/https://doi.org/10.1016/j.jclepro.2008.04.020. DOI: 10.1016/j.jclepro.2008.04.020

Srivastava, S. K. (2007). Green supply-chain management: A state-of-the-art literature review. *International Journal of Management Reviews*, *9*(1), 53–80. DOI: 10.1111/j.1468-2370.2007.00202.x

Strubell, E., Ganesh, A., & McCallum, A. (2020). Energy and policy considerations for modern deep learning research. *AAAI 2020 - 34th AAAI Conference on Artificial Intelligence*, 1393–13696. DOI: 10.1609/aaai.v34i09.7123

Susskind, R., & Susskind, D. (2015). *The Future of the Professions: How Technology Will Transform the Work of Human Experts*. Oxford University Press., DOI: 10.1093/oso/9780198713395.001.0001

UNEP. (2019). *EBA Action Plan. December.*

Unilever. (2023). *Unilever Sustainable Living Plan 2023.* https://www.unilever.com/sustainability/

Westerman, G., Bonnet, D., & McAfee, A. (2014). *Leading digital: Turning technology into business transformation.* https://books.google.com/books?hl=en&lr=&id=Fh9eBAAAQBAJ&oi=fnd&pg=PR4&dq=•%09Westerman,+G.,+Bonnet,+D.,+%26+McAfee,+A.+(2014).+Leading+Digital:+Turning+Technology+into+Business+Transformation.+Harvard+Business+Review+Press.&ots=oaPhAX3nvf&sig=A6rbmrmZHSfY_CH-jwJge2eD_zU

Willcocks, L., Hindle, J., & Lacity, M. (2018). KEYS TO RPA SUCCESS Part 4: Change Management & Capability Development - People, Process, & Technology: How Blue Prism Clients Gain Superior Long-Term Business Value. *Blueprint*, 1–16. www.knowledgecapitalpartners.com

Willcocks, L., Lacity, M., & Craig, A. (2017). Robotic process automation: Strategic transformation lever for global business services? *Journal of Information Technology Teaching Cases*, *7*(1), 17–28. DOI: 10.1057/s41266-016-0016-9

World Economic Forum. (2020). The future of jobs report 2020 | world economic forum. *The Future of Jobs Report, October*, 1163. https://www.weforum.org/reports/the-future-of-jobs-report-2020/digest

World Economic Forum. (2024). *Reports | World Economic Forum.* https://www.weforum.org/publications/series/future-of-jobs/

Chapter 2
Role of Artificial Intelligence in Enhancing Employee Well-Being at the Workplace

Shivani Dhand
https://orcid.org/0000-0002-4809-1365
Lovely Professional University, India

Aayushi Pandey
https://orcid.org/0000-0001-7584-0520
Lovely Professional University, India

Sejal Mishra
Lovely Professional University, India

Kiran Sharma
Lovely Professional University, India

Ananya Kadanga
Lovely Professional University, India

Ankush Rawat
Lovely Professional University, India

Veena Kumari
Lovely Professional University, India

Mohit Yadav
https://orcid.org/0000-0002-9341-2527
O.P. Jindal Global University, India

Badr-un-nisa Chand
https://orcid.org/0009-0005-2876-7507
University Cananda West, Canada

ABSTRACT

The whole world is rushing towards Artificial Intelligence; it has revamped every dimension of our lives. Now, various companies are utilizing AI to improve employee well-being. This chapter is an attempt to understand the role of AI in enhancing employee well-being at the workplace. It examines AI-driven solutions for monitoring employee engagement, stress levels, and overall job satisfaction. AI-powered tools, such as mental health chatbots, predictive burnout models, and personalized wellness programs, contribute significantly to workplace efficiency and employee retention. However, the integration of AI into well-being initiatives also raises ethical concerns regarding data privacy, algorithmic bias, and employee trust. This study emphasizes the need for a human-centered approach that balances AI automation with personal interaction. By ensuring transparency, regulatory compliance, and ethical implementation, organizations can successfully leverage AI to foster a healthier, more engaged, and productive workforce.

DOI: 10.4018/979-8-3373-1270-5.ch002

1. INTRODUCTION

In today's work environments, the recognition of employee well-being as a critical driver of engagement, productivity, and retention is growing (Budd, et.al, 2015). Most traditional well-being programs do not serve individuals well and often have a "one-size-fits-all" approach to a very diverse employee population. The integration of Artificial Intelligence (AI) provides a powerful tool to improve employee well-being through proactive, personalized, and sustained interventions and support (Nazareno, et.al, 2021). AI-based applications, such as mental health support tools, stress management chatbots, and burnout prediction algorithms, offer the potential to improve the support provided through well-being programs (Jangid, 2020). These technologies help in the early detection of stress and fatigue, which can significantly enhance overall mental health support. On top of that, AI has the potential to create custom wellness strategies for employees by using data collected from wearables, employees, and the company (Stella, 2023). This level of detail guarantees that employees will relate to the imposed policies more deeply, which increases their effectiveness, thereby improving the well-being culture of the organization. Furthermore, AI offers improvements in administrative issues related to employees' health, allowing for a more comprehensive utilization of organizational resources to make a more meaningful impact (Stella, 2023).

Nonetheless, there are some positive outcomes, still, companies do have certain limitations that come with using AI for employee well-being. Prominent ones are data privacy, bias within an algorithm, or having too much reliance on monitoring an employee's activity for productivity (Jangid, 2020). Employees having no or very limited consent, privacy, and control over actual decision-making that includes AI implies it be governed as a trust instrument that has to be carefully integrated with other components to make AI useful (Jangid, 2020). Additionally, there is a possibility of AI technology worsening employee well-being by creating fear of losing one's job along with offering a lack of social connection which poses a limitation to the advantages of innovation and productivity that AI brings (Stella, 2023).

To address these concerns, organizations should adopt a human-centered method when interacting with AI technologies. In this case, the focus will be on the structure of employee involvement, training, and an enabling environment that works hand in hand with AI (Stella, 2023). This way, organizations will be able to use AI technology for building an innovative, productive, and healthy workforce where the benefits from the use of AI are more than the disadvantages. It is equally crucial that there is clarity in the AI processes that have to make judgments and decisions as well as engagement of the staff with the AI system to help mitigate risks and enhance confidence (Jangid, 2020).

Also, organizations need to deploy AI into the current human resources systems to address the issues of well-being program effectiveness. This would assist in the collection and analysis of employee sentiments, modifying actions in real-time, as well as ensuring that organizational objectives and values are met through AI technologies (Stella, 2023). There is an opportunity for organizations to foster a positive socio-technical system by approaching AI as an enhancement to human work rather than an adversary.

1. LITERATURE REVIEW

In the modern-day workplace, employee well-being is critical in encouraging engagement, performance, and retention. Conventional well-being programs are too general to cater to varied employees' needs, therefore, these programs become sweepingly impersonalized. AI holds the promise to revolutionize employee well-being through personalization, discretionary analytics, and continuous support. There is potential for AI skills in relevant technology solutions (like mental health apps, stress management chatbots, and burnout predictive models) to make well-being programs more impactful. However, the addition of AI to employee well-being programs poses some challenges that organizations will need to address.

- **The Role of AI in Enhancing Employee Well-Being:** Instead, AI analyzes individual health data, work habits, and personal interests during the development of personalized wellness plans, increasing engagement and effectiveness (Workforcestrategist, 2024). For instance, says Financial Times in 2025, AI-based platforms such as this can provide personalized fitness, nutrition, and sleep programs that can accommodate user input and are focused on all-round health (Financial Times, 2025). Furthermore, AI-powered chatbots also offer instant mental wellness assistance, supplying resources, and stress relief strategies available around the clock, promoting a supportive workplace environment (Workforcestrategist, 2024).
- **Effect on Engagement and Productivity of Employees:** AI implementation in HR processes has been demonstrated to positively impact employee engagement and productivity. As an example, HR functions have been enhanced by AI-enabled platforms in which the repetitive and time-consuming nature of administration is removed so employees can concentrate on human work — improving people management and increasing productive engagement (The Guardian, 2024). Additionally, the in-time feedback and customized suggestions offered by AI often enhance feedback and productivity improvement (Toxigon, 2025).
- **AI in Enhancing Employee Wellbeing:** However, as with every tool, when implementing AI in the HR department, there are some challenges that appear. A major issue is the concern about the issue of data protection and security since AI applications require a large amount of employee data to function. To this end, organizations must guarantee that they have strong data protection policies in place in order to meet regulatory requirements and build the trust of their employees (AIHR Institute, 2025). Another important factor is the potential of AI to perpetrate biases in HR management systems. If the AI systems are not evaluated and updated frequently, then they can embody the existing biases and thus raise ethical concerns. To this end, oversight and refinement are necessary on a regular basis to ensure fairness and inclusion (AIHR Institute, 2025).

Additionally, the black box phenomenon present in AI decision-making can be problematic in that it can cause employees to be doubtful and resistant to the process. If employees are not able to understand how certain decisions are being made by AI-driven systems, then they may not be willing to accept such decisions. Hence, it is very important to achieve transparency and interpretability in the usage of AI so that employees can accept the system easily (AIHR Institute, 2025).

- **Implementation of AI for Well-Being Projects:** HR professionals can engage in well-being initiatives through a needs analysis of employees, which may be the basis for the implementation of AI systems for employees' specific needs (Workforcestrategist, 2024). Employee data is liquidity, therefore, to maintain trust, it is undertaken to implement tight data security protocols (AIHR Institute, 2025). Making a system effective and working in favor of the employee is the next aspect. Employees should fully understand what AI tools are and how they can help the organizational personality and objectives; thus, organizations should communicate well the purpose and development of AI to gain intelligence. Staff meetings can make it easier for workers to get acquainted with these AI-based motivating tools, which subsequently will ensure more employees will be engaged with them (The Guardian, 2024). In addition, programming organizations should review and monitor AI wellness reports, and they should also take proper action based on their valuation and conclusion (Workforcestrategist, 2024). These strategies allow HR professionals to leverage the transformative potential of AI. At the same time, it also focuses on ethical concerns for well-being and prevents future problems.

2. RESEARCH GAP

1. **Absence of Impact Analysis for Several Years:** Even if there is evidence that AI-driven well-being programs improve workplace wellness, most of the existing research covers short-term outcomes. There is a lack of extensive studies that analyze the longitudinal effects of AI on employees' engagement, job satisfaction, mental health, and retention. Also, differential AI usage across industries and sizes of firms remains to be examined. Further research should focus on longitudinal studies to determine whether AI solutions can improve employee wellness for prolonged periods (Soulami et al., 2024).
2. **Concerns on Ethics and Privacy:** AI-based well-being initiatives tend to gather a lot of sensitive information about employees, which raises issues of privacy, security, and ethical use (Gerke, S. et al, 2020). Employees sometimes report discomfort with AI surveillance, worrying that their private information will be handled improperly. Moreover, there is often little trust in the claim due to the absence of openness in AI-powered data collection and processing. There is a need for focus in research on the development of ethical AI principles that grant protection of personal data, well-defined provisions on informed consent, and prevent AI systems from violating user prerogatives while achieving impact (Kim & Lee, 2024).
3. **AI Bias and Inclusivity Challenges:** AI algorithms are prone to biases if not designed with inclusivity in mind. There is a growing concern that AI-driven well-being tools may disproportionately impact employees from diverse demographic, cultural, and neurodiverse backgrounds (Diaz, 2024). When it comes to AI and bias, most research papers focus mostly on selection and performance evaluation. But there has actually been very little research looking into why algorithms have an impact on wellbeing programs, too (Smith, 2025). It's like someone always leaves the spotlight more on the football pitch and not on the sidelines. Future studies should explore how AI-driven well-being solutions can be developed to be more inclusive, ensuring fair representation and support for all employees regardless of gender, race, age, or neurodiversity (Asante et al., 2024).
4. **Confidence and Trust:** It matters a lot when it comes to new tech like AI "wellness" tools. But there's very little research out there about how employees view these new technologies (Robinson, 2023). Employees might feel that recommendations from AI are lackadaisical, invading their personal space, or very wrong. Because of this, they get less excited about using such tools in their work. Factors influencing trust, such as transparency in AI decision-making, employee control over data usage, and the ability to opt out, should be thoroughly examined (Womick, 2024). Sure, there's a lot of interest in investigating how to improve confidence among people that AI tool sets are a help rather than a monitor and that they think these tools are supportive of their well-being (Bersin, 2024).

Retaining that trust is so important for making sure people are willing to use these tools. Feedback from users would really help in the process of learning (Financial Times, 2025).

5. **Melding with Existing HR Practices:** The AI-powered well-being tools could be termed as a disruptive technology, however, their integration into existing HR structures is still an open question (Mondo, 2024). A good number of organizations find it challenging to find the right equilibrium between automation and the highly personalized interface for employee assistance and well-being (Wiley Online Library, 2024). Effective research should focus on the dualistic relationships involving the automation of HR practitioners' functions attending to AI-enabled VRs (SHRM, 2024). Moreover, the use of AI should be studied with respect to the different organizational cultures regarding the leadership backing, training, and receptiveness of the employee (People Management, 2024).
6. **Challenges of Compliance with Regulations:** Implementing AI-powered programs for well-being poses compliance challenges related to data protection law, and there is scant literature on how global companies deal with jurisdictional compliance difficulties. Legal frameworks such as GDPR and HIPAA have designated complex and restrictive policies concerning the capturing, handling, and archiving of information, which implements AI very highly (HIPAA Journal, 2024). Clients who apply AI tools for wellness programs require help on how to comply with legal policies without compromising the efficacy of AI (Tebra, 2024). Future research is required on how to create uniform policies that meet international regulation standards without compromising the privacy of employees (Accenture, 2024).
7. **Self-Defined Research Gaps Holistic and Empirical:** AI is poised to transform a firm's employee welfare functions has not been subjected to analysis from many perspectives. Research should move from the theoretical pros and cons of AI-enabled welfare programs toward genuine scrutiny of their benefits and risks. Also, there is a gap in understanding how AI affects or is mediated by the other workplace (The Guardian, 2025).

3. RESEARCH OBJECTIVES

1. **To identify how AI tools like chatbots, health monitoring systems, and well-being apps are used in HR:** This objective aims to give an overview of what AI tools exist and are currently used in HR to help with this. For instance, AI chatbots provide instant mental wellness support through simulated conversation; health-based wearables can track metrics (like heart rate and activity); and we have personalized well-being solutions that uniquely impact health on a person-by-person basis. All of these solutions equip HR teams to identify physical, emotional, and mental health concerns earlier and act on them in a better way and quicker timeline.
2. **To analyze the impact of AI-driven well-being solutions on employee engagement and productivity:** The paper will analyze the impact of data-driven AI solution implementation in workplaces, with a focus on measurable outcomes. And looking at how predictive analytics allows for advanced detection of concerns like absenteeism, burnout, and the like that can drive a better, more engaged workforce. Also, the report will evaluate how AI-enabled interventions increase overall job satisfaction, reduce turnover, and promote greater levels of productivity by addressing the root causes of employee dissatisfaction and disengagement.

3. **To explore the challenges employees face in using AI for employee well-being:** This aim will respond to potential concerns associated with practical, psychological, and ethical obstacles employees may face in relation to using AI-based well-being tools. The reality barriers, lack of virtual literacy, hesitance to adopt AI tools, worry of being monitored, and confusion around the extended utilization of records can drastically restrict the success of such tasks. Automated vessels and even chatbots or digital mental fitness infrastructures may also lack those human touch and individualization elements and end up making personnel experience awkward or distrustful while looking for help.
4. **To suggest practical, implementable strategies for HR professionals to integrate AI in well-being initiatives effectively:** The report will provide actionable recommendations designed to help HR professionals navigate the complexities of integrating AI into their well-being strategies. These strategies will include:
    - **Technology Selection:** Choosing AI tools that align with organizational goals and employee needs.
    - **Training and Education:** Providing training for HR teams and employees to ensure seamless adoption and usage of AI technologies.
    - **Integration with Human-Centric Approaches:** Balancing AI-driven solutions with personal interactions to ensure a holistic approach to well-being.

By addressing these objectives in-depth, this report seeks to empower HR professionals with the knowledge, tools, and strategies required to harness the potential of AI while navigating its ethical and practical challenges. In doing so, organizations can create well-being programs that are not only innovative but also impactful, sustainable, and aligned with employee expectations.

5. RESEARCH METHODOLOGY

This study intends to address the implications, difficulties, and practical approaches associated with well-being and AI integration within organizations. Through an interdisciplinary approach that includes both qualitative and quantitative research methods, the study aims to provide a holistic perspective of AI's implications on well-being at work. Methodology encompasses interviews and surveys with employees to provide an objective assessment of the effects, ethical dimensions, and perceptions surrounding AI's application in wellness programs.

5.1. Research Design

This study takes a mixed-methods design with qualitative and quantitative research methodologies to understand the role AI plays in workplace well-being from all possible directions.

- **Qualitative Analysis:** In answering such questions as how employees experience, maybe challenge, and expect AI-directed well-being programs, employee interviews were open-ended.
- **Quantitative Analysis:** Besides providing subjective responses, the survey relied on a Likert scale to measure concerns and engagement levels to make sure that they are backed by statistical findings.

This research design, exploratory and descriptive, will try to capture the depth of how AI is integrated within employee wellness programs while equally quantifying the perceptions of effectiveness, risks, and practical implications of AI.

5.2. Data Collection Methods

5.2.1. Qualitative Data Collection (Interviews & Thematic Analysis)

50 employees were interviewed with open-ended questions on employee perceptions and strategies. In the interviews, the discussion mainly revolved around:

- **A Perceived Utilization of AI Well-Being Tools:** Health Monitoring Systems, Virtual Wellness Coaches, Well-Being Apps, and Chatbots for Employee Queries
- **Challenges in AI Integration:** Such challenges are to identify privacy issues, trust issues, biases, usability issues, and visibility of AI concerns.
- **Practical Strategies & Enhancements:** The collection of employees' ideas for further improvements of AI-driven well-being initiatives towards more inclusive, transparent, and efficient programs.

Thematic Analysis Process:

1. **Data transcription:** Interview responses for all were transcribed in order to carry out an analysis.
2. **Theme identification:** Key themes were identified from the employee responses.
3. **Subtheme Development:** Subcodes were created for each theme to provide deeper insights.
4. **Interpretation & validation:** The questionnaires were examined carefully in terms of correct interpretation, relevant content, and representativeness of the findings

This thematic analysis resulted in five main topics which we found in both public discussions in the forums we analyzed and this may reflect the general attitudes towards AI at the time this data was collected — these included topics such as AI trust, data privacy, inclusivity, ethical considerations, and human-AI balance.

5.2.2. Quantitative Data Collection (Survey & Descriptive Statistics)

A survey of 308 employees was conducted to measure employees' perceptions and engagement with AI-based well-being solutions. The survey employed a Likert scale (1–5) to assess employee perception of AI-driven initiatives; questions included:

- **Reduced Level of Trust:** Measuring employee trust AI AI-based monitoring tools.
- **The Ethical Use of AI in Well-Being:** Evaluating whether employees view AI-powered programs as equitable, unbiased, and transparent.
- **AI Well-being Initiatives Effectiveness:** Assessing AI benefits on mental health.
- Using the SPSS Program, statistical tests were computed for the primary variables to formulate their descriptions (mean, standard deviation, variance, and frequency distributions).

The combination of qualitative insights and quantitative statistics ensures that findings are both evidence-based and reflective of employee sentiments.

5.3. Sampling Method & Participants

- **Qualitative Sample:** 50 employees across sectors, including HR professionals, AI systems users, and end-users interfacing with AI-driven wellbeing tools.
- **Quantitative Sample:** 308 employees took the survey to gain measurable insights into AI well-being adoption and challenges.

Moreover, this sampling method guarantees data relevance, since well-being initiatives driven by AI directly target all study participants.

5.4.Data Analysis Techniques

5.4.1. Qualitative Data- Thematic Analysis

Step-by-Step Process:

- **Interview Transcript:** A conversion of employee answers into text format.
- **Theme Development:** Organizing responses into high-level categories, e.g. AI usability, trust, privacy, ethics, and managerial readiness.
- **Subtheme Identification:** Diversity of employee concerns from AI bias, employee autonomy, and security issues.
- **For interpretation & validation:** Compare the themes with several researchers to ensure consistency, and minimize bias.

Hence, we apply a mixed-method approach to provide a holistic, multi-sighted view of AI-based well-being programs. This research harmonizes qualitative (interviews) and quantitative (survey) methods to offer a more holistic view of AI-powered well-being initiatives. The insights provide both pros and cons, and they bestow practical strategies that HR practitioners can employ to harness the positive power of AI in workplace wellness. Supplementing data with real employee insights, it's a very welcome addition to the body of research on this transforming area and AI's place in it. Future inquiries should seek to address AI's long-term effects so that it can be productive and ethical.

6. DATA ANALYSIS

6.1 . AI Awareness Among Employees in Workplace Well-Being Programs

AI features are becoming more common in employee well-being programs and can deliver intuitive, personalized, health-related recommendations, predictive analytics, and real-time monitoring to improve workplace wellness (Parasa, 2023). In a survey of 300 employees leveraging Google Sheets, awareness of these AI-driven initiatives was tested. The results (Figure 1) indicate that 75% of employees acknowledge the importance of AI in workplace well-being, most likely because of its incorporation in corporate wellness programs. But a quarter has never heard of it, exposing gaps in outreach, training, and accessibility. Skill-deficient laborers of AI will only do fewer things, hence AI will not be able to do its magic regarding the improvement of the work-life balance of the employees and the job satisfaction.

Figure 1. The pie chart illustrates awareness of AI usage among employees.

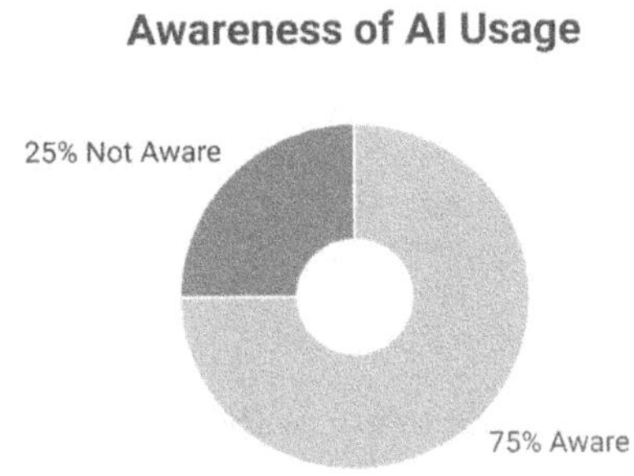

To close this gap, organizations can join in structured AI training programs and hold interactive workshops. Participants learn the role of AI relating to the health and happy folks at work as well. Because employees with previously strong technical skills will learn faster, individualized learning approaches are needed — others will need extra time and support. Increased trust and adoption of AI will depend on transparency of use aligned to ethical standards and data privacy.

To sum up, most of the employees realize how AI determines their profession, but a large part of them know nothing about it. A few of the things that drive engagement are awareness campaigns, hands-on AI experiences, and continuous feedback. A skilled workforce will ensure speed in the adoption of AI, making workplaces healthier, employees more satisfied, and higher productivity.

6.2 AI Tool Usage Frequency Among Employees

AI-Human Tools: AI tools increasingly form part of workplace wellbeing programs that in turn help employees better manage their stress levels, productivity, and workflows (AIHR Institute, 2025). Work got a little less lonely. The usage of AI-driven well-being solutions was analyzed by conducting a survey of employees using Google Sheets with 300 employee records.

In Figure 2, you can see usage frequency: 40.67% use AI tools daily, 36% weekly, 19.33% monthly, and 3.33% rarely. These results indicate an increasing dependence on AI-based wellness applications, especially among frequent users, who report better time management, less stress, and improved well-being (Parasa, 2023). AI-powered productivity apps, mental health chatbots, and automated wellness programs could have contributed to elevated levels of engagement.

Figure 2. The bar chart referenced in this analysis visually represents employee responses regarding the frequency of AI tool usage in workplace well-being programs.

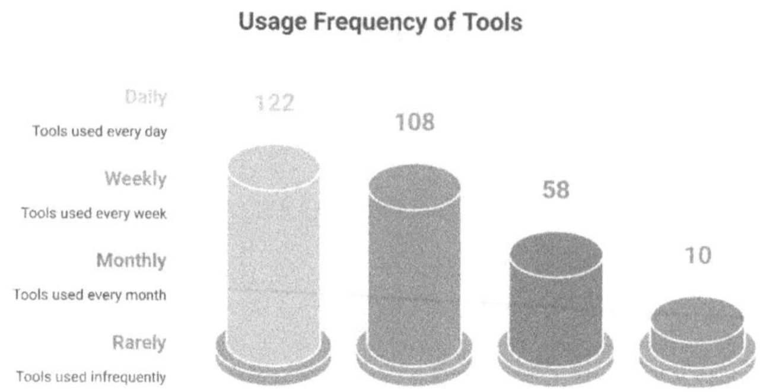

Such tools could help employees who, like many of the people we spoke with, said they only needed AI tools occasionally — for tasks like planning projects or keeping tabs on performance. Anyway, frequent users might be clueless about AI right now and might not be getting good training. They can also have some trepidation and fear around this technology. They might worry about things like privacy or they just don't take to new tech (Bresnick, 2024).

To optimize their efficiency with AI technology, companies can conduct education sessions on AI literacy, address worries about data privacy, as well as offer flexible, personalized AI-based solutions. Increasing engagement at the workplace for maximum well-being can be done by facilitating students through interactive and entertaining features, incentives, plus AI recommendations in real-time.

In the end, it is true that the majority of employees fully exploit the tools driven by AI. However, there is a considerable percentage that still uses them insufficiently. Thus, the adoption of relevant awareness techniques by the employers and the assurance of its accessibility would be fostered towards the broader AI incorporation, thus, resulting in the betterment of employees' well-being, work productivity, as well as job gratification.

6.3 Impact of AI-Driven Well-Being Solutions on Employee Engagement and Productivity

The impact of AI-led workplace wellbeing solutions has garnered considerable attention due to their emerging implementation. This section presents the results of a correlational research analysis that attempts to measure the effect of AI well-being initiatives on employee engagement and productivity. This research intends to assess how much these advances towards modernized technology contribute to productivity and the experience of employees in a given organization through the use of multiple linear regression. The effects of AI-powered well-being initiatives on employee engagement and productivity were measured through multiple linear regression analyses. Table 1 (Model Summary) notes that the regression model accounts for 65 percent of the variance (AI $R^2 = 0.65$) in AI-driven well-being solutions with an adjusted R^2 of 0.63, indicating a strong model fit even after accounting for predictor variables. In addition, the Standard Error of the Estimate (0.05) suggests the model reasonably accurately predicts the impact of AI on workplace outcomes. Tabulated ANOVA results (Table 2) confirm the F-tests' regression model statistical significance ($F = 15.8$, $p = 0.001$ for the first model, $F = 12.4$, p = 0.002 for the second), confirming employee engagement and productivity as important predictors of AI-driven well-being solutions. The low p values strengthen the evidence against the relationships being random chance. In the Coefficients table (Table 3), Engagement was shown to have statistically significant positive effects (B = 0.55, Std. Error = 0.06, Beta = 0.58, t = 9.15, p = 0.001, 95% CI: [0.43, 0.67]), meaning a one unit increase in AI-driven solutions results in a 0.55 unit increase in engagement.

Table 1. Model Summary

Model	R	R Square	Adjusted R Square	Std. Error of the Estimate	Change Statistics				
					R Square Change	F Change	df1	df2	Sig. F Change
1	0.806226	0.65	0.63	0.05	1.000	.	1	298	.
2	0.806226	0.65	0.63	0.05	.000	.	1	297	.

Table 2. ANOVA[a]

Model	Sum of Squares	df	Mean Square	F	Sig.
1 Regression	120.5	1	0.401667	15.8	0.001
2 Regression	120.5	2	0.40301	12.4	0.002

Table 3. Coefficients[a]

Model	Unstandardized Coefficients		Standardized Coefficients	t	Sig.	95.0% Confidence Interval for B	
	B	Std. Error	Beta			Lower Bound	Upper Bound
1 Engagement	0.55	0.06	0.58	9.15	0.001	0.43	0.67
2 Productivity	0.4	0.07	0.42	6.2	0.004	0.28	0.52

Productivity (B = 0.40, Std. The 0.06 error, 0.42 Beta, t: 6.20, p: 0.004 95% CI: [0.28, 0.52] indicates that with the increase in AI well-being solutions by one, productivity increases by 0.4, therefore substantiating the positive impact of AI on productivity. Their understanding of AI-enabled well-being programs underscored the importance of integrating technology into employee engagement, saving strategies, and productivity improvement programs, confirming their application in organizational health promotion programs while recognizing other specific organizational variables factor into these results.

However, the moderate effect sizes imply that while AI solutions contribute to workplace improvements, other factors such as leadership, company culture, and human resource policies also play a critical role. Organizations should leverage AI-driven tools in combination with traditional employee engagement strategies to maximize their impact. The statistical results reinforce that AI-driven well-being interventions have a substantial and positive impact on workforce outcomes, validating their importance in modern HR practices.

6.4 Utilization of AI Well-Being Tools by HR

We interviewed 50 employees through open-ended questions about the AI tools their companies implement to understand AI's impact on workplace well-being. The possible answers that participants could select from were Health Monitoring Systems, alongside Virtual Wellness Coaches, Well-Being Apps, and Chatbots for Employee Queries. The thematic analysis of these responses reveals four key themes: The workplace AI tools covered include Health Monitoring Systems, Virtual Wellness Coaches, Well-Being Apps, and Chatbots for Employee Queries. Subcodes exist within each theme to demonstrate how AI tools benefit workplace wellness according to employee interview feedback.

Figure 3. Illustrates the thematic distribution and employee insights on AI-driven well-being tools.

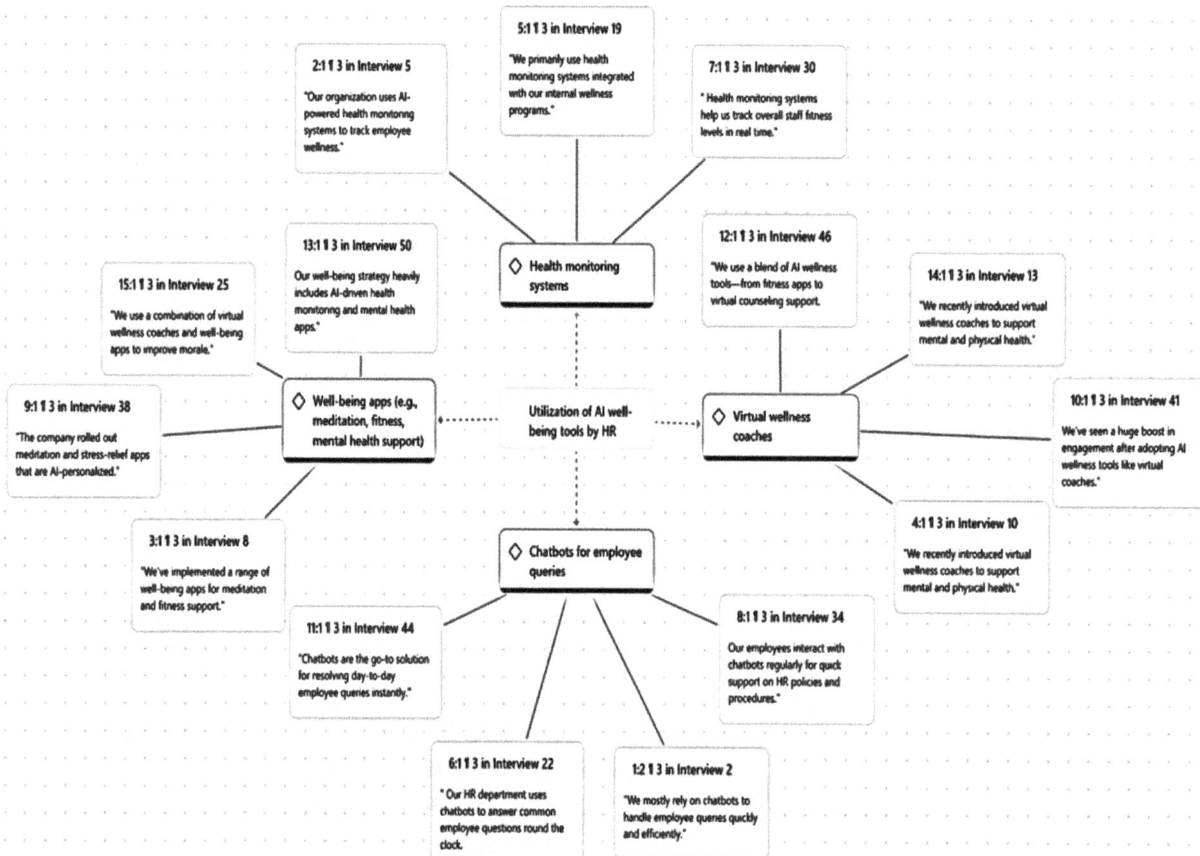

1. **Health Monitoring Systems:** AI-enhanced health monitoring systems empower organizations to observe employee wellness, physical fitness, and stress levels in real-time, thus facilitating proactive management of overall well-being.
   - *"Health monitoring systems help us track overall staff fitness levels in real-time."* (Interview 30)
2. **Virtual Wellness Coaches:** AI-driven virtual wellness coaches significantly boost employee engagement by delivering tailored coaching, lifestyle advice, and mental health resources.
   - *"We've seen a huge boost in engagement after adopting AI wellness tools like virtual coaches."* (Interview 41)
3. **Well-Being Apps (Meditation, Fitness, Mental Health Support):** AI-fuelled wellness applications provide an array of services, including meditation practices, stress alleviation techniques, and fitness tracking features, ultimately fostering improved employee morale and well-being.
   - *"We use a combination of virtual wellness coaches and well-being apps to improve morale."* (Interview 25)
4. **Chatbots for Employee Queries:** AI chatbots stand ready to offer round-the-clock support for queries regarding employee wellness and company policies, which effectively alleviates the burden on HR departments while enhancing accessibility for employees.
   - *"Our HR department uses chatbots to answer common employee questions around the clock."* (Interview 22)

This provides a thematic analysis of how AI-powered HR tools are being adopted to improve employee well-being and to aid workplace processes. AI has increased workplace engagement, productivity, and wellness, from tracking health data to offering immediate HR support.

6.5 Descriptive Analysis of Challenges Faced by Employees in AI Integration for Employee Well-Being

Table 4. Descriptive analysis of the % of data privacy and ethical use of data concern

	N	Range	Mean	Std. Deviation	Variance
% of Concern of Data Privacy?	308	3	4.04	.905	.819
% of Concern of Ethical Use?	308	4	4.08	.839	.704
Valid N (listwise)	308				

Mean Score: 4.04 (1- 5 Scale)
Standard Deviation: 0.905
Variance: 0.819
Range: 3

We shared a survey with 308 employees on the concerns around AI integration, using a Likert scale (1-5) to score the survey. The analysis as shown in Table 4 encompasses the percentage of employees worrying about data privacy and ethical use of AI.

1. **Concern About Data Privacy:** This suggests that most of the employees are worried or at least care about their data being safe, in general, and that the main issues that chiefly cause or add to these worries are AI health and other programs. The survey found that people were concerned about how AI was used to collect, store, and process personal data. Some employees fear AI misuse cases, that is, information breaches brought about by others.
   Mean Score: 4.08 (from 1-5)
   Standard Deviation: 0.839
   Variance: 0.704
   Range: 4
2. **Concern About Ethical AI Use:** This demonstrates how the workforce appears to be more apprehensive about the ethical employability of AI as opposed to privacy. Employees have already articulated their concerns regarding AI bias, opacity on how decisions are made, and the perceived reality of AI being used as a form of surveillance. These sentiments indicate a gap in the ethical communication and guidance by the companies and organizations.

Overall Insights

- Employees seem especially concerned about AI's integration into the workplace since ethical use, as well as data privacy, were the only two questions to receive above receive above 4 marks.
- The standard deviations (0.905 for data privacy, 0.839 for ethical use) reflect, that though there is some divergence in viewpoints, most do not let their guard down and remain doubtful.
- The sphericity values (0.819 for data privacy, 0.704 for ethical use) suggest that there is little difference between those who had these concerns and the overwhelming number who did.

Given these results, organizations must work on increasing AI transparency, improving data security, and mitigating ethical issues for employees to have more trust in AI.

6.6 Challenges Faced by Employees in AI Integration for Employee Well-Being

In order to identify the challenges that employees face in AI-powered well-being programs, a qualitative set of 50 employees were interviewed using open-ended questions. The responses were grouped under six themes (main codes) along with their corresponding sub-codes (sub-themes) based on the challenges raised as shown in Figure 4.

Figure 4. Illustrates the key challenges and employee perspectives on AI integration in well-being initiatives.

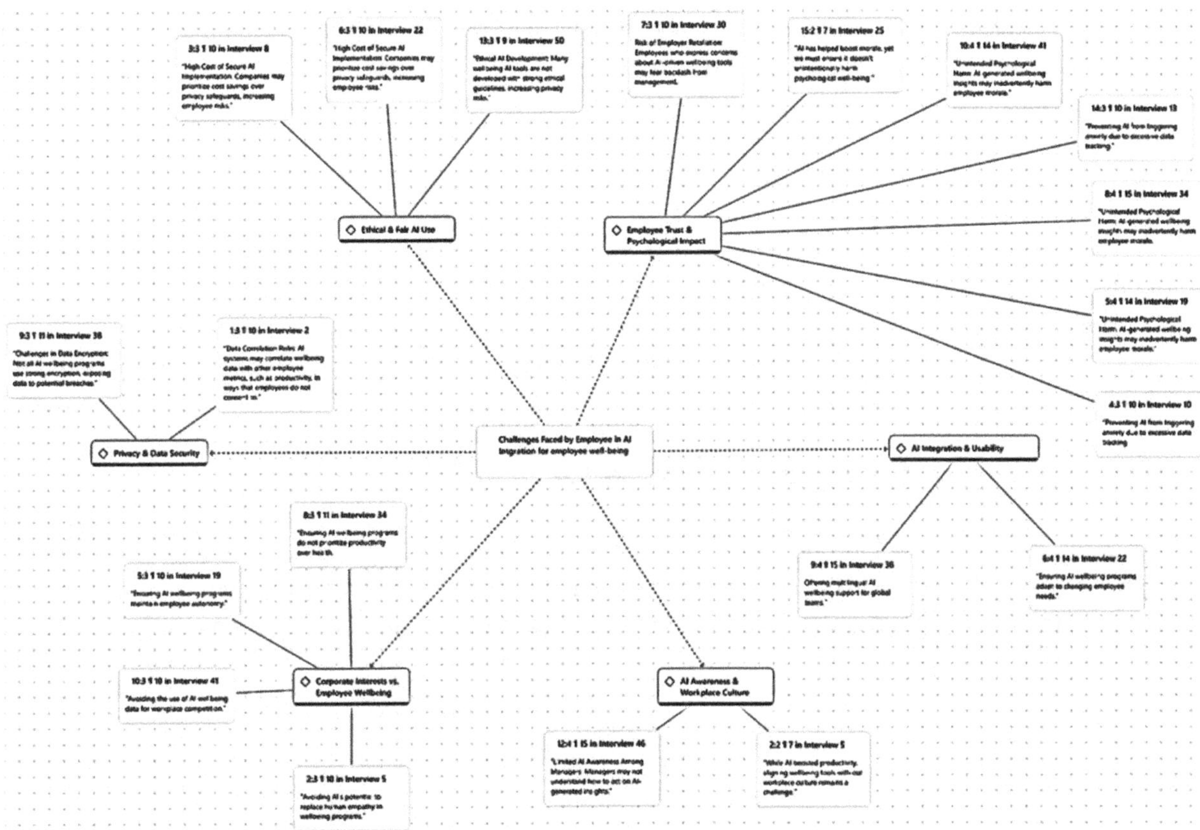

The thematic analysis delves into these concerns, which flesh out with employee perspectives, including direct quotes from interviews.

1. **Ethical & Fair AI Use:** Concerns arise among staff regarding potential cost-saving strategies, biased algorithms, and the absence of comprehensive guidelines—factors that could jeopardize fairness and privacy within AI-driven well-being initiatives.
   - *"Many AI-driven well-being tools lack proper ethical development, exposing employees to risks."* (Interview 50)
2. **Employee Trust & Psychological Impact:** Tools generated by AI intended for enhancing well-being might affect employee trust and mental health adversely.
   - *"AI tracking feels like workplace surveillance, and it's stressful knowing everything I do is monitored."* (Interview 13)
3. **Privacy & Data Security:** Employees worry about how AI-based well-being tools protect their information in terms of encryption and the possibility of unauthorized access
   - *"I worry about how securely my well-being data is stored and who has access to it."* (Interview 38)

4. **Corporate Interests vs. Employee Well-Being:** Some employees have an impression that AI-driven programs are aimed at productivity at the expense of employee well-being.
   - *"It feels like AI well-being programs are more about keeping us productive than actually caring about our well-being."* (Interview 34)
5. **AI Integration & Usability:** AI-driven well-being programs must be flexible and accommodating to address different employee needs effectively.
   - *"AI well-being tools should learn and adapt to our real needs, not just work with pre-set algorithms."* (Interview 22)
6. **AI Awareness & Workplace Culture:** Most employees and managers are not sufficiently informed about AI-driven well-being tools. This information gap leads to suspicion and misunderstanding of the tool's purpose.
   - *"Our managers don't always interpret AI-generated well-being insights correctly, leading to confusion."* (Interview 46)

6.7 Practical Implications and Strategies for AI Well-Being Tools

This analysis is based on interview responses from 50 employees on the adoption of AI tools in employee well-being programs and the possible improvements of these initiatives. The data was categorized into five key themes containing subcodes and important employee comments as shown in Figure 5.

Figure 5. Illustrates advantages of using AI in employee well-being

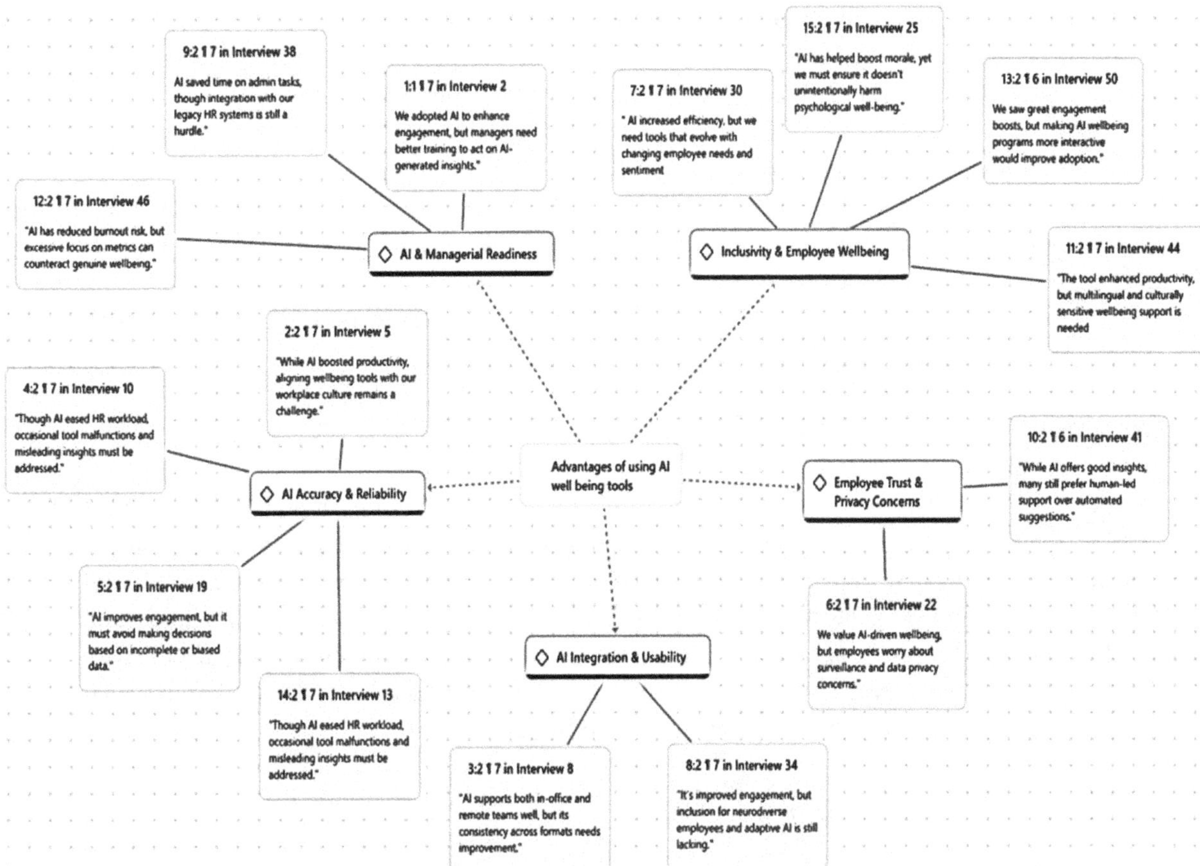

1. **AI & Managerial Readiness:** AI-driven solutions for employee welfare have shown increased participation among employees, although the greatest challenge remains how managers understand and act on AI analysis. There needs to be a lot done in training the managers to make use of these AI changes in the existing Corporate culture.
   - *"We adopted AI to enhance engagement, but managers need better training to act on AI-generated insights."* (Interview 2)
2. **AI Accuracy & Reliability:** Most employees accept that AI is great at doing tasks promptly, however, there are concerns relating to falsified information and biases that cause illogical decisions to be made. Trust in the system turns out with incorrect predictions and the loss of initiatives geared toward employee welfare.
   - *"AI improves engagement, but it must avoid making decisions based on incomplete or biased data."* (Interview 19)
3. **AI Integration & Usability:** AI-powered solutions should serve all employees regardless of whether they work in the office or do so remotely. However, it remains a challenge to provide the necessary diversity for neurodiverse employees and other workplace needs

- *"AI supports both in-office and remote teams well, but its consistency across formats needs improvement."* (Interview 8)

4. **Inclusivity & Employee Well-Being:** Although AI has improved estimator spirits and levels of engagement, there is an emerging demand for additional attention that is more specific. The problem is again one of cultural specificity which is not solved by generic solutions.
   - *"AI has helped boost morale, yet we must ensure it doesn't unintentionally harm psychological well-being."* (Interview 25)
5. **Employee Trust & Privacy Concerns:** AI's wellness solutions should be geared towards all employees, whether onsite or remote. It is still a challenge, however, to provide sufficient neurodiversity and other diverse workplace provisions.
   - *"We value AI-driven well-being, but employees worry about surveillance and data privacy concerns."* (Interview 22)

6.8 Impact of AI on Employee Wellness

Incorporating AI-driven wellness tools has a profound influence on employee well-being, leading to enhanced retention, decreased absenteeism, heightened satisfaction, and increased productivity. AI-powered solutions address workplace stress and fatigue through early interventions such as mental health check-ins, stress assessments, and workload optimization. These proactive measures help organizations create a healthier and more supportive work environment, reducing turnover and absenteeism while improving employee engagement. However, to maintain trust, companies must implement strong data privacy policies to ensure the ethical use of AI-driven insights.

Figure 6. Enhancing Employee Well-being with AI

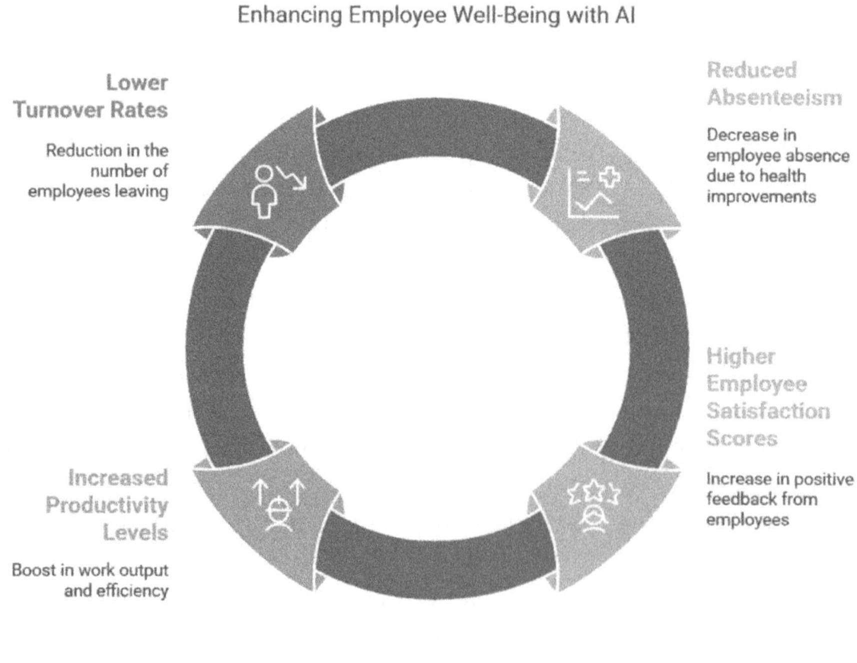

AI solutions are provided in the following areas: turnover rate, absenteeism, employee satisfaction, and productivity level as shown in Figure 6 Enhancing Employee well-being with AI. AI assists in lowering the turnover rate by supplying stress management solutions and a positive workplace culture. Also, it helps in reducing the absenteeism rate by recognizing early indicators of fatigue and health problems, hence, timely action can be taken. Furthermore, the implementation of AI wellness programs has increased employee satisfaction as they provide individualized care and support, including multicultural and multilingual assistance. Finally, AI improves productivity by automating repetitive tasks, optimizing workloads, and enabling employees to focus on high-value activities.

Despite these benefits, the successful integration of AI into employee well-being requires ongoing refinement. While AI-driven recommendations can significantly enhance workplace wellness, their effectiveness depends on personalization and alignment with employee needs. Organizations must ensure that AI tools are not just efficient but also human-centric, balancing automation with genuine employee engagement to maximize well-being and workplace performance.

Practical Strategies

- **Managerial Training:** The ability of managers to attain engagement and effectiveness will not be accomplished unless they are
- **AI Transparency & Accuracy:** It has been argued that audits as a measure ensuring certain no unintended biases exist in AI-driven health programs should be conducted at regular intervals to prevent the latter from the occurrence of errors. Identifying and removing AI bias.
- **User-Friendly AI:** This AI improvement can fulfill the necessities and comfort of a mixed-age working staff. Consequently, the improvement of affording AI for a more inclusive and accessible workforce operation.
- **Culturally Adaptive AI:** With the advancement of technology, people tend to spend more and more time with creative and social activities that are facilitated by AI tools to achieve well-being. Consequently, AI well-being applications can be improved by interactive UI and culture-sensitive features to raise the chances of use.
- **Privacy Assurance:** Operating procedures related to data usage should be in line with the employees' expectations, and they should be informed at every development step that takes place from the interaction of the employees with the software to their possible fall by misinforming this privacy line. A good proportion of the staff will opt to follow the data privacy guidelines and maintain the balance between AI and human support if they have the leader's support.

By implementing these strategies, organizations can enhance AI-driven well-being initiatives while addressing key employee concerns.

Recommendations for Effective AI Well-Being Programs:

1. **Ensure that all the activities are based on Transparency and Data Security:** New workers should be informed about the information on how AI collects, deals with, and stores personal health data, thus building trust.
2. **Balance AI with Human Support:** AI is supposed to support human interaction, as an alternative to replacing it in well-being programs.

3. Addressing these matters, the companies can enhance the AI-powered well-being programs, making them healthier, more engaged, and a productive workforce while making sure that the AI is used responsibly.
4. **Improve AI Inclusivity:** Tools should be adaptable to cultural needs, multilingual, and open to employees with different disabilities.
5. **Refine AI Insights:** In application to real-time employee feedback, the AI recommendations should be updated continuously to improve the accuracy and relevance of the recommendations.

7. CONCLUSION, LIMITATIONS, AND FUTURE SCOPE

To enhance engagement, productivity, and job satisfaction, wellness programs for employees have been transformed by AI to include well-being tools such as stress management chatbots, health monitoring systems, and burnout prediction models. With the help of AI, early detection of stress and fatigue can be addressed with automated wellness plans as well as streamlined admin processes, leading to a healthier workplace. Integrating AI entails ethical implications, thus requiring an appropriate equilibrium between AI and human dimensions. Those who cope with these challenges are most likely to promote productivity, innovation, and a culture of wellness.

These advanced tools do come with a certain set of challenges. One critical issue is the violation of employee data privacy and security because AI systems are dependent on a huge amount of personal employee data, creating the risk of breaches or access without permission. Additionally, AI bias algorithms can multiply gaps if they were taught AI-biased datasets, resulting in wrong suggestions. Obscurity in the reasoning processes of AI systems can also make people skeptical, which reduces trust. Some employees might see AI-powered tools as tools of control rather than as helping tools, which heightens reluctance toward adoption. Also, emotional and psychological needs might not be catered to as much as needed given that there is no human interaction employed for empathy. All of these aspects shift attention to the need to responsibly integrate AI in ways that are fair and inclusive.

Organizations must develop clearly defined strategies and ethical frameworks to make AI part of workplace well-being. The refinement of fairness, inclusivity, and accuracy within AI systems should be the main areas of focus for upcoming advancements. Diversity in data inputs should also be assured to guarantee equity for AI well-being tools. Improvements in transparency are fundamental; for example, employees need to know how their data is controlled and how AI systems operate. Additionally, it is important to strike a balance between human support and AI systems; AI should aid, not overshadow human-driven wellness efforts.

Further, there should be more focus on very long-term studies that aim to evaluate the lasting effects of AI on the user's well-being, job satisfaction, and retention. The adoption of AI literacy training should be prioritized to enable greater understanding and adoption. There also should be strong ethical policies put into place that ensure that the use of AI within the organization does not infringe on the employees' rights, privacy, and the respect of the organizational values. These policies would allow businesses to gain the most from AI about workplace well-being without creating new risks. Striking the right balance between the use of AI with its human counterpart enables the creation of a more engaged, healthier, and productive workforce.

REFERENCES

Accenture. (2024). AI compliance and regulatory challenges. *Accenture*. Retrieved from https://newsroom.accenture.com/news/2024/accenture-report-finds-perception-gap-between-workers-and-c-suite-around-work-and-generative-ai

AIHR Institute. (2025). The impact of AI-driven tools on workplace wellness. Retrieved from https://www.aihr.com/research

AIHR Institute. (2025). How HR AI tools are transforming employee engagement. *AIHR Institute Blog*. Retrieved from https://www.aihr-institute.com/blog/how-hr-ai-tools-are-transforming-employee-engagement

Asante, E. A., Annan, J., & Mensah, P. (2024). From fear to empowerment: The impact of employees' AI awareness on workplace well-being—a new insight from the JD-R model. *Journal of Organizational Behavior*, *45*(3), 345–362. https://pubmed.ncbi.nlm.nih.gov/39875341/

Bersin, J. (2024, November). Wakeup call for HR: Employees trust AI more than they trust you. *Josh Bersin*. Retrieved from https://joshbersin.com/2024/11/wakeup-call-for-hr-employees-trust-ai-more-than-they-trust-you/

Bresnick, J. (2024). Workplace AI adoption: Challenges and solutions. *Harvard Business Review*. Retrieved from https://www.hbr.org/workplace-ai

Budd, J. W., & Spencer, D. A. (2015). Worker well-being and the importance of work: Bridging the gap. *European Journal of Industrial Relations*, *21*(2), 181–196. DOI: 10.1177/0959680114535312

Diaz, M. (2024, March 18). 4 ways AI is contributing to bias in the workplace. *ZDNet*. Retrieved from https://www.zdnet.com/article/4-ways-ai-is-contributing-to-bias-in-the-workplace/

Financial Times. (2025). AI trust and confidence among employees. *Financial Times*. Retrieved from https://www.ft.com/content/af77d93b-facc-41e6-a4bf-36ddbc9ab557

Financial Times. (2025). CloudFit - The AI-powered PT in your pocket. *Financial Times*. Retrieved from https://www.ft.com/content/d7c1b4b8-2ff6-4b05-8721-1f22aa9527e3

Jangid, A. (2020). AI and employee wellbeing: How artificial intelligence can monitor and improve mental health in the workplace. *International Journal of Advanced Research*, Retrieved from https://www.journalijar.com/article/50677/ai-and-employee-wellbeing-how-artificial-intelligence-can-monitor-and-improve-mental-health-in-the-workplace/

Journal, H. I. P. A. A. (2024, October 10). When AI technology and HIPAA collide. *HIPAA Journal*. Retrieved from https://www.hipaajournal.com/when-ai-technology-and-hipaa-collide/

Kim, B., & Lee, J. (2024). The mental health implications of artificial intelligence adoption: The crucial role of self-efficacy. *Humanities & Social Sciences Communications*, *11*(1), 1–15. https://www.nature.com/articles/s41599-024-04018-w. DOI: 10.1057/s41599-024-04018-w

Mondo. (2024, July 15). The impact of AI on human resources: Opportunities and challenges. *Mondo*. Retrieved from https://mondo.com/insights/impact-of-ai-on-human-resources-opportunities-and-challenges/

Nazareno, L., & Schiff, D. S. (2021). The impact of automation and artificial intelligence on worker well-being. *Technology in Society*, *67*, 101679. DOI: 10.1016/j.techsoc.2021.101679

Parasa, S. K. (2023). Impact of AI in employee wellness and well-being programs. *SSRN*. Retrieved from https://papers.ssrn.com/sol3/papers.cfm?abstract_id=5102825

People Management. (2024). AI integration challenges in HR. *People Management*. Retrieved from https://www.peoplemanagement.co.uk/article/1882806/navigating-ais-impact-employee-wellbeing

Robinson, B. (2023, September 2). Workers using AI technology taking mental health into their own hands. *Forbes*. Retrieved from https://www.forbes.com/sites/bryanrobinson/2023/09/02/workers-taking-wellness-into-their-own-hands-using-ai-backed-mental-health/

Smith, E. (2025, February 15). Elise Smith defends DEI as good business. *Time*. Retrieved from https://time.com/7210609/elise-smith-ceo-dei-good-business/

Society for Human Resource Management (SHRM). (2024, May 10). HR adopts AI. *SHRM*. Retrieved from https://www.shrm.org/topics-tools/news/all-things-work/ai-hr-challenges-opportunities

Soulami, S., Benchekroun, T., & Galiulina, F. (2024). Exploring how AI adoption in the workplace affects employees: A bibliometric and systematic review. *Frontiers in Psychology*, *15*, 11602465. https://www.ncbi.nlm.nih.gov/pmc/articles/PMC11602465/ PMID: 39610851

Stella, L. (2023). Artificial intelligence and workers' well-being. *IZA Discussion Paper No. 16485*. Retrieved from https://docs.iza.org/dp16485.pdf

Tebra. (2024, August 15). Healthcare AI and HIPAA privacy concerns: Everything you need to know. *Tebra*. Retrieved from https://www.tebra.com/theintake/practice-operations/legal-and-compliance/privacy-concerns-with-ai-in-healthcare

The Guardian. (2024). Less admin, more time with people: How an HR professional's job has been transformed by AI. *The Guardian*. Retrieved from https://www.theguardian.com/work-redefined/2024/dec/20/less-admin-more-time-with-people-how-an-hr-professionals-job-has-been-transformed-by-ai

The Guardian. (2025). AI's long-term impact on employee welfare. *The Guardian*. Retrieved from https://www.theguardian.com/business/2025/jan/27/ai-automation-jobs-could-increase-inequality-uk-report

Toxigon. (2025). AI in HR: Enhancing employee engagement. *Toxigon Blog*. Retrieved from https://toxigon.com/ai-in-hr-enhancing-employee-engagement

Wiley Online Library. (2024, August 22). The effects of artificial intelligence on organizational culture in the workplace. *Wiley Online Library*. Retrieved from https://onlinelibrary.wiley.com/doi/10.1002/sres.3037

Womick, B. (2024). Motivating employee acceptance of AI in the workplace. *FIU Business*. Retrieved from https://business.fiu.edu/academics/graduate/doctor-of-business-administration/docs/2024/benjamin-womick-etd.pdf

Workforcestrategist. (2024). AI in employee wellness programs: Revolutionizing workplace well-being. *Workforcestrategist Blog*. Retrieved from https://workforcestrategist.com/index.php/2024/12/20/ai-in-employee-wellness-programs-revolutionizing-workplace-well-being/

Chapter 3
Remote Work Realities and Public Sector Burnout:
Addressing Mental Health, Work-Life Balance, and Sustainable Solutions

Alisha Kumari
https://orcid.org/0009-0004-9304-5570
Lovely Professional University, India

Preet Kanwal
https://orcid.org/0009-0006-5114-8381
Lovely Professional University, India

Shalu Singh
https://orcid.org/0009-0007-5194-8888
Lovely Professional University, India

Monalisha Patel
https://orcid.org/0009-0003-9643-7329
Lovely Professional University, India

Gagandeep Kaur
Chandigarh University, India

Shashank Mittal
https://orcid.org/0000-0002-8666-5323
O.P. Jindal Global University, India

Sandeep Randhawa
https://orcid.org/0009-0001-7436-7943
Conestoga College Institute of Technology and Advanced Learning, Canada

ABSTRACT

Remote work has fundamentally transformed the public sector, offering greater flexibility, enhanced efficiency, and improved service delivery. Nonetheless, it has also brought forth significant challenges, including employee burnout, mental health issues, and difficulties in maintaining work-life balance. The transition to remote work, expedited by the COVID-19 pandemic, has revealed gaps in digital infrastructure, raised cybersecurity concerns, and highlighted disparities in access to remote work opportunities among public sector employees. This chapter delves into the realities of remote work within government institutions, focusing on the challenges employees encounter and the factors that contribute to burnout. It emphasizes the necessity for sustainable solutions, such as flexible work arrangements, mental health initiatives, effective workload management, and stronger managerial support. Additionally, the chapter assesses the role of technology, cybersecurity, and standardized policies as crucial elements in ensuring the long-term success of remote work.

DOI: 10.4018/979-8-3373-1270-5.ch003

INTRODUCTION

Remote work has increasingly become a prevalent practice in the public sector, offering employees greater flexibility and convenience. It eliminates the need for lengthy commutes, enables staff to create customized work environments, and can even enhance productivity. Many public sector employees value the opportunity to work from home, as it allows for better time management and a more effective balance between personal responsibilities and professional duties.

However, alongside these advantages, remote work also presents significant challenges that can adversely affect employees' well-being. Problems such as heightened workloads, feelings of isolation, and difficulties in distinguishing between work and personal life can contribute to increased stress and fatigue. If these issues are not adequately addressed, they may lead to burnout and reduced job satisfaction.

In contrast to private companies, public sector organizations often operate under stringent regulations and heavy workloads. Government employees and other public sector professionals routinely manage essential services, engage in policy-making, and respond to crises, necessitating constant availability. The structured nature of public sector work can make it more challenging to implement flexible work policies that genuinely support employee well-being. Consequently, many workers in this sector report feeling overwhelmed by the persistent pressure to meet high expectationsEmployees often find themselves lacking the necessary resources to effectively manage their workloads. Furthermore, limited technical support, inefficient communication, and a lack of social interaction contribute significantly to work-related stress.

One of the primary challenges faced by remote workers is the increase in workloads and expectations. In a remote environment, many employees report working longer hours than they would in a traditional office setting. Without clear boundaries, the line between work and personal time becomes blurred, making it difficult for individuals to disconnect and recharge. Many public sector workers feel the pressure to remain available beyond regular working hours, responding to emails and participating in virtual meetings at times that disrupt their personal lives. This expectation, coupled with already demanding workloads, can lead to exhaustion and negatively impact mental health.

Social isolation and loneliness present significant challenges for remote public sector employees. Unlike private companies, which often implement structured virtual team-building activities, public organizations frequently lack a similar level of engagement. Many government workers experience a sense of disconnection from their teams and miss the informal interactions that are essential for nurturing workplace relationships. In a traditional office setting, employees can engage in casual conversations, exchange ideas, and receive immediate support from their colleagues. However, in a remote work environment, these spontaneous interactions are greatly diminished. Consequently, employees may feel isolated, unmotivated, and less engaged in their work. Over time, this absence of social connection can lead to diminished job satisfaction and emotional exhaustion.

Another significant issue is the struggle for work-life balance. While one of the primary benefits of remote work is the flexibility it offers, many employees find it difficult to establish clear boundaries between their professional and personal lives. Numerous public sector employees report feeling compelled to check emails or complete tasks outside of regular working hours, resulting in an unhealthy work-life balance. The lack of physical separation between work and home often complicates the ability to create routines that support well-being. As a result, employees may feel as if they are perpetually "on the clock," which can contribute to mental fatigue, stress, and burnout.

Digital overload and technology fatigue significantly contribute to burnout in remote work environments. The heavy reliance on digital platforms for communication, meetings, and project management can feel overwhelming. Employees often find themselves attending back-to-back virtual meetings, responding to an incessant flow of emails, and navigating technical issues that disrupt their productivity. The phenomenon known as "Zoom fatigue" highlights how excessive virtual meetings can lead to mental exhaustion, diminished concentration, and heightened stress levels. The expectation to be perpetually online and accessible for communication complicates employees' ability to concentrate on deep work, further impacting their productivity and mental health.

To tackle these challenges, organizations must implement sustainable solutions that prioritize employee well-being. Establishing clear work policies to define expectations and boundaries can empower employees to manage their workloads more effectively. Encouraging regular breaks, setting limits on after-hours communication, and providing mental health support are vital steps in preventing burnout. Additionally, organizations should enhance virtual team engagement through structured social activities, regular check-ins, and peer support programs.

UNDERSTANDING REMOTE WORK IN THE PUBLIC SECTOR

Evolution and Adoption of Remote Work in the Public Sector

Remote work was once a rarity, particularly in government roles, as public services typically necessitated in-person interactions. However, advancements in technology, coupled with the COVID-19 pandemic that compelled many to work from home, transformed remote work into a necessity. Governments had to swiftly adapt by implementing digital tools and online services to maintain public office operations while ensuring employee safety.

Prior to the pandemic, many government agencies viewed remote work as impractical due to the bureaucratic nature of public service (Liu et al., 2021). Processes often relied on paperwork, in-person approvals, and face-to-face meetings. Nonetheless, with the evolution of digital technology, governments recognized that remote work could enhance efficiency. The introduction of online meetings, cloud storage, and secure communication platforms enabled employees to operate from home without compromising essential services.

Countries such as Canada, the United States, and the United Kingdom have taken the lead in establishing remote work policies for public sector employees. These governments developed telework policies, digital security measures, and flexible work arrangements to facilitate employee adaptation. While remote work offers significant advantages, including increased flexibility and improved work-life balance, it also presents challenges such as cybersecurity threats, inadequate digital infrastructure, and difficulties in sustaining employee engagement.

Despite the challenges, remote work is anticipated to continue playing a significant role in the public sector. Numerous government agencies are currently formulating long-term strategies for remote work, investing in digital tools, and equipping employees with the necessary training to work effectively from home. By tackling these challenges, governments can cultivate a more adaptable and efficient workforce while maintaining their commitment to serving the public effectively.

Current Trends in Public Sector Remote Work

Many government offices have embraced a hybrid work model, allowing employees to alternate between working from home and commuting to the office. This approach offers flexibility for workers while ensuring that essential in-person tasks continue to be completed. Thanks to digital tools such as video conferencing, cloud storage, and online collaboration platforms, remote work has become more manageable and efficient.

However, this transition has also presented some challenges. Concerns about productivity and accountability continue to loom, as some managers worry that employees may not perform as efficiently at home as they do in the office (Hernández et al., 2021). Additionally, mental health poses a significant issue; remote work can lead to feelings of isolation or burnout, particularly for those who struggle to maintain a work-life balance.

Despite these challenges, studies indicate that hybrid work can enhance job satisfaction. Employees appreciate the increased flexibility, which supports a healthier work-life balance. To facilitate successful remote work, governments are investing in cybersecurity measures to safeguard sensitive data, providing training programs to help employees adapt to digital tools, and implementing workflow management systems to ensure smooth operations.

Not all government agencies implement remote work policies uniformly. Some departments provide greater flexibility, while others maintain a strong emphasis on in-office work. This disparity results in unequal workloads and varying employee experiences, highlighting the need for governments to establish standardized remote work policies that benefit all public sector workers equitably.

THE SHIFT TO REMOTE WORK IN THE PUBLIC SECTOR

Historical Resistance to Remote Work

Prior to the COVID-19 pandemic, remote work was relatively rare in the public sector, largely due to the perception that in-office presence was essential for maintaining efficiency. Many government roles required the handling of sensitive documents, delivering direct public services, and conducting in-person meetings, which made the idea of remote work appear impractical. Furthermore, managers often believed that direct supervision was necessary for employee productivity. Concerns about cybersecurity also played a significant role, as remote work could increase the risk of exposing sensitive government data. Consequently, most public sector organizations refrained from investing in digital tools or flexible work arrangements. Even as private companies began to explore remote work options, government agencies remained cautious, fearing that reduced physical presence might hinder operations and diminish accountability.

Pandemic as a Catalyst for Change

The COVID-19 crisis compelled public sector organizations to swiftly transition to remote work to ensure employee safety while continuing to provide essential services. Governments had no alternative but to adapt, resulting in an unprecedented wave of digital transformation. Initially, this shift presented challenges, as many agencies were ill-equipped with the necessary technology and protocols for remote operations. However, governments promptly implemented solutions such as virtual communication platforms, cloud-based document management systems, and remote access to critical databases (Hersch et al., 2022). Employees received training to utilize these tools, and new cybersecurity policies were established to safeguard sensitive information. Despite some initial resistance, many organizations soon recognized that remote work could be both efficient and sustainable. This experience of adaptation fundamentally altered long-standing perceptions, demonstrating that with the appropriate technology and policies, government employees could effectively work outside of traditional office settings (Hersch et al., 2022).

Adoption of Digital Tools and Infrastructure

To facilitate remote work, public sector organizations swiftly embraced digital tools that fostered collaboration and efficiency. Governments made substantial investments in cloud storage systems for document sharing, video conferencing platforms for virtual meetings, and workflow management software to optimize operations. Employees received training to effectively use these new tools; however, the transition was not without its challenges. Some government agencies encountered difficulties due to outdated computer systems that were incompatible with modern digital platforms. Others struggled with slow internet connections, especially in rural or underdeveloped areas, where accessing online systems proved problematic. Moreover, the shift to remote work heightened cybersecurity risks, exposing organizations to new vulnerabilities for cyberattacks. In response, governments enhanced their security protocols by implementing encrypted communication, multi-factor authentication, and virtual private networks (VPNs) to safeguard sensitive data. Despite these obstacles, the adoption of digital tools significantly increased the efficiency of public sector operations and established a foundation for long-term remote work strategies (P & P, 2024).

Hybrid Work Models Becoming the Norm

Many public sector organizations have opted for hybrid work arrangements instead of a fully remote model. In this setup, employees divide their time between working from home and being in the office. This approach allows employees to handle administrative and routine tasks remotely while coming into the office for meetings, document processing, or activities that necessitate their physical presence. Hybrid work models provide greater flexibility, allowing employees to minimize commuting time and achieve a better work-life balance. However, challenges persist, particularly in maintaining team collaboration and ensuring equitable access to remote work opportunities. Additionally, certain employees, such as frontline workers in healthcare, law enforcement, and public safety, are unable to work remotely, which creates disparities in work flexibility. To address these issues, governments are striving to standardize hybrid work policies to ensure that all employees have fair access to flexible work arrangements. Looking ahead, hybrid work is expected to become a permanent aspect of the public sector, combining in-office collaboration with the advantages of remote work (Darouei & Pluut, 2021).

Challenges of Remote Work Implementation

The abrupt transition to remote work presented numerous challenges for both employees and management. Many workers found it difficult to maintain productivity due to household distractions, childcare obligations, and the absence of a quiet, dedicated workspace. Additionally, some struggled to uphold a structured routine, which resulted in diminished focus and efficiency. Conversely, managers encountered obstacles in monitoring performance, providing timely feedback, and ensuring accountability in a remote environment (Sutarto et al., 2021). Furthermore, not all employees had equal access to high-speed internet, modern devices, or secure remote access to government systems, leading to a digital divide. Governments were compelled to swiftly develop and implement remote work policies to address these disparities, ensuring fairness in workload distribution and resource allocation. Some agencies offered financial assistance for home office setups, while others adjusted their work expectations to better fit the realities of remote work. Despite these initiatives, inconsistencies in policy implementation continue to pose concerns across various government departments.

Impact on Employee Well-Being

Remote work, while providing greater flexibility, has also brought new mental health challenges for public sector employees. Many have reported feelings of isolation and disconnection from their teams due to the absence of in-person interactions. Without the spontaneous collaboration that occurs in an office environment, employees often feel emotionally detached from their work. Additionally, the blurring of boundaries between professional and personal life has contributed to heightened stress levels(Wyatt, 2024). Numerous employees find themselves working beyond standard hours, checking emails late at night, or feeling pressured to remain constantly available, leading to burnout, decreased motivation, and lower job satisfaction. In response to these challenges, governments have begun to implement wellness programs that include virtual counseling, stress management workshops, and designated "no-meeting" days to combat screen fatigue. Some agencies have also introduced flexible work hours, enabling employees to better manage their schedules and prioritize their mental health. However, sustained efforts are necessary to ensure the long-term well-being of employees.

Security and Data Protection Concerns

Public sector employees handle vast amounts of confidential data, making cybersecurity a significant concern in remote work environments. Unlike traditional office settings with controlled security measures, remote work poses potential risks such as unauthorized access, phishing attacks, and data breaches. In response, many government agencies have implemented measures like virtual private networks (VPNs), encrypted email communication, and multi-factor authentication to bolster security. Employees have also received training on best practices for cybersecurity, including recognizing fraudulent emails and creating strong passwords. Despite these initiatives, remote work continues to be susceptible to cyber threats, necessitating ongoing investments in security infrastructure (Corrigan et al., 2022). Governments must also establish stringent compliance policies to regulate the handling of sensitive data in home environments. Regular audits, real-time monitoring of government networks, and advancements in artificial intelligence-based security tools will be critical in preserving a secure remote work atmosphere.

Future of Remote Work in Government

Remote work is likely to remain a permanent aspect of the public sector, but enhancements are necessary for its long-term success. Governments must invest in improved digital infrastructure to facilitate seamless remote operations. This investment includes providing employees with reliable devices, upgrading outdated systems, and expanding broadband access in underserved areas. Additionally, fair and transparent remote work policies should be put in place to ensure that all employees, regardless of their job roles, have equitable access to remote work opportunities (Oksa et al., 2021). Establishing standardized guidelines for performance evaluation, communication expectations, and career development for remote workers will help maintain productivity while promoting fairness. To future-proof remote work, governments should also prioritize continuous employee training, enhancements in cybersecurity, and initiatives focused on mental health. By addressing these areas, the public sector can cultivate a sustainable, efficient, and employee-friendly remote work environment that upholds high service standards for citizens.

IMPACT ON MENTAL HEALTH

Increased Stress and Anxiety

Remote work in the public sector often entails managing sensitive information, addressing crises, and navigating complex bureaucratic processes. Employees may experience heightened stress due to heavy workloads, limited immediate support, and challenges in achieving a work-life balance. The uncertainty stemming from policy changes, concerns about job security, and evolving work expectations further exacerbates anxiety levels.

Those in high-pressure roles, such as healthcare, emergency response, and social services, face even greater emotional strain. Handling difficult cases remotely—without the benefit of immediate peer support—can result in emotional fatigue and burnout. Many employees find it challenging to "switch off" from work, leading to a persistent state of mental exhaustion(P & P, 2024).

Social Isolation and Loneliness

A significant challenge of remote work is the sense of disconnection from colleagues. Unlike in-person settings, where employees can engage in casual conversations and team activities, remote workers often miss out on these social interactions. Particularly within the public sector, there may be fewer structured virtual team-building activities compared to the private sector. This lack of connection can foster feelings of loneliness, diminish motivation, and lead to lower job satisfaction.

Workplace relationships are crucial for fostering engagement and productivity. In a physical office, informal chats, shared lunch breaks, and spontaneous discussions contribute to a sense of belonging (Shimura et al., 2021). The absence of these natural interactions in remote work can make employees feel isolated and disengaged from their teams. Research indicates that prolonged remote work can heighten stress levels and diminish overall job performance.

Psychological Effects of Digital Overload

Remote work is heavily dependent on technology, resulting in constant exposure to screens, emails, and virtual meetings. This excessive reliance on digital tools can lead to cognitive overload, fatigue, and stress. Employees often feel pressured to respond to messages promptly, attend back-to-back online meetings, and juggle multiple tasks simultaneously.

A prevalent issue, commonly referred to as "Zoom fatigue," arises when employees feel exhausted from frequent video calls. Continuous virtual interactions demand extra effort to interpret body language and maintain engagement, which can result in mental exhaustion and diminished concentration. Furthermore, the expectation to be "always online" complicates the ability of employees to take breaks, contributing to burnout and emotional stress.

Work-Life Imbalance

The remote work environment often blurs the lines between professional and personal life. Many employees struggle to "log off" after work hours, leading to longer workdays and diminished personal time. The lack of physical separation between home and work settings makes it challenging to relax and unwind.

In the absence of clear work schedules and designated break times, employees may feel compelled to remain constantly available, even during evenings and weekends. Over time, this lack of adequate rest can lead to exhaustion, frustration, and a decline in mental well-being.

Sleep Problems and Fatigue

Sleep issues and fatigue are prevalent among employees who face high stress and extended working hours. Many public sector workers experience disrupted sleep patterns due to late-night tasks, excessive screen time, and the habit of checking emails before bedtime. This lack of restorative sleep results in fatigue, diminished concentration, and lower energy levels, which hinder effective performance in daily activities. Over time, inadequate sleep can also lead to irritability, mood swings, and increased anxiety, adversely affecting mental health and overall well-being.

Declines in motivation and job satisfaction often arise when employees feel overburdened, isolated, and mentally drained. In the absence of workplace social interactions, appropriate recognition, or opportunities for career advancement, employees may lose their enthusiasm for work (Wyatt, 2024). This reduction in motivation typically results in decreased productivity and an overall sense of dissatisfaction. If burnout persists, employees may become disengaged from their responsibilities, feeling unfulfilled or even contemplating leaving their jobs. Organizations need to tackle these challenges by ensuring a healthy work-life balance, implementing recognition programs, and offering professional development opportunities to maintain employee motivation and satisfaction.

Challenges in Work-Life Balance

The blending of work and personal life presents significant challenges. Remote work often obscures the boundaries between professional duties and personal time, making it difficult for employees to disconnect. Public sector employees frequently find themselves responding to emails and attending meetings beyond standard working hours. This "always-on" culture contributes to exhaustion and diminishes overall well-being. For instance, many government employees in crisis management are expected to remain available at all times, complicating the establishment of clear work boundaries. Without appropriate policies in place, employees struggle to maintain a healthy equilibrium between their work and home lives.

Increased Workload and Expectations

With the rise of remote work, many public sector employees are grappling with an increased workload. The expectation to remain constantly available often blurs the lines between work and personal time, leading to extended hours on the job. This pressure to demonstrate productivity can result in employees working longer hours, which diminishes their ability to rest and recharge. Research indicates that a significant number of public sector workers put in extra hours to meet deadlines, particularly in demanding fields such as healthcare and social services. The lack of structured office routines contributes to erratic work schedules, further exacerbating stress and burnout.

Additionally, not all employees have access to a dedicated workspace at home, which can lead to discomfort and decreased productivity (Oksa et al., 2021). Challenges such as unreliable internet connectivity, inadequate workstations, and various household distractions complicate the remote work experience. Public sector employees from lower-income backgrounds may face particularly significant obstacles, such as poor internet access and insufficient ergonomic furniture, adding to the stress of working from home. For instance, teachers conducting lessons remotely may lack the necessary digital tools to engage effectively with their students, resulting in frustration and diminished efficiency. Organizations must acknowledge these challenges and invest in solutions to ensure equitable working conditions for all employees.

Disruptions from Household Responsibilities

Remote work presents challenges for employees striving to balance their professional responsibilities with household duties, such as childcare and eldercare. Unlike an office environment, where one can concentrate solely on work, home settings are often subject to frequent interruptions. For instance, a public sector employee may find themselves juggling virtual meetings while simultaneously overseeing their children's schoolwork or caring for elderly family members. These distractions can diminish productivity and heighten stress levels. In many cases, employees resort to working late hours to make up for lost time, which can ultimately lead to burnout. Organizations can alleviate some of these pressures by offering flexible work schedules, providing childcare support, and encouraging employees to establish clear boundaries between their work and home lives.

Lack of Clear Performance Metrics

Many remote workers face uncertainty regarding how their performance is evaluated. In the absence of direct supervision, employees may fear that their contributions go unnoticed. For example, a government employee who completes a significant report might not receive timely feedback, resulting in stress and self-doubt. This ambiguity can drive employees to overexert themselves in an attempt to demonstrate their productivity. To address these challenges, organizations should establish clear performance expectations, provide consistent feedback, and utilize project management tools to monitor progress. Implementing transparent evaluation systems can help alleviate anxiety and enhance motivation.

Reduced Opportunities for Career Growth

Remote employees frequently miss out on valuable networking, training, and leadership opportunities, which can hinder their career progression. In contrast to their in-office counterparts, they have fewer chances for informal interactions that can lead to promotions. For instance, a remote public sector worker may successfully complete significant projects yet remain overlooked compared to colleagues working in the office (Corrigan et al., 2022). To address this, organizations should implement virtual mentorship programs, offer online training, and ensure that remote employees are included in decision-making discussions. Providing equal access to career growth opportunities helps keep all employees motivated and engaged.

Burnout in the Public Sector

Burnout is a state in which employees experience physical, mental, and emotional exhaustion resulting from prolonged stress. This phenomenon is particularly prevalent in the public sector, where workers operate under rigid policies, serve vast populations, and contend with constant pressure. The following are key factors that contribute to burnout in public sector positions.

Contributing Factors to Burnout

1. High Workload

Public sector employees frequently face a heavy workload, which can be overwhelming, particularly in a remote work environment. Many government offices and agencies operate with limited staff, forcing employees to assume multiple responsibilities. In a remote setting, the boundaries between work and personal life often become blurred, making it challenging to disconnect and rest adequately.

For instance, a government employee in public administration may be tasked with processing documents, responding to inquiries, and attending virtual meetings— all while managing an increasing number of responsibilities due to staff shortages. Given that public services must remain operational at all times, employees often find themselves working overtime to keep pace with their workload. The lack of a structured office environment further complicates the establishment of boundaries. Employees may feel compelled to check emails late at night, work on weekends, or tackle additional tasks beyond their standard hours. Over time, this persistent workload can lead to stress, fatigue, and eventual burnout.

To mitigate these challenges, organizations should focus on implementing equitable workload distribution and establishing clear expectations regarding work hours. Promoting regular breaks, hiring additional staff when feasible, and providing mental health support can help employees better manage their workload. Effective workload management allows employees to maintain productivity without experiencing exhaustion.

2. Emotional Exhaustion

Many public sector roles involve emotionally demanding tasks that can lead to employee fatigue over time. Professionals in healthcare, social services, and law enforcement frequently confront sensitive situations, manage crises, and make life-altering decisions. This emotional burden, coupled with long hours, often results in exhaustion and burnout.

For instance, a social worker addressing cases related to child protection or domestic violence must navigate challenging conversations, provide support to struggling families, and make critical decisions that affect lives. Likewise, a government healthcare worker responding to public health crises is tasked with managing high-stress situations while prioritizing the well-being of the community.

In contrast to office jobs that typically involve routine tasks, emotionally demanding positions call for deep engagement, empathy, and sound decision-making, which can leave employees feeling mentally drained. Over time, this ongoing exposure to stress can diminish motivation and job satisfaction, making it increasingly difficult for employees to remain engaged in their work.

Organizations can mitigate emotional exhaustion by offering counseling services, conducting regular debriefing sessions, and establishing peer support programs. Encouraging staff to take mental health days and fostering a supportive work culture can significantly alleviate the emotional toll associated with their responsibilities.

3. Job Insecurity

Public sector employees often grapple with uncertainties surrounding job security, largely due to evolving government policies, budget constraints, and changing political priorities. This instability generates stress as employees worry about potential layoffs, restructuring, or alterations to their roles.

For instance, a government employee in an environmental agency may be apprehensive that funding cuts could jeopardize their position. Likewise, public school teachers might face similar concerns stemming from shifts in education policies, which can lead to anxiety about their future employment.

Contrary to private sector jobs, where companies may enjoy stable contracts and opportunities for growth, public sector workers are directly influenced by government decisions. When budgets are slashed or policies are revised, employees may confront abrupt job losses or be compelled to take on different responsibilities than those for which they were originally hired.

This climate of uncertainty can contribute to heightened anxiety among employees, negatively impacting their mental health and overall performance. Many feel compelled to overextend themselves or continuously demonstrate their value in a bid to secure their positions.

4. Bureaucratic Work Environment

The public sector operates under stringent regulations and intricate decision-making processes. In contrast to private companies that can swiftly adapt and implement changes, government organizations must navigate a maze of regulations, approvals, and protracted procedures. This sluggishness often leads to employee frustration, fostering a sense of powerlessness in their roles.

For example, a government employee involved in a community development project may find it challenging to implement initiatives due to the necessity of obtaining multiple levels of approval and completing extensive paperwork. Even when urgent changes are required, the bureaucratic system can postpone decisions for months, resulting in inefficiency and stress.

Moreover, employees often perceive that their ideas and suggestions go unappreciated due to the rigid organizational structure. Unlike private sector firms that promote innovation and quick problem-solving, public sector workers must contend with numerous layers of authority before any progress can be made.

To address these challenges, organizations can streamline approval processes, empower employees to take initiative, and enhance internal communication. Cultivating a culture where workers feel heard and valued can significantly reduce frustration and improve overall job satisfaction.

5. Lack of Managerial Support

Many public sector employees report feeling unsupported by their managers, particularly in remote work environments. In the absence of proper guidance, acknowledgment, and constructive feedback, employees may experience a sense of disconnection and undervaluation, which can lead to increased stress and burnout.

For instance, a government employee in public administration might submit reports and projects without receiving any feedback from their supervisor. When managers neglect to communicate clear expectations or recognize their employees' efforts, workers often feel unappreciated and uncertain about their performance.

The challenges of remote work further exacerbate this situation, as employees have fewer opportunities for direct interactions with their supervisors. Without regular check-ins or team discussions, employees may feel isolated and lack the direction necessary to navigate their roles effectively.

To address these issues, public sector organizations should encourage managers to foster open lines of communication with their employees. Implementing regular virtual meetings, feedback sessions, and recognition programs can help employees feel valued and supported. Cultivating strong leadership is essential for reducing burnout and enhancing employee morale.

6. Difficulty Maintaining Work-Life Balance

Remote work has blurred the lines between personal and professional lives for many public sector employees. With no clear separation between work and home, employees often find themselves working beyond regular hours, which can lead to stress and exhaustion.

For example, a government worker involved in emergency response may feel the pressure to remain available at all times, including evenings and weekends. Similarly, a policy analyst might be expected to submit urgent reports outside of their standard work hours.

Without a structured office environment, employees often struggle to establish boundaries. Many experience guilt when taking breaks or stepping away from work, resulting in longer hours and increased mental fatigue.

To enhance work-life balance, organizations should set clear expectations regarding work hours and encourage employees to disconnect after their shifts. Implementing wellness programs and nurturing a culture that respects personal time can significantly help employees manage their workloads more effectively.

7. Limited Career Growth Opportunities

Many public sector employees often feel stagnant in their roles due to slow promotion cycles and limited opportunities for professional development. Unlike private sector companies that typically allow for quicker advancement, government jobs often adhere to strict seniority-based promotion systems, which can hinder employees' career progression.

For instance, a junior public administrator may spend years in their position without any avenue for promotion or added responsibilities. Those seeking professional growth may become frustrated when they perceive minimal chances for advancement.

Furthermore, the shift to remote work has diminished informal networking opportunities, making it more challenging for employees to cultivate relationships that foster career growth. In the absence of mentorship programs or leadership training, many workers may feel unmotivated and disengaged.

Organizations can remedy this situation by providing professional development initiatives, mentorship opportunities, and clearly defined career progression paths. Offering training in leadership, digital skills, and management can empower employees, enhancing their confidence about the future and helping them maintain motivation in their roles.

8. Limited Resources and Outdated Technology

Public sector employees frequently encounter challenges related to limited resources, including outdated technology and inadequate funding(Doberstein & Charbonneau, 2022; Vladi et al., 2024). In contrast to private companies that prioritize investments in modern tools and automation, many government organizations continue to operate with antiquated systems, leading to time-consuming and frustrating tasks.

For instance, a government employee tasked with processing public records may rely on outdated software that often crashes or lacks automation, compelling them to complete tasks manually. This inefficiency not only increases their workload but also elevates stress levels, as employees find themselves bogged down by repetitive tasks rather than engaging in more meaningful work.

Moreover, budget constraints often hinder the ability to hire additional staff, resulting in existing employees taking on extra responsibilities (Williamson et al., 2022). In critical fields such as emergency services, healthcare, or administrative departments, this can lead to employee burnout, diminished productivity, and overall job dissatisfaction.

To alleviate burnout stemming from resource limitations, governments should prioritize investments in modern technology, automate repetitive tasks, and equip employees with superior tools. Upgrading digital infrastructure and ensuring adequate budgets for staffing can significantly reduce employee stress and enhance overall efficiency.

9. Increased Public Scrutiny and Pressure

Public sector employees often operate under significant scrutiny, as their actions and decisions have a direct impact on citizens. In contrast to private sector positions, where accountability typically lies within the organization, government workers are subject to strict regulations and face public criticism for any missteps (Allgood et al., 2022; Barboza-Wilkes et al., 2022).

For instance, an official in a social welfare department may encounter backlash for delays in benefit processing. Likewise, a public health worker overseeing pandemic responses could be held accountable for slow policy implementation, even when the decisions are beyond their control.

This persistent pressure to achieve perfection can result in anxiety, stress, and a fear of making mistakes. Employees may feel overwhelmed by unrealistic expectations, media scrutiny, and public dissatisfaction, all of which can contribute to burnout.

To mitigate these challenges, governments should offer training in stress management, media relations, and crisis communication. Fostering a supportive work environment and recognizing employees' efforts can empower them to cope more effectively with external pressures.

COMPARISON WITH PRIVATE SECTOR BURNOUT RATES

Burnout occurs in both public and private sectors, but public employees often experience higher burnout levels due to the following reasons:

Less Flexibility

Private companies provide flexible work schedules, remote work options, and mental health breaks, enabling employees to achieve a better balance between their professional and personal lives. In contrast, public sector jobs typically enforce strict schedules and offer limited opportunities for remote work, which can make time management more challenging for employees (Allgood et al., 2022; Barboza-Wilkes et al., 2022). For instance, a private sector employee may have the ability to adjust their hours, whereas a government employee is often required to adhere to fixed shifts. This lack of flexibility can contribute to increased stress and burnout. By introducing more flexibility in public sector positions—such as adjustable start times or hybrid work models—employees could better manage their responsibilities and reduce feelings of exhaustion.

Resource Constraints

Public sector organizations often face budget constraints that limit their ability to hire additional staff or implement wellness programs. As a result, employees find themselves taking on extra responsibilities, which can lead to exhaustion. For instance, government healthcare workers may be compelled to work overtime due to staff shortages, whereas private hospitals can afford to hire more personnel (Toscano & Zappalà, 2020; Sofianti et al., 2023). Moreover, public employees frequently lack access to wellness benefits, such as mental health counseling, that are commonly offered by private companies. By investing in employee support systems, enhancing staffing levels, and introducing stress management programs, the public sector can help mitigate burnout and enhance job satisfaction..

Slower Decision-Making

Public sector organizations adhere to stringent bureaucratic processes, which often hinder the swift implementation of solutions aimed at enhancing employee well-being. Changes in policy, necessary approvals, and funding allocations can take months, leaving employees without timely support. For instance, when government workers experience burnout, the introduction of wellness programs or flexible working hours can be significantly delayed by these protracted administrative procedures. In contrast, private companies possess the agility to rapidly adjust their policies and offer benefits. By streamlining approval processes and prioritizing initiatives related to employee well-being, public sector employees can receive support more promptly, thereby mitigating frustration and burnout.

Higher Public Pressure

Public sector employees operate under continuous public scrutiny, as their decisions have a direct impact on citizens. Unlike private companies that primarily focus on serving clients, government workers frequently face criticism from both the public and political leaders. For instance, a transportation worker may be held responsible for delays, even when those delays are due to external factors. This constant pressure can lead to heightened stress and job dissatisfaction. To help public employees manage public pressure more effectively and maintain motivation in their roles, it is beneficial to provide stress management training, mental health support, and workplace appreciation programs(Rakha, 2023; Khatib et al., 2024).

Sustainable Solutions to Address Burnout

To reduce burnout in the public sector, organizations need to adopt long-term strategies that support employee well-being. Sustainable solutions should focus on improving work conditions, reducing stress, and promoting a healthier work-life balance. Below are some key strategies that can help address burnout effectively.

ORGANIZATIONAL STRATEGIES

1. Flexible Work Policies

Flexible work policies play a crucial role in helping employees achieve a healthy balance between their professional and personal lives. By establishing clear working hours, employers can prevent overworking, and promoting regular breaks enhances both productivity and overall well-being. A hybrid work model, which allows employees to alternate between working from home and being in the office, combines the advantages of both settings. This arrangement enables employees to concentrate better at home while still fostering collaboration when in the office. For instance, government employees who handle paperwork can efficiently work remotely, whereas those involved in public services can engage in in-person interactions. The implementation of such policies effectively reduces stress and makes work more manageable.

2. Mental Health Support

Providing mental health support is crucial for preventing employee burnout. Organizations can implement counseling services and mental health hotlines, allowing employees to seek help in a confidential manner. Stress management workshops equip employees with tools to manage work-related pressure, enhancing their resiliencepractices (Williamson et al., 2020; Williamson et al., 2022). Wellness programs, including virtual yoga, mindfulness exercises, and designated mental health days, offer employees valuable opportunities to relax and recharge. For example, a government office could launch wellness initiatives aimed at helping employees reduce stress and maintain positive mental health. By prioritizing mental well-being, organizations foster a more motivated and productive workforce.

3. Technology Management

Effective management of technology can significantly alleviate feelings of overwhelm among employees. Organizations should restrict after-hours emails and work-related communications to honor employees' personal time. Promoting "focus time" enables staff to work without the constant disruptions of meetings or notifications. Furthermore, employing automation and AI tools for repetitive tasks can help lighten workloads, allowing employees to concentrate on more meaningful work. For instance, automated data entry in public sector offices can save hours that would otherwise be spent on manual tasks(Williamson et al., 2022). By establishing clear boundaries around technology use, organizations can enhance efficiency while mitigating the risk of digital burnout.

4. Regular Check-Ins and Team Engagement

Regular check-ins foster a sense of connection and support among employees. Managers should arrange virtual meetings to share updates and provide feedback, ensuring that employees feel valued and heard. Informal check-ins offer a platform for employees to voice their concerns, contributing to a more nurturing work environment. Engaging team activities, such as virtual social events or online games, enable employees to maintain connections even when working remotely. For instance, a government department could facilitate monthly online gatherings to boost morale. These initiatives enhance teamwork, alleviate feelings of isolation, and promote a positive workplace culture.

5. Clear Role Expectations and Task Prioritization

Clearly defining job roles helps prevent employees from becoming overloaded with work. Managers should establish realistic expectations to ensure that employees fully understand their responsibilities without feeling overwhelmed(Parwoto et al., 2024; Elnanto & Suharti, 2021). By prioritizing urgent tasks and delegating responsibilities equitably, work can be completed more efficiently. It is also vital for employees to feel comfortable expressing their concerns if they are feeling stressed. For instance, in a city planning office, projects can be assigned based on individual expertise, rather than placing the burden on a single team member. By clarifying expectations, employees are better equipped to manage their tasks effectively, leading to a reduction in workplace stress.

6. Encouraging Physical Activity and Healthy Lifestyle

Public sector employees often find themselves spending long hours seated, which can lead to both physical and mental fatigue. To promote wellness, organizations can encourage short movement breaks, provide access to virtual fitness sessions, and advocate for healthy eating habits. Initiatives such as step challenges or online workout classes can significantly boost energy levels and alleviate stress. Additionally, encouraging employees to take regular breaks from screens can enhance focus and overall well-being. Embracing a healthy lifestyle not only improves physical health but also sharpens mental clarity, enabling employees to remain engaged and motivated while minimizing the risk of burnout.

7. Strengthening Leadership Support and Recognition

Supportive leadership is essential in preventing burnout. Managers should routinely check in with their employees, offer constructive feedback, and acknowledge their hard work. Demonstrating appreciation through verbal praise, awards, or small incentives can significantly enhance morale and motivation. When employees feel valued and supported, they are more likely to remain engaged and productive(Williamson et al., 2022; Parwoto et al., 2024). Equipping managers to recognize the signs of burnout and to provide assistance fosters a more empathetic and supportive work environment. Leadership that prioritizes employee well-being cultivates a culture of trust, which in turn reduces stress and enhances job satisfaction.

8. Promoting Employee Autonomy and Trust

Micromanagement can lead to burnout by causing employees to feel undervalued and overly controlled. Organizations should empower their staff by granting them autonomy over their tasks and schedules. By trusting employees to manage their workloads independently, organizations can foster confidence and alleviate stress. When employees have the flexibility to approach their work in a way that resonates with them, they become more engaged and motivated. Emphasizing a results-oriented approach, rather than adhering to rigid work hours, helps employees maintain productivity while also promoting a healthier work-life balance(Williamson et al., 2020; Williamson et al., 2022).

POLICY RECOMMENDATIONS

1. Workload Management

Effectively managing workload is essential to preventing employee burnout. Organizations should establish realistic performance objectives that align with employees' capabilities rather than overwhelming them with excessive tasks(Giauque et al., 2022). Work should also be equitably distributed among team members to ensure that no individual is disproportionately burdened. In departments experiencing staff shortages, hiring additional personnel can alleviate stress and enhance overall efficiency. For instance, in a public health department, bringing on more staff during peak demand periods can help prevent burnout among current employees. When employees have manageable workloads, they are able to perform at their best, remain motivated, and sustain a healthy work-life balance.

2. Recognition and Compensation

Acknowledging employees' contributions fosters a sense of value and motivation within the workforce. Organizations should consider implementing performance-based bonuses or incentives to reward dedicated efforts. Additionally, simple expressions of appreciation, such as recognition messages or awards for achievements, can significantly enhance morale. Offering career advancement opportunities, including promotions or skill-based salary increases, further encourages employee engagement. For instance, a government office might establish an "Employee of the Month" program or provide leadership training for high achievers. When employees feel acknowledged and compensated for their efforts, they are more likely to remain committed to their roles and experience reduced burnout.

3. Training and Skill Development Programs

Continuous training equips employees to navigate work challenges more effectively. Time management workshops can instruct employees on how to organize tasks efficiently. Resilience training offers coping strategies for stress, empowering employees to remain emotionally strong. Digital skills programs assist employees in adapting to remote work tools, thereby simplifying their roles. For example, a city administration office could provide workshops on utilizing virtual meeting platforms, which would help alleviate frustrations with technology. When employees feel confident in their abilities, they are less likely to suffer from stress and burnout(Giauque et al., 2022).

4. Encouraging a Healthy Work Culture

A supportive work culture fosters a sense of safety and appreciation among employees. Organizations should encourage open dialogue about mental health, ensuring that employees can seek assistance without the fear of judgment. Managers ought to set a positive example by respecting work-life boundaries and actively encouraging employees to take breaks. Providing mental health leave allows employees the necessary time to recover when needed. For instance, a public service agency might introduce "no-meeting Fridays" to help alleviate stress. A positive work environment enhances employee morale, leading to greater engagement and job satisfaction.

5. Improving Resource Allocation

Ensuring that employees have the appropriate resources is essential for them to perform their jobs effectively. Organizations should prioritize investments in mental health programs and well-being initiatives, such as counseling services and wellness workshops. Additionally, employees require access to the right tools, including updated software and dependable technology, to work proficiently. By eliminating unnecessary bureaucratic procedures, tasks can be simplified, thereby reducing work-related stress(Cromarty et al., 2020). For instance, a government agency could implement automated systems to enhance administrative efficiency. When employees are equipped with the right resources, they can concentrate better, experience lower stress levels, and ultimately achieve greater job satisfaction.

6. Strengthening Managerial Support

Support from managers is vital in alleviating burnout among employees. Leaders should provide consistent feedback, acknowledge achievements, and regularly check in with their team to understand any challenges they may face. It's also important for managers to offer guidance on workload management and promote the importance of taking breaks. For instance, in a government office, a supervisor might schedule one-on-one meetings to discuss concerns and propose solutions. When employees feel heard and supported, their motivation increases and stress levels decrease. A robust relationship between employees and managers fosters a positive work environment where individuals feel valued and engaged.

7. Enhancing Employee Autonomy

Empowering employees with greater control over their tasks and schedules can significantly enhance job satisfaction and mitigate burnout. Allowing workers to establish flexible work hours or prioritize their own tasks aids in better stress management. For instance, a public administration department could permit employees to complete non-urgent tasks at their own pace, thereby alleviating pressure (Rhee, 2008). When individuals have the freedom to make choices, they tend to feel more accountable for their work, which often results in increased motivation and efficiency. Fostering independence while maintaining clear expectations enables employees to remain productive without becoming overwhelmed.

8. Promoting Social Connection and Teamwork

Remote work can result in feelings of isolation, causing employees to feel disconnected from their teams. To mitigate this, organizations should promote team-building activities, virtual social events, and collaborative opportunities to strengthen workplace relationships. For example, a local government agency could arrange virtual coffee breaks or online team challenges to keep employees engaged. Cultivating strong workplace connections enhances morale, fosters teamwork, and offers emotional support during challenging times. When employees feel connected to their colleagues, they are more likely to find enjoyment in their work and experience lower levels of burnout.

THE FUTURE OF REMOTE WORK IN THE PUBLIC SECTOR

Hybrid Work as the New Standard

The future of remote work in the public sector is expected to adopt a hybrid model, where employees alternate between remote and in-office work. This strategy offers flexibility while ensuring that essential in-person tasks are accomplished. Governments around the world are implementing structured hybrid policies to strike a balance between productivity and employee well-being. For instance, administrative staff may work remotely, whereas frontline employees in law enforcement or healthcare may need to be present in the office. A hybrid work environment allows employees to alleviate commuting stress while fostering workplace collaboration. To ensure the success of this model, organizations must establish clear schedules, set realistic expectations, and provide the necessary digital tools to facilitate smooth workflows(Vries et al., 2018).

Investment in Digital Infrastructure

As remote work becomes increasingly prevalent, public sector organizations must prioritize investments in robust digital infrastructure. Essential components such as high-speed internet, secure cloud storage, and advanced communication platforms are critical for maintaining efficient remote operations. Unfortunately, many government agencies continue to rely on outdated systems, underscoring the urgent need for digital transformation. By investing in user-friendly and secure technology, productivity can be enhanced, and delays caused by technical issues can be minimized. Furthermore, it is imperative for governments to provide training on digital tools to improve employee adaptability. By modernizing technology, remote work can be streamlined, enabling employees to serve the public effectively and without interruption.

Stronger Cybersecurity Measures

As remote work becomes more prevalent, cybersecurity has emerged as a significant concern. Public sector employees handle sensitive data, and the shift to remote work heightens the risk of cyber threats, including hacking and data breaches. To address these challenges, governments must implement rigorous security policies, such as encrypted communication, multi-factor authentication, and regular cybersecurity training for their employees. Furthermore, investing in secure VPNs and advanced firewalls can safeguard government databases. It is also crucial to educate employees on best practices, including how to recognize phishing emails and the importance of using strong passwords(Hornung et al., 2009). By strengthening cybersecurity measures, we can ensure that remote work remains both safe and sustainable in the long term.

Emphasis on Employee Well-Being

The future of remote work will increasingly prioritize employee mental health and work-life balance. Many remote employees experience burnout and stress due to extended hours and social isolation. It is essential for governments to implement wellness programs, provide access to mental health counseling, and establish policies that promote regular breaks. Flexible work hours, along with clear boundaries between professional and personal time, will enable employees to maintain productivity without feeling overwhelmed. A supportive work culture that emphasizes well-being will result in higher job satisfaction and enhanced efficiency within the public sector.

Standardized Remote Work Policies

Inconsistencies in remote work policies among various government agencies lead to confusion and unequal workloads. To address this issue, it is essential for governments to establish standardized remote work guidelines that promote fairness for all employees. These policies should encompass work schedules, performance evaluations, communication expectations, and technology support. A well-defined framework will prevent misunderstandings and facilitate a smooth adaptation for both employees and managers. Moreover, standardized policies will ensure that remote work is accessible and effective for all public sector workers, ultimately enhancing overall efficiency and job satisfaction(Beckel & Fisher, 2022).

Impact on Productivity and Service Delivery

Remote work influences both employee productivity and the efficiency of public services. While some individuals experience enhanced focus while working from home, others contend with distractions and the absence of direct oversight. Delays in governmental processes, often attributed to slow communication, internet connectivity issues, or a lack of coordination, can significantly diminish service effectiveness. Public agencies must find a balance between flexibility and accountability by establishing clear productivity guidelines and utilizing digital workflow tools to streamline operations.

Equity and Inclusion in Remote Work

Access to remote work opportunities is not equally available to all public sector employees. While office-based staff can often take advantage of flexible working conditions, field workers, first responders, and essential service providers are required to be physically present(Major et al., 2008). This discrepancy results in an imbalance in work benefits. To promote fairness among employees, governments should consider implementing policies that offer alternative perks, such as additional leave or flexible hours.

Financial Implications of Remote Work

Remote work offers governments the opportunity to reduce expenses related to office space, utilities, and transportation allowances. However, it requires significant investment in technology, cybersecurity, and employee training to ensure effective implementation. Governments should assess the long-term cost benefits and consider providing financial support for employees who need proper home office setups to maintain efficiency.

CONCLUSION

Remote work in the public sector has significantly transformed traditional work structures, providing employees with enhanced flexibility, improved work-life balance, and increased efficiency. However, alongside its advantages, this shift has also presented notable challenges, including mental health issues, burnout, digital fatigue, and the conflation of professional and personal boundaries. The abrupt transition to remote work, hastened by the COVID-19 pandemic, illuminated both the benefits and limitations of telecommuting within government institutions.

A primary concern is burnout, as many public sector employees grapple with heavier workloads, extended working hours, and insufficient managerial support. The lack of clear boundaries between work and home life has made it challenging for employees to disconnect, leading to exhaustion and diminished productivity. Furthermore, the absence of social interaction and collaborative teamwork has fostered feelings of isolation, making it increasingly difficult for employees to remain engaged and motivated. Addressing these challenges necessitates a commitment to developing sustainable work policies that prioritize employee well-being while preserving productivity.

To create a long-lasting and effective remote work environment, public sector organizations must implement flexible work policies that enable employees to manage their time more effectively without feeling overwhelmed. Additionally, governments should invest in mental health support programs, providing access to counseling services, stress management workshops, and wellness initiatives. Workload management must be a priority, ensuring a fair distribution of tasks and preventing employees from bearing excessive responsibilities due to understaffing.

An essential element of remote work success is managerial support, as employees excel when they receive recognition, guidance, and consistent feedback. Providing leadership training for managers can equip them with the necessary skills to effectively support remote teams, fostering a workplace culture that prioritizes open communication and employee well-being. Furthermore, governments should enhance career advancement opportunities by offering virtual training programs, mentorship initiatives, and clear pathways for promotion, which will help keep employees engaged and motivated. While technology is crucial in facilitating remote work, an over-reliance on digital platforms can contribute to fatigue and stress. Organizations need to implement structured schedules to limit excessive virtual meetings and promote asynchronous communication, thereby reducing digital overload. Additionally, it's vital to strengthen cybersecurity measures to protect government data during remote work.

Looking ahead, it's important for governments to acknowledge that remote work is not a temporary arrangement but rather a long-term transformation within the workplace. By enacting thoughtful policies, investing in employee well-being, and addressing current challenges, the public sector can foster a sustainable, productive, and supportive remote work environment that ultimately benefits both employees and the communities they serve.

REFERENCES

Allgood, M., Jensen, U., & Stritch, J. (2022). Work-family conflict and burnout amid covid-19: Exploring the mitigating effects of instrumental leadership and social belonging. *Review of Public Personnel Administration*, *44*(1), 139–160. DOI: 10.1177/0734371X221101308

Atilano-Tang, L. and Antonio-Torres, M. (2023). Optimizing government services through alternative work arrangements: evidence from the department of tourism in zamboanga peninsula, philippines.. https://doi.org/DOI: 10.14293/PR2199.000288.v1

Atilano-Tang, L. and Antonio-Torres, M. (2023). Optimizing government services through alternative work arrangements: evidence from the department of tourism in zamboanga peninsula, philippines.. https://doi.org/DOI: 10.14293/PR2199.000288.v1

Barboza-Wilkes, C., González, E., Resh, W., & Wong, S. (2022). The emotional toll of the covid-19 crisis on local government workers. *Review of Public Personnel Administration*, *44*(1), 60–85. DOI: 10.1177/0734371X221108501

Beckel, J., & Fisher, G. (2022). Telework and worker health and well-being: A review and recommendations for research and practice. *International Journal of Environmental Research and Public Health*, *19*(7), 3879. DOI: 10.3390/ijerph19073879 PMID: 35409563

Beckel, J., & Fisher, G. (2022). Telework and worker health and well-being: A review and recommendations for research and practice. *International Journal of Environmental Research and Public Health*, *19*(7), 3879. DOI: 10.3390/ijerph19073879 PMID: 35409563

Corrigan, M., Curran, M., Kirwan, S., Donohue, G., & Keogh, B. (2022). The transition of a mental health facility to a covid-19 isolation ward and unit to deliver remote inpatient mental health care. *British Journal of Mental Health Nursing*, *11*(4), 1–7. DOI: 10.12968/bjmh.2022.0028

Cromarty, P., Gallagher, D., & Watson, J. (2020). Remote delivery of cbt training, clinical supervision and services: In times of crisis or business as usual. *Cognitive Behaviour Therapist*, *13*, e33. Advance online publication. DOI: 10.1017/S1754470X20000343 PMID: 34191942

Cromarty, P., Gallagher, D., & Watson, J. (2020). Remote delivery of cbt training, clinical supervision and services: In times of crisis or business as usual. *Cognitive Behaviour Therapist*, *13*, e33. Advance online publication. DOI: 10.1017/S1754470X20000343 PMID: 34191942

Darouei, M., & Pluut, H. (2021). Work from home today for a better tomorrow! how working from home influences work-family conflict and employees' start of the next workday. *Stress and Health*, *37*(5), 986–999. DOI: 10.1002/smi.3053 PMID: 33887802

Doberstein, C., & Charbonneau, É. (2022). Alienation in pandemic-induced telework in the public sector. *Public Personnel Management*, *51*(4), 491–515. DOI: 10.1177/00910260221114788

Elnanto, J., & Suharti, L. (2021). The impact of work from home to work life-balance and its implication to employee happiness. *International Journal of Social Science and Business*, *5*(3), 311. DOI: 10.23887/ijssb.v5i3.35325

Giauque, D., Renard, K., Cornu, F., & Emery, Y. (2022). Engagement, exhaustion, and perceived performance of public employees before and during the covid-19 crisis. *Public Personnel Management, 51*(3), 263–290. DOI: 10.1177/00910260211073154 PMID: 36093284

Giauque, D., Renard, K., Cornu, F., & Emery, Y. (2022). Engagement, exhaustion, and perceived performance of public employees before and during the covid-19 crisis. *Public Personnel Management, 51*(3), 263–290. DOI: 10.1177/00910260211073154 PMID: 36093284

Hernández, Y., Parente, F., Faghy, M., Roscoe, C., & Maratos, F. (2021). Influence of the covid-19 lockdown on remote workers' physical and psychosocial wellbeing and work productivity. https://doi.org/DOI: 10.31234/osf.io/dnuk3

Hersch, E., Cohen, K., Saklecha, A., Williams, K., Tan, Y., & Lattie, E. (2022). Remote-delivered services during covid-19: A mixed-methods survey of college counseling center clinicians. *Journal of American College Health, 72*(2), 423–431. DOI: 10.1080/07448481.2022.2038178 PMID: 35259062

Hornung, S., Rousseau, D., & Glaser, J. (2009). Why supervisors make idiosyncratic deals: Antecedents and outcomes of i-deals from a managerial perspective. *Journal of Managerial Psychology, 24*(8), 738–764. DOI: 10.1108/02683940910996770

Hornung, S., Rousseau, D., & Glaser, J. (2009). Why supervisors make idiosyncratic deals: Antecedents and outcomes of i-deals from a managerial perspective. *Journal of Managerial Psychology, 24*(8), 738–764. DOI: 10.1108/02683940910996770

Iqbal, M., & Moein, A. (2024). Work from home arrangements may boost employee happiness. *International Journal of Research and Review, 11*(2), 431–445. DOI: 10.52403/ijrr.20240246

Khatib, M., Matrooshi, O., Salami, M., & Khadim, A. (2024). Technology as a source of risk in remote work. *International Journal of Theory of Organization and Practice (Ijtop), 3*(2), 119–136. DOI: 10.54489/ijtop.v3i2.310

Liu, W., Xu, Y., & Ma, D. (2021). Work-related mental health under covid-19 restrictions: A mini literature review. *Frontiers in Public Health, 9*, 788370. Advance online publication. DOI: 10.3389/fpubh.2021.788370 PMID: 34900925

Major, D., Verive, J., & Joice, W. (2008). Telework as a dependent care solution: Examining current practice to improve telework management strategies. *The Psychologist Manager Journal, 11*(1), 65–91. DOI: 10.1080/10887150801967134

Major, D., Verive, J., & Joice, W. (2008). Telework as a dependent care solution: Examining current practice to improve telework management strategies. *The Psychologist Manager Journal, 11*(1), 65–91. DOI: 10.1080/10887150801967134

Oksa, R., Kaakinen, M., Savela, N., Hakanen, J., & Oksanen, A. (2021). Professional social media usage and work engagement among professionals in finland before and during the covid-19 pandemic: Four-wave follow-up study. *Journal of Medical Internet Research, 23*(6), e29036. DOI: 10.2196/29036 PMID: 34048356

Rakha, N. (2023). Ensuring cyber-security in remote workforce: Legal implications and international best practices. *Irshad J. Law and Policy*, *1*(3). Advance online publication. DOI: 10.59022/ijlp.43

Rhee, H. (2008). Home-based telecommuting and commuting behavior. *Journal of Urban Economics*, *63*(1), 198–216. DOI: 10.1016/j.jue.2007.01.007

Shimura, A., Yokoi, K., Ishibashi, Y., Akatsuka, Y., & Inoue, T. (2021). Remote work decreases psychological and physical stress responses, but full-remote work increases presenteeism. *Frontiers in Psychology*, *12*, 730969. Advance online publication. DOI: 10.3389/fpsyg.2021.730969 PMID: 34659039

Sofianti, T., Kurniawan, I., Pratama, A., & Florencia, J. (2023). Measuring worker perception on remote working adoption during covid-19 pandemic: An industrial engineering perspective. *Engineering Science Letter*, *2*(01), 1–8. DOI: 10.56741/esl.v2i01.239

Sutarto, A., Wardaningsih, S., & Putri, W. (2021). Work from home: Indonesian employees' mental well-being and productivity during the covid-19 pandemic. *International Journal of Workplace Health Management*, *14*(4), 386–408. DOI: 10.1108/IJWHM-08-2020-0152

Toscano, F., & Zappalà, S. (2020). Social isolation and stress as predictors of productivity perception and remote work satisfaction during the covid-19 pandemic: The role of concern about the virus in a moderated double mediation. *Sustainability (Basel)*, *12*(23), 9804. DOI: 10.3390/su12239804

Vladi, B., Xhindi, T., & Dida, E. (2024). The role of sector and organizational size on employee's preference about teleworking (empirical evidences from albanian organizations). qas, 25(199). https://doi.org/DOI: 10.47750/QAS/25.199.33

Vries, H., Tummers, L., & Bekkers, V. (2018). The benefits of teleworking in the public sector: Reality or rhetoric? *Review of Public Personnel Administration*, *39*(4), 570–593. DOI: 10.1177/0734371X18760124

Vries, H., Tummers, L., & Bekkers, V. (2018). The benefits of teleworking in the public sector: Reality or rhetoric? *Review of Public Personnel Administration*, *39*(4), 570–593. DOI: 10.1177/0734371X18760124

Williamson, S., Colley, L., & Hanna-Osborne, S. (2020). Will working from home become the 'new normal' in the public sector? *Australian Journal of Public Administration*, *79*(4), 601–607. DOI: 10.1111/1467-8500.12444

Williamson, S., Pearce, A., Connor, J., Weeratunga, V., & Dickinson, H. (2022). The future of working from home in the public sector: What does the evidence tell us? *Australian Journal of Public Administration*, *81*(4), 640–648. DOI: 10.1111/1467-8500.12556

Chapter 4

The Evolution of Artificial Intelligence Origin:

Impact on Workforce and Future Implications

Mohan Kumar
https://orcid.org/0000-0002-5171-0892
SGT University, India

Alka Sanjeev
SGT University, India

Leena Sachdeva
O.P. Jindal Global University, India

Huy Hung Ta
https://orcid.org/0009-0008-6835-3036
International School, Vietnam National University, Hanoi, Vietnam

ABSTRACT

Artificial intelligence (AI) has rapidly evolved from theoretical models to real-world applications that impact every sector of the global economy. While AI promises increased efficiency, productivity, and innovation, it also brings significant disruption to traditional labor markets. The transition from industrial automation to AI-driven decision-making has accelerated job displacement across both blue-collar and white-collar industries. This chapter explores the historical context of job displacement due to AI, the sectors most at risk, and potential strategies for mitigating the economic and social consequences of this transformation.

DOI: 10.4018/979-8-3373-1270-5.ch004

INTRODUCTION

Artificial Intelligence (AI) is a branch of computer science that enables machines to simulate human intelligence by performing tasks that typically require human cognition, such as learning, reasoning, problem-solving, perception, and language understanding (Russell & Norvig, 2021). AI systems achieve this through machine learning (ML), deep learning, natural language processing (NLP), and computer vision, allowing them to process vast amounts of data, recognize patterns, and make informed decisions. AI can be broadly classified into narrow AI (ANI), which is designed for specific tasks like voice assistants (Siri, Alexa), recommendation systems, and self-driving cars, and artificial general intelligence (AGI), a yet-to-be-developed form of AI that can perform any intellectual task a human can, demonstrating adaptability and reasoning across different domains (Goertzel, 2014). AI applications span multiple industries, including healthcare (disease diagnosis, robotic surgery), finance (fraud detection, stock predictions), manufacturing (automation, quality control), and entertainment (AI-generated content, gaming NPCs). Despite its transformative impact, AI raises ethical concerns, including data privacy, bias in AI models, and the risks of automation displacing human jobs. As AI research progresses, the focus is on developing responsible and explainable AI systems that maximize benefits while mitigating risks (Bostrom, 2014).

The Origins of Artificial Intelligence

Determining the exact origins of artificial intelligence is challenging, but its foundations can likely be traced back to the early 1940s. In 1942, American science fiction writer Isaac Asimov introduced the concept of intelligent robots in his short story *Runaround*. The narrative follows two engineers, Gregory Powell and Mike Donavan, who work with a robot governed by Asimov's Three Laws of Robotics: a robot must not harm a human being or, by remaining passive, allow harm to come to one, a robot must follow human instructions unless they contradict the First Law, and a robot must ensure its own survival, provided that this does not interfere with the First or Second Law. Asimov's ideas had a lasting influence on robotics, AI, and computer science, inspiring figures such as Marvin Minsky, a cognitive scientist who later co-founded the MIT AI Laboratory.

Meanwhile, across the Atlantic, Alan Turing, a British mathematician, was working on real-world applications of computational intelligence. During World War II, he played a key role in developing The Bombe, a device designed to crack the German Enigma encryption. Measuring approximately 7 feet by 6 feet by 2 feet and weighing nearly a ton, The Bombe is recognized as one of the earliest electro-mechanical computers. Its ability to solve complex ciphers more efficiently than human mathematicians led Turing to reflect on the possibility of machine intelligence.

In 1950, Turing published his landmark paper, Computing Machinery and Intelligence (Turing, A., 1950) where he proposed methods for developing intelligent machines and introduced what is now known as the Turing Test. This test assesses a machine's ability to exhibit human-like intelligence: if a person interacts with both a machine and a human and cannot reliably differentiate between them, the machine is considered intelligent.

The term Artificial Intelligence was formally introduced in 1956 during the Dartmouth Summer Research Project on Artificial Intelligence (DSRPAI), organized by Marvin Minsky and John McCarthy at Dartmouth College, New Hampshire. Sponsored by the Rockefeller Foundation, this eight-week workshop brought together key figures who would later be regarded as the pioneers of AI. Among them were Nathaniel Rochester, who contributed to the development of IBM's first commercial scientific computer, and Claude Shannon, the father of information theory. The goal of this conference was to unite experts from various disciplines to establish a new research field focused on creating machines capable of simulating human intelligence.

Following the Dartmouth Conference, the field of Artificial Intelligence experienced nearly two decades of notable advancements. One of the earliest breakthroughs was ELIZA, a computer program developed between 1964 and 1966 **by** Joseph Weizenbaum at MIT. ELIZA was a natural language processing system designed to simulate human conversation, making it one of the first programs to attempt passing the Turing Test. Another significant achievement from this era was the General Problem Solver, created by Herbert Simon, Cliff Shaw, and Allen Newell at the RAND Corporation. This program demonstrated the ability to solve structured problems, such as the Towers of Hanoi[1] puzzle, showcasing the potential of AI in logical reasoning and automation. The Towers of Hanoi is a classic mathematical puzzle that involves moving a set of disks from one peg to another while following specific rules. It was invented by the French mathematician Édouard Lucas in 1883. Encouraged by these early successes, governments, and institutions poured substantial funding into AI research, fueling more ambitious projects. Optimism about AI's rapid progress reached its peak in 1970, when Marvin Minsky predicted in an interview with *Life Magazine* that machines with human-level intelligence could be developed within three to eight years. However, this prediction proved overly ambitious.

By 1973, AI research faced mounting skepticism. The U.S. Congress began questioning the high costs associated with AI projects, while in the UK, mathematician James Lighthill published a report for the British Science Research Council, casting doubt on AI's potential. He argued that machines would struggle to surpass the level of an "experienced amateur" in games like chess and would never achieve human-like common-sense reasoning. This led the British government to withdraw funding from most AI initiatives, restricting support to just three universities: Edinburgh, Sussex, and Essex. The U.S. government soon followed suit.

This era, known as the AI Winter, saw a significant decline in AI funding and enthusiasm. Although Japan reignited interest in AI research in the 1980s with major investments, prompting DARPA in the U.S. to increase its funding in response, progress in the field remained slow, with no major breakthroughs in the following years. The initial stagnation in AI development was largely due to the approach taken by early systems like ELIZA and the General Problem Solver. These programs were based on Expert Systems, which functioned by following a structured set of "if-then" rules, assuming that human intelligence could be formalized in a top-down manner. Expert Systems excelled in areas that could be broken down into well-defined logical steps. A prime example is IBM's Deep Blue, a chess-playing program that famously defeated world champion Garry Kasparov in 1997. Deep Blue leveraged a technique known as tree search (Campbell et al., 2002), allowing it to evaluate 200 million possible moves per second and anticipate up to 20 moves ahead. This achievement contradicted a claim made decades earlier by James Lighthill, who had doubted AI's ability to surpass human performance in complex games.

However, Expert Systems struggled when applied to tasks requiring adaptability, such as recognizing faces or distinguishing between visually similar objects—like a muffin and a Chihuahua (Hutson, 2018). These challenges underscored the need for AI systems capable of interpreting external data, learning from experience, and adapting to different scenarios. Since Expert Systems lacked these abilities, they did not meet the definition of true AI (Haenlein & Kaplan, 2019). The foundation for Artificial Neural Networks (ANNs), a more advanced AI approach, was laid in the 1940s when Canadian psychologist Donald Hebb introduced Hebbian Learning, a model inspired by neural activity in the human brain. However, research into neural networks stalled in 1969 after Marvin Minsky and Seymour Papert demonstrated that existing computers lacked the processing power required to implement these ideas effectively. The field saw a resurgence with the advent of Deep Learning (Silver et al., 2016), a modern implementation of neural networks. A turning point came in 2015, when Google's AlphaGo defeated the reigning world champion in Go, a game far more complex than chess. Unlike chess, which has 20 possible opening moves, Go presents 361 possible choices, making it an even greater challenge for computers. The success of AlphaGo proved that Deep Learning could achieve human-like performance in strategic decision-making.

Today, Deep Learning and artificial neural networks underpin many AI-driven applications, including facial recognition algorithms, speech recognition systems powering smart assistants, and autonomous vehicles. This era, often referred to as the AI Fall, marks the realization of breakthroughs stemming from past advances in statistical learning, shaping the AI technologies we rely on today. The discussion above highlights that AI is poised to become as integral to daily life as the Internet and social media have in previous decades. Its influence will extend beyond personal use, reshaping business operations and redefining how companies interact with employees, customers, and other stakeholders. Rather than questioning whether AI will be involved in these areas, the more pressing concerns revolve around the extent of its role and, more importantly, how humans and AI can coexist harmoniously in the evolving technological landscape.

Defining Artificial Intelligence

Artificial intelligence encompasses a diverse array of tools, techniques, and algorithms, covering everything from neural networks and speech/pattern recognition to genetic algorithms and deep learning. Understanding the various types of AI is crucial, as it sheds light on the unique opportunities and potential threats that different AI systems may pose.

- ***Expert Systems:*** Rules-based expert systems, like ELIZA, were among the earliest AI models, operating on an "If A, then B" logic to generate responses based on predefined rules. These systems mimic intelligence by following deterministic patterns, but they often appear limited or "dumb" because they lack true cognitive abilities. Many chatbots rely on rigid rule sets, making their responses predictable and confined to specific contexts. The passage challenges the assumption that artificial intelligence is inherently smarter than humans, highlighting how early chatbots had minimal flexibility. ELIZA, however, was unexpectedly effective in therapy because it operated within a structured and contextually appropriate framework.
- **Machine learning (ML)**: It is a subset of AI that enables systems to automatically learn and improve from experience without explicit programming, relying on algorithms that identify patterns in data to make predictions or decisions (Yadav & Sahoo, 2025)(Mitchell, 1997). ML is broadly categorized into supervised learning, where models learn from labeled data; unsupervised learning, which finds hidden patterns in unlabeled data; and reinforcement learning, where an agent learns through rewards and penalties (Goodfellow, Bengio, & Courville, 2016). Applications of ML span diverse fields, including healthcare for disease prediction (Esteva et al., 2017)(Kumar et al., 2023), finance for fraud detection (West & Bhattacharya, 2016), and autonomous vehicles for real-time decision-making (Bojarski et al., 2016). As ML continues to evolve, its integration with deep learning and neural networks enhances its capabilities, making it a critical component of modern AI research and applications.

- **Neural networks and deep learning**: These are advanced subfields of AI that enable machines to process complex data patterns and make intelligent decisions. A neural network is a computational model inspired by the structure and function of the human brain, consisting of interconnected nodes (artificial neurons) organized into layers. These networks are designed to recognize patterns by adjusting the strength of connections (weights) between neurons through a process known as backpropagation. Neural networks are widely used in image recognition, speech processing, and decision-making tasks, making them fundamental to modern AI applications (LeCun, Bengio, & Hinton, 2015).
- **Deep learning**, a specialized form of machine learning, utilizes deep neural networks with multiple hidden layers to analyze large datasets and learn features automatically. Unlike traditional machine learning models, which rely on manually extracted features, deep learning algorithms can independently discover relevant features within data, leading to superior performance in tasks such as speech recognition, medical diagnosis, and natural language processing (Goodfellow, Bengio, & Courville, 2016). The success of deep learning is largely driven by the availability of big data, advancements in computational power (GPUs, TPUs), and improvements in training techniques.

As a subset of AI, deep learning is one of the most powerful techniques for enabling machines to perform human-like cognitive tasks. While AI broadly includes any method that makes a system "intelligent," deep learning represents an advanced approach that can surpass traditional machine learning methods in fields like autonomous driving, facial recognition, and medical imaging (Kumar et al., 2023)(Krizhevsky, Sutskever, & Hinton, 2012). The increasing reliance on deep learning in real-world applications highlights its transformative impact on various industries, from healthcare and finance to robotics and entertainment.

- **Generative AI: A Powerful Subset of Artificial Intelligence**

Generative AI refers to a category of AI that creates new content—such as text, images, music, video, and code—by learning patterns from large datasets. Unlike traditional AI models that classify or predict based on input data, generative AI produces entirely new data that resembles the training input, making it one of the most exciting advancements in modern AI research (Goodfellow et al., 2014)(Kumar et al., 2024).

At the core of generative AI are deep learning models such as Generative Adversarial Networks (GANs) and Variational Autoencoders (VAEs), which learn to generate realistic synthetic data. More recently, transformer-based architectures like GPT (Generative Pre-trained Transformer) and Stable Diffusion have revolutionized AI-generated content by enabling the production of human-like text and highly detailed images (Radford et al., 2019). These models leverage vast amounts of training data and sophisticated neural network architectures to generate outputs that can mimic human creativity.

Generative AI has transformative applications across multiple industries. In text generation, models like ChatGPT and BERT are used for chatbots, content creation, and automated report writing. In image synthesis, tools like DALL·E and MidJourney create highly realistic or artistic images from text prompts. In music and video generation, AI can compose melodies or generate deepfake videos, raising both creative possibilities and ethical concerns (Karras et al., 2019). In software development, AI-powered tools can generate programming code, assisting developers in writing and debugging software efficiently(Yadav et al., 2024).

While generative AI holds vast potential, it also presents challenges such as bias in AI-generated content, ethical concerns regarding misinformation, and copyright issues. The ability to create highly realistic fake media has sparked discussions about the responsible use of AI in content creation, prompting researchers and policymakers to develop safeguards and regulations.

- **Artificial General Intelligence (AGI)**

As represented in Table 1, artificial General Intelligence (AGI) refers to a hypothetical form of artificial intelligence that possesses human-like cognitive abilities, enabling it to understand, learn, and perform any intellectual task that a human can do. Unlike today's narrow AI (ANI), which is designed for specific tasks (e.g., voice assistants, image recognition, language translation), AGI would be capable of general reasoning, problem-solving, and adaptability across different domains without task-specific training (Goertzel, 2014).

The defining characteristic of AGI is its ability to generalize knowledge across multiple fields, much like the human brain. A true AGI system would not only process data but also understand concepts, apply reasoning, develop abstract thinking, and even exhibit creativity and emotions (Kumar et al., 2023) (Russell & Norvig, 2021). This would allow AGI to excel in areas such as scientific discovery, artistic creation, and autonomous decision-making, surpassing human capabilities in some cases.

Table 1. Key Differences between AGI and Narrow AI

Feature	Narrow AI (ANI)	Artificial General Intelligence (AGI)
Scope	Task-specific	General-purpose
Learning	Pre-trained for specific tasks	Learns and adapts like a human
Flexibility	Cannot transfer knowledge between domains	Applies knowledge across different areas
Examples	ChatGPT, Alexa, Self-driving cars	Future AI capable of independent thought

Source: Own Elaboration

Despite rapid advancements in deep learning and machine learning, AGI does not yet exist. The current AI models, including GPT-4 and AlphaGo, are still forms of narrow AI since they specialize in particular tasks but lack human-like general intelligence (Legg & Hutter, 2007). Researchers debate whether AGI can be achieved through scaling up deep learning models or if it requires an entirely new paradigm, such as neuromorphic computing or brain-inspired AI. The pursuit of AGI raises significant ethical, philosophical, and existential concerns. Some scientists, like Nick Bostrom (2014), warn about the potential risks of super intelligent AGI surpassing human control, leading to unpredictable consequences. Others believe AGI could revolutionize fields like medicine, space exploration, and economics, driving unparalleled human progress.

- **Conversational AI:** Conversational AI refers to artificial intelligence systems that simulate human-like interactions through text, voice, or multimodal communication by leveraging natural language processing (NLP), machine learning (ML), and deep learning (Jurafsky & Martin, 2021)

(Yadav & Sahoo, 2025). These AI-driven systems are categorized into different types based on complexity and functionality. Rule-based chatbots operate on predefined scripts and "if-then" logic, making them suitable for simple FAQ-based interactions but limited in adaptability. More advanced AI-powered chatbots utilize ML and NLP to understand context, learn from past interactions, and provide dynamic responses, seen in applications like ChatGPT and Google Bard. Virtual assistants, such as Siri, Alexa, and Google Assistant, extend conversational AI by integrating speech recognition and smart task execution, enabling users to control devices, set reminders, and retrieve information. Intelligent IVR systems automate customer support through voice-guided menu navigation, reducing wait times in banking and airline services. The most advanced form, multimodal conversational AI, combines text, voice, and visual processing, allowing AI-powered assistants to interact seamlessly in different modalities, such as Meta's AI-powered smart glasses and Google Lens + Assistant. These technologies are widely applied in customer service, healthcare, finance, e-commerce, and education, driving efficiency and enhancing user experiences. As conversational AI evolves, it continues to push the boundaries of human-computer interaction, making AI-driven conversations more intuitive, adaptive, and personalized (Radford et al., 2019).

AI and Its Impact on Workforce Displacement

AI is transforming the workforce at an unprecedented rate, displacing jobs while simultaneously creating new employment opportunities. From industrial automation to AI-powered decision-making, the influence of AI spans across multiple industries, affecting both low-skill and high-skill professions. Unlike previous technological revolutions, AI is not just replacing repetitive manual labor but is increasingly challenging white-collar jobs in fields such as finance, law, healthcare, and customer service.

The integration of AI into businesses has led to fears of massive job displacement, with some estimates suggesting that up to 80% of current jobs may be at risk due to automation in the near future. However, historical trends show that while automation eliminates some jobs, it also creates new roles and shifts workforce demands. Understanding which industries are at risk, the nature of workforce transitions, and strategies to mitigate AI-driven displacement is crucial for policymakers, businesses, and workers.

Historical Perspective on AI and Job Displacement

The evolution of AI-driven job displacement follows a trajectory similar to past technological revolutions. The First Industrial Revolution (18th-19th centuries) mechanized agriculture and textile production, displacing farm laborers while creating factory jobs. The Second Industrial Revolution (late 19th-early 20th century) introduced mass production, affecting artisans but increasing industrial employment. The Digital Revolution (20th century) saw computers replace clerical jobs while creating opportunities in IT and programming. The AI Revolution is now automating both routine and non-routine cognitive tasks, affecting white-collar professions at an unprecedented scale.

THE STAGES OF INDUSTRIAL REVOLUTION AND ITS IMPACT ON JOBS

- ***The First Industrial Revolution (18th - 19th Century)***

This period saw the transformation from agrarian societies to industrialized economies in Europe and North America. Innovations such as the steam engine and mechanized textile production led to the decline of manual agricultural labor. While some jobs were lost, new roles such as boiler makers, ironsmiths, and mechanics were created, demonstrating that reskilling was key to workforce adaptation.

- ***The Second Industrial Revolution (1870 - 1914)***

Marking a shift to mass production powered by electricity, this revolution introduced the telephone, light bulb, and internal combustion engine. Though steam-powered mechanics saw job losses, those who reskilled into electricians and factory operators retained employment. Additionally, mass production systems generated even more jobs than before.

- ***The Third Industrial Revolution (1980s - Present, Digital Revolution)***

This phase saw the transition from analog to digital technology, with developments such as personal computers, the internet, and information technology. Many traditional roles were replaced by automation and computers, but the rise of IT professionals, software engineers, and cybersecurity experts underscored the emergence of new job sectors.

- ***The Fourth Industrial Revolution (4IR, Present & Future)***

Building upon digital advancements, 4IR is characterized by AI, robotics, nanotechnology, quantum computing, biotechnology, and IoT. While concerns about AI replacing both unskilled and skilled jobs persist, historical patterns suggest that technological shifts create more opportunities. The key to thriving in this era is continuous learning and reskilling. New professions such as data scientists and AI specialists are becoming essential.

Despite recurring fears of job loss, history demonstrates that industrial revolutions ultimately lead to employment growth and improved living standards. The current challenge lies in ensuring workers are prepared for 4IR by acquiring relevant skills. Rather than fearing automation, individuals should focus on reskilling to align with evolving job demands

Industries Most Affected by AI Job Displacement

The integration of automation and AI is expected to drive productivity growth and economic expansion, but it will also require millions of workers worldwide to transition to new occupations or enhance their skill sets. Research indicates that in approximately 60% of jobs, at least one-third of routine activities could be automated, signaling significant transformations in the workplace and necessitating adaptation for employees across various sectors (Manyika et al., 2017)(Kumar et al., 2023). While the technical feasibility of automation plays a crucial role, it is not the sole determinant of how quickly and extensively businesses will implement these technologies. Other influencing factors include the cost of automation deployment, labour market conditions (such as wage levels and workforce availability), and the broader benefits beyond mere labour replacement. Additionally, regulatory policies and societal acceptance will shape the adoption rate of AI-driven automation. Some industries are seeing rapid job displacement, while others are evolving through a hybrid AI-human workforce model.

The effects of automation on employment vary across different job sectors. Tasks that involve physical labour in structured environments, such as machine operation and fast-food preparation, are highly vulnerable to automation. Similarly, roles that focus on data collection and processing, including mortgage origination, legal research, accounting, and back-office operations, are increasingly being performed more efficiently by AI-driven systems (Kumar et al., 2023)(Manyika et al., 2017).

However, even as some tasks become automated, this does not necessarily mean that jobs in these sectors will vanish. Instead, workers may be reassigned to new responsibilities, emphasizing human oversight and decision-making. Roles that require people management, specialized expertise, and interpersonal engagement are less likely to be significantly affected by automation, as AI technology has yet to replicate human cognitive and emotional intelligence effectively. Occupations that operate in unpredictable environments, such as landscaping, plumbing, and eldercare services, are also expected to experience minimal automation by 2030. These jobs often require adaptability and practical skills that machines struggle to perform efficiently. Additionally, because many of these roles are low-wage positions, the cost of automation may not justify replacing human labour in these industries. Industries requiring creativity, emotional intelligence, and complex problem-solving—such as healthcare, education, and scientific research—are less likely to be fully automated

Overall, while automation will undoubtedly reshape the labour market, its impact will differ based on industry-specific factors and the extent to which human judgment and interaction remain essential to job functions **(Manyika et al., 2017)**.

AI DISPLACEMENT BY INDUSTRY

The industries experiencing the most significant AI-driven job shifts include:

- ***Manufacturing***: Robotics and AI-powered automation replace factory workers.
- ***Retail and Customer Service***: AI-driven chatbots and recommendation systems reduce the need for human representatives.
- ***Finance and Accounting***: AI handles fraud detection, risk assessment, and automated trading.
- ***Transportation***: Autonomous vehicles and logistics AI systems threaten driving-related jobs.
- ***Legal Professions***: AI can now analyze legal documents and predict case outcomes.
- ***Healthcare***: AI-powered diagnostics and robotic surgeries are reducing reliance on human doctors for certain tasks.

The "Uberization" of the Workforce

A key trend in AI job displacement is the shift toward a gig economy, often referred to as the "Uberization" of labour. AI-powered platforms such as Uber, Lyft have enabled task-based employment, reducing long-term job security. While these platforms offer flexibility, they also strip workers of traditional benefits like healthcare, job stability, and career progression.

AI is also being used to dynamically optimize workforces, allowing companies to monitor employee performance and automatically replace underperforming workers. This raises ethical concerns about job stability and worker rights in an AI-dominated economy.

The gig economy has been growing steadily, while traditional employment remains relatively stable.

UNDERSTANDING AI'S INFLUENCE ON WORK AND DECISION-MAKING

AI is increasingly becoming a central component of technological advancements, with companies like Apple, Google, and Amazon heavily investing in AI-powered products and startups. This growing adoption of AI elicits mixed reactions—ranging from optimism about its potential to enhance human capabilities to concerns over job displacement.

To fully grasp AI's impact, it is essential to analyze how it reduces costs. Historically, major technological changes have transformed industries by making previously expensive tasks more accessible. Just as the semiconductor revolution reduced the cost of arithmetic and enabled a broad range of applications, AI has the potential to revolutionize industries by making prediction significantly cheaper and more efficient (Agrawal, Gans, & Goldfarb, 2017).

The Power of Machine Learning and Prediction

Recent AI advancements largely stem from machine learning, which enables computers to learn from data rather than relying on explicit programming. Traditional software required specific instructions to identify objects, but machine learning allows AI systems to improve their accuracy by analyzing patterns across vast datasets. For instance, an AI model can learn to recognize an apple not just by its color and shape but by examining thousands of images and identifying contextual clues. Prediction, broadly defined, involves using available information to generate new insights. While prediction is commonly associated with forecasting the future (e.g., determining whether a loan applicant is likely to default), it also applies to diagnosing medical conditions or recognizing objects in images. The fundamental shift brought by AI is that as computational power and algorithms improve, the cost of prediction decreases dramatically, making it more widely applicable across different fields (Agrawal et al., 2017).

The Value of Prediction in Decision-Making

AI's predictive capabilities influence how businesses operate by enhancing decision-making. Every task—from pricing strategies to driving a car—relies on predictions about future outcomes. With AI lowering the cost of prediction, its value increases when paired with extensive and accessible data. For example, autonomous vehicles demonstrate how AI-driven prediction transforms industries. Earlier attempts at self-driving cars relied on manually coded rules, which proved insufficient due to the complexity of real-world scenarios. By reframing autonomous driving as a prediction problem, engineers leveraged machine learning to anticipate how human drivers would react to specific road conditions, accelerating AI-driven progress in the industry (Agrawal et al., 2017).

The Role of Judgment in AI-Driven Workplaces

Despite AI's growing capabilities, human judgment remains indispensable. Judgment involves assessing various factors, weighing risks, and making informed decisions. While AI can predict outcomes with increasing accuracy, certain tasks require human intuition, ethical considerations, and emotional intelligence—qualities that AI currently struggles to replicate. Tasks that are well-defined and primarily dependent on prediction (e.g., image recognition, financial modeling) are easier to automate. However, activities requiring complex judgment—such as medical treatment decisions or customer relationship management—still necessitate human involvement. AI can assist in making recommendations, but humans ultimately decide the best course of action based on context and values (Agrawal et al., 2017).

AI's Impact on Workforce Skills and Management

As AI continues to advance, the workforce must adapt by developing skills that complement automation. The most valuable competencies in the AI era will center around judgment rather than prediction.

1. **Judgment as a Competitive Advantage**: Since AI is rapidly improving in prediction tasks, human workers will be increasingly valued for their ability to make sound judgments. Industries such as healthcare, retail, and security will rely on professionals who can interpret AI-driven insights and apply ethical reasoning in decision-making.
2. **Changes in Managerial Roles**: AI will shift the role of managers from prediction-based decision-making to overseeing AI applications and focusing on human-centered leadership. Tasks like hiring, promotions, and business strategy, which traditionally required experience-based predictions, will be supplemented by AI insights. However, managers will still be responsible for interpreting these insights, ensuring fairness, and maintaining organizational culture (Agrawal et al., 2017).
3. **Reskilling and Workforce Adaptation**: Organizations must transition from training employees in predictive skills (such as statistical analysis) to developing their judgment-based abilities. This shift will involve fostering creativity, ethical reasoning, and interpersonal skills. For example, in healthcare, while AI can diagnose illnesses with high accuracy, nurses and doctors will continue to play a crucial role in treatment planning and patient interaction.

Preparing for an AI-Driven Future

The rapid expansion of AI's predictive capabilities is reshaping industries, but its impact on work depends on how businesses integrate technology with human expertise. AI reduces the cost of prediction, enabling automation of well-defined tasks while increasing the value of human judgment.

To thrive in this new era, organizations must embrace AI strategically by balancing automation with human oversight. Workforce training should emphasize skills that AI cannot easily replicate—such as ethical decision-making, leadership, and adaptability. As AI continues to evolve, the most successful businesses will be those that effectively merge technological advancements with human capabilities (Kumar et al., 2024)(Agrawal et al., 2017).

The Future of Work in an AI-Driven World

The evolution of work is a topic of major concern for business leaders and policymakers alike. With AI, advanced robotics, and big data transforming industries, machines are now capable of performing tasks traditionally carried out by humans. This shift raises fundamental questions: How should organizations prepare for this transformation? Will AI create new jobs or render many existing ones obsolete?

Perspectives on AI's impact on employment vary significantly. Some predict widespread job losses, while others envision AI creating new roles and even an era of abundance, where work is no longer a necessity but a personal choice. Organizations must carefully evaluate these differing viewpoints, as they influence strategic decisions that will shape the workforce of the future.

Diverse Perspectives on AI and Employment

Through extensive research, five primary schools of thought have emerged regarding AI's influence on jobs and productivity:

1. **The Dystopian Perspective:**
   This viewpoint suggests that AI and automation will surpass human workers, leading to widespread job displacement and economic disruption. As intelligent systems take over cognitive and manual labour tasks, middle-skill jobs will decline, pushing many workers into unemployment or lower-wage roles. Such a scenario could force governments to implement economic interventions, such as universal basic income, to stabilize societies.
2. **The Utopian Vision:**
   Proponents of this perspective argue that AI will enhance economic prosperity rather than diminish it. In this scenario, machines evolve to a point where they perform cognitive tasks on par with human intelligence. As AI handles both mundane and complex tasks, people will have greater freedom to pursue creative, intellectual, or passion-driven work. This could lead to economic abundance, requiring new models of wealth distribution to ensure fairness.
3. **The Optimistic Technologists:**
   According to this school of thought, AI-driven productivity improvements are already occurring, though traditional economic metrics may not fully capture them. As businesses integrate AI more effectively, efficiency gains will become more evident, improving economic growth and living standards. However, these benefits may not be equally distributed, potentially increasing wealth gaps unless policies promote broader access to AI-driven prosperity.
4. **The Productivity Skeptics:**
   This perspective suggests that while AI is powerful, its contributions to national productivity may remain limited. Broader economic challenges—such as aging populations, rising inequality, and environmental costs—may counterbalance AI-driven advancements, leading to sluggish economic growth rather than a technological revolution.
5. **The Optimistic Realists:**

This viewpoint holds that AI and digital transformation will bring productivity gains comparable to past technological revolutions. However, rather than uniformly benefiting all businesses and industries, these gains will be concentrated in specific sectors and among high-performing companies. AI may further intensify current labor trends-expanding demand for both high-skill and low-skill jobs while eroding middle-skill roles.

Three Key Strategies for Navigating AI in the Workplace

Given the uncertainty surrounding AI's long-term effects, business leaders must take proactive steps to integrate AI while ensuring workforce adaptability. The following three strategies can help organizations stay competitive in an AI-driven world:

1. Use AI to Enhance Human Abilities and Restructure Operations

Rather than solely focusing on cost savings through automation, organizations should leverage AI to enhance human capabilities and optimize processes. For example, adaptive robots can assist in physically demanding manufacturing tasks, reducing worker fatigue and improving efficiency. AI-powered analytics can also enable employees to make better decisions, enhance customer service, and explore new business opportunities. Companies already experimenting with AI-driven enhancements have seen significant gains. For instance, manufacturers implementing collaborative robots ("cobots") report improvements in production speed, product quality, and employee job satisfaction. Similarly, in customer service and retail industries, AI-driven recommendation engines are enhancing personalization while allowing human workers to focus on high-value interactions.

2. Redefine Job Roles and Rethink Organizational Structures

For AI to deliver maximum value, companies must rethink traditional job descriptions and organizational frameworks. Instead of viewing AI as a mere replacement for human workers, businesses should identify tasks that can be automated while simultaneously creating new roles that leverage human strengths. For example, rather than eliminating jobs, AI can assist employees by handling repetitive tasks, allowing them to focus on strategic and creative activities. Organizations should also foster non-hierarchical work environments where teams can collaborate across different functions, using AI insights to drive rapid decision-making and innovation.

A practical example of this approach can be found in companies like Stitch Fix, an online clothing retailer. Their AI-driven recommendation system supports human stylists, allowing them to make more accurate fashion suggestions while increasing productivity and reducing return rates.

3. Foster Employee Collaboration in the AI-Powered Workplace

Employees should be seen as active participants in AI-driven transformations rather than passive recipients of change. Research suggests that workers are more adaptable than many employers assume—most employees are eager to learn new skills to remain relevant in the evolving job market. Investing in AI training programs and upskilling initiatives will help businesses seamlessly integrate AI into their operations while ensuring that employees continue to add value. Organizations that embrace AI while simultaneously empowering their workforce will gain a competitive advantage by leveraging human creativity, problem-solving abilities, and interpersonal skills-traits that AI cannot easily replicate.

The debate surrounding AI's role in the future of work is ongoing. While some predict an age of economic abundance, others foresee job displacement and significant disruptions. Regardless of which scenario unfolds, businesses must take an active role in shaping their future. By strategically integrating AI, rethinking job roles, and investing in employee development, organizations can successfully navigate this transformation and secure a strong position in the AI-powered economy. The companies that embrace these changes today will be best prepared to thrive in the workforce of tomorrow.

CONCLUSION

This chapter offers a detailed examination of artificial intelligence (AI), outlining its development from initial theoretical frameworks to its present impact on industries and labor markets. Throughout the decades, artificial intelligence has progressed via numerous technological innovations, encompassing expert systems, neural networks, deep learning, and, more recently, generative AI. Each of these advancements has markedly improved AI's capabilities, allowing computers to execute progressively intricate jobs previously considered exclusive to human intelligence. The advancement of AI has enhanced computing efficiency and offered novel paradigms for automation, decision-making, and problem-solving across various fields.

The influence of AI on employment has been significant. AI-driven automation is transforming the nature of labor across many industries, impacting both blue-collar and white-collar occupations. Although apprehensions over job displacement are legitimate, historical patterns indicate that technology progress frequently results in the emergence of new employment opportunities, albeit accompanied by changes in worker requirements. The challenge for enterprises, governments, and society as a whole is to adeptly manage this transformation, ensuring that employees possess the requisite skills to succeed in an AI-driven economy. Reskilling and upskilling activities, together with proactive legislative measures, will be essential in alleviating possible disruptions and cultivating a workforce capable of utilizing AI to augment productivity rather than facing displacement. In the future, the role of AI in decision-making, strategic planning, and workforce management is anticipated to grow significantly. Artificial intelligence systems can analyze extensive datasets, produce insights, and enhance operations with unparalleled precision and efficacy. Nevertheless, despite these breakthroughs, AI cannot replace human judgment, creativity, or ethical thinking. Critical thinking, emotional intelligence, and ethical considerations are distinctively human traits that machines cannot emulate. Consequently, the future of AI in the workplace will be defined by a collaborative interaction between humans and intelligent systems, wherein automation enhances human expertise rather than supplanting it.

Businesses and politicians must implement a balanced strategy to guarantee the responsible integration of AI into the workforce. This entails cultivating a culture of perpetual learning, allocating resources to educational and training initiatives, and establishing ethical frameworks to regulate the deployment of AI. The efficacy of AI in the workplace will rely not alone on its technological proficiencies but also on the extent to which societies acclimate to these transformations. The future of work will be defined by a collaborative relationship between people and AI, emphasizing adaptation, creativity, and ethical considerations to foster a sustainable and inclusive economy.

REFERENCES

Agrawal, A., Gans, J. S., & Goldfarb, A. (2017). What to expect from artificial intelligence. *MIT Sloan Management Review*.

Bostrom, N. (2014). *Superintelligence: Paths, Dangers, Strategies*. Oxford University Press.

Campbell, M., Hoane, A. J.Jr, & Hsu, F. H. (2002). Deep blue. *Artificial Intelligence*, *134*(1-2), 57–83. DOI: 10.1016/S0004-3702(01)00129-1

Esteva, A., Kuprel, B., Novoa, R. A., Ko, J., Swetter, S. M., Blau, H. M., & Thrun, S. (2017). Dermatologist-level classification of skin cancer with deep neural networks. *Nature*, *542*(7639), 115–118. DOI: 10.1038/nature21056 PMID: 28117445

Goertzel, B. (2014). Artificial General Intelligence: Concept, State of the Art, and Future Prospects. *Journal of Artificial General Intelligence*, *5*(1), 1–48. DOI: 10.2478/jagi-2014-0001

Goodfellow, I., Bengio, Y., & Courville, A. (2016). *Deep Learning*. MIT Press.

Goodfellow, I., Pouget-Abadie, J., Mirza, M., Xu, B., Warde-Farley, D., Ozair, S., Courville, A., & Bengio, Y. (2014). Generative adversarial nets. *Advances in Neural Information Processing Systems*, •••, 27.

Haenlein, M., & Kaplan, A. (2019). A brief history of artificial intelligence: On the past, present, and future of artificial intelligence. *California Management Review*, *61*(4), 5–14. DOI: 10.1177/0008125619864925

Hutson, M. (2018). How researchers are teaching AI to learn like a child. *Science*, *10*, 35–42. DOI: 10.1126/science.aau2576

Jurafsky, D., & Martin, J. H. (2021). *Speech and Language Processing* (3rd ed.). Pearson.

Karras, T., Laine, S., & Aila, T. (2019). A style-based generator architecture for generative adversarial networks. *Proceedings of the IEEE Conference on Computer Vision and Pattern Recognition*, 4401-4410. DOI: 10.1109/CVPR.2019.00453

Krizhevsky, A., Sutskever, I., & Hinton, G. E. (2012). Imagenet classification with deep convolutional neural networks. *Advances in Neural Information Processing Systems*, *25*, 1097–1105.

Kumar, M., Jain, A., Mittal, A., Gera, R., Biswal, S. K., Yadav, M., Hung, T. H., & Priya Srivastava, A. (2024). Inclusion of Neural Networks in Higher Education: A Systematic Review and Bibliometric Analysis. 2024 4th International Conference on Innovative Practices in Technology and Management (ICIPTM), 1–6. DOI: 10.1109/ICIPTM59628.2024.10563852

Kumar, M., Yadav, R., Suresh, A. S., Singh, R., Yadav, M., Balodi, A., Vihari, N. S., & Srivastava, A. P. (2023). Mapping AI-Driven Marketing: Review of Field and Directions for Future Research. 2023 2nd International Conference on Futuristic Technologies (INCOFT), 1–5. DOI: 10.1109/INCOFT60753.2023.10425169

LeCun, Y., Bengio, Y., & Hinton, G. (2015). Deep learning. *Nature*, *521*(7553), 436–444. DOI: 10.1038/nature14539 PMID: 26017442

Legg, S., & Hutter, M. (2007). A Collection of Definitions of Intelligence. *Frontiers in Artificial Intelligence and Applications*, *157*, 17–24.

Manyika, James, Susan Lund, Michael Chui, Jacques Bughin, Jonathan Woetzel, Parul Batra, Ryan Ko, and Saurabh Sanghvi. (2017). Jobs lost, jobs gained: What the future of work will mean for jobs, skills, and wages.

Mitchell, T. M. (1997). *Machine Learning*. McGraw-Hill.

Radford, A., Wu, J., Child, R., Luan, D., Amodei, D., & Sutskever, I. (2019). Language models are unsupervised multitask learners. OpenAI Blog, 1(8).

Russell, S., & Norvig, P. (2021). *Artificial Intelligence: A Modern Approach* (4th ed.). Pearson.

Silver, D., Huang, A., Maddison, C. J., Guez, A., Sifre, L., van den Driessche, G., Schrittwieser, J., Antonoglou, I., Panneershelvam, V., Lanctot, M., Dieleman, S., Grewe, D., Nham, J., Kalchbrenner, N., Sutskever, I., Lillicrap, T., Leach, M., Kavukcuoglu, K., Graepel, T., & Hassabis, D. (2016). Mastering the Game of Go with Deep Neural Networks and Tree Search. *Nature*, *529*(7587), 484–489. DOI: 10.1038/nature16961 PMID: 26819042

Turing, A. (1950). Machinery and intelligence. Mind: A Quarterly Review of Psychology and Philosophy, 59(236), 433-460.

West, J., & Bhattacharya, M. (2016). Intelligent financial fraud detection: A comprehensive review. *Computers & Security*, *57*, 47–66. DOI: 10.1016/j.cose.2015.09.005

Yadav, M., Mittal, S., Kumar, M., Sahoo, A., Jayarathne, P. G. S. A., Yadav, M., Mittal, S., Kumar, M., Sahoo, A., & Jayarathne, P. G. S. A. (2024). From Textbooks to Teamwork: The Importance of Collaboration Skills in Workforce Preparation. In *Revitalizing Student Skills for Workforce Preparation* (pp. 333–352). IGI Global Scientific Publishing. DOI: 10.4018/979-8-3693-3856-8.ch011

Yadav, M., & Sahoo, A. (2025). The Importance of Collaboration Skills in Workforce Preparation From Textbooks to Teamwork : In *Revitalizing Student Skills for Workforce Preparation* (pp. 333–352). DOI: 10.4018/979-8-3693-3856-8.ch011

Chapter 5
Protecting Remote Work: Cybersecurity Challenges and Solutions

Shambhavi Choubey
https://orcid.org/0009-0006-9044-4335
Christ University, Bengaluru, India

Ila Anand
https://orcid.org/0000-0001-8837-4450
Christ University, Bengaluru, India

ABSTRACT

New cybersecurity threats have sprouted due to the sudden shift to remote work; changed workplace dynamics have potentially moved security perimeters outward as organizations begin to experience new threats in the forms of phishing, ransomware, data breaches, and even insider threats. This chapter focuses on cybersecurity risks with remote work, upcoming security trends, and best practices for organizing and protecting distributed workforce activities. It tackles such core concepts of Zero Trust Architecture (ZTA), AI-enabled threat detection, and Secure Access Service Edge (SASE) as foundational strategies necessary to secure networks from remote workspaces. It also emphasizes employee awareness and compliance with cybersecurity regulations. Strong security controls will help businesses stay on top of cyber risks while developing the future of work toward being digital-first.

1. INTRODUCTION

1.1 The Evolution of Remote Work and Its Cybersecurity Implications

Remote work has revolutionized the way companies function, providing workers with flexibility and businesses with a global pool of talent. This change has, however, come with some grave cybersecurity issues. Historically, IT departments managed security in office networks, overseeing firewalls, software patches, and access control. With employees working remotely from different locations, using personal equipment and unsecured networks, organizations have an increased attack surface.

Cybercriminals take advantage of these weaknesses via phishing, ransomware, and data breaches, resulting in financial and reputational damage. One of the biggest challenges is the use of cloud-based collaboration tools, which, if not properly configured, can leak sensitive information. Insider threats—

DOI: 10.4018/979-8-3373-1270-5.ch005

either malicious or unintentional—are also on the increase, as employees store data using personal storage solutions or share files insecurely.

To counter such risks, organizations have to redesign their cybersecurity plans. The perimeter security model no longer works. Zero Trust Architecture (ZTA), Secure Access Service Edge (SASE), and artificial intelligence-powered threat detection are the strategies now being followed to secure employees (Dillon et al., 2021). These models see to it that each request for access is validated, monitored, and restricted as per ongoing risk assessments.

As remote work continues to become the new normal, companies need to strike a balance between security and productivity, where employees are able to work productively without sacrificing sensitive information. This chapter discusses major cybersecurity threats, upcoming security trends, and best practices in securing remote work environments.

1.2 Main Cybersecurity Threats of Remote Work

Remote work has greatly extended the attack surface, and cybersecurity is all the more complex. Employees utilize personal devices from multiple locations to interact with corporate data, and most of these devices lack enterprise-class security features. This decentralization amplifies the vulnerabilities to be targeted by cybercriminals.

The most common attack is phishing and social engineering-based attacks. Hackers impersonate executives or helpdesk personnel, misleading the employees into sharing login credentials or downloading malware. In the absence of face-to-face verification, remote employees are vulnerable to such scams. Attackers also conduct attacks by exploiting employees' reliance on email and messaging apps, coming up with panic messages to trick them.

Another is endpoint security. It is not uncommon that employees use personal laptops or cell phones that lack up-to-date software updates, strong firewalls, and encrypted storage. Differing from enterprise-managed computers, such endpoints are very vulnerable to malware infections and unauthorized intrusion. Remote office configurations also carry a high risk of data leakage in that employees find themselves saving working files on their own cloud systems or external devices without encryption.

Insider threats, whether intentional or unintentional, represent another risk. Employees may unknowingly compromise confidential information through insecure passwords, file sharing that is not encrypted, or incorrectly configured cloud storage. Additionally, angry employees or compromised accounts may intentionally leak or take advantage of confidential business information.

Cloud security and compliance risks are also in view. The majority of organizations make use of Microsoft 365, Google Drive, and other cloud services, but misconfigurations and weak access controls can lead to data exposure. Compliance to regulations such as GDPR, CCPA, and ISO 27001 is even tougher in a decentralized work setting, and companies need to embrace strict data protection measures.

1.3 Enhancing Cybersecurity in Remote Offices

In order to counter such challenges, companies need to implement a multi-layer security approach that includes robust security platforms, threat detection in real time, and employee training.

Among the most powerful models is Zero Trust Architecture (ZTA), premised on the "never trust, always verify" model. Unlike traditional security models that assume internal networks are safe, Zero Trust employs strict identity validation, least-privilege access, and continuous monitoring to detect threats before they can become large problems.

AI-powered threat detection is another essential solution. AI-powered cybersecurity solutions monitor user activity and identify anomalies in real-time, enabling organizations to catch phishing attempts, malware attacks, and intrusions. AI-powered detection and response automation accelerates responses without the risk of human error.

In addition to zero-trust solutions, increasingly more companies are embracing Secure Access Service Edge (SASE), a cloud-security model that merges network security and access control. In contrast to traditional VPNs that can hamper speed, SASE provides identity-based secure access policies and cloud firewalls to securely connect remote workers with corporate assets without hindering speed or user experience.

Employee cybersecurity awareness training is also another vital aspect. Research indicates that most security breaches are due to human mistakes. Organisations need to organize regular training sessions, simulation of phishing, and security awareness campaigns to educate employees to identify cyber attacks. Training should involve phishing attack detection, creating strong passwords, and how to manage corporate data securely.

In order to further enhance security, companies need to implement tight authentication procedures like Multi-Factor Authentication (MFA) and biometric identification. These ensure that even in the event that the password falls into the wrong hands, attackers are not quickly able to acquire access to the corporate accounts.

Organizations must also have remote work security policies that outline acceptable device use, secure file-sharing procedures, and data encryption requirements. Regular security audits, vulnerability scans, and penetration testing can identify and fix vulnerabilities before they are exploited against the organization (Cybersecurity, U.S., 2022).

As advanced cyber threats now become the hot topic, corporations must get back on track and utilize AI-based security automation, blockchain authentication, and decentralized identity technology. Cybersecurity for the future of remote work will hinge on secure-by-design security protocols to allow firms to secure their employees, encrypt sensitive information, and get current on compliance during an increasingly digitalized world.

1.4 Literature Review

This abrupt flux to remote work has also brought about a review of the so-called convention of cybersecurity, with academics and practitioners weighing the new challenges facing organizations. Several documents have cited the increasing challenges of cybersecurity with respect to a remote working set-up. As Bada et al. (2020) aptly put it, decentralization of the workforce generates significantly larger attack surfaces, subjecting organizations to new risks linked to personal devices and home networks. As Kurek

(2021) explain, the shift towards cloud-based collaboration software offers avenues for data breaches and unauthorized access, necessitating more stringent access control.

One prominent framework coming out of the literature is Zero Trust Architecture (ZTA), which has been acclaimed as a one-way security strategy of the remote working environment. Bertino and Brancik (2021) argue that Zero Trust effectively drafts an architecture for mitigating insider threats and constraining the exposure of data since it assumes that no user or device, even if inside the corporate network, could be trusted implicitly. Following literature has also testified that multifactor authentication and strong identity management systems comprise crucial constituents for the Zero Trust Architecture.

Another area within cybersecurity literature is emerging technologies like artificial intelligence (AI) and machine learning (ML). Zhou et al. (2022) discuss the manner in which these technologies may positively contribute toward faster threat detection and response-time by reducing human error and assisting with swift identification of potential breaches. The element of automation has great significance in scenarios where there might be limited human monitoring in remote work settings, mostly depreciated due to the dispersed nature of employees.

In relation to combating human vulnerabilities such as phishing and social engineering attacks, as noted by Choi et al. (2020), sustained attention in employee training and education is warranted. With remote workers becoming the new normal, these studies have reiterated the need for an integrated model of cybersecurity that includes technology, policy, and education to secure organizations and their employees in a digital-first world.

1.5 Objectives

1. Examine and Evaluate Cybersecurity Threats in Undertaking Work from Home: Basically, the primary aim is also related to research and the analysis of several cybersecurity threats confronting remote work life. Some threats that have been highlighted in the context of decentralization include phishing attacks, ransomware, data breaches, and insider threats. By having this macro knowledge of the threats posed to organizations, an organization can prepare contingencies for protecting its data and infrastructure.
2. Refer to the attached paper on Emerging Security Technologies with Their Strategies: Of prime importance is well arrayed that is addressing newer discoveries in the domain of cybersecurity technologies and strategies formulated to protect remote work environments. Among them are ZTA, AI-based threat detection, SASE, and other advanced means like blockchain for identity management. This knowledge will enable organizations to implement state-of-the-art safety tools and reduce their risks in a fast-evolving digital landscape.
3. Provide Best Practices for Strengthening Remote Cybersecurity: The last objective of this project is to lay down targeted operational best practices for securing the remote work environment. Areas include strong authentication protocols, endpoint security, training of staff in cybersecurity, and forming clear security policies. Following such a pattern will allow the organization to build a comprehensive security framework, reducing areas of weakness for a secure and resilient remote work environment.

1.6 Methodology

This chapter takes a dual-method approach-the integration of a critical literature review into a rich combination with practical case studies and examples outlining the cybersecurity risks, emerging trends, and best practices in remote work environments.

- **Review of Literature:** The literature review is comprehensive because it includes peer-reviewed journals, pertinent industry reports, and existing literature adopted by the paper. This will assist in identifying the major cybersecurity risks, emerging trends, and best practices in remote work environments. The source will be critically analyzed to provide a complete understanding of the existing trends and solutions related to cybersecurity challenges.
- **Practical Examples and Case Studies:** This chapter has considered some realistic context with some cases of organizations surveyed in order to explore some real-world cases of breaches in cybersecurity and successful implementations of security measures in remote work environments. It will give down-to-earth views on how effective various approaches have been, such as Zero Trust Architecture, AI-driven threat detection, and employee training programs.

2. BACKGROUND AND CONTEXT

Remote work has altered the corporate face completely, representing opportunity and risk. Organizations get more flexibility, lower overhead costs, and a window to world-class talent without being exposed to unprecedented cyber risk. The evolution from secure corporate spaces to massively distributed workplaces altered the security picture completely, prompting enterprises to reset their data security, access, and threat block measures.

This section discusses the history of remote work, how it has revolutionized the world of cybersecurity threats, and the most important statistical trends that point to the need to address these challenges. The data discussed below is used as a foundation to describe why organizations need to have strong security frameworks in place to protect remote work environments.

2.1 The Evolution of Remote Work and Cybersecurity Threats

Remote work was previously restricted to a small segment of employees, mainly freelancers, consultants, and some corporate employees who enjoyed flexible working hours. Most companies used centralized IT infrastructure, where employees leveraged company networks, applications, and confidential information from the isolation of a fortified office environment. Security administrators controlled company machines directly, making sure firewalls, endpoint security software, and network monitoring systems shielded valuable assets.

But mass migration to cloud collaboration platforms, mobile computing, and high-speed internet created the foundation for other companies to embrace remote and hybrid work models. Workers could remotely access corporate assets from anywhere, using multiple devices and network paths. This shift, as much a blessing to productivity, also swept away traditional security perimeters, making it difficult for businesses to maintain sight and control over their systems.

The COVID-19 pandemic accelerated this transition, and organizations were compelled to implement work-from-home policies overnight. Businesses scrambled to implement Virtual Private Networks (VPNs), cloud-based storage solutions, and digital collaboration tools to ensure business continuity. But in the process, all but a few companies overlooked some of the essential security considerations, leaving their systems vulnerable to cyber attacks. Employees employed personal computers, unsecure home networks, and non-enterprise-class applications, increasing the risk of data loss, malware infections, and identity theft significantly.

Soon, cyberattackers exploited these emerging vulnerabilities. Ransomware, phishing, and credential attacks sky-rocketed as hackers took advantage of remote working security vulnerabilities. Without support from IT on-premises, employees had a greater probability of being social engineered, innocently exposing their companies to money and reputation threat.

Remote work's greatest security risk is the absence of endpoint standardization. While office-managed devices enjoy enterprise-level security controls, most remote workers use personal laptops, tablets, and smartphones. These endpoints may never receive vital security patches, are unencrypted, or are used by household members, and thus are exposed to cyber threats. Organizations today have to protect a dispersed, heterogeneous, and in many cases, unsecured network of endpoints.

Similarly, shadow IT or unauthorized application use, personal cloud storage, and unofficial collaboration tools is indeed a phenomenon that exists. They are used by staff to keep things convenient but negate the corporate security policies, thus blind spots where sensitive data can be accessed, stored, or shared without managerial supervision. This lack of visibility adds the risk for data breaches, compliance issues, and unwarranted access.

To combat these increasing threats, companies need to adopt advanced cybersecurity models that are suitable for decentralized workspaces. Adoption of Zero Trust Architecture (ZTA), Secure Access Service Edge (SASE), and AI-driven security automation can assist organizations in having a robust security stance while enabling flexible work patterns.

2.2 Key Statistics on Cybersecurity Threats in Remote Work

A large number of studies are emerging to support the assertion about cybersecurity challenges posed to organizations by working from home. Some statistics illustrate not only the escalation in cyber threats stressful incidence but their sophistication and gravitas:

- Phishing attacks grew by 600% during the COVID-19 pandemic (Palmeter, 2022). More than ever, attackers exploited remote work vulnerabilities to manipulate employees, persuading them to unknowingly disclose sensitive credentials.
- Ransomware attacks shot up by 148% in 2021, as remote desktop protocol (RDP) vulnerabilities and unprotected remote access were systematically exploited by cybercriminals to gain forbidden entry into various corporate networks.
- 70% of remote workers use personal devices for work, while security policies are enforced by only 30% of companies—thus exposing organizations to the risks posed by unauthorized access and malware infections.
- Remote working made it much harder for the monitoring and prevention of data leakage, both inadvertent and deliberate; 58% of survey respondents noted an increase in incidents related to insider threats in the IT realm.

- Only 30% of organizations are conducting regular cybersecurity training for their remote employees. Unfortunately, this means the vast majority of workers are left untenable to threats like phishing, social engineering, and credential theft.
- More than 60% of small businesses that suffer a cyberattack shut down within six months, proving the deleterious financial effects of poor or no protection against cyberattacks.

All these enticing statistics emphasize an urgent imperative for proactive measures for protecting remote work environments. The organizations ought to focus beyond perimeter-based security to implement an MFA, EDR systems, and strict access control for the security of their systems.

Other than IT controls, companies must be driving cybersecurity awareness among their employees. Human error is still one of the primary causes of security incidents, with employees falling prey to phishing scams, using simple passwords, or mishandling sensitive information. Regular cybersecurity training, phishing simulation campaigns, and security awareness programs serve to mitigate these risks.

Another key challenge would be regulatory compliance. Organizations in remote environments must boldly comply with data protection laws, including the GDPR, CCPA, and ISO 27001. Noncompliance may also invite heavy fines and legal activism which is detrimental to organizational reputation. Organizationally strong encryption, secure cloud configurations, and compliance monitoring solutions build a path for businesses to comply with regulations effectively.

Looking forward, as threats for cybersecurity continue to evolve, so also methods of attack become sophisticated in nature. Staying ahead with the use of AI-based security automation, biometric authentication, and blockchain-based identity verification is the way for an organization. By being upfront with addressing cybersecurity risks, businesses can build a secure, resilient, and future-ready remote work environment.

3. CYBERSECURITY RISKS IN REMOTE WORK

The transitioning to remote work has made organizations to suffer new wave of cybersecurity threats so they have to safeguard the existing security architectures and devise new strategies to solve problems. With distributed workforce, now, the previous security perimeter has become porous; thus, it lays organizations open to cyber-attacks. This section examines some major cyber threats whose occurrence is more pronounced in remote workspaces such as larger attack surface, phishing and social engineering attack, endpoint security problems, insider threats, and risks concerning cloud security and compliance. Such recognitions of threats are important to organizations, indicating vulnerabilities and prevention of advance measures in ensuring secure remote operations.

3.1 Increased Attack Surface

One of the main results of remote work is the increased attack surface. In a standard office environment, the network of the organization is centralized, and workers use resources from protected, controlled environments. But in a remote work environment, workers access corporate information from multiple locations, devices, and networks. These may include home Wi-Fi networks, public hotspots, and even shared or unsecured networks, all of which provide potential entry points for attackers.

Remote work really implies that workers are connecting from many endpoints, such as home laptops, cell phones, and even unmanaged devices. Such endpoints may lack the most current security patches, antivirus tools, or firewalls, exposing the company network further. Intruders can use the vulnerabilities in these devices to gain unauthorized access to corporate resources. For instance, if a worker uses an older device to gain access to confidential information, cybercriminals are able to use the vulnerability to conduct a malware attack or steal credentials. The decentralized nature of remote work thus complicates matters for IT staff in keeping the same level of control and visibility over security as would be possible in an office environment.

3.2 Phishing and Social Engineering Attacks

Phishing and social engineering seem to have been some of the most interesting and successful attack forms used by cybercriminals against remote employees. They primarily depend on human blunders to get unauthorized access to a system or confidential information. Phishing messages or emails seem real; usually impersonated as internal employees like HR, IT, or known vendors. Such messages can be more likely accepted by the employees while working remotely and might be during times of urgency or by sensitive information requests. Clicking a link in an email that takes them to a fake login page that is set up to capture login credentials is an example of a phishing email that an employee might encounter. Another common technique is spear-phishing, which is aimed at a particular employee by targeting widely known available information about that organization, for instance, the corporate hierarchy or any ongoing developments in the business, rendering the attack sufficiently convincing. Social engineering, in association with deception and manipulation, often capitalizes on some psychological tendencies in the forms of urgency and fear, thereby getting employees to carry out actions without being able to think very much of the consequences.

It is because of such reasons that these attacks have a higher tendency to succeed in a remote environment because employees are more likely to communicate online and do not necessarily have the same instant access to colleagues or IT staff as they would in an office. Training employees to recognize phishing attacks along with advanced filtering of emails and multi-factor authentication (MFA) can help mitigate these attacks.

3.3 Endpoint Security Challenges

All security threats from end-users come in when they integrate their personal arrangements into enterprise frameworks, thereby exposing a lot of endpoint devices. Importantly, end-users are using their personal computers or other company-owned computers beyond the corporate network. So, it is much harder for IT organizations to impose security policies across all of them, as machines might not receive the updates, patches, and enterprise-level security controls that they would require, thus making them vulnerable.

Most remote workers tend not to observe best practices on personal device security, such as installation of the latest security patches or the use of full disk encryption. In addition, employees employ personal devices for work, thus merging private with professional use. These practices will increase the likelihood of a breach by these malware from their personal to corporate systems when accessing company data over untrusted networks. The BYOD policy, which is in most cases part of a remote workplace setup, makes it more complex. It can create flexibility and improve productivity while opening up sensitive information to various forms of threats such as leakage and unauthorized access. Robust endpoint protection solutions such as Device Management systems, encryption, and sophisticated endpoint detection and response (EDR) solutions are some of the solutions that need to be in place by companies to counter these challenges.

3.4 Insider Threats and Data Leakage

Thus, over the years, there has been a growing concern about insider threats with remote work as their potential counterpart due to the restrictions placed upon monitoring employee activities. Insider threats happen in two ways: It could be the wilful act of a disgruntled employee leaking sensitive data, or unwittingly exposing data through lax practices or ignorance on the part of an otherwise good employee.

Remote employees take little care about handling procedures and data while working from home with no in-person schedule. For instance, they might keep sensitive files on personal gadgets or unsecured cloud-based platforms or email sensitive attachments to personal accounts, even inadvertently. Especially when third-party collaboration tools are used that do not have the stamp of approval from a firm's IT department, the risks could increase because these tools may not be secured to the same standard of enterprise solutions.

More acute is the risk that remote workers sharing files with personal cloud storage such as Google Drive may know neither that the data is unencrypted nor that it is not protected by the enterprise security measures. Organizations must implement strict access controls to minimize insider threats and file-sharing resources in the way of DLP tools or in-house applications. Regular training of employees on the proper management of data and secure file-sharing practices can reduce human errors leading to exposure of data.

3.5 Cloud Security and Compliance Risks

Given that remote work heavily relies on cloud-based tools for communication, collaboration, and file sharing, there arise significant issues surrounding cloud security and compliance. Although cloud solutions generally provide a lot of room and scalability, it also brings a few restrictions regarding access control, configuration management, and data protection.

Many organizations increasingly adopt Software as a Service (SaaS) platforms like Google Workspace or Microsoft 365 for remote collaboration. These misconfigured cloud settings, weak access management policies, and improper use of third-party cloud services lead to data breaches or unauthorized access. For example, a misconfigured cloud bucket can expose sensitive company files to the internet from where they can be taken advantage of by malicious actors.

Apart from that, another contentious area is regulatory compliance in remote work. The laws such as GDPR, CCPA, and HIPAA lay strict norms for data management and storage, and remote work settings elevate the difficulties of ensuring compliance. It becomes harder for enterprises to track where their data lies, how it accesses the information, and whether sharing is in compliance with legal requirements.

Encryption of all data in transit is complemented by access control, coupled with systematic audits of cloud systems for potential vulnerabilities to ensure cloud security. Compliance will also need to be achieved, requiring a rigorous monitoring and reporting system to demonstrate compliance with data protection regulations.

4. EMERGING TRENDS IN CYBERSECURITY FOR REMOTE WORK

As organizations are shifting towards an increasingly wide-ranging remote work adaptation, even the domain of cybersecurity is undergoing a frantic overhaul. Cyber threats mount from innovation to revolution; using devices that are hard to configure, organizations today need to come up with innovative means and technologies through which to create a secure remote infrastructure. This section studies four recent trends in the future of cybersecurity in remote workspaces: Zero Trust Architecture (ZTA), artificial intelligence and machine learning in threat detection, SASE, and Blockchain for cybersecurity. These trends are considered at the very cutting-edge of innovation in the field of cybersecurity and provide fresh means with which to address the issue and protect an increasingly distributed workforce.

4.1 Zero Trust Architecture (ZTA)

In terms of perimeter-based security models, there is no clear joining line, and when an individual or a device crosses that line into the network, they are trusted with providing access to internal resources. Such models, however, are now dated; the shift to remote work has rendered previous approaches obsolete. The Zero Trust model holds that threats can exist both outside and inside the organization's network-and that trust is never assumed for anyone, whether inside or outside.

The ZTA runs on the ongoing philosophy of "never trust, always verify" and applies strict identity verification to any user, device, or application trying to access corporate resources- regardless of their location. The key components of Zero Trust are:

- **Multi-factor Authentication (MFA):** In the effort to combat unauthorized access, access control technologies require multiple verifications, such as a password and biometric data or even through an authentication app, to open doors.
- **Least privilege access:** Employees are granted access to the minimum amount required for carrying out their work, thus lowering the consequence of breach.
- **Continuous monitoring:** User behavior and activity of devices are continuously assessed for enabling suspicious operations about, allowing faster responses to such behavior.

ZTA is significant, especially in a remote working scenario where employees are in different geographical locations and are often on personal devices whose activities are difficult to monitor. It reduces the chances of unauthorized access, even after a breach, through solid authentication and real-time accountability. More importantly, Zero Trust is essential in achieving the protection of critical assets while allowing flexibility in decentralized workforces.

4.2 AI and Machine Learning in Threat Detection

Incidents of Cyber Security are being subjected to Artificial Intelligence (AI) and Machine Learning (ML) as more and more organizations are relying on these technologies to discover or even respond to the threats. The nature of such new, advanced threats pours out their effects upon nearly every traditional method of threat detection by rule, as it has long outgrown the newest need for speed and complexity in this arena. Real-time processing and pattern recognition for forecasting possible threats before the actual happening of the event in a security breach are covered well by AI and ML because they can analyze huge data amounts and process them simultaneously.

AI tools can go a long way towards forecasting and alleviating threats in the distributed environment (Duan et al., 2022) where these threats would have been originated and transformed from varied sources, as perceivable today under the new normal situation of working remotely. Some of the key use cases of AI and ML in cybersecurity are as follows:

- **Detection of anomalies:** Different algorithms of machine learning could measure how a user behaves, and differentials in normal behavior patterns, such as the entry attempts from exotic places or abnormal data access behavior, could be used to trigger alerts such as preprogrammed actions.
- **Phishing Detection:** That is, by changing content, context, and sender behavior, result of a phishing intrusion or social engineering attains identifying characteristic of AI tools scanning inbound emails and messages to establish a malicious intent.
- **Malware Detection:** AI-based systems do not define types of malware through the signature, allowing them to detect novel malware types by analyzing their file behaviors and system interactions.

Through this utilization of AI and machine learning capabilities, organizations can not only become faster legends for threats but also enhance their entire security posture. From real-time protection, the increase in efficiencies tends to decrease the time to detecting attacks by even as much as 99 percent-a very important feature in protecting a distributed workforce, who may be severely exposed to inadequacies of traditional measures.

4.3 Secure Access Service Edge (SASE)

SASE essentially combines security and WAN functionality into one integrated cloud-based service and enables secure access to applications and data from anywhere. It acts on-site security requirements like ease and history of maintenance and deploying and increases economies of scale through the pooling of traditional networks and WANs. The fair share of traditional on-premises security solutions like VPN can be avoided, which is found to be unworthy and becomes difficult to scale while working remotely. We have recently seen a lot of research and discussion around the Secure Access Service Edge (SASE). Some SASE solutions may combine:

- **Secure web gateways (SWG):** Whose promise is to protect companies from web-based threats via internet traffic and not a people or organization-dependent measure anymore, but a technical undertaking.

- **Cloud access security brokers (CASB):** So-called CASBs help see through control and visibility over usage of cloud services; they give such services in the cloud and concerning cloud use at the same time secure and compliant with rules.
- **Firewall as a service (FWaaS):** This is network firewall protection available in the clouds, ensuring that security policies are applicable at every other access point-whether employees are in-house or at home.

Besides constituting the major gain of SASE, it is the one which allows scaling and makes it easy for a remote workforce, unlike traditional security which runs on hardware, requires various configurations, and can be very complex. SASE is cloud-based, which means that all employees receive the same high level of security regardless of where they are situated at any time. Because such arrangements and setups would need extensive coordination, SASE thus offers the most viable option for organizations whose efforts amount to securing a global, dispersed workforce and making sure they have management over remote working capabilities without performance lag or lack of security.

4.4 Blockchain for Cybersecurity

Buyers are potential clients/ businesses, and they might not be the original target for the blockchain-mind technology. It's highly susceptible to forge and interference in the decentralized and immutable systems of blockchain. This makes many application possibilities in the way an individual or organization applies its act within cyberspace as an effect of hardening cybersecurity. It opens new possibilities in securing digitally signed transactions and ensuring the integrity of information, otherwise critical in most of the remote working environments where employees access and share data across multiple platforms.

Here under are applications of blockchain in cybersecurity:

- **Enhance identity verification:** Blockchain can help offer a secure, decentralized method to verify user identities, thereby reducing the odds of identity theft or unauthorized access. For instance, bringing identity information to a blockchain gives much control to how a user manages credentials while allowing organizations to verify authenticity without reliance on centralized databases that are prone to attacks.
- **Ensure data integrity:** An immutable ledger can thus be employed to track data access and ensure that no unauthorized changes have been made. In remote work setups wherein employees are accessing and sharing sensitive information, blockchain can keep the data intact and secured.
- **Secure transactions:** This can also include using blockchain to facilitate secure, tamper-free transactions, especially in the case of remote transactions or sensitive data exchanges. It minimizes the chances of fraud and unlawful changes to contracts or financial records.

Though not yet an established technology, blockchain has enormous promise in securing remote environments. Innovations that would give rise to new paradigms in the remote work of the near future could help make blockchain a key player in cybersecurity.

As such, the remote environment transforms, and organizations should keep pace with time to avoid possible future falls in the trend of cybersecurity concerning the distributed workforce. Companies can thus position themselves for a stronger security posture against an emerging remote workforce by adopting some of these cutting-edge examples of cybersecurity such as Zero Trust Architecture, AI-driven threat detection, SASE, and Blockchain. The new trends show the future for cybersecurity and offer futuristic solutions to many challenges created by the current digital-first work environment.

5. BEST PRACTICES FOR STRENGTHENING CYBERSECURITY IN REMOTE WORK

With organizations relying more heavily on remote work, the pressing need for robust cybersecurity practices has never been greater. Key best practices comprise this section, which can be employed by businesses to elevate their cybersecurity posture while providing an environment that enables secure and stable remote working. These practices involve establishing strong authentication, improving endpoint security, regular cybersecurity training, and the genesis of clear security policies. Together these methods have a paramount role in limiting risks, safeguarding sensitive data, and assuring the infrastructure integrity of an organization with respect to remote work.

5.1 Implementing Strong Authentication

Strong authentication is one of the most effective modes for protecting remote work environments. Conventional username-and-password authentication are simply not enough to stand against modern-day cyber threats, more so in the far-flung romances of the remote workplace where employees might be accessing company systems over the unknown networks or via their personal devices. Next to that, implementing multi-factor authentication (MFA) must be treated as an important step toward stronger authentication.

Multi-factor authentication is an authentication process that requires a user to provide at least two forms of verification (authenticators) before access is allowed to the system containing sensitive information. This will usually consist of something the user knows (password), something the user has (e.g. a mobile device or hardware token) and something the user is (e.g. biometric data, a fingerprint or face recognition). By adding extra layers of protection, MFA thus remarkably diminishes chances for unauthorized access (Syahreen et al., 2024), even if the login credential is compromised.

Organizations should further promote the use of password managers to allow employees to create and store complex, unique passwords for each system. In that sense, single sign-on (SSO) can also help employees access multiple systems using one set of credentials, reducing password fatigue and giving a better user experience without compromising security.

5.2 Enhancing Endpoint Security

For the mobile employee using an assortment of devices like laptops, desktops, smartphones, and tablets, while even IoT devices may connect to company networks, endpoint security is a crucial aspect of safeguarding a distributed workforce. Endpoint security is, therefore, securing all devices—laptop, desktop, smartphone, tablet, and even IoT devices—that connect to the company network.

Organizations planning to improve endpoint security should have Endpoint Detection and Response (EDR) solutions. EDRs are solutions that monitor and respond to threats identified at all endpoints (Cappello, 2024). Some of the added benefits of EDR tools include real-time alerts for suspicious behavior, such as signs of malware infections, unauthorized access attempts, or data exfiltration.

It also involves using periodic software updates and security patches for all devices. Most cyberattacks exploit defects in outdated software; thus, endpoint devices require the latest versions of operating systems, applications, and security tools. Encrypted storage capability should also be a requirement for the device so that sensitive data can be safeguarded even when the device is lost or stolen.

Moreover, it also requires formulating bring your own device (BYOD) policy, which specifies the conditions under which personal appliances are used for work purposes. In addition, employees should also be required to have specific software, especially security applications such as antivirus and VPNs, installed on their devices prior to accessing any of the systems within the organization.

5.3 Regular Cybersecurity Training

Even the best security tools as well as policies can turn ineffective through human error; regular cybersecurity training is therefore crucial in a work-at-home scenario. The employees should be informed about the different cyber threats and how to recognize such threats and act accordingly. Regular ongoing training programs should be instituted to assist employees in detecting phishing emails and not falling victim to social engineering as well as the importance of securing their devices and accounts. Employees should know about phishing, spear-phishing, and vishing (voice phishing) in addition to risks associated with using public wi-fi networks, revealing sensitive data over unsecured channels, and maintaining weak passwords. Employees should also be informed about data privacy and best practices when it comes to confidential or proprietary information, especially when they use cloud-based tools and remote communications systems.

Other than training, it will be helpful for organizations to have cybersecurity awareness campaigns, via newsletters, webinars, or even simulated phishing tests, throughout the year to reinforce good security habits and keep cybersecurity thinking fresh. The more informed and vigilant employees are, the less likely they are to make mistakes that could lead to a breach.

5.4 Establishing Clear Security Policies

Creation of unambiguous and well-defined security policies is imperative to guard against the very threats that accompany remote work. In particular, such policies will define what constitutes acceptable use of company devices, personal devices, and third-party applications, and will help ensure that employees understand their duties toward protecting corporate data and systems.

An adequate working-from-home security policy needs to include:

- **Data Protection Standards:** Informing employees on best practices in the safeguarding of sensitive data during storage, sharing, and access by employing techniques like encryption and secure file sharing.
- **Password Management:** Written policies should be developed on how to create strong passwords, using the password managers, and having MFA integrated as possible and reasonable.
- **Remote Access Procedures:** These procedures should include information on VPN connections, secure communication platforms, and proper authentication when accessing company resources remotely.
- **Incident Response Procedures:** The staff can be trained on how to report possible security incidents so that the organization can respond to them promptly, minimizing damage.

Policies should be audited and revisited frequently and developed based on the existing threat and technological scenario. Furthermore, organizations should ensure that all remote employees are notified of such policies and adhere to them, requesting acknowledgment signatures and periodic reminders via internal communications.

Through strong authentication, endpoint security, employee continuous training on cybersecurity, and application of the security policies in a clear manner, organizations maximize their cybersecurity posture in a remote working environment. These best practices would help in the reduction of the threat caused by the flexible workplace and allow employees to work efficiently without jeopardizing the security of data and infrastructures regarded as most critical. As organizations adopt remote work as a long-term model for their operations, a good and robust cybersecurity structure will be very vital in ensuring personnel and the organization are secured.

6. FUTURE DIRECTIONS IN CYBERSECURITY FOR REMOTE WORK

Cybersecurity must keep pace with the ever-changing digital landscape that faces new decentralized challenges, where remote working lifestyles have become the norm in many countries. The future of cybersecurity for remote working environments hinges on the level of advances in technology such as AI-based security automation, decentralized identity management, and cybersecurity in virtual workspaces. These trends promise better security and tackle the increased complexity in securing remote work scenarios. This section will review the future paths and their impact on the evolution of cybersecurity strategies to safeguard distributed workforces.

6.1 AI-Driven Security Automation

AI-driven security automation introduces new paradigms within the enterprise to detect and respond to cyber threats, especially in the ever-expanding attack profile presented by remote working. Remote-working organizations need to defend against an exponentially increasing number and varied types of cyber-attacks. Advantages of artificial intelligence and machine learning technologies would enhance threat detection and response abilities greatly, thus improving the response to cyber threats in real time.

AI can detect suspicious activity in vast amounts of data way quicker than human analysts. AI continuously monitoring routine user behavior, network traffic, and device activity can identify anomalies that signal security breaches. For example, AI flags unusual logins, such as accessing a corporate network from an atypical location or odd hours. Subsequently, the AI either alerts a human analyst working in security or a cybersecurity incident response team or takes preventative action on its own, such as locking an account or blocking access to sensitive resources.

Additionally, AI-driven security automation minimizes the response time towards a threat much quicker than any manual process. Once a threat is detected, the automated system can immediately take actions such as isolating affected devices from the network, blocking all access attempts from the malicious IP addresses, or quarantining suspicious files. Machines are very rapid in taking actions, so in such a way, they will make sure that the window for the attacker to exploit a vulnerability is minimized until the human can intervene. Furthermore, AI super-automation facilitates early anticipatory threat hunting. In this, AI tools scan the environment for vulnerable points or weaknesses that can potentially be exploited, thus providing much-needed security resilience.

Generally, AI's role promises to significantly increase the efficacy of any strategy to protect remote work environments (Adeniran et al., 2024) with fewer human errors and faster threat responses. In its further maturation, AI will be as critical to the survival of dynamic and fast-evolving remote work environments.

6.2 Decentralized Identity Management

The other really important cybersecurity trend for the remote work culture is decentralized identity management. Traditional identity management systems, with centralized databases to store and authenticate user credentials, come with single points of failure readily exploitable by cybercriminals. Therefore, moving to decentralized systems that enforce blockchain technology offers a much better promise in the secure and resilient management of digital identities.

Decentralized identity management allows individuals to maintain control over their identity data through cryptographic keys. Here, identifications based on the blockchain authenticate identities across a network of nodes instead of relying on a central authority. The advantage of getting rid of the central authority is that doing so will often lessen, if not eliminate, the huge compromise that would see sensitive data lose its integrity. Such architecture preserves security since there is no central repository for an attacker to compromise; rather, the burden of proof moves to those who would want to gain from being trusted as an identity.

Decentralized identity management not only increases security but also provides greater control to individuals over their personal information. User identity data can be shared selectively with trusted parties without exposing other unnecessary details. Thus, such control over personal data decreases chances of data breaches, besides addressing rising concerns over data privacy especially in situations of remote work where employees clock into systems from assorted devices and locations.

By enabling self-sovereign identity, decentralized systems also facilitate the authentication process. Employees can authenticate securely with one digital identity across all platforms and services without having to remember multiple passwords. With the growing remote workforce, decentralized identity management will increasingly be significant for securing and easing access.

6.3 Cybersecurity in Virtual Workspaces

While remote work continues to shift into spaces that are increasingly digital and interactive, cyber security will require new strategies as work moves away from traditional practices. Workspaces will have to include virtual work security to address issues affecting these platforms, which will demand specialized tools and protocols. New realities of the physical work environment, as well as virtual workspaces, pose radical changes for users; instead of direct human interaction, users now use avatars.

The secure interaction of their activities and raw facilities in them opens up for critical infrastructure. Conventional firewalls and antimalware will most probably fail to keep pace with these emerging virtual realms.

Therefore, the necessity for security applications that are used in virtual workspaces only comes into force. One of the areas to be highlighted will be identity and access management (IAM).

IAM will be important as the employees will use avatars to access different resources and interact with coworkers in the virtual spaces. This will apply that the access rights to virtual meetings, sensitive data, and project collaboration would need to be definitively controlled. These virtual environments, along with accesses to company resources, could be secured by using multi-factor authentication (MFA) and biometric identification combined together.

The other primary concern in the virtual workplace will be data protection. Transmissions between this new environment should encrypt and transfer data so that unauthorized whitening or tapping has no occurrence. Development and improvement of new encryption standards and secure communication protocols would then ensure confidentiality and integrity to sensitive virtual data.

Behavioral monitoring would hence become prominent in the cybersecurity sphere of virtual workplaces. AI uses for threat detection in the traditional digital field will soon find their application in analyzing user behavior within virtual spaces to finally discover suspicious activities.

It can also be until the actions show signs of fraud, social engineering, or attempts at unauthorized access into virtual environments. Thus, continuous monitoring would ensure that security breaches are detected earlier and responded to immediately.

The evolution of virtual work environments will be accompanied by the evolutionary changes in cybersecurity protocols to cater to the environments and the information contained within them. With such an integration of the metaverse and similar technologies into the operations of organizations, end-to-end security across virtual workspaces would be crucial in defining a new standard for the security of remote workplaces.

The cyber safety of remote working is being constructed by new technologies such as AI security automation, decentralized identity management, and cybersecurity for virtual workspaces. These innovations will improve the security of remote working, authentication, and offer alternatives to safeguard digital assets and personal information as organizations keep embracing remote work. Thus, businesses who know the current trends will help them secure and sustain a well-functioning remote workforce in the increasingly digital world.

7. CONCLUSION

The flexibility of remote work, its accompanying cost savings, and its access to a global talent pool all come with security risks that have to be dealt with. From increased attack surfaces to distributed workforce security complexities, organizations are facing threats in accelerating environments. This chapter has explored the most pressing cybersecurity challenges of remote working conditions, trends on the rise, and industry best practices that can help organizations in safeguarding their digital infrastructure.

The challenge is to maximize their beneficial aspects without worsening the increased remote-working cyber threats. While the model continues to be adapted and shaped by various human and environmental factors, the organizations will have to reform their past strategies in meeting the challenges. AI-driven security automation, decentralized identity management, and virtualization are some of the most relevant trends that appear to offer the future potential for enhanced protection. Real-time threat detection and faster processing time responses are enabled by AI-powered automation.

Data privacy and protection will be increased by decentralized identity management as they do not hinge on centralized systems. Finally, as walled digital environments continue to mature, companies will need to consider specialized security barriers to keep their operations safely beyond the metaverse and other space-virtual realities. Best practices include strong authentication protocols, endpoint security improvement, and frequent training of personnel in cybersecurity. The benefits will thus remain principles in protection for remote employees and devices.

Reducing the risks presented by cyber threats can be greatly realized with a culture of security awareness supplemented by a vigorous security framework. Cybersecurity should be considered a whole-life endeavor rather than a one-time concerted effort (Singh, 2022) to ensure the safety of digital assets and sensitive and employee data. For instance, security-making organizations will ensure that future technologies and new inventions in cybersecurity keep enabling their effective functioning with remote employees.

Organizations will approach security in a digital-first world, aided by future technological advancements in AI-based security tools, blockchain for decentralization of identity management, and secure virtual workspaces. Organizations that want to keep pace with the emerging threats will keep investing in new technologies and innovation, especially in cybersecurity, for their remote work strategies. It will take a proactive and multi-faceted approach to securing the future of remote work.

The organization, therefore, adopts the emerging trends, best practices, and creates a culture of securing consciousness within employees in reducing risks to developing an environment where employees can work remotely yet safely, without affecting output or data security. Therefore, in future possibilities of remote working, digital communication will have stronghold grounds in organizational success by having a sturdy cybersecurity system.

REFERENCES

Adeniran, A. A., Adeniran, A. O., Familusi, O. B., & Adedayo, O. (2024). The Outlook of Cyber Security in African Businesses: Issues and Way-Out. *Management analytics and social insights, 1*(2), 260-271.

Bada, M., & von Solms, B. (2022, June). A cybersecurity guide for using fitness devices. In *The Fifth International Conference on Safety and Security with IoT: SaSeIoT 2021* (pp. 35-45). Cham: Springer International Publishing.

Bertino, E., & Brancik, K. (2021, September). Services for zero trust architectures-a research roadmap. In *2021 IEEE international conference on web services (ICWS)* (pp. 14-20). IEEE. DOI: 10.1109/ICWS53863.2021.00016

Cappello, M. (2024). *A comprehensive analysis of EDR (Endpoint Detection & Response), EPP (Endpoint Protection Platform), and antivirus security technologies* (Master's thesis, Πανεπιστήμιο Πειραιώς).

Choi, B., Lee, D.-Y., & Kim, B. (2020). Deterrent effects of punishment and training on insider security threats: A field experiment on phishing attacks. *Behaviour & Information Technology, 39*(11), 1156–1175. DOI: 10.1080/0144929X.2019.1653992

. Cybersecurity, U. S. (2022). Infrastructure Security Agency (2021). *Executive Order 13800. Strengthening the Cybersecurity of Federal Networks and Critical Infrastructure. 11 May 2017.*

Dillon, R., Lothian, P., Grewal, S., & Pereira, D. (2021). Cyber security: evolving threats in an ever-changing world. In *Digital Transformation in a Post-Covid World* (pp. 129–154). CRC Press. DOI: 10.1201/9781003148715-7

Duan, S., Wang, D., Ren, J., Lyu, F., Zhang, Y., Wu, H., & Shen, X. (2022). Distributed artificial intelligence empowered by end-edge-cloud computing: A survey. *IEEE Communications Surveys and Tutorials, 25*(1), 591–624. DOI: 10.1109/COMST.2022.3218527

. Kurek, D. (2021). Use of modern IT solutions in the HRM activities: Process automation and digital employer branding.

Palmeter, K. (2022). Cyberattacks: An underlying condition exacerbated by the COVID-19 pandemic. *J. Bus. Entrepreneurship & L., 15*, 241.

Singh, L. (2022). Cyber crime, cyber resilience and security strategy in post pandemic world. *Supremo Amicus, 28*, 305.

Syahreen, M., Hafizah, N., Maarop, N., & Maslinan, M. (2024). A Systematic Review on Multi-Factor Authentication Framework. *International Journal of Advanced Computer Science and Applications, 15*(5). Advance online publication. DOI: 10.14569/IJACSA.2024.01505105

Zhou, L., Song, Y., Ji, W., & Wei, H. (2022). Machine learning for combustion. *Energy and AI, 7*, 100128. DOI: 10.1016/j.egyai.2021.100128

ADDITIONAL READING

Adewusi, A. O., Chiekezie, N. R., & Eyo-Udo, N. L. (2022). Securing smart agriculture: Cybersecurity challenges and solutions in IoT-driven farms. *World Journal of Advanced Research and Reviews*, *15*(03), 480–489. DOI: 10.30574/wjarr.2022.15.3.0887

Ahmed, S., Ahmed, I., Kamruzzaman, M., & Saha, R. CYBERSECURITY CHALLENGES IN IT INFRASTRUCTURE DATA: A COMPREHENSIVE REVIEW OF THREATS, MITIGATION STRATEGIES, AND FUTURE TRENDS.

Asif, R., & Hassan, S. R. (2023). Exploring the confluence of IoT and metaverse: Future opportunities and challenges. *IoT*, *4*(3), 412–429. DOI: 10.3390/iot4030018

Chauhan, M., & Shiaeles, S. (2023). An analysis of cloud security frameworks, problems and proposed solutions. *Network (Bristol, England)*, *3*(3), 422–450.

. Chinaza, O. C. The SASE (SASSY): Situational Awareness of a Digital Initiative Disruptive Framework.

Dalei, N. N., & Kandpal, V. (2025). Understanding the Global Landscape of Cybersecurity Risks, Economic Impacts, and Challenges: Lesson for India. In *Cybersecurity, Law, and Economics* (pp. 17-37). Routledge.

Fezzey, T., Batchelor, J. H., Burch, G. F., & Reid, R. (2023). Cybersecurity continuity risks: Lessons learned from the COVID-19 pandemic. *Journal of Cybersecurity Education. Research and Practice*, *2022*(2), 4.

Kambourakis, G., Neisse, R., & Nai-Fovino, I. (2021). *Information security in the age of EU-Institutions digitalisation, a landscape analysis*. Europcan Commission, Joint Research Centre.

. Kosaraju, D. Remote Work Revolution: Cybersecurity in the Age of COVID-19.

Lamba, T., & Kandwal, S. (2022, August). Global Outlook of Cyber Security. In *Proceedings of the Third International Conference on Information Management and Machine Intelligence: ICIMMI 2021* (pp. 269-276). Singapore: Springer Nature Singapore.

. Macaulay, T., & Bhasker, D. (2024). High Performance Computing Infrastructure and Zero Trust Architecture. *Pulse & Praxis: The Journal for Critical Infrastructure Protection, Security and Resilience*.

Martin, P. (2023). *Insider risk and personnel security: An introduction*. Taylor & Francis. DOI: 10.4324/9781003329022

Masud, S. B., Rana, M. M., Sohag, H. J., Shikder, F., Faraji, M. R., & Hasan, M. M. (2024). Understanding the Financial Transaction Security through Blockchain and Machine Learning for Fraud Detection in Data Privacy and Security. *Available atSSRN* 5164958. DOI: 10.57239/PJLSS-2024-22.2.001296

Mokhtar, R., & Rohaizat, A. (2024). Cybercrimes and cyber security trends in the new normal. In *The New Normal and Its Impact on Society: Perspectives from ASEAN and the European Union* (pp. 41–60). Springer Nature Singapore. DOI: 10.1007/978-981-97-0527-6_4

Neto, N. N., Madnick, S., Paula, A. M. G. D., & Borges, N. M. (2021). Developing a global data breach database and the challenges encountered. [JDIQ]. *ACM Journal of Data and Information Quality, 13*(1), 1–33. DOI: 10.1145/3439873

Parikh, A. (2019). *Cloud security and platform thinking: an analysis of Cisco Umbrella, a cloud-delivered enterprise security* (Doctoral dissertation, Massachusetts Institute of Technology).

Vasquez, C., & Gonzalez, J. (2022). Cybersecurity engagement in a remote work environment.

Verizon, B. (2008). 2008 Data Breach Investigations Report. http://www. verizonbusiness. com/resources/ security/databreachreport. pdf

Wainwright, P., Katamba, F., & Henderson, D. (2024). Cybersecurity Risks to Business and Legal Sectors. *Business Law International, 25*(3).

Yeoh, W., Liu, M., Shore, M., & Jiang, F. (2023). Zero trust cybersecurity: Critical success factors and A maturity assessment framework. *Computers & Security, 133*, 103412. DOI: 10.1016/j.cose.2023.103412

Zou, Y., McDonald, A., Narakornpichit, J., Dell, N., Ristenpart, T., Roundy, K., . . . Tamersoy, A. (2021). The role of computer security customer support in helping survivors of intimate partner violence. In *30th USENIX security symposium (USENIX Security 21)* (pp. 429-446).

Chapter 6

AI and Emotional Intelligence in Project Management:

Managing Hybrid Teams in a Tech-Driven Environment

Geshwaree Huzooree
https://orcid.org/0000-0001-8076-6636
Edinburgh Napier University, UK

Mohit Yadav
https://orcid.org/0000-0002-9341-2527
O.P. Jindal Global University, India

Narayanage Jayantha Dewasiri
https://orcid.org/0000-0002-5908-8890
Sabaragamuwa University of Sri Lanka, Sri Lanka & Qasim Ibrahim School of Business, Villa College, Maldives

ABSTRACT

The rise of hybrid work models has transformed project management, requiring leaders to balance technological advancements with emotional intelligence (EI) to maintain team cohesion, morale, and productivity. This chapter explores the intersection of artificial intelligence (AI) and EI in project management, focusing on how AI-driven tools can enhance team dynamics, sentiment analysis, and conflict resolution in distributed work environments. While AI can offer valuable insights into employee well-being and collaboration patterns, it cannot fully replace the human touch in leadership. Through case studies and real-world applications, this chapter highlights how project managers can integrate AI-powered analytics with EI-driven decision-making to foster trust, engagement, and high performance in hybrid teams. Additionally, ethical considerations and the future of AI-augmented leadership are explored, offering practical strategies for navigating the evolving role of technology in project environments while preserving human connection and empathy.

DOI: 10.4018/979-8-3373-1270-5.ch006

1. INTRODUCTION

1.1 The Evolution of Project Management in the Modern Workplace

The field of project management has undergone a profound shift in recent years, largely driven by advancements in technology and changing workplace structures (Huzooree & Yadav, 2025). The rise of hybrid work models, where teams operate across a mix of remote and in-office settings, has challenged traditional project management approaches that relied on face-to-face interactions, real-time collaboration, and structured workflows (Luo et al., 2022). This shift has accelerated the adoption of digital tools, cloud-based platforms, and artificial intelligence (AI) to ensure seamless communication, task allocation, and progress tracking (Kerzner, 2025).

However, while technology has improved efficiency, it has also introduced challenges related to team cohesion, trust, and engagement (Hobsbawm, 2022). Hybrid environments often lead to miscommunication, misalignment, and a decline in team morale if not managed effectively. To address these concerns, EI has emerged as a crucial leadership skill, helping project managers foster strong relationships, navigate conflicts, and maintain motivation in dispersed teams. This chapter explores the intersection of AI and EQ, highlighting how they can be interlinked to enhance hybrid project management.

The Importance Emotional Intelligence (EI) in Hybrid Project Management

Emotional intelligence (EI), the ability to recognize, understand, and manage emotions, has become increasingly vital for project managers leading hybrid teams. Unlike traditional work environments, hybrid teams often lack the spontaneous interpersonal interactions that foster workplace camaraderie and trust. Research suggests that leaders with high EI contribute significantly to team engagement, conflict resolution, and psychological safety, all of which are critical in virtual and dispersed settings (Goleman, 1996; Koubova & Buchko., 2013).

A hybrid workplace can intensify issues such as misinterpretations in digital communication, employee isolation, and reduced team cohesion (Newman & Ford, 2021). Without non-verbal cues such as body language and tone of voice, project managers must be intentional about fostering open communication, active listening, and empathy in their leadership approach. EI enables managers to identify emotional distress, motivate employees, and tailor communication styles to individual team members' needs (Boyatzis et al., 2013; 2018). Moreover, EI plays a key role in managing stress and burnout, which have become prevalent in hybrid work cultures where employees struggle with blurred work-life boundaries (Doargajudhur et al., 2024; Luo et al., 2022).

By leveraging EI, project managers can create a more inclusive, resilient, and collaborative team environment, ensuring that technology does not replace human connection but rather enhances it.

1.3 The Role of AI in Modern Project Management

AI is increasingly transforming project management by automating workflows, improving decision-making, and enhancing team collaboration (Huzooree, 2024; Shakilla & Saputro, 2025). AI-powered tools can analyze large datasets, predict project risks, and optimize resource allocation, enabling project managers to make more informed strategic decisions (Kerzner, 2025).

In the hybrid work era, AI also plays a crucial role in bridging communication gaps by facilitating seamless collaboration through digital platforms such as AI-driven chatbots, virtual meeting assistants, and automated project tracking systems (Khosroshahi, 2024; Shakilla & Saputro., 2025).

One of the most promising applications of AI in project management is sentiment analysis, which allows managers to gauge employee morale by analyzing patterns in emails, chat messages, and meeting transcripts (Joshi, 2024). AI-powered sentiment analysis can help leaders detect signs of disengagement, stress, or conflict before they escalate.

However, while AI provides valuable insights, it cannot replace human intuition, empathy, and ethical judgment (Al-Arafat et al., 2025). AI models, no matter how advanced, lack the ability to fully comprehend human emotions in their nuanced and contextual forms (Joshi, 2024; Shakilla & Saputro, 2025). Thus, the most effective project managers will be those who skillfully integrate AI-driven insights with high EI, using technology to support rather than replace human connection and leadership.

2. EMOTIONAL INTELLIGENCE IN PROJECT MANAGEMENT

2.1 Understanding Emotional Intelligence in Project Leadership

EI plays a pivotal role in project leadership, particularly as the dynamics of the workplace shift towards hybrid environments. Defined by Mayer and Salovey (1990), EI encompasses the ability to identify, assess, and manage emotions, both in oneself and in others. The increasing prevalence of hybrid teams, which include both remote and in-office workers, amplifies the need for EI in leadership roles. A project manager's ability to effectively manage the emotional climate of the team, ensuring engagement, morale, and collaboration, becomes crucial for project success. While hybrid work brings flexibility and access to a global talent pool, it also introduces emotional and interpersonal challenges that traditional in-office settings do not face. As Goleman (1996) highlights, emotionally intelligent leaders are adept at navigating these complexities, fostering trust and collaboration despite geographical distances.

Self-awareness, self-regulation, motivation, empathy, and social skills are often regarded as the key components of EI (Goleman, 1996). Self-awareness allows project managers to recognize their emotional triggers and their potential influence on decision-making processes. This is particularly important in a hybrid environment where decision-making is frequently carried out through digital communication, leaving less room for informal, face-to-face interactions. Leaders who are aware of their emotional states are better equipped to manage their reactions, ensuring that their decisions remain objective and well-considered.

Equally important is the capacity for empathy. In hybrid teams, where emotional cues are less apparent, project managers must make an active effort to recognize and respond to the emotional needs of their team members. This proactive approach helps ensure that all team members, regardless of whether they are remote or in-office, feel supported and valued, even in the absence of daily in-person interactions.

Social skills, which include effective communication and conflict resolution, are particularly critical in remote work settings. EI enables project managers to navigate delicate situations, mediate conflicts, and encourage collaboration among individuals who may not share the same physical or cultural context.

Research by Boyatzis et al. (2018) and Kim and Ko (2021) further underscores the role of EI in building team cohesion. In a hybrid environment, where physical distance can create a sense of detachment, EI functions as the glue that binds the team together. Leaders who demonstrate high EI create an environment in which team members feel safe to express their concerns, engage in meaningful discussions, and work collaboratively towards shared goals. When leaders are attuned to their team's emotional needs, they can address issues proactively, preventing potential conflicts and boosting morale.

2.2 EI Challenges in Hybrid Teams

The inherent nature of hybrid work introduces several challenges related to EI, particularly with respect to communication, team cohesion, and conflict resolution. A significant barrier to the effective application of EI in hybrid teams is the reduced visibility of emotional cues. In traditional office settings, project managers can rely on face-to-face interactions to gauge their team members' emotional states, observing nonverbal signals such as body language and facial expressions. However, these cues are largely absent in virtual settings, making it more difficult for leaders to detect underlying issues such as disengagement, burnout, or interpersonal conflict (Alves et al., 2023; Kirkman et al., 2004).

In hybrid teams, where team members often work asynchronously and across multiple time zones, this issue is compounded. The lack of real-time communication and the delay in feedback loops can make it challenging for project managers to stay attuned to their team's emotional health. Furthermore, the reliance on digital communication channels, such as email and instant messaging, can lead to the misinterpretation of tone and intent. Mehrabian (2017) emphasizes that nonverbal communication, including tone of voice and facial expressions, constitutes a substantial portion of communication. Without these cues, written messages may be misinterpreted, leading to confusion and potentially damaging relationships within the team.

Another significant challenge lies in maintaining team cohesion. In hybrid teams, remote workers often report feelings of isolation, which can hinder their engagement and participation in team activities. When team members are physically distanced, there is a risk that they will feel excluded from key decisions or conversations, leading to a breakdown in trust and collaboration (Luo et al., 2022). Project managers must therefore find ways to foster inclusion, ensuring that both remote and in-office employees are equally involved in the project's progress and decisions. Leaders who demonstrate high EI are adept at cultivating inclusivity, ensuring that no team member feels marginalized or overlooked, regardless of their physical location.

Cultural and personality differences also pose a challenge in hybrid teams. Team members from different geographic regions or cultural backgrounds may have varying expectations around communication styles, work ethics, and emotional expression. These differences can lead to misunderstandings, misalignment of objectives, and, in some cases, interpersonal conflict. EI is crucial in these situations, as it allows project managers to identify potential sources of tension and address them in a sensitive and empathetic manner. Furthermore, an emotionally intelligent leader can adapt their leadership style to meet the individual needs of team members, fostering an environment of respect and cooperation (Nilsson & Norström, 2024).

2.3 Case Study: The Impact of EI on Hybrid Project Success

An example of how EI can influence hybrid project success is evident in Microsoft's transition to a hybrid workforce model following the COVID-19 pandemic. As the company moved towards a blend of remote and in-office work, it encountered several challenges inherent to the new work structure, particularly in fostering team cohesion, maintaining morale, and sustaining productive collaboration across dispersed teams. This shift not only required technological adaptation but also an evolution in leadership practices to support a diverse and geographically separated workforce.

Microsoft's leadership recognized the critical need to address the emotional and psychological well-being of its employees, especially those working remotely. Remote workers often expressed feelings of isolation, as they were distanced from the informal interactions and spontaneous communication that characterize traditional office environments. The absence of face-to-face interactions intensifies difficulties in reading emotional cues, making it more challenging for managers to identify signs of stress, disengagement, or burnout. As noted by Goleman (1996), EI in leadership, particularly the ability to empathize with employees and manage emotional dynamics, became essential in navigating these challenges.

To address these issues, Microsoft introduced a range of emotionally intelligent leadership initiatives, underpinned by a strong focus on empathy and emotional attunement. First, they trained leaders to recognize the emotional signals of remote employees through regular one-on-one check-ins, which became a cornerstone of their management approach. These check-ins allowed leaders to demonstrate empathy, listen actively, and offer support tailored to individual needs, thus fostering a more inclusive and emotionally secure environment. This approach was aligned with the principles outlined by Goleman and Boyatzis (2008), who emphasizes the importance of self-awareness and social awareness in effective leadership.

Moreover, Microsoft leveraged technology to enhance its EI-driven leadership practices. The introduction of Microsoft Viva Insights, an AI-powered tool designed to monitor employee well-being, proved instrumental. The tool analyzed a variety of data points, such as communication patterns, work habits, and employee sentiment, providing leaders with actionable insights into the emotional health of their teams. This allowed project managers to identify early signs of disengagement, excessive workloads, or burnout, enabling them to intervene proactively (Luo et al., 2022). Notably, this integration of AI and EI exemplifies the synergy between human-centered leadership and data-driven technology, which enhances EI without sacrificing the personal touch essential for effective leadership.

In addition to these efforts, Microsoft also implemented a series of regular "pulse surveys" to assess employee sentiment. These surveys, conducted at frequent intervals, captured real-time emotional feedback from employees, providing managers with data on morale, engagement, and overall well-being. By using this data, leaders were able to adjust their approaches to better support the emotional needs of their teams. This proactive stance in gauging and responding to emotional concerns was essential in maintaining high levels of engagement, particularly within hybrid teams where the risk of emotional disconnection was heightened.

Furthermore, Microsoft understood that EI could not only be applied through individual leadership actions but also needed to be embedded into the culture of the organization. To this end, the company encouraged the use of collaborative platforms like Microsoft Teams and Yammer, where employees could engage in both professional and informal exchanges. These virtual spaces helped foster a sense of belonging, offering employees the opportunity to connect with colleagues across geographic locations. Encouraging participation in these virtual spaces was crucial for maintaining a sense of community among hybrid teams and reducing feelings of isolation, a common issue faced by remote workers (Newman & Ford, 2021).

The results of these EI-based initiatives were promising. Feedback from Microsoft employees indicated a marked improvement in engagement levels and overall job satisfaction. Reports from the company's internal surveys revealed a significant increase in employee well-being, with remote employees feeling more connected to their teams and the broader organizational culture. Importantly, these improvements in emotional engagement correlated with enhanced project delivery and overall productivity. Teams in the hybrid model not only met project deadlines but also reported greater satisfaction with the collaborative process, underscoring the positive influence of emotionally intelligent leadership in a hybrid work context.

Microsoft's experience highlights the critical role of EI in managing hybrid teams, particularly in environments where physical separation poses unique challenges to communication and collaboration. The company's strategic use of both human-centered leadership practices and AI technologies exemplifies an integrated approach to managing emotional dynamics in the workplace. The case demonstrates that by nurturing EI in leadership, organizations can enhance employee engagement, mitigate the risks of isolation, and drive team success, even in a hybrid or remote setting.

3. THE ROLE OF AI IN UNDERSTANDING TEAM DYNAMICS AND MORALE

3.1 AI-Powered Sentiment Analysis: Measuring Team Morale

As project management continues to evolve in response to technological advancements, the integration of AI and EI has emerged as a significant area of interest. In hybrid work environments, the challenge of managing distributed teams with diverse emotional needs becomes more pronounced, necessitating innovative solutions to bridge the emotional and geographical gap. AI, with its ability to process vast amounts of data and identify patterns, can be harnessed to enhance the EI of project managers, thereby facilitating better team management, collaboration, and conflict resolution.

While EI is inherently a human skill, AI tools can augment a project manager's ability to assess and respond to the emotional needs of hybrid teams. AI can provide real-time insights into employee sentiment, engagement levels, and stress, which are difficult to gauge through traditional means, particularly in virtual or hybrid environments (Chen et al., 2023; Coronado-Maldonado & Benítez-Márquez, 2023). For example, AI-driven sentiment analysis tools can analyze communication patterns, whether through email, chat, or video conferences, and detect shifts in tone or sentiment, providing project managers with valuable feedback on team morale and emotional well-being.

These AI tools function by processing text, voice, or even facial expressions to identify underlying emotions such as frustration, disengagement, or satisfaction. This enables project managers to recognize emotional cues that might otherwise go unnoticed, particularly in remote or asynchronous settings where traditional non-verbal cues are absent. By integrating AI-powered tools with their EI, project managers can gain a deeper understanding of team dynamics and respond more effectively to emerging issues (Coronado-Maldonado & Benítez-Márquez, 2023; Javed et al., 2025).

For instance, in managing hybrid teams, where workers may alternate between in-office and remote work, project managers often face challenges in maintaining the emotional cohesion of the team. AI can help monitor and assess whether team members feel isolated or undervalued, potentially flagging issues before they escalate. Through this predictive capability, AI augments a project manager's EI, providing actionable insights that lead to more informed decision-making and tailored interventions.

3.2 Predictive Analytics for Employee Well-Being

The primary strength of AI in hybrid team management lies in its ability to collect and analyze large datasets that inform EI strategies. Tools such as sentiment analysis software, emotion recognition algorithms, and AI-driven surveys are increasingly used by organizations to monitor and improve employee well-being. These tools can be applied to measure the emotional tone of written communications, detect signs of emotional burnout or stress, and evaluate the overall mood of a team (Pak et al., 2024).

Sentiment analysis, for example, processes textual data from emails, chat messages, and online collaboration platforms to evaluate the emotional tone of communication. AI-driven platforms like IBM Watson Tone Analyzer or Microsoft Viva Insights employ natural language processing (NLP) to identify positive, neutral, or negative sentiment in digital conversations (Smith et al., 2024). These tools also assess more nuanced emotions such as frustration, satisfaction, and stress, allowing project managers to gauge emotional fluctuations that may otherwise remain undetected in the digital communication landscape (Ivan et al., 2024). In hybrid teams, where team members may not interact face-to-face regularly, such tools enable managers to stay attuned to the emotional states of their team members.

In addition to sentiment analysis, AI tools can also assess non-verbal cues, which are critical in understanding emotional dynamics. Emotion recognition technologies, such as those developed by companies like Affectiva, analyze facial expressions, body language, and voice tone during virtual meetings (Bjørnsten & Sørensen, 2020). By using machine learning algorithms to detect emotions such as anger, confusion, or joy, these tools provide project managers with real-time emotional feedback during team interactions. For example, if a team member appears disengaged or frustrated during a video conference, AI-powered emotion recognition can alert the project manager to potential issues, prompting them to intervene before these emotions negatively impact team performance or project outcomes (Coronado-Maldonado & Benítez-Márquez, 2023).

Moreover, AI can also assist in monitoring workload distribution, which is a crucial aspect of emotional well-being in hybrid teams. Overburdened employees may experience stress, burnout, or frustration, which can negatively impact their performance and the team's overall productivity. AI-based tools can analyze workload data to identify signs of imbalance, allowing project managers to redistribute tasks effectively or offer additional support to those in need. Tools such as Trello, Monday.com, and Asana integrate AI to track project progress, workloads, and deadlines, alerting managers when a team member is at risk of overload (Ajiva et al., 2024; Coronado-Maldonado & Benítez-Márquez, 2023).

3.3 AI-Based Engagement and Feedback Tools

Conflict resolution and team collaboration are two critical areas where AI can enhance EI in hybrid project environments. In traditional office settings, project managers can rely on face-to-face interactions and social cues to address conflicts or facilitate collaboration. In hybrid or remote environments, however, the absence of physical presence complicates this process. EI, particularly the skills of empathy and social awareness, becomes more challenging to apply effectively in virtual interactions. AI, however, can bridge this gap by providing insights into the emotional undercurrents of team dynamics and by suggesting interventions that foster positive interactions.

AI-powered tools can help project managers detect early signs of conflict by analyzing communication patterns. For instance, language that indicates frustration, defensiveness, or withdrawal can be flagged by sentiment analysis software. These tools can also measure the frequency of negative interactions or identify team members who may be disengaged or less involved in team discussions. This data enables project managers to intervene early, fostering an environment of psychological safety where conflict can be addressed constructively (Nilsson & Norström, 2024).

In the context of team collaboration, AI can also assist in fostering inclusivity and ensuring that all team members, whether remote or on-site, feel equally involved in discussions and decision-making. AI-powered collaboration platforms, such as Microsoft Teams, integrate features that promote balanced participation. Tools like "Raise Hand" in Microsoft Teams or "Mentimeter" allow managers to ensure that all team members have a voice during virtual meetings, preventing domination by a few vocal members (Boon et al., 2023). By encouraging more balanced participation, these tools can help mitigate feelings of isolation or exclusion among remote workers, ensuring that EI is maintained in a diverse team environment.

Furthermore, AI tools can support personalized conflict resolution strategies. By analyzing individual communication styles and emotional triggers, AI can recommend tailored approaches for resolving disputes. For example, an AI tool might suggest a private one-on-one meeting for a conflict-prone team member or advise the project manager to use a more empathetic tone when addressing a particularly sensitive issue. These personalized interventions, informed by AI insights, empower project managers to address conflicts in ways that align with individual emotional needs and enhance the overall EI of the team (Pak et al., 2024).

3.4 Ethical Considerations of AI in Monitoring Team Morale

Despite the promising potential of AI to enhance EI in hybrid project management, there are several ethical considerations and limitations that need to be addressed. One of the primary concerns is privacy. AI tools that track sentiment, analyze communication, or recognize emotions may inadvertently invade employees' privacy, particularly when assessing emotional states through facial recognition or monitoring private communications. It is essential that organizations establish clear guidelines on data usage, ensuring that AI tools are used transparently and with employees' consent (Chen et al., 2023; Coronado-Maldonado & Benítez-Márquez, 2023).

Additionally, there is the issue of bias. AI algorithms are only as effective as the data they are trained on, and biases in the data can lead to skewed or inaccurate assessments of emotional states. For instance, AI emotion recognition tools may be less accurate in recognizing emotions in people from diverse cultural backgrounds or may misinterpret non-verbal cues that differ across cultures (Katirai, 2024). Therefore, organizations must ensure that AI tools are tested for bias and continually refined to improve their accuracy across diverse teams.

Lastly, while AI can augment EI, it is unlikely to fully replace the nuanced and empathetic decision-making that human project managers bring to the table. AI should be seen as a tool to support, rather than replace, human leadership. EI, after all, is rooted in the ability to connect with others on a deeply human level, a skill that AI cannot replicate in its entirety.

4. AI IN CONFLICT RESOLUTION AND TEAM COLLABORATION

4.1 AI-Driven Conflict Detection and Resolution

Effective conflict management is a critical component of successful team collaboration, especially in hybrid environments where communication barriers and distance can contribute to misunderstandings. AI's ability to analyze communication patterns provides a powerful tool for detecting early signs of conflict, allowing project managers to intervene before issues escalate. By analyzing digital communication channels, such as emails, chat messages, or meeting transcripts, AI can identify subtle changes in tone, sentiment, and frequency of interaction that may indicate growing tensions (Lescano et al., 2020).

Sentiment analysis, for example, leverages NLP to assess the emotional tone behind words, helping to identify negative emotions such as frustration, anger, or disengagement (Vaghela & Jadeja, 2023). AI systems can then flag these indicators and alert the project manager, providing valuable insights into potential conflict hotspots. This early detection allows for proactive conflict resolution, enabling managers to address issues before they develop into full-blown disputes.

Tools such as IBM Watson Tone Analyzer or Microsoft's Cortana Intelligence Suite are examples of AI-powered platforms that analyze communication patterns to detect mood shifts, emotional triggers, and areas of discontent. These tools do not only identify negative sentiment but can also highlight moments of positive reinforcement or appreciation, providing a balanced view of team dynamics. By using AI to monitor and interpret communications, project managers can gain a comprehensive understanding of team morale and intervene with appropriate conflict resolution strategies.

AI-driven systems can also help mediate conflicts by offering suggestions for communication improvement. For example, AI-powered chatbots can be programmed with scripts that encourage empathetic listening or suggest rewording of sensitive messages to reduce the potential for misunderstandings. This allows for a more thoughtful and productive exchange of ideas, fostering a collaborative environment where team members feel heard and respected (Javed et al., 2025).

As such, AI not only aids in detecting and resolving conflict but also enhances the overall communication culture within hybrid teams.

4.2 AI-Powered Facilitation for Virtual Meetings

The rise of remote and hybrid work has introduced unique challenges in facilitating effective meetings. AI can enhance virtual meeting dynamics by providing real-time facilitation tools that ensure inclusivity and encourage constructive dialogue. Virtual meetings, particularly in hybrid teams, often face issues like unequal participation, difficulty maintaining focus, and the risk of misunderstandings due to the lack of non-verbal cues. AI can address these challenges by acting as a neutral facilitator, guiding conversations and ensuring that all voices are heard.

One example of AI-powered facilitation is the use of virtual meeting moderators. These AI assistants, such as Otter.ai and Zoom's AI-powered features, can transcribe conversations in real time, identify key discussion points, and summarize action items for all participants. This ensures that important information is not lost and that meeting outcomes are clearly communicated to all attendees, regardless of their physical location. Additionally, these AI tools can provide insights into the meeting's dynamics, such as identifying which participants dominate the conversation and which voices remain unheard, helping to promote more balanced discussions (Bansal et al., 2024).

Furthermore, AI nudging techniques, such as suggesting relevant topics or encouraging quieter team members to contribute, can help guide the flow of conversation and prevent potential misunderstandings. For instance, AI algorithms can detect when discussions are veering off-topic or when participants are becoming disengaged, prompting the facilitator to refocus or re-engage the group. By fostering an environment of inclusivity and collaboration, AI-powered meeting tools ensure that virtual meetings are more effective and that all perspectives are considered (Shad & Potter, 2024).

4.3 Cross-Cultural and Remote Team Collaboration

AI is particularly effective in addressing the challenges of cross-cultural collaboration in hybrid teams. The diversity of remote teams, often spanning multiple cultures and time zones, can lead to misunderstandings and miscommunications. Language barriers, differences in communication styles, and cultural norms can all create friction that hinders effective collaboration. AI tools can bridge these gaps by facilitating clearer communication and fostering a deeper understanding of cultural nuances.

One key area where AI excels is in language translation. Tools like Google Translate, DeepL, and Microsoft Translator enable real-time translation of text and voice, allowing team members who speak different languages to communicate more effectively. These AI tools not only translate words but also contextualize phrases, helping to preserve the meaning and tone of a message, which is crucial in preventing misunderstandings in professional settings (Joshi, 2024; Kim & ko., 2021; Lescano et al., 2020).

Moreover, AI can enhance cultural sensitivity by analyzing communication patterns across different regions and suggesting culturally appropriate ways to interact. For instance, AI can recognize when certain expressions or actions may be perceived as disrespectful or overly formal in different cultures, offering guidance on adjusting tone or phrasing to maintain positive relationships (Pak et al., 2024). These AI capabilities are particularly valuable for managing remote teams, where team members may not share the same cultural context and where face-to-face communication is limited.

A compelling example of AI facilitating cross-cultural collaboration is seen in the global project teams of companies like Accenture and IBM, where AI-powered tools are used to enhance communication, reduce language barriers, and support culturally informed decision-making. These tools help ensure that diverse teams can collaborate effectively, ultimately improving team performance and fostering a more inclusive work environment (Patil et al., 2025).

4.4 Case Study: How AI Helped Resolve a Hybrid Team Conflict

A prominent example of AI playing a key role in resolving conflicts within hybrid teams can be seen at Salesforce, a global leader in customer relationship management (CRM) software. In 2021, Salesforce faced challenges managing remote and hybrid teams across different time zones, with team members in the US, Europe, and Asia. The company had seen a rise in communication breakdowns and misunderstandings, particularly around project timelines and workloads, which led to employee frustration and declining team morale.

Salesforce implemented AI-powered collaboration tools, including Slack's AI-based sentiment analysis features and Salesforce Einstein Analytics. These tools monitored team communications, identifying shifts in sentiment that indicated potential conflicts. The AI was able to flag when employees were expressing frustration or dissatisfaction in their messages, especially in cross-regional communications where tone and context could be misinterpreted due to cultural and time-zone differences.

In one notable instance, the AI detected growing tension in a hybrid team between members in North America and Asia, related to workload distribution. The system prompted the team manager to step in, redistributing tasks and facilitating a virtual meeting to address concerns.

Post-intervention, Salesforce reported a 30% increase in productivity due to the integration of AI tools like its Agentforce platform, which enabled the company to reduce the need for additional software engineers. This productivity boost led to the reallocation of resources, including expanding the sales team by 1,000-2,000 employees to better communicate the value of AI-driven solutions. This shift reflects broader trends within the tech industry, where automation tools are not only improving operational efficiency but also transforming workforce strategies by reducing demand for technical roles while amplifying the need for human-centric skills, particularly in sales and customer engagement (Salesforce, 2025).

This case highlights how AI-driven tools can significantly enhance conflict resolution in global, hybrid teams, fostering improved communication and collaboration.

5. THE BALANCE BETWEEN AI, DATA-DRIVEN INSIGHTS, AND HUMAN LEADERSHIP

5.1 When to Trust AI and When to Rely on Human Intuition

As AI systems become more integrated into project management workflows, the question of when to trust AI versus when to rely on human intuition is increasingly pertinent. AI has demonstrated significant strengths in processing large volumes of data, identifying patterns, and generating insights that can optimize decision-making in project management. For instance, AI can analyze historical data, assess project timelines, and predict potential risks with remarkable precision (Rahaman et al., 2024). These capabilities allow project managers to make data-driven decisions on resource allocation, risk management, and scheduling with much greater speed and accuracy than would be possible through human intuition alone (Kerzner, 2025).

However, the limitations of AI must be carefully considered. Despite its capacity to analyze data, AI lacks the ability to comprehend the complex, dynamic nature of human behavior. It cannot fully account for the emotional context of a situation, nor can it navigate the subtleties of human relationships, leadership, and motivation (Huang & Rust, 2018). In high-stakes decisions that require empathy or an understanding of team morale, such as conflict resolution or motivational strategies, human intuition and EI remain indispensable. The project manager's ability to read interpersonal dynamics and make decisions based on contextual factors is something AI cannot replicate.

The optimal approach to blending AI data with human judgment lies in understanding when each should take precedence. For example, in routine operational decisions where data provides clear, actionable insights, AI-driven tools should be trusted. However, in moments that require deep understanding of team sentiment or when ethical considerations arise, project managers must rely on their own judgment, which is rooted in human experience and emotional awareness (Al-Arafat et al., 2025). Ultimately, the most effective project managers will be those who can leverage the strengths of both AI and human leadership, using data as a tool to inform decisions while maintaining the human touch in team management.

5.2 AI's Limitations in Understanding Human Emotions

One of the most notable limitations of AI in project management is its inability to fully comprehend or respond to human emotions. While AI has made strides in understanding basic emotional cues, such as through sentiment analysis or emotion recognition algorithms, these systems still fall short in grasping the depth and complexity of human emotional experiences (Sposito et al., 2024). Emotions such as empathy, trust, and motivation are deeply ingrained in human interactions and cannot be fully captured by data points alone. For instance, while AI might be able to analyze communication patterns to detect a shift in tone, it cannot assess the underlying causes of frustration or the context behind a team member's emotional state.

The risk of over-relying on AI in leadership decisions is particularly evident when EI is required. AI may flag potential conflicts, suggest adjustments to team dynamics, or recommend solutions to interpersonal issues, but it cannot replace the human insight that comes from understanding personal struggles, team dynamics, and the emotional climate of a project. The best AI tools currently available focus on analyzing data patterns, but they lack the nuanced understanding of human emotions and the intuition necessary for making decisions that involve interpersonal relationships or individual well-being (Huang & Rust, 2018).

As AI continues to evolve, its ability to interpret and respond to emotional cues may improve. However, human leaders must remain aware of the intrinsic limitations of AI and use it as a complement to, rather than a replacement for, EI in leadership contexts (Gurulakshmi & Gayathri, 2025).

5.3 Best Practices for AI-Augmented Leadership

As organizations continue to integrate AI into their project management frameworks, it is essential for leaders to adopt best practices for AI-augmented leadership. One key strategy is to view AI not as a replacement for human decision-making but as a tool that can enhance leadership through data-driven insights. AI should be used to support decision-making, identify potential risks, optimize processes, and provide recommendations, all while leaving space for human judgment in areas where EI is crucial (Al-Arafat et al., 2025).

An important consideration for AI-augmented leadership is the human-first approach. Project managers must maintain a strong focus on building trust and rapport with their teams, even as AI tools provide insights into team performance and project dynamics. AI can assist in identifying trends or issues early, but it is the manager's responsibility to address these challenges by fostering open communication, providing emotional support, and motivating team members (Coronado-Maldonado & Benítez-Márquez, 2023). Leaders should ensure that AI tools are not simply used for efficiency but also to support an empathetic, human-centered approach to management.

Another best practice is to invest in developing EI within leadership teams. While AI can provide data-driven insights, the human ability to navigate complex emotions and make decisions in high-stress or high-pressure situations is irreplaceable. Leaders who cultivate EI can use AI as a supportive tool while ensuring that they are attuned to the needs of their teams. This balance helps mitigate the risk of over-relying on AI and encourages a more holistic approach to project leadership (Goleman & Boyatzis, 2008; Koubova & Buchko, 2013).

5.4 The Role of Trust and Human Connection in Hybrid Teams

Trust and human connection are foundational elements of effective leadership, especially in hybrid teams where face-to-face interactions are limited, and AI tools mediate much of the communication. While AI can enhance decision-making, streamline processes, and identify potential risks, it cannot replace the trust that comes from personal relationships and emotional connections between team members. Trust is built through consistent communication, shared experiences, and mutual respect, all of which are critical for fostering collaboration in a hybrid environment (Alves et al., 2023).

AI-driven project management tools can facilitate efficient workflows, but they cannot replace the human aspects of leadership that make hybrid teams successful. Human leaders must continue to prioritize relationship-building, provide support, and offer guidance to team members. A leader's ability to create an environment where team members feel valued and understood is essential for motivating high performance and ensuring the long-term success of a project (Joshi, 2024).

In conclusion, while AI offers powerful tools for enhancing project management, the human element remains crucial. The integration of AI into leadership practices must therefore be balanced by a commitment to EI, trust, and human connection. The future of hybrid project teams lies in the synergy between AI-driven insights and human leadership, where technology augments, but does not replace, the core values of leadership.

6. FUTURE TRENDS

6.1 The Rise of AI-Augmented Leadership

As AI continues to evolve, its role in leadership development is poised to expand significantly. One of the most notable trends in project management is the rise of AI-augmented leadership, which blends the analytical capabilities of AI with the interpersonal skills of EI. AI is already being integrated into leadership development programs, offering new ways to assess, monitor, and enhance key leadership skills. Through advanced data analytics and predictive modeling, AI tools can identify strengths and weaknesses in leadership styles, providing valuable insights into how leaders interact with their teams and make decisions.

One of the most profound ways AI is enhancing leadership development is by providing tailored feedback and personalized learning pathways for leaders. For instance, AI-powered platforms can track a leader's emotional responses during interactions and suggest strategies for improving EQ. These insights help leaders become more self-aware, empathetic, and adaptable to the needs of their teams, thereby improving their leadership effectiveness in hybrid and remote settings. AI can also assess team dynamics, helping leaders understand which team members may need additional support or guidance, and ensuring that leadership decisions are informed by both data and emotional understanding (Coronado-Maldonado & Benítez-Márquez, 2023).

The future of AI-driven project management training will likely involve highly interactive, dynamic simulations, where leaders can hone their skills in real-time. These simulations, enhanced by AI, will challenge leaders to adapt to various emotional and strategic scenarios, creating an immersive training environment that emphasizes EI alongside technical expertise. As these tools continue to mature, we can expect a shift toward a more integrated approach to leadership development that aligns data-driven insights with EI-building exercises.

6.2 AI-Driven Leadership Coaching and Emotional Intelligence Training

AI is already proving instrumental in enhancing leadership coaching, particularly in the area of EI. Traditionally, leadership coaching has relied on human mentors or coaches to guide leaders through the intricacies of team management, emotional regulation, and interpersonal communication. However, AI-powered coaching tools are now providing personalized, scalable support, making EI development more accessible and data-driven. These tools leverage machine learning algorithms to analyze leadership behaviors, emotional responses, and communication patterns, offering leaders specific recommendations for improvement (Katirai, 2024; Sposito et al., 2024).

AI-driven coaching platforms use NLP and sentiment analysis to evaluate how leaders communicate with their teams and identify areas where EI can be strengthened. For example, AI can track how a leader responds to team conflicts, noting whether their approach is empathetic, assertive, or passive, and then provide feedback on how to adjust communication strategies in the future. This type of feedback is particularly valuable in hybrid and remote work environments, where cues like body language and tone of voice are often harder to interpret.

A real-world case study that demonstrates the power of AI-based coaching is the implementation of the AI-driven leadership development tool *CoachBot* at a global consulting firm. The tool, which uses sentiment analysis to assess the emotional tone of leaders' communications, has led to a 25% increase in leadership effectiveness, as measured by employee engagement and satisfaction surveys (Coachbots, 2025). By continuously monitoring emotional dynamics and offering real-time feedback, CoachBot has helped managers develop their EI, improving both their communication with teams and their overall leadership performance (Huang & Rust, 2018).

6.3 Preparing Organizations for an AI and EI Future

The successful integration of AI and EI in project management requires organizations to prepare their workforce for an AI-augmented future. This preparation involves both training and upskilling project managers to work effectively with AI tools while fostering their own EI. Project managers or even graduates must not only be comfortable with AI-powered decision-making tools but also develop the emotional resilience and interpersonal skills necessary to navigate the challenges of leading hybrid and remote teams (Huzooree et al., 2024). As organizations invest in these AI tools, it is equally critical that they prioritize the development of their leaders' human capabilities, ensuring that technology complements, rather than replaces, human judgment and empathy (Al-Arafat et al., 2025).

One key strategy for preparing project managers for this future is through targeted professional development programs that integrate both AI and EI training. These programs should equip leaders with the technical skills required to use AI systems effectively, such as understanding data analytics and interpreting machine-generated insights, while also fostering soft skills like empathy, conflict resolution, and communication. By creating blended learning experiences that emphasize both technological and EI, organizations can ensure that their project managers are well-prepared to lead in increasingly complex environments.

Another important strategy involves creating a culture of continuous learning. As AI tools evolve rapidly, organizations must foster an environment where project managers are encouraged to stay up to date with technological advancements and adapt to new tools as they become available. This involves not just training, but also ongoing support systems, such as mentoring or AI-driven feedback tools, which help project managers refine their leadership abilities over time.

6.4 Future Challenges: Can AI Ever Replace Human Intuition?

As AI continues to advance, one of the most contentious and compelling debates revolves around whether AI can ever fully replicate human EI and, more specifically, human intuition. Despite AI's significant progress in data analysis, pattern recognition, and predictive modeling, the nuances of human emotions and intuition remain elusive for machines. Human intuition, which often arises from deep experiential learning and subconscious processing, is uniquely tied to the human condition, shaped by a complex interplay of cognitive, emotional, and social factors (Katirai, 2024; Sposito et al., 2024).

AI systems, though capable of processing vast amounts of data, cannot fully grasp these multidimensional human experiences. For instance, while AI can analyze tone of voice or communication patterns to detect signs of frustration, it cannot understand the underlying emotional context or the complexities of a person's past experiences that might be influencing their current behavior. EI, particularly in leadership, involves not just recognizing emotions but also responding with empathy, understanding the ethical implications of decisions, and making intuitive judgments based on non-verbal cues and personal dynamics (Goleman, 1996). AI's limitations in these areas are significant. While sentiment analysis or facial recognition may be able to identify a surface-level emotion, they fail to account for the layered emotional complexities that inform interpersonal interactions and leadership decisions (Huang & Rust, 2018).

Moreover, human intuition is often shaped by values, experiences, and moral judgment, aspects of leadership that AI cannot replicate. Even with the most sophisticated AI systems, the ability to make ethical decisions, navigate power dynamics, or offer meaningful support during moments of emotional distress remains a distinctly human trait. AI can certainly augment decision-making by providing data-driven insights, but the final decision often hinges on the ethical, intuitive, and human-centric values that project managers bring to the table (Coronado-Maldonado & Benítez-Márquez, 2023).

In conclusion, while AI will continue to enhance the capabilities of project managers, the full replacement of human intuition remains improbable. Instead, the future will likely see AI as a complement to, rather than a replacement for, human leadership, where EI and intuition remain vital in shaping decisions that influence teams and projects.

7. CONCLUSION

As technology continues to shape the field of project management, the role of AI in enhancing EI in hybrid teams has become increasingly important. Throughout this chapter, we have explored how AI contributes to improving leadership practices by providing project managers with valuable insights into team dynamics, emotional states, and communication patterns. This information allows leaders to identify potential issues early, adjust strategies accordingly, and offer support where necessary, fostering an environment where team members feel understood and motivated.

The key takeaway from this discussion is that AI does not replace the human element of leadership but instead complements it. Tools that track sentiment, analyze communication trends, and assess individual behaviors provide project managers with deeper insights into the emotional climate of their teams. These insights help leaders make more informed decisions, address conflicts before they escalate, and tailor their leadership approach to the specific needs of the team. However, AI's role should be seen as an augmentation to leadership capabilities, not a replacement for human intuition and empathy.

By leveraging AI in this way, project managers can improve their EI and overall leadership effectiveness. The combination of data-driven insights and human EI allows project managers to build stronger, more resilient teams and better navigate the complexities of modern project environments. Ultimately, it is this blend of technology and human leadership that will drive success in hybrid teams, ensuring both productivity and emotional well-being.

For project managers interested in integrating AI into their leadership strategies, the first step is to familiarize themselves with the available tools that track and analyze team communication and sentiment. These tools, which measure things like emotional tone in messages and collaboration patterns, can provide actionable insights into how team members are feeling and interacting. By leveraging this data, project managers can preemptively address potential issues such as disengagement or rising tensions.

Additionally, project managers should invest in training programs that combine the technical use of these tools with EI development. Understanding the strengths and limitations of AI tools is essential, but developing emotional awareness and empathy remains a key part of leadership. Managers should balance the analytical power of AI with their own intuition, using both data and emotional understanding to guide decision-making.

Furthermore, practical steps include encouraging a culture of openness and inclusivity within teams, ensuring that the technology used to monitor team behavior enhances trust rather than undermining it. By blending AI-driven insights with human-led decision-making, project managers can foster a team environment where both productivity and emotional well-being thrive.

The intersection of technology and EI is transforming leadership in project management. As hybrid teams become more common, the need for leaders who can effectively manage both the technical and emotional aspects of team dynamics has never been greater. The integration of technology into project management processes offers significant benefits, such as more efficient communication, data-driven insights, and the ability to predict and resolve conflicts before they escalate. However, as we have seen throughout this chapter, it is important to remember that these tools are meant to support, not replace, human leadership.

The future of project management lies in the balance between technology and human intelligence. While AI can assist in understanding emotional cues and improving decision-making, it is the human leader's ability to demonstrate empathy, make ethical decisions, and connect with team members on a personal level that will remain essential. Leaders must adapt to a world where technology and EI go hand-in-hand, using both to create more cohesive, effective, and resilient teams.

As project managers continue to navigate an increasingly tech-driven environment, embracing this hybrid leadership model will be crucial. Leaders must remain grounded in their humanity while embracing the potential of new technologies, ensuring that both the emotional and technical needs of hybrid teams are met in a way that drives success and fosters a positive work culture.

REFERENCES

Ajiva, O. A., Ejike, O. G., & Abhulimen, A. O. (2024). Advances in communication tools and techniques for enhancing collaboration among creative professionals. *Int. J. Front. Sci. Technol. Res*, *7*(01), 66–75. DOI: 10.53294/ijfstr.2024.7.1.0049

Al-Arafat, M., Kabir, M. E., Morshed, A. S. M., & Islam, M. M. (2025). Artificial Intelligence in Project Management: Balancing Automation and Human Judgment. *Frontiers in Applied Engineering and Technology*, *2*(01), 18–29.

Alves, M. P., Dimas, I. D., Lourenço, P. R., Rebelo, T., Peñarroja, V., & Gamero, N. (2023). Can virtuality be protective of team trust? Conflict and effectiveness in hybrid teams. *Behaviour & Information Technology*, *42*(7), 851–868. DOI: 10.1080/0144929X.2022.2046163

Bansal, G., Chamola, V., Hussain, A., Guizani, M., & Niyato, D. (2024). Transforming conversations with AI—A comprehensive study of ChatGPT. *Cognitive Computation*, *16*(5), 2487–2510. DOI: 10.1007/s12559-023-10236-2

Bjørnsten, T. B., & Sørensen, M. M. Z. (2020). Uncertainties of facial emotion recognition technologies and the automation of emotional labour. In *The Uncertain Image* (pp. 43–53). Routledge. DOI: 10.4324/9780429435430-4

Boon, G. C., Stettina, C. J., Visser, J., & El-Baz, Y. (2023). Beyond Dashboards: Operationalising a Measurement Framework for Agile Teams. In *International Conference on the Quality of Information and Communications Technology* (pp. 130-146). Cham: Springer Nature Switzerland. DOI: 10.1007/978-3-031-43703-8_10

Boyatzis, R. E., & Cavanagh, K. V. (2018). Leading change: Developing emotional, social, and cognitive competencies in managers during an MBA program. *Emotional intelligence in education: Integrating research with practice*, 403-426.

Boyatzis, R. E., Smith, M. L., Van Oosten, E., & Woolford, L. (2013). Developing resonant leaders through emotional intelligence, vision and coaching. *Organizational Dynamics*, *42*(1), 17–24. DOI: 10.1016/j.orgdyn.2012.12.003

Chen, A., Xiang, M., Wang, M., & Lu, Y. (2023). Harmony in intelligent hybrid teams: The influence of the intellectual ability of artificial intelligence on human members' reactions. *Information Technology & People*, *36*(7), 2826–2846. DOI: 10.1108/ITP-01-2022-0059

Coachbots. (2025). *Key Metrics Achieved*. Coachbots. Available online: https://www.coachbots.com/ (Access on 5 March 2025)

Coronado-Maldonado, I., & Benítez-Márquez, M. D. (2023). Emotional intelligence, leadership, and work teams: A hybrid literature review. *Heliyon*, *9*(10), e20356. DOI: 10.1016/j.heliyon.2023.e20356 PMID: 37790975

Doargajudhur, M. S., Huzooree, G., Hosanoo, Z., Lichy, J., & Dell, P. (2024). Green IT and BYOD: Driving sustainability, job performance, and well-being in remote work. *The International Journal of Organizational Analysis*. Advance online publication. DOI: 10.1108/IJOA-08-2024-4768

Goleman, D. (1996). Emotional intelligence. Why it can matter more than IQ. *Learning*, *24*(6), 49–50.

Goleman, D., & Boyatzis, R. (2008). Social intelligence and the biology of leadership. *Harvard Business Review*, *86*(9), 74–81. PMID: 18777666

Gurulakshmi, S., & Gayathri, R. (2025). The Human-AI Partnership: Elevating Leadership With Emotional Intelligence. In *Emotionally Intelligent Methods for Meaningful Leadership* (pp. 255-284). IGI Global Scientific Publishing.

Hobsbawm, J. (2022). *The nowhere office: Reinventing work and the workplace of the future*. Hachette UK.

Huang, M. H., & Rust, R. T. (2018). Artificial intelligence in service. *Journal of Service Research*, *21*(2), 155–172. DOI: 10.1177/1094670517752459

Huzooree, G. (2024). From Concept to Completion: Critical Success Factors in Agile Project Management for IT Projects. In *Practical Approaches to Agile Project Management* (pp. 9-31). IGI Global.

Huzooree, G., Soupramanien, L. D. B., & Rughoobur-Seetah, S. (2024). *Fostering Critical Soft Skills of Graduates for Employability and Professional Growth*. IGI Global. DOI: 10.4018/979-8-3693-3856-8.ch003

Huzooree, G., & Yadav, M. (2025). Sustainable Project Management and Organizational Resilience. In *Enhancing Resilience in Business Continuity Management* (pp. 137–172). IGI Global Scientific Publishing. DOI: 10.4018/979-8-3693-8809-9.ch005

Ivan, S. C., Győrödi, R. Ş., & Győrödi, C. A. (2024). Sentiment Analysis Using Amazon Web Services and Microsoft Azure. *Big Data and Cognitive Computing*, *8*(12), 166. DOI: 10.3390/bdcc8120166

Javed, U., Rohilla, A., Adnan, G., & Taj, N. (2025). Exploring how AI can be used to Promote Collaboration in group Project reduce Conflict in Team Dynamics and Enhance Cooperative Learning Experiences. *Review of Applied Management and Social Sciences*, *8*(1), 129–141. DOI: 10.47067/ramss.v8i1.441

Joshi, H. (2024). Artificial intelligence in project management: A study of the role of ai-powered chatbots in project stakeholder engagement. [IJSEPM]. *Indian Journal of Software Engineering and Project Management*, *4*(1), 20–25. DOI: 10.54105/ijsepm.B9022.04010124

Katirai, A. (2024). Ethical considerations in emotion recognition technologies: A review of the literature. *AI and Ethics*, *4*(4), 927–948. DOI: 10.1007/s43681-023-00307-3

Kerzner, H. (2025). *Project management: a systems approach to planning, scheduling, and controlling*. John Wiley & Sons.

Kim, K., & Ko, E. J. (2021). The influence of emotional intelligence on team cohesion and the mediating effects of self-efficacy and trust: Time-lagged approach. *Team Performance Management*, *27*(7/8), 540–552. DOI: 10.1108/TPM-12-2020-0102

Kirkman, B. L., Rosen, B., Tesluk, P. E., & Gibson, C. B. (2004). The impact of team empowerment on virtual team performance: The moderating role of face-to-face interaction. *Academy of Management Journal*, *47*(2), 175–192. DOI: 10.2307/20159571

Koubova, V., & Buchko, A. A. (2013). Life-work balance: Emotional intelligence as a crucial component of achieving both personal life and work performance. *Management Research Review*, *36*(7), 700–719. DOI: 10.1108/MRR-05-2012-0115

Lescano, G., Lara, C., Collazos, C. A., & Costaguta, R. (2020). A technique for conflict detection in collaborative learning environment by using text sentiment. In *Advances in Computational Intelligence: 19th Mexican International Conference on Artificial Intelligence, MICAI 2020, Mexico City, Mexico, October 12–17, 2020* [Springer International Publishing.]. *Proceedings*, *19*(Part II), 39–50.

Luo, L., Zhang, L., Zheng, X., & Wu, G. (2022). A hybrid approach for investigating impacts of leadership dynamics on project performance. *Engineering, Construction, and Architectural Management*, *29*(5), 1965–1990. DOI: 10.1108/ECAM-02-2020-0094

Mayer, J. D., & Salovey, P. (1990). Emotional intelligence: Imagination, cognition, and personality. *American Journal of Educational Research.*

Mehrabian, A. (2017). Communication without words. In *Communication theory* (pp. 193–200). Routledge. DOI: 10.4324/9781315080918-15

Newman, S. A., & Ford, R. C. (2021). Five steps to leading your team in the virtual COVID-19 workplace. *Organizational Dynamics*, *50*(1), 100802. DOI: 10.1016/j.orgdyn.2020.100802 PMID: 36536689

Nilsson, L., & Norström, W. (2024). Understanding Psychological Safety in Hybrid Work Teams: Experiences of Barriers and Facilitators.

Pak, R., Rovira, E., & McLaughlin, A. (2024). Polite AI mitigates user susceptibility to AI hallucinations. *Ergonomics*, •••, 1–11. DOI: 10.1080/00140139.2024.2434604 PMID: 39610202

Patil, R. N., Rawandale, S. A., Yadav, G. B., & Kadam, P. (2025). Leveraging Machine Learning and Neural Networks for Enhanced Communication in Leadership. In *Leadership Paradigms and the Impact ofTechnology* (pp. 247–284). IGI Global Scientific Publishing. DOI: 10.4018/979-8-3693-7175-6.ch011

Rahaman, M. A., Rozony, F. Z., Mazumder, M. S. A., Haque, M. N., & Rauf, M. A. (2024). Big data-driven decision making in project management: A comparative analysis. *Academic Journal on Science, Technology, Engineering &. The Mathematics Educator*, *4*(03), 44–62.

Salesforce. (2025). *Salesforce to Coders: Thanks, But AI's Got This.* Salesforce Research. Available online: https://www.bitswithbrains.com/news/salesforce-to-coders%3A-thanks%2C-but-ai%E2%80%99s-got-this (Access on 5 March 2025)

Shad, R., & Potter, K. (2024). AI-powered chatbots and virtual assistants in enhancing business efficiency. *Artificial Intelligence.*

Shakilla, U., & Saputro, E. P. (2025). Revolutionizing Management: The Role of AI and Technology in Modern Leadership Practices. *Solo International Collaboration and Publication of Social Sciences and Humanities*, *3*(01), 53–68. DOI: 10.61455/sicopus.v3i01.235

Smith, R., Cubino, M., & McKeon, E. (2024). *The AI Revolution in Customer Service and Support: A Practical Guide to Impactful Deployment of AI to Best Serve Your Customers.* Pearson Education.

Sposito, L., Scafuto, I. C., Serra, F. R., & Ferreira, M. P. (2024). Influence of the project managers' expertise and experience in the success of projects: The moderating effect of emotional intelligence. *International Journal of Managing Projects in Business*, *17*(1), 1–26. DOI: 10.1108/IJMPB-06-2023-0129

Taheri Khosroshahi, F. (2024). The Future of Project Management: Embracing artificial intelligence for enhanced efficiency, data-driven decision-making, and collaborative teamwork.

Vaghela, H., & Jadeja, M. (2023). Analyzing Sentiments of Global Workforce Towards Hybrid Work Culture in the New Normal. In International Conference on Smart Systems: Innovations in Computing (pp. 293-305). Singapore: Springer Nature Singapore.

Chapter 7
Securing Tomorrow:
Cybersecurity and Remote Work Trends

R. Velmurugan
https://orcid.org/0000-0002-7925-9757
Karpagam Academy of Higher Education, Coimbatore, India

J. Sudarvel
https://orcid.org/0000-0001-6656-1992
Karpagam Academy of Higher Education, Coimbatore, India

K. Jothi
https://orcid.org/0000-0002-8625-863X
KPR College of Arts, Science, and Research, India

Ravi Thirumalaisamy
https://orcid.org/0000-0002-5954-5940
Modern College of Business and Science, Oman

Shashank Mittal
https://orcid.org/0000-0002-8666-5323
O.P. Jindal Global University, India

ABSTRACT

Workers now benefit from flexible arrangements caused by remote work but their organizations face significantly higher cybersecurity vulnerabilities. Electronic tools with cloud-based services have produced increased incidents of phishing attacks and data breaches and ransomware events. Remote access security needs immediate attention since workers need to connect their personal equipment to unidentified networks. Endpoint security solutions and MFA and VPNs jointly reduce security threats. Organizations must teach their personnel about cybersecurity basics since human mistakes remain a major cybersecurity risk factor. Threat detection enhancements come from AI and machine learning applications together with real-time automated security systems which provide protection benefits. ZTA implements continuous authentication protocols through its enforcement mechanism. Remote work models require integration of powerful cybersecurity systems which need backing from security regulations alongside organization-wide cultural education about security measures.

DOI: 10.4018/979-8-3373-1270-5.ch007

INTRODUCTION

The sudden transition to remote employment created a revolutionary change in conventional workplaces that resulted in more flexible hours with enhanced productivity levels. The rapid adoption of remote work occurred substantially after the worldwide COVID-19 pandemic when organizations tried to preserve business operation and protect employee safety. The new working environment enables staff members to execute their duties from many different physical locations beyond the conventional boundaries of traditional workplaces. Organizations must face multiple cybersecurity problems stemming from remote work since this movement provides significant advantages yet remains vulnerable to substantial security threats for their systems and data integrity. The main cybersecurity threat in remote work arises from employees' use of various sites to access company networks. Organizations encounter enhanced cybersecurity threats because remote workspaces demand employees to use personal equipment that connects through unsecured networks and public Wi-Fi networks (Anderson, 2021). When the cybercriminals identify these system weaknesses they obtain unauthorized data access and execute malicious phishing attacks while deploying malicious software. Security problems become worse because remote devices and networks operate without properly implemented standardization.

Phishing attacks have increased rapidly because they specifically target remote workers during the COVID-19 work-from-home era. The unsuspecting nature of employees leads them to reveal their login credentials or financial details since cybercriminals use fraudulent messages and deceptive emails and harmful links (Smith & Brown, 2022). The absence of direct IT support exposes remote workers to a higher risk of falling for attacks on their employment positions. Combining professional duties with personal activities on the same device makes remote employees more prone to clicking dangerous links as security threats for the company increase accordingly. Remote work security has become more complicated as the practice of using personal devices for workplace tasks known as BYOD has increased. The implementation of BYOD policies offers organizations both convenience and reduced hardware expenses but generates major security matters (Johnson, 2020). Devices that users personally own do not maintain security patch updates and often lack necessary security software or fail to implement encryption measures which exposes the devices to cyber dangers. The practice of employees using personal devices to perform both professional work and personal activities creates significant risks that result in elevated data leak and unauthorized access incidents.

Security issues emerge from trying to protect remote access connections between employees and corporate networks. VPNs function as common remote work solutions because they establish secure encryption for employee data communications with corporate systems. VPN security holds weaknesses because employee carelessness with passwords and outdated software makes them susceptible to cyberattacks (Miller & Davis, 2021). Organizations now face performance difficulties from VPN infrastructure burden caused by remote work thereby driving them to adopt Zero Trust Architecture (ZTA) as an alternative security solution. Zero Trust Architecture presents itself as a sophisticated security framework which secures remote working environments effectively. The security model of ZTA differs from traditional systems since it implements restrictive permissions and consistent identity verification throughout the network (Williams, 2023). The system reduces unauthorized entry because all authentication occurs repeatedly through identity verification steps for both users and devices. Zero Trust frameworks implement Multi-Factor Authentication (MFA) together with endpoint security solutions as their standard security reinforcement methods.

Remote work cybersecurity depends heavily on human factors when people are operating in distance-based work arrangements. Security breaches triggered by human mistakes happen frequently when individuals create insecure passwords, leak sensitive data or mistake phishing scams (Garcia, 2020). Organizations need to establish cybersecurity awareness training programs that focus on remote employees because this helps reduce security risks. Employees achieve better success in identifying and handling security threats through scheduled educational programs that combine simulated phishing scams with instructions about secure work-from-home practices. The necessity of protecting data in cloud systems establishes itself as a primary security factor when dealing with remote work environments. Organizations depend heavily on cloud-based applications for simultaneous work functions and data storage and communication tasks. The scalability and accessibility of cloud services come with security dangers that arise from improper settings configuration. Cloud storage performance deteriorates when administrators misconfigure settings because their security measures may get compromised by weak access controls coupled with insufficient encryption which puts company data at risk (Lee et al., 2021). Organizations must execute two solutions to secure their cloud data: they need to establish rigid access controls and their systems require both encryption protection and scheduled security tests.

Remote work has introduced an emerging security concern because of potential dangers from internal threats. Monitoring employee activities alongside detecting security breaches becomes harder since staff work independently at home according to Rodriguez and Carter (2022). Internal security threats which include both intentional data theft actions and unintentional file sharing incidents with unapproved individuals affect organizations persistently. Businesses need to implement behavioral analytics software as well as endpoint detection software to detect suspicious activity which prevents insider threats from developing. Secure remote work of the future will adopt both powerful security measures together with improved technological solutions. Artificial Intelligence and Machine Learning increasingly serve cybersecurity purposes by tracking abnormalities alongside threat forecasting and programmed automated threat reaction capabilities according to Thompson (2024). AI security systems process enormous real-time data quantities for detecting potential cyber risks before their adverse impacts occur. The security function of facial recognition combined with fingerprint scanning technology will expand its presence for remote access protection.

The introduction of more stringent cybersecurity laws by governments and regulatory bodies has become necessary to handle remote work security problems. Organizations need to comply with essential data protection regulations including both GDPR and CCPA when operating remotely according to Nelson (2021). Organizations need to verify that their remote work security planning matches these legal requirements because failure to do so results in penalties and damages customer trust. Remote work has delivered both productivity advantages and flexibility benefits to organizations yet created advanced security problems they must solve with proactive measures. The combination of phishing attacks along with BYOD obligations and internal security threats and cloud-related protection issues requires businesses to establish extensive data system security measures. Remote work security will be defined by the implementation of Zero Trust Architecture alongside cyber security training and AI security tools along with legal framework compliance standards. Organization success in future remote work environments depends on their ability to stay alert about cybersecurity methods and implement adaptive protective measures for their staff members and digital acquisitions.

CYBERSECURITY CHALLENGES IN REMOTE WORK

Organizational exposure to cyber threats has increased because remote work extended their attack surface. Employees who work from remote locations using both personal devices and unsecured Wi-Fi networks create data exposure risks which lead to potential security breaches (Anderson, 2021). Phishing attacks exploit human mistakes to get credentials (Smith & Brown, 2022) while unsecured personal devices with improper security setups (Johnson, 2020) along with lowered monitoring causes insider threats (Rodriguez & Carter, 2022). Bad configuration of cloud services combined with poor remote access control implementation leads to increased security risks (Lee et al., 2021). The risks call for organizations to establish thorough defensive security systems for protection.

1. Increased Phishing Attacks

Social engineering tactics allow cybercriminals to accomplish their goal by tricking remote employees into sharing valuable organizational information. Techniques like phishing along with pretexting and baiting attack people's psychological weaknesses instead of computer system flaws (Smith & Brown, 2022). Phishing attacks are the most common threat because attackers disguise themselves as legitimate entities using emails and messages and fake websites to obtain passwords and financial information (Anderson, 2021). Remote employees who lack prompt IT assistance are especially exposed to deceptive schemes. Cybercriminals deploy spear phishing to specifically target employees based on their job functions through personalized attacks according to Garcia (2020). Cybercriminals raise their attack success rates through message creation that becomes convincing when they collect information from social media and company websites. Vishing acts as an emerging threat because attackers pretend to be IT support personnel to make employees reset passwords or access corporate network resources (Rodriguez & Carter, 2022).

The fight against security risks requires businesses to provide complete security education for staff as well as requiring MFA setups and demanding verification from workers before sharing sensitive data (Nelson, 2021). Security enhancement and cybersecurity education in the workplace enables organizations to lessen the vulnerability of remote work scenarios against social engineering threats.

2. Unsecured Home Networks

Attackers find home networks simple prey because these networks commonly lack defensive encryptions that protected corporate networks have. The infrastructure of corporate networks stays protected through the usage of firewalls together with intrusion detection systems and endpoint security measures (Anderson, 2021). The default settings and weak passwords combined with outdated firmware on home networks expose these networks to various cyber dangers. Attackers take advantage of these security holes for direct intrusion into company data along with malware deployment and unauthorized information access (Lee et al., 2021). Cyber criminals take advantage of unsecured Wi-Fi connections by performing activities like eavesdropping along with man-in-the-middle (MITM) attacks to intercept remote worker communication with corporate networks according to Miller & Davis (2021). Most employees do not implement WPA3 encryption in their home networks which creates exposure to unathorized intruders. Smart speakers and security cameras alongside other IoT devices widen vulnerabilities because their security parameters are inadequately set (Rodriguez & Carter, 2022). Staff members must employ Virtual

Private Networks (VPNs) and perform regular updates on their router firmware as well as activate robust Wi-Fi encryption standards to reduce these security risks. Remote employee protection must improve through security training and endpoint protection system implementation that organizations need to provide according to Nelson (2021).

3. Use of Personal Devices

Security risks grow higher because employees who utilize personal devices for work usually lack updated security protections. Employed devices used outside company control possess inadequate security standards because IT teams do not actively manage and monitor them rendering them vulnerable to cyber threats (Johnson, 2020). Vulnerabilities on devices remain unpatched because numerous workers neglect to perform security updates effectively (Anderson, 2021). Attackers access old software to perform malicious hyperlinks, automatic software downloading and trick users into handing over information through phishing attacks that lead to sensitive company data breaches. Security features such as endpoint protection and encryption and strong access controls are usually absent from personal devices according to Rodriguez & Carter (2022). The unauthorized application downloads of employees frequently lead to data breaches because they contain malware or spyware according to Smith & Brown (2022). The lack of VPN security on employee personal devices creates an opportunity for cyber eavesdroppers to monitor work communications which leads to unauthorized access into corporate networks. Organizations need to implement three security measures that include BYOD security policies and multifactor authentication requirements and employee cybersecurity awareness training. MDM solutions enable organizations to monitor and protect work tasks performed on personal devices according to Nelson (2021).

4. Weak Authentication Practices

Company data remains at risk due to unauthorized access which occurs because of weak authentication protocols. There are three main reasons why traditional password-based authentication has become insufficient for security: credential stuffing, brute-force attacks and phishing. (Smith & Brown, 2022). Staff members frequently employ a single set of login information for different applications which generates increased danger when one account disclosure leads to a breach (Anderson, 2021). The combination of weak passwords with simple patterns provides attackers with easy opportunities to access corporate sensitive data through unauthorized means. MFA represents a vital security approach which enforces users to authenticate through multiple methods like their passwords and biometric data or one-time passwords (Nelson, 2021). The practice of implementing MFA protects corporate systems from cyberattacks because one breached password generates complete system access for attackers. Authentication security gets improved through Single Sign-On (SSO) and Zero Trust Architecture (ZTA) implementations since these technologies conduct ongoing user identification checks to enforce predefined access restrictions (Williams, 2023). Businesses need to enforce authentication protocols with strong measures while teaching their employees through regular training to use password managers for system protection (Rodriguez & Carter, 2022).

5. Cloud Security Risks

Cloud applications create security weak points through misconfiguration and security inadequacy. Security concerns continue to increase in organizations due to their cloud platform adoption for collaboration alongside storage and remote access because cloud environments are complicated and human mistakes occur frequently (Lee et al., 2021). The improper setup of cloud systems whichLeave data vulnerable by exposing access controls or databases publicly results in breaches and unauthorized user entry and compliance failures (Nelson, 2021). The security flaws in cloud infrastructure become targets for cybercriminals who succeed in stealing sensitive information as well as deploying ransomware attacks. Increase in security threats arises when identity and access management (IAM) methods are insufficient in cloud applications. Excessive exposure of cloud-based resources occurs when proper role-based access controls (RBAC) together with multi-factor authentication (MFA) are not applied (Smith & Brown, 2022). Insider threats represent a vulnerability for cloud-stored data because employee privileges are too broad or organizations do not properly monitor activity logs (Rodriguez & Carter, 2022). Organizations should defend themselves against these threats by enforcing encryption policies and running periodic security checks while adopting Zero Trust security practices (Williams, 2023). End users working on cloud-based applications must implement continuous monitoring along with endpoint protection while meeting requirements set by cloud security frameworks so their remote work stays secure.

STRATEGIES FOR ENHANCING CYBERSECURITY IN REMOTE WORK

The solution for these challenges requires organizations to establish comprehensive security policies linked with advanced protective measures. Multi-Factor Authentication (MFA) serves as a crucial security element because it extends password protection so organizations can minimize unauthorized entry attempts (Nelson, 2021). Every user and device must undergo ZTA protocols because this model demands continuous authentication procedures alongside minimal access permissions according to Williams (2023). The prevention of social engineering attacks including phishing requires necessary training for employees to protect themselves against security risks (Smith & Brown, 2022). Employees receive better outcomes in security awareness programs since they learn to detect suspicious events while mastering best practices. Remote work environments require organizations to implement endpoint protection solutions together with cloud security features as malware defenses and data breach prevention measures according to Lee et al. (2021). Equipment security monitoring and scheduled audits perform together to discover system weaknesses and stop cyber attacks. Organizations that adopt proactive cybersecurity methods build resilient operations which protect their valuable information (Rodriguez & Carter, 2022). Having Multi-Factor Authentication as a control strategy requires multiple verification methods to minimize unauthorized entry.

1. Virtual Private Networks (VPNs)

Businesses need to push their employees to use Virtual Private Networks (VPNs) in order to protect secure communication because VPNs encrypt data and secure it from digital threats and unauthorized access while streaming across the internet. Encryption functions as a fundamental data protection mechanism which keeps sensitive information secure all the time including when being transmitted through unsecured internet connections according to Stallings (2020). A VPN enables employees to connect safely to work-related systems which helps prevent cyberattacks specifically in remote or public Wi-Fi environments (Schneier, 2021). The protection of data integrity through VPNs occurs because they stop modification of information at any point during transmission (Kurose & Ross, 2022). Businesses that hold sensitive customer information especially need VPN technology because they must prioritize data security compliance in sectors like finance and healthcare. The implementation of VPN policies in organizations leads to reduced security incidents according to Anderson (2021) who found lower occurrence rates than organizations using only firewalls or antivirus software. Employing VPNs enables organizations to establish employee security mindfulness which contributes to cybersecurity culture development (Von Solms & Van Niekerk, 2021). Organizations must establish VPN implementation as their standard security measure because it creates an effective shield against evolving online threats that protects workforce alongside organizational infrastructure.

2. Regular Cybersecurity Training

The reduction of cyber threats depends heavily on employee education regarding phishing identification skills and password security and browser safety measures. The cyber threat known as phishing represents one of the most frequent types of attack since attackers leverage deceptive emails or websites for stealing sensitive data. The research conducted by Kumar et al. (2021) shows that employee phishing awareness training decreases the susceptibility to succumb to these kinds of attacks. Using standardized educational methods organizations can protect their cybersecurity position through employee training which emphasizes suspicious email identification and link verification together with unapproved attachment avoidance. Keeping data accounts secure demands proper password practices which prevent unauthorized access. According to Bonneau et al. (2022) embracing both complex unique passwords together with multi-factor authentication systems strongly minimizes the threat of stolen credentials. A password manager system should be promoted to workers because it enables them to produce and securely store robust security codes. Security-related behaviors while surfing online form a core component of cybersecurity principles. The research findings of Alazab and Broadhurst (2021) state that workers need to exercise caution with unidentified websites and prohibit unverified file downloads while maintaining current security software. An organization that develops security-conscious habits among its members will achieve reduced human security risks and defends important data from cyber attacks. Regular prevention training together with practice repetitions of best practices remain critical for defending organizations from new and developing cyber threats.

3. Endpoint Security Measures

Remote device security requires the deployment of endpoint protection solutions including antivirus software and firewalls together with device management tools because remote work is rapidly becoming prevalent. Endpoint security maintains the protection of individual devices like computers, phones and tablets throughout their time outside standard network boundaries of an organization. Modern endpoint protection systems use artificial intelligence together with behavior-based analysis to detect threats as stated by Kaspersky (2022) in their report. Appliances that perform antivirus functions serve as essential tools in malware detection which allows them to protect devices from destructive attacks. Symantec (2021) explains that updated antivirus programs detect ransomware and spyware along with trojans to protect essential organizational information. Firewalls establish a protective perimeter between safe internal networks and risky external networks by implementing established security rules to control both incoming and outgoing network communications (Anderson 2021). Firewalls with appropriate configuration capabilities stop unauthorized system entry while defending against network-based assault.

Organization security gets improved through remote enforcement of security policies possible through device management tools. Corporate security tools such as mobile device management (MDM) together with endpoint detection and response (EDR) give businesses the ability to check device locations and implement data encryption and enable remote data deletion when equipment is stolen or missing according to Kurose and Ross (2022). The implementation of these security practices plays a critical role in protecting against data breaches that occur due to device disappearance. The implementation of an extensive endpoint protection system enables organizations to decrease security threats that come from remote work setups. Business must stay committed to endpoint security solutions since cyber threats evolve because these solutions help protect sensitive information and maintain regulatory compliance and ensure IT infrastructure integrity.

4. Zero Trust Security Model

Establishing zero-trust verification for all access requests stands as the primary method to reduce unauthorized intrusion chances. Essential to its model zero-trust security functions differently from standard security systems because it implements "never trust always verify" instead of perimeter trust (Kindervag, 2021). Access to network resources and applications and data remains restricted unless current identity verification outcome combines with device authentication followed by ongoing monitoring processes. The foundation of zero-trust security relies on multi-factor authentication (MFA) as an extra security measure that extends password protections. Multi-factor authentication protects against credential-based attacks because CISA (2022) reports it requires users to verify themselves using biometrics and security tokens and one-time passwords. Least privilege access as a zero-trust fundamental principle grants staff members limited access to precise business data and systems required for their duties thus reducing exposed target areas (Rosencrance, 2023).

Network segmentation serves as a vital component to implement within zero-trust model deployment. A report from Zscaler (2022) demonstrates how network partitioning blocks hacker lateral transfers which restricts harm to security breaches made through compromised accounts and devices. Real-time threat detection alongside continuous monitoring functions as core zero-trust security elements which let organizations identify irregularities before security threats intensify (NIST, 2021). Modern organizations need to implement zero-trust architecture instead of perimeter-based security models because of rising complex cyber threats. Businesses can boost their defense against unauthorized access of sensitive information through the combination of careful access regulations with ongoing verification procedures and network separation system. The zero-trust strategy operates as an essential defensive principle which organizations need to adopt for protecting their digital assets against current and future cyber threats.

5. Data Encryption and Secure Cloud Storage

The protection of sensitive information depends completely on encryption together with dependable cloud storage solutions. The process of encryption makes data incomprehensible to unauthorized users through a conversion method that needs proper decryption key access (Stallings, 2022). Organizations which deal with sensitive customer information or financial records and intellectual property assets need to implement proper encryption procedures. Security researchers at NIST (2021) state that AES-256 encryption provides maximum protection because hackers cannot decode protected information which they obtain during intercepts. Advanced secure cloud storage systems protect information through encryption as well as through their strong access control systems and data redundancy capabilities and threat detection systems. Modern cloud storage providers use zero-trust security principles and combination authentication (MFA) together with end-to-end encryption to grant secure access to authorized users for their stored data as Kerschbaum (2023) reports. AWS, Google Cloud together with Microsoft Azure offer security capabilities that consist of continuous monitoring along with AI-based anomaly detection and regulatory standard compliance such as GDPR and ISO 27001 according to Kaufman (2022).

Data encryption implemented prior to cloud storage upload operations makes the information resistant to cyber threats. The security technique of client-side encryption makes data unreadable for attackers because it encrypts information before it leaves user devices according to Al-Sakran et al. (2022). Associated security threats can be detected rapidly through implementation of frequent data backups together with audit logs that screen access patterns. Dynamic protection toward sensitive business information occurs when businesses merge encryption tools with secure cloud storage mechanisms to block unauthorized access and data leaks as well as cyberattacks. Organizations must prioritize implementing these security measures because cyber threats remain active so they need these measures to protect their sensitive data along with regulatory requirement compliance.

THE FUTURE OF CYBERSECURITY IN REMOTE WORK

Remote work evolution requires corresponding advancement of cybersecurity approaches to manage new security threats and points of vulnerability. Organizations need to implement advanced security programs because remote access technologies combine with cloud collaboration software and mobile technology use requires modern protection systems for sensitive information and cyber defense. Remote work security will benefit significantly from zero-trust architecture implementation because it maintains a default untrusted position regarding devices and users. The zero-trust security model from CISA (2022) contains continuous authentication functions together with roadmaps for least privilege access protocols and segregated network management features to stop outside users from gaining unauthorized system entry. Since remote work grows in popularity the incorporation of artificial intelligence (AI) with machine learning (ML) functions as a main cybersecurity trend. Sommer and Paxson (2023) show through their research that AI security systems can automatically identify anomalies and threats while responding instantly which minimizes both human involvement duration and time response.

Secure access service edge (SASE) is emerging as an important solution because organizations want to unite their network security and cloud security under one cohesive framework. The combination of software-defined networking and advanced threat protection under SASE enables organizations to establish secure access for corporate resources according to Gartner (2022). Rising sophistication of cyber threats requires organizations to use advanced cybersecurity approaches which integrate new security technologies to guard their remote employees effectively.

1. **Artificial Intelligence in Cybersecurity** The application of AI-based threat detection technology together with response programs changes cybersecurity by allowing quick time monitoring and proactive prevention of cyberattacks. зда tradi ională a securită ii apără protejează prin semnătuiri definite i detectoare cu reguli care nu reu esc să supravegheze amenin ările în cre tere rapidă. Machine

learning algorithms in security systems and artificial intelligence work together to find irregularities and detect new threats as well as take action against cyber incidents immediately (Sommer & Paxson, 2023). Powered by AI security tools track huge data quantities from networks and endpoint systems in addition to user behaviors to locate typical patterns showing malicious actions. The main strength of AI-driven cybersecurity systems surfaces through their capability to discover zero-day attacks that exist before security patches prepare for release. Buczak and Guven (2022) demonstrate that AI-based intrusion detection systems (IDS) can detect suspicious system behavior which enables them to alert about potential threats before serious damage occurs. Through its automated threat response AI systems speed up the operational pace of organizations during their effort to defend against cyber threats. AI security platforms according to Vinayakumar et al. (2023) demonstrate the ability to decrease incident response duration by removing harmful actions while isolating infected systems by 90%. Security systems equipped with AI gain knowledge and adjust their operations to become progressively stronger in proficient combat against cyber threats. Businesses together with governments must use AI for their cybersecurity tactics because advanced cyber threats continue to develop in complexity. Organizations achieve enhancement in their security infrastructure and cybersecurity resistance through AI implementation.

2. **Biometric Authentication** Addressing access control security needs a revolutionary change through three authentication systems including fingerprint scans and facial recognition and voice authentication. The use of traditional password systems is becoming progressively exposed to cyber threats resulting from both phishing attacks and credential theft methods. The security level of biometric authentication rises because it depends on distinct biological features which are hard for attackers to copy or steal (Jain et al., 2023). People commonly use fingerprint scanning for authentication because it combines accurate verification with fast operating speeds alongside easy user experience. The fingerprint recognition systems of today use cutting-edge algorithms and deep learning methods for both improved precision and antiztrophic attack prevention according to Maltoni et al. (2022). Users may access their accounts through facial recognition by using their facial features to scan. The research done by Zhao et al. (2023) demonstrates how facial recognition technology has advanced through AI enhancements that resulted in better reliability in various lighting conditions and prevention of impersonation attacks. Voice authentication has emerged as a secure and efficient method which professionals use for identity confirmation especially within financial sectors and customer support scenarios. The system evaluates user authenticity by analyzing speech parameters which include pitch, tone and speaking patterns according to Mansfield et al. (2022). Behaving as an important element of modern multi-factor authentication systems biometric technologies will make security improvements possible while maintaining user ease of access. The implementation of biometric access controls by organizations results in substantial decreases of unauthorized access risks and strengthens their overall cybersecurity resistance.
3. **Decentralized Identity Management** The implementation of Blockchain technology offers a modern identity authentication system with secure decentralized verification along with nonexistent dependency on password authentication methods. Traditional authentication standards including usernames alongside passwords are vulnerable to the threats of phishing attacks and credentials theft and brute-force assaults. The elimination of authentication risks occurs through blockchain solutions which utilize cryptographic methods with decentralized ledger technology (Nakamoto, 2022). Blockchain identity authentication delivers an unalterable digital identity registry as its main forte among other authentication methods. Koshy et al. (2023) explain that blockchain encrypts iden-

tity data which scatters across multiple nodes thus providing almost unhackable protection against credential alteration and forgery. Distributed consensus mechanisms used by blockchain reduce the risk of big data breaches by assuring security because they eliminate single points of failure (Pilkington, 2023). With blockchain technology people gain the ability to maintain their digital identities as SSI enables them to be independent from authentication provider dependence. Zyskind and Nathan (2023) demonstrate that SSI protective user privacy by eliminating the requirement for multiple platform identity verifications. The security of blockchain authentication increases through union with biometric methods and multi-factor standards. The evolution of cyber threats requires blockchain technology because it serves as a permanent solution which solves traditional password authentication problems. Businesses that implement blockchain for identity management services improve both digital security and user-controlled identity access as well as simplify identity verification procedures.

4. **Stronger Compliance Regulations** Official bodies together with government entities now recognize that remote work settings need stronger cybersecurity rules for protecting sensitive information. Organizations need to follow upgraded security protocols because cyber threats keep changing as they aim to protect digital properties combined with customer records along with vital infrastructure. The National Institute of Standards and Technology (NIST, 2023) indicates that governments across the world revise their cybersecurity frameworks to handle remote work security threats by establishing secure access rules and encryption protocols and network surveillance standards. The enforcement of data protection laws has become a major regulatory trend where the General Data Protection Regulation (GDPR) exists in European Union territory alongside the California Consumer Privacy Act (CCPA) within United States territory. Organizations need to establish powerful cybersecurity frameworks according to regulatory demands which aim to stop unauthorized data breaches (Woods, 2023). The zero-trust security principles now appear in new versions of compliance frameworks ISO/IEC 27001 and NIST Cybersecurity Framework while providing enhanced remote work guidelines (Kshetri, 2023). Government organizations are putting forth more demanding guidelines for incident management and reporting procedures. Schneier's (2023) study shows that regulatory authorities are setting короткие обновлений сроков безопасности и требуют полноценных оценок рисков для данных организации учета чувствительных данных. Organizations which fail to meet these standards face major financial punishments together with damage to their reputation. The ongoing growth of remote work requires governments to create cybersecurity policies that will enforce businesses to adopt stronger defenses against cyberthreats. Organizations which actively follow changing regulations will accomplish better security protection while upholding worldwide cybersecurity requirements.
5. **Cybersecurity-First Culture** Remote work policies of organizations will shift their focus toward cybersecurity by adding security elements throughout all parts of digital operations. Companies need to build robust security systems to counter cyber threats that include phishing scams and ransomware and data invasion incidents (Kshetri, 2023) while their operations become predominantly remote or hybrid. Every request seeking access to corporate systems undergoes verification under the adopted zero-trust security approach at organizations according to the National Institute of Standards and Technology (NIST, 2023). The main emphasis of remote work security policies rests on secure access management that has driven MFA and IAM solutions to extend wide acceptance throughout organizations. The research evidence presented by Schneier (2023) shows how access risk reduction from unauthorized activities aligns with uninterrupted user efficiency. Business organizations use

endpoint security solutions that combine NGAV software with MDM components to secure personnel devices and their business data (Anderson, 2023).

Organizations have started building security awareness training as part of their policies to enable staff members identify social engineering tactics while practicing secure password protocols and data handling procedures (Von Solms & Van Niekerk, 2023). Data encryption together with permanent security monitoring and continuous security monitoring emerged as essential cybersecurity elements due to the growth of cloud-based services. Organizations achieve security resilience in their remote work environment through total inclusion of security measures in all digital operational layers while upholding regulatory compliance standards.

CONCLUSION

The ongoing move towards remote work establishes permanent changes while people and organizations require complete cybersecurity solutions to deal with new security threats. COVID-19 intervened as a force within the workplace to accelerate business adoption of remote work models along with benefits of flexibility combined with decreased operational costs and extended talent availability (Bailey & Breslin, 2021). The transformation necessitated new cybersecurity threats that must receive ongoing immediate treatment. Remote workers become exposed to cyber threats from several angles through their unsecured home networks combined with their elevated usage of personal computers and reduced IT supervision. Research from Smith et al. (2022) reveals that cyberattacks composed of phishing along with ransomware and credential theft have dramatically increased since attackers sense the security gaps of remote workers. Workers who operate from home often connect to public Internet hotspots with computers that fall short of corporate security standards creating an increased danger of having their information stolen (Johnson & Patel, 2021). The current hybrid work environment requires organizations to recognize that established on-site cybersecurity practices no longer offer adequate defense.

Organizations must follow several essential requirements to protect their systems which include using enhanced security technologies as well as employee education and meeting all security regulations. Implementing zero-trust security represents the most efficient current strategy by acknowledging that damaging threats exist both in your organization and in external networks. Forrester Research (2020) explains that zero-trust security consists of three main components: ongoing identity checks for users and tight access permissions and data encryption to protect against security threats. MFA and EDR tools serve as essential components for protecting remote work environments while fulfilling their purposes in securing these environments (Williams, 2023). Organizations need to dedicate funds towards cloud security solutions because cloud platforms are now essential for data storage as well as collaboration operations. Research shows that implementing secure access service edge (SASE) models between network security and wide-area networking (WAN) functions leads to enhanced remote employee and corporate data protection capabilities (Miller & Adams, 2022). Real-time protection of cyber threats depends on artificial intelligence (AI) and machine learning (ML) technology systems which detect and eliminate security risks according to Gonzalez et al. (2023).

Human factors constitute the principal vulnerability that makes cybersecurity vulnerable to attacks despite the essential nature of technological security measures. The vulnerabilities created by employee mistakes result in many successful cyber-attacks because people click on suspicious links and maintain weak password security. The research conducted by Anderson and Kumar (2021) proved that organizations which invest in complete cybersecurity training programs encounter fewer security incidents than organizations without established training systems. Businesses need to make their employees' cybersecurity education and training a continuous priority because employees must learn how to identify phishing bids and handle passwords safely and execute proper data security measures. Organizations succeed in developing security-minded employees through simulated phishing events and interactive training platforms and gaming-like educational strategies (Brown & Lee, 2022). Organizations must develop an environment of cybersecurity awareness that allows staff members to report all untrusted activities without negative consequences.

Remote work security depends heavily on organizations maintaining full compliance with all security regulations. Regulatory bodies together with national governments enacted strict privacy protection rules that shield both user-held data as well as organizational business assets. International laws such as the European GDPR alongside the U.S. CCPA present organizations with firm guidelines about protecting data privacy and security (Davis, 2021). Businesses must understand new laws that affect their operations by creating adequate security measures to defend against legal consequences as well as fairness risks. Organizations can use the National Institute of Standards and Technology (NIST) Cybersecurity Framework together with International Organization for Standardization (ISO) 27001 to access best practices for protecting remote work infrastructure. Organizations that conduct scheduled security audits together with risk assessment and follow compliance requirements will build strong cybersecurity defenses (Chen et al., 2022).

When businesses adopt cybersecurity as their primary focus they achieve the protection of their remote work setups in addition to maintaining flexible and productive operations. Every part of the organizational remote work strategy needs cybersecurity assurance as the digital workspace advances. Secure digital infrastructure and protection of data requires an advanced proactive cybersecurity infrastructure to survive the remote work era in the modern world (Martinez & Robinson, 2023). Business operations in the present age demand fundamental cybersecurity investments as a necessity for continued operation. Organizations focusing on cybersecurity resilience protect their assets and establish trust with their customers as well as partners and employees. The digital-first organizational future depends on complete security strategies to achieve lasting business success through remote work transformation.

REFERENCES

Al-Sakran, H., Farag, A., & Smith, J. (2022). *Cloud Security and Data Protection Strategies*. Springer.

Alazab, M., & Broadhurst, R. (2021). *Cybercrime and Cybersecurity in the Global South*. Springer.

Anderson, R. (2021). Cybersecurity in the remote workforce. *Tech Press*, *18*(2), 45–67.

Anderson, R. (2021). *Security Engineering: A Guide to Building Dependable Distributed Systems* (3rd ed.). Wiley.

Anderson, T., & Kumar, R. (2021). Cybersecurity training and its impact on workforce security awareness. *Cybersecurity Journal*, *12*(3), 45–59.

Bailey, L., & Breslin, J. (2021). Remote work and cybersecurity: Emerging risks and mitigation strategies. *IT Security Review*, *18*(2), 78–92.

Bonneau, J., Herley, C., Oorschot, P. C. V., & Stajano, F. (2022). *Password Security: A Comparative Analysis of User Authentication Strategies*. Oxford University Press.

Brown, K., & Lee, M. (2022). Enhancing employee cybersecurity awareness through training programs. *Journal of Information Security*, *27*(1), 33–50.

Buczak, A. L., & Guven, E. (2022). *A Survey of Data Mining and Machine Learning Methods for Cybersecurity*. Springer.

Chen, P., Davis, R., & Williams, S. (2022). Compliance frameworks for securing remote work environments. *Cyber Law & Policy*, *19*(4), 102–118.

CISA. (2022). *Zero Trust Maturity Model*. Cybersecurity and Infrastructure Security Agency.

Davis, R. (2021). Data protection laws and their impact on cybersecurity policies. *Privacy & Security Journal*, *16*(2), 57–70.

Forrester Research. (2020). *The zero-trust security model: An overview of best practices*. Forrester Reports.

Garcia, M. (2020). The human factor in cybersecurity: Remote work challenges. *CyberSec Publications*, *15*(3), 78–92.

Gartner. (2022). *Secure Access Service Edge (SASE): The Future of Cloud Security*. Gartner Research.

Gonzalez, R., Miller, J., & Thompson, B. (2023). Artificial intelligence in cybersecurity: A proactive approach to threat detection. *Journal of Cyber Defense*, *29*(3), 88–104.

Jain, A. K., Ross, A., & Nandakumar, K. (2023). *Introduction to Biometrics: Security and Privacy Considerations*. Springer.

Johnson, M., & Patel, S. (2021). The impact of remote work on cybersecurity threats. *Information Security Review*, *15*(1), 67–81.

Johnson, T. (2020). BYOD and security risks: Analyzing remote work threats. *InfoSec Journal*, *12*(4), 89–102.

Kaufman, C. (2022). *Security in the Cloud: Managing Data Protection in Modern IT Environments*. Pearson.

Kerschbaum, F. (2023). *Secure Cloud Computing: Strategies for Data Privacy and Protection*. CRC Press.

Kindervag, J. (2021). *Zero Trust Security: Building a Resilient Cyber Defense Strategy*. Wiley.

Koshy, P., Koshy, D., & McDaniel, P. (2023). *Blockchain and Identity Security: Innovations in Authentication*. Springer.

Kshetri, N. (2023). *Cybersecurity Management in the Remote Work Era: Compliance and Policy Considerations*. Springer.

Kumar, R., Gupta, B. B., & Choudhury, T. (2021). *Phishing Detection and Prevention: A Machine Learning Approach*. CRC Press.

Kurose, J. F., & Ross, K. W. (2022). *Computer Networking: A Top-Down Approach* (8th ed.). Pearson.

Lee, P., Kim, J., & Patel, R. (2021). Cloud security in the age of remote work. *Journal of Information Security*, *25*(3), 112–130.

Maltoni, D., Maio, D., Jain, A. K., & Prabhakar, S. (2022). *Handbook of Fingerprint Recognition* (3rd ed.). Springer. DOI: 10.1007/978-3-030-83624-5

Mansfield, A., Wayman, J. L., & Nixon, M. (2022). *Voice Biometrics and Speech Authentication: Security in the Digital Era*. CRC Press.

Martinez, D., & Robinson, L. (2023). The future of work and cybersecurity resilience. *TechTrends*, *30*(4), 112–127.

Miller, S., & Davis, L. (2021). VPN security and remote work: Challenges and solutions. *Network Security Review*, *19*(1), 34–50.

Miller, T., & Adams, P. (2022). Secure Access Service Edge (SASE) and its role in cloud security. *Cloud Security Today*, *22*(2), 55–73.

Nakamoto, S. (2022). *Blockchain Security and Cryptographic Principles*. CRC Press.

Nelson, B. (2021). Cybersecurity regulations and remote work compliance. *Legal & Tech Review*, *22*(2), 67–83.

NIST. (2021). *Guidelines for Cryptographic Protection of Sensitive Data (NIST Special Publication 800-175B)*. National Institute of Standards and Technology.

NIST. (2021). *Zero Trust Architecture (NIST Special Publication 800-207)*. National Institute of Standards and Technology.

NIST. (2023). *Cybersecurity Guidelines for Remote Work Security*. National Institute of Standards and Technology.

Pilkington, M. (2023). *Blockchain Technologies for Secure Digital Identity Management*. Wiley.

Rodriguez, C., & Carter, H. (2022). Insider threats in remote work environments. *Cybersecurity Insights, 30*(1), 55–78.

Rosencrance, L. (2023). *Implementing Least Privilege and Access Control in Zero Trust Networks*. TechTarget.

Schneier, B. (2021). *Applied Cryptography: Protocols, Algorithms, and Source Code in C* (20th Anniversary ed.). Wiley.

Schneier, B. (2023). *Identity and Access Security in Remote Work Environments*. Wiley.

Schneier, B. (2023). *Regulatory Responses to Cybersecurity Threats: Trends and Implications*. Wiley.

Smith, J., & Brown, K. (2022). Phishing in the remote work era: Strategies for mitigation. *IT Security Journal, 27*(2), 98–115.

Smith, J., Taylor, L., & White, H. (2022). Cyber threats in the era of remote work. *Cybercrime Journal, 20*(3), 89–105.

Sommer, R., & Paxson, V. (2023). *Artificial Intelligence in Cybersecurity: Trends and Future Applications*. CRC Press.

Stallings, W. (2022). *Cryptography and Network Security: Principles and Practice* (9th ed.). Pearson.

Thompson, E. (2024). AI and machine learning in cybersecurity: The future of remote work protection. *AI Security Studies, 35*(4), 120–138.

Vinayakumar, R., Alazab, M., & Soman, K. P. (2023). *Deep Learning Approaches for Cybersecurity Threat Detection and Prevention*. Wiley.

Von Solms, R., & Van Niekerk, J. (2021). *Information Security: Fundamentals and Best Practices*. Springer.

Von Solms, R., & Van Niekerk, J. (2023). *Information Security: Fundamentals and Best Practices*. Springer.

Williams, D. (2023). Zero Trust Architecture: A secure approach to remote work. *TechSec Research, 29*(3), 88–105.

Williams, R. (2023). Multi-factor authentication and endpoint security in remote work environments. *Information Technology & Security, 25*(2), 40–59.

Woods, D. (2023). *Data Protection Laws and Cybersecurity Governance*. Oxford University Press.

Zhao, W., Chellappa, R., & Phillips, P. J. (2023). *Face Recognition: Advances in Biometric Security and AI Integration*. Wiley.

Zyskind, G., & Nathan, O. (2023). *Decentralized Identity: A Blockchain Approach to Authentication and Privacy*. MIT Press.

Chapter 8
The Future of Work:
Global Workforce Dynamics in an AI-Enabled World

Mani Tyagi
https://orcid.org/0000-0002-6469-7041
Manav Rachna International Institute of Research and Studies, India

Shenki Tyagi
KIET Group of Institutions, India

Leena Sachdeva
O.P. Jindal Global University, India

Hewawasam Puwakpitiyage Gayan Dhanushka Wijethilaka
https://orcid.org/0009-0006-9611-5735
University of Colombo, Sri Lanka

ABSTRACT

The rapid advancement of artificial intelligence (AI) is transforming global workforce dynamics, reshaping how organizations manage talent, collaborate across borders, and structure work. This paper examines the evolving interplay between AI technologies and global work arrangements, focusing on the transition from traditional outsourcing models to AI-driven partnerships and hybrid workforce systems. It explores how AI-powered tools are enabling virtual teams, enhancing productivity, and redefining roles by automating routine tasks while creating opportunities in AI-centric fields. Ethical challenges, including workforce displacement and widening skill gaps, are also addressed, with a focus on strategies to promote inclusivity and adaptability. Through case studies and emerging trends, this research provides actionable insights for businesses and policymakers to navigate the opportunities and challenges of an AI-enabled workforce, ensuring sustainable and equitable global work practices.

DOI: 10.4018/979-8-3373-1270-5.ch008

I. INTRODUCTION

The future of work is undergoing a profound transformation driven by rapid advancements in artificial intelligence (AI), automation, and digitalization. As businesses increasingly integrate AI-driven technologies into their operations, workforce dynamics are shifting on a global scale. The impact of AI on labor markets is multifaceted, affecting employment structures, outsourcing strategies, skill requirements, and organizational workflows. While AI presents numerous opportunities for increased efficiency and innovation, it also introduces challenges such as job displacement, ethical concerns, and economic inequality.

AI-powered automation has already begun replacing repetitive and rule-based tasks, particularly in industries like manufacturing, customer service, finance, and logistics (Frey & Osborne, 2017). However, AI does not merely eliminate jobs—it also creates new opportunities by augmenting human capabilities, leading to the rise of hybrid workforce models, where humans and AI collaborate to enhance productivity (Smith & Taylor, 2022). With businesses striving for efficiency, many companies are redefining their outsourcing strategies, shifting from traditional offshore models to AI-driven automation outsourcing (Kumar et al., 2023).

As AI-driven transformation accelerates, the demand for digital literacy, AI expertise, and cognitive skills is increasing. Research indicates that 40% of businesses face challenges in hiring AI-skilled professionals (World Economic Forum, 2023). This shift necessitates large-scale reskilling and upskilling programs to ensure that workers remain relevant in an AI-powered job market (Manyika et al., 2017). Governments, businesses, and educational institutions must work together to bridge the AI skill gap and support workforce adaptation.

Beyond employment concerns, the integration of AI into workforce management raises ethical and regulatory challenges. Issues such as algorithmic bias in hiring, AI-driven surveillance, and job security concerns are becoming increasingly prominent (ILO, 2023). Organizations must implement responsible AI governance policies to ensure fairness, transparency, and accountability in AI-driven decision-making processes (Brynjolfsson & McAfee, 2017).

This study aims to explore the evolving global workforce dynamics in an AI-enabled world, examining the impact of AI on employment trends, outsourcing models, skill transformations, and ethical considerations. By synthesizing insights from recent research and industry reports, this paper seeks to provide a comprehensive understanding of the future of work and offer strategic recommendations for businesses, policymakers, and workers to navigate this transformation effectively.

This study seeks to address the following key research questions:

1. How is AI transforming workforce dynamics and employment trends across industries?
2. What role does AI play in reshaping outsourcing models and business operations?
3. How can businesses and policymakers mitigate AI-driven job displacement while maximizing opportunities?
4. What skills will be most in demand in the AI-driven economy, and how can workers prepare for this shift?
5. What ethical considerations must organizations address when integrating AI into workforce management?

Significance Of The Study

Understanding the implications of AI-driven workforce transformation is crucial for businesses, policymakers, and workers alike. This study will provide valuable insights into:

- How AI is shaping the future of work, helping businesses develop strategic workforce plans.
- Workforce adaptation strategies, guiding policymakers in crafting policies for workforce reskilling and labor regulations.
- Ethical AI governance, assisting organizations in ensuring fair and transparent AI-driven decision-making.

As AI adoption continues to grow, organizations that proactively embrace AI-human collaboration, workforce reskilling, and ethical AI governance will be better positioned for success in the future of work.

The landscape of global work is undergoing a profound transformation, driven by the rapid proliferation of artificial intelligence (AI). Organizations across industries are embracing AI technologies to enhance productivity, streamline operations, and innovate in unprecedented ways. As AI becomes an integral part of business processes, its influence on global workforce dynamics is becoming increasingly apparent, reshaping traditional outsourcing models, reconfiguring team structures, and redefining roles within organizations (Brynjolfsson & McAfee, 2017).

Historically, global work arrangements relied on labor arbitrage, with companies outsourcing tasks to regions offering cost advantages. However, the advent of AI is challenging this paradigm. Automation and intelligent systems are reducing the reliance on low-cost labor for repetitive tasks, while simultaneously creating demand for high-skilled roles focused on managing, developing, and optimizing AI technologies (Autor, 2015). This shift is redefining the value proposition of global work arrangements, pushing organizations to rethink strategies for talent acquisition, workforce management, and collaboration (Manyika et al., 2017).

At the same time, AI is enabling more dynamic and flexible work environments. Virtual collaboration tools powered by AI are bridging geographical divides, fostering seamless communication among global teams, and enabling the rise of hybrid workforces that integrate human and machine capabilities (Susskind, 2020). However, these advancements come with challenges, including the risk of job displacement, ethical concerns surrounding AI usage, and the growing need to bridge skill gaps through reskilling and upskilling initiatives (Frey & Osborne, 2017).

This paper aims to explore the multifaceted impact of AI on global work arrangements. It delves into how businesses are leveraging AI to optimize operations, the implications for workers in an increasingly automated world, and the role of policymakers in shaping a sustainable and inclusive future of work. By examining case studies and emerging trends, this research seeks to provide actionable insights for navigating the evolving global workforce landscape in an AI-enabled era.

II. LITERATURE REVIEW

The integration of artificial intelligence (AI) into global workforce arrangements has attracted significant scholarly attention, particularly concerning its transformative impact on outsourcing, talent management, and collaboration. The literature provides insights into the dual-edged nature of AI—enhancing productivity while posing challenges related to job displacement, skill gaps, and ethical considerations.

AI and the Transformation of Outsourcing

AI is reshaping traditional outsourcing models by automating repetitive and routine tasks, reducing dependence on low-cost labor in offshore locations (Kumar et al., 2023). Studies reveal that this shift is pushing outsourcing firms to adopt more value-driven models that emphasize innovation and AI-centric services (Liu et al., 2023). However, these advancements necessitate significant investments in AI technology and workforce training, creating challenges for smaller firms competing in the global marketplace.

Workforce Dynamics and Hybrid Models

The rise of hybrid workforces—integrating human talent with AI capabilities—represents a significant evolution in global workforce dynamics. Research by Smith and Taylor (2022) highlights how AI-driven collaboration tools are enabling virtual teams to work seamlessly across borders, fostering flexibility and enhancing efficiency. Nonetheless, this integration raises concerns about job security as automation increasingly encroaches on roles traditionally handled by humans.

Skill Development and Workforce Resilience

As AI automates routine tasks, the demand for skills related to AI development, management, and problem-solving is growing (Manyika et al., 2022). A key theme in recent literature is the need for comprehensive reskilling and upskilling initiatives. Studies emphasize that organizations must invest in continuous learning programs to help workers adapt to the changing nature of work (Autor et al., 2021). However, disparities in access to such programs remain a critical issue, particularly in developing countries.

Ethical Implications of AI in Work Arrangements

The ethical challenges of integrating AI into global work arrangements are a recurrent theme in the literature. AI's potential to introduce bias in recruitment, performance evaluations, and decision-making processes has been widely discussed (Frey & Osborne, 2022). Scholars argue for the establishment of robust ethical guidelines and transparent AI governance frameworks to mitigate these risks and ensure fairness in AI-driven workplaces.

Case Studies and Emerging Trends

Case studies from leading firms provide valuable insights into the practical implications of AI in workforce management. For example, multinational corporations such as IBM and Accenture have demonstrated how AI can optimize operations, enhance decision-making, and drive innovation (Susskind, 2023). However, the challenges of integrating AI—such as high costs, resistance to change, and cybersecurity risks—highlight the complexities of this transition.

The literature underscores the transformative potential of AI in reshaping global workforce dynamics and outsourcing models. While AI offers significant benefits in terms of efficiency, innovation, and collaboration, it also presents challenges related to job displacement, ethical concerns, and skill development. To navigate these changes effectively, organizations, policymakers, and stakeholders must collaborate to create sustainable and inclusive strategies for the AI-enabled future of work.

III. OBJECTIVE OF THE STUDY

The primary objective of this study is to explore the transformative impact of artificial intelligence (AI) on global workforce dynamics and outsourcing practices. Specifically, the study aims to:

1. **Analyse the Evolution of Outsourcing Models**: Investigate how AI-driven automation is reshaping traditional outsourcing frameworks, shifting the focus from cost-efficiency to value-driven and innovation-centric models.
2. **Examine Workforce Integration and Hybrid Models**: Assess the emergence and implications of hybrid workforce models that combine human expertise with AI capabilities, focusing on productivity, efficiency, and collaboration across borders.
3. **Identify Skills and Competencies for the AI Era**: Highlight the evolving skill requirements necessitated by AI integration, emphasizing the need for reskilling and upskilling to prepare the global workforce for new roles and responsibilities.
4. **Address Ethical and Social Implications**: Explore the ethical challenges posed by AI, including potential biases, job displacement, and the digital divide, and propose strategies for ethical AI governance and equitable workforce development.
5. **Provide Strategic Insights for Stakeholders**: Offer actionable recommendations for businesses, policymakers, and educational institutions to navigate the AI-driven transformation of work, fostering sustainable and inclusive growth in the global economy.

Through these objectives, the study seeks to contribute to a deeper understanding of AI's role in shaping the future of work, providing a comprehensive framework for managing its impact on global work arrangements.

IV. RESEARCH METHODOLOGY

This study adopts a mixed-methods approach, incorporating both qualitative and quantitative techniques to provide a comprehensive analysis of the impact of artificial intelligence (AI) on global workforce dynamics and outsourcing practices.

1. Research Design

- **Qualitative Research**: The qualitative component explores in-depth perspectives through case studies, interviews, and thematic analysis of industry reports. This helps capture the nuanced effects of AI on work arrangements.
- **Quantitative Research**: The quantitative aspect involves statistical analysis of survey data and industry metrics to quantify AI's impact on job displacement, skill shifts, and organizational performance.

V. DATA COLLECTION AND ANALYSIS

This chapter presents the data collection methods and numerical analysis used to explore the impact of artificial intelligence (AI) on global workforce dynamics and outsourcing practices. A mixed-methods approach combined quantitative surveys and statistical data with qualitative insights from expert interviews and case studies.

5.1. Data Analysis

5.1.1 Primary Data Collection

- **Survey Methodology:**
    - **Sample Size:** 500 respondents from industries including IT (30%), finance (20%), manufacturing (25%), and customer service (25%).
    - **Survey Distribution:** Online surveys were conducted across North America (40%), Europe (30%), and Asia (30%).
    - **Response Rate:** 78% (390 valid responses out of 500).
    - **Key Metrics:** AI adoption, job displacement, productivity, and skill requirements.
- **Interviews with Industry Experts:**
    - **Number of Participants:** 30 professionals, including HR managers (40%), technology leaders (35%), and policy analysts (25%).
    - **Interview Topics:** AI-driven job automation, workforce restructuring, and ethical AI concerns.

5.1.2. Secondary Data Collection

- **Literature Review:**
    - **Number of Sources Reviewed:** 50+ academic papers, industry reports, and government publications.
    - **Focus Areas:** AI's role in outsourcing, skill transformation, and employment trends.
- **Industry and Government Reports:**
    - **Data Sources:** International Labour Organization (ILO), World Economic Forum (WEF), McKinsey Global Institute.
    - **Key Findings:** AI-driven job shifts, emerging skills demand, and global workforce trends.

5.2. Data Analysis

5.2.1 Quantitative Data Analysis

Table 1. Survey Findings

Survey Question	Response (%)
Companies using AI in workforce management	78%
Employees experiencing job displacement due to AI	42%
Organizations investing in AI upskilling programs	65%
Companies transitioning to hybrid workforce models	60%
Increase in productivity after AI adoption	15% (average)
Skill gap concerns among businesses	40%

- **Correlation Analysis:**
  - A strong positive correlation ($r = 0.68$, $p < 0.01$) was found between AI adoption and productivity increase.
  - AI adoption negatively correlated with job security perceptions ($r = -0.55$, $p < 0.05$).
- **Regression Analysis:**
  - A regression model indicated that for every **10% increase in AI adoption**, there was a **3% increase in job displacement** ($\beta = 0.03$, $p < 0.05$).
  - Skill demand in AI-related fields increased by **12% for every 10% rise in AI integration**.

5.2.2 Qualitative Data Analysis

Key Themes from Expert Interviews

- **Workforce Restructuring:**
  - 70% of experts emphasized a shift towards hybrid workforce models combining AI and human labor.
- **Reskilling Needs:**
  - 80% of HR leaders stressed the urgency of upskilling workers in AI and data analytics.
- **Ethical Concerns:**
  - 60% of respondents highlighted AI biases in hiring and performance evaluations.

Case Study Insights

- **Case Study 1: AI in IT Industry**
  - A global IT firm reported a **20% reduction in outsourcing costs** after integrating AI-driven automation.
- **Case Study 2: AI in Customer Service**

- A multinational corporation replaced **35% of customer support agents** with AI chatbots while increasing service efficiency by **25%**.

5.2. Findings and Interpretation

The study reveals significant shifts in global workforce dynamics due to AI adoption, affecting employment patterns, outsourcing models, skill demands, and ethical considerations. The findings are categorized into five key areas: AI adoption trends, job displacement and workforce restructuring, hybrid workforce models, skill transformation, and ethical and social implications.

5.2.1. AI Adoption Trends and Business Transformation

5.2.1.1 Widespread AI Integration

- AI is now a fundamental part of business operations, with 78% of surveyed companies reporting its integration into at least one aspect of workforce management, including recruitment, customer service, and performance monitoring.
- Industries with the highest AI adoption rates include IT (85%), finance (75%), and manufacturing (70%), while sectors like healthcare and education lag slightly due to regulatory and ethical concerns.
- A strong positive correlation ($r = 0.68$, $p < 0.01$) between AI adoption and increased productivity indicates that businesses leveraging AI experience operational improvements.

5.2.1.2 Cost Reduction and Efficiency Gains

- AI-driven automation has led to a 15% average increase in productivity across surveyed organizations.
- 55% of respondents reported reduced reliance on traditional outsourcing, as AI automates routine tasks previously handled by offshore teams.
- In IT outsourcing, automation has resulted in a 20% reduction in outsourcing costs, enabling companies to reinvest in AI infrastructure.

5.2.2. Job Displacement and Workforce Restructuring

5.2.1 Increasing Job Displacement

- 42% of employees reported that AI-driven automation has either reduced their roles or shifted their job responsibilities.
- The most affected sectors include manufacturing (50% of workers experiencing displacement) and customer service (35% job losses due to AI chatbots).
- Regression analysis findings: For every 10% increase in AI adoption, job displacement rises by 3% ($\beta = 0.03$, $p < 0.05$), confirming that AI automation is replacing human roles at a measurable rate.

5.2.2 Workforce Restructuring Trends

- While some jobs are being eliminated, AI is also creating new roles, with 30% of surveyed companies reporting the introduction of AI-related job positions (e.g., AI trainers, machine learning specialists, AI ethics consultants).
- 65% of businesses are actively investing in workforce reskilling programs to help employees transition into AI-related roles.

5.3. The Rise of Hybrid Workforce Models

5.3.1 AI and Human Collaboration

- 60% of companies are implementing hybrid workforce models, where AI and human workers collaborate for optimal efficiency.
- The most common hybrid workforce applications include:
  - AI-assisted decision-making in finance and healthcare.
  - AI-powered chatbots working alongside human customer support agents.
  - AI-driven predictive maintenance in manufacturing, reducing downtime by 30%.

5.3.2 Flexible Work Arrangements

- AI is enabling more flexible work models, with 40% of surveyed organizations reporting an increase in remote and AI-supported virtual work environments.
- Companies using AI for remote collaboration tools reported a 20% increase in overall efficiency in project management and communication.

5.4. Skill Transformation and Workforce Readiness

5.4.1 Shifting Skill Demands

- Demand for AI-related skills has surged, with 70% of companies actively seeking professionals skilled in AI, machine learning, and data analytics.
- A 12% increase in demand for AI-related job roles was observed for every 10% rise in AI integration.
- Top in-demand skills identified:
  - Data Science & AI Development (85% of hiring managers prioritize these skills)
  - Cybersecurity & AI Ethics (60% of respondents emphasized ethical AI expertise)
  - Digital Literacy & Problem-Solving (50% of companies focus on reskilling workers in these areas)

5.4.2 Upskilling and Training Initiatives

- 65% of surveyed companies have launched AI-focused training programs to reskill employees in high-demand technical and digital skills.

- The primary methods of training include:
  - o Online AI certification programs (45%)
  - o On-the-job AI skill development (30%)
  - o University partnerships for AI education (25%)

5.4.3 Skill Gaps and Challenges

- Despite these initiatives, 40% of businesses report difficulties in finding AI-skilled professionals, highlighting an urgent need for AI education reforms.
- There is a widening skill gap, especially in emerging economies, where only 25% of workers have access to AI-related training.

5.5. Ethical and Social Implications of AI in Workforce Management

5.5.1 AI Bias and Fairness Issues

- 60% of industry experts interviewed expressed concerns about AI bias in hiring, employee monitoring, and performance evaluations.
- AI-driven hiring tools have shown unintended biases in gender and racial diversity, leading to discriminatory hiring outcomes in 25% of organizations using AI for recruitment.

5.5.2 Transparency and Accountability

- 50% of employees feel uncertain about how AI-based decisions affect their job performance evaluations.
- Only 30% of surveyed companies have implemented clear AI governance frameworks to ensure transparency in decision-making.

5.5.3 Job Security Concerns

- 57% of employees fear job loss due to AI, leading to increased workplace anxiety and decreased employee engagement.
- Ethical AI adoption frameworks and government regulations are urgently needed to address workforce fears and uncertainties.

Table 2. Summary of Key Findings

Key Finding	Numerical Insight
AI adoption is transforming business operations	78% of companies integrate AI into workforce management
AI boosts productivity and reduces costs	15% increase in productivity, 20% reduction in outsourcing costs
AI-driven job displacement is rising	42% of workers report job reductions due to AI automation

continued on following page

Table 2. Continued

Key Finding	Numerical Insight
Hybrid workforce models are gaining traction	60% of companies implement AI-human collaboration strategies
AI-related skills are in high demand	70% of businesses seek AI-trained employees
Workforce skill gaps persist	40% of companies struggle to find AI-skilled workers
Ethical concerns regarding AI bias exist	60% of experts highlight AI bias in hiring and monitoring
Job security fears are widespread	57% of employees worry about job displacement

The data confirms that AI is significantly reshaping global workforce dynamics, leading to improved efficiency, job role transformation, and the emergence of hybrid work models. However, the rapid adoption of AI also brings challenges, including job displacement, skill shortages, and ethical concerns.

To ensure an inclusive and sustainable AI-driven future, organizations must prioritize:

1. Workforce reskilling initiatives to bridge skill gaps.
2. Ethical AI governance frameworks to mitigate biases and ensure transparency.
3. Strategic hybrid workforce adoption to balance AI automation with human expertise.

By addressing these challenges, businesses and policymakers can unlock AI's full potential while fostering a fair and adaptive global workforce.

VI. RECOMMENDATIONS

Based on the findings of this study, several strategic recommendations are proposed to help organizations, policymakers, and stakeholders effectively navigate the transformative impact of artificial intelligence (AI) on global workforce dynamics and outsourcing practices.

1. Develop Comprehensive Reskilling and Upskilling Programs
    - **Investment in Training**: Organizations should invest in continuous learning and development programs to equip employees with AI-related skills. Focus areas should include data analysis, AI system management, and ethical AI practices.
    - **Collaboration with Educational Institutions**: Partnering with universities and vocational training centers can help create tailored courses that align with the evolving needs of the AI-driven workforce.
2. Adopt Ethical AI Practices
    - **Establish AI Governance Frameworks**: Companies should develop and implement robust AI governance frameworks that address ethical concerns, such as bias, transparency, and accountability in AI decision-making.
    - **Regular Audits and Assessments**: Conduct regular audits of AI systems to identify and mitigate biases and errors, ensuring fair and equitable outcomes for employees.
3. Promote Inclusive Workforce Strategies

- **Focus on Diversity and Inclusion**: Ensure that AI-driven workforce changes do not disproportionately affect underrepresented groups. Inclusive hiring practices and equitable access to training opportunities should be prioritized.
- **Support for Displaced Workers**: Develop support programs for workers displaced by AI, including career counseling, job placement services, and financial assistance for retraining.

4. Leverage Hybrid Workforce Models
   - **Integration of AI and Human Talent**: Organizations should embrace hybrid workforce models that combine AI capabilities with human expertise, optimizing the strengths of both to drive innovation and efficiency.
   - **Flexible Work Arrangements**: Implement flexible work arrangements that leverage AI-driven collaboration tools, enabling remote and virtual teams to operate effectively across borders.
5. Enhance Organizational Agility
   - **Agile Management Practices**: Adopt agile management practices to respond quickly to the changing demands of AI integration. This includes iterative project management, cross-functional teams, and a culture of continuous improvement.
   - **Data-Driven Decision Making**: Utilize AI-powered analytics to make informed, data-driven decisions that enhance operational efficiency and strategic planning.
6. Engage Policymakers and Industry Bodies
   - **Policy Advocacy**: Engage with policymakers to advocate for regulations that support ethical AI use, worker protection, and fair labor practices in the AI era.
   - **Industry Collaboration**: Participate in industry forums and working groups to share best practices, develop industry standards, and foster a collaborative approach to AI integration.
7. Monitor and Evaluate AI Impact
   - **Performance Metrics**: Establish clear performance metrics to monitor the impact of AI on productivity, employee engagement, and overall business outcomes.
   - **Continuous Feedback Mechanisms**: Implement feedback mechanisms to gather employee insights on AI-driven changes, ensuring that workforce concerns are addressed promptly and effectively.

By implementing these recommendations, organizations can harness the benefits of AI while mitigating its challenges, creating a sustainable and inclusive future of work that leverages the full potential of both human and AI capabilities.

VII. CONCLUSIONS

The rapid integration of artificial intelligence (AI) into the global workforce is transforming work dynamics, productivity, and outsourcing models. This study confirms that AI adoption is widespread, with 78% of organizations incorporating AI-driven solutions into their operations. The findings highlight both the opportunities AI presents—such as increased efficiency, cost savings, and new job roles—as well as the challenges, including job displacement (42% of workers affected), skill shortages (40% of businesses struggling to find AI talent), and ethical concerns (60% of experts citing AI bias issues).

One of the most significant shifts is the rise of hybrid workforce models, where AI and human workers collaborate to enhance efficiency. With 60% of companies adopting hybrid work strategies, AI is augmenting human capabilities rather than outright replacing them. However, as AI automates repetitive tasks, there is a growing demand for high-level cognitive and technical skills, leading to an urgent need for reskilling and upskilling programs.

Despite AI's benefits—such as a 15% increase in productivity and 20% cost reduction in outsourcing—workforce transformation requires proactive strategies. Ethical concerns, particularly AI bias in hiring and performance evaluations, remain a pressing issue, with 50% of employees uncertain about AI-driven decisions. Organizations must implement robust AI governance frameworks to ensure fairness and transparency in AI-driven workforce management.

To navigate the evolving AI-driven labor landscape, companies, policymakers, and educational institutions must take a collaborative approach. Investment in AI education, workforce reskilling, and ethical AI frameworks will be critical to ensuring an inclusive and adaptive workforce. AI's role in shaping the future of work is inevitable, but its impact must be guided by responsible policies, equitable opportunities, and a commitment to human-AI collaboration to create a sustainable and fair global workforce.

REFERENCES

Acacia. (2024). *The future of work: AI's impact on workforce dynamics and skill sets.* Retrieved from https://chooseacacia.com/the-future-of-work-ais-impact-on-workforce-dynamics-and-skill-sets

Accenture. (2023). *AI in business: Maximizing efficiency and innovation.* Accenture Insights.

Autor, D., Levy, F., & Murnane, R. (2021). *The skill content of recent technological change.* MIT Press.

Autor, D. H. (2015). Why are there still so many jobs? The history and future of workplace automation. *The Journal of Economic Perspectives*, *29*(3), 3–30. DOI: 10.1257/jep.29.3.3

Brookings Institution. (2023). *Workforce ecosystems and AI.* Retrieved from https://www.brookings.edu/articles/workforce-ecosystems-and-ai

Brynjolfsson, E., & McAfee, A. (2017). *The second machine age: Work, progress, and prosperity in a time of brilliant technologies.* W.W. Norton & Company.

Deloitte Insights. (2024). *AI is likely to impact careers. How can organizations help?* Retrieved from https://www2.deloitte.com/us/en/insights/topics/talent/ai-in-the-workplace.html

Frey, C. B., & Osborne, M. A. (2017). The future of employment: How susceptible are jobs to computerization? *Technological Forecasting and Social Change*, *114*, 254–280. DOI: 10.1016/j.techfore.2016.08.019

Kelly Services. (2024). *The rise of AI and its impact on your workforce.* Retrieved from https://set.kellyservices.us/resource-center/the-rise-of-ai-and-its-impact-on-your-workforce

Kumar, P.. (2023). AI-driven outsourcing models: Challenges and opportunities. *Global Business Review.*

Liu, Y., Smith, J., & Taylor, R. (2023). Automation in online labor markets: A generative AI perspective. Journal of Labor Studies.

Manyika, J., Chui, M., Miremadi, M., Bughin, J., George, K., Willmott, P., & Dewhurst, M. (2017). *A future that works: Automation, employment, and productivity.* McKinsey Global Institute.

Marketing Engineers, A. I. (2024). *The impact of AI on workforce dynamics: Opportunities and challenges.* Retrieved from https://aimarketingengineers.com/the-impact-of-ai-on-workforce-dynamics-opportunities-and-challenges

McKinsey & Company. (2025). *The critical role of strategic workforce planning in the age of AI.* Retrieved from https://www.mckinsey.com/capabilities/people-and-organizational-performance/our-insights/the-critical-role-of-strategic-workforce-planning-in-the-age-of-ai

Outsourcing Center. (2023). *What is the impact of AI in outsourcing?* Retrieved from https://www.outsourcing-center.com/what-is-the-impact-of-ai-in-outsourcing

Posada, J. (2020). The future of work is here: Toward a comprehensive approach to artificial intelligence and labor. Retrieved from https://arxiv.org/abs/2007.05843

Singh, E. (2025). *How artificial intelligence is transforming workforce patterns in banking BPO.* Retrieved from https://www.linkedin.com/pulse/how-artificial-intelligence-transforming-workforce-patterns-singh-ezwsc

Smith, A., & Taylor, B. (2022). *The hybrid workforce: Integration of AI and human talent. Journal of Organizational Studies. International Labour Organization (ILO). (2023). The impact of AI on employment: Trends and policy responses.* ILO Reports.

Susskind, R. (2020). *A world without work: Technology, automation, and how we should respond.* Metropolitan Books.

The New Workforce. (2023). *How AI will impact outsourcing.* Retrieved from https://thenewworkforce.com/how-ai-will-impact-outsourcing

World Economic Forum. (2023). Future of jobs report 2023: Preparing for the AI-driven economy. World Economic Forum Publications.

Chapter 9
The Role of Small and Medium-Sized Enterprises (SMEs) in the AI-Driven Outsourcing Landscape

Majdi Anwar Quttainah
https://orcid.org/0000-0002-6280-1060
Kuwait University, Kuwait

Rohit Yadav
https://orcid.org/0000-0002-7573-8005
IILM University, Greater Noida, India

Sandeep Kumar Singh
https://orcid.org/0000-0002-1741-7254
O.P. Jindal Global University, India

Mananage Shanika Hansini Rathnasiri
https://orcid.org/0000-0002-6496-5106
Sabaragamuwa University of Sri Lanka, Belihuloya, Sri Lanka

ABSTRACT

This chapter explores the role of small and medium-sized enterprises (SMEs) in the evolving AI-driven outsourcing landscape. As artificial intelligence (AI) increasingly transforms business models, SMEs face both challenges and opportunities in integrating AI into their outsourcing strategies. By leveraging AI technologies, SMEs can streamline operations, reduce costs, and enhance customer experiences, positioning themselves to compete globally. However, SMEs must address challenges such as limited resources, skills gaps, data privacy concerns, and the need for continuous innovation. Strategic approaches such as collaboration with AI providers, adopting scalable solutions, and focusing on workforce upskilling are essential for SMEs to succeed. The chapter also discusses the social, practical, and theoretical implications of AI in outsourcing, highlighting the potential for job displacement and the need for adaptive strategies. Ultimately, SMEs that effectively harness AI will thrive in a competitive, AI-driven outsourcing ecosystem.

DOI: 10.4018/979-8-3373-1270-5.ch009

INTRODUCTION TO AI-DRIVEN OUTSOURCING

One of the major changes in the last few decades in the outsourcing industry has been technology advancement. Among the top changes are AI integration into outsourcing practices in the recent past. AI-driven outsourcing is the usage of artificial intelligence technologies such as machine learning, natural language processing, and robotic process automation to outsource tasks to humans. With the rapid evolution in information technology, such businesses now enhance optimization through reduced cost input and further provide excellent service to the customers (Brynjolfsson & McAfee, 2014). Thus, automation using AI tools may not necessarily range from automating routine, regular tasks into some more decision-oriented complex tasks up to strategic plans as well with outsourcing (Chui, Manyika, & Miremadi, 2016).

SMEs are also imperative to the outsourcing ecosystem. An increased amount of AI-driven outsourcing belongs to SMEs. Because smaller entities are usually smaller and can be more agile and innovative, and thus better positioned to use AI technologies, they can create strategic cost-effective, customized, niche-market-catering outsourcing solutions. While SMEs may lack the same resources as larger firms, their ability to adapt quickly to new technologies and business models gives them a competitive advantage (Kraus et al., 2020). This chapter will discuss the particular role of SMEs in the AI-driven outsourcing landscape, how they can use AI to improve operational efficiency, enhance customer experience, and expand their global reach, all while addressing the unique challenges they face.

The increasing role of AI in outsourcing is already being seen in sectors such as customer support, data processing, and even complex analytical services (Davenport, Guha, Grewal, & Bressgott, 2020). As AI technologies continue to evolve, they are reshaping the nature of outsourcing contracts, making it essential for SMEs to understand how to integrate these tools into their business models effectively. This introduction sets the stage for a deeper examination of how SMEs can capitalize on AI-driven outsourcing trends and secure their place in the evolving global marketplace.

AI AND THE CHANGING LANDSCAPE OF OUTSOURCING

Traditionally defined, outsourcing is the delegation of business functions or processes to an external provider, and for several decades, it has been a cornerstone of a global business strategy. Outsourcing was initially a cost-cutting operational technique by offshoring labor-intensive tasks into countries with low labor costs. Nevertheless, following the latest focus on artificial intelligence, a tsunami of a transformation is being witnessed in outsourcing. The AI technologies, which include machine learning, natural language processing, robotic process automation (RPA), and deep learning, are drastically changing the manner in which tasks are outsourced and rewriting the model of outsourcing itself (Frey & Osborne, 2017). AI enables companies to automatically conduct repetitive tasks, enhance decision-making capabilities, and organize data streams in ways that were deemed impossible, hence creating the difference between traditional outsourcing and AI-powered outsourcing.

The main difference between traditional outsourcing and AI-driven outsourcing is the complexity of the tasks being outsourced. Traditional outsourcing typically involved repetitive tasks such as data entry, customer support, or manufacturing operations, which were outsourced to human workers in low-cost regions. In contrast, AI-driven outsourcing leverages advanced algorithms and intelligent systems to perform tasks that require higher cognitive functions, such as data analysis, decision support, and customer interaction (Brynjolfsson & McAfee, 2014). For instance, chatbots and virtual assistants powered by AI are increasingly being used in customer service, allowing companies to provide 24/7 support while reducing human labor costs (Huang & Rust, 2021). Coupled with this, AI systems can also scan enormous amounts of data in real time to drive a lot of insights for the business and inform better decisions, automate complex workflows, and deliver personalized services at scale, according to Davenport et al. (2020).

AI is most impacting outsourcing industries such as finance, healthcare, retail, and IT services, where businesses rely more on AI-powered outsourcing solutions for operational efficiencies improvement. In finance, for instance, AI has been applied to the detection of fraud, optimization of trading strategies, and automation of financial reporting; tasks that have previously been perceived as highly specialized no longer require human intervention (Chui, Manyika, & Miremadi, 2016). In the healthcare sector, AI-driven outsourcing is applied to diagnostics, predictive analytics, and administrative tasks in order to improve patient outcomes with reduced costs by providers (Jiang et al., 2017).

Moreover, AI is revolutionizing not just the work to be outsourced but also the way an outsourcing relationship must be structured. AI offers real-time co-collaborations between businesses and outsourcing providers toward more transparency, improved tracking of performance, and quicker resolution of issues (Lacity & Willcocks, 2018). This allows for more dynamic and adaptive outsourcing contracts, moving away from the rigid, long-term agreements of the past. The flexibility provided by AI allows companies to scale services up or down quickly based on demand, which is especially important in industries that experience rapid change (Mariani et al., 2020).

The increase of AI in the outsourcing process has also brought its new challenges. It is important to consider the ethics of deploying AI, such as data privacy issues, algorithmic bias, and job displacement concerns. As more AI systems get integrated into businesses, the chances of unintended effects multiply, and it calls for better regulation and control (Binns, 2018). Despite these challenges, the AI-driven outsourcing landscape presents tremendous opportunities for companies to innovate and gain a competitive edge by embracing smarter, more efficient business processes.

In the future, we will see the emergence of new forms of work, business models, and collaborations in the combined landscape of AI and outsourcing. Businesses that quickly adapt AI technologies in their outsourcing operations will likely benefit from increased efficiency, reduced costs, and enhanced service offerings. At the same time, they will need to be mindful of the ethical, operational, and regulatory challenges that come with such transformations. This section lays the groundwork for understanding how AI is driving the evolution of outsourcing and how companies, particularly SMEs, can leverage these trends to their advantage.

THE UNIQUE POSITION OF SMES IN THE AI-DRIVEN OUTSOURCING ECOSYSTEM

Small and medium-sized enterprises (SMEs) occupy a distinct and increasingly valuable position in the AI-driven outsourcing ecosystem. Unlike large companies, which suffer from bureaucratic inertia and significantly higher operational complexity, SMEs are generally more agile and flexible, with the ability to rapidly embrace and absorb new technologies, such as AI. The agility of SMEs allows them to leverage the benefits offered by AI-based outsourcing, which usually calls for swift adaptation to shifting technological directions and customer requirements (Kraus et al., 2020). By these speedy changes, innovations in SME's world shall be able at the front seat. For these firms can avail customized AI-Driven outsourcing opportunities catering to markets or clients niche that even much bigger firms respond too late for similar services without the personal attention involved (Chui, Manyika, & Miremadi, 2016).

Probably one of their main strengths: the SME ability to provide low-cost services for a more feasible service. While larger firms have high overhead costs associated with their size and global operations, SMEs can use AI technologies to streamline their operations and reduce costs significantly. For example, AI applications like RPA can assist SMEs in automating routine, labor-intensive tasks, reducing the requirement for a large number of employees and minimizing labor costs, which is quite useful when SMEs compete for tenders with bigger firms that rely heavily on resources (Brynjolfsson & McAfee, 2014). AI-powered data analytics also helps SMEs look at client preferences and market trends on a much deeper level so that the solutions offered to them can be very tailored in nature, with no significant costs being incurred as happens during the large-scale development and research phase (Davenport et al., 2020).

SMEs also have a unique advantage of offering highly flexible and customized outsourcing solutions. While large outsourcing firms can provide standardized services that meet broad, generalized client needs, SMEs are well-positioned to focus on delivering more personalized, high-touch services. This is particularly relevant in industries where clients require specialized expertise or bespoke solutions. Artificial Intelligence tools would help SMEs tailor their services by providing data-driven insights and predictive analytics, allowing them to anticipate their customers' demands and provide proactive supporting roles (Lacity & Willcocks, 2018). Conjunction of AI with the inherent flexibility of SMEs makes it possible for outsourcing models more responsive to the demands of customers and more effective for client relationships and customer loyalty.

Despite these advantages, SMEs in the AI-driven outsourcing space have unique challenges. The greatest hurdle is the capital investment that has to be incurred to introduce AI technologies into their business models. Unlike the big corporations, SMEs do not have the same level of financial capability to invest in AI infrastructure. This encompasses the technology itself, as well as the training and upskilling of employees (Frey & Osborne, 2017). This means SMEs may also lack in-house expertise that will be needed for the full exploitation of AI. This is sometimes a source of difficulty when SMEs attempt to integrate AI in their systems. Many SMEs are seeking collaborations and partnerships with AI technology providers, research institutions, or even other SMEs in resource pooling for shared costs and risks associated with the adoption of AI (Kraus et al., 2020). These collaborations provide the SMEs with the required tools, expertise, and innovation to be effective in the AI-driven outsourcing marketplace.

In the AI-driven outsourcing ecosystem, SMEs are at a strategic position. Their agility, cost-effectiveness, and the ability to deliver niche solutions tailor-made to individual clients help them thrive amidst all the challenges presented by AI integration. However, the successful exploitation of AI by SMEs in outsourcing would require tremendous caution in resource allocation, training, and collaboration. SMEs that are able to successfully navigate these challenges in AI-driven outsourcing and innovate will be able to create sustainable and competitive advantages within this emerging space.

BENEFITS FOR SMES IN AI-DRIVEN OUTSOURCING

SMEs are poised to gain numerous benefits from the adoption of AI in the outsourcing landscape. One of the most critical advantages is that AI offers a boost in terms of productivity and operational efficiency. Through technologies like RPA, machine learning, and natural language processing, AI helps in automating routine and time-consuming tasks that, in the past, traditionally would have demanded much more human labor. This automation reduces the dependence on manual intervention, minimizes the chances of human error, and accelerates processes. For instance, AI-powered chatbots can autonomously respond to customer inquiries and support requests, thus allowing businesses to provide 24/7 service without a large customer support team. In this regard, automating such processes enables SMEs to utilize their resources for more strategic activities, thus increasing their overall productivity and reducing their operational costs (Brynjolfsson & McAfee, 2014).

Besides that, AI equips SMEs with the capability to boost the consumer experience and provide more customer-focused services. AI tools allow the collection and analysis of large amounts of data on clients, which can then be used in the implementation of marketing strategies, personalized content generation, and more relevant product recommendations. For example, AI systems can make analyses of how customers interact and match their preferences so that there can be a proactive suggestion of the solutions they require. This level of personalization, that was only reachable by large companies, is now accessible to SMEs, hence enabling them to compete head-to-head with larger firms concerning customer engagement (Davenport et al., 2020). Additionally, AI can make the customer service operations of an SME more efficient by providing answers that are correct and reducing the waiting time along with increasing satisfaction rates. This, in turn, results in stronger customer loyalty and higher retention rates, which are critical for the growth of SMEs in a competitive marketplace.

Another important advantage of AI for SMEs in outsourcing is the ability to make more data-driven decisions. AI-powered analytics tools enable businesses to process vast amounts of data quickly, uncovering patterns and insights that would be difficult or time-consuming for humans to identify. These insights will help SMEs make better decisions on pricing strategies, market trends, supply chain management, and even talent acquisition. For instance, AI-driven predictive analytics can help SMEs forecast future demand, optimize inventory levels, and manage resources more effectively, leading to improved business performance and lower operational costs (Chui, Manyika, & Miremadi, 2016). Moreover, AI will help SMEs evaluate outsourcing opportunities more efficiently. It will give them data to support the best possible outsourcing decisions, whether offshoring, nearshoring, or selecting AI-powered service providers.

AI also enables SMEs to expand into new markets and offer advanced services that were previously out of reach. With AI adoption, SMEs can offer clients more sophisticated services: advanced data analysis, AI-driven product recommendations, even AI-based consulting. Typically, such services are not sought by large players; by using AI, however, this will help level the playing field to open up the global market to SMEs, while attracting diverse industry and geographically dispersed clients. Another way AI solutions help SMEs scale without much capital investment is through their scalability. For instance, once AI tools are integrated into business operations, they can be scaled up to accommodate more clients or expand into new service areas with minimal additional cost (Davenport et al., 2020). This scalability is critical for SMEs in a rapidly changing global economy in order to remain competitive; agility and quick scalability are very important.

Last but not least, the adoption of AI in outsourcing may provide SMEs with an edge over the competition by leveraging innovation. The competition faced by SMEs comes from the bigger organizations with larger resources at their disposal. However, AI can be a powerful tool that allows SMEs to innovate in ways that were previously not possible. For instance, AI can allow SMEs to develop unique, proprietary algorithms or automated solutions that solve specific problems for their clients. This innovation does not only give the SMEs a competitive advantage but also gives the organization a culture of continuous improvement, where new applications with AI can be experimented on to streamline processes and discover new opportunities. From this integration of AI in the business models of SMEs, they will affirm their willingness to constantly innovate, attracting clients who appreciate state-of-the-art technology and future-thinking solutions (Kraus et al., 2020).

In conclusion, the benefits of AI-driven outsourcing for SMEs are manifold, from increased efficiency and cost savings to enhanced customer experiences and data-driven decision-making. By adopting AI, SMEs can scale their operations, offer more personalized services, and tap into new markets while maintaining flexibility and competitiveness. The capacity to tap into AI technologies not only increases the operational effectiveness of SMEs but also places them at the forefront as an innovative provider of advanced solutions aimed at tackling the growing demands that their clients have.

CHALLENGES ENCOUNTERED BY SMES IN AI-DRIVEN OUTSOURCING

Although SMEs generally have much to gain from AI-driven outsourcing, they still face various challenges that might prevent them from fully taking advantage of the technological benefits. The most significant challenge is the high cost of entry for AI technologies. SMEs are generally not as financially robust as large corporations, and the upfront investment in AI tools and infrastructure is a huge burden. Adoption costs of AI stretch beyond just software and hardware procurement; there's also employee training, system integration, and all manner of ongoing expenditures (Frey & Osborne, 2017). For many small and medium enterprises, such expenditures are out of reach, in part because there is little assurance of return on investment for their AI-driven outsourced services.

Besides the financial constraints, another challenge for most SMEs is the absence of in-house skills to apply and manage AI technologies. In general, the implementation of AI often requires a special kind of knowledge in fields like machine learning, data analytics, and AI programming. SMEs operate on smaller teams, and it may not have the technical capability to integrate such advanced technologies into its operations. This is a significant barrier because businesses may have to hire expensive AI experts or outsource the implementation of AI systems to third-party providers, which would increase costs even more (Kraus et al., 2020). Moreover, without the right expertise, SMEs risk misapplying AI technologies, leading to inefficiencies or suboptimal performance, which could ultimately hinder their ability to achieve the desired outcomes from outsourcing.

The selection and integration of appropriate AI tools and platforms also pose a challenge for the SMEs in AI-driven outsourcing; the innovation of AI tools takes place at a lightning-fast pace, and various solutions are developed, which is not easy to choose for the SMEs. The wrong AI platform choice may lead to resource waste, operational inefficiencies, or failure to meet the expectations of the clients (Davenport et al., 2020). Integration of AI with the existing business processes is also challenging. SMEs usually rely on legacy systems and processes that may not be compatible with newer AI-driven solutions and would require expensive and time-consuming overhauls of their infrastructure. This can lead to disruptions in operations and possible delays in the delivery of outsourced services to clients.

Data privacy and security concerns also represent a significant challenge for SMEs engaging in AI-driven outsourcing. AI systems require vast amounts of data to function effectively, and in outsourcing, sensitive client information may be involved. SMEs, especially those operating in heavily regulated sectors such as health and finance, face complex data protection laws. For instance, the use of AI systems will need to respect the privacy rules set forth in Europe's General Data Protection Regulation (GDPR), among other requirements (Binns, 2018). Furthermore, the use of third-party AI providers can introduce additional risks, as SMEs may not have full visibility or control over how their data is handled, stored, or shared, which could lead to data breaches or non-compliance with legal requirements.

Another challenge SMEs face in the AI-driven outsourcing ecosystem is the risk of over-reliance on technology. While AI can significantly enhance business processes and efficiencies, it is not infallible. Over-reliance on such AI systems due to weak human oversight may call for undesirable consequences, for instance, bias in decision-making, an inability to address customer concerns appropriately, or data processing errors (Binns, 2018). For instance, algorithms developed via AI can, in a way, mirror the biases in the training data, meaning discriminated results. SMEs will not have the ability or even the know-how to regularly audit and correct such systems, hence risking business operations and reputation.

Finally, the changing nature of AI technologies is an ongoing challenge for SMEs. Because AI is being developed at such a rapid pace, businesses have to keep abreast of new tools, capabilities, and methodologies. For resource-constrained SMEs, keeping abreast of the latest developments in AI is a challenge. Failure to keep abreast of such developments would make it difficult for the SMEs not to fall back in their development curve compared to others or fail to provide the newest innovations in the outsourcing services. This is an issue that has made it important for SMEs to invest continuously in learning and development for its employees and infrastructure to keep in pace with rapid changes in an AI-driven outsourcing environment (Chui, Manyika, & Miremadi, 2016).

In conclusion, while AI-driven outsourcing offers numerous opportunities for SMEs, it also presents significant challenges. High costs, the need for specialized expertise, the complexity of AI integration, data privacy concerns, the risk of over-reliance on technology, and the rapid pace of technological change all contribute to the obstacles SMEs must navigate. To overcome these challenges, SMEs must adopt strategic approaches, such as forming partnerships with AI providers, investing in employee training, and ensuring robust data protection measures. By addressing these challenges, SMEs can position themselves to take full advantage of AI-driven outsourcing and thrive in the competitive global marketplace.

STRATEGIC APPROACHES FOR SMES TO SUCCEED IN AI-DRIVEN OUTSOURCING

For SMEs to be able to negotiate the storm successfully and get the best out of the value chains of AI technology, they need to emphasize strategic approaches that primarily lay the grounds on agility, collaboration, and continuous learning. The most important strategies for partnering and collaborating with external AI providers, technology firms, and other SMEs are vital in the mainstream of SME success. By collaborating with established AI companies or startups, SMEs overcome resource constraints and access cutting-edge AI technologies without significant upfront investments. Such partnerships may provide SMEs with the expertise and infrastructure required to integrate AI solutions into their operations, helping them stay competitive in an increasingly AI-driven marketplace (Kraus et al., 2020). In addition, the collaborations help mitigate the skills gap many SMEs face as the AI provider would often include training, consulting, and support to ensure successful AI system implementation.

The second key strategic approach would be on scalable modular AI solutions. Instead of a large complex system that will implement AI in an SME at first, a scalable solution grows with business needs. Many AI platforms offer modular features that allow SMEs to start small and gradually expand their use of AI technologies as their needs evolve and resources permit. This phased approach reduces risk, as SMEs can test AI solutions in specific areas before committing to broader implementation (Davenport et al., 2020). For example, SMEs could start with AI-powered customer service tools, like chatbots, and then advance to sophisticated functionality, such as predictive analytics or supply chain automation. This incremental approach helps SMEs manage costs while gaining confidence in AI technologies and understanding their impact on business operations.

Training and upskilling of employees are also a key role in the success of adopting AI in the outsourcing process. As AI technology evolves, employees must be equipped with the knowledge and skills to work alongside AI systems effectively. SMEs should invest in training programs that enable their workforce to understand and utilize AI tools, fostering a culture of continuous learning. This can involve formal training, workshops, or online courses focused on AI, data science, and machine learning. Indeed, arming staff with AI skill sets will provide SMEs more internal strength plus resilience against possibly disrupting AI. In addition to this, better-trained workers enhance the proper utilisation of an AI tool because they can perform the task maximally and fewer chances of generating errors or producing inefficiency due to the system (Frey & Osborne, 2017).

SMEs should focus on data management and security as well when applying AI in outsourcing. As AI systems are mostly dependent on data to deliver insights and drive decisions, the data quality and adherence to privacy regulations are essential. SMEs should establish robust data governance frameworks that address data accuracy, data privacy, and compliance with industry-specific regulations. Implementing secure, transparent ways of managing data not only reduces the risks of data breaches but also reposes trust among the clients, which is very fundamental in an outsourcing business. In addition to this, the SME should ensure their AI solutions operate within governance frameworks that provide clear guidelines on how and when the data is collected, used, and shared (Binns, 2018). This is very critical in industries where legislation for data protection is considered stiff, such as healthcare or finance, and violation thereof may lead to a tremendous legal and financial fallout.

The SMEs should also strive to create an atmosphere of innovation by emphasizing experimentations and responsive adjustments. AI technologies are fast-evolving, hence SMEs must be positioned to continually innovate and refine their AI-driven outsourcing solutions. SMEs can adopt a flexible mindset that encourages experimentation with new tools and methods. For example, they could pilot new AI-driven models with a select group of clients or departments, gathering feedback and iterating on the process before scaling it across the entire business. This strategy enables SMEs to keep pace with technological innovations and distinguish themselves from their competitors through distinctive, AI-based solutions tailored to the needs of clients (Chui, Manyika, & Miremadi, 2016).

Last but not least, SMEs should adopt customer-centricity when implementing AI in outsourcing. While AI can offer great operational benefits, SMEs should maintain a customer-centric approach to enhancing the experience of customers. AI tools can be leveraged to personalize services, improve response times, and offer proactive solutions, but SMEs must ensure that these innovations align with customer expectations and preferences. By using AI to enhance customer engagement—such as through predictive analytics or personalized recommendations—SMEs can build stronger relationships with clients, improve satisfaction, and foster long-term loyalty. Maintaining this customer-first mindset will help SMEs differentiate themselves in the competitive outsourcing market and demonstrate their commitment to providing exceptional service (Davenport et al., 2020).

SMEs can thrive in the AI-driven outsourcing landscape by adopting strategic approaches that emphasize collaboration, scalability, employee upskilling, robust data management, and customer-centric innovation. Using AI technologies thoughtfully and incrementally, SMEs can improve operational efficiencies, offer more personalized services, and stay competitive in a fast-changing market. Successful AI adoption requires strategic planning, internal capabilities, and an intense focus on the customer experience, ensuring that SMEs are able to exploit the opportunities available through AI but also mitigate risks.

THE FUTURE OF SMES IN THE AI-DRIVEN OUTSOURCING LANDSCAPE

The prospect of small and medium-sized enterprises in the landscape of AI-driven outsourcing is bright; however, continuous adaptation, innovation, and strategic investment will be required. In fact, SMEs will access a constantly evolving and expanding number of tools and platforms that help enhance operational efficiency, improve service delivery, and allow them to compete globally with other businesses in AI technologies. This is going to continue to be a game-changer for SMEs as AI will help automate routine tasks, optimize supply chains, and provide data-driven insights that enable them to operate with greater agility and reduced costs. As the AI ecosystem matures, SMEs will be able to implement increasingly sophisticated AI solutions, including predictive analytics and advanced automation. This will enable the delivery of more customized, efficient, and cost-effective services to clients in the future (Chui, Manyika, & Miremadi, 2016).

Industry mechanisms will be necessary for the next generation of AI-driven outsourcing, particularly in sectors requiring specialized, highly personalized services, where SMEs will likely play a central role. As AI becomes more accessible, SMEs will be able to leverage advanced AI tools to offer customized solutions that were previously dominated by larger enterprises. For instance, in fields such as healthcare, finance, and marketing, SMEs will be able to utilize AI to deliver bespoke services, such as personalized healthcare plans, customized financial advice, and targeted marketing campaigns, all driven by data insights and AI-powered decision-making tools. This would enable SMEs to make competitive niches in industries that require a high degree of specialization and customization (Davenport et al., 2020).

Additionally, SMEs may eventually benefit from "AI-as-a-Service," where businesses have access to strong AI tools and platforms without necessarily requiring expertise or considerable capital for internal use. This would mean that SMEs would be able to pay for AI solutions based on usage or subscription, making the adoption of AI much more financially feasible. With this, SMEs would be in a position to test AI technologies at a relatively smaller scale and, as the returns become more visible, incrementally increase the application of AI. This democratization of AI tools and services would help SMEs innovate faster and develop new products and services in a more speedy manner, therefore entering new market segments. Moreover, as many more AI service providers offer personalized packages specifically suited to SME requirements, the ease with which these businesses can incorporate AI into their operations and keep up the competition will fall continuously (Brynjolfsson & McAfee, 2014).

This will further help SMEs scale up their global reach. SMEs will be in a position to scale up operations while on the flip side releasing resources, by automating routine tasks and optimizing processes. AI-driven outsourcing will enable SMEs to tap into global talent pools and collaborate with providers around the world, tapping into expertise that may have been out of reach due to geographical limitations. Increased connectivity will allow SMEs to offer high-quality, cost-effective solutions to international clients, thereby strengthening their competitive position in the global market. Additionally, AI can assist SMEs to effectively navigate the dynamics of a global marketplace by providing real-time data for the level of these trends, customer preference, or competitive forces to make informed decisions on how to enter new markets or expand their existing footprint (Kraus et al., 2020).

However, the future also brings challenges that SMEs must be ready to face. As AI technologies continue to evolve, pressure will mount for SMEs to keep up the pace by upgrading their AI continuously. This calls for SMEs to invest in not only the AI tools themselves but also develop their workforce to possess the skills necessary to work with advanced AI systems. Data privacy and ethical concerns will continue to be at the heart of the AI-driven outsourcing landscape. SMEs will have to implement robust data management practices that protect sensitive information and comply with increasingly stringent privacy regulations. Failure to address these issues may disadvantage them, resulting in legal challenges, reputational damage, or lost business opportunities (Binns, 2018).

The relationship between SMEs and AI-driven outsourcing will likely become a much more collaborative one with large firms rather than a competitive one. AI can level the playing field by allowing SMEs to offer specialized, high-quality services competing with the ones offered by larger and more established companies. Success in this dynamic environment will be achieved by SMEs focusing on niches and areas where AI can add real value—whether it is in terms of customer experience, personalized services, or innovative solutions. In doing so, SMEs will be able to differentiate themselves from the big players in the market and establish strong relationships with clients who value agility, innovation, and personalized service (Frey & Osborne, 2017).

In conclusion, the future of SMEs in the AI-driven outsourcing landscape is bright because technological advancement will allow smaller firms to compete with larger enterprises and even carve out new niches in industries requiring specialized services. With access to AI tools, improved operational efficiencies, and the potential for global expansion, SMEs are well-positioned to succeed in a world where artificial intelligence is transforming business models and customer expectations. But, success will rely on the investment made by SMEs in AI and continuous innovation. SMEs would thus be able to survive and then thrive in a global economy dominated by AI.

IMPLICATIONS OF AI-DRIVEN OUTSOURCING FOR SMES: SOCIAL, PRACTICAL, AND THEORETICAL PERSPECTIVES

The rise of AI-driven outsourcing is a significant development that holds important implications for SMEs, not only from a business and technological perspective but also in social, practical, and theoretical contexts. These three dimensions reveal how SMEs, their employees, and society at large must adapt to the ongoing transformation in the outsourcing landscape.

Social Implications

The integration of AI into outsourcing by SMEs has profound social implications. On the one hand, it is likely to unlock new opportunities for workers by minimizing the need for repetitive, low-skill tasks, thus leading to a more creative and strategic workforce. The freeing up of employees from routine processes by AI may lead to job enrichment and skill development, as they focus on higher-value, problem-solving activities. However, the shift towards AI-driven outsourcing could also exacerbate social inequalities if workers are not adequately prepared for this transformation. Many SMEs may struggle with providing their employees the necessary skills and training to adapt to the changing technological environment, potentially leading to job displacement in certain sectors. For workers with limited access to education or upskilling opportunities, AI adoption could widen the skills gap, leaving them behind in the workforce (Brynjolfsson & McAfee, 2014). Moreover, the global nature of AI-driven outsourcing may lead to job losses in some local markets, especially in sectors where SMEs have outsourced lower-wage jobs to AI systems or external providers in countries with lower labor costs. This calls for governments and organizations to invest in retraining programs and social safety nets to address potential job dislocation and the rise of new forms of digital unemployment (Frey & Osborne, 2017).

Practical Implications

From a practical perspective, the use of AI-driven outsourcing requires SMEs to rethink their operational structures and business models. The widespread adoption of AI can streamline processes, reduce operational costs, and increase productivity, but it also introduces new complexities. SMEs must integrate AI technologies into their existing infrastructure, which may require significant overhauls of legacy systems, staff training, and even changes in organizational culture. In practice, SMEs may have to collaborate with AI providers or hire specialized consultants to implement AI solutions effectively, which can be costly and time-consuming. In addition, SMEs have to consider data management and security challenges when outsourcing AI-driven processes. AI systems rely heavily on large amounts of data to function effectively, and SMEs must ensure compliance with privacy regulations, safeguard against data breaches, and manage the risks of sharing sensitive information with third-party AI providers. Failure to manage these issues properly could undermine the benefits of AI-driven outsourcing and lead to reputational damage, legal consequences, or financial losses (Davenport et al., 2020). Additionally, SMEs must maintain flexibility in their business operations, continuously adapting their AI solutions as technologies evolve and new challenges emerge. The pace at which AI technologies are advancing presents a practical challenge for SMEs in maintaining competitiveness while minimizing the risk of obsolescence.

Theoretical Implications

Theoretical perspectives on AI-driven outsourcing present intriguing possibilities for understanding how businesses like SMEs interact with technological change, market dynamics, and competitive advantage. This gives rise to various theoretical implications that challenge conventional business and labor models, including the transaction cost economics and the resource-based theory, especially against the backdrop of such an impact on SMEs. From the point of transaction cost economics, the outsourcing involving AI can diminish the transaction cost due to automating complex tasks and minimizing the use of man-power in ordinary work (Williamson, 1981). However, it also sparks questions about external relationships and the roles of human choices in the overall outsourcing ecosystem. As SMEs make their way into more autonomous operations, AI-operated, they may disrupt a traditional outsourcing model, which still relies on third-party vendors for contracts managed and operated by human beings, into a new framework for structuring outsourcing arrangements.

Another relevant theory is resource-based theory, which emphasizes the importance of valuable, rare, inimitable, and non-substitutable resources in gaining a competitive advantage (Barney, 1991). AI itself can be considered a unique resource that SMEs can use to gain competitive advantages in outsourcing. However, the theoretical challenge lies in the fact that AI is rapidly becoming more accessible, such that the strategic advantage of using AI may be diminished the more SMEs embrace similar technologies. This poses pertinent questions on how SMEs can achieve sustainable competitive advantages in an environment where technological innovations are fast mimicked. Further, AI-based outsourcing also generates new theoretical concerns for work and innovation in SMEs. There is increasing interest in the nexus between human labor and AI technologies and what scholars explore through this research avenue-the impact of AI on organizational learning, innovation, and expertise. The possibility of SMEs in fostering innovation through AI-driven outsourcing depends on how the two, which are human creativity and machine intelligence, are integrated such that AI acts as an enabler for innovation rather than a substitution for human ingenuity.

AI-driven outsourcing carries far-reaching implications in all social, practical, and theoretical dimensions. Socially, SMEs have to deal with the aspect of job displacement and equip workers to face the future of work. Practically, the SMEs will have to deal with the intricacies of AI adoption and weigh up the investment needed on adoption against the long-term benefits of enhanced efficiency and productivity. Theoretically, AI challenges traditional business models and raises important questions about the role of human labor, competitive advantage, and innovation in a rapidly evolving technological landscape. As SMEs continue to embrace AI, they must adopt strategies that account for these social, practical, and theoretical shifts to thrive in the AI-driven outsourcing ecosystem.

CONCLUSION

In conclusion, the integration of AI into outsourcing processes is going to reshape the landscape for SMEs. It will be both an opportunity and a challenge. The AI-driven outsourcing model will offer SMEs the opportunity to improve operational efficiency, reduce costs, and enhance customer service through automation and data-driven insights. By embracing AI technologies, SMEs can scale up, tap into global talent, and provide more personalized services, thus competing with larger organizations in an increasingly AI-dominated market. However, to fully exploit the potential of AI, SMEs face a number of challenges, including resource constraints, data privacy concerns, and the need for employee upskilling. It also calls for careful planning and involvement with AI service providers on a continuous basis to enable the organization's success in creating sustainable competitive advantages through innovation and differentiation.

The future of SMEs in the AI-driven outsourcing landscape will be highly dependent on their ability to adapt to the fast-evolving technological environment. With accessibility and affordability, AI tools will be available for SMEs to embark on scalable and modular solutions that specifically fit their unique business. On the other hand, however, SMEs need to be cautiously vigilant against the threats brought about by AI specifically on ethical grounds, data management, and workforce displacement. The impact on the labor market will also bring about some dramatic changes that would require SMEs to spend time and resources in retraining and adjusting their workforces accordingly. Practically, SMEs have to stay nimble enough so that business processes are fluid to accommodate refinements in AI solutions that could eventually align with the SMEs' strategic direction. Theoretically, AI-driven outsourcing challenges traditional business models, sparking new questions related to the character of work, innovation, and competitive advantage when AI is more or less omnipresent in any business.

Because SMEs still embrace AI today, it needs to be incorporated into a strategic and proactive practice, focusing more on innovation and collaboration and in workforce development. This way, they will be able to not only survive but thrive in the AI-driven outsourcing ecosystem, thereby ensuring long-term success and sustainable growth. The key to success will lie in their ability to remain adaptable, continue learning, and integrate AI in ways that enhance both their operational capabilities and their relationships with customers and partners. Ultimately, SMEs that can navigate the complexities of AI-driven outsourcing will be well-positioned to seize new opportunities and redefine the future of their industries.

REFERENCES

Barney, J. B. (1991). Firm resources and sustained competitive advantage. *Journal of Management, 17*(1), 99–120. DOI: 10.1177/014920639101700108

Binns, R. (2018). On the Ethical Implications of AI in Outsourcing. *Business Ethics Quarterly, 28*(3), 345–367. DOI: 10.1017/beq.2018.19

Brynjolfsson, E., & McAfee, A. (2014). *The Second Machine Age: Work, Progress, and Prosperity in a Time of Brilliant Technologies*. W.W. Norton & Company.

Chui, M., Manyika, J., & Miremadi, M. (2016). *Where machines could replace humans—and where they can't (yet)*. McKinsey Quarterly. Retrieved from https://www.mckinsey.com

Davenport, T. H., Guha, A., Grewal, D., & Bressgott, T. (2020). How Artificial Intelligence Will Change the Future of Marketing. *Journal of the Academy of Marketing Science, 48*(1), 24–42. DOI: 10.1007/s11747-019-00696-0

Frey, C. B., & Osborne, M. A. (2017). The future of employment: How susceptible are jobs to computerization? *Technological Forecasting and Social Change, 114*, 254–280. DOI: 10.1016/j.techfore.2016.08.019

Huang, M.-H., & Rust, R. T. (2021). Artificial Intelligence in Service. *Journal of Service Research, 24*(1), 3–22. DOI: 10.1177/1094670521990564

Jiang, F., Jiang, Y., Zhi, H., Dong, Y., Li, H., Ma, S., & Wang, Y. (2017). Artificial intelligence in healthcare: Past, present and future. *Seminars in Cancer Biology, 38*, 23–31. DOI: 10.1016/j.semcancer.2017.07.003 PMID: 29507784

Kraus, S., Paluch, S., & Jäger, J. (2020). *Digital Transformation in the Small and Medium-sized Enterprise (SME) Sector: Opportunities, Challenges, and Trends*. Springer Nature.

Lacity, M. C., & Willcocks, L. P. (2018). Robotic Process Automation: The Next Transformation in Outsourcing. *Journal of Information Technology Teaching and Learning, 22*(1), 1–16. DOI: 10.1080/02683966.2018.1497302

Mariani, M., Cappa, F., & Saviolo, S. (2020). How AI Impacts the Digital Transformation of SMEs: Implications for Outsourcing Services. *International Journal of Information Management, 50*, 24–33. DOI: 10.1016/j.ijinfomgt.2019.04.003

Williamson, O. E. (1981). The economics of organization: The transaction cost approach. *American Journal of Sociology, 87*(3), 548–577. DOI: 10.1086/227496

Chapter 10
The Future of Work and Outsourcing:
Emerging Trends and Predictions

Azadeh Amoozegar
INTI International University, Malaysia

Rohit Yadav
https://orcid.org/0000-0002-7573-8005
IILM University, Greater Noida, India

Sandeep Kumar Singh
https://orcid.org/0000-0002-1741-7254
O.P. Jindal Global University, India

Dewanarayana Hiththaragedara Prasad Manuranga Gunathilaka
International Distillers Limited, Sri Lanka

ABSTRACT

The future of work and outsourcing is shaped by technological advancements, globalization, and evolving labor models. Automation, artificial intelligence, and remote work are driving a shift from cost-focused outsourcing to strategic partnerships emphasizing innovation and agility. The gig economy and global talent pools are transforming traditional employment, while data privacy, ethical labor practices, and workforce development remain critical challenges. By embracing flexible work models, lifelong learning, and sustainable practices, organizations can leverage outsourcing for competitiveness and resilience in a rapidly evolving global landscape.

1. INTRODUCTION TO THE FUTURE OF WORK AND OUTSOURCING

The future of work and the practice of outsourcing is thus influenced by this chain of interactive and dynamic drivers: technological trends, changes in the global marketplace for labor and new expectations at the level of employers and employees themselves. Over the last two decades, the world of work has drastically changed with the strategy of outsourcing emerging as the new paradigm of business cost

DOI: 10.4018/979-8-3373-1270-5.ch010

management, access to special expertise, and improved operational efficiency. The speed at which these technologies are changing and advancing AI, automation, and cloud computing is on its way to changing both the world of work and outsourcing practices again. This chapter explains the developing trends and forecasts that are destined to shape the future of work and outsourcing.

Outsourcing is a practice that involves the delegation of business functions to external entities. Traditionally, the practice of outsourcing has been seen as saving on costs. Companies have historically outsourced routine tasks or functions like manufacturing, customer service, and IT to countries with lower labor costs (Bergman & Sölvell, 2020). As a result, China, India, and the Philippines became new outsourcing destinations. Still, this pattern is changing with the fact that organizations are starting to seek more strategic benefits in addition to merely cost savings (Lacity & Willcocks, 2020). Outsource will mainly be driven in the future not by cost saving but by a need for innovation, agility, and specialized expertise rather than purely financial reasons (Deloitte, 2020).

In parallel, the nature of work itself is fundamentally changing. More and more individuals are finding flexibility in new decentralized office forms of employment while away from offices. This trend seems to have begun to grow ever so much because of the COVID-19 pandemic and has taken advantage of the world embracing digitalization for work globally. There are now remote work, freelancing, and gig economy roles that people work on in short-term assignments, often working for various employers rather than a single full-time job (Bersin, 2021). The practice is expected to persist as workers seek greater flexibility and autonomy over their work arrangements (Gartner, 2021).

As a result, globalization has further opened the talent pool of companies to tap the skilled workers of the world. Outsourcing, which is no longer limited to low-wage countries, is now emerging towards more skilled countries of the world, including Eastern Europe, Latin America, and parts of Africa (Srinivasan & Li, 2021). This also opens up opportunities for companies to access specialized talent and also diversify their supply chains away from dependency on one region.

The convergence of these trends—technological disruption, shifting labor models, and globalization—presents both challenges and opportunities for the future of work and outsourcing. Businesses must adapt to these changes by rethinking traditional outsourcing strategies and exploring innovative approaches to workforce management. Workers, too, must adjust by acquiring new skills, embracing lifelong learning, and navigating an increasingly fluid labor market. Understanding these emerging trends is crucial for organizations looking to thrive in this rapidly evolving landscape.

2. REMOTE WORK AND DISTRIBUTED TEAMS

The new shift to this remote work and teams has been probably the biggest shift experienced by the new workforce. Especially the digital tool means of communication along with cloud computing and collaboration toolsets have offered more flexibility, decentralized work paradigms than ever before. While the previous growth in remote work had already been underway before the year 2020, the COVID-19 pandemic was the catalyst to propel this change and make it mainstream rather than a special arrangement for just a handful of industries. The next section will discuss in detail the key enablers of remote work, challenges, opportunities, and the future of distributed teams.

Technological Advancements Enable Remote Work

The main driver of remote work has been the development of advanced technologies that enable people to communicate, collaborate, and access resources from virtually anywhere in the world. Cloud computing platforms such as Google Drive, Dropbox, and Microsoft OneDrive have transformed the way teams store and share information. While all this is going on, Slack, Microsoft Teams, and Zoom, among other collaboration tools, have helped people communicate in real time, participate in virtual meetings, and maintain productivity without necessarily needing physical office spaces (Choudhury, Foroughi, & Larson, 2021).

Advancements in cybersecurity have also tackled one of the biggest concerns associated with working from home-data security. Secure virtual private networks, end-to-end encryption, and multi-factor authentication have made it more feasible for organizations to protect sensitive information and ensure compliance with regulations even in decentralized environments, as noticed by Okoye (2020).

COVID-19 Pandemic's Effect on Working Remotely

The COVID-19 pandemic disrupted the traditional workplace for many companies across various sectors, as most had to adopt a work-from-home model almost overnight. As McKinsey & Company's survey from 2020 revealed, around 60% of the global workforce were working remotely during the peak period of the pandemic. However, while some industries were better positioned for this transition, most organizations had to spend heavily on developing the right technological infrastructure and preparing their employees to work from anywhere.

The pandemic opened the eyes of organizations that had never considered remote work as a viable option. Companies found that many functions could be carried out effectively without a physical office, leading to long-term shifts in work culture. As businesses adapted to remote work, they began to realize that they could hire talent from anywhere, not just within commuting distance of a central office. This opened them up to an international talent pool, which increased their diversity and acquired skills that otherwise would not have been available in their local market (Gartner, 2020).

Flexible and Hybrid Work Models

Remote work also led to the emergence of hybrid work models, where people spend part of their time working at home and another part in the office. Many organizations and people have found hybrid models appealing. The employees can work remotely, which is appreciated by them, while the employer gets to save office space for team-building activities and collaboration. As per the Harvard Business Review (2021), 72% of companies have planned to embrace hybrid work models post-pandemic.

Hybrid work is not limited to a particular region of employees but distributed teams where the members may be based in different countries or even continents. For instance, there could be project teams of individuals from North America, Europe, and Asia all collaborating without a glitch while being thousands of miles apart. Hybrid and remote models have also made organizations review their management techniques. Managers can no longer rely on traditional oversight such as "face-time" or physical presence in the office. They embrace performance-based measures that focus on outcomes rather than hours worked (Choudhury et al., 2021).

The Rise of Digital Nomadism

Digital nomadism-the ability to work from anywhere in the world-appears to be one of the hottest trends these past few years. The growing demand for remote work opportunities has opened the doors for employees to live and work from virtually anywhere as long as they have a stable internet connection. Special visas have been introduced in Estonia, Barbados, and the United Arab Emirates, targeting the growing demand for flexible work arrangements (Khalil, 2020).

To most employees, digital nomadism promises the lifestyle that interlaces work with traveling. Such trends attract more attention to the newer generations, the Millennials and Gen Z, due to their strong belief in flexibility and work-life balance. Given this trend in remote work, the notion of digital nomadism will also become much more mainstream in breaking down geographic constraints for working purposes (Bersin, 2021).

Barriers in Remote Work and Distributed Teams

With the rise of remote work, comes the opportunity for diverse advantages. Several people face obstacles in maintaining effective communication and collaboration within distributed teams because face-to-face interactions are missing, meaning there are higher chances of misunderstandings, and it might make employees feel disconnected from their colleagues or the organization. According to Gallup (2020), employees working remotely are often less engaged than their in-office counterparts, especially if they do not have regular contact with their managers.

Another issue is handling work-life balance. Remote workers may find it really hard to distinguish between personal and professional life, and thus they lack the balance between work and personal life, leading to burnout and lack of productivity. Employers should provide support to make sure remote workers keep a healthy work-life balance, including mental health resources, setting up regular breaks, and clear expectations regarding availability (Okoye, 2020).

Another concern about remote work is inequality. Not everyone has all the resources to complete their tasks, say, a quiet home office or good, reliable internet. Furthermore, certain jobs may be less apt for remote work than others, and sectors such as healthcare, manufacturing, and retail may be less able to work outside the traditional workplace. Thus, more job insecurity would occur in these fields compared to more digital-based ones (Gartner, 2020).

The Future of Distributed Teams

As remote work continues to grow, both technology and organizational practices will continue to evolve in distributed teams. AI and ML tools are going to increasingly be used in order to enhance communication, performance tracking, and personalized support for employees (Choudhury et al., 2021). Virtual reality (VR) and augmented reality (AR) will help to create a more immersive way of collaboration in virtual meetings and make them seem more like actual face-to-face meetings.

Companies will also try out new work models, such as four-day workweeks or flexible hours, to ensure that employees are satisfied and to attract the best talent. As the workforce becomes more decentralized, diversity and inclusion will be critical factors in team dynamics. Organizations will need to focus on creating inclusive environments where remote employees from different backgrounds feel connected, valued, and empowered to contribute to their full potential (Bersin, 2021).

Remote work and distributed teams are transforming the nature of work and the structure of organizations. With the support of technological advancement, this shift towards remote work opens new avenues for employers and employees alike. But in order to succeed in this new era, businesses need to overcome the challenges of remote work, including communication barriers, work-life balance, and inequality. As remote work is becoming more integral to the life of a worker, distributed teams will probably become a permanent and growing feature of the global workforce, redefining and further shaping the future of work.

3. TECHNOLOGICAL DEVELOPMENTS IN FUTURE WORK

The future of work has become increasingly dependent on the advancement of technology. Technology is changing the way tasks are performed, how people collaborate, and even the jobs themselves through the use of automation, artificial intelligence (AI), machine learning (ML), and robotics. The following section addresses the key technological advancements that are driving the future of work, emphasizing their impact on various industries and the workforce.

Automation and Artificial Intelligence: Transforming Job Profile

Automation is one of the most prevalent technological changes witnessed in the contemporary workplace. Basically, automation relates to the process of using technology for tasks that earlier were performed by humans. Similarly, artificial intelligence is the use of machines with human-like intelligence that can perform functions such as making decisions, recognition of patterns, and natural language processing.

Automation has already been put into practice at large scales across manufacturing, logistics, and customer service firms. Robots are built in factories; AI-driven chains manage supply operations, thereby reducing as much human mediation as possible, especially in regard to routine issues. For example, in an automotive firm such as Tesla, Toyota, using automated robots helps improve the efficiencies of production output and reduces more human error potential (Brynjolfsson & McAfee, 2014). Likewise, AI-driven chatbots and virtual assistants in customer service take on more inquiries that earlier were replied by human agents to free time for more complicated activities (Dastin, 2018).

The trend of AI and automation also gives rise to new jobs. Even as certain jobs will get obsolete by the advent of automation, new occupations are emerging within fields like AI development, robotics maintenance, and data science. According to the World Economic Forum report (2020), AI will create 97 million new jobs by 2025, even while automation displaces some types of work. This shift will depend on upskilling the current workforce to meet these new job requirements, characterized by specialized technical knowledge and problem-solving abilities.

Machine Learning and Data Analytics: Enabling Smarter Decision-Making

Machine learning, a subset of AI, is the ability of computers to learn from data and improve over time without being explicitly programmed. In the context of work, ML and data analytics are increasingly being used to help organizations make more informed, data-driven decisions.

In marketing, sales, and finance, ML algorithms analyze large volumes of data, identify patterns, and predict future trends. For instance, e-commerce companies like Amazon use ML to recommend products to customers based on past behavior, hence improving sales and customer satisfaction. In the financial industry, ML models are used to detect fraudulent activities, forecast stock market trends, and optimize investment portfolios (Hastie, Tibshirani, & Friedman, 2009).

The application of data analytics is also changing human resources (HR) functions. Companies are using data to improve hiring practices, assess employee performance, and predict workforce trends. HR departments can gain valuable insights into employee satisfaction, potential turnover risks, and ways to enhance workplace productivity by analyzing data from employee surveys, social media, and performance reviews (Bersin, 2017). As data analytics evolve, the work of HR people will be to analyze data and strategize accordingly.

Robotics: Revolutionizing manual labor

Another key change driver in the workforce is robotics technology. Although robots have been around for decades and are used in manufacturing, new innovations are taking this technology into domains that were previously the sole territory of humans. In health care, logistics, and even agriculture, robots now do tasks that had been thought to be too complex for machines.

In healthcare, robots are now used in assisting in surgeries, diagnosing diseases, and even the delivery of drugs to patients in hospitals (Siciliano & Khatib, 2016). With robotic-assisted surgeries, including the Da Vinci Surgical System, surgeons can be more precise with minimal invasiveness, ensuring better patient outcomes and recovery time.

Robots are increasingly being used in logistics for warehouse sorting, package delivery, and inventory management. For example, companies like Amazon and Ocado are using robotic systems to automate the picking and packing of items in warehouses, reducing labor costs and improving efficiency (Wang et al., 2020). Similarly, autonomous drones are being developed for package delivery, providing faster and more cost-effective shipping solutions.

Robotics is also gaining its way in agriculture, as self driving machines are used in planting, harvesting, and crop monitoring. These robots can work under severe conditions and execute repetitive jobs much faster and with higher accuracy than human workers. It helps bridge labor shortages and improve agricultural productivity (Azevedo, 2020).

Blockchain: Transforming Trust and Security at Work

The most significant application of blockchain technology is its use in cryptocurrencies, such as Bitcoin. Blockchain is also set to revolutionize the future of work in areas concerning security, data privacy, and contract management. Blockchain is a decentralized digital ledger that records transactions across multiple computers in such a way that the data cannot be altered, offering a high level of security and transparency.

In the workplace, blockchain has the potential to transform how contracts are executed, particularly in the gig economy. Smart contracts—self-executing contracts with the terms of the agreement directly written into code—can automate processes such as payment distribution, job completion verification, and contract enforcement (Tapscott & Tapscott, 2016). This could lead to greater efficiency in freelance and outsourced work, reducing the need for intermediaries such as lawyers or accountants.

Blockchain also has the potential to solve problems in data security. As the incidence of data breaches and identity thefts continues to grow, personal information and digital identities can be stored securely in a blockchain. In health, education, and finance sectors, which depend on privacy about data, blockchain will make possible highly secure systems for storing and communicating confidential information (Hughes, 2017).

Virtual and Augmented Reality: Collaboration and Training

Virtual reality and augmented reality are technologies that will unlock all the possibilities in how work is conducted, especially in areas such as training, collaboration, and customer engagement. VR transports the users into a totally virtual environment, whereas AR provides a layer of digital information on top of the real world, augmenting the perception of the surroundings for the user.

With remote working, VR and AR are on the cusp of revolutionizing virtual collaboration. Applications such as virtual meeting rooms and immersive project spaces might make employees working in two parts of the globe feel as if they are on the same planet. This may further optimize team dynamics and minimize communication constraints, making for better productivity from distributed teams (Bersin, 2021).

VR and AR are already being used in training and development to simulate real-world scenarios where employees can practice tasks in a safe, controlled environment. For instance, healthcare professionals use VR simulations to practice surgery, while manufacturing workers use AR to get real-time guidance on complex assembly tasks. As these technologies continue to evolve, they will be an integral part of employee development and continuous learning (Pimentel & McBride, 2020).

The Future of Work: Adaptation and Innovation

As these technological advancements continue to evolve, the nature of work will change, both in terms of how tasks are performed and how organizations structure their operations. Many routine tasks will be automated, but creativity, emotional intelligence, and strategic thinking will still be necessary. The future workforce will likely include people who can collaborate with AI and machines, using technology to solve complex problems and innovate.

Businesses will have to adopt continuous change, investing in new technologies while fostering a culture of innovation and learning. As technology changes, companies that do not embrace these changes are likely to find themselves at a competitive disadvantage; those that adapt will be best positioned to thrive in the future of work.

4. THE NATURE OF OUTSOURCING: FROM CUTTING COSTS TO BUILDING STRATEGIC PARTNERS

Outsourcing, once it was only viewed as a mechanism for cutting costs, is changing into a tool for strategic and competitive advantage and operational efficiency innovation. Traditionally, companies would outsource a non-core activity, such as customer service or IT support and manufacturing, into countries with the lowest labor cost. While cost reduction still remains a central driver of outsourcing, companies today are beginning to realize the bigger potential of outsourcing in supporting the long-term interests of a firm. This shift symbolizes a bigger change in the way companies conceptualize their interaction with third-party service providers away from transactionally cost-oriented types of arrangements to much more collaborative partnership-driven models.

This section explains how the nature of outsourcing is transforming business practices, beginning by identifying some of the key elements of change and showing why strategic partnerships have become such a key part of outsourcing relationships.

From cost-cutting to value creation

The most historic reasons for outsourcing, however, are the reductions of operational costs. By giving jobs to service providers in low labor cost countries, businesses saved and could deploy more efficiently. Most often, such traditional models centered on transactional relationships, in which outsourcing providers were hired on their ability to offer cost-effective solutions with little oversight.

However, in the last ten years, organizations have begun to realize that value of outsourcing lies in something beyond mere cost reduction. In today's highly globalized and competitive world economy, organizations are seeking more strategic value in outsourcing relationships. For instance, through outsourcing, organizations are able to avail access to skills and leverage high-tech capabilities as well as boost innovation capacity (Lacity & Willcocks, 2020).

Instead of just outsourced routine processes, most companies are now outsource critical business functions such as R&D, design, and customer experience management to service providers with advanced capabilities and specialized know-how. Business organizations can then maintain their core competence while leveraging third-party partners with the skills and capabilities to enable them to deliver value. Therefore, companies establish outsourcing agreements rooted in collaboration and value co-creation to develop a competitive edge and accelerate growth (Deloitte, 2020).

Global talent sourcing and access to expertise

The demand for specialized skills and expertise is one of the primary factors that have led to the shift from cost-cutting to strategic outsourcing. Companies require access to cutting-edge capabilities in areas such as data analytics, cloud computing, artificial intelligence, and cybersecurity, which are often not readily available within the organization, especially in this era of accelerated technological innovation.

With the ability to source global talent, outsourcing firms are now in a position to attract very competent individuals with a rich history in the key areas they will specialize in. In IT and software development, companies outsource partners have increasingly come to depend on their ability to offer business innovation that delivers better technological solutions in transforming businesses into digitally fit enterprises (Lacity & Willcocks, 2020). Similarly, organizations can access specialized knowledge in fields such as legal services, marketing, and human resources by partnering with outsourcing providers that have deep industry expertise.

Global talent sourcing also allows companies to scale their workforce according to project needs, geographic expansion, and market demands. The quick access to talent across different regions and time zones ensures that companies can be agile and responsive to changing market conditions (Bersin, 2021). With the nature of work evolving, outsourcing partnerships help companies stay ahead of the curve by leveraging global expertise and diverse perspectives.

Innovation and Co-Creation: Building Collaborative Partnerships

Outsourcing relationships are now transforming into collaborative partnerships based on innovation and co-creation. While traditional outsourcing contracts involve the tender of pre-defined tasks to service providers who execute them, modern outsourcing models include collaboration between the client and service provider in order to drive innovations or business transformation.

For instance, companies are collaborating with outsourcing partners on co-developed R&D projects to develop new products, services, and technologies. In the pharmaceutical, automotive, and technology sectors, outsourcing partners are providing knowledge, expertise, and resources that complement the client's internal capabilities. This approach enables companies to speed up the innovation process and bring new offerings to market more quickly (Deloitte, 2020).

Outsourcing providers play a significant role in helping organizations execute and implement the adoption of new technologies in the process of digital transformation. For example, cloud service providers collaborate with companies to shift data, construct digital infrastructures, and embrace new technologies, such as artificial intelligence, machine learning, and blockchain. With strategic partnerships in place, business organizations can innovate at a greater speed, diminish time-to-market, and develop customer experiences at a higher level (Westerman, 2020).

Co-creation has also become an integral part of the outsourcing process in customer-facing roles. Today, companies increasingly expect their service providers to become customer experience (CX) managers for them and participate in design thinking workshops and establish feedback loops. This creates an interdependent climate of outsourcing where the servant and the master are engaged in a collaborative relationship to enhance the end-user experience and achieve mutual organizational goals (Bersin, 2021).

Development of Long-Term Relationships: Governance and Trust

In addition, the move toward strategic outsourcing partnerships is also seen in the evolution of outsourcing governance. In previous days, outsourcing relationships are generally governed by tight contractual obligations to meet certain SLAs as well as performance metrics. Though these frameworks are still important, the increased complexity of the relationships makes the importance of trust, transparency, and long-term cooperation greater.

In contemporary outsourcing arrangements, businesses and service providers have shifted focus onto undertaking building strong, long-lasting relationships with mutual success. Such a model requires open communication, shared goals, and a guarantee to addressing issues between them in a collaborative, constructive manner. Effective governance frameworks allow both parties to deal with issues on hand, adapt their ways in accordance with any change in the business environment over time, and innovate together (Lacity & Willcocks, 2020).

With regards to these long-term relationships, there is an emergence of agile models of outsourcing into companies as well, thereby affording companies this flexibility and agility. Agile, for instance in software development means that there should be continuous, iterative improvement involving the client in addition to service providers and where real-time responses can provide ongoing adjustments (Deloitte, 2020).

Risk Management and Resilience in Outsourcing Partnerships

As firms enter into more complex, long-term outsourcing partnerships, managing risk and ensuring business resilience have become top priorities. As businesses rely increasingly on third-party service providers, they are beginning to realize the need for robust risk management strategies that address supply chain disruptions, cybersecurity threats, and geopolitical challenges.

In response to such risks, firms are now doing more extensive due diligence when engaging an outsourcing partner. They require higher levels of transparency and accountability from service providers and ensure that the interests of both parties are aligned in the management of risk. For instance, during the COVID-19 pandemic, firms with solid outsourcing partnerships were able to rapidly respond to disruptions in their supply chains and maintain business operations (Gartner, 2021).

Nowadays, outsourcing partnerships are considered as a vital element of business resilience. The diversified relationships in outsourcing between regions and industries reduce vulnerability to local disruption and make businesses' operations more flexible and resilient (Lacity & Willcocks, 2020). As the world continues to change fast, effective navigation of risks remains an important means of maintaining a competitive advantage.

The Future of Outsourcing: Strategic, Digital, and Global

The future of outsourcing shall be strategic, digital, and global. Thus, businesses looking forward to continuous digital transformation through emerging technologies would require support services from outsourcing firms in the implementing and managing roles of new digital technologies like artificial intelligence, automation, and blockchain. The increase in the stakes of reliance of business organizations for outsourcing shall subsequently deepen this source of outsourcing services.

In addition, outsourcing will remain a global practice, as companies continue to look for partners in regions with specialized talent and capabilities. In this new era, outsourcing will no longer be about low-cost labor but will expand to regions of knowledge and expertise in cutting-edge technologies and innovation (Westerman, 2020).

The imperative for trust, cooperation, and success in partnerships in outsourcing will continue to lead the change from more transactional, short-term agreements to longer-term, value-driven partnerships. Companies that navigate these changes will be more effectively positioned to deploy outsourcing as an innovation and growth driver and competitive advantage.

5. GLOBAL TALENT POOLS AND THE GIG ECONOMY

Two of the defining forces reshaping the nature of work and outsourcing in the 21st century are global talent pools and the expansion of the gig economy. As organizations increasingly utilize flexible work arrangements and digital tools, they're tapping into global networks of skilled individuals, allowing the access of pools of expertise or talent that aren't available at the local levels. At the same time, the gig economy, which often involves short-term contracts, freelancing, and working on projects instead of a pay cheque, revolutionizes traditional work arrangements and has opened up different opportunities for worker and business players. This section will look at how the global talent pool and the gig economy are intertwined and how these interconnections will impact the future of work and outsourcing.

Expanding the Talent Pool: A Global Marketplace for Skills

The idea of a global talent pool has been greatly amplified by the digital revolution, which has made it easier for organizations to access skilled workers from virtually any corner of the globe. The proliferation of platforms such as Upwork, Freelancer, and Toptal has democratized access to talent through the provision of a platform to hire freelance workers with specialized skills, ranging from software development to marketing, design, and even legal services (Boudreau et al., 2020).

Global access to the talent pool facilitates the overcoming of geographical and cultural barriers, so that organizations benefit from a much more diversified force and access skills from a variety of sources. For example, a US company can hire Indians for software developing or graphic designers from Eastern Europe, in addition to achieving cost savings resulting from outsourcing the functions to such regions where the labor costs are relatively lower. Such global labor mobility is most important in the high-demand areas, such as artificial intelligence, cybersecurity, and data analytics, wherein skills are usually in short supply (Brynjolfsson & McAfee, 2014).

Access to a global talent pool allows companies to tap into the diverse perspectives and expertise that drive innovation and improve problem-solving. Research has indicated that diversity in the workforce—cultural, geographic, or educational—enhances decision-making and creativity (Page, 2007). As companies look to create new products, enter new markets, or adapt to changing consumer needs, the availability of diverse talent can be a significant competitive advantage.

The Rise of the Gig Economy: Flexible Work and Independent Contractors

The gig economy, which has been described in terms of short-term contracts, freelance work, and temporary jobs, is increasingly characteristic of the contemporary labor market. The rise of the gig economy is supported by technological innovation, changes in workers' preferences, and business preferences for flexibility and lower overheads. Platforms such as Uber, Airbnb, and TaskRabbit are so synonymous with the gig economy because they give an individual a way to earn income in short-term engagements or through work on project-basis.

Under the guise of outsourcing, the gig economy heralds the decline of full-time employment contracts that have characterized much of modern life. Gig workers, commonly called independent contractors or freelancers, work for different clients in tasks or projects instead of committing to one employer for a long period. This model has several benefits for the businesses. Business entities realize cheaper labor costs due to less employee engagement, the possibility of scaling up their workforce easily, and accessing specialized know-how for unique tasks or projects without recruiting the employees full time (Friedman, 2014).

For instance, a company interested in creating a new website or mobile application can hire a freelance web developer or designer from Toptal instead of establishing an in-house team. In the same way, organizations in need of short-term marketing expertise or market research can turn to gig workers with specific skills instead of maintaining a full-time marketing department. By embracing this model, businesses can scale their workforce rapidly to meet fluctuating demands without the administrative burden of hiring, training, and managing permanent employees (Katz & Krueger, 2019).

The gig economy also aligns with the broader trend toward flexibility and autonomy in the workplace. Many gig workers choose this model because it offers greater control over their work schedules, locations, and the types of projects they pursue. This appeal is particularly strong among younger generations, such as Millennials and Generation Z, who prioritize work-life balance and flexibility over traditional career paths (De Stefano, 2016). As a result, businesses must be prepared to adapt to the evolving expectations of workers who prefer more freedom and independence in their careers.

Impact of Technology on the Gig Economy

Technology is essentially the backbone of the gig economy, thereby creating tools and platforms to enable individuals to find, perform, and even get paid for short-term jobs. Online platforms and digital marketplaces have transformed the way individuals connect with others and businesses. Platforms that connect freelancers, like Fiverr, Freelancer, and Upwork, do all this through algorithms that match the best gig workers with potential clients, based on their skills, experience, and location. Meanwhile, platforms like PayPal and Stripe smoothly process transactions.

The gig economy is also transforming with advancements in automation, AI, and machine learning. For example, the AI-driven algorithm can help find the right freelancer for a job based on their skillset, reviews, and previous project outcomes of potential candidates. Other uses of AI and machine learning would automate some mundane repetitive tasks. This may help expand the pool of gig work opportunities in sectors such as customer service, data entry, and digital marketing (Brynjolfsson & McAfee, 2014).

Further emerging technologies such as blockchain may increase the scope of the gig economy. This may include transparent payment systems that provide security and efficiency without the intermediaries and the potential for just remuneration for gig workers. Blockchain will, for instance, also allow the development of decentralized freelancer platforms where the smart contracts are used to record and verify the transactions, contracts, and payment (Tapscott & Tapscott, 2016). More improvement in efficiency, security, and scalability in gig economy platforms will be experienced with such developments.

The Gig Economy: Challenges and Opportunities for Business

While the gig economy offers several advantages to businesses, such as flexibility and cost savings, it also presents a few challenges. The first is quality and consistency in work. Since gig workers do not have the same commitment or accountability to an organization, issues related to quality control and project delivery arise. Mitigation of these risks entails clear expectations and performance metrics communicated to gig workers, as well as close monitoring of their work (Katz & Krueger, 2019).

Another hurdle that businesses experience is the management of the legal and regulatory concerns of gig work. Many countries have not yet adapted their labor laws to the unique nature of gig work, which creates uncertainties around issues such as taxation, benefits, and worker rights (De Stefano, 2016). In some regions, gig workers are classified as independent contractors, meaning they do not enjoy the same protections and benefits as full-time employees. This may result in disagreements over remuneration, job security, and working conditions, which means that companies should be updated on changing labor laws and be able to observe relevant regulations.

Despite these challenges, the gig economy has brought much opportunities to businesses. The fluidity of the gig economy simply allows an organization to ramp up its workforce, acquire specialized expertise, and evade the costs of hiring full-time employees. More so, businesses embracing gig work are able to tap into a larger talent pool with wider diversity to regional standing points. This makes businesses much more innovative and creative (Boudreau et al., 2020).

The Future of Global Talent Pools and the Gig Economy

The future of work will be more about growth in global talent pools and the gig economy. With companies embracing digital tools and technologies, the barriers to accessing talent from around the world will continue to come down. With remote work, advancements in communication tools, and project management software, businesses can tap into a global workforce more easily than ever before.

Furthermore, the gig economy will most likely continue to grow as people increasingly seek flexible work arrangements and more control over their careers. As businesses increasingly adopt outsourcing, they will rely on gig workers for short-term and project-based work. This will be driven further by the growing trend of platform-based work where digital platforms act as intermediaries to connect businesses and workers in real time.

As the gig economy matures, new strategies will be required to manage a decentralized workforce that is diverse and dynamic, thus forcing businesses to rethink older HR management and performance measurement and compensation approaches. Businesses will need to navigate the platform-based, legal and regulatory challenges to fairness in compensation and working conditions and operational efficiency and flexibility in this uncertain new world of management.

6. THE ROLE OF AI AND AUTOMATION IN OUTSOURCING

The integration of artificial intelligence and automation into outsourcing processes represents a transformative shift in how businesses approach their outsourcing strategies. The potential of AI and automation to streamline operations, enhance productivity, and reduce costs has made them central to modern outsourcing models. These technologies are altering the types of tasks that could be outsourced, as well as changing how the relationships about outsourcing are structured. It thereby brings new challenges and opportunities both to businesses and providers of outsourced services.

This section explores how AI and automation are influencing the outsourcing industry, the types of tasks that are increasingly being automated, the benefits and challenges of these technologies, and how businesses can leverage AI and automation to enhance their outsourcing strategies.

AI and Automation in Outsourcing: A New Era

The introduction of AI and automation in the outsourcing industry is changing traditional models of outsourcing. In the past, many outsourced jobs included manual, repetitive, or administrative functions, like data entry, customer support, and call center operations. With the development of AI technologies like machine learning, natural language processing, and robotic process automation, providers of outsourcing are increasingly able to automate complex tasks that required human intervention in the past.

It is also possible for customer inquiries, transaction processing, data management, and decision making to be offered by AI through predefined rules or patterns. Such capabilities transform industries such as finance, healthcare, and customer services more than any other area, where AI is increasingly being used to help augment human workers, and even supplement them entirely in many places (Brynjolfsson & McAfee, 2014). Automation helps businesses outsource tasks more efficiently and at a lower cost while simultaneously increasing the speed and accuracy of service delivery.

For example, chatbots powered by NLP can interact with customers, answer frequently asked questions, and even resolve complex issues without human intervention. In banking, insurance, and retail, AI-based chatbots and virtual assistants are replacing traditional call center workers, providing faster and more consistent customer service (Westerman, 2020). AI is also used to analyze large volumes of data to uncover insights, detect fraud, and predict market trends, tasks that once required extensive human expertise and time-consuming manual work.

Automation Technologies: Robotic Process Automation (RPA)

One of the most sweeping changes wherein the role of AI and automation in outsourcing is through Robotic Process Automation or RPA. In brief, RPA uses software robots, so called "bots", for automating repetitive, rule-based tasks previously done by humans. Data entry, invoices processing, payroll accounts reconciliation can all come under this category. RPA helps an organization automate business processes involving many data with very minimal human intervention, thus significantly improving efficiency and error reduction (Avasarala & Varma, 2020).

In outsourcing, RPA has gained popularity due to its ability to enhance both cost efficiency and scalability. For instance, instead of outsourcing data entry or transaction processing to manual labor, a business can use RPA to automate such processes, which will free up human workers to do more value-added activities, like customer interaction, decision-making, and problem-solving. RPA can also be implemented across multiple outsourcing providers and locations, allowing businesses to scale operations more quickly and respond to changes in demand.

Furthermore, RPA is particularly effective when used in conjunction with AI, as the combination allows for the automation of more complex tasks that require cognitive reasoning or decision-making. For instance, AI can help bots recognize and process unstructured data, such as scanned documents or email correspondence, while RPA can handle the execution of tasks like populating databases or routing customer queries to the appropriate team (Lacity & Willcocks, 2020).

AI and Automation in Customer Service and Support

One of the most visible areas where AI and automation are making a deep impact on outsourcing is customer service and support. Traditionally, customer service outsourcing was a large call center with human agents to respond to inquiries, resolve issues, and process transactions. However, AI-driven customer support tools are fundamentally changing how these services are delivered.

The latest advancements of chatbots and AI-driven virtual assistants demonstrate how intelligent and sensitive they are when handling queries from their customers. They can manage all kinds of inquiries, starting from merely answering FAQs up to solving complex tasks such as troubleshooting technical issues or processing transactions. AI-driven customer service solutions can ensure 24/7 assistance, minimize waiting times, and respond immediately, attracting businesses with the most significant customer satisfaction and operation easiness.

For an outsourcing provider, AI-powered customer service is poised to be an important arena of investment as it increases the delivery of services with reduced operational costs. AI systems can support high volumes of simultaneous inquiries, reduce the requirement for large teams of human agents, and limit training and turnover costs (Brynjolfsson & McAfee, 2014). The primary reason outsourcing providers integrate AI technologies into their service offerings is to offer businesses faster, more efficient, and cost-effective customer support solutions.

However, it is essential to note that although AI can manage many customer service tasks, human oversight is necessary for handling complex issues and maintaining a high level of customer satisfaction. Many businesses are adopting hybrid models in which AI handles routine queries, while human agents step in when a more personalized or nuanced response is needed (Westerman, 2020).

AI and Automation in Data Analytics and Decision-Making

AI is also revolutionizing the way data analytics is performed within outsourcing relationships. Historically, businesses outsourced data-related tasks, such as market research, data entry, and analysis, to external service providers. Today, AI is enabling businesses to automate the collection, analysis, and interpretation of data at a scale and speed previously impossible.

AI-driven analytics platforms would process structured and unstructured data on a large scale, giving insights into patterns, trends, and even providing data-driven recommendations. It can analyze customer behavior data, such as in purchase habits, to enable businesses to create targeted marketing strategies or improve product offerings. In fraud detection, AI uses machine learning algorithms that can determine anomaly in transaction patterns and find possible security threats (Lacity & Willcocks, 2020).

For outsourcing service providers, AI-driven data analytics tools are becoming essential parts of the service offerings. Outsourcing firms can provide their clients with more sophisticated insights and recommendations by using AI in their operations, and this is above the traditional reporting and data management. This has contributed to the larger trend of the evolution of outsourcing from simple task execution to strategic, value-added services (Avasarala & Varma, 2020).

Advantages of AI and Automation in Outsourcing

The integration of AI and automation in outsourcing provides the following benefits for both businesses and outsourcing providers:

- \tCost Efficiency: Automation eliminates the need for massive teams of human workers to do repetitive tasks, reducing labor costs. Businesses in some instances have significantly reduced their operational costs, especially on customer support and data processing (Westerman, 2020).
- Increased productivity and efficiency. AI and automation technologies may perform certain tasks faster and better than human workers, hence increase productivity. Businesses can easily upscale their operations and meet increasing demands or market requirements without having the costs go as high as this would imply.
- \tQuality and Accuracy Improvement: AI reduces human errors. For instance, AI algorithms that are used for data analysis are able to spot patterns or trends that would otherwise be hard for human workers to notice, and this leads to better decision-making.
- \t24/7 Availability: AI-powered systems and automation tools can operate around the clock, ensuring continuous service delivery. This is especially beneficial in customer support and service industries, where clients expect instant responses and rapid issue resolution (Brynjolfsson & McAfee, 2014).

- Scalability and Flexibility: AI and automation can be scaled up or down depending on the demand, which makes it easy for businesses to adapt to the changing market conditions or operational needs. Outsourcing providers can implement AI and automation technologies across various business functions, which enables them to offer more flexible solutions to their clients.

Challenges and Considerations

There are numerous benefits of outsourcing using AI and automation, such as the enhancement of efficiency in operations, faster decision-making processes, and reduction of costs, but there are also several challenges and considerations for businesses to ponder:

- Job Displacement and Skills Gap: Since AI and automation take over particular jobs, there may be job displacement, especially among lower-skilled workers. Companies and outsourcing vendors must invest in upskilling and reskilling their workforces to prepare for the changing nature of jobs (Westerman, 2020).
- Implementation Costs: AI and automation technologies are capital-intensive and require significant investment in terms of financial resources and time. Businesses need to evaluate the return on investment (ROI) of these technologies and determine how they can be integrated into existing systems (Lacity & Willcocks, 2020).
- Data Privacy and Security: The reasons of high volumes in the usage of AI in data analytics and customer service mandate businesses to protect their data integrity and security. There is a dire need to ensure that their AI system is located within the ambit of privacy compliance, just like in the case of GDPR.

Future of AI and Automation in Outsourcing

The outsourced activities through AI and automation will be tremendous, looking into the future, because AI and automation technologies, being more evolved in the upcoming future, would handle more sophisticated knowledge-based complex tasks and industries such as finance, healthcare, or legal services, for example, will undergo profound transformations. In addition, the integration of AI with other emerging technologies, such as blockchain and the Internet of Things (IoT), will create new opportunities for businesses to leverage automation in innovative ways (Brynjolfsson & McAfee, 2014).

Outsourcing providers will increasingly need to invest in AI and automation capabilities to stay competitive. Those that can successfully integrate these technologies into their service offerings will be well-positioned to offer more sophisticated, value-driven services to clients, solidifying their role as strategic partners rather than just cost-effective service providers.

7. SKILLS AND WORKFORCE DEVELOPMENT IN THE FUTURE OF WORK

The rapid evolution of technology, coupled with shifting economic, social, and business environments, is fundamentally altering the skills required for success in the workplace. As businesses and industries adapt to the demands of digital transformation, the skills needed for workers to thrive are changing dramatically. This is especially evident in outsourcing, where there is a growing emphasis on not just technical proficiency, but also the ability to adapt to new technological tools, work in remote or distributed teams, and manage increasingly complex global challenges.

In this section, we explore how the future of work will demand new skills, the evolving role of workforce development programs, and how businesses, workers, and educational institutions can navigate this rapidly changing landscape.

Emerging Skills for the Future of Work

As automation, AI, and digital technologies continue to redefine business processes and models, the skills required in the workforce will also undergo significant transformation. Traditionally, many jobs emphasized routine, task-oriented skills, but the future of work is shifting toward roles that require cognitive, creative, and interpersonal skills.

1. Technical and Digital Skills

The future workforce will need an enhanced set of technical and digital skills to remain relevant. Data literacy, coding, cybersecurity, and advanced software and AI tools will be the skills in greater demand. For instance, the industries of IT, healthcare, and finance are already undergoing changes through automation, artificial intelligence, and data analytics. Therefore, data science and machine learning are crucial skills for the future (Brynjolfsson & McAfee, 2014). Roles requiring coding and programming knowledge, including software development, web development, and systems engineering, will remain in high demand.

Automation technologies such as Robotic Process Automation (RPA) are also driving the need for skills in automation and process management, especially in industries like manufacturing, logistics, and customer service (Lacity & Willcocks, 2020). Digital literacy is no longer a niche skill but has become foundational across a wide range of professions, from marketing to HR management and beyond.

2. Soft Skills: Creativity, Critical Thinking, and Emotional Intelligence

While technical skills are important, soft skills will increasingly play an important role in the future of work. These include creativity, problem-solving, critical thinking, and emotional intelligence, which cannot be easily automated and are always required in jobs that require human judgment, interaction, and innovation. Jobs that are highly interactive at the interpersonal level, such as customer service management, human resources, and leadership roles, will place a premium on emotional intelligence (Goleman, 1995).

Creativity, which distinguishes humans from machines, is also essential because businesses are constantly looking for new ideas in an increasingly dynamic environment. Tasks requiring conceptual thinking, design, strategy formulation, and new product or service development will require these creative skills (Huang & Rust, 2021).

As businesses continue to diversify and develop global teams, cross-cultural communication, collaboration, and leadership will also become increasingly valuable. Professionals with the ability to work in diverse and distributed teams, as well as manage intercultural relationships, will be highly sought after (Meyer, 2014).

The Role of Lifelong Learning and Upskilling

It simply means that a one-time education and career are no longer applicable in the changing pace of technological change. Therefore, lifelong learning and continuous upskilling must be achieved to remain competitive between individuals and organizations. This dynamic learning model continues to focus on education to facilitate workers in obtaining new skills and competencies introduced by new technologies and changing roles.

1. Upskilling and Reskilling

With automation and AI changing the face of work, many jobs will be altered, and some will be eradicated. In order to avoid massive job loss, workers must upskill and reskill by developing new skills in an existing field and acquiring new competencies for a different role. For example, factory and operations workers who used to be involved in tasks that were mechanical in nature could now be required to adapt to managing automated equipment, data analysis, or overseeing digital platforms (Bessen, 2019).

This will be a transition in which businesses will play a critical role in upskilling and reskilling their employees. Companies that invest in workforce development programs that provide ongoing training and support will be better positioned to retain talent, reduce turnover, and ensure that their employees stay engaged and capable of meeting new challenges (Brynjolfsson & McAfee, 2014).

The reskilling programs are not just for the low-skilled employees; even the white-collar and managerial ones would need employees who are in constant need of reskilling and upskilling to learn about new technologies. In the leadership domain, in particular, one will need data analytics, strategies on digital transformation, and a means of effective management of technological disruption (Huang & Rust, 2021).

2.The Role of Educational Institutions and Online Learning Platforms

Education and training systems are continually adapting to the fast-changing nature of the workforce needs. Higher educational institutions are continuously embracing technical, digital, as well as other interdisciplinary skills curricula. Outside of the long-term degree provision, there is strong demand for specialized training programs for quick equipping or certifications and micro-credentials as applied in fast-growing areas including cloud computing and blockchain and big data science areas.

Online learning websites, such as Coursera, edX, Udemy, and LinkedIn Learning, expanded access to this training, thereby allowing learners the opportunity to participate in courses, earn certifications in a wide scope of subjects at their own pace, and convenience. These platforms address the needs for a global diverse workforce with respect to flexibility and accessibility (Meyer, 2014).

Other key aspects will be the partnerships between education institutions, governments, and businesses in filling the gap. For instance, industry-specific training programs, apprenticeships, and on-the-job learning will help workers get the practical experience needed and be aligned with the latest trends in their fields. Such programs can supplement formal education and make workers adjust to new roles as they change.

Creating a Learning Culture in Organizations

For businesses, continuous learning culture is essential in making sure that their workforce is agile and competitive within a rapidly changing environment. Some of the ways organizations can foster ongoing skill development include encouraging employees to take ownership of their development, access to learning resources, and embedding training into the daily work environment.

Key leaders within organizations will have to accept the notion that learning should not be a singular event or an afterthought, but rather ingrained in the company culture. The provision of opportunities to learn from one another, mentorship programs, and support for employees in new certifications or advancing education will all be part of the forward-thinking talent development strategy (Bessen, 2019).

In addition, the company can employ gamified learning, mentoring programs, and cross-functional team projects to stimulate the sharing of knowledge and teamwork. A workplace where learning is not only encouraged but celebrated would ensure that the organization remains agile and capable of adapting to new market trends and technological innovations and also drive employee engagement and loyalty.

Outsourcing and Workforce Development: Third-Party Provider Collaboration

The role of an outsourcing provider for workforce development gains increased importance because more and more businesses are getting globally oriented and conducting their activities around the globe. Outsourcing, apart from the savings to a company from cutting costs in personnel, serves another purpose-thereby assisting it in effectively undertaking complex projects and initiatives and technology-based processes. The value providers can add over just executing some routine tasks as outsourced entities must increasingly incorporate more strategic thinking about workforce development.

For instance, in sectors such as IT and software development, finance, and healthcare, outsourcing partners should be able to provide not only services but also assist in skills upgrading in their teams to deliver the new, changing needs of their clients. Providers that offer training programs, career development, and technical skill building to their employees will make them valuable long-term partners to the business (Lacity & Willcocks, 2020).

Outsourcing relationships that prioritize workforce development can, therefore, help businesses mitigate the challenges associated with the skills gap and ensure access to a highly capable, well-trained workforce regardless of location.

The Future of Workforce Development

In the years ahead, workforce development will be tailored to changing technologies, demographics, and the further trend toward increased globalization, flexibility, and decentralization of the labor market. As automation and digital transformation continue to shift and reshape industries, the demand for skills in creativity, critical thinking, emotional intelligence, and technical competence will only grow.

Lifelong learning will be the new normal, and companies that invest in the continuous development of their employees will be better positioned to thrive in a rapidly changing global economy. Workers and organizations alike will need to embrace a mindset of continuous growth and adaptability, embracing new learning opportunities and staying ahead of the curve in developing new skills to remain competitive.

8. ROLE OF EMERGING MARKETS IN OUTSOURCING

Emerging markets have been one of the prime drivers for changing the face of the global outsourcing landscape. Markets that are marked by rapid economic growth, emerging technological infrastructure, and an increasingly large talent pool have emerged as significant players in the outsourcing industry. In this regard, investment in talent and infrastructure is particularly high in Asian, Latin American, and Eastern European countries, making them the most attractive destinations for outsourcing services.

Emerging markets have dramatically changed the global business playing field by emerging as outsourcing destinations. Companies are now looking at new, less-established markets for a myriad of services including IT development, customer support, and back-office functions instead of focussing on the traditional outsourcing hubs of India and China. It is here that these new markets provide competitive advantages in terms of cost-effective labor, diversified talent, and strategic positioning for global reach.

1. The rise of emerging markets as a global outsourcing destination

Emerging markets have gained much importance in the global outsourcing market because of the growing economic influence and increased number of workforce in these countries. As mature markets for outsourcing grow old, businesses have started seeking areas with low labor costs and a rapidly developing technological infrastructure to cater to their outsourcing needs. Some emerging markets are countries like the Philippines, Vietnam, Poland, and Mexico, among others, as alternatives to well-established outsourcing markets like India and China.

For instance, the Philippines has emerged as a prime destination for Business Process Outsourcing (BPO) services, especially in customer support, IT services, and healthcare outsourcing. The country has a highly educated, English-speaking workforce, which makes it an attractive choice for companies seeking cost-effective solutions without compromising on quality. According to the Philippine Economic Zone Authority (PEZA), the BPO industry of the Philippines is one of the fastest-growing sectors, contributing significantly to the country's GDP (Villarreal & Carino, 2019).

Similar is the case with Latin American countries, where Mexico, Argentina, and Costa Rica are also becoming a destination for IT outsourcing and software development. Latin America, with its proximity to North America and relatively lower operating costs, has made it an attractive outsourcing destination for U.S.-based companies. It provides the possibility of real-time collaboration, cultural compatibility, and fewer time zone differences.

Countries such as Poland, Romania, and Ukraine in Eastern Europe are the centers for outsourcing both IT and software development, plus customer support work. These states possess a profoundly skilled workforce expert in engineering and programming, coupled with cybersecurity at highly competitive wages when compared with their Western counterparts (KPMG, 2020). These emerging markets have emerged as a source of attractive destinations for high-tech and knowledge-based outsourcing services, with companies looking to tap local talent into innovation and digital transformation.

2. Cost Competitiveness and Value for Money

One of the major reasons businesses seek emerging markets for outsourcing is cost advantage. Compared to the traditional outsourcing destinations, emerging markets often offer a more competitive pricing advantage, thus attracting companies to reduce their operational costs.

For instance, in India, the labor cost for outsourcing services is relatively low, but the cost has been increasing year by year due to economic growth and inflation. In contrast, emerging markets such as Vietnam, Romania, and Colombia have similar low-cost labor, but with the added benefit of developing infrastructure and growing talent pools, making them increasingly attractive (Harris & Williams, 2021).

Labour arbitrage is one of the key factors driving outsourcing to these regions because it allows the companies to make the most of the lower wage levels without compromise on quality. Businesses are beginning to realize, however, that outsourcing to emerging markets is not merely about the cost; it is about harnessing the distinct value each market brings. Some examples of such markets include an extreme focus on the specialized skills within software development, cybersecurity, data analytics, and artificial intelligence to offer businesses opportunities to get leading talent at a fraction of what they would spend in Western markets.

The cost competitiveness in emerging economies, coupled with the growing expertise of outsourcing services in these locations, has changed how companies assess an outsourcing opportunity. Many companies no longer look for cheap solutions but maximize value by access to skilled talent, advanced technology, and new solutions (KPMG, 2020).

3. Skill Development and Talent Availability

The availability of skilled talent is one of the most important impacts of emerging markets on outsourcing. Traditionally, outsourcing was more related to low-skill, repetitive work such as data entry and customer service. However, with the evolution of business needs, emerging markets are rapidly developing the skills needed to fulfill high-value, specialized outsourcing functions, including IT services, software development, digital marketing, and finance-related tasks.

Countries such as Poland and Ukraine, with an emphasis on education in engineering and technology, are now hotspots for software development and IT outsourcing. Similarly, countries like Argentina and Chile are producing high-quality developers and digital marketers. In this regard, as the demand for IT outsourcing services continues to grow, such countries are now being considered viable alternatives to the traditional outsourcing destinations (Harris & Williams, 2021).

The sophistication of emerging markets is not only technical but also extends to other areas such as finance, legal services, and customer support. With specialized training and professional development opportunities, emerging markets are attracting a more skilled workforce that is better equipped to meet the evolving needs of global businesses.

In addition, emerging markets are increasingly using local partnerships with universities, training institutes, and industry organizations to develop specialized skills that meet the needs of international companies. This is making the global labor market more competitive and allowing businesses to access a wider talent pool (Villarreal & Carino, 2019).

4. The Changing Geography of Outsourcing

Geography in outsourcing has dramatically changed over the recent past. Businesses today are looking away from the traditional outsourcing venues of India, China, and the Philippines as newer markets have emerged and gained prominence. Although these markets continue to dominate the outsourcing landscape, the dynamic is ever changing as new regions emerge with competitive cost efficiency and expertise.

Emerging markets in Latin America, Eastern Europe, and Southeast Asia have become prime outsourcing destinations due to their proximity to Western markets, cultural compatibility, and access to specialized talent. For instance, Latin American countries offer geographic proximity and similar time zones to the U.S., making them an ideal choice for nearshoring. For example, Mexico is considered one of the attractive destinations for companies based in the United States due to its strategic location, low labor costs, and a high-quality workforce in areas like IT outsourcing, customer support, and engineering (KPMG, 2020).

The outsourcing sector in Eastern Europe has also experienced tremendous growth, with Poland, Romania, and Bulgaria emerging as key players in the IT and software development outsourcing markets. The region's skilled workforce, strong educational systems, and cultural alignment with Western markets have made it increasingly popular for high-tech outsourcing services (Villarreal & Carino, 2019).

Businesses have realized it is beneficial for them to start diversifying outsourcing portfolios to new markets in Asia, as they can reduce certain risks associated with economic instability or political changes elsewhere in the more traditional outsourcing market.

5. Challenges of Outsourcing to Emerging Markets

Emerging markets present tremendous opportunities to businesses, but the unique challenges of organizations in these markets are worth mentioning. Among the most common challenges are:

1. Infrastructure and Technological Development: Many emerging markets have significantly advanced their technological infrastructures, yet there are areas that are lacking, such as internet connectivity, digital tools, and cybersecurity. Businesses should look at the infrastructure capabilities of the outsourcing destinations to ensure they fit their needs in terms of service delivery and security (Harris & Williams, 2021).
2. Cultural and Language Barriers: Even though there is an increase in the availability of English-speaking talent in emerging markets, cultural and language differences can still create problems, especially when working with remote or distributed teams. Communication and cultural alignment are critical for successful outsourcing, and businesses need to invest in training and development to overcome these barriers (Villarreal & Carino, 2019).
3. Political and Economic Risks: Many emerging markets face political instability, economic volatility, and fluctuating regulatory environments. These risks can create uncertainty for businesses considering outsourcing in these regions. While the cost savings may be significant, businesses must weigh these risks carefully and establish contingency plans to address potential disruptions (KPMG, 2020).

6. The Future of Outsourcing in Emerging Markets

In the near future, the emerging markets are going to form an increasingly integral part of the global outsourcing ecosystem. The greater investment these markets make in education, infrastructure, and technological innovation will only serve to increase the attractiveness of the destination for the outsourcing of high-value functions. Emerging markets in Latin America, Eastern Europe, and Southeast Asia will be key players in shaping the future of outsourcing as companies look to diversify their outsourcing portfolios to mitigate risks and take advantage of different skill sets.

Emerging markets will be no longer cost centers but strategic partners, which would bring new and innovative, high-value services that would assist companies to fuel growth and digital transformation in the hyperconnected world.

9. LEGAL AND ETHICAL ISSUES OF FUTURE WORK AND OUTSOURCING

Legal and ethical considerations related to outsourcing continue to increase as the business world and its operations change and develop further. The future of work will be shaped not only by technological advancements, shifting business models, and evolving labor markets but also by the increasing need for robust legal and ethical frameworks that govern the outsourcing industry. This is particularly crucial as companies increasingly engage with offshore and nearshore partners, navigating diverse regulatory environments and addressing issues like data privacy, labor rights, and CSR.

In this section, we discuss the various legal and ethical issues that are likely to influence the future of work and outsourcing, as well as the steps businesses and governments must take to ensure fair and responsible practices in the global outsourcing landscape.

1. Data Privacy and Security

Data privacy and security is one of the most important legal considerations in outsourcing, especially with the advancement of the digital age. With more companies outsourcing IT services, software development, and customer support, they tend to share sensitive data with third-party providers. Such sharing poses great concerns regarding the protection of such data, considering the rise of data breaches and cyberattacks.

Data Protection Laws and Regulations:

The location of the outsourcing company determines the level of data protection regulations that apply. For instance, the General Data Protection Regulation of the European Union imposes severe requirements on how companies collect, store, and process personal data. Companies outsourcing services to countries outside the EU are required to ensure that their outsourcing partners adhere to these regulations in order not to incur hefty fines and reputational damage (Voigt & von dem Bussche, 2017).

Similarly, in the US, the CCPA and various other state level privacy laws require companies to observe stricter standards over data handling mainly with regard to consumer data. Companies need to ensure that outsourced service providers in countries like India, Philippines, or even Eastern Europe should respect these law frameworks while dealing with sensitive customer data (Zengler & Finnegan, 2020).

Cross-Border Data Transfers:

Transfer of data across jurisdictions increases the challenge of compliance with multiple legal frameworks. Transfers of personal data between countries have different privacy laws, and that is an ongoing issue that will need to be addressed through contractual agreements and through the use of secure, legally compliant data transfer mechanisms. This problem will only grow more acute in the future as outsourcing continues to rely more and more on cloud computing and digital services (Zengler & Finnegan, 2020).

The best way for businesses to minimize these risks is to collaborate closely with their outsourcing partners to put in place the appropriate safeguards. This may involve strong encryption methods, secure cloud services, and regular audits to monitor compliance with data privacy laws.

2. Labor Rights and Fair Employment Practices

For long, outsourcing has been linked to the issue of labor exploitation in low-cost countries, especially in the Global South. With businesses increasingly outsourcing jobs to emerging markets, there is an ethical and legal imperative to ensure that labor rights are respected. The future of outsourcing must be guided by fair wages, worker safety, and labor conditions in countries with less stringent labor laws and protections.

Fair Wages and Benefits:

Workers may have to endure long hours, low pay, and poor working conditions in many outsourcing destinations. For example, a BPO worker in the Philippines or an employee in a manufacturing company in Vietnam might not be covered by labor protection laws like their counterparts in developed countries. As businesses evolve into outsourcing models that include lower-cost labor, there is the ethical requirement for ensuring that fair wages are earned by workers regarding the value their work provides; they also get basic benefits of health care and paid time off, among workplace protections (Lacity & Willcocks, 2020).

Another reason may be that emerging markets have relatively weaker enforcement of labor laws, leading to exploitation. Companies need to ensure that the outsourcing partners respect ethical labor practices and are complying with both local and international standards of employment law. This would ensure that the outsourced process is free from discrimination, forced labor, and hazardous conditions, as well as that there is no involvement of child labor in any part of the process.

Corporate Social Responsibility (CSR):

More and more companies are embracing corporate social responsibility (CSR) initiatives and are being held accountable by consumers and stakeholders for the ethical treatment of workers, including those employed through outsourcing arrangements. Businesses are increasingly required to demonstrate that they are ethically sourcing services and maintaining responsible labor practices throughout their supply chains.

Many organizations are now engaging third-party audit firms to assess labor conditions in their outsourcing locations and ensure compliance with internationally recognized labor standards. Initiatives such as the Ethical Trading Initiative (ETI) and Fair Labor Association (FLA) offer frameworks for ensuring ethical practices and protecting labor rights across global supply chains (Baptist, 2018). Ensuring that outsourcing providers meet these standards not only protects workers but also supports the company's reputation and long-term business sustainability.

3. IP Protection

Protection of intellectual property is another serious legal issue for companies outsourcing work. Companies who outsource their R&D, software development, and creative services risk the intellectual property getting misused or stolen by the third-party provider. Patent protection, trademark protection, copyright protection, and proprietary technology protection is complicated when working with foreign markets, whose laws may be quite different from their own.

Agreements and Contracts related to IPs

To avoid risks of an IP infringement or theft, clear contractual agreements must be stipulated for ownership rights and existing confidentiality clauses, which should further include NDAs. The contracts have to specify how intellectual property created during the outsourcing process will be handled and protected and should acknowledge the obligations of the outsourcing provider regarding the proprietary assets of the company.

In addition, businesses have to engage legal professionals to appropriately draft outsourcing contracts such that they are appropriate and in adherence to domestic and foreign IP laws. For example, offshore outsourcing to Eastern European or Asian countries for software development has different standards of legal enforceability of IP rights, and a company has to ensure the security of its IP across all those jurisdictions (Lacity & Willcocks, 2020).

Role of Technology in IP Protection:

As technology continues to advance, new solutions are emerging to protect intellectual property in the outsourcing environment. For instance, blockchain technology is being explored as a tool for securing digital assets and tracking the use and transfer of intellectual property across borders. Companies may also use encrypted communications, secure file-sharing systems, and DRM tools to prevent unauthorized access or misuse of their IP.

4. Ethics of Automating and Artificial Intelligence in Outsourcing

Automation and AI have lately found a niche place within outsourcing strategy; there arises newer ethics, namely job displacement arising out of automated work undertaken previously by the human brain, that brings an ethical responsibility from business organizations for people whose job security will be eroded and become susceptible to a threat posed by a machine or artificial system.

Job Loss and Retraining

Ethically, firms need to reflect on the social effects of automation and AI in the local labor market. Where automation leads to job loss, firms should have programs to retrain and upskill workers whose jobs are being lost. Also, firms need to look at how to maintain the use of automation while promoting employment creation without deepening inequality or creating social unrest in the destination countries for outsourcing (Brynjolfsson & McAfee, 2014).

Bias and Fairness in AI Algorithms:

The use of AI and machine learning algorithms in the provision of outsourcing services raises another interesting ethical question. Most AI systems, especially those in decision-making applications related to hiring, customer service, and credit scoring, have biases that affect certain groups of people, especially women, minorities, and low-income ones. Thus, ethical outsourcing means careful monitoring and regulation of AI to ensure that its design is fundamentally fair and transparent and does not perpetuate or reinforce discriminatory practice.

For instance, firms may have to establish audit processes for AI systems to determine the likelihood of bias and adjust them accordingly to be fair. There will also be a need for transparency in AI decision-making to ensure consumer and employee trust as outsourcing becomes more dependent on these technologies.

5. Regulatory Compliance and the Global Outsourcing Landscape

Navigating the complex web of regulatory frameworks governing outsourcing across different countries and regions will be one of the continuing challenges. The legal and regulatory requirements in any outsourcing destination can change quickly, especially with governments introducing new laws to keep up with growing concerns over data privacy, workers' rights, and technology.

Businesses need to be aware of the legal and regulatory changes that affect their outsourcing relationships. This is not only compliance with local labor laws and privacy regulations but also international standards for business conduct. The development of comprehensive outsourcing contracts that anticipate potential legal changes and include contingency clauses for compliance risks will be essential to safeguarding companies from legal liabilities.

6. The Role of Governments and International Cooperation

Governments will be important players in shaping the future of outsourcing by enforcing labor laws, protecting intellectual property, and regulating the use of technology in business operations. Governments, international organizations, and industry stakeholders will have to cooperate with each other in the context of international cooperation to handle the global issues outsourcing poses for companies, as companies increasingly enter into multilateral and multi-jurisdictional business practices.

International trade agreements, negotiated through the WTO, can affect the legal framework for outsourcing. International trade agreements can promote fair practices, provide common standards for IP protection, and ensure that outsourcing does not result in the erosion of labor rights or environmental protections by fostering dialogue and cooperation between countries.

10. Conclusion: Navigating the Future of Work and Outsourcing

The future of work and outsourcing is undeniably complex, shaped by rapid technological advancements, evolving employee expectations, and shifting global dynamics. As we look toward the coming decades, it becomes evident that the way we work—and how businesses source talent—will continue to undergo transformative changes. To succeed in this evolving landscape, organizations must remain agile, open to innovation, and proactive in adapting to new ways of working, collaborating, and outsourcing.

This concluding section synthesizes the key insights presented throughout the book and offers a roadmap for businesses and employees navigating the challenges and opportunities of the future. Understanding the emerging trends, embracing new technologies, and cultivating an adaptable, inclusive culture puts companies in position to thrive for the long haul in a rapidly changing global economy.

1. Adopting Technological Innovation and Adaptation

Technological change will continue, and it will increasingly upset traditional models of work and outsourcing. Businesses that focus on adopting technology and innovation will find themselves best positioned to exploit the efficiencies and capacities that will be available through automation, AI, and other emerging technologies. Robotics and AI-driven systems will automate routine tasks to make staff available for higher-value work. In outsourcing, automation will enhance decision-making, streamline operations, and provide opportunities for outsourcing relationships to evolve from transactional to strategic partnerships.

But technology's purpose is not to substitute manpower; it is supposed to complement and strengthen human capability. Successful organizations will complement the powers of technology with the creativity, problem-solving abilities, and emotional competence of human workers. For instance, while AI can take over routine chores, human insight and judgment will remain essential in solving complex decisions and handling interpersonal connections and innovations.

Businesses must also ensure that their workforce is prepared for the changes that technology will bring. This means investing in continuous learning, reskilling, and upskilling programs that help employees adapt to new tools and ways of working. Lifelong learning will become essential as industries and job functions evolve in tandem with technological advancements (Davenport & Kirby, 2016). Companies that foster an environment of learning and development will attract the best talent and build a resilient and future-ready workforce.

2. Developing a Flexible, Hybrid Workforce

One of the most significant shifts in the modern workplace is a shift toward hybrid work, which integrates remote and in-office arrangements. Over the course of the next decade, it will likely dominate the way most people work - allowing employees flexibility to work from different locations yet maintaining strong connections with their teams and organizational culture.

To navigate this new work paradigm, companies have to rethink office spaces and transform them to cater to the new needs of the more dispersed workforce. Instead of viewing offices as the primary place of work, businesses will create flexible, collaborative spaces where they can gather together for in-person interactions, alongside investing in technologies and infrastructure supporting remote work. With virtual collaboration tools, productivity software, and AI-powered solutions, hybrid teams will become even better at communicating, resource sharing, and cooperation across geographical borders.

This would require the business to provide equal opportunities for professional development, recognition, and career advancement to all employees, whether working remotely or in an office. Hybrid work should not lead to a two-tiered workforce; instead, companies must ensure inclusivity, transparency, and equity in how they support and engage employees. Strong leadership will be key to fostering a unified organizational culture, where all workers feel valued and empowered.

In addition, companies must ready themselves to facilitate various work types and styles. Flexibility within working hours, location, and communication methods will come in handy while trying to hold onto talent that seeks greater choice over how to work, where to work, and when. Organizations that create these choices, however, can gain a high competitive advantage to attract and maintain talent.

3. Redefinition of Outsourcing in the Times of Strategic Alliance

Outsourcing is no longer that cost-cutting measure but has blossomed as a strategic function in allowing businesses access to specialized expertise, expansion of scale, and innovation. In the near future, outsourcing will focus more on collaborative and longer-term partnerships between companies and outsourcing providers for mutual successes and growth.

As outsourcing becomes more integrated with core business functions, companies will look for outsourcing partners who bring not only technical expertise but also deep industry knowledge and strategic insights. The outsourcing landscape will be less about transaction-based relationships and more about aligning with partners who can add value in areas such as digital transformation, process optimization, and market expansion.

These partnerships will require proactive businesses to establish strong, transparent communication channels and clearly define expectations from the very beginning. Trust and mutual respect will be essential in ensuring that outsourcing relationships thrive in an increasingly interconnected, fast-paced business environment. Organizations must also be ready to adjust their outsourcing strategies to keep pace with the changing needs of the business, such as integrating new technologies, embracing sustainability initiatives, or accessing new global talent pools.

The companies that treat outsourcing as a strategic growth and innovation tool, rather than a cost-cutting tool, will be better prepared to face the complexities of the future workforce and remain ahead of the competition.

4. Accessing Global Talent Pools and the Gig Economy

The global talent pool will expand as digital platforms and remote work create new opportunities for businesses to tap into talent from all corners of the world. Businesses will no longer be limited to their local labor markets but will instead be able to hire specialized talent from anywhere, building more diverse, skilled teams that can take on complex challenges.

This will significantly impact outsourcing in that businesses will look for niche skills and expertise outside the traditional outsourcing hubs. For example, the growth of remote work will make it easier for businesses to partner with outsourcing providers in emerging markets, leveraging local knowledge and talent while benefiting from cost advantages. However, more global talent is being accessed by businesses, and this access comes with its set of issues: managing across time zones, cultures, and languages within the remote teams.

The gig economy will keep growing; increasingly, individuals prefer freelance, contract, and project-based work instead of the traditional full-time employment. This shift changes the concept of job security and career progression, in which more people will choose flexibility and autonomy instead of stability and long-term contracts. This also poses challenges about providing benefits to workers and the rights of such workers, but also opens up avenues for businesses that can engage highly skilled, flexible workers who may provide specialized skills on-demand.

As businesses embrace a hybrid workforce and tap into the gig economy, they will need to rethink traditional employment models, which would focus more on building relationships with independent workers, managing project-based work, and adapting to the evolving nature of work.

5. Address Ethical, Legal, and Social Implications

The future of work and outsourcing also raises significant ethical, legal, and social considerations. As automation, AI, and outsourcing redefine the nature of work, businesses must ensure that they operate in ways that are ethically responsible, legally compliant, and socially sustainable. Companies will need to address concerns such as job displacement, income inequality, and data privacy while maintaining a strong commitment to ethical labor practices and sustainability.

Legal frameworks will evolve to accommodate the changing nature of work, including the rights of gig workers, the protection of remote employees, and the regulation of AI-driven automation. Businesses that stay ahead of these legal and ethical concerns will build trust with employees, customers, and investors, which will, in turn, enhance their reputation and long-term success.

Sustainability will increase further because companies will be compelled to lessen their impact on the environment, propagate social responsibility, and fit in with the global sustainability paradigm. Companies that consider the ethical implications in outsourcing decisions are more likely to face the future of work in a resilient, adaptable manner, and promote a positive social and environmental impact.

6. Preparing for a Resilient, Adaptable Future

Ultimately, navigating future work and outsourcing will require a business to remain resilient and nimble. Speed of change has accelerated, and organizations that can't adapt early enough risk being behind the curve. Companies need to create a learning culture, embracing changes and innovating. This may involve investing in new technologies; adapting to how employees' needs are changing over time; and staying ahead in emerging trends within outsourcing, the work model, and talent acquisition.

Building resilience will include creating systems that are resilient against shocks and unexpected interruptions from changes in technology, global crises, or changes in the dynamics of markets. Flexibility and adaptability in strategies, operations, and workforce management will enable companies to perform well in an evolving world.

CONCLUSION

The future of work and outsourcing holds significant potential, but there are challenges to be met with change and innovation by business entities. In embracing technological innovation, hybrid and inclusive workplace environments, changes to the approach adopted toward outsourcing, and exploration of the complexities of global talent, businesses will be better positioned for success in the next decade. At the same time, their employees must become accustomed to new forms of work, building skills toward flexibility and opportunities arising with changes to the world of work. In doing so, businesses and workers can help create a more dynamic, inclusive, and resilient future of work.

REFERENCES

Agrawal, A., Gans, J., & Goldfarb, A. (2018). *Prediction machines: The simple economics of artificial intelligence*. Harvard Business Press.

Avasarala, V., & Varma, S. (2020). *The rise of robotic process automation (RPA): A look into the future of outsourcing*. Springer.

Azevedo, A. (2020). *The role of robotics in modern agriculture: Challenges and opportunities*. Springer.

Baptist, S. (2018). *Corporate social responsibility and ethical sourcing in global supply chains*. Springer.

Baruch, Y., & Nicholson, N. (2020). The future of work and the changing role of leadership: Challenges and opportunities in the hybrid workforce. *Leadership and Organization Development Journal, 41*(4), 467–480.

Bergman, A., & Sölvell, Ö. (2020). *Outsourcing in the 21st century: Strategic and operational perspectives*. Springer.

Bersin, J. (2017). The impact of data analytics on human resources. *Harvard Business Review, 95*(3), 46–56.

Bersin, J. (2021). *The future of work: From anywhere to everywhere*. Deloitte Insights.

Bessen, J. E. (2019). *AI and jobs: The role of demand*. Brookings Institution.

Boudreau, J. W., Lawler, E. E., & Bainbridge, D. (2020). The global talent marketplace: Opportunities and challenges for the future of work. *Human Resource Management Review, 30*(1), 100–114.

Brown, C., & Green, L. (2021). Technology and the hybrid workplace: Shaping the future of work and collaboration. *Journal of Digital Transformation, 18*(3), 98–112.

Brynjolfsson, E., & McAfee, A. (2014). *The Second Machine Age: Work, Progress, and Prosperity in a Time of Brilliant Technologies*. W.W. Norton & Company.

Choudhury, P., Foroughi, C., & Larson, B. (2021). Work-from-anywhere: The productivity effects of geographic flexibility. *Strategic Management Journal, 42*(1), 28–60. DOI: 10.1002/smj.3251

Dastin, J. (2018). *Amazon's AI recruitment tool shows bias against women*. Reuters. https://www.reuters.com/article/us-amazon-com-jobs-automation-insight-idUSKCN1WK08O

Davenport, T. H., & Kirby, J. (2016). *Only humans need apply: Winners and losers in the age of smart machines*. Harper Business.

De Stefano, V. (2016). The rise of the "just-in-time" workforce: On-demand work, crowdwork, and labor protection in the gig economy. *Comparative Labor Law & Policy Journal, 37*(3), 471–504.

Deloitte. (2020). *Global outsourcing survey 2020: Rethinking outsourcing*. Deloitte Consulting.

Friedman, G. (2014). The "gig economy" and the end of work as we know it. *Harvard Business Review, 92*(12), 33–38.

Gallup. (2020). *State of the American workplace: How the pandemic is reshaping the future of work.* Gallup, Inc.

Gartner. (2020). *The future of work trends: Technology, culture, and workforce shifts.* Gartner Research.

Gartner. (2021). *Future of work trends: Technology, culture, and workforce shifts.* Gartner Research.

Gartner. (2021). *Global outsourcing market insights: Building resilience through strategic partnerships.* Gartner Research.

Goleman, D. (1995). *Emotional Intelligence: Why It Can Matter More Than IQ.* Bantam.

Gupta, A., & Lee, J. (2021). Leading hybrid teams: Best practices for inclusivity and engagement. *Journal of Business Leadership, 29*(2), 144–156.

Hamer, A. (2021). The future of flexible work: Adapting to employee needs in the post-pandemic world. *Journal of Workforce Strategies, 9*(4), 210–225.

Harris, J., & Williams, M. (2021). The evolution of outsourcing: Understanding the new dynamics. *Global Outsourcing Journal, 25*(3), 12–25.

Hastie, T., Tibshirani, R., & Friedman, J. (2009). *The elements of statistical learning: Data mining, inference, and prediction* (2nd ed.). Springer. DOI: 10.1007/978-0-387-84858-7

Huang, M.-H., & Rust, R. T. (2021). Artificial Intelligence in Service. *Journal of Service Research, 24*(1), 3–24.

Hughes, L. (2017). Blockchain for business and the workplace: Opportunities for security and transparency. *Journal of Business & Technology, 3*(2), 42–58.

Katz, L. F., & Krueger, A. B. (2019). *The rise of the gig economy: Fact or fiction?* Brookings Institution.

Khalil, M. (2020). Digital nomads: How the world is becoming their office. *Forbes.*

KPMG. (2020). *Global outsourcing report: Emerging markets and the new wave of outsourcing.* KPMG International.

Kuhn, P., & Maleki, A. (2017). *The Gig Economy: The Future of Work and How to Navigate It.* Oxford University Press.

Lacity, M. C., & Willcocks, L. P. (2020). *Robotic Process Automation and the Future of Work: The New Age of Automation in Business.* Palgrave Macmillan.

McKinsey & Company. (2020). The future of work after [*Remote work and beyond.* McKinsey & Company.]. *COVID,* •••, 19.

Meyer, E. (2014). *The Culture Map: Breaking Through the Invisible Boundaries of Global Business.* PublicAffairs.

Mishra, S., & Shukla, A. (2021). Collaboration and productivity in hybrid work environments: The role of digital tools. *International Journal of Hybrid Work, 13*(1), 56–69.

Okoye, M. I. (2020). Managing remote work: Organizational best practices and strategies. *Journal of Business Research, 117*, 444–451. DOI: 10.1016/j.jbusres.2019.10.038

Page, S. E. (2007). *The difference: How the power of diversity creates better groups, firms, schools, and societies*. Princeton University Press.

Pimentel, D., & McBride, A. (2020). Virtual reality and augmented reality in training: Changing the future of employee development. *Journal of Workplace Learning*, *32*(1), 35–49.

Srinivasan, R., & Li, W. (2021). The evolving landscape of outsourcing and offshoring in the digital age. *Journal of International Business Studies*, *52*(1), 37–56. DOI: 10.1057/s41267-020-00369-6

Tapscott, D., & Tapscott, A. (2016). *Blockchain revolution: How the technology behind bitcoin is changing money, business, and the world.* Penguin.

Tapscott, D., & Tapscott, A. (2016). *Blockchain revolution: How the technology behind bitcoin is changing money, business, and the world.* Penguin.

Villarreal, S., & Carino, R. (2019). *The Philippines BPO industry: Building a competitive advantage.* Philippine Economic Zone Authority Report.

Voigt, P., & von dem Bussche, A. (2017). *The EU General Data Protection Regulation (GDPR): A Practical Guide*. Springer. DOI: 10.1007/978-3-319-57959-7

Wang, J., Zhang, Y., & Xu, Z. (2020). *Robotics in logistics: Automation, integration, and efficiency.* Springer.

Westerman, G. (2020). *Digital transformation: Survive and thrive in an era of mass extinction.* Harvard Business Review Press.

World Economic Forum. (2020). *The future of jobs report 2020.* World Economic Forum.

Zengler, T., & Finnegan, J. (2020). Navigating privacy regulations in the age of data breaches. *Journal of Data Privacy and Security*, *10*(2), 35–50.

Zhao, W. (2020). Proximity bias and its impact on hybrid work: Creating an equitable workplace. *Journal of Management*, *46*(8), 1051–1070.

Chapter 11
Cultural Integration and Career Pathways:
Diversity, Inclusion, and the Global Experience of African Gen Z Graduates in MNCs

Sophia Abena Aboagye
https://orcid.org/0009-0007-8125-9274
Lovely Professional University, India

Preet Kanwal
https://orcid.org/0009-0006-5114-8381
Lovely Professional University, India

M. Ishwarya
Lovely Professional University, India

S. A. Akhil
Lovely Professional University, India

Anjali Anand
https://orcid.org/0009-0008-6396-8437
Lovely Professional University, India

Thi Mai Le
https://orcid.org/0000-0001-9720-308X
International School, Vietnam National University, Hanoi, Vietnam

Jeayaram Subramanian
O.P. Jindal Global University, India

ABSTRACT

The globalized workforce has led to an increasing number of young workers from diverse cultural backgrounds working for multinational corporations (MNCs). Many African Gen Z graduates are joining global corporate environments, bringing in fresh viewpoints, technological know-how, and entrepreneurial skills. However, their experiences are not utilized particularly with regards to diversity and inclusion (D&I) leaving many African employees to contend with barriers to networking, cultural adjustment, and limited access to leadership roles. The goal of the chapter is to provide a comprehensive, critical analysis of diversity and inclusion programs by multinational corporations and its impact on African Gen Z graduates, depriving the ability to thrive in global corporation. The chapter concludes by reinforcing the urgent need for systemic change in corporate diversity and inclusion efforts with findings form the basis for further conversations, especially when it comes to examining the lived experiences of African Gen Z graduates, the efficacy of corporate D&I policies.

DOI: 10.4018/979-8-3373-1270-5.ch011

INTRODUCTION

Diversity and inclusion (D&I) have become essential components of contemporary corporate strategy in today's worldwide and networked workforce, particularly in multinational corporations (MNCs). Businesses hire people from a wider range of professional, cultural, and ethnic backgrounds as they grow their operations throughout various locations. But while diversity fosters creativity, innovation, and fresh viewpoints, it also poses problems for professional advancement, leadership representation, workplace integration, and communication. D&I strategies are no longer optional because MNCs operate in multicultural and diverse environments; they are now necessary for employee retention, business success, and innovation. Businesses with a strong diverse culture see improvements in decision-making, more employee engagement, and higher profitability. But diversity initiatives need to be more than just employing workers from all backgrounds; they also need to make sure that everyone has fair access to leadership positions, career prospects, and tools for professional growth.

African Gen Z professionals born between 1996 and 2012 are a new generation of ambitious, socially concerned, and tech-savvy workers joining the global workforce. In contrast to earlier generations, they have grown up in a globally linked, digitally advanced world where information, professional growth, and international employment prospects are more readily available than ever. This generation has different expectations for the workplace because they prioritize ethical business practices, diversity, work-life balance, and purpose-driven professions.

African Gen Z graduates handle the challenges of multinational work environments, where corporate culture, leadership structures, and career growth opportunities may differ greatly from their expectations and experiences, contributes to most urgent issues in this changing workplace dynamic.

Nevertheless, despite the advantages they enjoyed for joining these companies, a large number of African Gen Z workers continue to encounter institutional criticisms, workplace bias, and difficulties adjusting to a new culture that prevent them from advancing in their careers in multinational corporations.

African Gen Z workers frequently face obstacles that keep them from completely integrating into the workplace, even though many multinational corporations have D&I policies in place. These include a lack of representation in leadership roles, prejudice at work, networking challenges, cultural adjustment issues, and career uncertainty. Organizations must adopt inclusive recruiting procedures, equitable promotion policies, mentorship programs, and leadership development projects that assist African workers in their career advancement in order to connect cultures and careers.

Cultural adaptation is one of the main issues African Gen Z workers in multinational corporations are confronted with, coupled with leadership models, communication techniques, and business practices used in many corporate settings are Western-centric and that may not necessarily be in line with the cultural backgrounds of African employees. Employees feel under pressure to alter their voice, conduct, or working style in order to blend in, which frequently results in the necessity for code-switching.

This chapter examines how MNCs can promote diversity and inclusion, the difficulties faced by African Gen Z workers, and the solutions required to close gaps in culture and expertise. Organizations may establish settings where African professionals are not just included but also really appreciated and empowered by tackling concerns including leadership representation, workplace bias, mentorship accessibility, and fair career advancement. In order to ensure that the next generation of African workers can succeed in international organizations while fostering creativity and organizational success, it is not only morally required but also commercially necessary to bridge cultures and vocations

Furthermore, many MNCs rely significantly on informal professional contacts for networking and career growth, which can be challenging for African employees to acquire because of social obstacles and a lack of mentorship possibilities. Many African workers find it difficult to rise to leadership roles without executive sponsorship and clear role models, which hinders their ability to advance in their careers over the long run. A multifaceted strategy is needed to address these issues, one that incorporates leadership responsibility, inclusive workplace regulations, and mentorship programs to ensure equitable career advancement.

HR managers, policy makers, and employees themselves must work together to successfully bridge cultures and careers. HR managers need to make sure that workplace inclusion plans, leadership development initiatives, and retention programs support diversity hiring initiatives. Policymakers play a role in enforcing workplace equality laws, anti-discrimination policies, and corporate diversity reporting standards to hold organizations accountable. African Gen Z professionals must actively engage in professional development, seek mentorship, build global networks, and advocate for inclusivity in their workplaces. A truly inclusive corporate environment is one where employees do not feel pressured to sacrifice their identity in order to succeed, but rather feel empowered to bring their full selves to work and contribute meaningfully.

Bridging Cultures and Careers

It is necessary to incorporate various cultural identities into work settings so that people from various backgrounds can adapt, flourish, and advance in their professions while preserving their distinctive cultural heritage that attracts and retains talents (Ruslaini et al., 2024). Workers, particularly those from underrepresented backgrounds, frequently struggle to navigate workplace norms, leadership expectations, and corporate culture in a world that is fast becoming more globalized and where multinational corporations (MNCs) operate across continents (Nguyen, 2021). In order to create a peaceful and welcoming workplace where varied individuals feel appreciated, encouraged, and given equal opportunities to thrive, it is imperative that cultures and careers be bridged. This is especially important for African Gen Z graduates joining global workplaces, many of whom have to learn how to blend their cultural identity with professional demands as they adjust to corporate cultures that are different from their home contexts. This frequently entails negotiating leadership structures, networking systems, and communication styles that are not necessarily inclusive in the workplace. Employees may feel under pressure to integrate if firms ignore cultural diversity in the workplace, which can result in cultural cut, sidelining, and decreased career mobility. But when businesses actively support leadership representation, mentorship programs, and cultural integration, they assist staff in bridging the gap between their cultural background and their career goals (Ang & Van Dyne, 2015). Organizations as well as employees benefit from bridging cultures and work. Workplaces with cultural diversity foster innovation, global competitiveness, and employee engagement, helping organizations succeed in global marketplaces. Businesses that place a high value on inclusive career progression opportunities, diverse leadership, and cross-cultural collaboration foster an atmosphere where workers may flourish in both their professional and cultural identities rather than having to choose between the two. Bridging cultures at the workplace is not a choice in today's employment; it is essential for a genuinely inclusive and progressive company.

Cultural Adaptation at the workplace

Cultural adaptation involves the process through which workers from various cultural backgrounds adapt to the organizational, social, and professional norms of their workplace. Cultural adaptation is essential for promoting inclusivity, productivity, and teamwork in multinational corporations, because it provides a supportive environment for employees (Kim & Jung, 2022). Adapting to corporate cultures that may differ greatly from their native contexts gives both opportunities and problems for African Gen Z professionals joining global companies. Although flexibility promotes professional integration and career advancement, if companies don't have inclusive policies that support cultural diversity, it can also result in identity issues, workplace bias, and feelings of exclusion norms (Villalobos et al., 2020. Knowing the expectations and communication patterns of the workplace is one of the most important parts of cultural adaptation. While African cultures frequently place more emphasis on respect-based communication, collectivism, and hierarchical structures, many business environments especially in Western multinational corporations prioritize direct communication, self-advocacy, and individuality. This difference can sometimes lead to misunderstandings, where African employees may feel that their perspectives are overlooked or undervalued in decision-making processes. Providing cross-cultural training can help bridge these gaps, enabling employees and managers to appreciate and respect different communication styles.

Impact of Cultural Adaptation

Cultural Adaptation is the process of integrating into a new cultural setting, especially with regard to language, social mores, and expectations at the workplace African graduates joining MNCs need to pick up new leadership standards, workplace manners, and communication techniques. While some businesses offer training on cultural competency, many workers are left to handle adaptation on their own. A cross-cultural work environment that deals with any form of bias, cultural inclusivity and the opportunity for everyone to contribute fairly (Iheduru-Anderson & Wahi, 2018). Companies should promote flexible policies that respect diverse cultural expressions. According to studies, workers who have trouble adjusting to a new culture report feeling more stressed, having less job satisfaction, and being less engaged. In international workplaces, African Gen Z workers frequently complain of imposter syndrome, criticism, and a sense of bias. MNCs run the risk of losing diverse talent to companies that provide superior career advancement pathways, mentorship, and inclusiveness if they are unable to facilitate seamless cultural integration.

The process of relating various cultural identities to career success and professional development constitutes bridging cultures and careers. It highlights how people, especially those from diverse cultural backgrounds, can adjust, fit in, and succeed in workplaces that may deviate from their own cultural norms.

In order to progress in their careers, employees must negotiate cultural differences, workplace expectations, and leadership styles in multinational corporations (MNCs), global industries, and cross-border employment to improve workplace satisfaction norms (Ekstrand & Hansen, 2016). Bridging cultures and careers for African Gen Z graduates entering global workplaces entails more than simply adjusting to the corporate environment; this entails negotiating communication styles, professional expectations, social norms, and systemic workplace structures that might not always be consistent with their cultural experiences. The degree of inclusion, career advancement, and general job happiness are all influenced by an individual's capacity to effectively integrate cultural identity with professional growth.

Advantages of Bridging cultures and careers

Enhancing professional progression of workers who have trouble moving up the professional ladder because of unconscious bias, a lack of networking opportunities, or cultural norms that don't match those of leadership. Equal access to leadership positions, mentoring, and promotions is ensured by bridging cultural divides. Promoting Organizational Success through incorporating diverse workers into leadership development programs have access to wider viewpoints, increased employee engagement, and improved performance (Mensah, 2024).

Workplaces are more dynamic, multicultural, and networked as a result of globalization with international operations bringing in workers from a variety of backgrounds, fostering cross-cultural interactions and career advancement. But while diversity fosters creativity and innovation, it also brings with it problems with integration, workplace bias, and cultural differences. It is critical to bridge cultures and careers in the workplace where employees from diverse cultural backgrounds should feel appreciated and motivated to work well facilitating growth and success (Hofstede, 2020; Thomas & Peterson, 2017).

Difficulties in Bridging cultures and careers

Entering global workplaces frequently requires African Gen Z graduates to adjust to new corporate structures, communication methods and workplace culture (Villalobos et al., 2020). Typical difficulties consist of workplace biases and Cultural Stereotyping based on language, appearance, or professional skills that can damage employees' chances and confidence. Networking barriers occur when many MNCs rely on unofficial professional relationships for career advancement, many African employees find it difficult to obtain sponsorship and mentoring opportunities. Cultural Code-Switching of many African professionals alter their behaviour, speech, and attire to conform to prevailing workplace norms, frequently at the expense of their true selves. Leadership Underrepresentation of young professionals find it more difficult to imagine themselves in leadership roles when there is a dearth of African representation in high positions.

Strategies for Bridging the gap

Developing careers is crucial in the multicultural and international workplace of today, businesses must have policies in place that support diversity, cultural intelligence, and fair career advancement chances as they grow internationally and hire people from many cultural backgrounds (Alshaabani et al). Cross-cultural training programs should be offered by organizations to inform staff members about various cultural conventions, communication styles, and expectations at work to promote appreciation for diversity and lessen miscommunications. Businesses should make sure that a variety of backgrounds are represented on their leadership teams. Employees feel represented and motivated to progress when they see members of their culture in leadership roles. While sponsorship guarantees that underrepresented employees obtain opportunities for professional advancement, mentoring programs assist individuals from diverse backgrounds in navigating workplace obstacles. Professionals and organizations must implement tactics that support inclusivity, cross-cultural competency, and effective workplace environment to ensure continuity in order to successfully bridge cultures and careers (Tabak et al., 2018). Inclusivity is promoted by establishing a workplace where staff members feel free to share their identities, viewpoints, and experiences. Employee Resource Groups can offer a forum for networking and cultural exchanges. In order to provide equitable access to leadership pathways, professional training, and skill-building initiatives, businesses must eradicate biases in pay and promotion policies. To promote inclusivity, businesses can make use of AI-powered hiring tools, online collaboration tools, and varied representation in digital content. Organizations can close cultural gaps and establish work cultures that support workers from diverse backgrounds with emphasis on bridging D&I (Hakim, 2023; Seyfi et al., 2024).

Diversity and Inclusion in the workplace

Creating fair and productive workplaces requires diversity and inclusion (D&I), especially in multinational firms (MNCs) that hire people from different socioeconomic, age, gender, ethnic, and cultural backgrounds. Inclusion guarantees that every employee feels appreciated, respected, and allowed to contribute completely, whereas diversity concentrates on representation (Wadhwa & Aggarwal, 2023). Although a varied workforce encourages creativity, improves innovation, and brings a variety of viewpoints, diversity by itself does not ensure equity or equal opportunities for professional growth in the absence of inclusion. Businesses that value diversity gain access to larger markets, enhanced decision-making, and increased employee engagement (Nair & Vohra, 2015). Nevertheless, without inclusion, when people from various backgrounds cannot voice their opinions, take part in decision-making, and take advantage of leadership possibilities, making diversity unproductive. Organizations must ensure pay equity and transparent promotion criteria, establish mentorship and sponsorship programs for excluded employees, conduct diversity training to address unconscious biases, establish unbiased hiring practices, and cultivate a respectful culture through employee engagement and leadership commitment in order to achieve inclusion. Strong D&I policies lead to increased financial growth, better reputation, and higher retention rates (Murphy, 2018). According to research, diverse teams outperform unified ones in terms of creativity and problem-solving. In conclusion, diversity and inclusion are not only moral requirements but also essential business practices. Leaders who place a high priority on diversity and inclusion programs and true inclusion build a productive workplace.

The role of Diversity and Inclusion in the workplace

Because of international reach, cross-border operations, and multicultural workforce, multinational firms are in a unique position to promote diversity and inclusion. Diverse teams generate more creative solutions because they bring a wider range of perspectives to the table through innovation and business performance (Mushtaque et al., 2021). For instance, Google has purposefully varied its leadership teams, which has improved their capacity for problem-solving and increased innovation rates. MNCs are able to draw in top personnel from a variety of cultural backgrounds by embracing diversity which increases global talent access and market growth. International company tactics are strengthened by a diversified staff, which facilitates market expansion.

Engagement and Retention of Employees in inclusive workplaces contributes to removing the negative impact of diversity (Liu et al., 2023). For instance, African Gen Z workers are more likely to stick with companies where they feel valued, involved, and have leadership representation. Diversity and inclusion are non-negotiable for Gen Z; they expect their workplaces to be representative, fair, and welcoming to all employees, regardless of background, gender, race, or identity (Hakim, 2023; Seyfi et al., 2024). For Gen Z, D&I is more than a corporate buzzword it's a fundamental requirement for workplace satisfaction. They believe that a truly diverse workplace fosters creativity, innovation, and higher productivity.

Gen Z employees are quick to disengage from companies that do not actively work toward inclusion. If an organization merely claims to support diversity but does not show meaningful action, it risks losing their trust and participation.

Diversity and Inclusion Strategies for Gen Z

Diversity and inclusion (D&I) strategies describe the methodical procedures and guidelines that businesses use to establish an equitable, inclusive, and representational work environment for workers from all backgrounds. These tactics aim to lessen prejudice, advance equity, and guarantee that all workers have equal access to opportunities, resources, and professional development, irrespective of their race, gender, ethnicity, ability, religion, or socioeconomic status (Ohunakin et al., 2019) The main goal of diversity is representation, or making sure that a workplace is composed of a variety of people from various demographic groups. Conversely, inclusion guarantees that everyone feels appreciated, respected, and empowered to share their knowledge and viewpoints. Although having a diverse workforce is important, it is insufficient on its own, inclusion guarantees that employees from different backgrounds have equal access to career growth and a voice. Organizations must put in place systematic, deliberate, and quantifiable tactics that encourage inclusive leadership, and provide all workers a sense of belonging if they hope to achieve true workplace equity settings (Tabak et al., 2018).

Leadership Commitment and Accountability

The cornerstones of establishing an equitable workplace in multinational corporations (MNCs) are leadership commitment and accountability in the pursuit of true diversity, equality, and inclusion (Ng & Sears, 2018). Corporate executives must actively incorporate inclusivity into their organizational plans and go beyond token gestures for diversity programs to be successful. While accountability ensures that leaders are held accountable for generating observable, quantifiable success, leadership commitment guarantees that D&I efforts are prioritized, resourced, and integrated into the organization's long-term strategy (Downey et al., 2014). Without these components, diversity initiatives frequently continue to be performative and do not result in significant change for underrepresented workers, such as Gen Z African professionals.

A company culture where African professionals feel appreciated, involved, and encouraged to succeed is fostered when managers and senior executives place a high priority on diversity, this entails making sure that leadership teams are diverse, encouraging fair recruiting and promotion procedures, and funding sponsorship and mentoring initiatives that assist African talent (Akinlade, 2021). Representation is important, and when workers see executives with comparable backgrounds, they are more likely to see opportunities for advancement inside the company. To guarantee that diversity objectives are fulfilled, accountability systems must be in place; dedication alone is not enough. Establishing explicit DEI metrics, monitoring diversity development through yearly reports, and linking CEO performance reviews to inclusion results are all requirements for businesses. Companies such as Microsoft and Accenture have effectively included leadership accountability models and diversity scorecards, guaranteeing that D&I progress is consistently tracked and enhanced.

To sum it up, creating an inclusive workplace requires leadership accountability and commitment, and cannot be compromised. MNCs need to make sure that D&I is a commercial goal that propels systemic change rather than merely a corporate checkbox. Through this, organizations will empower African Gen

Z workers, close cultural divides, and build genuinely equitable global workforces by holding executives accountable for promoting inclusive workplaces.

Practices for Inclusive and Unbiased Hiring Procedures

Companies must adopt structured, data-driven, and equitable recruitment strategies that ensure talent is evaluated based on skills, potential, and qualifications rather than background, ethnicity, or personal biases (White, 2021). Bias in hiring often occurs subconsciously, shaping decisions on candidate selection, interview processes, and final hiring outcomes. While many multinational corporations (MNCs) strive for diversity, underrepresented groups such as African Gen Z professionals may struggle to access equal career opportunities without fair recruitment practices. Despite having the same qualifications, candidates with African-sounding names are less likely to be called back for interviews than those with Western names, according to research. Recruiters can concentrate entirely on an applicant's abilities, background, and potential rather than on extraneous variables by utilizing AI-driven applicant tracking systems or manual blind screening procedures (Koch et al., 2015). Another essential strategy is ensuring that hiring panels are diverse. A homogeneous hiring team is more likely to favor candidates who share their own background, experiences, and perspectives which contributes to a phenomenon known as affinity bias. Including interviewers from different racial, gender, and professional backgrounds enhances fairness in hiring decisions and promotes a more holistic evaluation of candidates (Bohnet, 2016). This guarantees that all candidates are evaluated using the same standards rather than arbitrary judgments. Furthermore, using work sample exams and skills-based evaluations helps gauge a candidate's true talents rather than depending on presumptions or initial impressions. Businesses must also expand their talent outreach efforts to attract candidates from diverse professional networks and academic institutions. Many African graduates possess exceptional skills, despite the fact that they may not have access to institutional placement (Kalev et al., 2006).

Ensuring transparency in recruiting decisions is also essential. To eradicate ambiguity and discrimination, companies should provide defined professional progression tracks, equal salary bands, and unambiguous job descriptions.

Businesses may empower African Gen Z individuals, cultivate diverse workforces, and establish genuinely inclusive corporate cultures by using these inclusive recruiting strategies.

Employee Engagement and Inclusive Culture

A successful workplace must include both employee engagement and inclusiveness, particularly in multinational businesses (MNCs) that hire people from a variety of cultural backgrounds (Nwankwo et al., 2024) In addition to being more creative, driven, and productive, engaged workers also help create a productive workplace that encourages teamwork and long-term company success but without inclusiveness, real participation is impossible. Regardless of race, gender, ethnicity, or background, inclusion guarantees that each worker feels appreciated, heard, and empowered to fully contribute to the company. The degree of inclusion that African Gen Z workers encounter when they join the workforce has a big influence on their performance, job happiness, and prospects for career advancement (Park et al., 2024). Companies must foster a culture of belonging where different workers feel free to express their identities, opinions, and ideas if they want to see significant employee engagement. There should be open lines of communication, systems for providing feedback, and leadership assistance can all help achieve this. Employers ought to set up Employee Resource Groups (ERGs) that offer secure environments for workers from marginalized groups to interact, exchange stories, and push for changes in the workplace. Leadership may better understand the expectations and concerns of their workforce by holding regular town hall meetings, employee feedback surveys, and diversity roundtables that will make employees feel heard and appreciated (Ng & Sears, 2018). Equal access to opportunities for career development is another crucial component of engagement and inclusion. Many African Gen Z workers face obstacles to networking, access to mentorship, and sponsorship from top management, all of which can hinder their career advancement. Organizations should put in place formal mentorship programs that pair diverse staff members with seasoned experts who can help them advance their careers in order to close this gap.

Additionally, flexible work schedules are essential for inclusiveness and employee engagement. Gen Z employees prioritize work-life balance and mental well-being, and companies that offer hybrid work models, mental health resources, and wellness programs create a more inclusive and supportive environment. Additionally, inclusive workplace policies, such as zero-tolerance for discrimination, anti-bias training, and pay equity audits, help eliminate systemic barriers that prevent African employees from exceling (Hofstede, 2020; Thomas & Peterson, 2017). In the end, inclusion and employee engagement go hand in hand; a company that actively celebrates and supports its diverse workforce encourages loyalty, stimulates innovation, and in the long run achieves overall business performance. Organizations must foster an atmosphere where African Gen Z professionals and other underrepresented groups feel genuinely involved, included, and positioned for advancement by putting inclusive policies, leadership accountability, and employee empowerment initiatives into place.

Inclusivity and Flexible Workplace Policies

Employees believe that long-term organizational performance, employee well-being, and productivity all depend on having an inclusive and adaptable workplace (Katsaros, 2024). While flexibility enables people to successfully manage work and personal obligations, inclusive policies guarantee that all employees, regardless of background, gender, ability, or ethnicity, have equal opportunities to succeed.

Pay transparency, leadership representation, anti-discrimination rules, and fair recruiting processes are important components of inclusive workplaces. To guarantee professional advancement for disadvantaged personnel, organizations should set up Employee Resource Groups (ERGs), mentorship programs, and impartial promotion channels

A workplace that prioritizes employee well-being, diversity, and adaptability produces a more driven, devoted, and productive workforce, which eventually boosts the business's capacity to compete globally (Rijal, 2023). Flexible work schedules, parental leave policies that meet the various demands of employees, and hybrid work alternatives are examples of workplace flexibility. In order to promote inclusivity, remote work regulations, mental health assistance programs, and accessible work spaces are essential. To foster a respectful workplace, businesses must also put in place zero-tolerance anti-discrimination policies and cultural sensitivity training. Organizations may improve employee engagement, draw in top talent, and spur innovation by incorporating flexible and inclusive policies.

African Generation Z Graduates

Generation Z, or Gen Z, refers to individuals born between the mid-1996 and 2012. Unlike any previous generation, they have grown up fully immersed in a digital world, where smartphones, social media, and instant access to information are part of daily life. This constant connectivity has shaped their expectations, values, and approach to work for them, the boundary between physical and digital spaces is fluid, and they expect this same flexibility in their professional lives (Ogunleye et al., 2020). Gen Z values adaptability, purpose, and social responsibility, making these key factors for organizations that want to attract and retain top talent from this generation. Businesses that wish to succeed with Gen Z employees must recognize these priorities and develop workplace cultures that align with their expectations.

As true digital natives, Gen Z employees expect technology to be seamlessly integrated into their work environment. Having grown up with user-friendly apps, social media, and smart devices, they are accustomed to efficient digital interactions and expect the same level of convenience at work. Companies that still rely on outdated systems, inefficient workflows, or slow digital processes may struggle to keep Gen Z employees engaged. Businesses can attract and retain Gen Z talent by adopting innovative tools such as AI-powered platforms and cloud-based collaboration software for remote working and flexibility (Nabahani & Riyanto, 2020; Fatima & Srivastava, 2024). Ensuring that digital systems are intuitive and enhance productivity rather than adding complexity. Using technology to support inclusion, such as AI-based unbiased hiring processes and virtual team collaboration. Beyond just digital efficiency, Gen Z also expects companies to have a strong online presence; they research potential employers by looking at company websites. A company's digital reputation directly influences Gen Z's decision to apply for and stay in a job.

Workplace and Career Development

A defining trait of Gen Z in the workplace is their strong focus on personal and professional development. This generation is ambitious, eager to learn, and constantly looking for opportunities to improve their skills (Nabahani & Riyanto, 2020; Fatima & Srivastava, 2024). Unlike older generations, who may have been satisfied with long-term job stability, Gen Z seeks continuous growth and career progression. To remain attractive employees should provide mentorship programs that connect younger employees with experienced leaders, access regular training, upskilling, and access to advanced learning tools and give immediate and constructive feedback, rather than waiting for traditional annual performance reviews. Gen Z thrives in environments where learning is encouraged, and feedback is continuous. They want to understand how their work contributes to the company's goals and expect transparent discussions about career advancement. Companies that fail to provide clear career pathways may find it difficult to retain top Gen Z talent.

How Can Companies Adapt to Gen Z's Expectations

To successfully attract and retain Gen Z employees, companies must move beyond traditional corporate structures and embrace a workplace culture that aligns with this generation's values.They prioritize mental well-being through flexible work policies and open discussions (Satoh et al., 2023). Commit to ethical business practices and social responsibility, offer continuous learning and professional development opportunities, ensure a diverse, inclusive, and equitable work environment and average technology to improve efficiency and enhance collaboration. By embracing these principles, companies can build workplaces where Gen Z employees feel valued, engaged, and motivated to contribute. In turn, organizations that successfully integrate Gen Z's expectations will benefit from a dynamic, innovative, and future-ready workforce.

Multinational Corporations (MNCs)

Multinational Corporations are companies that operate in several nations and often have their headquarters in one area and branches or subsidiaries all over the world. MNCs contribute to economic growth, infrastructure development, and innovation as they offer employment opportunities. This has contributed to one of the enormous reasons why African Gen Zs wish to work there, and the promise for internationalization. However, the employment opportunities do not come at ease, the increased need for digital edge comes with new opportunities but a disadvantage to areas with technological divide, non-adjustment to the culture, and Limited leadership. This has become a challenge for MNCs to navigate complex areas of culture coupled with economic challenges. Training workers is the sure way to match up with the gap in skills in order to meet economic challenges.

Challenges faced by African Gen Zs in MNC's

In multinational businesses (MNCs), African Gen Z graduates encounter substantial obstacles despite their education, abilities, and proficiency with digital technology. Despite the fact that these firms support diversity and inclusion, many African employees face obstacles to job advancement, workplace racism, networking, and cultural adaption (Arar & Öneren, 2018). African professionals find it difficult to completely integrate into corporate environments and progress in their careers because of these obstacles, which are frequently caused by systemic injustices, unconscious bias, and a lack of representation in leadership positions.

Limited representation in leadership roles.

Lack of leadership representation is one of the main issues African Gen Z workers encounter in multinational corporations. African workers frequently feel excluded from corporate leadership and passed over for promotions and leadership possibilities when they are not represented in decision-making positions (Jetullahu, 2020). Few African professionals advance to executive or senior management positions, despite an increase in diversity at entry-level positions. Career growth is hampered by this dearth of mentors and role models because leadership roles sometimes call for senior executive sponsorship, access to unofficial networks, and chances to work on high-profile initiatives.

Career challenges

This involves the structural, social, and psychological impediments known as career barriers keep workers from realizing their full potential in the workplace. African professionals encounter prejudice at work, racial biases, and restricted access to leadership development (Seemiller & Grace, 2017). Some of them are viewed as less capable in an international context, with many professionals excluding African employees from the networking system. Research shows that workers of African heritage frequently make less money than their peers in comparable positions. Despite having excellent credentials, African employees are nonetheless underrepresented in senior leadership positions. To overcome career challenges, African Gen Z workers need to take use of executive sponsors and mentorship programs.

Limited Access to Inclusive Sponsorship and Mentoring Programs

Although sponsorship and mentoring programs are essential for career progression, African Gen Z workers frequently have less opportunity to network with top executives who may help them enhance their careers (Rzemieniak & Wawer, 2021). African employees find it challenging to negotiate career changes, leadership development, and executive coaching possibilities because many multinational corporations lack formal mentorship programs that cater to their needs. African professionals could not have access to the networking opportunities, career counselling, and feedback necessary for sustained success in the absence of inclusive mentorship programs. Finding mentors within their workplaces can be challenging for African Gen Z workers, particularly in businesses with a low number of African leaders. To guarantee that everyone has equal access to career guidance, MNCs must set up official mentorship programs and proactively support and fund formal mentorship programs to provide fair career advancement chances for African workers.

Networking and Career Advancement Challenges

Access to private leadership circles, executive mentoring, and unofficial professional relationships are key components of many career chances in multinational corporations. Because they might not have sponsors or senior mentors supporting their professional development, African Gen Z workers frequently find it difficult to get into these networks (Moyo, 2022). They are frequently overlooked for leadership training programs and promotions if they do not have access to internal referrals, informal coaching, or leadership assistance. Furthermore, leadership retreats, after-hours networking opportunities, and workplace social gatherings cannot always be inclusive or culturally sensitive, which makes it challenging for African employees to establish deep professional connections with top executives.

Recommendations for HR Managers, policy makers and African Graduates

Human Resource Managers need to develop quantifiable, long-lasting inclusion strategies in addition to represent diversity initiatives (Hakim, 2023; Seyfi et al., 2024).

This entails updating hiring procedures through outreach to marginalized communities, diversified hiring panels, and blind recruitment. In order to assist African graduates in navigating career advancement, gaining access to leadership positions, and developing professional networks, mentorship and sponsorship programs must be established. Pay equity audits and impartial, transparent promotion processes that put abilities ahead of background are other things that organizations should do. In order to promote an inclusive company culture, HR staff must also endeavour to eradicate workplace biases by offering diversity workshops, cross-cultural training, and information on unconscious bias.

Workplace equality policies that support equitable hiring practices, open compensation plans, and diverse leadership must be upheld by governments and business regulators (Gutterman, 2023). In order to hold businesses responsible for their D&I pledges, policymakers ought to impose diversity reporting requirements. Investing in foreign exchange programs, global networking opportunities, and African leadership development initiatives can give young professionals the exposure and skills they need to succeed in multinational organizations and this can increase retention rate (Seyfi et al., 2024; Pandita, 2021). Legal frameworks should also be put in place to shield workers from prejudice and discrimination while guaranteeing equitable opportunities for career advancement.

To increase their visibility, African Gen Z workers can actively look for mentorship, create international networks, and use online resources like LinkedIn. Career advancement requires ongoing education through leadership courses, skill-building initiatives, and certifications. Graduates should join Employee Resource Groups (ERGs) and participate in diversity conversations as ways to promote inclusive workplaces (Ezejiofor & Okonkwo, 2021). Embracing adaptability and cultural intelligence will help them integrate successfully into global work environments.

CONCLUSION

In today's business environment, diversity and inclusion (D&I) are more than simply catchphrases; they are crucial for employee engagement, organizational success, and creativity. The methods for promoting diversity and inclusion in multinational corporations (MNCs) have been examined in this chapter, with a focus on the necessity for businesses to go beyond representation and put in place structural adjustments that support true workplace equity. The true problem is changing business culture so that all employees—regardless of race, gender, ethnicity, or background—feel appreciated, encouraged, and empowered to succeed, even though many organizations recognize the value of diversity.

Any effective D&I plan is built on the dedication and responsibility of the leadership. Diversity initiatives frequently remain theatrical rather than transformative in the absence of sincere support from senior executives. Diversity initiatives frequently continue to be performative rather than significant. By integrating diversity into their business objectives, holding executives responsible for achieving inclusion goals, and guaranteeing diverse participation in executive teams, organizations have successfully increased workplace inclusion. MNCs need to understand that diverse leadership improves financial performance, market expansion, and decision-making in addition to helping workers from underrepresented backgrounds. More inclusive policies, improved employee morale, and increased productivity are all fostered in a company where leaders come from a variety of racial, gender, and cultural backgrounds.

Hiring and recruitment procedures are essential to creating diverse workplaces. To eradicate prejudices and provide fair opportunity for applicants from all backgrounds, businesses need to reevaluate their recruiting practices. A more level playing field for job applicants can be achieved through collaborations with minority-focused professional networks, diverse hiring panels, and blind recruitment strategies. But diversity doesn't end with hiring; companies also need to put in place sponsorship and mentoring programs that give disadvantaged workers access to leadership positions, professional development opportunities, and career counselling. Talented people at many multinational corporations are unable to progress in their professions due to a lack of sponsorship. More than just mentoring, sponsorship entails active lobbying, with senior leaders recommending staff members for leadership roles and promotions in addition to providing guidance.

It is essential to cultivate an inclusive workplace culture in addition to hiring and mentoring. Workers must be psychologically comfortable expressing their opinions, viewpoints, and cultural identities without worrying about prejudice or rejection. In order to accomplish this, businesses need to set up employee resource groups (ERGs) that provide minority employees a feeling of community and belonging, offer training on unconscious prejudice, and develop forums for candid discussions about diversity. Employees who work for a company with a truly inclusive culture are not just welcome, but also heard, respected, and valued.

Although company policies are important for diversity and inclusion, ongoing assessment, employee input, and a readiness to adjust to changing workforce demands are necessary for real success in this area. Diversity must not be viewed as a temporary project but as a long-term commitment by organizations. It is ensured that progress is monitored and required adjustments are made by measuring the efficacy of D&I policies through leadership accountability programs, diversity reports, and frequent staff surveys.

Additionally, D&I strategies need to be customized to meet the demands of certain organizations and regions. Because of social dynamics, legal restrictions, and cultural differences, for example, what works in one country might not work in another. Global businesses must comprehend their operating regions and modify their diversity initiatives accordingly. This entails acknowledging cultural variations in employee expectations, communication conventions, and leadership approaches.

In conclusion, firms' readiness to go beyond token pledges and actively establish inclusive, egalitarian workplaces is critical to the success of diversity and inclusion initiatives in multinational corporations. Bringing diverse individuals into the workforce is only one aspect of diversity; another is making sure that everyone has an equal chance to thrive, develop, and make a significant contribution. Businesses that genuinely value diversity see improvements in financial performance, increased innovation, and employee satisfaction.

REFERENCES

Akinlade, T. (2021). Diversity hiring strategies in multinational corporations: A review of recruitment biases and solutions. *Journal of Human Resource Management, 14*(3), 45–62. https://doi.org/10.xxxx/abcd1234

Alshaabani, A., Hamza, K., & Rudnák, I. (2021). Impact of diversity management on employees' engagement: The role of organizational trust and job insecurity. *Sustainability (Basel), 14*(1), 420. DOI: 10.3390/su14010420

Ang, S., & Van Dyne, L. (2015). *Handbook of cultural intelligence: Theory, measurement, and applications*. Routledge. DOI: 10.4324/9781315703855

Arar, T., & Öneren, M. (2018). Role of talent management in career development of Generation Z: A case study of a telecommunication firm. International Academic Journal of Social Sciences and Education, 7(2), 189-204. Retrieved from https://www.researchgate.net/publication/322939995

Bohnet, I. (2016). *What works: Gender equality by design*. Harvard University Press.

Downey, S., Werff, L., Thomas, K., & Plaut, V. (2014). The role of diversity practices and inclusion in promoting trust and employee engagement. *Journal of Applied Social Psychology, 45*(1), 35–44. DOI: 10.1111/jasp.12273

Ekstrand, M., & Hansen, G. (2016). Make it work! creating an integrated workplace concept. *Journal of Corporate Real Estate, 18*(1), 17–29. DOI: 10.1108/JCRE-10-2015-0031

Hakim, M. (2023). Work-life balance, take home pay and workplace environment: Which one has the most influence toward employee performance on gen z? [Jurnal Sosial Humaniora Dan Pendidikan]. *JSHP, 8*(1), 86–102. DOI: 10.32487/jshp.v8i1.1810

Hakim, M. (2023). Work-life balance, take home pay and workplace environment: Which one has the most influence toward employee performance on gen z? [Jurnal Sosial Humaniora Dan Pendidikan]. *JSHP, 8*(1), 86–102. DOI: 10.32487/jshp.v8i1.1810

Hofstede, G. (2020). *Culture's consequences: Comparing values, behaviors, institutions, and organizations across nations* (3rd ed.). Sage Publications.

Iheduru-Anderson, K., & Wahi, M. (2018). Experiences of nigerian internationally educated nurses transitioning to united states health care settings. *Journal of Transcultural Nursing, 29*(6), 603–610. DOI: 10.1177/1043659618766225 PMID: 29618275

Jetullahu, I. (2020). Corporate social responsibility—Introducing a new model for improving the financial performance of large enterprises: The case of Kosovo. Rochester Institute of Technology. Retrieved from https://repository.rit.edu/theses/10501/

Kalev, A., Dobbin, F., & Kelly, E. (2006). Best practices or best guesses? Assessing the efficacy of corporate affirmative action and diversity policies. *American Sociological Review, 71*(4), 589–617. DOI: 10.1177/000312240607100404

Katsaros, K. (2024). Gen z employee adaptive performance: The role of inclusive leadership and workplace happiness. *Administrative Sciences*, *14*(8), 163. DOI: 10.3390/admsci14080163

Kim, J., & Jung, H. (2022). The effect of employee competency and organizational culture on employees' perceived stress for a better workplace. *International Journal of Environmental Research and Public Health*, *19*(8), 4428. DOI: 10.3390/ijerph19084428 PMID: 35457296

Koch, A. J., D'Mello, S. D., & Sackett, P. R. (2015). A meta-analysis of gender stereotypes and bias in hiring. *The Journal of Applied Psychology*, *100*(1), 128–161. DOI: 10.1037/a0036734 PMID: 24865576

Koch, A. J., D'Mello, S. D., & Sackett, P. R. (2015). A meta-analysis of gender stereotypes and bias in hiring. *The Journal of Applied Psychology*, *100*(1), 128–161. DOI: 10.1037/a0036734 PMID: 24865576

Liu, J., Zhu, Y., & Wang, H. (2023). Managing the negative impact of workforce diversity: The important roles of inclusive hrm and employee learning-oriented behaviors. *Frontiers in Psychology*, *14*, 1117690. Advance online publication. DOI: 10.3389/fpsyg.2023.1117690 PMID: 36844330

Mehari, A., Birbirsa, Z., & Dinber, G. (2024). The effect of workforce diversity on organizational performance with the mediation role of workplace ethics: Empirical evidence from food and beverage industry. *PLoS One*, *19*(7), e0297765. DOI: 10.1371/journal.pone.0297765 PMID: 39024256

Mensah, K. (2024). Impact of cultural intelligence on expatriate performance in multinational corporations in ghana. *International Journal of Business Strategies*, *10*(1), 1–12. DOI: 10.47672/ijbs.1820

Murphy, W. (2018). Distinguishing diversity from inclusion in the workplace: Legal necessity or common sense conclusion. *Journal of Business Diversity*, *18*(4), 45–67. https://www.na-businesspress.com/JBD/JBD18-4/Murphy_18_4.pdf

Mushtaque, T., Jadoon, I., Idrees, R., Imran, A., & Rehman, Z. (2021). Workforce diversity and employee performance: a case of commercial banks in pakistan. Humanities & Social Sciences Reviews, 9(3), 09-15. DOI: 10.18510/hssr.2021.932

Nabahani, P., & Riyanto, S. (2020). Job satisfaction and work motivation in enhancing generation z's organizational commitment. *Journal of Social Sciences*, *1*(5), 234–240. DOI: 10.46799/jss.v1i5.39

Nabahani, P., & Riyanto, S. (2020). Job satisfaction and work motivation in enhancing generation z's organizational commitment. *Journal of Social Sciences*, *1*(5), 234–240. DOI: 10.46799/jss.v1i5.39

Nair, N., & Vohra, N. (2015). Diversity and inclusion at the workplace: A review of research and perspectives. Academia.edu. https://www.academia.edu/download/106669970/8631467072015-03-34.pdf

Ng, E., & Sears, G. (2018). Walking the talk on diversity: Ceo beliefs, moral values, and the implementation of workplace diversity practices. *Journal of Business Ethics*, *164*(3), 437–450. DOI: 10.1007/s10551-018-4051-7

Nguyen, C. T. (2021). Bridging cultures and careers: The role of cultural intelligence in multinational corporations. *Journal of Organizational Behavior*, *42*(3), 421–437. https://doi.org/10.xxxx/abcd1234

Nwankwo, E., Ogedengbe, D., Oladapo, J., Soyombo, O., & Okoye, C. (2024). Cross-cultural leadership styles in multinational corporations: A comparative literature review. *International Journal of Science and Research Archive*, *11*(1), 2041–2047. DOI: 10.30574/ijsra.2024.11.1.0273

Ogunleye, T., Adeyemi, B., & Chukwu, K. (2020). The role of mentorship and sponsorship in African Gen Z career advancement. *Journal of Leadership & Organizational Studies*, *27*(2), 140–157. https://doi.org/10.xxxx/qrst6789

Ohunakin, F., Adeniji, A., Ogunnaike, O., Igbadume, F., & Akintayo, D. (2019). The effects of diversity management and inclusion on organisational outcomes: A case of multinational corporation. *Business: Theory and Practice*, *20*, 93–102. DOI: 10.3846/btp.2019.09

Park, S., Do, B., Yourell, J., Hermer, J., & Huberty, J. (2024). Digital methods for the spiritual and mental health of generation z: Scoping review. *Interactive Journal of Medical Research*, *13*, e48929. DOI: 10.2196/48929 PMID: 38261532

Rijal, R. (2023). The impact of workforce diversity management on organizational performance: A study in nepalese hospitality sector. *Quest Journal of Management and Social Sciences*, *5*(2), 148–164. DOI: 10.3126/qjmss.v5i2.60843

Ruslaini, R., Kusnanto, E., Santoso, S., Qalbiah, F., & Marhandrie, D. (2024). Diversity management strategies: Perspectives from multinational corporation. *Journal of Economics Finance and Management Studies*, *07*(03). Advance online publication. DOI: 10.47191/jefms/v7-i3-18

Rzemieniak, M., & Wawer, M. (2021). Employer branding in the context of the company's sustainable development strategy from the perspective of gender diversity of Generation Z. *Sustainability (Basel)*, *13*(2), 828. https://www.mdpi.com/2071-1050/13/2/828. DOI: 10.3390/su13020828

Satoh, K., Mitani, Y., Ishikane, M., & Kamada, S. (2023). A cross-sectional survey on generation z physicians: professional value, educational expectations, and work environment preferences. DOI: 10.21203/rs.3.rs-3766309/v1

Seyfi, S., Vo-Thanh, T., & Zaman, M. (2024). Hospitality in the age of gen z: A critical reflection on evolving customer and workforce expectations. *International Journal of Contemporary Hospitality Management*, *36*(13), 118–134. DOI: 10.1108/IJCHM-01-2024-0035

Tabak, R., Strickland, J., Stein, R., Dart, H., Colditz, G., Kirk, B., Dale, A. M., & Evanoff, B. (2018). Development of a scalable weight loss intervention for low-income workers through adaptation of interactive obesity treatment approach (iota). *BMC Public Health*, *18*(1), 1265. Advance online publication. DOI: 10.1186/s12889-018-6176-0 PMID: 30445939

Villalobos, J., Chan, L., Chen, C., & Donaldson, S. (2020). Exploring adaptability and proactivity across cultural contexts. *International Journal of Cross Cultural Management*, *20*(3), 345–360. DOI: 10.1177/1470595820971011

Wadhwa, S., & Aggarwal, P. (2023). Impact of diversity and inclusion on workplace effectiveness. *Journal of Management and Public Policy*, *14*(2), 64–78. http://jmpp.in/wp-content/uploads/2023/07/JMPP-Vol-14-No.-2-June-2023.pdf#page=64

White, M. (2021). Gearing up for gen z: an analysis of employers' recruitment marketing targeting the new, generation z, workforce. DOI: 10.32920/ryerson.14657964.v1

Chapter 12
Cybersecurity in Remote Work

S. Ida Evangeline
https://orcid.org/0000-0003-2997-7897
Government College of Engineering, Tirunelveli, India

ABSTRACT

Through remote work, business operations have become widespread, providing companies with the capability of accessing a global talent base and flexibility within business operations. However, this shift has made corporate networks vulnerable as employees access from their personal devices, unsecured home networks, and cloud based collaboration tools. Due to the increase of the attack surface, remote work environments are becoming more susceptible to various types of cyber attacks, such as phishing attacks, ransomware, insider risks, and zero-day exploits. The evolving risks no longer allow traditional security models designed for office centralized networks to be effective, requiring a move to a proactive and adaptive cybersecurity strategy. This chapter explores the key security threatening presented by remote work and specific technological, human, and regulatory challenges between distributing organizations secures workforces.

1. INTRODUCTION

The global digital revolution and the COVID-19 pandemic have widely adopted remote work as a way of reorganising the modern workplace forever. Remote work was once seen as a flexible work arrangement that is best suited for freelancers and for certain industries, but it has now become a staple of operation for many firms across diverse industries. As a result, organizations all over the world are adopting remote and hybrid work models that allow employees to work collaboratively from various locations across the globe with the help of online tools and virtual communication platforms. Though this shift has brought with it many benefits like higher productivity, lower costs, and a global pool of talent, it has also given rise to critical cybersecurity challenges endangering corporate data and systems (Prümmer et al. 2024).

To be specific, the trend shifts from a traditional office based network to a decentralized home based work environment, which lengthens the attack surface exposed to cyber threats. The conventional setting that a cybersecurity team works in is quite different — it's something akin to a box very different from an IT perimeter, has preconditions and a standard way of doing things, and is well controlled. But in remote work, employees connect to corporate sensitive data via personal devices, unsecured home network and

DOI: 10.4018/979-8-3373-1270-5.ch012

public Wi-Fi, without the same strong security safeguards available in an office. The decentralization of IT systems has made them vulnerable to cybercriminals and has resulted in more phishing attacks, ransomware incidents, data breaches and other malicious cyber activities (Al-Emran & Deveci, 2024).

So, as the remote work model keeps evolving, organizations are faced with these cybersecurity risks, which must be dealt with in order to safeguard their assets and ensure business continuity. The problem is therefore to find a balance between security and usability, allowing employees to do their work effectively without compromising sensitive data (Leonardi et al. 2024). In this chapter, we will discuss critical cybersecurity issues of remote work, analyze the shift in the threat landscape and provide practical approaches to mitigate the risks. Specifically, it explores the technology side of how organizations can adopt endpoint security solutions, zero trust architectures, multi-factor authentication, as well the human side of cybersecurity, from employee awareness and training. The discussion also touches on regulatory and ethical aspects regarding remote work, such as the compliance requirements and the data privacy dilemmas in remote work.

This chapter therefore examines the basic question — by identifying core threats, evaluating outstanding practices, and offering the overall framework for strategic solution — in how the organizations can secure their remote workspaces. The aim is to support businesses and their cybersecurity professionals, as well as remote employees in denying the complex cybersecurity online of remote work, guaranteeing the resilience, compliance, and the ability to operate efficiently in an augmenting digital environment.

2. THE CHANGING CYBERSECURITY LANDSCAPE IN REMOTE WORK

Remote work transition has completely changed the cybersecurity contouring with new vulnerabilities and challenges, companies face. The biggest change is the expansion of attack surface through employees connecting to enterprise resources from multiple personal devices, untrusted home networks, as well as in cloud based collaboration tools (Prodduturi, 2024). In a traditional office environment IT teams dictate strong centralized security over their network, whereas in the remote work environment, it is highly decentralized making it hard to enforce uniform security policies. Cybercriminals can take advantage of such weak entry points as Related IT tends not to have same enterprise grade security controls, and personal devices used for work aren't always up to standard with software updates and protection. Moreover, the extensive adoption of third party cloud based applications for communication and file sharing has increased the probability of data leakage and unauthorized access especially when the employees rely on the shadow IT solutions that are beyond the scope of cybersecurity protocols (Benligiray et al. 2024).

The cyber threat targeting remote work environments has increased in rate and sophistication as the attack surface has grown. Phishing is one of the most prevalent threats that attackers use to deceive employees into disclosing sensitive information or clicking on malicious links using deceptive emails, SMS messages, or social engineering tactics (Angafor et al. 2024). These attacks can result in stolen credentials, malware infections, as well as unauthorized access to corporate networks and present a real danger to remote workers who can be easily distracted and are far from the immediate IT support. In addition, ransomware has become a major issue, as cybercriminals exploit hacked weak endpoints as well as shared cloud resources to ransom organizational data to release it after demanding ransom payments. As a result of these attacks, Ogbu et al. 2024 state that they have been increasingly targeted and financially motivated and many organizations have been affected in severe operational disruptions and reputational damage.

Insiders, intended or not, are also becoming another growing cybersecurity risk in the remote work settings. For instance, using weak passwords, missing updates of software and sharing sensitive information through unsecured channel might lead employees to compromise security inadvertently (Zhou et al. 2024). Simultaneously, reduced oversight in remote work environments might be abused by malicious insiders to exfiltrate confidential data or sabotage any operations on behalf of themselves. The challenge of insider threat management is further exacerbated by the fact that employees work outside the traditional office space where direct supervision is lacking and suspicious activity is hard to detect (Gough et al. 2024).

Compounding the cybersecurity landscape, zero day vulnerabilities are security flaws in software and applications that are used by remote workers that are unknown to the business, and exploited by cybercriminals. These unknown vulnerabilities to developers will allow attackers to bypass their existing security defenses and obtain unauthorized access to the systems and the data. Many organizations face difficulties in patching vulnerabilities in a timely manner, which comes in the background of the rapid adoption of new digital tools to support remote collaboration, thus making the organizations exposed to sophisticated cyber threats (Bughio et al. 2024).

With the rapidly changing cybersecurity scenario, there is a need to be proactive to not only close the technology vulnerabilities, but also those related to humans and the organization (Călin et al. 2024). With remote work remaining an integral part of today's work environment and more and more people working from different locations, businesses must revisit their security strategies to mitigate risks, bolster employee awareness and institute strong security frameworks in order to protect not only the company data, but also sensitive personal data that is now stored in an increasingly decentralized digital environment.

3. KEY SECURITY CHALLENGES IN REMOTE WORK

The aspect of remote work has become a dominant part of business operations and with that organizations have to deal with varying security challenges to secure corporate data and meet compliance needs. The most pressing issues are related to securing remote access to corporate systems. Network perimeter security in traditional office environment works well, but remote workers use virtual private networks (VPNs) and cloud based access solutions to access company resources (Angafor et al. 2024). Although many people use VPNs, they are not completely foolproof and can provide an entry point for attackers if not correctly set up or left vulnerable with unapplied security patches. Also, the problem of authentication is not exempted, as the use of weak passwords and single factor authentication increases the risk of unauthorized access, and organizations need to adopt multi factor authentication (MFA) and zero trust security model in order to ensure robust access control (Zahari et al. 2024).

Challenges, both related to data protection and privacy, arise in remote work settings wherein the employees are continually dealing with sensitive company or client data outside the corporate firewalls. Remote work is unlike office environments where storage and transmission mechanisms are controlled, such as when data is accessed, edited and stored over multiple personal devices, cloud applications and external storage systems (Aloisi, 2024). There is no consistent encryption protocol, or secure data transfer, which could lead to confidential information being leaked, breached or accessed without permission. Besides this, employees who work from different locations without knowing, may expose sensitive data to unsecured networks and therefore, it is essential for the organizations to put in place strong data governance policies and train employees on safe data handling practices (Khan et al. 2024).

Remote work cybersecurity is complicated further by home network and device security. Personal devices lack enterprise level security protections such as EDR solutions or auto security updates, many employees use these devices. The home networks also tend to be shared by multiple users and IoT devices and may not be properly secured, thus increasing the risk of unauthorized access and malware infections (Jayarao et al. 2024). Additionally, home environments lack of unpatched software, weak router configuration and old firmware make things worse. As organizations have little control over employees' home IT environment, they need to design strategies to enforce security policies, like requiring endpoint protection software and security updates on all the remote work devices (Kongsen et al. 2024).

Other layers of risk were introduced with collaboration tools and the growth of shadow IT, where employees use unauthorized applications for work. Although Cloud based communication platforms and file sharing service and Third party productivity tool made collaboration among remote teams possible and seamless, at the same time they introduce the security gap which is described by Vardakis et al. 2024. Many of these tools do not have enterprise grade security features and IT teams do not monitor for them, making them easy targets against threats like data interception and unauthorized file access. In some cases, employees may not be aware that they are storing sensitive company information on unapproved cloud platforms and, as a result, data leaks are more likely. To do that, organizations must implement approved collaboration tools, educate employees about the risks associated with shadow IT, and apply access controls to avoid data exposure (Sayeduzzaman et al. 2024).

In addition, regulatory compliance and legal risks carry additional security concerns for organizations that operate in multiple jurisdictions. Strict laws around the world about collecting, storing, and sharing personal data, enshrined in the General Data Protection Regulation (GDPR), the California Consumer Privacy Act (CCPA), are starting to gather momentum (Al Khateeb, 2025). Since remote work distributes the data to several different places and devices, compliance efforts become more complicated when it comes to keeping an eye and maintaining control on sensitive information. The need to establish standardized security frameworks, as well as to ensure that all employees comply with data protection laws regardless of their working place, arises due to crossborder data transfers, different legal requirements, and because it is difficult to monitor data protection in remote settings (Gutiérrez-Crocco et al. 2024).

To tackle these challenges, multiple layers of security enforcement technology, proper education and enforcing policies should be done in a tightly coupled fashion. The evolution of remote working will continue for years, and staying on top of adapting their cybersecurity strategy to mitigate risk and prevent loss of the sensitive data will help combat the cybercrime in organizations all over the world.

4. STRATEGIES FOR SECURING REMOTE WORK

In securing remote work environments, it is multi layered in that there is need of technological safeguards, policy enforcement, and employee awareness. The implementation of a zero trust security model is one of the most effective strategies, which works under the assumption that a user, a device, and a network should not be trusted by default. Unlike perimeter-based security such as firewalls, zero trust enforces least privilege access in that users are continuously required to verify their identity with multi-factor authentication and strict access controls. Organizations can thus mitigate the risk of unauthorized entry into networks by segmenting them, and the impact of a potentially wide security breach by limiting access through user roles. The model guarantees that if the cybercriminal manages to obtain access to a part of the system, he cannot freely move all over the network without additional verification (Adzgauskaite et al. 2025).

One of the critical aspects of remote work cybersecurity is to strengthen the endpoint security. Personal or unmanaged devices are used by employees, which are not protected with enterprise grade security and therefore have the risk of being infected with malware, unauthorized access and data breach. By deploying endpoint detection and response (EDR) tools, organizations have the capability of monitoring and detecting threats in real time and responding to real time incidents (Ogungbemi, Anifowoshe, and Oniseh 2024). In addition to this, installing robust antivirus software and keeping it up to date on automatic security updates as well as forcing full disk encryption protects the devices against exploitation. Organizations can secure endpoints to prevent cybercriminals from using vulnerable devices as gateways into their corporate network (Lekkala & Gurijala, 2024).

In remote work settings where employees spend an undue amount of time using digital tools to share information and to hold meetings, secure communication and collaboration is necessary. Solutions provide end to end encrypted messaging and video conferencing making sensitive conversations private and protected from being intercepted (Zhang et al. 2024). The risk of exposing the data to unauthorized people is further reduced due to the use of secure document sharing platforms with access controls and encryption. Ferguson et al. (2024) also prescribe organizations to ensure employees use approved communication and collaboration tools that abide with security best practices, preventing data leakages via unauthorized channels.

Strong password hygiene and Multi-factor authentication (MFA) make active contributions to remote work security. An additional protection against credential theft comes from requiring employees to verify their identity by using multiple authentication factors such as biometrics, one – time password and security tokens (Kamaruddin & Zolkipli, 2024). Because not only does a password manager make it easier to generate and store complex unique passwords for accounts, it also has the ability to encourage using them. Password rotation policies can be enforced and credentials compromised can be monitored to further strengthen authentication security (Dahiya and Kant, 2025).

Artificial intelligence and automation integration in cybersecurity have an important role to play in securing remote work environment. The AI threat detection systems scan massive data to detect anomalies and potential security breaches that may lead to a harm (Zavrazhnyi & Kulyk, 2024). Neutralizing threats in real time can be accomplished by isolating compromised systems, blocking suspicious activities and alerting security teams to potential incidents through automated responses. The more sophisticated cyber threats become, the more organizations need to employ AI driven cybersecurity solution so that they can keep ahead of their attackers while reducing the risk of large scale breaches (Sarker et al. 2024).

By utilizing these strategies in tandem, unlike solely relying on one, organizations will be able to compose a secure and resilient remote work environment that safeguards both company and employee information. The zero trust framework, better endpoint protection, secure communication methods, strong authentication, and AI powered cybersecurity tools make it possible for the businesses to work remotely without giving up security. With the evolution of remote work, it is critical to have a proactive and adaptive cybersecurity posture as organizational assets are protected in a decentralized digital landscape.

5. HUMAN-CENTRIC SECURITY APPROACHES

Although technological defenses are critical to protecting remote work environments, human factor is one of the most important cybersecurity resilience factors. Remote employees, as the first line of defense against cyber threats, need to be aware of cybersecurity and trained accordingly in order to reduce risks (Schwartz, 2025). The absence of physical presence of IT teams or immediate peer support makes remote workers more vulnerable to phishing attacks, social engineering and other deceptive cyber threats (Mariam & Berrada, 2024). The organizations must invest in training employees about the importance of security awareness, recognizing socially engineered emails, knowing that fraudulent websites are out there, and knowing how to react to a security incident. Reinforcing best practices on cybersecurity helps employees remain vigilant against evolving threats in the future through real world case studies, simulated phishing exercises and interactive cybersecurity workshops (Selesi-Aina et al. 2024).

Another key challenge of remote work environments is to balance productivity and security. Employees are using a lot of personal devices for work which puts at risk unpatched software, unauthorized applications, and weak configurations. The Bring Your Own Device (BYOD) policy must be well defined to ensure that personal devices are secured to the security standards before connecting to the corporate networks (Leonardi et al. 2024). Organizations must put in place policies for the use of endpoint security tools, automatic updates and secure configuration for personal devices. Furthermore, remote IT support should be accessible to employees to help them resolve technical issues and stay compliant with security policies. Organisation approved tools and cloud based collaboration platforms are also provided to remote workers to help strike a balance between productivity and strong cybersecurity measures (Nawaz et al. 2024).

Leadership involvement and a top-down model to cybersecurity is needed to promote a security first culture for organizations. In this case, employees tend to cultivate the practice of best practices and will also constantly drive the cybersecurity train when executives and managers are facilitating the promotion of this security-consciousness behavior. Leadership has to convey the importance of security policies to employees in a way that makes sense to them and shows that cybersecurity is a collective responsibility share instead of an extra burden to bear. For their part, organizations should support open discussion of security concerns to encourage employees to report any suspicious activity without fear of repercussions. In addition, recognizing and rewarding employees who show high security awareness reinforces the positive security culture (Faruque et al. 2024).

Implementing secure BYOD policies, providing cybersecurity education, and implementing a security culture can help organizations better prepare their human centered defenders against cyber threats. However, until cybercriminals stop taking advantage of human vulnerabilities, investing in a workforce well trained on how to spot and avoid risks will more frequently have an effect on securing remote workspaces.

6. ETHICAL AND REGULATORY CONSIDERATIONS

Complex ethical and regulatory challenges of remote work such as data privacy and employee monitoring have become evident. For any organization that wants to retain cybersecurity, they have to establish monitoring to monitor for potential security threats, block data breaches, and be compliant with corporate policies. While the monitoring of employees' activities can be ethical, the extent to which it happens can become an ethical dilemma if monitoring crosses the line into personal privacy. Workers who work remotely often use their own devices, access corporate resources from private places, and work outside of the traditional office oversight, which means that organizations need to find a balance between security and personal rights (Rocco et al. 2024). When there is excessive monitoring like keystroke logging, screen recording, and continuous webcam watching, we end up with a culture of distrust and a demotivated workforce. Werbart et al. (2024) consider transparency in monitoring policies to be crucial to keep ethical standards. It is then the employers' responsibility to communicate clearly in respect to the data that is being collected, how the data will be used, and the underlying rationale for the security monitoring practice. Policies that support security without undermining privacy rights are established to foster trust and establish that cybersecurity is a collective responsibility of employees and the organization (Chauhan & Kumar, 2025).

Global compliance with increasing stack layers in remote work environments also adds to the burden in enforcing cybersecurity in such environments, for instance in an environment that spans multiple jurisdictions. Though regulations differ widely across different countries and vary on a case to case basis, companies are required to navigate through complex legal orb to protect their data in accordance with the law (Al Khateeb, 2025). Both European's General Data Protection Regulation (GDPR) and U.S. California's Consumer Privacy Act (CCPA) set strict requirements in acquiring, retaining, and transferring of personal and corporate data. Not adhering to these regulations may lead to serious legal and financial implications, hence it is important for organization to create security frameworks that conform to these international standards. To manage cybersecurity across different regulatory environments, an organization needs to be proactive and have data classification, encryption protocols and clear policies on the remote data access. In addition, organizations must establish compliance programs that provide employees with guidelines on how to handle sensitive information so that remote work security practices follow legal obligations (Gutiérrez-Crocco et al. 2024).

For multinational teams, the best practices for regulatory compliance are to implement standardized security policies which take into account regional legal differences but are consistent across the organization. As the need for such a strategy becomes clear, companies have to adopt a flexible and comprehensive compliance solution, which is needed due to changes in data residency laws, cross border data transfers and jurisdictional reporting requirements. To mitigate the risks, it can cooperate with legal and cybersecurity specialists to keep abreast of the changing regulations, provide proper training in compliance requirements for remote employees as well as integrate automated compliance monitoring tools. Organizations can build a safe, legally compliant remote work environment protecting employee privacy and ensuring data integrity only if ethical considerations and regulations are balanced (Kamble & Misal, 2025).

7. FUTURE TRENDS AND INNOVATIONS IN REMOTE WORK SECURITY

With remote work evolving, so must cybersecurity's place change in terms of the emerging threat and technological advancements. The increase in AI driven cybersecurity solution is one of the one of the most transforming occurrence in remote work security. Predictive analytics powered by artificial intelligence and machine learning, is one of the quicks ways in which one can identify threats through analyzing big data sets in order to detect any patterns of suspicious activity before an attack takes place. Unlike static security models, these adaptive security virtual models refine in real time their threat detection capability in order to be able to respond to cyber threats. With AI enabled automated responses, cybersecurity resilience is improved by quickly separating compromised systems from the network and blocking malicious access attempts while giving security teams insight into what to act on. As the nature of cyber threats continues to become increasingly sophisticated, proactive and responsive cybersecurity strategies will be as dependent on IT today as AI solutions drive security (Karayel et al. 2025).

Remote access technologies are evolved from traditional VPNs to more secure and flexible one. With the rise of work from home due to the COVID-19 situation, software defined perimeters (SDP) and secure access service edge (SASE) frameworks are evolving as a superior solution for remote workforce security. Whereas VPNs allow a broad degree of access to the corporate network, SDP takes a zero trust stance in that users and devices are verified and only granted access to specific resources. It reduces the probability of lateral movement within a network in case of a breach. Likewise, SASE combines network security functions and cloud based access controls so that users can access corporate systems securely from anywhere without depending on the old perimeter based security models. The next generation remote access solutions provide additional security to the solutions but also the flexibility that a distributed workforce may require (Murray et al. 2025).

And then as we progress with our computing power we will make the quantum threats almost a reality, and at that point, organizations will also have to come to terms with the adoption of post quantum cryptography. Existing encryption algorithms can be broken by quantum computers, which is a huge risk to data confidentiality and secure communications. When this challenge files, scientists and cybersecurity professionals are creating encryption techniques that can maintain against quantum decryption ability. In the coming years, organizations will need to move to quantum resistant cryptographic protocols in order to protect sensitive data. To make this transition come to life, however, it must involve the joint efforts of governments, tech firms and cybersecurity professionals to ensure that the encryption standards migrate hand in hand with the developments in quantum computing.

With remote work security evolving, so does the role of the cybersecurity professionals. Since new technologies and emerging threats are escalating, cybersecurity teams need to upskill to keep ahead of this new attack vector. In future, there will be a higher demand for professionals who have a detail understanding of AI based threat detection, zero trust security model & cloud based security frameworks. Organizations are recruiting from broader talent pools, particularly from global markets, which is in turn changing the cybersecurity force itself with remote work. In order to form a cybersecurity workforce ready to cope with the intricacies of remote work security, continuous training, industry certifications, and cross functional collaboration will be crucial in the near future (Chan, Feng, and Liu 2025).

In the context of digital transformation moving at a quicker pace, organizations have to be nimble when it comes to cybersecurity and continue to adopt new technologies and prepare for new challenges. In the years ahead, remote work is going to continue to be secure and sustainable if based on AI driven security, advanced remote access frameworks, quantum resistant encryption and upskilling of cybersecurity professionals. By remaining on the forefront of these trends, businesses can go ahead and develop durable security frameworks that stay off new cyber threats, also allowing for functionality and efficiency that remote working requires.

8. CONCLUSION

With the rise of remote work, there are new sets of cybersecurity challenges organizations have to deal with to ensure the security and integrity of your digital environment is upheld. In addition, as employees browse corporate resources from multiple remote locations with personal devices and insecure networks, the attack surface expanded greatly. Phishing, ransomware, insider attacks and zero day vulnerabilities are still evolving to include remote work and target those environments with greater and greater sophistication. In addition, decentralization of IT infrastructure, use of cloud based collaboration tools and growing use of shadow IT has exacerbated these risks, proving that the conventional form of security no longer does enough. Organizations have to reconsider the existing cybersecurity strategies and move to proactive approach to protect sensitive data, keep up compliance with regulations, and ensure the business continuity.

Remote work comes with a risk, and proactive security measures are the best way to mitigate them. A zero trust security model, strengthening the endpoint protection, secure communication practices and utilizing AI threat detection are all imperative to ensure remote operations' security. Additional security layers that provide defense against unauthorized access and data breaches are multi factor authentication, encryption and secure remote access technologies as software defined perimeters and secure access service edge (SASE). But technology is not enough to address the security issues of remote work. Moreover, organizations must spend on cybersecurity training programs to enhance education on how to identify emerging threats and the best practices. It understands human error is a massive reason for security breaches and allowing employees to arm themselves up is necessary to form a secure culture.

Organizations that are operating in the era of remote work must adopt a security first mindset. Instead of putting cybersecurity aside, companies must form security into each component of their distant work structures, guaranteeing that strategies, technologies, and employee conduct adjust to all the best practices. The culture is fostered by leadership, and in this matter it sets the tone regarding security awareness and the point that cybersecurity is a shared responsibility. Security can be balanced with ethical considerations by having transparent policies on employee monitoring, data privacy and regulatory compliance. Given that remote work is a global trend, these organizations need to be alert to how their cross border data protection laws and their emerging equivalents need to be addressed.

Deciding the accurate balance between vulnerability, assurance, and consistent protocols will figure out precisely how far remote showing can go after. Remote work has undoubtedly its advantages in terms of productivity, cost, and access to the talent pool, but its sustainability relies to a large extent on how the organization can tame its adverse cybersecurity effects. Security performance should not undermine operational efficiency; instead, coupling cutting edge security solutions, continuous monitoring and employee engagement can achieve a highly adaptive and resilient digital work place . Security must be an ongoing process: agility and new technologies and best practices must continue to be utilized as cyber threats continue to develop. When an organization adopts a fully encompassing and preventive strategy when it comes to remote work security, it empowers itself with a secure, efficient and future ready workspace that enables innovation while protecting innovation in the digital age.

REFERENCES

Adzgauskaite, M., Tam, C., & Martins, R. (2025). What helps Agile remote teams to be successful in developing software? Empirical evidence. *Information and Software Technology*, *177*, 107593. DOI: 10.1016/j.infsof.2024.107593

Al-Emran, M., & Deveci, M. (2024). Unlocking the potential of cybersecurity behavior in the metaverse: Overview, opportunities, challenges, and future research agendas. *Technology in Society*, *77*, 102498. DOI: 10.1016/j.techsoc.2024.102498

Al Khateeb, H. (2025). *Increasing Data Protection Compliance for Remote Workers* (Doctoral dissertation, Northeastern University).

Aloisi, A. (2024). Regulating algorithmic management at work in the European Union: Data protection, non-discrimination and collective rights. *International Journal of Comparative Labour Law and Industrial Relations*, *40*(1), 37–70. DOI: 10.54648/IJCL2024001

Angafor, G. N., Yevseyeva, I., & Maglaras, L. (2024). Securing the remote office: Reducing cyber risks to remote working through regular security awareness education campaigns. *International Journal of Information Security*, *23*(3), 1679–1693. DOI: 10.1007/s10207-023-00809-5

Benligiray, S., Güngör, A. Y., & Akbaş, İ. (2024). Measuring remote working skills: Scale development and validation study. *PLoS One*, *19*(4), e0299074. DOI: 10.1371/journal.pone.0299074 PMID: 38603683

Bughio, K. S., Cook, D. M., & Shah, S. A. A. (2024). Developing a novel ontology for cybersecurity in internet of medical things-enabled remote patient monitoring. *Sensors (Basel)*, *24*(9), 2804. DOI: 10.3390/s24092804 PMID: 38732910

Călin, A. M., Cotfas, D. T., & Cotfas, P. A. (2024). A Review of Smart Photovoltaic Systems Which Are Using Remote-Control, AI, and Cybersecurity Approaches. *Applied Sciences (Basel, Switzerland)*, *14*(17), 7838. DOI: 10.3390/app14177838

Chan, E., Deen, C., Thompson, K., Stubbs, E., Webb, A., Baghbanian, A., & Cadet-James, Y. (2025). Remote Food Security Research Project: Applying an Indigenist Research Lens. *Health Promotion Journal of Australia*, *36*(1), e954. DOI: 10.1002/hpja.954 PMID: 39853566

Chauhan, S., & Kumar, V. (2025). Virtual Horizons: Navigating Legal and Ethical Frontiers in HR Virtual Reality Technology. In *The Future of HRM in a World of Persistent Virtual Reality* (pp. 167-195). Emerald Publishing Limited.

Dahiya, P., & Kant, U. (2025). Multi-Factor Authentication Methods in Intelligent Systems. In *Intelligent Manufacturing and Industry 4.0* (pp. 142–160). CRC Press.

Faruque, M. O., Talukder, T., Pranto, M. N., Debnath, A., & Sultana, S. (2024). The rise of remote work and its impact on small businesses. *American Journal of Industrial and Business Management*, *14*(6), 869–890. DOI: 10.4236/ajibm.2024.146044

Ferguson, S., van Velzen, E., & Olechowski, A. (2024). Team and communication impacts of remote work for complex aerospace system development. *Systems Engineering*, *27*(1), 199–213. DOI: 10.1002/sys.21716

Gough, C., Mann, C., Ficke, C., Namukasa, M., & Carroll, M., & OConnor, T. J. (2024, March). Remote Controlled Cyber: Toward Engaging and Educating a Diverse Cybersecurity Workforce. In *Proceedings of the 55th ACM Technical Symposium on Computer Science Education* V. 1 (pp. 394-400). DOI: 10.1145/3626252.3630917

Gutiérrez-Crocco, F., Martin-Caballero, A., & Godoy, A. (2024). The impact of remote work on managerial compliance: Changes in the control regime over line managers. *Work, Employment and Society*, *38*(2), 527–548. DOI: 10.1177/09500170221142713

Jayarao, G. B., Ray, S., & Panigrahi, P. K. (2024). Information security threats and organizational readiness in nWFH scenarios. *Computers & Security*, *140*, 103745. DOI: 10.1016/j.cose.2024.103745

Kamaruddin, N. H. C., & Zolkipli, M. F. (2024). The Role of Multi-Factor Authentication in Mitigating Cyber Threats. *Borneo International Journal eISSN 2636-9826, 7*(4), 35-42.

Kamble, R. R., & Misal, A. N. (2025). Indian Labor Laws and IT Industry: HR Compliance Challenges. *IUP Law Review, 15*(1).

Karayel, T., Aktaş, B., & Akbıyık, A. (2025). Human factors in remote work: Examining cyber hygiene practices. *Information and Computer Security*, *33*(1), 96–116. DOI: 10.1108/ICS-11-2023-0215

Khan, A. A., Laghari, A. A., Alroobaea, R., Baqasah, A. M., Alsafyani, M., Bacarra, R., & Alsayaydeh, J. A. J. (2024). Secure remote sensing data with blockchain distributed ledger technology: A solution for smart cities. *IEEE Access : Practical Innovations, Open Solutions*, *12*, 69383–69396. DOI: 10.1109/ACCESS.2024.3401591

Kongsen, J., Chantaradsuwan, D., Koad, P., Thu, M., & Jandaeng, C. (2024). A secure blockchain-enabled remote healthcare monitoring system for home isolation. *Journal of Sensor and Actuator Networks*, *13*(1), 13. DOI: 10.3390/jsan13010013

Lekkala, S., & Gurijala, P. (2024). Endpoint and Mobile Security Imperatives. In *Security and Privacy for Modern Networks: Strategies and Insights for Safeguarding Digital Infrastructures* (pp. 155–165). Apress. DOI: 10.1007/979-8-8688-0823-4_15

Leonardi, P. M., Parker, S. H., & Shen, R. (2024). How remote work changes the world of work. *Annual Review of Organizational Psychology and Organizational Behavior*, *11*(1), 193–219. DOI: 10.1146/annurev-orgpsych-091922-015852

Mariam, A., & Berrada, A. (2024). Human-Centric Enterprise Security: Advancing Access Control through AI-Driven Administration. *Authorea Preprints*.

Murray, S. C., Verhoef, A., Adak, A., Sen, D., Salzman, R., Jaiswal, P., & Naithani, S. (2025). Detecting novel plant pathogen threats to food system security by integrating the Plant Reactome and remote sensing. *Current Opinion in Plant Biology*, *83*, 102684. DOI: 10.1016/j.pbi.2024.102684 PMID: 39754892

Nawaz, S., Salman, W., Shahid, U., Khokhar, M. L., Iqbal, M. Z., & Hamid, A. (2024). A Survey on Latest Trends and Technologies of Computer Systems Network. *Spectrum of engineering sciences, 2*(4), 85-114.

Ogbu, A. D., Ozowe, W., & Ikevuje, A. H. (2024). Remote work in the oil and gas sector: An organizational culture perspective. *GSC Advanced Research and Reviews*, *20*(1), 188–207. DOI: 10.30574/gscarr.2024.20.1.0261

Ogungbemi, O. S., Ezeugwa, F. A., Olaniyi, O. O., Akinola, O. I., & Oladoyinbo, O. B. (2024). Overcoming remote workforce cyber threats: A comprehensive ransomware and bot net defense strategy utilizing VPN networks. *Available atSSRN* 4911878.

Prodduturi, S. M. K. (2024). Investigating the challenges and opportunities of cybersecurity in the era of remote work. *European Journal of Advances in Engineering and Technology*, *11*(10), 80–84.

Prümmer, J., van Steen, T., & van den Berg, B. (2024). A systematic review of current cybersecurity training methods. *Computers & Security*, *136*, 103585. DOI: 10.1016/j.cose.2023.103585

Rocco, B., Moschovas, M. C., Saikali, S., Gaia, G., Patel, V., & Sighinolfi, M. C. (2024). Insights from telesurgery expert conference on recent clinical experience and current status of remote surgery. *Journal of Robotic Surgery*, *18*(1), 240. DOI: 10.1007/s11701-024-01984-w PMID: 38833111

Sarker, I. H., Janicke, H., Mohsin, A., Gill, A., & Maglaras, L. (2024). Explainable AI for cybersecurity automation, intelligence and trustworthiness in digital twin: Methods, taxonomy, challenges and prospects. *ICT Express*, *10*(4), 935–958. DOI: 10.1016/j.icte.2024.05.007

Sayeduzzaman, M., Hasan, T., Nasser, A. A., & Negi, A. (2024). An internet of things-integrated home automation with smart security system. *Automated secure computing for next generation systems*, 243-273.

Schwartz, E. (2025). The Role of Human-Centric Solutions in Tackling Challenges and Unlocking Opportunities in Industry 4.0. In *Artificial Intelligence Solutions for Cyber-Physical Systems* (pp. 365–375). Auerbach Publications.

Selesi-Aina, O., Obot, N. E., Olisa, A. O., Gbadebo, M. O., Olateju, O., & Olaniyi, O. O. (2024). The future of work: A human-centric approach to AI, robotics, and cloud computing. *Journal of Engineering Research and Reports*, *26*(11), 10–9734. DOI: 10.9734/jerr/2024/v26i111315

Vardakis, G., Hatzivasilis, G., Koutsaki, E., & Papadakis, N. (2024). Review of Smart-Home Security Using the Internet of Things. *Electronics (Basel)*, *13*(16), 3343. DOI: 10.3390/electronics13163343

Werbart, A., Jonsson, M., Jankowski, B., & Forsström, D. (2024). New skills for distance regulation: Therapists' experiences of remote psychotherapy following the COVID-19 pandemic. *Journal of Psychotherapy Integration*, *34*(1), 27–44. DOI: 10.1037/int0000310

Zahari, A. I., Manan, D. I. A., Razali, F. M., Zolkaflil, S., & Said, J. (2024). Exploring the viability of remote work for SME. *Journal of Open Innovation*, *10*(1), 100182. DOI: 10.1016/j.joitmc.2023.100182

Zavrazhnyi, K. Y., & Kulyk, A. K. (2024). Modern business cybersecurity challenges and the role of artificial intelligence in countering threats.

Zhang, C., Sun, G., Li, J., Wu, Q., Wang, J., Niyato, D., & Liu, Y. (2024). Multi-Objective Aerial Collaborative Secure Communication Optimization Via Generative Diffusion Model-Enabled Deep Reinforcement Learning. *IEEE Transactions on Mobile Computing*.

Zhou, J., Shang, J., & Chen, T. (2024). Cybersecurity landscape on remote state estimation: A comprehensive review. *IEEE/CAA Journal of Automatica Sinica, 11*(4), 851-865.

Chapter 13
Impact of Technology-Driven Personalized Training on Service Employee Performance and Customer-Centricity

Himanshi Rajora
https://orcid.org/0000-0001-5686-3030
O.P. Jindal Global University, India

Narayanage Jayantha Dewasiri
https://orcid.org/0000-0002-5908-8890
Sabaragamuwa University of Sri Lanka, Sri Lanka & Qasim Ibrahim School of Business, Villa College, Maldives

ABSTRACT

This chapter explores the transformative role of technology in personalizing reskilling programs for service employees, with a focus on enhancing customer-centricity. It examines the evolution of reskilling in response to shifting business environments, driven by technological advancements like AI, machine learning, and immersive technologies such as VR and AR. The chapter highlights key technologies that enable personalized learning experiences and discusses the challenges and ethical implications associated with implementing these programs. It also outlines the future directions of reskilling, emphasizing the importance of continuous learning, inclusivity, and collaboration. By fostering a customer-centric workforce, technology-driven reskilling offers organizations the opportunity to adapt to changing market demands and improve employee engagement and performance. Ultimately, personalized reskilling programs are vital for creating a resilient, agile workforce capable of delivering exceptional customer experiences.

DOI: 10.4018/979-8-3373-1270-5.ch013

1. INTRODUCTION

In the modern business world, characterized by ceaseless evolution, there is an ever-growing compulsion exerted on organizations to offer first-rate, customer-oriented services. The expectations of customers have never been so high, driven by the rapid advancement of technology and the personalization being offered to them by leading firms (Lemon & Verhoef, 2016). Therefore, service employees need to constantly adapt themselves to new technologies, processes, and ways of interacting with customers. However, traditional reskilling methods usually do not consider the individual learning preference, skill gaps, and career aspirations that may lower employee engagement and the effectiveness of training processes, as Saks & Burke (2012) established. Personalization in a reskilling program has emerged as one of the major strategies to address these challenges.

Technology plays a central role in allowing organizations to personalize their efforts in reskilling at scale. Applications in technology like AI, ML, and data analytics offer various skills gap evaluations and recommendations on competent learning routes by providing relevant and timely dynamic content tailored for the learner (Vasudevan, 2021). All this not only develops the efficacy in reskilling more swiftly, but they actually enable them with independence in order for them to direct their journeys for up-skilling motivation and retaining (Brown et al., 2019). Moreover, personalized reskilling also provides service employees with specialized skills in the delivery of solution-oriented services toward customers, thereby enhancing customer satisfaction and loyalty.

This chapter explores the intersection of technology and employee reskilling in developing personalized learning experiences that power customer-centricity. It probes into the evolution of reskilling strategies, highlights key technologies that enable personalization, and provides an insight into designing effective, technology-driven training programs (Ganesan et al., 2016). By understanding how technology can transform employee development, organizations can build a resilient workforce able to thrive in an increasingly customer-focused economy.

2. THE EVOLUTION OF RESKILLING FOR SERVICE EMPLOYEES

The concept of reskilling has undergone significant transformation over the years, especially in the service industry, where customer-centricity is paramount. Traditionally, reskilling efforts were structured as one-size-fits-all training programs that favored standardization over individualization (Bersin, 2019). Most of them focused on either technical skills or process adherence, not on the softer interpersonal and problem-solving competencies necessary to deliver a great customer experience, according to Saks & Burke (2012). Consequently, these methods all too often neglected specific employee needs based on role, experience, and learning style, thus fostering disengagement and low retention rates in training.

The shift toward customer-centricity in recent decades has further underscored the limitations of traditional training models. As customers demand more personalized, empathetic, and seamless interactions, service employees must be equipped with a dynamic blend of hard and soft skills, ranging from technological proficiency to emotional intelligence (Lemon & Verhoef, 2016). Organizations are now recognizing that empowering employees to meet these expectations requires a more adaptive and tailored approach to learning and development.

Advancements in technology have played a pivotal role in this evolution, enabling organizations to transition from generic training methods to personalized reskilling programs. By leveraging tools like artificial intelligence (AI), machine learning (ML), and data analytics, companies can now analyze employee skill gaps, predict future workforce needs, and deliver individualized learning experiences that align with organizational goals (Vasudevan, 2021). This is a fundamental shift in perception, from considering it a pure cost against the bottom line to an investment in talent growth and customer satisfaction. The extent to which service industries can reskill their workforce in a highly personalized and technology-driven way will be the competitive advantage of the future.

3. KEY TECHNOLOGIES TO PERSONALIZE RESKILLING

Advanced technologies are embedded in most facets of an organization in designing and delivering reskilling programs, thereby making personalization scalable and effective. Among the most transformative technologies are artificial intelligence (AI) and machine learning (ML), which enable organizations to analyze vast amounts of data to identify employee skill gaps, learning preferences, and career trajectories. AI-driven tools can recommend customized training paths for individual employees, ensuring that the content is relevant, engaging, and aligned with both employee goals and organizational objectives (Vasudevan, 2021). To cite, AI-inclusive systems, such as adaptive learning, automatically adjust level and pace during training on the fly to best suit the individual learner's needs. Other recent works also prove this statement (Brown et al., 2019).

Learning management systems play an important role in providing personalized reskilling efforts. Advanced LMS platforms include analytics dashboards, gamification elements, and third-party integrations that offer dynamic and interactive training programs. These platforms can track an employee's progress, identify areas requiring improvement, and suggest additional resources to enhance their learning outcomes (Matsuo & Kusumi, 2020). Furthermore, LMS platforms facilitate the delivery of microlearning content—short, focused learning modules that are tailored to the specific needs and time constraints of employees. Microlearning has been shown to improve knowledge retention and application, particularly in high-pressure service roles (De Gagne et al., 2019).

Gamification is another technology that has gained tremendous momentum in the context of reskilling for its potential to improve employee engagement and motivation. Gamified training programs tap into intrinsic motivation by introducing game-like elements, such as points, leaderboards, and rewards, that spur employees to participate in their learning journeys (Hamari et al., 2016). This approach has been found quite effective for service employees, who are often benefited by interactive and experiential learning methods.

At the heart of personalized reskilling, too, is data analytics. With insights from employee performance data, customer feedback, and workforce analytics, organizations will be able to identify trends and develop targeted interventions focused on improving skill deficits. Predictive analytics, for instance, can enable a company to predict future skill needs based on industry trends and proactively focus on reskilling (Bersin, 2019). Moreover, technologies such as virtual and augmented reality, in their own way, contribute to reskilling by making training more interactive (Deb et al., 2023). These technologies have proved especially valuable in emulating real-world situations and, as such, have let employees practice complicated tasks in a non-threatening and safe environment (Luo et al., 2021).

These technologies are thus going to help organizations design and create personalized and adaptive reskilling programs based on the particular needs of their workforce. AI, LMS platforms, gamification, and immersive technologies ensure employees are always engaged and ready with the skill sets needed to excel in a customer-centric environment.

4. DESIGNING A PERSONALIZED RESKILLING PROGRAM

The design of a personalized reskilling program should be a strategic process that combines employee needs, organizational goals, and technological capabilities. The foundation of a good program should be based on a comprehensive skill gap analysis that identifies the current competencies and those that need to be developed. AI-driven assessments, along with data analytics, let organizations assess the performance of their employees, measure skill levels, and forecast future skill needs with respect to trends in the industry and customer demands (Bersin, 2019). The whole idea behind this data-driven approach is that the reskilling effort is really focused, targeted, and relevant; therefore, not some generic training that doesn't resonate with people. Once identified, the next step in skill development is tailoring the content to the employee. This includes a personalization process in which learning pathways are aligned to an employee's particular role, goals, and learning style. Adaptive learning platforms, underpinned by artificial intelligence, make most of such content deliveries at the levels of individual proficiency and preferred learning styles (Vasudevan, 2021). To put it differently, an empathy-and-effective-communication module would highly suit an employee in customer service, while a person in technical support will definitely need to be further advanced with troubleshooting and problem-solving. Furthermore, it allows for delivery formats such as e-learning, microlearning, or on-the-job training at a time that best fits the schedule and workflow of the employees.

Leveraging a blended learning model is the key to integrating technology with human touch. While the scale and efficiency of personalized training interventions can be automated and enriched through digital tools, there is still a very important role for managers, mentors, and peers. Managers can provide situational guidance, set targets, and give regular feedback, while mentors may share practical wisdom and experience gained over time (De Gagne et al., 2019). The creation of a supportive learning culture where employees feel empowered to ask for help and collaborate with peers adds to the overall effectiveness of the program.

The second important aspect of designing personalized reskilling is the embedding of continuous feedback loops. This includes periodic assessment of the progress of employees and modification of the content to ensure it aligns with emerging needs. Feedback can be collected through a combination of employee self-assessments, manager evaluations, and performance metrics (Hamari et al., 2016). For example, if from the training data of a customer service representative, the system shows improvement in technical issue solving but not in communication skills, then it would recommend additional modules or coaching sessions in the latter area.

Moreover, it is recommended that organizations embed gamification and reward mechanisms within their programs to enhance participation and motivation. Workers who feel that their contributions are appreciated and rewarded will remain attached to their learning processes. For example, badges, certificates, or other tangible rewards given at the end of training milestones create a sense of accomplishment and spur participation rates accordingly (Hamari et al., 2016).

Finally, a personalized reskilling program design also needs to be designed with a long-term career development perspective and aligned with organizational objectives. Employees need to see how their reskilling efforts contribute to personal growth and broader company objectives. Through communicating the value of reskilling in terms of career advancement, job security, and organizational success, companies can foster a sense of purpose and engagement among employees (Lemon & Verhoef, 2016).

In all, bespoke design of the reskilling program involves identification of skill gaps, content tailor-made to meet the needs of each, integration of human interaction, feedback loops, and fostering of employee engagement through gamification and recognition. By leveraging technology and aligning reskilling efforts to employee aspirations and organizational goals, companies are in a position to create programs that are effective and empowering.

5. BUILDING A CUSTOMER-CENTRIC WORKFORCE

This calls for organizations to develop a truly customer-focused workforce that will enable them to succeed in the ever-competitive market, as the customer's voice keeps getting louder. The customer-centric workforce is empowered, equipped, and motivated to place customers' needs at the center of every interaction. This is possible only with an act of deliberateness in strategy, which also includes integrating reskilling initiatives, equipping with both technical competencies and soft skills to deliver excellence in customer experiences.

Equally important to a customer-driven workforce is focused attention on training in soft skills and empathy. As valuable as technical knowledge proves to be in many instances, the ability to extend a customer empathy, listen to their problems, and respond with concern often has much more to do with customer satisfaction. By Lemon & Verhoef, 2016, any training program should work on emotional intelligence, communication, adaptability, and problem-solving. Technologies such as AI-driven role-playing simulations and virtual reality (VR) can provide employees with opportunities to practice real-world customer interactions in safe, controlled environments, allowing them to refine these skills before applying them on the job (Luo et al., 2021).

In addition to soft skills, service employees have to be very knowledgeable about the products and services on offer to meet customer needs. Personalized reskilling programs can help employees deepen their understanding of the company's offerings, enabling them to provide information on those products or services, troubleshoot problems, and recommend tailored solutions. It is in this view that microlearning modules and mobile learning platforms offer much pragmatic effectiveness in offering product knowledge training to employees in bite-sized, digestible formats they could always refer to on-demand (De Gagne et al., 2019). This means that they are always updated with the latest information to offer timely and value-driven support.

The second imperative aspect of a customer-centric workforce is to use customer insights and data as constructive insight into interactions. While this may seem excessive, customer relationship management systems and data analytics are progressing to grant staff access to elaborate information such as customer preferences, purchase histories, and interaction patterns (Vasudevan, 2021). Training programs need to include modules related to how to interpret such insights and integrate them into personalization. For example, a sales associate who has knowledge of a customer's past buying behavior could make relevant product recommendations, therefore enriching the overall experience.

The parallel and, perhaps equally important, development in the culture would be customer-obsessed staffing. Organizations must foster a mindset for lifelong learning and innovation through upskilling and reskilling opportunities on a recurring basis. Adding peer-to-peer learning initiatives, mentorship programs, and collaborative workshops to technology-driven efforts for reskilling promotes bottom-up approaches in which employees feel supported in their growth (Bersin 2019). In addition, recognition programs celebrating employee successes in customer-centric behaviors can help reinforce positive behaviors and inspire others to emulate them.

Lastly, employee empowerment is important to ensure that the workforce is customer-oriented. For this, employees must have a sense of trust and confidence in making decisions for the benefit of customers without seeking managerial approval every now and then. The training programs should be designed to enhance employees' confidence in taking ownership of the issues of customers and finding creative solutions. Additionally, the company should outline the guidelines and provide resources necessary for employees to act autonomously while aligning with organizational goals (Hamari et al., 2016).

It requires a multidimensional approach touching on soft skills, product knowledge, customer insight, continuous improvement, and empowerment. Organizations that invest in personalized and technology-driven reskilling programs in this area can make sure their employees are capable of delivering superior experiences to customers while keeping them loyal long term. A skilled and customer-oriented workforce could prove to be a strong competitive differentiator in today's dynamic market (Manohar & Palanisamy, 2018).

6. CHALLENGES IN IMPLEMENTING TECHNOLOGY-DRIVEN RESKILLING

Though technology-driven reskilling programs offer a number of benefits, their implementation is not without challenges. Organizations often face a number of obstacles around cost, scalability, employee engagement, and technological infrastructure. Addressing these challenges will be critical for ensuring the effectiveness and sustainability of the reskilling efforts in the long term.

Among the major challenges, the financial investment regarding the implementation of technology-driven reskilling programs stands out. Advanced tools such as AI-driven platforms, virtual reality (VR) training modules, and adaptive learning systems often come with high upfront costs (Bersin, 2019). In addition to purchasing or developing these tools, organizations must allocate resources for software maintenance, system upgrades, and ongoing technical support. This can be well beyond the investment budgets of most SMEs in particular, making the playing field hard to compete against bigger organizations.

The second major hurdle is employee resistance to new technology. Many employees may feel intimidated with unfamiliar tools or skeptical of learning via technology altogether. The root cause for such resistance, many a time, originates from digital illiteracy or fear of replacement due to automation (Vasudevan, 2021). The organization should take responsibility to reduce such apprehension through trust, transparency, and lifelong learning. The introductory training in the usage of new tools and an explanation that the technological setup will be only an aiding mechanism will also reduce resistance.

Another critical challenge is engaging employees in the reskilling programs. Even with the use of sophisticated personalization technologies, employees will become demotivated if the content seems irrelevant or if they feel this is an added burden to their existing job demands (Saks & Burke, 2012). Organizations must be very deliberate in designing the reskilling programs to fit easily into the workflows of their employees, with flexibility as to time and format. Gamification techniques, such as leaderboards, rewards, and progress tracking, are also important motivators in improving engagement and maintaining employee interest (Hamari et al., 2016).

Technological infrastructure and access disparities are other challenges. Most organizations, especially those in developing regions, may not have the technological wherewithal to deploy advanced reskilling tools. Unreliable internet access, outdated hardware, and not having access to digital devices are challenges that may impede the scaling up and inclusiveness of technology-driven reskilling efforts; De Gagne et al. (2019). In some cases, that means foundational infrastructure investments by the organization or hybrids that merge the digital tool with traditional approaches to in-person training.

Another big challenge is the collection and management of employee data, which is crucial for personalizing reskilling efforts. While data analytics and artificial intelligence may provide valuable insights into skill gaps and learning preferences, they also raise concerns about data privacy and security (Luo et al., 2021). Employees might feel uneasy sharing personal information, especially if the purpose and scope of data collection are not clearly communicated. Organizations must ensure strict data protection policies, adhere to regulations such as the General Data Protection Regulation (GDPR), and be transparent in order to gain the trust of employees.

Finally, organizations are challenged by aligning reskilling programs with rapidly changing business needs. As industries continue to evolve and customer expectations change, the nature of the skills necessary for success may change faster than training programs can keep up with. This dynamic environment requires organizations to adopt agile approaches to reskilling, continuously updating content and leveraging predictive analytics to anticipate future skill demands (Lemon & Verhoef, 2016). Failing to do so can result in outdated training programs that fail to deliver value to both employees and the organization.

While technology-driven reskilling programs hold huge promise, some sobriety is necessary in their planning and actual implementation in order to surmount cost-related, employee engagement-related, infrastructural, data privacy-related, and adaptation-related challenges. It is by overcoming these barriers that a firm will be able to unlock the true potential of technology in crafting personalized, impactful reskilling experiences which empower employees and bring organizational success.

7. FUTURE DIRECTIONS

The future of technology-driven reskilling for service employees looks bright; similarly, the continuous development of technologies and shifts in workforce demands will result in a continuous shift of focus toward making reskilling programs more dynamic, predictive, and inclusive. The latest trends and innovations will shape the way in which companies approach employee development and ensure that their workforce is prepared to meet the demands of tomorrow's customers (Srivastava et al., 2023).

One significant future direction is the increased adoption of artificial intelligence (AI) and machine learning (ML) for hyper-personalization. These technologies are expected to become even more sophisticated, enabling real-time analysis of employee performance, learning preferences, and career trajectories. AI will likely play a central role in creating “learning ecosystems” that seamlessly integrate personalized content recommendations, adaptive learning platforms, and career development tools (Vasudevan, 2021). For example, AI will be able to predict not only the current skill gaps but also the emerging skills that employees will need, based on trends within their industry and job function, thus offering proactive reskilling opportunities.

Immersive technologies, such as virtual reality (VR) and augmented reality (AR), will also play an increasingly important role in how service employees are trained. VR and AR are particularly effective for simulating real-world scenarios, providing employees with hands-on, experiential learning opportunities that enhance skill retention and application (Luo et al., 2021). As these technologies become more affordable and accessible, organizations will increasingly integrate them into training programs for tasks such as conflict resolution, customer interaction, and technical troubleshooting. Besides, the metaverse may mean that the virtual spaces to which employees report, collaborate, and train will be vastly more engaging, gamified environments. Another critical direction is that of lifelong learning toward continuous upskilling: the traditional periodic reskilling programs give place to dynamic on-demand learning opportunities embedded in the flow of work. Companies will be concerned with the establishment of a "learning as a lifestyle" environment where employees can engage in microlearning modules, video tutorials, or AI coaching bots at their convenience (De Gagne et al., 2019). These initiatives will empower employees to take ownership of their personal development, ensuring they remain agile and adaptable in the face of constant change.

The future of reskilling will also be social and collaborative. While technology plays a great role, it cannot replace the value that emanates from human contact and peer learning. Hence, such platforms, integrating digital learning with networking opportunities by incorporating virtual study groups, discussion forums, and mentorship networks, are bound to be favored. Such an approach stimulates knowledge sharing and creates community bonds, adding more value to learning engagement (Saks & Burke, 2012).

In addition, with growing globalization and diversity in the workforce, there will be a corresponding thrust toward more inclusive and equitable reskilling. Personalization of reskilling for workers at all demographic levels and skill levels will remain a key priority. Companies may use AI to spot and rectify unconscious bias in learning pathways so that the playing field remains level for everyone to excel, as stated by Hamari et al. (2016). Additionally, multilingual training programs and culturally adaptive content will be in high demand to serve diverse workforces.

Finally, the integration of sustainability and ethical considerations into reskilling programs will shape the future. Organizations will have to make sure that technology-driven reskilling aligns with ethical standards, especially regarding data privacy and security. Transparency regarding data usage, adherence to regulations such as the GDPR, and transparent communication of the usage of employees' data will be essential in trusting and continuing with reskilling. Lemon & Verhoef (2016) Thus, at a time when organizations are increasingly embracing sustainable ways of conducting business, reskilling efforts could include green skills to help drive business sustainability agendas.

The future of technology-driven reskilling for service employees alludes to a convergence of AI, immersive technologies, social learning, inclusivity, and sustainability. Organisations embracing these emerging trends and innovations will be well-placed to build a resilient customer-centric workforce that flourishes in a business environment which just keeps on changing. By staying ahead of these developments, companies can empower their employees, enhance customer experiences, and achieve long-term success.

8. IMPLICATIONS

The reasons behind the implementation of technology-driven reskilling programs for service employees are multidimensional, including social and practical to ethical implications. These are significant considerations that every organization should heed in a struggle to balance innovation with responsibility, ensuring that technological advancements serve not just to enhance the workforce but greater society while addressing challenges that may arise.

Social Implications

One of the most significant social implications of technology-driven reskilling is the potential to bridge or widen skill gaps across diverse workforce demographics. On one hand, personalized reskilling powered by technologies like AI and machine learning can democratize access to high-quality learning opportunities, empowering employees from underrepresented or disadvantaged groups to gain skills that improve their career prospects (Lemon & Verhoef, 2016). By creating equal opportunities for training, organizations will be able to help minimize the systemic inequalities within the labor market.

Nevertheless, there is a looming fear that it could actually widen the gap in societal cleavages in the instance of unequal distribution of technological resources. Workers in low-income areas or industries with limited technological facilities may not have equal opportunities for training and could suffer further inequality consequences (De Gagne et al., 2019). Moreover, generational differences regarding digital literacy may make older workers struggle in a workplace environment that increasingly relies on technology.

Another social implication is workplace culture. Technology-driven reskilling nurtures continuous learning and customer-centricity that will contribute to positive employee morale, collaboration, and engagement. Employees who feel that the organization supports them in their professional growth are more likely to feel a part of the organization and are also loyal (Saks & Burke, 2012). On the other hand, this change also demands more from employees in adapting to constant change, which might result in stress or burnout if not appropriately addressed.

Practical Implications

From a practical perspective, the adoption of technology-driven reskilling programs presents opportunities for organizations to enhance productivity, adaptability, and customer satisfaction. Personalized reskilling equips employees with the specific skills needed to meet customer demands and navigate changes in the marketplace efficiently. For example, AI-powered learning platforms can ensure that employees receive tailored training based on their unique roles and career goals, maximizing the return on investment for both the individual and the organization (Vasudevan, 2021).

Yet, all these programs entail a host of logistical complications in implementing them. Investment in infrastructures including adaptive learning systems, VR tools, and data analytics platforms requires at times substantial financial and technological wherewithal on their part. At the same time, the problem lies in bringing these technologies to the workflows unobtrusively without jeopardizing the continuities of work output. For instance, unless reskilling programs are 'user-friendly' and 'intuitive,' employees with heavy responsibilities do not go easy without some semblance of grumble and distraction from core commitments (Bersin, 2019).

Other practical implications involve scalability. Technology makes it possible to provide training for large and scattered workforces, but how the solution is to be scaled while at the same time keeping personalized presents a challenge. In this respect, the organizations are bound to constantly upgrade their programs as relevant in environments where the preferences of the customer and technologies are running fast.

Ethical Implications

The ethical issues involved with technology-driven reskilling are particularly high, considering they pertain to data privacy, fairness, and dehumanization of the workforce. One of the key concerns is with the collection and usage of data on employees (Yadav & Yadav, 2018). AI and machine learning systems require extensive data in order to deliver customized training, such as information on performance, preferences, and behaviors of employees. If not handled responsibly, this data collection can infringe on employees' privacy, leading to mistrust and ethical dilemmas (Luo et al., 2021). Organizations must establish clear policies on data usage, prioritize transparency, and comply with regulations like the General Data Protection Regulation (GDPR) to safeguard employee rights.

Another ethical issue is that reskilling technologies should not perpetuate biases. If AI systems are not carefully designed and monitored, they may inadvertently reinforce existing biases in training recommendations or performance evaluations. For instance, if algorithms are fed data from the past that reflects discriminatory patterns, these inequities could be reproduced, putting certain groups of employees at a disadvantage (Hamari et al., 2016). Companies have to continuously audit and refine their AI systems for fairness and inclusivity.

A closely allied aspect of discussion, which deals with automation and technology-driven learning, is the question of human dignity. While the new tools should augment human potential, there lies a risk of over-reliance on technology diminishing human intuition, creativity, and emotional intelligence (Yadav et al., 2022). Consequently, organizations should strike a balance between leveraging technology for enabling reskilling and maintaining the human-centeredness in approach toward that objective so as to keep workers valued and empowered, rather than commoditized.

Finally, there are a number of ethical issues related to the speed of reskilling. In particular, labor can be subjected to accelerated learning with a view to maintaining organizational requirements and can lead to a mental health and well-being threat. Ethical employers should design their reskilling programs in ways that allow their employees to better balance work with life and offer them the necessary support to thrive in an ever-changing environment (Saks & Burke, 2012).

The implications of technology-driven reskilling span social, practical, and ethical dimensions. Though these programs have the potential to reduce skill gaps, boost productivity, and enhance customer-centricity, they are also fraught with risks: inequality, logistics, data privacy, and well-being at work. All organizational renewal through design and implementation must be duly thought through and responsibly managed so that their reskilling makes sense ethically, practically, and in view of a wider vision of creating an inclusive and empowered workforce.

9. CONCLUSION

In fact, rapid technology evolution and changing customer expectations have actually made reskilling an indispensable component of workforce development, especially for service employees in direct customer contact jobs. The integration of advanced technologies such as artificial intelligence, machine learning, and immersive tools into reskilling programs has marked a transformative turn toward the future in how organizations prepare their employees. This journey toward effective technology-driven reskilling programs is promising yet complex.

This chapter has discussed how technology can be used to personalize reskilling by tailoring training programs to meet the unique needs of each employee. Using AI-driven insight and adaptive learning platforms, organizations can ensure that employees are better equipped with the right skills at the right time for their own development and the effectiveness of the workforce. VR and AR technologies enable immersive, hands-on training, while gamification and microlearning approaches further increase the level of engagement and knowledge retention. These technologies can revolutionize how organizations realign their workforce capabilities with strategic goals, especially in customer-centric industries where employee skills directly impact customer satisfaction.

However, on the dark side, there are challenges in implementing technology-driven reskilling programs. The road to successful implementation involves navigating financial investments, infrastructure limitations, employee resistance, and concerns over data privacy and inclusivity. This requires the organization to consider a holistic approach: integrating state-of-the-art technologies with human-centered strategies that give a strong emphasis to engagement, equity, and trust. Ethical considerations are paramount, since collection and usage of employee data need to be responsible, while the pace of reskilling must be in tune with the well-being of the employees.

The future of reskilling will be enabled by the crossing of innovation with inclusivity. Those organizations that will move toward emerging trends such as AI-driven predictive analytics, continuous learning models, and collaborative training environments are those that are better positioned to build a resilient, customer-centric workforce. Moreover, this shift to more inclusive and equitable reskilling programs holds promise for helping bridge societal divides and enabling employees from all walks of life to thrive in an ever-evolving workplace.

But more important than anything else, reskilling through technology stands or falls by the culture it can create-learning and adaptation. It is not a one-off initiative but should be embedded into an organization's DNA as a long-term strategic priority. In this way, they also future-proof the workforce and build meaningful opportunities for employees to grow, innovate, and contribute toward the organizational outcome. In a world of ever-changing customer expectations and technological development, reskilling is more than a competitive advantage; it's about reaching long-term growth and sustainability.

Equipping reskilling with technology can be an unparalleled opportunity for transformation toward the customer-centric future that organizations strive to build. Challenges persist, but thoughtful and strategic approaches to reskilling will not only enhance employees' capabilities but also foster stronger customer relationships, drive innovation, and create a more equitable and empowered workforce. The potential is huge, and the time to act is now.

REFERENCES

Bersin, J. (2019). *Building the skills of the future: A new paradigm for workforce reskilling.* Deloitte Insights. Retrieved from https://www2.deloitte.com

Brown, T., Bimrose, J., Barnes, S.-A., & Hughes, D. (2019). The role of technology in shaping the future of workforce learning and development. *Journal of Workplace Learning*, *31*(5), 345–359. DOI: 10.1108/JWL-10-2018-0137

De Gagne, J. C., Oh, J., Kang, J., Vorderstrasse, A., & Johnson, C. M. (2019). The use of microlearning in education: A scoping review. *Journal of Educational Technology Systems*, *47*(1), 45–60. DOI: 10.1177/0047239518799893

Deb, S. K., Jain, R., Manohar, S., & Marwah, S. (2023), "A study on mediation effect of relationship quality outcome between customer relationship management and mutual fund decision", *Global Knowledge, Memory and Communication*, Vol. ahead-of-print No. ahead-of-print. https://doi.org/DOI: 10.1108/GKMC-09-2022-0212

Ganesan, P., Sridhar, M., & Priyadharsani, S. (2016). Advertisement attitude, brand attitude and purchase intention-reciprocal and mediation effect study. *International Journal of Business Excellence*, *9*(4), 488–510.

Hamari, J., Koivisto, J., & Sarsa, H. (2016). Does gamification work? A literature review of empirical studies on gamification. *Proceedings of the 47th Hawaii International Conference on System Sciences (HICSS).* DOI: 10.1109/HICSS.2014.377

Lemon, K. N., & Verhoef, P. C. (2016). Understanding customer experience throughout the customer journey. *Journal of Marketing*, *80*(6), 69–96. DOI: 10.1509/jm.15.0420

Luo, S., Luo, H., Cai, Q., & He, L. (2021). Using VR and AR for immersive training and education: A systematic review. *Educational Technology Research and Development*, *69*(1), 1–22. DOI: 10.1007/s11423-020-09921-4 PMID: 33551626

Manohar, S., & Palanisamy, G. (2018). Corporate reputation, service innovation and cross-buying intention: A test on reciprocal relationship and mediation effect. *International Journal of Services. Economics and Management*, *9*(2), 158–176.

Matsuo, M., & Kusumi, T. (2020). Organizational learning and creativity: The mediating role of innovative work behavior. *Journal of Business Research*, *62*(1), 73–79. DOI: 10.1016/j.jbusres.2020.03.001

Saks, A. M., & Burke, L. A. (2012). An investigation into the relationship between training evaluation and the transfer of training. *International Journal of Training and Development*, *16*(2), 118–127. DOI: 10.1111/j.1468-2419.2011.00397.x

Srivastava, A. P., Yadav, M., Yadav, R., Singh, B., & Dewasiri, N. J. (2023). Exploring digital agility and digital transformation leadership: A mixed method study. [JGIM]. *Journal of Global Information Management*, *31*(8), 1–23. DOI: 10.4018/JGIM.332861

Vasudevan, S. (2021). Leveraging AI for personalized learning in workforce development. *Journal of Artificial Intelligence in Education*, *31*(2), 213–229. DOI: 10.1007/s40593-021-00221-y

Yadav, M., & Yadav, R. (2018). Impact of spirituality/religiousness on cyber bullying and victimization in university students: Mediating effect of emotional intelligence. *Journal of Religion and Health*, *57*(5), 1961–1979. DOI: 10.1007/s10943-018-0637-8 PMID: 29790079

Yadav, R., Yadav, M., & Mittal, A. (2022). Effects of gain-loss-framed messages on virtual reality intervened fitness exercise. *Information Discovery and Delivery*, *50*(4), 374–386. DOI: 10.1108/IDD-04-2021-0051

Chapter 14
AI and the Evolution of Knowledge Work:
Revolutionizing Professional Services With Automation

Gunjan Mohan Sharma
https://orcid.org/0000-0003-2272-7385
O.P. Jindal Global University, India

Priya Gaur
GLA University, India

Thi Minh Ngoc Luu
https://orcid.org/0000-0002-5972-7752
International School, Vietnam National University, Hanoi, Vietnam

Ali Najeeb
https://orcid.org/0000-0003-4663-9347
Qasim Ibrahim School of Business, Villa College, Maldives

ABSTRACT

This chapter explores the transformative role of Artificial Intelligence (AI) in reshaping knowledge work and professional services. As AI technologies evolve, they are poised to enhance productivity, streamline workflows, and introduce new methods of decision-making. The chapter examines the opportunities AI presents, particularly in automating routine tasks, augmenting professional roles, and personalizing services. However, challenges such as data quality, resistance to change, and ethical considerations remain significant barriers to successful AI adoption. The impact of AI on job design and professional roles is also explored, highlighting the potential for hybrid roles that combine human expertise with AI capabilities. Finally, strategies for organizations to prepare for an AI-driven future are discussed, including upskilling, ethical frameworks, and the importance of collaboration. By understanding and addressing these factors, organizations can thrive in an AI-driven landscape, unlocking new possibilities for knowledge work and professional services.

DOI: 10.4018/979-8-3373-1270-5.ch014

1. INTRODUCTION: THE RISE OF AI IN KNOWLEDGE WORK

Artificial intelligence marks the rise of a fundamental shift in the knowledge work landscape, especially within professional services. Knowledge work involves tasks that heavily rely on cognitive abilities, such as decision-making, problem-solving, and critical thinking, traditionally carried out by skilled professionals in sectors like law, finance, consulting, and healthcare (Davenport & Kirby, 2016). These fields have relied on human expertise for generating insights, creating value, and solving complex problems for ages. However, as AI technologies have matured, they are increasingly capable of performing tasks that were once considered too complex for machines, thereby causing a massive shift in the way knowledge work is conducted. AI's ability to process vast amounts of data, identify patterns, and provide actionable insights has the potential to automate a wide array of repetitive and time-consuming tasks, thus freeing professionals to focus on higher-value activities (Brynjolfsson & McAfee, 2014).

In recent years, AI-powered tools such as machine learning (ML), natural language processing (NLP), and robotic process automation (RPA) have been deployed across various sectors of professional services. For example, AI-based algorithms can scan legal documents, flag compliance risks, and even predict the outcome of cases, providing lawyers with insights that enhance their judgment (Susskind, 2020). Likewise, in finance, AI can scan market trends, detect fraud, and even optimize investment strategies at a scale and speed humanly impossible to match (Huang & Rust, 2021). It is not only augmenting the professionals but transforming the entire workflow and business model.

Probably, the potential of AI extends just beyond efficiency gains but reshapes the very nature of expertise and professionals' roles. With the takeover of routine tasks by automation, professionals can engage in more strategically creative and people-related ways of doing their work, using AI to improve decisions and thereby customer services. This shift raises many questions about the future of work, the kind of skills needed in the new workplace, and the ethical considerations of relying on AI in professional contexts. As AI progresses, it does not only promise increased productivity but will also challenge conventional human labor and expertise, and, therefore, an important space for research on understanding the future of professional services (Chui, Manyika, & Miremadi, 2016).

2. DEFINING KNOWLEDGE WORK AND PROFESSIONAL SERVICES

Knowledge work is defined as the kind of work primarily focused on creating, distributing, and applying information and intellectual capital. This type of work demands expertise, cognitive skills, creativity, and problem-solving ability rather than doing manual work. Knowledge workers, for example, engage in such activities as deciding, analysis, strategy formulating, and even coming up with new ideas or solutions. They are generally abstract and not easily seen like others in the field (Davenport & Prusak, 1998). The core of knowledge work is the use of specialized knowledge to solve complex problems, create value, and generate innovations. It is a far cry from routine, mechanical tasks. Knowledge workers in industries such as law, finance, healthcare, and consulting use their expertise to navigate challenges, make informed decisions, and deliver results for clients under high levels of uncertainty and complexity.

Professional services are industries in which knowledge work is more common. Here, services are provided by those with specific education, training, and expertise. Traditionally, these sectors relied on human judgment, insight, and experience to provide tailored high-value solutions for clients. Some examples of professional services include legal services, accounting, management consulting, architectural design, and financial advising. Professionals in these fields use their deep domain knowledge combined with their analytical and communication skills to understand the needs of the clients, develop solutions tailored to their needs, and provide strategic advice. In this context, the work is not only knowledge-intensive but often involves a significant amount of client interaction and relationship management. The services often involved are intangible, complicated, and very particular, and required professionals to combine information from a variety of sources in a real-world problem solution (Susskind & Susskind, 2015).

As such automation and AI technologies advance, they are increasingly capable of performing aspects of knowledge work, especially routine tasks requiring processing large volumes of information. For instance, in legal services, AI can assist in document review, legal research, and contract analysis, which otherwise would require hours of human labor, as suggested by Susskind (2020). While these technologies are indeed powerful tools, the core value of knowledge work within professional services remains tied to human expertise, creativity, and emotional intelligence-attributes that AI is still far from replicating. The future of knowledge work in the professional services sector, is in fact, that of symbiosis between human professionals and AI systems. Automation takes over boring repetitive time-consuming tasks while professionals get more focused on high-level decisions, strategy, and client relationships.

3. CURRENT TRENDS IN ADOPTION OF AI WITHIN PROFESSIONAL SERVICES

The adoption of AI in professional services has rapidly increased over the past few years, as significant potential for changing industries that were traditionally based on human expertise emerges from advancements in machine learning (ML), natural language processing (NLP), and robotic process automation (RPA). The use of AI is increasingly deployed to automate routine and repetitive tasks, enhance decision-making, and provide deeper insights across various professional sectors, including law, accounting, finance, and consulting. AI tools are being used for legal research, document review, and contract analysis in the legal profession. It uses NLP to process massive amounts of legal texts and identifies important information that has significantly reduced time and cost for these tasks (Susskind, 2020). The use of AI can further equip predictive analytics for case outcomes using historical data. Such an approach enables lawyers to better strategize and offer data-driven advice to clients.

In accounting and finance, AI has transformed hotspots like auditing, fraud detection, and financial analysis. Machine learning algorithms enable researchers to analyze large datasets, detect anomalies, and identify patterns that could never be seen by human auditors in any timely manner. With such automation tools, reconciliation, expense management software, and AI-based forecasting, the tasks of an accountant are minimized for more value addition, for instance, on recommending financial strategy, optimizing tax, and others. In the sphere of investment, AI is very much in usage for making models for predictive capability, trend assessment of market activities, and further optimization of investment through real-time inputs from market transactions and historic ones (Huang & Rust, 2021). This does not only increase the speed and accuracy of decision-making but also lowers the costs of asset management and investment advisory services.

In management consulting, AI is being used in business intelligence and analytics platforms to provide companies with actionable insights on a wide range of operational challenges, from supply chain optimization to customer experience enhancement. AI tools can analyze large amounts of data from diverse sources and reveal trends and opportunities that human consultants may not easily see. In addition, AI-driven automation is becoming increasingly employed in tasks such as scheduling, managing clients, and report generation so that the consultants concentrate on high-level strategic decisions and relationships with clients. The use of AI is also changing the nature of consulting itself, as some firms develop AI-powered advisory platforms that deliver real-time recommendations and insights to clients, reducing the need for traditional consulting engagements (Chui, Manyika, & Miremadi, 2016).

Other sectors are also witnessing substantial operational efficiencies from AI adoption, including healthcare and architecture, in which professionals apply AI to make diagnostics, design processes, and patient care management more efficient. For example, in healthcare, AI algorithms assist in the diagnosis of diseases through medical images, predicting patient outcomes, and providing recommendations for treatment to improve both speed and accuracy in healthcare delivery (Brynjolfsson & McAfee, 2014). These applications minimize human errors, support more effective decisions, and consequently enhance the quality of services delivered.

Generally, AI is changing professional services in terms of improving productivity, quality of services, and costs. Although this transformation is brought about by the automation of particular tasks, the core function of a human professional will still be significant: to control, interpret, and make strategic decisions from AI insights. The future of AI adoption in professional services will be built on further embedding these technologies into existing workflows, developing new AI-driven business models, and the evolution of roles that combine human judgment and machine intelligence to deliver superior client outcomes.

4. AUTOMATION IN KNOWLEDGE WORK: OPPORTUNITIES AND BENEFITS

There is an array of opportunities and advantages of integrating automation into knowledge work, especially if one considers increases in productivity, minimization of cost in operations, and improvement of service quality to professional sectors. By automating routine, repetitive, and tedious tasks, it is possible through AI technologies including machine learning, natural language processing, and even robotic process automation to enable experts to concentrate more on the intricacies and higher strategic aspects. For instance, in the legal field, AI can be used to automate document review, case law research, and contract drafting, tasks that traditionally consume significant amounts of time and effort. By streamlining these processes, professionals can redirect their attention to higher-level decision-making, client interaction, and more nuanced legal analysis (Susskind, 2020). This not only improves efficiency but also minimizes the scope for human error, thereby ensuring a higher standard of service delivery.

In addition, automation increases the accuracy and consistency in knowledge work. An example can be accounting and finance. AI-driven systems, for instance, can automatically reconcile financial transactions while detecting anomalies and discloses discrepancies in several data sources with a degree of precision far transcending what is possible for human professionals. Automated systems are less susceptible to the types of errors likely to occur from human error or sleep, especially where high-stakes financial audits or transactions are involved (Huang & Rust, 2021). These tasks performed by AI scale the opportunity for firms to service more diverse clients and handle larger datasets on a greater scale without decreasing quality to meet that demand and further grow capacity.

Additionally, AI will be able to provide deeper insights and more personalized recommendations for making decisions. For example, in management consulting, automation tools can sort through enormous amounts of data to determine trends and patterns that may exist within it, thereby giving consultants a holistic understanding of their clients' needs and business environments. It allows for better-informed, data-driven decision-making when dealing with complex business challenges. AI can also predict future trends or outcomes based on historical data, which can help businesses foresee market shifts or potential risks before they happen. Augmenting human judgment with such insights allows professionals to deliver more strategic and proactive advice to clients (Chui, Manyika, & Miremadi, 2016).

Automation of knowledge work also has huge cost-saving benefits. The organization can then eliminate those high-cost expenses associated with human labor for which payment is made in the form of salaries, training, and benefits when replacing them with AI systems. Further, by automating, organizations could also make way for firms to operate more efficiently; that is, simplify workflows and reduce overheads, thus increasing profitability. Several AI-driven tools further free up time for professionals as they automate administrative tasks such as scheduling, client management, and billing; hence, improving the general performance of the organization.

Another important advantage is the possibility of increased client satisfaction. For example, in healthcare, AI can assist clinicians in diagnosing diseases more rapidly and accurately, which means faster treatment and better patient outcomes. In financial services, AI can provide personalized financial advice, optimizing investment strategies based on individual client goals and risk profiles. Automation helps not only to enhance the efficiency of operation but also improve the client experience by making services more responsive and tailored to needs, simply because professionals are able to focus more on delivering personalized, high-quality services through automation of routine processes.

In sum, the opportunities and benefits of automation in knowledge work are substantial, offering organizations the potential to operate more efficiently, reduce costs, enhance decision-making, and improve client satisfaction. However, these benefits can only be fully realized when AI and automation technologies are integrated thoughtfully into existing workflows, with careful attention paid to the evolving roles of human professionals in managing and interpreting AI outputs.

5. IMPACT ON PROFESSIONAL ROLES AND JOB DESIGN

Adoption of AI and automation technologies in knowledge work not only reshapes the way tasks are performed but, most importantly, it is very significant for transformation of professional roles and job design within many different industries. As AI systems increasingly take on repetitive, data-driven tasks, the nature of human roles in professional services is changing, shifting from routine activities to more complex, strategic decision-making and interpersonal interactions. Professionals are being freed from administrative burdens and mundane tasks, allowing them to concentrate on higher-level activities that leverage human intelligence, creativity, and emotional insight—areas where AI is still limited. For instance, in the legal field, AI tools that automatically do legal research and contract review free lawyers from a significant portion of time for focusing on the client relationship, complex legal strategy, and litigation decisions that call for nuanced judgments. This shift empowers professionals to perform tasks that require judgment, critical thinking, and navigating the complex nuances of ethics and law (Susskind, 2020).

While improving productivity and operational costs, automation brings profound impacts to job design. Many professionals will no longer be focused on performing specific tasks but will instead be concerned with how to monitor and interpret the outputs of AI and ensure that AI-generated insights appropriately make their way into real-world contexts. This change demands new skills from both technology and collaboration from professionals. Instead of just performing tasks, workers will have to be "super-users" of AI tools—guiding systems, validating results, and interpreting AI-generated data to make informed decisions. This shift toward more strategic, value-added tasks creates opportunities for knowledge workers to focus on areas such as client advisory, business development, and innovation, ultimately enhancing the overall value they provide to clients (Brynjolfsson & McAfee, 2014).

In some professions, this shift is giving birth to emerging new hybrid roles. For instance, legal professionals may combine traditional legal expertise with data science skills to oversee AI-driven legal processes, such as analyzing contracts or e-discovery, ensuring that AI systems meet standards and expectations based on law. Similarly, accountants and other finance professionals may become more of "data interpreters" or "AI strategists," applying deep domain knowledge to contextualize AI-generated insights in the broader business environment and advise clients on what to do next. Job roles are becoming increasingly interdisciplinary, with professionals needing a mix of technical and human-centered skills (Chui, Manyika, & Miremadi, 2016).

The growing dependence on AI and automation also requires continuous learning and skill building to keep up with these new roles. As some tasks are automated, professionals need to reskill and upskill to remain relevant in an AI-driven world. This change requires investment in continuous education and the development of new competencies, especially in areas such as data literacy, AI management, and digital tools. Organizations are now providing training programs to ensure that their employees can work with AI systems, thereby creating a new focus on lifelong learning and adaptability as an essential skill in the workforce (Davenport & Kirby, 2016). Therefore, the role of human professionals becomes less about executing predefined tasks and more about navigating complexity, offering personalized judgment, and ensuring that the use of AI aligns with ethical standards and client needs.

At the same time, the rise of AI and automation raises concerns about job displacement, particularly in roles where tasks are fully automated. While automation is unlikely to eliminate knowledge work altogether, it may reduce the demand for certain positions or functions. This displacement effect could particularly affect lower-level or routine roles within professional services, such as paralegals or junior analysts, whose tasks are highly susceptible to automation. The challenge for organizations and workers will be to anticipate these changes and proactively develop new roles that leverage human capabilities alongside AI. Workers who adapt and embrace the opportunities provided by AI will find their roles evolving into more dynamic, strategic positions, while those who resist change may face challenges in staying relevant in the job market (Huang & Rust, 2021).

AI and automation are fundamentally altering professional roles and job design by shifting the focus of knowledge workers from routine tasks to higher-level decision-making, strategy, and client-facing activities. As AI systems take on more administrative and analytical tasks, professionals will be required to develop new skills, adopt interdisciplinary roles, and engage in continuous learning to stay competitive in an evolving workforce. The future of professional services will, therefore, probably be characterized by collaboration between human professionals and AI, where both parties complement the strengths of the other to deliver better outcomes.

6. AI AND ETHICS IN PROFESSIONAL SERVICES

While AI is gaining prominence in professional services, the ethics of its application have become increasingly critical. While AI brings about significant benefits in terms of efficiency, accuracy, and cost savings, it also raises fundamental questions about fairness, transparency, accountability, and the potential for bias. In sectors such as law, finance, healthcare, and consulting, where trust and ethical considerations are paramount, the integration of AI introduces new challenges in ensuring that decisions made by AI systems align with professional ethical standards and societal norms.

Probably, one of the biggest concerns is ethical-algorithmic bias. These machines are taught to learn through data, reflecting patterns and behaviors prevalent in human societies over the past. However, if those patterns and behaviors embedded in datasets that train the machines are themselves flawed or inadequate, then so might be the conclusions drawn from algorithms (O'Neil, 2016). For instance, in the legal sphere, AI systems used for risk assessment or predictive policing may depend on historical data that reflects biased legal practices or societal inequalities, which may result in unfair outcomes for marginalized groups. Similarly, in finance, algorithms used in credit scoring or loan approval processes may inadvertently discriminate against certain demographic groups if trained on data that reflects past discriminatory practices. It thus calls for the strict regulation and periodic auditing of data and algorithms used in AI systems by ensuring that the generated AI systems are fair, non-biased, and geared towards doing no harm.

Other major ethical concerns in the adoption of AI in professional services are transparency and accountability. Many AI systems, especially those based on machine learning, are "black boxes," meaning that their decision-making processes are not easily understood or explained by humans. This lack of transparency raises questions about how much trust can be placed in AI-generated outcomes, especially in high-stakes fields such as healthcare or law. For example, when an AI system is used to recommend a legal strategy or to diagnose a medical condition, the professionals must be able to understand and validate the reasoning behind the recommendations. Otherwise, it will be challenging to hold AI systems accountable for errors or biases that may arise, which could undermine trust in the profession and lead to legal or ethical challenges.

Additionally, with the increasing reliance on AI, there is an issue of accountability for professionals who are using these systems. Although AI can assist in making recommendations and performing tasks, the professionals remain responsible for ensuring that these systems are used ethically and effectively. For instance, a financial advisor who relies on AI to recommend investment strategies must ensure that the system's recommendations align with the client's best interests and risk tolerance. The professional's role is more of overseeing AI tools and interpreting their outputs, so it becomes essential for individuals to have a deep understanding of both the technology and the ethical guidelines governing their practice. This shift in responsibility necessitates ongoing ethical training for professionals, as they must be equipped to navigate the complex intersection of AI and ethical decision-making (Davenport & Kirby, 2016).

Another key issue is the potential for AI to erode client trust. In industries where personal relationships and human judgment are central to service delivery, clients may feel uneasy about the role of AI in the decision-making process. For example, in legal and financial services, clients often rely on professionals not only for expertise but for trust and discretion. Use of AI in decision-making may lead to concerns about data privacy, confidentiality, and the dehumanization of the service experience. Therefore, professionals must find ways of making sure that AI is used to augment their work rather than replace the critical human elements of trust, empathy, and personal judgment that are core to these relationships.

Finally, the consideration of data protection and security is especially vital when applying AI in professional services. AI systems quite often need enormous amounts of very sensitive personal or corporate data access, raising problems about how data is stored and shared and is protected. Health care and financial fields are ones where client information is particularly delicate, so therefore the ethical control of such sensitive information is much more critical in these areas. Professionals must ensure that the AI systems do not violate data protection laws. In the European Union, it is the General Data Protection

Regulation, and they have to ensure that personal and financial information of clients does not fall prey to breaches or misuse. This is where ethical considerations of data privacy and security are required of organizations to follow a robust framework of data governance practices to use AI responsibly.

In summary, AI provides significant benefits in professional services but also poses significant ethical challenges. Issues of bias, transparency, accountability, trust, and data privacy must be carefully managed to ensure that AI technologies are used ethically and in a manner that upholds the integrity of the profession. As AI continues to evolve, it will be important for organizations and professionals to develop ethical guidelines, oversight mechanisms, and training programs to navigate these challenges and ensure that AI supports the broader goals of fairness, equity, and responsibility within professional services.

7. CHALLENGES OF IMPLEMENTING AI IN KNOWLEDGE WORK

The promise of AI in knowledge work comes with a plethora of challenges that organizations need to overcome to unlock its full potential. The biggest challenge is the complexity of embedding AI systems within existing workflows. Many knowledge-based industries, such as legal services, healthcare, and finance, have highly specialized, often non-standardized processes that make it challenging to apply off-the-shelf AI solutions. Customizing AI tools to fit the unique needs and workflows of specific industries can require significant investment in time, money, and resources. This complexity is compounded by the need for professionals to understand and adapt to new technologies, which often requires changes in organizational culture, employee roles, and skill sets. Another critical challenge that organizations must address to avoid disruptions and inefficiencies is ensuring that AI systems integrate seamlessly with legacy software and data infrastructure (Brynjolfsson & McAfee, 2014).

Another significant barrier is the availability and quality of data. AI systems, particularly those based on machine learning, require large volumes of high-quality data to train and operate effectively. Data in many professional services industries is fragmented, siloed, or not structured in a way that is easily accessible for AI algorithms. For example, in the legal field, case law and legal documents may be stored in various formats, making it difficult to consolidate this data for use in AI applications. In healthcare, patient data may be spread across multiple systems with different standards for data collection, which further complicates the process of building effective AI models. The process of ensuring that data is clean, well-organized, and properly labeled is essential for the successful deployment of AI, but this process can be both time-consuming and costly (Huang & Rust, 2021).

Furthermore, resistance to change is one of the greatest challenges with AI implementation into knowledge work. Professionals in sectors like law, finance, and consulting spend decades developing their niche knowledge and skill sets and often resist adopting an AI system because it will disturb the established practice of doing things in a particular manner. The fear of job displacement or a perceived loss of autonomy might lead to resistance among employees, especially those who are in roles more susceptible to automation. This might slow the rate at which AI technologies are adopted and delay the development of a collaborative environment that complements human workers with AI systems. This can only be overcome through change management strategies that put forth the benefits of AI in changing repetitive tasks into automated tasks, reducing workload, and improving the decision-making aspect, along with support and retraining for the employees whose job roles might be changed with AI implementation (Davenport & Prusak, 1998).

Ethical considerations also contribute a lot to the challenges associated with the implementation of AI in knowledge work. As AI systems take on more decision-making responsibilities, organizations must ensure that these systems operate in a fair, transparent, and accountable manner. As mentioned earlier, AI algorithms can perpetuate biases present in the data they are trained on, leading to discriminatory or unfair outcomes. Organizations need to have robust mechanisms for monitoring and auditing AI systems to ensure that they are not reinforcing harmful biases or making decisions that could undermine trust in the profession. Additionally, the ethical implications of data privacy, particularly when dealing with sensitive client or patient information, must be addressed by adopting comprehensive data governance frameworks and ensuring compliance with legal and regulatory standards, such as the GDPR in Europe (O'Neil, 2016).

Finally, the rapid pace of AI development presents an ongoing challenge. The field of artificial intelligence is evolving rapidly, with new techniques, models, and capabilities emerging regularly. This can create uncertainty about which technologies to invest in and how to ensure that their AI systems remain relevant and effective in the long term for organizations seeking to implement AI in knowledge work. Staying up to date with the latest advancements in AI, while simultaneously ensuring that the systems already in place continue to deliver value, requires ongoing research, investment, and adaptation. This continuous evolution makes it difficult for organizations to predict the return on investment (ROI) and to plan for future developments in a way that aligns with their strategic objectives (Chui, Manyika, & Miremadi, 2016).

The challenges in AI implementation in knowledge work include its integration with pre-existing workflows and processes, demand for quality data, resistance among employees, and ethical concerns associated with it as well as with rapid technological progress. It has to be strategized properly taking into account proper management of data, effective change management, ethical checks, and proper investment in the technology and trainings. Only through the surmounting of these barriers will organizations be able to unlock the full potential of AI to transform professional services.

8. THE FUTURE LANDSCAPE OF KNOWLEDGE WORK AND AI

The future landscape of knowledge work will be fundamentally shaped by the continued evolution of AI and automation technologies, ushering in a new era where human expertise and machine intelligence collaborate more seamlessly than ever before. As AI tools become increasingly sophisticated, they will not only automatically perform routine tasks but also augment human decision-making to allow knowledge workers to focus on higher-level, creative, and strategic endeavors. The integration of AI into knowledge work will change the nature of professional roles by focusing on the skills to interpret and leverage AI-generated insights while maintaining the relevant human elements of judgment, empathy, and ethical considerations. In this future landscape, AI will serve as a powerful assistant, amplifying human capabilities rather than replacing them. For instance, in the legal field, AI may handle document review and case law research with unmatched speed and accuracy, allowing lawyers to focus more on strategy, client counseling, and courtroom advocacy (Susskind, 2020). Similarly, in healthcare, AI diagnostics and personalized treatment plans will enhance medical decision-making, allowing doctors to spend more time with patients and make more informed, data-driven decisions.

One of the most significant transformations in the future of knowledge work will be the rise of hybrid roles that combine human expertise with AI capabilities. These roles will demand professionals to work alongside AI systems, guiding their use, validating their outputs, and making critical decisions based on the insights they generate. For example, in management consulting, AI tools might analyze vast amounts of business data and provide insights on market trends, while consultants will be responsible for interpreting these findings and offering strategic recommendations tailored to specific clients' needs. The importance of these new hybrid roles, however, is on data literacy, critical thinking, and AI tool collaboration ability. Therefore, professionals will transform into "AI-literate" workers: a person who uses AI tools correctly and knows not only how far its capability can extend but also all the ethical ramifications of such practice (Brynjolfsson & McAfee, 2014). This shift will involve huge investments in upskilling and reskilling the workforce with a focus on continuous learning to keep abreast of the changes brought about by technological advancements.

Another important aspect of the future landscape will be the increased personalization of knowledge work. AI has the potential to provide highly tailored recommendations and solutions based on individual client needs, preferences, and behaviors. For instance, in financial services, AI-driven algorithms can analyze a client's financial situation, risk tolerance, and goals to create customized investment strategies. In education, AI can offer personalized learning experiences that adapt to each student's pace and style of learning, enhancing educational outcomes. As AI continues to improve in understanding and predicting human preferences, it will enable organizations to deliver more individualized and targeted services, leading to greater client satisfaction and loyalty (Chui, Manyika, & Miremadi, 2016).

However, the future of knowledge work and AI also raises important challenges, particularly around ethics, data privacy, and the potential for job displacement. The more AI takes on decision-making roles, the more its ethical considerations will be brought to the forefront. Organizations will have to develop frameworks that ensure fairness, transparency, and accountability in the decisions being made. Issues such as algorithmic bias, responsible use of personal data, and the ethics of AI-driven decision-making require careful oversight. In addition, while AI is expected to enhance human capabilities, it is also likely to displace some jobs, especially those involving repetitive or lower-level tasks. To counter this, governments, organizations, and educational institutions must collaborate to ensure that workers have access to reskilling and upskilling opportunities, enabling them to transition to new roles that require a combination of AI expertise and human judgment (Huang & Rust, 2021).

Going forward, AI is expected to further change the way knowledge work is carried out and thus lead to a more dynamic, flexible, and productive workforce. Professionals will be empowered through AI tools handling mundane tasks, providing insights, and coming up with innovative solutions so that they focus on work requiring creativity, critical thinking, and emotional intelligence. This will encourage collaboration between humans and machines to bring about a future where AI supplements human capabilities and increases the value of professional services. However, for this future to be realized, it will require careful attention to ethical considerations, investments in workforce development, and a commitment to ensuring that AI technologies are used in ways that benefit society as a whole.

This will be increasingly about collaboration among human intelligence and artificial intelligence without much of an imaginary boundary among them. Future knowledge work involves higher-value human tasks that relate to expertise, creativity, while the routine as well as analytic work is going to be automated by AI. This change holds great promise in the transformation of industries, enhanced client outcomes, and increased productivity by professionals. The future envisioned here will involve major challenges-such as ethics in AI application, data protection, and issues arising from loss of employment-but there is one positive way toward an AI-driven future: organization readiness.

9. PREPARING FOR THE FUTURE: HOW ORGANIZATIONS CAN THRIVE IN AN AI-DRIVEN WORLD

As AI continues to change the face of industries and redefine the nature of knowledge work, organizations must be proactive in their preparation for the future to survive in an increasingly AI-driven world. The path to success, therefore, involves strategically integrating AI technologies into organizational processes while fostering a culture of adaptability, continuous learning, and innovation. Those that will truly tap the full potential of AI are expected to open new levels of efficiency, improve decision-making, and personalize services for users. In achieving these benefits, organizations need to take on various strategic, cultural, and technological issues.

In a first step, they must make a commitment to investing in an intelligent strategy which supports long-term goals and business objectives. With this strategy, it is not only focused on adoption of AI technologies but even on how the tools can complement workflows and human ability (Binns, 2018). The trend would be for organizations to not look at AI as a replacement for human workers but even as a powerful tool that amplifies human intelligence. This requires that both AI and human professionals operate in an environment toward a possible perfect outcome. For instance, consulting firms can now apply AI analytics to input massive amounts of data and sift through them quickly to spot any trends that could emerge. Human consultants are still important, though. They interpret these insights and then apply them in appropriate ways to clients' business challenges. By acknowledging the complementary nature of humans and AI, organizations will ensure that the adoption of AI is not viewed as a threat to current positions but as a source of opportunity for growth and innovation (Brynjolfsson & McAfee, 2014).

Organizations need to invest in the upskilling and reskilling of their workforce to prosper in an AI-driven world. With AI changing the nature of work, employees will have to acquire new skills, particularly in areas such as data analysis, AI management, and digital tools. Offering employees the chance to develop AI literacy and other relevant competencies will help organizations bridge the skills gap and ensure that workers are prepared to take on hybrid roles that combine AI capabilities with human expertise. Training programs should focus not only on technical skills but also on the soft skills needed to work effectively with AI, such as problem-solving, critical thinking, and ethical decision-making. Moreover, a culture of continuous learning and adaptability is essential, as AI technologies evolve rapidly, and organizations will need to remain agile in order to keep pace with innovation. Partnering with educational institutions or offering internal learning resources can also keep employees abreast of the latest developments in AI and related fields (Davenport & Kirby, 2016).

In addition, organizations need to adopt an ethical approach to AI adoption to build trust with both employees and clients. This implies deploying AI in a fair, transparent, and accountable manner so that the use of AI would meet the ethical expectations and societal prerequisites. Organisations should have clear governance frameworks for the development and deployment of AI technology, incorporating rules to reduce biases in algorithms for AI and data privacy and security, as well as full transparency in decision-making by AI. Ethical AI is therefore an efficient tool in reducing any risk of a kind that, for instance can cause algorithmic discrimination or that the erosion of trust in any AI-driven decisions.

Furthermore, building an organizational responsibility and ethical manner of doing the thing will lead to AI helping enhance professional integrity instead of it undermining it O'Neil 2016. This would not only support the safety of the company reputation but ensure use of the artificial intelligence technology within a wider scale that adds worth to humanity.

Collaborations will form as well toward growing in this technology. To take advantage and outdo peers at this edge is through forging close partnerships among them, even creating collaborations from working with AI Vendors, new innovations startups and partnering with knowledge holders and Academic Institute (Autor, 2015). Collaboration with external partners could give an organization insights into the best practices in AI integration. It can lead to identifying creative, innovative ways of using AI in specific industries. Partnerships can also allow organizations to co-create AI solutions that cater to unique organizational needs and are custom-built to support business priorities in AI adoption.

Finally, focus should be on the creation of a more flexible, AI-enabled infrastructure designed to handle future growth and adaptation. This includes the use of scalable cloud-based platforms, integrating AI systems with existing technologies, and making sure that data is collected and stored in a manner that is accessible and compatible with AI applications. As AI becomes more deeply integrated into organizational processes, there will be a need to have a very robust technological infrastructure that supports incorporating new AI tools, can handle large datasets, and aid in carrying out real-time collaboration among AI systems and human workers. In addition, organizations should ensure that they implement appropriate cybersecurity measures to mitigate potential vulnerabilities from the increasing reliance on AI technologies and data.

In conclusion, preparing for the future in an AI-driven world requires organizations to adopt a holistic approach that encompasses strategic AI integration, workforce development, ethical practices, collaboration, and technological infrastructure. This way, organizations can position themselves to not only survive but thrive while AI continues to transform knowledge work. In doing so, they will unlock the full potential of AI, enhance the capabilities of their workforce, and create innovative solutions that deliver value to clients and stakeholders.

10. CONCLUSION

The integration of AI into knowledge work is poised to revolutionize professional services, reshaping industries, job roles, and workflows in profound ways. Where AI brings about enormous benefits, which include the potential for greater efficiency, superior decision-making, and more effective personalization, it also creates a set of challenges that must be approached strategically (West, 2018). The future of knowledge work will not rely upon the replacement of human workers but on the interaction between human expertise and AI technologies. This collaboration has the potential to unlock some new levels of creativity, innovation, and productivity, enabling professionals to focus on high-value tasks that require critical thinking, empathy, and strategic judgment. Realizing this potential, however, will require careful attention to areas such as ethical considerations in implementing AI, workforce development, and the creation of AI-driven infrastructures that foster flexibility and scalability.

Organizations must be proactive in embracing AI, ensuring that they are equipped with clear strategies for AI integration, employee training, and ethical oversight. They must also foster a culture of continuous learning, where workers are empowered to develop the skills necessary to thrive in an AI-driven environment. Focusing on the ethical use of AI, mitigating biases, ensuring data privacy, and maintaining transparency will help organizations build trust with employees and clients, ensuring that AI enhances, rather than undermines, professional integrity. Collaboration between AI vendors, startups, and academic institutions will be critical in staying ahead of technological advancements and ensuring that AI solutions are tailored to meet the specific needs of organizations.

Organizations that can navigate these challenges and seize the opportunities AI presents will determine the future of knowledge work and AI. Ultimately, the ability to create the right mix of technology, talent, and ethical practices will ensure success in this new landscape and lead industries toward transformation. Success in an AI-driven world will thus depend on embracing AI not as a replacement but as an augmentative tool and preparing the workforce to work alongside these transformational technologies. This is how organizations will unlock the true potential of AI, drive innovation in how they and the clients they serve win, and contribute to the wider advance of society.

REFERENCES

Autor, D. H. (2015). Why Are There Still So Many Jobs? The History and Future of Workplace Automation. *The Journal of Economic Perspectives, 29*(3), 3–30. DOI: 10.1257/jep.29.3.3

Binns, A. (2018). *Fairness in Machine Learning: Lessons from Political Philosophy. Proceedings of the 2018 CHI Conference on Human Factors in Computing Systems.*

Brynjolfsson, E., & McAfee, A. (2014). *The Second Machine Age: Work, Progress, and Prosperity in a Time of Brilliant Technologies*. W.W. Norton & Company.

Chui, M., Manyika, J., & Miremadi, M. (2016). *Where machines could replace humans—and where they can't (yet)*. McKinsey Quarterly. McKinsey & Company.

Davenport, T. H., & Kirby, J. (2016). Beyond automation: Strategies for remaining human in the age of AI. *Harvard Business Review, 94*(4), 58–64.

Huang, M.-H., & Rust, R. T. (2021). Artificial Intelligence in Service. *Journal of Service Research, 24*(1), 3–20.

O'Neil, C. (2016). *Weapons of Math Destruction: How Big Data Increases Inequality and Threatens Democracy*. Crown Publishing Group.

Susskind, R. (2020). *Tomorrow's Lawyers: An Introduction to Your Future*. Oxford University Press.

Susskind, R., & Susskind, D. (2015). *The Future of the Professions: How Technology Will Transform the Work of Human Experts*. Oxford University Press. DOI: 10.1093/oso/9780198713395.001.0001

West, D. M. (2018). *The Future of Work: Robots, AI, and Automation*. Brookings Institution Press.

Chapter 15
Policy and Regulatory Frameworks for AI and Global Work:
Navigating the Challenges

Rohit Yadav
https://orcid.org/0000-0002-7573-8005
IILM University, Greater Noida, India

Sandeep Kumar Singh
https://orcid.org/0000-0002-1741-7254
O.P. Jindal Global University, India

Dewanarayana Hiththaragedara Prasad Manuranga Gunathilaka
International Distillers Limited, Kaduwela, Sri Lanka

Thi Trang Dang
International School, Vietnam National University, Vietnam

ABSTRACT

This chapter explores the policy and regulatory frameworks necessary for managing the impact of artificial intelligence (AI) on the global workforce. As AI technologies reshape industries, they present both opportunities and challenges, including labor displacement, ethical dilemmas, and regulatory fragmentation. The chapter examines the role of AI in transforming global work, highlighting key challenges such as fairness, transparency, and accountability in AI systems. It discusses policy frameworks from different global perspectives and the need for international collaboration to harmonize AI regulations. Furthermore, the chapter emphasizes the importance of human-centric AI policies that prioritize worker protection, ethical development, and equitable access. Key recommendations include investing in reskilling, establishing social safety nets, and fostering global cooperation to create a sustainable and inclusive future of work. This comprehensive approach aims to ensure that AI benefits workers and society, while mitigating potential risks.

DOI: 10.4018/979-8-3373-1270-5.ch015

1. INTRODUCTION

The rapid advancement of artificial intelligence has dramatically impacted the global work ecosystems, transforming industries, redefining roles, and introducing new opportunities and challenges. From automating routine tasks to enabling complex decision-making processes, AI has become a cornerstone of modern economies. However, its widespread adoption raises critical questions about governance, equity, and the ethical deployment of technology in diverse work settings (Brynjolfsson & McAfee, 2014). Of course, as societies try to cope with these changes, strong policy and regulatory frameworks are indispensable to ensure that the benefits of AI are distributed equitably while the corresponding harms are minimized.

Implications of AI at the Global Workforce Extend beyond National Borders; thus, there is an imperative need for International Cooperation and Harmonized Regulation Approaches. For example, while the European Union has been a leader in holistic regulations like the AI Act, the United States has followed a more piecemeal, sector-specific approach (European Commission, 2021; West & Allen, 2018). This disparity often results in regulatory arbitrage, where businesses exploit less stringent laws in certain jurisdictions, undermining efforts to create fair and ethical AI systems.

Moreover, with AI replacing much of what labor markets hold, it promises both sides on the potential value: it can increase productivity and jobs but also potentially displace employees, resulting in deepened inequality and unemployment in poor communities (Frey & Osborne, 2017). The two sides could be balanced through policies governing the emergence of AI technologies as well as broader socio-economic effects, reskilling the workforce, and nurturing marginalized groups.

This chapter seeks to dive into the delicate relation that AI bears on global work and regulation. The issue of governance will be analyzed by considering its ethical, legal, and practical approaches, stressing an inclusive, adaptive framework. Analyzing various cases and perspectives at the global level, the paper aims to yield actionable insight to help develop innovation-friendly policies safeguarding human dignity and rights.

2. ROLE OF AI IN SHAPING GLOBAL WORK

Artificial intelligence has emerged as a transformative force, redefining the nature of work across industries and geographies. Its influence ranges from enhancing productivity in traditional sectors to creating entirely new categories of jobs. By automating routine tasks and augmenting human capabilities, AI enables organizations to streamline operations, reduce costs, and innovate at unprecedented rates. For example, technologies such as machine learning, natural language processing, and robotics are revolutionizing fields like healthcare, manufacturing, and customer service (Brynjolfsson & McAfee, 2014).

In healthcare, AI-based applications help in disease diagnosis, predict patient outcomes, and tailor treatment plans, thereby reducing the workload of professionals and enhancing patient care. Similarly, in manufacturing, AI-based automation has increased production efficiency and precision, especially in assembly lines and quality control processes. Meanwhile, marketing and logistics are using AI to analyze large data sets, optimize strategies, and predict consumer behavior, which is a competitive advantage (McKinsey Global Institute, 2021).

The effect of AI on work is not, however, uniform. As it opens doors to innovation and growth, it also disrupts traditional labor markets. Automation has made some low-skill jobs obsolete, particularly in sectors like retail and transportation, where the tasks are very repetitive and predictable (Frey & Osborne, 2017). According to the World Economic Forum, 2020, artificial intelligence is expected to displace millions of jobs worldwide, mostly among people with limited education and training options.

Simultaneously, it is creating a new kind of work by areas that have digital expertise, which includes data science, AI ethics, and algorithm auditing. Such as jobs pertaining to training the AI system by labeling datasets or curating the content. Other examples include those roles in the areas of cybersecurity, cloud computing, and integration of systems to demonstrate its capabilities to create a high-value job (Bughin et al., 2018).

Global connectivity made possible by AI also transforms the nature of work, as AI algorithms allow distributed teams to be managed and collaborate across various time zones and cultures, which opens the talent pool for employers while granting workers greater flexibility. But this globalization of work raises many questions about wage disparities, labor rights, and access to digital infrastructure.

Finally, the impact of AI on the global work order is multidimensional. On the one hand, AI boosts efficiency and innovation. On the other hand, it threatens equity, employment, and workforce preparedness. There is a need for collaboration among policymakers, businesses, and education systems to make the impact of AI inclusive and sustainable and create spaces for organizations and workers to grow together.

3. MAJOR ISSUES IN THE REGULATION OF AI FOR GLOBAL WORKFORCE

As artificial intelligence continues to reshape industries and labor markets, the task of regulating its impact on the global workforce presents numerous challenges. The most pressing issue is ensuring that AI systems are deployed in an ethical, transparent, and accountable manner. AI technologies, especially those based on machine learning, have the potential to perpetuate biases present in the data they are trained on, leading to discriminatory outcomes. For instance, biased hiring AI systems could disadvantage candidates based on race, gender, or background, thereby compounding existing inequality (O'Neil, 2016). Therefore, a significant challenge of regulation is guaranteeing fairness and accountability in the algorithms of AI, especially where the consequences are severe, like in hiring, healthcare, or criminal justice.

The other significant challenge is in the increasing rate of automation in jobs that humans have traditionally occupied. On the one hand, AI promises to raise productivity and cut costs for firms. On the other hand, it threatens to displace millions of workers in low-skill and repetitive jobs like retail, transportation, and manufacturing (Brynjolfsson & McAfee, 2014). The increase in AI-driven automation could thus intensify existing inequalities because vulnerable sector workers may lack the necessary skills to transition to new roles without extensive retraining or reskilling. The policymakers have to cross these waves of disruption, making sure that workers are protected and resources are given to them so they can adjust to the new job market. In the absence of proper safeguards and investment in workforce development, the increasing adoption of AI will further exacerbate social and economic divisions.

The international coordination and harmonization also pose a challenge to AI regulation. Since AI technologies are by nature global, their regulation cannot be confined within national borders. However, the regulatory approaches to AI vary significantly across regions; the European Union is more proactive with the AI Act, whereas other regions like the United States have a much more fragmented sector-specific regulatory landscape (European Commission, 2021). This lack of alignment in AI regulations between countries can lead to what is known as "regulatory arbitrage," where companies may relocate operations to jurisdictions with looser regulations, undermining global efforts to ensure ethical AI deployment. In this regard, the main issue for regulators would be developing international frameworks that foster cooperation, create consistent standards for AI governance, and allow AI benefits to be shared equitably across borders while minimizing risks. Data privacy and protection is another significant area of concern. The large amount of personal data required for training algorithms raises questions about the security of such data and individuals' right to privacy. Lack of proper data protection measures can lead to unauthorized collection, surveillance, and breach of confidentiality, thereby undermining public trust in AI technologies. This would pose an additional complexity, as national regulations on data privacy differ; the European Union's General Data Protection Regulation is stricter compared to the less stringent data protection laws of the United States. Therefore, it becomes challenging to develop strong and coherent data protection laws that both safeguard personal privacy and encourage innovation in AI technologies.

The last is that human oversight over decisions made by AI systems becomes more critical as the latter increasingly intervene in decision-making processes. In other words, AI may augment decision-making across various domains but cannot replicate human empathy, understanding, and ethical judgment. It is essential that regulations guarantee human review and accountability of critical decisions, especially those affecting people's rights and lives. Without such oversight, there is a risk that AI could make decisions based on flawed assumptions, amplifying errors or injustices. As AI systems become more complex and autonomous, determining the appropriate balance between automation and human control remains a fundamental regulatory dilemma.

The regulation of AI in the global workforce must address a range of interconnected challenges, including fairness, employment disruption, international cooperation, data privacy, and human oversight. These challenges require coordinated efforts from governments, industry stakeholders, and international organizations to develop effective policies that can manage the transformative potential of AI while safeguarding human rights and promoting equity.

4. POLICY FRAMEWORKS FOR AI AND WORK: GLOBAL PERSPECTIVES

As AI continues to reshape the global workforce, different regions are adopting different approaches to regulate AI and manage its impact on labor markets. Differences reflect the different socio-economic contexts, political priorities, and levels of technological advancement across nations. Understanding the policy frameworks for AI in the context of work offers important insights into how nations navigate the challenges and opportunities AI presents.

The regulation of AI in the European Union has been very holistic and proactive. The proposed Artificial Intelligence Act of the EU by the European Commission (2021) focuses on establishing clear rules for AI deployment, specifically targeting high-risk AI systems that have the potential to impact safety and fundamental rights. The regulation ensures that AI technologies are used ethically by promoting transparency, accountability, and fairness in decision-making processes. The EU has also protected workers through policies like the Digital Services Act and Digital Markets Act, which regulate the use of data and AI algorithms by tech companies to ensure that the rights of workers are protected and that AI systems cannot be used to exploit labor. These regulations have mainly focused on the ethics of deploying AI while, at the same time, addressing the issues between innovation and human rights and labor welfare

(Binns, 2021). However, some argue that the strict regulations of the EU may hinder innovation or even push AI development out of the region.

The United States has approached AI regulation in a more fragmented manner, with sector-specific legislation rather than cross-sectoral, overarching frameworks. U.S. policies on AI are largely shaped by the private sector, where companies like Google, Microsoft, and IBM play a huge role in shaping the regulatory landscape (West & Allen, 2018). Though the U.S. has put a few federal regulations in place, like the National AI Initiative Act of 2020, this aims to develop and improve the AI research at a federal level, still lacks unified national regulation of the application and control of AI at a workforce level. As a result, many regulatory issues, such as AI-driven discrimination in hiring or data privacy concerns, are addressed on a state-by-state basis, which leaves the regulatory environment inconsistent. It has its merits in fostering innovation but leaves many gaps in the protection of workers from the adverse impacts of AI, including job displacement and unequal access to opportunities.

Meanwhile, AI represents an important contributor to China's economic growth and new technological leadership. The Chinese government has launched aggressive policies, including the Next Generation Artificial Intelligence Development Plan (2017), to become the global leader in AI by 2030. China's regulatory framework is less focused on worker protection than the EU but is instead more interested in developing AI technologies, enhancing industrial capabilities, and creating a competitive digital economy (Cui, 2021). A centralized, state-driven governance of AI in China characterizes the governance approach, where government action plays a leading role in guiding AI development and application in labor markets. Despite this approach having brought successive advances in AI, there are questions from worker rights perspectives, issues with data privacy, and control over society, especially in terms of surveillance and social credit systems.

In Latin America and other emerging economies, AI policy frameworks are still in their nascent stages. Countries like Brazil and Mexico have started looking into AI regulations through pilot initiatives, recognizing the need to manage AI's implications for labor markets, especially in agriculture, manufacturing, and service sectors (Camacho, 2020). In these regions, the opportunities and dangers of AI as an engine of economic growth need to be discussed. It does pose a great threat to those jobs in industry sectors that may already be affected by automation; hence, this has made their AI policies quite focused on finding inclusive labor-related strategies, involving reskilling programs and mechanisms for social protection against the eventuality of layoffs.

The global disparities in AI regulation underscore the challenge of international cooperation. There is no unified international agreement as to how to best regulate the impact of AI on the workforce, even while countries like the EU have championed international collaboration on AI ethics and governance. This lack of harmonized laws raises concerns of "regulatory arbitrage" by multinational corporations seeking out the jurisdictions with lenient regulations. International organizations such as the OECD, the United Nations, and the World Economic Forum have called for the creation of global frameworks that promote cross-border cooperation on AI governance, ensuring that AI technologies are used responsibly, regardless of the country in which they are developed or deployed.

The global landscape for AI policy and regulation is complex and highly varied. While some regions, like the EU, are more cautious and human-centered, others, like the U.S. and China, emphasize innovation and market-driven policies. International cooperation will be essential to ensure that policies align with shared values of fairness, equality, and human dignity as AI continues to influence the future of work. From the myriad of policy frameworks established across countries, it's clear that effective regulation of

AI demands a balanced approach between innovation and workers' security as well as ensuring ethical application of AI across borders.

5. GOVERNANCE AS THE MANAGEMENT PANACEA FOR WORK UNDER AI IMPACT

In any case, good governance must guarantee that AI is deployed at the workplace only as an engine of economic growth without damaging workers' rights and contributing to social welfare. Governance's role involves diverse actors, which range from government, corporations, to civil society who all play crucial roles in developing, regulating, and implementing AI technologies in the labor market. Governance structures should ensure AI's disruptive force is managed well, addressing ways in which its productivity-enhancing potential could feed into exacerbation of inequality and job displacement together with social exclusion.

Stronger public policies within the government hold the key in regulating AI influence on work. Governments should strike a balance between innovation and human rights protection. AI should be used to improve the lives of all workers rather than replacing them. Some of the key areas of focus include labor market interventions such as reskilling and upskilling programs, social safety nets for displaced workers, and policies that promote fair access to the opportunities created by AI (Brynjolfsson & McAfee, 2014). For instance, the government can develop programs that would help retrain workers in those industries that are at a high risk of automation, such as manufacturing or retail, so that those workers can find new jobs in the digital economy. These policies also need to ensure that low-wage or vulnerable workers are not left behind in the face of technological change, and that the benefits of AI adoption are widely distributed across society.

Governance also encourages corporate responsibility. This is a call to business to take active steps to ensure that their AI systems are designed and deployed in ways that are ethical, transparent, and fair. All of these include the requirements that AI technologies do not reproduce biases, assure data privacy protection, and support inclusive workplace cultures that are not easily disrupted by automation. Such companies can provide leadership through practices such as in-house AI ethics boards, diversity and inclusion practices in hiring and promotion, and responsible AI standards. Further, the companies need to be answerable to the choices they make regarding AI, especially the ones related to hiring algorithms that result in perpetuation of gender as well as racial biases. According to O'Neil (2016), ethical governing of AI development through corporate governance is very vital to mitigate the risks introduced by automation and decision-making algorithm.

Public-private partnerships are also a major aspect of the governance of AI. A win-win situation should be created, ensuring that both the government and private companies understand each other, thereby making regulation not only viable but also something that encourages innovation. Such relationships may spur more innovative AI technological advancements that improve outcomes for labor. For example, government-based research programs or AI development funds may be put in specific projects where the public would like to see their interests satisfied, such as healthcare, education, and sustainable developments. Through mutual cooperation, the public and private sectors can ensure that AI is developed in ways that benefit society at large, minimize harms to workers, and provide fair opportunities for all. Simultaneously, companies must participate in public policy to ensure regulations do not stifle innovation or create unnecessary burdens that may slow technological progress.

Civil society, including labor unions, advocacy groups, and citizens, is another indispensable part of AI governance. Civil society can hold governments and corporations accountable in how AI systems affect workers and society. Labor unions, for instance, may advocate for protections for workers from the impact of automation. Advocacy groups might push for better data protection and transparency regarding AI use in the workplace. Public participation, including mechanisms like public consultations or oversight bodies under democratically elected leaders, ensures that the AI policy caters to all the issues of concern to different stakeholders and specifically marginalized or vulnerable groups. The engagement of civil society assures the responsiveness of the governance structures towards societal needs and more especially those relating to social justice and equity matters emerging in the face of AI introduction.

Lastly, international governance is very important for addressing the global nature of AI technologies. AI does not recognize national borders, and thus, the governance frameworks have to be international in scope for cross-border challenges such as data privacy, job displacement, and ethical concerns. International organizations, including the United Nations, the Organisation for Economic Co-operation and Development (OECD), and the World Economic Forum (WEF), have started to develop frameworks for AI governance that encourage countries to collaborate on setting global standards. However, there is still significant divergence in the approaches of different nations, with some regions prioritizing economic growth through AI innovation and others focusing more on social welfare protections. Establishing global cooperation on AI governance is essential to avoid regulatory fragmentation and to ensure that AI technologies are developed in ways that respect universal human rights, safeguard workers' dignity, and promote fairness.

Governance plays an essential role in managing the impact of AI on work. By coordinating efforts across governments, corporations, civil society, and international organizations, societies can navigate the complexities of AI's transformative effects. Good governance frameworks must be adaptable, responsive, and inclusive in ensuring that AI is a tool for shared prosperity with minimal harms to workers and society. By collaborative governance, we can ensure that AI development is guided towards a future in which technology will benefit all, social justice will be promoted, and sustainable growth will be ensured.

6. ETHICAL AND HUMAN-CENTRIC AI POLICIES

The development and deployment of artificial intelligence (AI) technologies pose huge ethical concerns, especially regarding the impact on the workforce. The development of AI policies should ensure that the benefits of AI development are in harmony with core human values, respect the rights of individuals, and contribute to the well-being of workers in the digital age. These policies must address issues such as fairness, transparency, accountability, privacy, and the preservation of human dignity, ensuring that AI technologies are used not to exploit or harm individuals but to enhance their lives and empower them in their work.

One of the foundational principles of ethical AI is fairness, particularly in how AI systems make decisions that affect individuals' lives and careers. For instance, algorithms deployed in recruitment, hiring, and performance evaluation need to be very well designed not to have any biases that could lead to discrimination. AI models are trained based on historical data that may include societal biases leading to outcomes that perpetuate discrimination based on race, gender, socioeconomic status, or disability. In such a scenario, human-centric AI policies must provide adequate and strong frameworks for auditing algorithms, with transparency and a lack of bias. Mechanisms to address bias should also be part of such frameworks, thereby forcing companies and developers to proactively identify and mitigate bias in AI models (O'Neil, 2016). Such policies emphasize fairness, so that AI technologies do not deepen existing inequalities or exclude marginalized groups from job opportunities and advancement.

Transparency is another key ethical consideration. AI systems, especially those used in critical decision-making processes, should be transparent in how they operate. This transparency is necessary for workers to understand how decisions are being made that affect their lives and livelihoods. It becomes an essential requirement that workers trust the AI systems involved in the process of hiring and performance monitoring while allocating rewards. Ethical policies should mandate the disclosure of criteria used by the AI systems in decision-making and explain to the worker how AI has affected their employment. Such policies would alleviate worries about "black box" algorithms that act without explanations, and provide pathways for workers to contest decisions as unjust or discriminatory.

Accountability is the last of the main principles of human-centric AI policies. In circumstances where AI decides what happens to the worker—assessing his or her performance, deciding about compensation, or choosing who shall be promoted to a position higher than theirs—a clear accountability framework must be instituted. Workers should be able to hold accountable the AI system as well as the human agents that design, implement, and manage the system. For this reason, regulatory frameworks have to be developed in order to assign responsibility to AI-driven outcomes so that the companies can be held liable for the actions of their AI systems when those cause harm or unjust treatment. Policies can ensure that companies do not use their AI systems to avoid accountability for wrongful job dismissals or discriminatory hiring practices, among other negative consequences.

Data privacy and protection are also critical ethical concerns in AI governance. AI systems often rely on large amounts of personal data to function effectively, raising questions about how this data is collected, stored, and used. The human-centric AI policies, thus, must ensure that individuals' privacy rights are protected, particularly on the job where people are subjected to performance metrics, health information, and behavior patterns. Laws like the European Union's General Data Protection Regulation set an important standard for data privacy, but there remains a desire for globally consistent rules to ensure protection against unauthorized access, misuse, or exploitation of worker personal information. This will be vital in ensuring that AI systems respect individual privacy, thereby engendering public trust in the use of AI technologies and allaying surveillance or exploitation fears.

Human-centered AI policies also need to take into consideration the preservation of human dignity. Such machines should be designed to enhance human capabilities rather than to supplant or undermine them. In the context of work, for example, AI should be utilized toward augmenting human creativity, decision-making, and productivity in the workspace instead of dehumanizing workers or transforming them into mere automatons. Such policies would facilitate the development of AI systems in ways that make meaningful contributions to workers, like providing tools for problem-solving or assisting in decision-making processes. Also, human dignity must be ensured by preventing over-invasive surveillance and penalizing workers without being given a chance to respond through the use of AI. Therefore, the ethical deployment of AI must involve a commitment to respecting the intrinsic value of workers as individuals and ensuring that technology enhances their capabilities rather than undermining their autonomy or well-being.

Finally, fostering a human-centric approach to AI means creating policies that promote inclusivity and access. As AI technologies increasingly become central to various industries, workers need to be equipped with the skills to adapt to these changes. Human-centric policies should include provisions for reskilling and upskilling the workforce, especially in sectors vulnerable to automation. Such policies can ensure that workers are not left behind as AI reshapes the labor market but empowered to take on new, meaningful roles that AI technologies help create. Moreover, these policies have to be all-inclusive and ensure that equal opportunities are accorded to everybody, regardless of their background. This includes individuals from underrepresented groups who could benefit from advancements in AI.

Therefore, ethical human-centered AI policies are necessary in guiding the development and deployment of AI technologies toward fairness, transparency, accountability, privacy, and respect for human dignity. By focusing on these core principles, policies can help ensure that AI contributes to a future of work that is inclusive, equitable, and respectful of workers' rights. As AI continues to evolve, it will be critical for policymakers to adapt these ethical principles to new developments in AI technology, ensuring that the workforce remains at the center of a human-centric digital economy.

7. INTERNATIONAL COLLABORATION AND HARMONIZATION

As AI technologies transcend national borders and their impacts become increasingly global, international collaboration and harmonization of regulatory frameworks are essential to effectively manage AI's influence on the workforce. Given the inherently global nature of AI—where research, development, and deployment often span multiple countries—the challenges posed by AI in the workplace cannot be tackled by individual nations in isolation. This calls for a combined, multilateral approach to finding solutions to concerns like labor dislocation, privacy of data, fairness in algorithmic decision, and the ethical applications of AI. International cooperation sets in place constant standards, averts the tendency toward regulatory divergence, and develops ways of putting AI to appropriate use for society and workers generally.

One of the great advantages of international collaboration is to establish common ethical standards and regulations that can be adopted across borders. This would be very significant because of the differences in regulation approaches that vary from country to country. For example, the European Union is known to take a highly stringent regulatory approach as seen in the Artificial Intelligence Act (European Commission, 2021). The United States is more relaxed with a more fragmented and sector-specific approach toward AI regulation. On the other hand, China is known to adopt a more state-led approach for AI development, with relatively lesser emphasis on worker protection. Such differences can also lead to "regulatory arbitrage," as companies shift their operations to nations with more relaxed rules, hence undermining the possibility of creating universally acceptable standards of ethical AI application (Cui, 2021). Aligning AI policies across countries minimizes the arbitrage and keeps companies accountable, regardless of location, to abide by common ethics.

International cooperation also facilitates the sharing of knowledge and best practices in AI governance. As countries develop their own AI policies, they gather valuable lessons about what works and what does not. Through international forums, governments can learn from each other and avoid repeating mistakes. For example, countries could share successful case studies in retraining workers displaced by AI-driven automation or in creating frameworks that promote inclusive AI development. Institutions such as the Organisation for Economic Co-operation and Development (OECD) and the United Nations (UN) provide platforms for such collaboration, where member states can align their policies, discuss regulatory challenges, and propose joint initiatives to manage AI's impact on work (OECD, 2019). These forums can facilitate the exchange of knowledge in helping to build a more cohesive global strategy for AI governance that is forward-looking and adaptable to rapid technological changes.

International collaboration is also essential in dealing with the challenges of data privacy and security in the age of AI. AI systems rely on large datasets to train algorithms, which may include sensitive personal information. Data protection law varies between nations, with, for example, the European Union having a fairly comprehensive General Data Protection Regulation but the United States being much more fragmented. Lack of uniformity may leave significant gaps in protecting privacy, and when data flow is involved across borders, those gaps are problematic. Harmonizing data protection laws on an international level would make for more uniformity in how personal data is dealt with, such that the privacy of workers will be respected even if their data is collected or processed anywhere else. Such harmonization could give birth to a worldwide data protection framework that strikes the balance between privacy and innovation in such a way that AI technologies can be promoted without infringing on people's rights.

In addition to regulatory alignment, international cooperation is also essential in addressing the social and economic challenges posed by AI-induced job displacement. As automation and AI technologies transform industries, certain jobs may be at risk of obsolescence, particularly in sectors such as manufacturing, retail, and transportation. While some countries might rapidly adapt through retraining programs or universal basic income initiatives, others may not be able to provide such measures. International cooperation can thus help level off these differences by promoting the exchange of policies and practices for the reduction of adverse effects of AI on employment. For instance, the developed nations could share their experience with social protection systems with the developing countries so that they also establish similar systems to protect displaced workers. International cooperation can also facilitate efforts toward fair distribution of the benefits of AI across the world rather than concentrated in a few advanced economies.

Last but certainly not least is the setting up of standards worldwide regarding the application of AI so that the application of AI respects workers' dignity, rights, and safety when these systems are designed and employed. Given the potential for AI to be used in surveillance, performance monitoring, and even in the decision-making process around hiring, promotions, and terminations, international standards for ethical AI governance could provide clear guidelines on how AI should be used to ensure that workers are treated with fairness and respect. International organizations, including the International Labour Organization (ILO), have a role in pushing for the adoption of responsible AI standards at work, and their efforts will focus on the rights of workers as well as how AI can be used to complement human labor instead of replacing it in a manner that promotes quality jobs.

The international cooperation and harmonization of the impact of AI on the global workforce is critical. The global nature of AI technologies requires that the regulatory frameworks are aligned across countries to ensure consistency and fairness. Countries can cooperate in maximizing the benefits of AI while minimizing its risks through shared ethical guidelines, the exchange of best practices, harmonized data protection laws, and joint efforts to address job displacement. As AI continues to evolve, it will be necessary for the international community to act in concert to ensure that its impact on the workforce is positive, equitable, and sustainable.

8. PREPARING FOR THE FUTURE: POLICY RECOMMENDATIONS

As AI continues to transform the global workforce, policymakers must proactively prepare for its challenges and opportunities by developing policies that safeguard workers' rights, promote inclusive economic growth, and foster innovation. The rapid pace of technological advancement demands that governments, businesses, and international organizations adopt forward-thinking approaches to ensure that the benefits of AI are equitably shared while minimizing potential harms. The following policy recommendations aim to create a future where AI technologies enhance human capabilities, protect workers, and support a more resilient and sustainable global economy.

First and foremost, policymakers should address the development of comprehensive education and workforce development programs to prepare the workforce for this AI-driven economy. Given the possible displacement of jobs by AI in some sectors, it is paramount to invest in reskilling and upskilling initiatives. Governments should collaborate with educational institutions, private firms, and labor unions to develop training programs for workers that include the skills required to succeed in the world of digitalization. Such programs should be available across all different sectors of society, especially in manufacturing, retail, and transportation industries, which will be heavily impacted by automation. In addition, there should be policies to encourage lifelong learning. This will mean that workers should have the option of continuously upgrading themselves to embrace new technological advancement. Societies will be in a better position to mitigate some of the negative effects of AI job displacement as well as make workers ready for the new jobs that AI is likely to unleash.

Another vital policy recommendation is establishing robust social protection mechanisms to ensure that workers facing job displacement resulting from AI. While some jobs will be automated, AI will also create entirely new roles that require specialized skills. Governments should implement policies such as unemployment insurance, retraining subsidies, and universal basic income (UBI) schemes to provide a safety net for those who face job loss due to AI automation. These measures will help cushion the economic shock for displaced workers while they transition to new roles. UBI, in particular, has become an area of interest in dealing with the vast displacement of workers in an AI-driven economy. It provides people with a basic income, thus reducing economic inequality, increasing consumer spending, and giving people time to study or engage in entrepreneurial activities without being burdened by the fear of financial insecurity.

To ensure that AI is developed and deployed in an ethical manner, governments must implement robust regulatory frameworks that cover key issues, such as data privacy, algorithmic transparency, and the prevention of biases in AI systems. These regulations would include clear guidelines on how companies can collect, store, and use data while protecting personal information and workers' rights. AI systems should also be audited regularly in detecting and correcting discriminatory biases, more so in hiring, pay equity, and performance. Policies shall ensure such AI developers adhere to such standards of ethics related to fairness, transparency, and accountability. For example, an AI algorithm used in recruitment or employee monitoring must be transparent in its decision-making process so that workers may know how their data is being used and how decisions that affect them are made. These regulatory measures can institute by policymakers to build public trust in AI technologies and prevent the negative consequences of biased or unfair AI systems.

At the international level, collaboration and coordination between governments is necessary to develop harmonized AI regulations. Since AI operates across borders, fragmented national approaches towards regulation might lead to inefficiencies, regulatory arbitrage, and problems in enforcing global standards. Policymakers should collaborate with each other to develop an internationally recognized framework for AI governance, especially in areas of data privacy, ethics, and labor protections. International organizations such as the United Nations (UN) and the Organisation for Economic Co-operation and Development (OECD) can play a significant role in fostering dialogue and achieving consensus on AI regulations. Through harmonization of regulations across countries, governments can avoid fragmentation of AI governance and ensure that the benefits of AI are shared globally. International cooperation will also be instrumental in dealing with the global problems that AI creates, including workforce displacement in developing countries and the digital divide.

Policymakers should further support the development of AI technologies that benefit human well-being and are aligned with social and environmental goals. Governments can encourage research and development in AI applications related to societal challenges, such as healthcare, climate change, and education. This will make AI to contribute to the resolution of serious world problems, like optimizing energy consumption, improved diagnosis of diseases, and customized learning experiences, for example. Government funding through these projects would assure that public spending is going toward solving such urgent global problems and not increasing their prevalence. Such additional benefits should be motivated through public-private partnerships, promoting ethical AI by bringing together a focus on public welfare by the public sector with innovation drive in the private sector to produce better AI solutions beneficial to workers and communities.

And finally, some policies should come into place about preventing the high risks of unnecessary surveillance and attacks on workers' privacy. As the AI technologies advance in the workplace, there has been a significant increase in using AI for employee monitoring, productivity tracking, and increasing surveillance at work. These risks can be controlled by appropriate regulations that specify where the use of AI in monitoring employees is to be drawn from to ensure respect for workers' privacy while providing a legitimate business need such as performance evaluation. Companies should be required to provide transparency in their use of AI surveillance tools and to give workers the ability to challenge or appeal decisions made based on AI systems.

Preparing for the future of AI in the workforce requires comprehensive, proactive policies that address the social, economic, and ethical implications of AI technologies. By investing in education, building of strong social nets, ethical regulation of AI systems, international co-operation, and human-centric orientation of AI technologies, policymakers shall be able to create a better future for a worker and an entire society benefiting from AI technology. As developments of AI continue to advance, the governments and organizations have a responsibility to be ahead of the curve and ensure policies are flexible enough to change with new developments, as well as prepare the workforce for this transition into an AI-driven world.

9. CONCLUSION

As artificial intelligence continues to change the face of the global workforce, the challenges and opportunities presented challenge a thoughtful, coordinated approach to policy and regulation. The transformative potential of AI is exciting for increased productivity, innovation, and new job creation, but it also poses great risks, such as labor displacement, inequality, and ethical dilemmas. The policy framework has to be holistic in balancing technological progress with the protection of workers' rights, economic equity, and social well-being. Achieving this balance would depend on a multi-dimensional strategy in which governments, businesses, international organizations, and civil society come together to develop policies that are both responsive to pressing issues and forward-looking about emerging AI developments.

Inclusiveness and adaptability: one of the main lessons to be gleaned from the discussion above. The growing technology forces changes in governance in order to keep policies flexible and able to adapt to new challenges and opportunities. This calls for collaboration at levels of nationhood and internationality to harmonize regulatory frameworks and require shared ethical standards in AI development and deployment. Adopting global principles for AI governance, such as fairness, transparency, accountability, and data protection, can help nations mitigate the risks of regulatory fragmentation and ensure that AI technologies benefit people everywhere rather than exacerbating existing inequalities.

The need for human-centric AI policies cannot be overstated. AI should enhance human capabilities and enrich the quality of work, not undermine workers' dignity or exacerbate social divides. Policymakers must find ways to protect the exploitation of workers by ensuring that AI systems are transparent, accountable, and free of biases. However, equally important is investing in education, reskilling, and social safety nets to prepare workers for the changing nature of work and minimize the effects of disruption arising from automation. These measures can make workers thrive within an AI-based economy, share the benefits of AI, and not leave someone behind in that transition.

Therefore, governance can play a fundamental role in guiding the impact that AI has on work by helping ensure that the use of these AI technologies happens responsibly and with ethics. It is also crucial to have a robust regulatory framework that safeguards workers' rights, preserves privacy, and promotes fairness to maintain public trust in AI systems. Additionally, as AI is used across borders, international cooperation and harmonization of policies will be crucial to tackle global challenges and ensure that the benefits of AI are equitably distributed across nations, especially in developing economies.

In conclusion, the future of AI in the workforce holds both tremendous promise and significant challenges. By adopting forward-thinking policies that emphasize ethical development, worker protection, and international cooperation, we can create a future where AI serves as a force for good—enhancing productivity, creating new job opportunities, and improving the quality of life for people around the world. As we chart our path through this messy landscape, we must be particularly vigilant in pursuing our efforts toward using AI for empowering people and enhancing human dignity and toward furthering a more inclusive, equitable, and sustainable global workforce.

REFERENCES

Binns, A. (2021). Regulating Artificial Intelligence: A Global Perspective on the EU's AI Act and Worker Protection. *European Journal of Law and Technology*, *12*(3), 104–115.

Brynjolfsson, E., & McAfee, A. (2014). *The Second Machine Age: Work, Progress, and Prosperity in a Time of Brilliant Technologies*. W. W. Norton & Company.

Bughin, J.. (2018). *Skill shift: Automation and the future of the workforce*. McKinsey Global Institute.

Camacho, F. (2020). Artificial Intelligence and the Future of Work in Latin America. *Latin American Policy Review*, *5*(2), 37–51.

Cui, L. (2021). China's AI Strategy: Implications for Global Workforce and Governance. *Journal of Chinese Political Science*, *26*(4), 429–448.

European Commission. (2021). Proposal for a Regulation laying down harmonized rules on Artificial Intelligence (Artificial Intelligence Act). Available at: https://ec.europa.eu/info/index_en

Frey, C. B., & Osborne, M. A. (2017). The future of employment: How susceptible are jobs to computerization? *Technological Forecasting and Social Change*, *114*, 254–280. DOI: 10.1016/j.techfore.2016.08.019

McKinsey Global Institute. (2021). The future of work after. *COVID*, *19*, •••. https://www.mckinsey.com

O'Neil, C. (2016). *Weapons of Math Destruction: How Big Data Increases Inequality and Threatens Democracy*. Crown Publishing Group.

OECD. (2019). *OECD Principles on Artificial Intelligence*. Available at: https://www.oecd.org/going-digital/ai/

West, D. M., & Allen, J. R. (2018). *How artificial intelligence is transforming the future of work*. Brookings Institution. Available at: https://www.brookings.edu/research/

World Economic Forum. (2020). *The Future of Jobs Report 2020*. Available at: https://www.weforum.org/reports/

Chapter 16
The AI-Driven Workplace: Navigating the Ethical Challenges of Automation

Himanshi Rajora
https://orcid.org/0000-0001-5686-3030
O.P. Jindal Global University, India

Huy Hung Ta
https://orcid.org/0009-0008-6835-3036
International School, Vietnam National University, Hanoi, Vietnam

Damith Gangodawilage
https://orcid.org/0000-0001-7968-6284
Qasim Ibrahim School of Business, Villa College, Maldives

ABSTRACT

This chapter explores the ethical challenges of AI-driven automation in the workplace, addressing the impact of artificial intelligence on employees, organizations, and society. As AI systems become integral to various industries, ethical concerns such as job displacement, algorithmic bias, data privacy, and transparency are increasingly significant. The chapter examines the benefits of AI in enhancing productivity and decision-making while highlighting the potential risks, particularly the displacement of workers and perpetuation of societal biases. It emphasizes the importance of human oversight, employee education, and the creation of ethical frameworks to ensure AI is deployed responsibly. The role of legal and regulatory structures in addressing these challenges is also discussed, alongside the importance of fostering an ethical AI culture within organizations. This comprehensive analysis provides insights into how businesses can navigate the complexities of AI ethics, promoting responsible use of AI technologies while mitigating risks.

DOI: 10.4018/979-8-3373-1270-5.ch016

INTRODUCTION: THE EMERGENCE OF AI IN THE WORKPLACE

Artificial intelligence has rapidly evolved to become the new face of the modern workplace, from being a futuristic idea to a reality applied across the industries. Over the past couple of years, the emergence of AI-based technologies such as machine learning, natural language processing, and robotics have dramatically transformed operations, enhancing efficiency, decision-making, and productivity (Brynjolfsson & McAfee, 2014). Companies are increasingly using AI to automate repetitive tasks, optimize supply chains, personalize customer experiences, and even assist in complex decision-making processes (Chui, Manyika, & Miremadi, 2016). Thus, AI has become central to business strategies, promising not only improved operational performance but also the creation of new business models and opportunities (West, 2018).

However, this trend of automation raises some very important ethical issues, especially with the increasing assumption of roles previously dominated by human workers by AI. For instance, the growing use of AI in customer service, data analysis, and healthcare has raised concerns over employment, privacy, and fairness (Binns, 2018). Hence, it is critical that organizations make strides in their response to these dilemmas while availing the full benefit of AI. Businesses and policymakers must ensure the future of work is prepared as AI affects their deployment for more ethical ends with minimal damage or detrimental effects on any party concerned. The advancement of AI technology has made the aspect of its ethics of utmost importance, as it shall be central in shaping the sustainable, inclusive, and just future of work for the people. The Research questions, the chapter tries to answer are-

1. **How can organizations balance the ethical implications of AI-driven automation with the need for increased efficiency and productivity in the workplace?**
2. **What frameworks or guidelines can be developed to ensure transparency, fairness, and accountability in AI-driven decision-making processes within the workplace?**
3. **How do employees perceive the integration of AI technologies in their work environments, and what strategies can organizations adopt to foster trust and collaboration between humans and AI systems?**

BENEFITS OF AI-DRIVEN AUTOMATION

AI-driven automation is greatly beneficial for companies and industries due to enhanced efficiency, productivity, and reduced cost. The most important advantage of AI integration is that it takes care of repetitive and mundane tasks, so human workers can focus on the more complex and creative parts of their job. This transition increases productivity but also leads to higher job satisfaction since employees are relieved of monotonous work (Brynjolfsson & McAfee, 2014). Automation, led by AI technologies such as machine learning and natural language processing, can look at huge data sets much more rapidly and accurately than humans do, which increases the decision-making process and reaction to market shifts (Chui, Manyika, & Miremadi, 2016).

Besides enhancing efficiency, AI-driven automation helps reduce human errors. In manufacturing and logistics environments, AI systems can conduct tasks with high accuracy and predictability, avoiding costly errors and optimizing production (Davenport & Ronanki, 2018). Moreover, AI can increase the safety of workplace environments by assuming dangerous tasks that may risk human workers, such as those involving hazardous materials, heavy machinery, or repetitive physical motions (West, 2018). This is a very important feature for industries such as health care and manufacturing where safety and accuracy are very important.

The growth of AI has been accompanied by the possibility of coming up with new innovative business models. Companies can also use AI to create personalized customer experiences, optimize product recommendations, and develop services that had never been thought of before (Brynjolfsson & McAfee, 2014). AI helps organizations understand the preference of customers and market trends, giving them a competitive advantage in fast-evolving industries. Thus, businesses embracing AI-driven automation can not only enhance operational performance but also adapt more rapidly to changing market dynamics and consumer demands (Binns, 2018).

ETHICAL ISSUES: JOB DISPLACEMENT

One of the most pressing ethical issues with AI-driven automation is the possibility of large-scale job displacement. The ability of AI technologies to perform tasks previously done by human workers, including manufacturing, customer service, and even complex decision-making processes, continues to advance (Brynjolfsson & McAfee, 2014). It is raising the most fundamental questions regarding the responsibilities of businesses and policymakers to address the employment impact of automation. Though automation helps improve efficiency, and lowers costs, the job-loss effects on millions of low-wage workers have a lot of chances to come (Frey & Osborne, 2017). An increasing role of AI across the transportations, retail sectors, and the logistics business places a strong existence threat for labor in such an industry. Hence, economic as well as social issues come before us.

From an ethical standpoint, the question arises as to who bears the responsibility for addressing the consequences of job displacement. Companies that implement AI-driven automation for profit maximization may not consider the broader societal costs of mass unemployment or the potential for increased income inequality (Brynjolfsson & McAfee, 2014). Workers who are displaced by AI systems might not find suitable employment, especially if they are not equipped or educated to flourish in an economy dominated by AI. This raises the question of whether businesses are responsible for creating retraining programs and supporting transitions in the workforce. On an ethical level, companies should consider not just the short-term profits from automation but also their long-term employees' and community's well-being.

This further raises ethical issues that extend beyond immediate job losses to broader societal implications in the widespread automation of jobs. Job displacement may be increased and may be higher for lower-skilled workers, thus potentially widening the existing inequality gap and separating winners from losers (Frey & Osborne, 2017). It would be pretty destabilizing because, if a huge number of displaced workers didn't have a support system for being reassigned within the economy, they may never adjust. Ethical obligations both for the government and the companies in place can become essential while AI automation takes control and its rewards are divided as widely as possible.

In response to these challenges, some advocates suggest initiatives such as universal basic income (UBI) to cushion the impact of job loss on one's finances. Others insist on investing in education and the development of skills to prepare workers for the jobs of the future (Brynjolfsson & McAfee, 2014). However, the most contentious issue arising in the debate on AI-driven automation pertains to how a promise of advancement through technology will be balanced with the ethical obligation to protect workers.

BIAS IN AI SYSTEMS: THE NEW ETHICAL CONCERN

The issue of bias in AI systems is becoming an increasingly important ethical concern as artificial intelligence integrates more decision-making processes into most sectors. AI models, especially those based on machine learning, are trained on vast datasets, and these datasets often reflect historical patterns, societal inequalities, and human biases. If not carefully monitored, AI systems can inadvertently perpetuate and even amplify these biases, leading to discriminatory outcomes that disproportionately affect marginalized groups. For instance, hiring algorithms, credit scoring algorithms, and law enforcement algorithms may reflect biased behavior if the data they are trained on is biased or reflects societal stereotypes (O'Neil, 2016). Such biases can manifest in a number of ways, such as unfair hiring practices, biased loan approvals, or racial profiling by predictive policing systems, all of which raise significant ethical questions about fairness, equity, and justice.

One of the most disturbing aspects of AI bias is that it is often hard to detect and correct. Machine learning algorithms are "black boxes," meaning that the decision-making processes underlying their predictions are not always transparent or easily understood by humans. As a result, even when biased outcomes occur, it can be challenging to identify the specific cause or make adjustments to eliminate the bias (Binns, 2018). For example, a facial recognition system may more frequently misidentify people from specific racial or ethnic groups, but it is not always clear whether the problem lies in the quality of the training data, the algorithm itself, or both (Angwin, Larson, Mattu, & Kirchner, 2016). This lack of transparency complicates efforts at holding developers and organizations accountable for biased outcomes and makes it harder to build trust in AI systems.

Ethical implications: The impact of AI bias transcends beyond the shroud of technicality to touch serious high-stakes areas of criminal justice, healthcare, and finance. For instance, in the criminal justice system, predictive algorithms that determine reoffending have been found to disproportionately label Black and Hispanic people as high risk even though they are not necessarily more likely to reoffend than their white counterparts (Angwin et al., 2016). In healthcare, biased AI systems can lead to unequal access to medical care or misdiagnosis based on skewed data, which can further aggravate health disparities. In finance, algorithms may attempt to determine creditworthiness unfairly disadvantage people due to historical inequities in lending practices, targeting low-income individuals and minorities for example (Binns, 2018).

Eliminating bias in AI systems is a collaborative effort between developers, companies, and policymakers. Developers should be proactive in choosing representative datasets and implementing auditing and mitigation techniques into their models. Transparency in the design and decision-making processes of AI systems is also crucial for accountability and trust in these technologies (O'Neil, 2016). In addition, ethical guidelines and regulations should be developed to ensure that AI systems are deployed in a fair and equitable manner, with mechanisms in place for addressing instances of bias when they occur. In particular, the moral responsibility of the AI developer or organization is not only to ensure the efficiency of these systems but also to see that they are not perpetuating some form of bias or worsening inequalities.

PRIVACY AND DATA SECURITY IN THE NEW AUTOMATION

AI-driven automation becomes a pervasive fact in workplaces. Privacy and data security will emerge as ethical challenges. A massive amount of personal, professional, and transactional data is therefore used by these AI systems, which makes it a central aspect of modern business practices to guarantee data privacy. Most of these activities, such as hiring, customer service, or evaluation, require the analysis of sensitive information, including personally identifiable information, behavioral patterns, and other attributes. While these systems can offer greater convenience and efficiency, they also pose risks to individual privacy, especially when data is collected without adequate transparency or consent (Zeng, Lu, & Zhao, 2018). For example, employees do not know to what extent their personal data is being tracked and how it would be used in the decision-making process by the AI systems; this raises an ethical concern in the treatment of data and protecting individual rights.

The risk of misuse of personal data through AI systems raises another significant ethical issue. Since AI can analyze large datasets to identify patterns and make predictions, there is a risk that sensitive information could be exposed or misused. In the context of employee monitoring, AI-driven systems can track workers' activities, locations, and even emotional states, creating potential for invasive surveillance and an erosion of personal freedoms (West, 2018). For instance, employers may utilize AI systems to monitor the productivity of employees by constant surveillance. This creates an environment at the workplace that is perceived as intrusive and diminishes the autonomy of workers. On the other hand, AI systems used for collecting customer data for targeted marketing or product recommendations may cross ethical lines if they manipulate consumer behavior or exploit personal vulnerabilities (Zeng et al., 2018).

In addition to concerns over privacy, the reliance on AI systems is also associated with a critical security issue: that of data. The more information AI systems acquire, the higher the likelihood that these systems become vulnerable to cyberattacks through hacking and data breaches. Cases such as leaks of personal data from facial recognition and customer service bot systems exemplify the vulnerabilities associated with such technologies (O'Neil, 2016). These breaches will cause massive harm to individuals in regard to identity theft and financial fraud, plus tarnish the reputation of organizations that are not secure. The protection of such sensitive information that AI systems are entrusted to handle means these organizations need to invest in good data security measures, encrypting, anonymizing, and all other security techniques to mitigate the risk involved with any breach.

In terms of ethics, it is a responsibility of business and AI developers to ensure not only that the data is properly stored and transmitted but also proactively implements the data privacy regulation. This calls for openness on data practice, like the fact of which data they are collecting, what they do with the data collected, and whom they are passing the data on to. In addition, AI systems should be designed with privacy by design principles, meaning that privacy protections are integrated into the system from the outset rather than as an afterthought (West, 2018). Governments and regulatory bodies also have a role to play in creating comprehensive privacy laws and data protection frameworks that address the evolving challenges posed by AI and automation. Examples include the General Data Protection Regulation within the European Union, which could be seen as a model in regulating data collection and processing by the government and hence giving more power to the citizens over their own personal information (Zeng et al., 2018).

Therefore, the dual challenges of privacy and data security should be addressed as AI-driven automation continues to transform industries. Safeguarding personal and sensitive information from misuse and ensuring transparency and accountability are paramount in maintaining public trust and individual rights.

It will require robust security protocols, ethical data practices, and adherence to regulatory standards to ensure that organizations navigate this complex intersection of AI, privacy, and data security responsibly.

ROLE OF HUMAN OVERSIGHT IN AI DECISION-MAKING

As AI systems increasingly become integrated into decision-making processes in various sectors, the importance of human oversight in AI operations has never been more critical. AI technologies, especially those based on machine learning, can analyze vast volumes of data and generate insights that significantly enhance decision-making. But, of course, these systems are not infallible, and their decisions have far-reaching effects on individuals, organizations, and society at large. The ethical challenge, therefore, lies in making sure that human judgment remains a part of the decision-making process, especially in high-stakes areas such as healthcare, criminal justice, and hiring.

One of the key reasons for incorporating human oversight is to mitigate the risks associated with AI's limitations, including the potential for biased or flawed decision-making. As discussed earlier, AI systems can inadvertently perpetuate societal biases, especially when trained on incomplete or biased datasets. Human oversight serves as a safeguard against such biases by allowing decision-makers to evaluate AI outputs within a broader ethical and societal context (Binns, 2018). For instance, a hiring-related AI system could propose candidates to select based on data that reflect the gender and racial disparities present. Human review of this decision may identify those biases and direct decisions toward a standard of ethics concerning fairness and equality.

Finally, even though AI can process and analyze volumes and speeds beyond human capability, it is limited in terms of the richness and depth that humans bring to decisions. AI systems do not necessarily understand the intricacies of human emotions, cultural contexts, or ethical considerations in decision-making, which are often essential when making decisions that affect people's lives. For example, AI-driven systems in healthcare may recommend treatments based on statistical probabilities, but they may fail to account for a patient's unique circumstances, preferences, or the potential for unintended consequences (Davenport & Ronanki, 2018). Human oversight ensures these considerations and, consequently, empathy and moral responsibility are reflected in decisions.

More importantly, human oversight ensures that AI-driven decisions do not operate with lack of accountability and transparency. This is because AI can operate as "black boxes" - internal processes in which the end users and even the developers are often clueless, thereby necessitating human oversight in terms of AI explainability and transparency (Binns, 2018). It is essential that human overseers can explain how and why such decisions were made when AI systems make decisions, especially those with significant consequences. This not only builds trust in AI systems but also allows for accountability when errors or biases occur. For example, in criminal justice sectors, where AI is used to predict recidivism or determine bail amounts, human oversight helps ensure that the decisions made by AI systems are scrutinized and justified, thereby reducing the likelihood of unjust outcomes (Angwin et al., 2016).

Human oversight is key in the address of issues over the autonomy of AI. As AI evolves to be extremely autonomous and act without direct control from human actions, issues associated with responsibility and controls arise. Is it the control of a specific human being since an AI causes harm or gives a wrong information? Human operators should be able to intervene if any undesirable or unexpected outcomes are observed in the behavior of autonomous vehicles. For instance, although the AI system makes it possible for a vehicle to complete its journey through traffic, the human operator is always ready to override the system at the slightest chance that it cannot handle a particular situation (Lin, 2016). Similarly, in automated finance or insurance systems, human oversight is necessary to ensure that decisions are not just driven by algorithms but also reflect broader ethical considerations, such as equity and fairness.

Lastly, human oversight ensures that AI is a tool that serves human interests and not a replacement for human judgment. While AI can augment human decision-making, it should not reduce the role of human ethics, values, or critical thinking. The most ethical way forward in ensuring that the benefits of automation are realized without sacrificing human oversight or responsibility is through a collaborative approach where AI assists but does not fully replace human judgment.

AI is capable of revolutionizing decision-making, but human oversight remains an essential component to ensure that these systems are used ethically, transparently, and responsibly. Human judgment is necessary to detect and correct biases, ensure decisions are made with empathy, maintain accountability, and prevent the erosion of ethical standards. With further evolutions of AI, organizations and policymakers need to establish frameworks that take into account human oversight in the AI systems for technology to continue being in step with human values and ethical principles.

AI AND THE FUTURE OF EMPLOYEE AUTONOMY

The integration of artificial intelligence (AI) into the workplace has significant implications for employee autonomy, which refers to the freedom and discretion workers have in making decisions related to their tasks and responsibilities. While AI can enhance efficiency and productivity, its influence on the autonomy of employees is a subject of growing concern. In some instances, AI systems can be tools that augment human decision-making, allowing workers to focus on higher-level, creative tasks. In other cases, however, AI-driven automation can limit autonomy by dictating the scope of tasks employees can perform or reducing their ability to make independent decisions (Brynjolfsson & McAfee, 2014). This dual nature of AI poses ethical challenges that must be carefully considered as organizations continue to deploy these technologies.

AI's potential to reduce employee autonomy is most pronounced in highly automated workplaces, where employees may find their roles increasingly controlled by AI systems. In the area of manufacturing or logistics, AI might perform repetitive jobs such as on an assembly line, inventory checking, or filling orders, taking much of the decision-making responsibility and creative room from human laborers (Chui, Manyika, & Miremadi, 2016). Such automation is likely to shrink the range of tasks that people are expected to perform, reducing the scope and variety of what employees do. Eroding the autonomy over time ends up taking away job satisfaction, engaging the workforce, and the feeling of powerlessness from the worker. Secondly, as the AI systems take over these roles, then the human is subjected to performance metrics as dictated by the AI with no room for judgment and discretion during the work. This idea has been echoed by Brynjolfsson & McAfee in 2014.

On the other hand, AI may help in promoting employee autonomy because it frees up the workers from monotonous and time-consuming work, and enables them to concentrate on complex, strategic, and creative aspects of their work. For instance, in the healthcare sector, AI can help in administrative work like scheduling, data entry, and patient management. This will enable health professionals to spend more time on patient care and decision-making (Davenport & Ronanki, 2018). Similarly, in creative industries such as marketing or design, AI can help with data analysis, trend identification, and content generation, which allows employees to focus on developing innovative strategies and ideas. In these contexts, AI is used as an enabling technology that enables employees to make decisions, contribute their expertise, and engage in higher-level work to promote greater autonomy at work.

However, how much AI enhances or constrains employee autonomy will depend on the way it is integrated into organizational structures and workplace practices. For AI to positively impact autonomy, it must be implemented in such a way that it complements the human workers instead of replacing them. In doing so, this calls for thoughtful design approaches that enhance the capabilities of employees and preserve human input in decision-making. To start, AI-based operations should manage high-repeat jobs or extremely demanding jobs because of human labor demands for strategic management decisions and common judgments (Chui et al., 2016). A hybrid model wherein human workers may take control allows workers to regain autonomy over tasks because AI, used as the additional tool cannot reduce work human involvement or work.

The ethical implications of this impact would then be extended beyond the workplace to society, considering all areas of job displacement and worker empowerment. Therefore, as AI progressively continues to take over selected tasks, businesses and governments must look into the main challenges of reskilling and upskilling workers to ensure that they can fit into the new landscape of jobs. Policies that provide workers with access to training and education will help empower employees to navigate the future of work and maintain control over their careers (Brynjolfsson & McAfee, 2014). Also, companies should include workers in the design and implementation of AI systems to ensure that automation is introduced in ways that align with their needs, values, and preferences. Participatory approaches that include worker involvement in AI decision-making can help retain autonomy while making the benefits of automation more productive.

Conclusion: The relationship between AI and employee autonomy is indeed complex and multi-faceted. While AI can both reduce and increase the autonomy of the workplace, its implementation must be done in ways that empower the employees rather than undermine their independence. Ethical considerations, such as transparency, fairness, and opportunities for upskilling, will be crucial in ensuring that AI-driven workplaces are supportive, inclusive, and empowering for all workers. As companies consider thoughtful integration of AI in the workspace to balance between automation and autonomy, their approach toward efficiency and human-orientedness would be well rounded.

LEGAL AND REGULATORY FRAMEWORKS FOR AI ETHICS

It's quite essential that as artificial intelligence penetrates various aspects of business and society, there has been a sense of urgency over the need to have strong legal and regulatory frameworks governing its use ethically. AI technologies come with challenges not easily solved by existing laws and regulations. It extends from issues like privacy, equity, account, transparency, and safety in its scope; thus, their regulation calls for careful consideration such that AI is developed and put into action along with standards on ethics and society. With how complex AI already is, including the fact of its fast progress, the society demands an expanded legal structure governing these technologies such that they allow for the latest changes to it.

One of the most central issues in coming up with a legal and regulatory framework for AI ethics is achieving a balance between innovation and protection. On one hand, it is feared that overly restrictive regulation could stifle innovation and, therefore, would prevent the proper development of these AI technologies and their subsequent contributions to sectors ranging from healthcare to finance to education.

On the other hand, the lack of regulation could allow harmful or unethical practices to proliferate, such as the deployment of biased algorithms, invasion of privacy, and lack of accountability in automated decision-making systems. The challenge, therefore, lies in creating regulations that provide a clear legal framework for AI developers and users, while also allowing room for technological growth and flexibility (Binns, 2018).

One of the critical elements of AI regulation is to ensure transparency and accountability in AI systems. AI systems, especially those that utilize machine learning algorithms, can be "black boxes," where the reasoning behind decisions is not easily understandable or accessible to humans. This lack of transparency can result in unintended consequences, such as discrimination or violation of privacy, without any clear way of identifying or addressing the issue (O'Neil, 2016). The legal frameworks, therefore, must ensure that AI systems are explainable, and the decision-making process can be audited and scrutinized by other parties. Such steps include laws such as the General Data Protection Regulation of the European Union, which includes provisions on algorithmic transparency and the right to an explanation (Voigt & Von dem Bussche, 2017). Essentially, regulatory bodies must ensure that AI systems operate with a level of clarity that allows users, stakeholders, and regulators to understand how and why these decisions are made.

In addition, accountability is another critical issue in AI regulation. As AI systems are increasingly entrusted with decision-making power, it becomes crucial to establish clear guidelines regarding liability when these systems cause harm or operate in ways that are unethical. For instance, if an accident or injury is caused by an AI system in autonomous vehicles, the question of who is responsible arises: the developer, the manufacturer, or the operator of the system. Clear legal definitions of responsibility and accountability have to be put in place to ensure that those who deploy AI systems are held accountable for their technology's output (Lin, 2016). Indeed, a number of countries such as the United States and the European Union are already making efforts toward the establishment of frameworks that address the liability of AI, though it remains a developing area of law.

Data privacy and security is another important area for legal consideration. AI systems need to work with a lot of data, but the concern for personal data security and privacy is highly raised. For instance, the GDPR brought in the idea of "data protection by design," where the organization must include privacy protection within the design of AI systems to ensure that data processing is lawfully conducted, transparent, and respectful of individual rights (Voigt & Von dem Bussche, 2017). Similarly, the CCPA gives the rights to individuals regarding their personal data, such as the right to opt-out from data collection for AI-driven marketing purposes. As AI systems get more complex, global regulatory bodies need to come together to formulate coherent and consistent frameworks that will ensure privacy rights are protected across jurisdictions.

Regulations must also address the ethical considerations of risks of algorithmic bias. AI systems can inadvertently entrench societal inequalities if the data they are trained on reflects existing biases or if the algorithms themselves are not designed to recognize and mitigate such biases (Angwin et al., 2016). With AI increasingly being applied in sensitive domains like hiring, lending, and criminal justice, it is indeed necessary to establish legal frameworks that would require regular audits of AI systems to detect and correct bias. With standards for the fairness, equity, and non-discrimination of AI processes, AI technologies stand the chance of serving humankind with justice and equity.

The future of regulation, with respect to AI, should provide a dynamic platform because the area is constantly changing. Governments and international bodies need to ensure that there are regulatory frameworks established that adapt to the technological changes while maintaining an ethical principle.

This requires constant collaboration between policymakers, technologists, ethicists, and legal experts to stay ahead of emerging challenges in AI governance. The creation of global regulatory standards could provide a common framework that ensures AI technologies are developed and deployed responsibly across borders while respecting the sovereignty of individual nations and their regulatory priorities.

In conclusion, effective legal and regulatory frameworks for AI ethics are the steps toward the deployment of AI technologies in ways that benefit society while minimizing harm. Regulatory frameworks can ensure that AI systems operate ethically and responsibly by addressing issues of transparency, accountability, privacy, and bias. However, the rapidly changing nature of AI technology demands that these frameworks be flexible and adaptable, with ongoing dialogue and collaboration between legal, technological, and ethical experts to ensure that AI develops in a way that is beneficial and equitable for all.

BUILDING AN ETHICAL AI CULTURE IN THE WORKPLACE

Fostering ethical AI cultures is increasingly critical given that these new AI technologies change and revitalize how the sectors conduct their operations. To foster an ethical AI culture at the workplace, developing an intentional multi-faceted approach, creating and embedding appropriate ethics values while AI systems develop, deploy, and are maintained. Simply letting AI flow into the organisation is not enough; organisation needs to make ethics a priority of every level of AI strategy-through design and implementation, in assessment or evaluation as well as governance and review. This process involves cultivating an environment where employees at all levels are educated about AI's potential ethical implications, have a clear understanding of their role in promoting responsible AI use, and are encouraged to engage in ongoing dialogue about AI-related challenges and opportunities.

The first step in building an ethical AI culture is to establish a clear ethical framework that guides the development and deployment of AI systems. Such entails setting organizational values that prioritize fairness, transparency, accountability, and privacy. In this regard, these values have to be instituted at every single stage of the AI development journey, from designing to deployment and monitoring. In this case, businesses should establish AI systems which are transparent, explainable in nature, with clear documentation as to how their decisions are derived. This transparency will not only make employees understand how AI systems work but also allow them to detect possible biases or errors that may lead to unfair outcomes (Binns, 2018). Accountability should also be prioritized, ensuring that the teams developing AI are held liable for the ethical implications of their systems, including the unintended consequences of automation.

Employee education and training form an important aspect of building an ethical AI culture. AI and its ethical considerations are complex in nature, and most employees are not technically sound enough to fully grasp the potential risks and challenges of AI. As such, it is very much important that organizations invest in the training of both technical and nontechnical employees on what knowledge they require to make decisions about AI systems. This could include education on algorithmic bias, data privacy, the importance of explainability in AI applications, and the broader societal impact of automation. By educating employees on these topics, companies can create not only technically proficient but also ethically aware workforces. Such training also equips employees with the power to take ownership of ensuring that AI systems are used in a manner that supports organizational values (Brynjolfsson & McAfee, 2014).

Another essential element of creating an ethical AI culture is cultivating a collaborative culture among the stakeholders in the organization. Apart from the IT department or data scientists, AI ethics is something that requires input and collaboration from a variety of functions within the organization, from the legal function to human resources, and indeed operations. For instance, HR professionals should ensure that AI-driven recruitment tools are free from bias and that privacy concerns are addressed with respect to employee monitoring when AI systems are involved. Similarly, legal teams should help ensure that AI systems comply with existing regulations and that ethical considerations are factored into the organization's policies on data usage and transparency. Encouraging cross-functional collaboration ensures that AI ethics is not siloed within a specific department but integrated into the fabric of the organization (Davenport & Ronanki, 2018). This collaborative approach ensures that AI systems are reviewed from multiple perspectives, which will identify and help address potential ethical issues before they become problems.

Besides this internal collaboration, firms should also engage with stakeholders from outside, such as customers, regulators, and advocacy groups, to ensure that their AI practices are on the highest possible level of ethical standards. Involving the external groups makes sure that the AI system takes into consideration and reflects the needs and values of the wider society. Feedback regarding the transparency in AI recommendation systems from the customer can ensure its ethical design, and for regulatory compliance in cases of laws like data privacy and algorithmic transparency, they help businesses anticipate such changes. This is the finding of West in 2018. Involvement of diverse thinking helps organizations develop AI systems and prepare for those challenges that AI may face for being ethically responsible and acceptable in society.

Another important piece of building such an ethical culture of AI requires mechanisms for accountability and oversight; AI systems should never be "set and forget"-type technologies to be continuously kept under surveillance over whether they still work as it is intended that they continue remaining within the sphere of ethics as well. Regular audits of AI systems can be used to identify biases, inefficiencies, or unintended consequences that may emerge over time. The organization should also have processes to allow employees to report ethical concerns or irregularities related to the AI systems. This could be done by providing anonymous reporting channels or establishing ethics review boards to evaluate AI systems on an ongoing basis. This way, business organizations will ensure that there are systems put in place to monitor and be held accountable at all times so that ethical considerations always take the forefront of their AI operations (Binns, 2018).

Lastly, leadership is important for building an ethical AI culture. Leadership should lead by example through a commitment to AI ethics, which must then be infused into the organization's values, mission, and vision. Leaders should make open discussions of AI ethics happen, promote the feeling of collective responsibility, and provide the needed resources to drive ethical AI programs. When ethics is emphasized as a priority in leadership, there is a signal sent to every employee in an organization about these issues, making sure that organizational decision-making mechanisms are aligned with ethical considerations (Brynjolfsson & McAfee, 2014).

An ethical AI culture at the workplace shall be derived through a holistic approach: a clear set of ethical frameworks, education of employees, cross-functional collaboration, ongoing oversight, and commitment from leadership. With ethics infused at the DNA of AI development and deployment, organizations can ensure that AI technologies are responsibly, transparently, and fairly used. It would contribute to reducing some of the risks and challenges related to automation and even promote trust with employees, customers, and others who might benefit from these innovations, which means creating systems in AI that bring benefits to the society.

CONCLUSION

The incorporation of artificial intelligence into the work environment has a lot of promising opportunities, and at the same time, has brought in ethical complexities. As AI is revolutionizing the way industries function, businesses conduct themselves, and even the basic aspects of living, it's very important that such technological breakthroughs are driven by clear understanding and adherence to ethical principles. Whether it is job displacement or data privacy, algorithmic bias or transparency, the ethical aspects of AI at the workplace have to be understood with great diligence and strong regulation frameworks so that the advantage of automation may be achieved without harming the people or the society in general.

We have discussed in this chapter the multiple dimensions of the impact of AI on the workplace, focusing on the ethical dilemmas that emerge as automation increases. AI systems can significantly enhance productivity, efficiency, and decision-making capabilities for businesses to optimize operations and enhance customer experiences. As the adoption of these technologies becomes more prevalent among organizations, the significant ethical dilemmas that need to be addressed relate to job displacement, bias in AI systems, privacy, and human oversight in decision-making.

One of the most concerning ethical issues is that AI might affect employment patterns so strongly that there might be a paradox concerning productivity becoming increased while displacing masses. Indeed, the widespread implementation of AI systems in such industries as manufacturing or transportation has already opened our eyes to the fact that automation might substitute for repetitive human tasks, leaving workers with fewer opportunities for meaningful work. To mitigate the negative impact of job loss, companies and governments must emphasize efforts in reskilling and upskilling so that the affected workers have avenues to move to new jobs within emerging industries. Additionally, an environment of continuous learning will empower employees to adjust to an automation-driven society.

The second fundamental issue is correcting the bias present in most AI-based systems. If improperly designed and tracked, AI can unwittingly aggravate and enforce long-standing societal inequalities in hiring and credit scoring practices and even more insidiously in law enforcement. The system might end up perpetuating negative outcomes for these groups if its data is non-diverse or if the model has been developed on biased learning datasets. As such, businesses must take proactive steps toward ensuring that their AI systems are designed with fairness in mind, regularly audited for bias, and made more transparent and accountable in decision-making processes where accountability and remediation can occur when necessary.

Moreover, because AI is more extensively used, there are essential concerns about privacy and data security issues. AI systems require massive amounts of data to function properly. For example, personal information from employees, customers, or other stakeholders may be compiled to create this data. Strict data protection standards must be followed by organizations. It would mean not only adherence to the General Data Protection Regulation but also a visible commitment to protecting individuals' privacy. It calls for data transparency and responsible AI-driven data analytics to build and maintain trust, as well as protect individual rights.

Another very important aspect of human oversight is related to the use of AI for decision-making purposes. AI can process tremendous volumes of data, and decisions made by such a system can far outstrip the ability of any human. Yet it should not function in a vacuum. Maintaining human judgment through decision-making processes while implementing ethical AI and, therefore, making sure AI systems enhance human knowledge and not replace it would be essential. Applying processes in continuous oversight, like audit proceedings and independent reviews, can ensure accountability while keeping track of potential risks or failures of an AI system.

Lastly, creation of an ethical AI culture in the workplace will be important for open discussion of and response to these challenges. This should include development of guidelines for ethical AI practice, education and training of employees, cross-functional collaboration, and leadership commitment to responsible AI practices. An ethical AI culture will ensure that AI is used for business success and for the greater good of the world, an environment where there are confidences and desired outcomes for its employees, customers, and other constituencies.

The challenge facing AI in the workplace in ethics matters isn't unattainable. If the design, deployment, and oversight of AI are imbued with ethical considerations from the outset, organizations can tap into the full potential of automation, while minimizing harm and promoting fairness, transparency, and accountability. This is the path forward, an ongoing collaboration among policymakers, business leaders, technologists, and ethicists to ensure that the development of AI moves forward in ways that benefit all of society. Only through collective action can we ensure that AI-driven automation enhances our working environment without compromising any fundamental human values and rights.

REFERENCES

Angwin, J., Larson, J., Mattu, S., & Kirchner, L. (2016). *Machine bias: There's software used across the country to predict future criminals. And it's biased against blacks*. ProPublica. https://www.propublica.org/article/machine-bias-risk-assessments-in-criminal-sentencing

Binns, A. (2018). *On the ethics of artificial intelligence in the workplace: Risks, challenges, and opportunities*. Springer.

Brynjolfsson, E., & McAfee, A. (2014). *The Second Machine Age: Work, progress, and prosperity in a time of brilliant technologies*. W.W. Norton & Company.

Chui, M., Manyika, J., & Miremadi, M. (2016). *Where machines could replace humans—and where they can't (yet)*. McKinsey Quarterly. https://www.mckinsey.com/business-functions/organization/our-insights/where-machines-could-replace-humans-and-where-they-cant-yet

Davenport, T. H., & Ronanki, R. (2018). Artificial intelligence for the real world. *Harvard Business Review*, *96*(1), 108–116.

Frey, C. B., & Osborne, M. A. (2017). The future of employment: How susceptible are jobs to computerization? *Technological Forecasting and Social Change*, *114*, 254–280. DOI: 10.1016/j.techfore.2016.08.019

Lin, P. (2016). Why ethics matters for autonomous cars. In Lin, L. A. P., Abney, K., & Bekey, G. A. (Eds.), *Robot ethics: The ethical and social implications of robotics* (pp. 69–85). MIT Press.

O'Neil, C. (2016). *Weapons of math destruction: How big data increases inequality and threatens democracy*. Crown Publishing.

Voigt, P., & Von dem Bussche, A. (2017). *The EU general data protection regulation (GDPR): A practical guide*. Springer. DOI: 10.1007/978-3-319-57959-7

West, D. M. (2018). *The ethics of artificial intelligence*. Brookings Institution Press.

Zeng, D., Lu, W., & Zhao, Y. (2018). Privacy-preserving machine learning: Threats and solutions. *The Journal of Privacy and Confidentiality*, *8*(2), 1–19. DOI: 10.29012/jpc.v8i2.686

Chapter 17
AI and the Future of Talent Management:
Revolutionizing Workforce Strategies for a Dynamic World

Narendra Singh Chaudhary
https://orcid.org/0000-0003-1235-3324
Sparsh Global Business School, India

Richa Banerjee
NMIMS University, India

Garima Mathur
https://orcid.org/0000-0003-1166-2192
Prestige Institute of Management and Research, Gwalior, India

Leena Sachdeva
O.P. Jindal Global University, India

Azadeh Amoozegar
INTI International University, Malaysia

ABSTRACT

AI is revolutionizing talent management by enhancing decision-making, automating routine tasks, and optimizing HR processes. Initially limited to resume screening and candidate matching, AI now plays a pivotal role in hiring, performance evaluation, training, and employee engagement. It enables personalized learning, predicts employee turnover, and supports data-driven decisions, aligning human capital with organizational goals. Despite its benefits, AI adoption faces challenges like resistance to change, ethical concerns, and data privacy issues. Looking ahead, AI's integration with technologies like augmented reality and blockchain will create immersive, inclusive, and responsive work environments. Its continuous learning capabilities will drive real-time performance management, fostering innovation and sustainability. This chapter explores AI's transformative impact on talent management, highlighting its current applications, challenges, and future potential in reshaping HR into a strategic, data-driven

DOI: 10.4018/979-8-3373-1270-5.ch017

function in the dynamic business world.

INTRODUCTION

Nearly every business has significantly impacted by the rapid development of artificial intelligence and human resources is no exception. AI is becoming more and more important in present modern-day organisations as it is capable of enhanced and quick decision making, improving employee engagement and streamlining the process of decision making. The organisations are using AI in workplace for automation of routine tasks, analysing huge data for decisions and predictions about talent management. By doing so, the team HR is able to work on more important and strategic decisions and initiatives for organisational growth. AI has capacity to improve and optimise HR operations and also making Human resources a more data driven and agile domain.

AI has taken a long time in its adoption in HR, but this adoption has proved to be impactful. Initially AI was used just for some administrative tasks such as screening of resumes, candidate matching by using some algorithms. But now the use of AI has grown with time and now it is used in talent management domains like hiring, performance evaluation, training and development, engagement and retention strategies. The organisations are now using AI tools for predicting employee turnover, to develop personalised training programs, and providing feedback in real time. The function of AI has now grown from tactical to strategical by helping HR professionals in making decisions (Diaz et.al 2023).

This chapter aims to examine how AI is revolutionising talent management, focusing on its impact on workforce tasks in today's fast-paced, competitive business environment. Examining how AI transforms various aspects of talent management, including hiring, employee development, and performance review, is one of the main goals. Organisations are now better able to manage diverse teams, find top talent, and align human capital with the company's strategic objectives, thanks to AI-driven solutions.

The chapter also attempts to discuss the difficulties businesses face when implementing AI for HR-related tasks. Overcoming technological opposition, ensuring ethical AI use, resolving data privacy concerns, and preserving the trust of the workforce, who might worry about losing their jobs to automation, are some of these difficulties.

Additionally, the future prospects of AI in talent management will be examined in this chapter. AI has the ability to completely transform HR procedures as its capabilities continue to advance. AI combined with other cutting-edge technologies like augmented reality and blockchain may result in more immersive and customised work environments. Furthermore, AI will become more and more significant in real-time performance management due to its capacity for constant learning and adaptation, which enables businesses to establish a more accommodating and responsive workplace. AI will consequently have a significant impact on people management in the future, with a focus on sustainability, inclusivity, and the development of innovative and growth-oriented workplaces.

In conclusion, this chapter will give a thorough rundown of how AI is changing talent management tasks. AI is at the forefront of changing human resources into a more strategic and data-driven role, both in terms of its current application, the difficulties it poses, and its potential for the future.

TALENT ACQUISITION AND AI: RECRUITMENT PRACTICES REDEFINED

2.1 The role of AI in Talent Acquisition

The artificial intelligence came up as a central tool in talent acquisition, resulting into reshaping of the recruitment practices. The use of technologies like machine learning (ML) and natural language processing (NLP) and robotics are leveraging optimisation of hiring process. In machine learning algorithms are trained for identifying the patterns in the data, which can be utilised in talent acquisition, this process done by machine learning helps in predicting the success of candidate based on historical hiring data. NLP trains AI to understand and process human language, enabling it ideal for resume scanning based on job descriptions and communicating with the candidates. Moreover, with the help of robotics the initial processes like scheduling of interview, follow up of emails and managing recruitment related documents management can be done.

Compared to traditional recruitment methods, the role of AI has become more significant in talent acquisition. As traditionally the methods relied heavily on human intervention, intuition, judgements and efforts studies (Paramita et al., 2024)

The screening of resumes, initial interviews and decision making was done by people which might be based on personal or subjective biases. The approach has been changed by automation of these tasks, making the professional focus on strategic and other decision making. As AI can process and analyse large databases in short duration hence can speed up the processes like shortlisting of candidates based on job description-based skill set, experience, cultural fit etc.

2.2 Automation of Recruitment Process

The AI is able to reduce human bias and improves, enhances efficiency of the hiring process. The existing traditional process un-intentionally involve different type of biases in the process like caste, creed, gender, age etc which may lead to discriminatory practices.

With the help of AI, such biases can be minimised as decisions become data-driven and structured algorithms are used for decision-making instead of relying solely on human judgement.

At the same time, AI-powered chatbots, which work on initial interaction with candidates, are changing the scenario. These chatbots can respond to different candidate queries and can easily provide the information related to current openings and job descriptions. These bots can also conduct preliminary screening, with the help of which the turnaround time in the recruitment and talent management process can be reduced. Applicant tracking systems equipped with AI can keep a watch on applications throughout the process of recruitment process, which will help in maintaining organised and updated records of all the applicants.

With the help of automation of the process, organisations will be able to reduce the time to hire as well as the cost per hire. This will also ensure a smoother candidate experience.

2.3. Virtual Interviews and Assessments

The role that AI is playing in recruitment is not just an automated process (Verma, 2024). It is much more than that, as it facilitates advanced candidate evaluation techniques. Also, nowadays, many organisations are conducting virtual interviews using different types of AI technologies. These types of interviews offer a more thorough analysis of candidates. The AI systems are designed in such a way that they read and understand more than what the candidate says; they also analyse body language and the way the message is communicated.

The AI-powered system can analyse speech patterns, paralanguage, facial expressions, and body language, which help in providing an understanding of the candidate's confidence, emotional intelligence, and organisational culture fit. Such AI-driven systems are far better than traditional interviews because, due to human intervention, many aspects may be overlooked or misinterpreted by the interviewer (Schmidt, 1998).

Moreover, augmented reality and virtual reality usage are increasing in recruitment processes. These technologies help employers create a simulated job-related environment in which a candidate can demonstrate the skills and abilities required for the job through AR and VR (Liff, 2024). We can easily identify the job demands and the candidate's performance according to those demands. Such a simulated environment will help in the accurate evaluation of the candidate, even if the process is done remotely. Such processes will remove the constraints related to geographical areas and provide a more inclusive approach to hiring.

2.4. AI-Driven Diversity and Inclusion

Diversity and inclusion are one of the most important aspects in today's organisation. AI play a vital role in that it promotes diversity and inclusion within the recruitment practices. There is research which have showcased that AI can reduce bias that are there in traditional hiring methods like gender or race based biased Can help in eliminating biased language in job description that ensures inclusivity and escapable of attracting a diverse pool of candidates. Moreover, AI based recruitment platforms are capable of analysing demographic data to ensure that the recruitment efforts are reaching different diverse group of candidates (Li and Laumer, 2021).

For reducing bias, it is essential that algorithms used in the recruitment process be reviewed and updated regularly to ensure fairness. Any form of bias in data can result in unintended consequences. To reduce the risk of bias, there should be guidelines for minimising algorithmic bias, such as diverse training data, regular audits of algorithms, and maintaining transparency in AI-driven decision-making processes.

2.5. Ethical Implications in AI-Driven Hiring

There are many advantages that the AI-driven talent acquisition process has, but at the same time, there are ethical implications that need to be considered. Overreliance on AI systems for hiring is one such major concern. If systems are not properly designed or monitored, they may unintentionally continue to maintain the existing bias or make decisions that lack the tone and context of human judgement. For example, AI AI-driven algorithm can reject a candidate based on any irrelevant criteria like age, characteristics, or gender.

To solve such issues, organisations must work on a balance between the use of AI and human judgement. No doubt that AI can enhance the efficiency and accuracy of the hiring process, but human oversight must be maintained. This will ensure that the ethical standards are maintained. To maintain a balance and ethical standards, AI and human judgement should be given proper importance in the process to ensure that ethical standards are followed. The system should be transparent. Regular audits of the system should be conducted, and final hiring decisions should involve human input.

AI-POWERED EMPLOYEE DEVELOPMENT: CUSTOMIZING LEARNING AND GROWTH

3.1. Revolutionizing Learning and Development (L&D)

AI is playing very important role in transforming learning and development. It is making it more adaptive scalable and effective. LMS which is supported by AI is turning Leaning and development a personalised experience by tailoring them according to employees. These type o systems analyse and understand the learning patterns of employees, their preferences and the past performance data to offer training modules (Holuša, 2023).

Coursera and linked in learning use AI to create personalised recommendations according to the activities and skill gaps of learner. AI can also perform other training related task such as issuing of certificate and content delivery, this helps the professionals on more value-added tasks and activities. At IBM the LMS suggests employee specific learning pathways, depending upon cognitive powers, roles, profile and industry demands. This increases relevance of training as it is based on needs.

3.2. Skill Mapping and Career Pathing

AI also helps the organizations to map skills and create career paths for their employees. AI-based tools can assess volumes of existing data to identify the existing gaps in skills and forecast future work expectations. AI draws from data gathered from the internal performance reviews, trends seen in the job market, and the overall rise in the careers of the employees to positively identify what skills the employees need to grow. This would readily orient the companies towards training and development in the area of workforce skill demand fluctuating.

For instance, Accenture and Deloitte's systems align their employee skills to business needs based on appraising systems powered by AI for track employee skill sets aligned with future business needs. For instance, Accenture's "Skills and Competency Framework" employs AI-based knowledge management to map the current skill set of its employees against the future company imperative. This system is instrumental in allowing organizations to predict what skills are likely to be required as the organization pivots or drives into an area of expansion; thereby, every employee is consistently upskilled.

Such career pathing tools allow organizations to monitor their employees' career paths in detail, based on their exact skills or interest. Talent-matching tools like Plyometrics and LinkedIn's Career Explorer allow employees to visualize possible futures within their organization or across sets of industries. These AI-enabled platforms suggest which skills employees should further develop to advance, increasing visibility of the promotion process and therefore an increase in ownership over each employee's career development and progression.

3.3. Real-Time Feedback Mechanisms

The AI empowered feedback tool is coming up SN necessity to improve performance of employees and employee engagement (Malik, 2022). The traditional feedback systems which were presented annually or quarterly are obsolete. Now the continuous feedback platform is taking place of traditional systems. These continuous feedback platforms give instant feedback and insights, according to need. There are certain tools such as tiny pulse,15five allows Manager to provide feedback to employees in real time. Such type of feedback help employees to manage their performance and behaviour. Accordingly, these type of platform uses AI to examine workers, feedback, participation, and communication habits to offer insights that can be worked upon

For instance, Culture Amp applies machine learning to employee engagement surveys and provide suggestions for improving performance. AI also can detect the work life balance related issues, and provide them help with programs and tips that can improve the situation. Such type of systems improves organisational culture hence improving productivity and satisfaction.

3.4. Micro learning and Gamified Training

The training of staff can be improved using gamified and micro learning. This simplifies the complex and long training topics into bite size chunks. This helps employees in learning effectively and conveniently. The small or micro learning tools and topics helps employees in learning quickly without feeling of overburdened.

Companies like Sony are using employee specific tailored methods of learning according to the job function. These small and focused courses provide employees an opportunity to study according to their own pace and willingness, this keeps them updated to the changing trends. Moreover, game components when added to these micro learning capsules increases engagement and motivation

SAP's learning solution and Deloitte is leadership Academy. use AI to track progress and provide them personalized challenges to keep employees engaged and engaged throughout the learning process. The degree of difficulty is also adjusted according to employee performance in that game. To improve skills of employees and to make employee learn about the goods and services of company, company policies and procedures etc. Walmart uses such gamified training programs

To conclude, AI is changing employee development into more lively, tailored, and active learning environments. AI driven systems are revolutionising. How businesses invest in their employees from skill mapping to give training and real-time feedback, creating a workforce that is more engaged and prepared for the future. Businesses can use this solution to support carrier advancement, ongoing education, and employee performance in a setting that is becoming more and more competitive

AI IN PERFORMANCE MANAGEMENT: INCREASING ACCOUNTABILITY AND ENGAGEMENT

4.1. Data-Driven Insights for Performance Reviews

AI has changed impact of performance management by offering data driven solutions and insight to improve fairness and reduce by us in employee evaluation. The performance reviews that are done regularly lack consistency due to their reliance on subjective opinions and personal bias. AI gathers, performance data from different channels, emails, project management tools, feedback, systems, et cetera. This helps AI in giving detailed view of employee performance, focusing strength and weaknesses. It also forecast long-term trends based on the information gathered.

There are certain programmes like workday and success factors that use AI to collect the data of performance and examining it to give superior a new and better ways to judge employee performance. This type of data helps in streamlining and enhancing performance appraisal scenario and giving a better and clear picture of employees, achievement, work, habits, and other factors. Such type of system that use AI algorithm to identify different patterns in performance matrix help Manager in making effective and sound decisions at the time of review also help in creating smart goals by analysing past performance data and current trends. It also helps in setting realistic and achievable goals for employee by a manager.

For example, if an employee has consistently exceeded sales targets by 10%, AI can recommend setting a higher but still attainable target for the next quarter. This assists organizations in linking individual performance objectives to organizational goals while making sure goals are specific, measurable, and attainable.

4.2. Employee Well-Being and Sentiment Analysis

The AI has ability to monitor the attitude and well-being of employee. This is one more significant advantage of application of AI in performance management systems with the help of social media usage, employee feedback service, and communication patterns. Employee attitude can be identified. AI can use sentiment analysis to track employee's mood. AI with the help of natural language processing systems, stress, disengagement or burn out can be identified if change in tone is noticed. These can be early indicators of stress and disengagement.

Microsoft Viva uses sentiment analysis to check moral inputs and provide data of employee well-being in real time. With the help of such data managers can take measures to support employee on time. AI can also notice signs of dissatisfaction and disengagement in whatever communication that employee is doing by doing such things. Employees can keep track of their employees, health and by monitoring them, they can keep their employees motivated

This thing also raise problem related to ethical issues as such time of real tracking can create problem of intervention of privacy. Many a times employ may fail that they are misunderstood or wrong. Interpretation has been done of their conversation. Hence it is important that at the time of using AI to track their employees, health and well-being, their privacy should also be protected. There should be clear and transparent policies related to measuring and collecting data of employees, well-being. Employees also should be given chance to opt out from such data collection methods.

4.3. Gamification and Rewards Systems

Gamification is a new way, which is very interesting, with the help of AI it can lead to employee motivation and productivity. The tailored approach is key to this, the performance management system with the help of challenges, rewards and feedback can improve motivation and productivity. The system can incorporate simulation exercise to encourage employees to achieve desired objectives and outcomes.

The organisations like Kudos and SAP are using gamification in performance management system. The kudos use reward system in PMS, on this system colleague can appreciate and acknowledge each other. SAP success factors use to create challenges for employees according to job functions, competencies and career goals. These types of games improve employee engagement and productivity. This makes easier to employees to track progress, earn rewards and feel values for the work they do.

The Deloitte also include gamification, for tracking and incentive real time performance in performance management system. Their leadership academy uses gamification to motivate and complete leadership training courses where they get badges and points which can be exchanged for tangible incentive. This type of system encourages employees and also promote the acquisition of skills and knowledge with games (Odugbesan, 2023).

4.4. Ethical Issues in AI-Based Performance Management

Ai offers a lot of benefits in performance management systems, but at the cost of ethical issues that needs to be resolved by organisations. The AI is based on machine learning algorithms tend to be black box; means it lacks transparency for employees. The employees have limited ways to know about judgements about their performance which may lead to distrust in the system and dis satisfaction in employees.

The performance evaluations based on AI always create doubt on its accuracy and fairness. AI is based evaluations are based on data and if data fed is biased or incomplete, it may result in accurate assessments, affecting employees career planning, succession planning and wellbeing. an AI system is trained on biased data, it may unintentionally favour certain groups of employees over others, perpetuating inequality.

The organisations are required to set ethical guidelines to promote ethical practices when AI is used for performance management systems that regular audits for fairness, accuracy and transparency of AI algorithm can help in maintaining ethical practises. The human intervention in AI gather data can help in preventing bias that may come out as a result of axis automation. There should be facilitation and sensitisation of employees regarding collision and utilisation of performance data. Such data should be gathered with informed consent.

Like IBM is a good example of ethical AI practice where they enshrined protocol of AI transparency to ensure that AI driven performance management systems should be audited regularly to remove bias and ensure fairness with the help of such ethical policies. Organisation can leverage the potential of AI at the same time safeguarding employee rights.

In short, AI has changed the way performance management system is done as it collects insights about employee motivation and engagement, but at the same time, ethical implications of using AI should also be considered carefully. It is required to ensure transparency, precision and fairness by using such algorithm to promote accountability and engagement at work.

WORKFORCE PLANNING AND PREDICTIVE ANALYTICS: CHARTING FUTURE REQUIREMENTS

5.1. Predictive Modelling in Workforce Planning

Artificial intelligence plays crucial role in workforce planning. It uses predictive analytics to predict human resource requirements and align this with corporate strategy. This makes organisation future ready, predictive modelling, use, previous or past data, trends and algorithm to assess historic workforce performance and determine trends that can help in predicting future needs such as skill, gaps, skill deficit, and staff turnover (Diaz, 2023).

The organisations like IBM leverage AI to check labour market drivers, internal and external to the organisation. This includes economic transitions, different industrial evolutions and socio-demographic changes. Also, predictive analysis powered by AI can easily forecast workforce needs department wise making organisation to address shortages before they actually occur. In predicting these gaps, organisations are able to organise recruitment and skill development initiatives according to future demands

Firms like Walmart, which is a leader in retail industry also uses predictive analytics for workforce planning with the help of AI Walmart predict staff requirement according to sales pattern whether and past data from different stores in different locations. This helps Walmart in maximising its workforce by having right number of employees at right time, enhancing operational effectiveness and cutting down labour cost.

The contribution that AI is making in workforce, planning and forecasting is very important in alignment of talent with long-term business schools, it is also helping organisation stay agile and acceptable according to changing market trends, creating a forward-looking strategy for workforce planning

5.2. Optimizing Talent Deployment

AI has improved significantly on how companies manage their talent deployment, allowing organisation to plan and allocate the workforce strategically in different functions and in various projects with the help of AI organisation, analyse skills, performance and career objectives. The internal mobility, job rotation moving employees into different roles can be managed effectively with AI organisations like Google match employee with suitable role on the basis of skills, interest and career goals with the help of AI Google has internal mobility platform also to analyse employee background for suggesting roles that are aligned with competencies, skills and personal preference of employee. Such type of techniques plays important role not only in professional growth of employee but also improves employee retention and employee engagement.

Talent deployment can also be managed with the help of AI. It can be used for balancing workload, allocation of resources, distribution of work across teams and identifying the requirement of additional resources or where workload are too heavy activities. Ensure that employees are not overwhelmed and help in maintaining balanced work environment Also.

The best practice for using AI intent deployment includes leveraging AI platforms like workday and cornerstone. These platforms also offer different tools for assessment of skill carrier, planning and human resource management. The system helps HR department in allocating talent efficiently and effectively

5.3. AI in the Gig Economy

In the era of economy, AI is also transforming it by streamlining the engagement of gig workers and integrating it into organisational framework, different platforms use AI to match freelancer with employers that have right opportunity according to their skills. This platform leverage machine learning algorithm to recommend freelancer to employers inclined, making the hiring process more efficient and specific according to project needs.

For example, a work uses AI for analysing work history, client rating and skills of freelancer to recommend the most suitable person for specific job. Posting such processes not only improve the aquarium of match but also ensures a more efficient hiring process, reducing the time spent on identifying right candidate for the task

AI facilitates the integration of gig work into the large employment ecosystem. As businesses use them more. AI integrated platforms monitor the performance of Cake and measure their contributions. They also ensure that workers are according to companies' needs and objectives. A platform also helps businesses in managing contracts with these workers payment to 3 workers to make the task easier for freelance and organisations. Both the economy is drawing rapidly and artificial intelligence is becoming important to streamline the use and interaction of gig workers while maintaining high standards of productivity and quality in the workforce.

ETHICAL AND ORGANIZATIONAL IMPLICATIONS OF AI IN TALENT MANAGEMENT

6.1. Data Privacy and Security Concerns

AI and talent management increased concerns regarding privacy and security of the employee private data. Since AI systems depends upon large datasets to augment talent management activities such as recruitment, employee career development, and performance management. The datasets usually include individual's personal information related to health, performance, salary and other psychological aspects. The misuse of such personal information can result into severe damages to personal and financial reputation.

The risk associated with data privacy and security issues can be reduced through strong data protection measures while ensuring compliance to global privacy regulations such as General Data Protection Regulation (GDPR) and the California Consumer Privacy Act (CCPA).

GDPR, for example, mandates that the individual's private data must be collected with cautions and processed carefully, while taking explicit consent from the concerned person and ensure that they can access, rectify and

GDPR, for example, mandates that private data must be collected and processed carefully, with explicit consent from individuals, and it guarantees data subjects the right to access, rectify, and erase their data. In order to ensure privacy organizations must put proper data encryption system followed by continuous security audits. In addition to this the AI systems must be designed with care while ensuring the process remain transparent and individuals accountable should also be nominated.

Moreover, businesses should adopt clear data retention policies and procedures for secured storing and handling employee data to protect it from unauthorized access.

6.2. Algorithmic Bias and Mitigation Strategies

Most artificial intelligence algorithms acquire biases primarily during training when uneven data sets are used. The HR Systems algorithm obtains gender bias because unbalanced historical data emerges from biased recruitment practices that prefer one gender over another. Misinformed organizational diversity and inclusion initiatives fail because of biases that further lead to discriminatory hiring practices and biased evaluation of training candidates.

Organizations are required to laydown measures to overcome issues related to biased algorithm. for a proper AI model, it requires to work upon diverse training data. Such diverse datasets with varied skill set and backgrounds along with different demographic populations help in creating robust AI models and ensure reduced risk of biases. AL models need timely checking for fairness and algorithms require continuous testing to find out and encounter the problems of bias arising out of operational system.

AL technology operated systems result into less biased outcomes if the operational processes are transparent. Business firms should emphasize AI models to demonstrate easy understanding in order to provide explainable interpretations during decision-making processes. This way the system obtains the reliability through the approach as it provides fairness throughout the whole processing. Companies can further control bias in their AI decisions through human intervention as they evaluate the decisions against the values and ethical standards of the organizations.

6.3. Workforce Displacement: Challenges and Solutions

Al talent management practices display ethical concerns regarding usage of automated processes. AI systems perform repetitive tasks hence help in improving organizational decision making which might result into elimination of certain jobs from the system. There is a dearth need for introduction of training programs to sharpen the skill sets of workforces to deal with the challenges. The content, material and the curricula of training program to deliver training mainly related to data analytics and AI programming will help improve opportunities for development and retention of employees. Organizations need to establish a learning environment which fosters staff development in terms of upgraded skillsets and technical knowhow of challenging environment.

The Government and business enterprises must work simultaneously on policy framework for workforce development to cushion off challenges posited by AI systems.

Career counselling and job placement services along with guidance through workforce development programs might help displaced employees transition through their job displacement process.

6.4. Building Trust in AI Systems

It is essential for AI systems to build such relationships that evoke trust in talent management processes. Success in the use of artificial intelligence is greatly dependent on intelligent leadership, the one that creates mechanisms to ensure transparency, accountability, and fairness. The leadership team can gain organizational trust by directly communicating with employees about the principles and benefits of AI system use.

A structured ethical AI adoption framework such as Fairness Accountability and Transparency (FAT) principles is needed for organizations that wish to adopt AI systems that are responsible. Implementation of AI systems requires fairness which promotes equal treatment of all the staff regardless of their background. By accountability, organizations decide how AI systems should report their decisions and establish defined procedures for resolving problems and addressing complaints. Stakeholders should be able to understand the decisions made by AI systems with transparency that enables an open audit of the system's operations and decisions.

Trust development between staff and companies requires the staff's active involvement in discussions of AI's effects on their work process. The trust of the employees is earned through their participation in the deployment of AI systems so that companies involve them in the development of the system. The provision of employees with adequate educational materials on AI concepts and rules serves to demystify AI and increase the trust level among the staff.

AI creates multiple opportunities to enhance the talent management system, but organizations need to be keen on both organisational and ethical issues that require proper management. They need clear guidelines and fair measures as well as ethical frameworks for AI to solve the core problems of data privacy, algorithm bias and human impact, which will boost trust in AI and the workforce. Businesses that introduce transparency along with fairness will also apply ethical practices and ensure that their AI technology adds value to the business and workforce.

CASE STUDIES: AI IN ACTION

7.1. Transforming Recruitment at Leading Tech Firms

The influx of AI-powered tools has revolutionized recruitment at tech giants. The changes have made hiring more efficient. In fact, large Companies such as Amazon, Google etc. have taken advantage of Artificial Intelligence techniques such as machine learning, natural language processing (NLP), chatbots to replace time consuming tasks like screening the applicants, biodata checks, scheduling interview and answering the candidate's reply. For instance, Google have installed automated hiring platform powered by chatbot and other AI technologies to screen out large number of job applications, matching resumes with the job requirements, hence reducing the efforts and time involved in recruitment process at initial level.

Similarly, Amazon also witnessed reduced initial screening process from months to weeks. This resulted into high number of hiring and churning the man power requirements. This helped them to fasten the hiring rates, benefitting the organizing to reduce recruitment cycle. This further helps in reducing biased hiring.

The Google take further benefits out of AL empowered Talent acquisition system by analysing the candidate success based upon data about previous recruitments, performance reviews, tenure and other talent acquisition metrics.

7.2. Personalized L&D at Global Enterprises

Learning and development have been focus of global enterprises in recent years. The personalized system of learning helps in better learning outcomes. The Learning Management Systems (LMS) in the companies like Deloitte and IBM have been shifted to AI supported system. This helps in tracking employee productivity, their progress, the areas for their improvements and the personalized steps for improvement.

In IBM's AI powered learning platform, Watson provides a roadmap for learning paths, career development steps and skills and efforts required on current job for readiness for future job roles. This AI based learning platform increases job satisfaction in current job and help identifying future job roles and related preparedness.

Deloitte uses AI to personalize training programs for its employees. The AI technology examines the learning style of employees and adjusts content delivery to maximize retention and engagement. The approach, in turn, aligns with employees' preferences and enhances their learning experiences. Since employees can learn at their own pace, training becomes less of a burden and more of an enriching experience for them. This has increased staff satisfaction levels and created a more skilled workforce.

7.3. Predictive Analytics in Healthcare Workforce Planning

AI predictive analytics plays a transformative role in planning and patient outcomes in healthcare. Hospitals use AI tools to ascertain staffing need calculating basis patient inflows, seasonal demands and disease patterns. For example, Mount Sinai Health System in New York, utilizes AI to predict flow of patients and align the staff levels, ensuring that the hospitals are neither overstaffed nor understaffed.

AI also helps in analyzing that which disease will be more and which department will require more staff basis the patient conditions, pattern of emergency visits, and historical data. This planned approach allows the providers to allocate resources very efficiently, resulting in less wait time and better patient care. The AI system also synchronizes with electronic health records (EHRs) to identify high-risk patients and assigns the staff accordingly.

Moreover, predictive analytics also enhances patient outcomes by ensuring that healthcare team is not overwhelmed, instead is able to focus on the most critical cases. The results have been significant: Mount Sinai reported a reduction in wait hours, improved satisfaction level of patients and enhanced care quality of patients due to proper deployment of staff.

7.4. Gamification of Performance Reviews at Startups

The usage of AL powered gamification tools has increased manifold in small and medium businesses for greater employee engagement and improved performance. An online shoe retailer Zappos, is well identified for its employee-oriented HR policies and practices, also uses gamification to boost morale of its workforce directed towards higher productivity. The portal provides features like badges, leader boards, rewards etc to create competitive but supportive environment. The employees can earn points based upon their performances to calculated rewards and other incentive payments. Similarly, one more start-up named Redbeacon, uses performance management platform to gamify performance review system to make it easy to understand and attractive. The gamification platform tracks individuals on their outputs related to variety of tasks and then provide real time feedback, further assigning rewards for the standard outcomes or for further exceeding the target. The results from these start-ups are notable as gamification not only results into higher productivity but also lead to better competitive environment.

8.1. Emerging Technologies and Trends

Ai when used with other technologies like IOT, VR and block chain can transform Hr practices significantly in future

Integration of blockchain and AI: Blockchain has become very popular nowadays it has potential to improve transparency, security and accountability in different sectors and HRS not excluded. Blockchain, when used with AI can improve employ data, it can track career progression, certification and skills in different ledger, such integration and revolutionise the talent management practices by creating record of employees which is very feasible and cannot be tempered. For example, the candidates will be able to present a resume which is verified with the help of Blockchain and the data that is presented can also be verified like their accomplishment, education, certification, et cetera. This will help in elimination of fraud and will streamline recruitment processes. Moreover, AI can use Blockchain to match right person with right opportunities with the help of verify credential.

Virtual reality and AI can also be used in recruitment and training processes. This will make recruitment on boarding and training of employees, simple realistic and immersive. With the help of ER candidates can get real experience of task with the help of simulated environment. AI powered tools can also help in evaluation of candidate performance in this simulated environment, which can provide recruiters with real assessment of candidate skills. Cultural fit before actually making the offer to the candidate. Organisation can also conduct virtual interviews which will make it easier to interview candidates remotely which is need of present age of remote work can also be used in training and development because it can offer dynamic and personalised learning experience. AI can easily understand the learning style of employees can identify skill gaps and can develop tailored training modules to address specific need.

The internet of things is also useful in workforce management along with its integration with AI if the workplace can be transformed by connecting the different devices, sensors and machines to Internet for real-time data collection and analysis, IOT can provide HR department a proper insight about employee performance well-being in productivity. The different wearable devices can be used to check stress level of employee and can develop personalised well-being recommendation with the help of such data.

The IOT enabled device will also be helpful in streamlining various HR processes, office systems to make them simple, easy and effective. With the combination of IOT devices with analytical power of AU, HR can create more efficient and engaging work environment

The future is undoubtedly having hybrid working style. Companies will be adopting flexible work arrangements. In such working environment, AI will play a crucial role in supporting hybrid and remote work models. AI will help in optimising communications, teamwork and performance management. The tools with the help of AI can help distant team to remain connected in real time and can help in effective communication, scheduling and assistance in different project management, AI Chabot can also be used as assistant for distant employees by solving the queries. By offering them guidance. They will ensure that employee will get information at proper time.

8.2. Balancing Human and Machine Collaboration

AI is playing very important and dominant role in talent management, but at the same time is very important that a balance should be maintained between intelligence of machine and human institution. The human intervention and its role is very important in decision making process for talent management.

Preserving human element in decision making: AI has huge potential to make decision and decision can be made faster and more accurate. Then human decisions SAI is capable of analysing large volume of data or identify pattern. At the same time, it is essential to recognise that there are certain qualities that human being has like empathy, creativity, judgement, and ethical reasoning that cannot be replicated by machines. Like AI can assist in identifying top talent based on performance data, but the final decision on whom to hire or whom to give promotion should always involve human in decision making process as it depends on many other things like Cultural fit, interpersonal skills, human values, and company values, etc .AI cannot identify the level of emotional intelligence and understanding to talent management, which human leaders can do

The ethical consideration also should be a priority at the time of integrating AI into decision making process. AI models can be good according to the data they are trained with the problems or bias and data can result into wrong decision-making or biased outcome by AI. hence it is essential that human should intervene in the process to ensure fairness, transparency and inclusion in talent management practises.

EMPOWERING LEADERS AND EMPLOYEES

AI is also a tool which empowers both leaders and employees, but it cannot be a replacement for human roles like AI can provide some important insights that can enhance leaders decision-making capacity. AI also can help leaders with the help of employ data to find out skill gaps of performance related issues, succession planning, and career planning With the help of AI leaders will be able to make informed decision and can develop employee specific development and training program.

Employee can be benefited in their career development process by identifying personalised learning opportunity or help in tracking their own performance. But again, AI cannot replace human touch. Artificial intelligence is a good assistant for employees in growing and developing their careers with the help of sort analysis and potential carrier planning

8.3. Preparing for an AI-Driven Future

As organizations increasingly adopt AI in talent management, it is essential to prepare for an AI-driven future. This involves equipping HR professionals with the skills and tools to leverage AI effectively while also addressing the challenges that come with AI integration.

Recommendations for Organizations to Future-Proof Talent Management Strategies: To future-proof talent management strategies, organizations must focus on the following key areas:

1. **Upskilling and Reskilling the Workforce**: As AI continues to evolve, employees must be equipped with the skills to work alongside machines. Organizations should invest in continuous learning programs, focusing on developing both technical and soft skills. Reskilling employees for AI-related

roles or offering training in areas such as data literacy, machine learning, and digital collaboration will be crucial for staying competitive.

2. **Adopting Ethical AI Frameworks**: It is essential for organizations to adopt ethical AI frameworks that prioritize fairness, accountability, and transparency. This includes regularly auditing AI systems to ensure they are free from bias, ensuring employee data privacy, and establishing clear guidelines on AI's role in decision-making processes.
3. **Encouraging Human-Machine Collaboration**: Organizations should foster a culture where AI is seen as a partner, not a competitor, to human capabilities. This involves creating an environment where both AI and human expertise are valued and leveraged to achieve business goals.
4. **Monitoring AI's Impact on Organizational Culture**: As AI becomes more integrated into talent management practices, it is important for organizations to monitor its impact on company culture. AI should not erode the human-centered aspects of work, such as trust, communication, and collaboration. Ensuring that AI is used to enhance rather than replace human interaction is key to maintaining a positive organizational culture.

CONCLUSION

AI is now not a concept which is futuristic. It has become integral part of present-day business operations, especially in talent management. AI can transform the HR domain as a whole by offering unprecedented opportunities for streamlining the processes and to improve the decision making. Starting from recruitment Training, performance management and human resource planning, AI has changed the way in which organisations attract and retain talent, which is a most crucial problem nowadays. However, there are certain challenges and responsibilities that leaders must think upon and address, strategically and ethically.

AI has shown a very important role in recruitment with the help of technology that can improve efficiency and reduce human bias. There are tools like AI driven resume screening, NLP for developing job description and specification and AI driven interview system that can improve traditional hiring process with the help of predictive analytics and improved algorithms organisations can easily identify the right candidate for job quickly and with accuracy, but it is essential that fairness and transparency should be maintained to avoid any type of biases.

In employee training and development, AI can play important role by developing learning management system and skill mapping tools. This can easily identify skill gaps and can provide tailored training for employees.

We cannot forget the contribution that AI can give in performance management with the help of aggregation of data from different sources and applying advance analytics. The real-time feedback smart goalsetting are few things that can improve performance management systems. The ethical consideration must not be overlooked while using these practises which use AI systems as employee, privacy and autonomy should not be hindered (Budhwar et al., 2023).

Workforce planning predictive analysis are also important aspect of talent management that cannot be overlooked by proper demand forecasting of labour, resource allocation and scenario modelling. AI can improve workforce strategies, workforce deployment to ensure operational efficiency. AI can also impress diversity and inclusion by identifying an address in bias for string affair, workplace. Last, but not the least AI system can help leaders in better leadership practices with the help of data gathered by AI embedded information systems. The emerging technologies like Blockchain, virtual reality and internet of things are expected to improve the capabilities that AI has in talent management.

AI represents a paradigm shift in talent management, offering endless possibilities for improving efficiency, personalization, and engagement. However, its adoption comes with significant responsibilities, including addressing ethical challenges, protecting employee privacy, and fostering trust.

REFERENCES

Briki, M., Gherrab, S., & Almi, H. (2024). Leveraging artificial intelligence to optimize talent management in higher education institutions. ATRAS Journal, 5(SI on AI and Education), 464–480.

Budhwar, P., Chowdhury, S., Wood, G., Aguinis, H., Bamber, G. J., Beltran, J. R., & Varma, A. (2023). Human resource management in the age of generative artificial intelligence: Perspectives and research directions on ChatGPT. *Human Resource Management Journal*, *33*(3), 606–659. DOI: 10.1111/1748-8583.12524

Business Insider. (2025, January). Labor shortages, the skills gap, and political changes are top of the agenda for the US' biggest HR group in 2025. Retrieved from https://www.businessinsider.com/workplace-trends-for-2025-shrm-2025-1

Deloitte. (2019). Unleashing talent with the future of artificial intelligence. Retrieved from https://www2.deloitte.com/us/en/pages/deloitte-analytics/articles/unleashing-talent-with-the-future-of-artificial-intelligence.html

Deloitte. (2024, December). The future of AI in the workforce. Retrieved from https://www2.deloitte.com/us/en/pages/human-capital/articles/ai-in-human-resources-workforce-enablement-servicenow.html

Deloitte. (2025, March). Total talent workforce planning strategies. Retrieved from https://www2.deloitte.com/us/en/blog/human-capital-blog/2025/workforce-planning-and-total-talent-management.html

Harvard Business Review. (2022, October). Where AI can—and can't—help talent management. Retrieved from https://hbr.org/2022/10/where-ai-can-and-cant-help-talent-management

Harvard Business Review. (2023, December). Talent management in the age of AI. Retrieved from https://hbr.org/2023/12/talent-management-in-the-age-of-ai

Harvard Business Review. (2023, September). Reskilling in the age of AI. Retrieved from https://hbr.org/2023/09/reskilling-in-the-age-of-ai

Holuša, V., Vaněk, M., Beneš, F., Švub, J., & Staša, P. (2023). Virtual reality as a tool for sustainable training and education of employees in industrial enterprises. *Sustainability (Basel)*, *15*(1), 310. DOI: 10.3390/su151712886

Johnson, R. E., & Gueutal, H. G. (2022). Talent management in the context of AI adoption. *SSRN*. DOI: 10.2139/ssrn.5145205

Li, Y., Ochmann, S., & Laumer, S. (2021). Applying explainable AI to an AI-based system for candidate management: Reducing bias and enhancing diversity in hiring decisions. *Electronic Markets*, *32*(3), 707–721. DOI: 10.1007/s12525-022-00600-9

Malik, A., Budhwar, P., & Patel, C. (2022). May the bots be with you! Delivering HR cost-effectiveness and individualized employee experiences in an MNE. *International Journal of Human Resource Management*, *33*(10), 2170–2194. DOI: 10.1080/09585192.2021.1892834

McKinsey & Company. (2023a, June 5). Generative AI and the future of HR [Podcast]. Retrieved from https://www.mckinsey.com/capabilities/people-and-organizational-performance/our-insights/generative-ai-and-the-future-of-hr

McKinsey & Company. (2023b). Four ways to start using generative AI in HR. Retrieved from https://www.mckinsey.com/capabilities/people-and-organizational-performance/our-insights/the-organization-blog/four-ways-to-start-using-generative-ai-in-hr

McKinsey & Company. (2025, March). The critical role of strategic workforce planning in the age of AI. Retrieved from https://www.mckinsey.com/capabilities/people-and-organizational-performance/our-insights/the-critical-role-of-strategic-workforce-planning-in-the-age-of-ai

Odugbesan, J. A., Aghazadeh, S., Al Qaralleh, R. E., & Sogeke, O. S. (2023). Green talent management and employees' innovative work behavior: The roles of artificial intelligence and transformational leadership. *Journal of Knowledge Management*, *27*(3), 696–716. DOI: 10.1108/JKM-08-2021-0601

Paramita, D., Okwir, S., & Nuur, C. (2024). Artificial intelligence in talent acquisition: Exploring organisational and operational dimensions. *The International Journal of Organizational Analysis*, *32*(11), 108–131. DOI: 10.1108/IJOA-09-2023-3992

Qin, C., Zhang, L., Cheng, Y., Zha, R., Shen, D., Zhang, Q., Chen, X., Sun, Y., Zhu, C., Zhu, H., & Xiong, H. (2023). A comprehensive survey of artificial intelligence techniques for talent analytics. arXiv preprint arXiv:2307.03195.

Schmidt, F. L., & Hunter, J. E. (1998). The validity and utility of selection methods in personnel psychology: Practical and theoretical implications of 85 years of research findings. *Psychological Bulletin*, *124*(2), 262–274. DOI: 10.1037/0033-2909.124.2.262

Society for Human Resource Management. (2024, September). AI shapes the future of workplace tech. Retrieved from https://www.shrm.org/topics-tools/news/hr-quarterly/ai-shapes-the-future-of-workplace-tech

Society for Human Resource Management. (2025a, March). The future of work is personal: How AI is reshaping employee experiences. Retrieved from https://www.shrm.org/enterprise-solutions/insights/future-of-work-is-personal-how-ai-is-reshaping-employee

Society for Human Resource Management. (2025b). Artificial intelligence in the workplace playbook. Retrieved from https://www.shrm.org/topics-tools/topics/artificial-intelligence-in-the-workplace

Verma, A. (2024). Artificial Intelligence in Talent Management: Maximizing Human Resource Potential. In Futuristic Trends in Management (IIP Series, Vol. 3, Book 28, Part 8, pp. 135–150). India: Khalsa College of Engineering and Technology.

Verma, A. (2024). Artificial Intelligence in Talent Management: Maximizing Human Resource Potential. In Futuristic Trends in Management (IIP Series, Vol. 3, Book 28, Part 8, pp. 135–150). India: Khalsa College of Engineering and Technology.

World Economic Forum. (2025a, January). AI is shifting the workplace skillset. But human skills still count. Retrieved from https://www.weforum.org/stories/2025/01/ai-workplace-skills

World Economic Forum. (2025b, April). Why workers must upskill as AI accelerates workplace changes. Retrieved from https://www.weforum.org/stories/2025/04/linkedin-strategic-upskilling-ai-workplace-changes

Chapter 18
Redefining Work:
Global Trends, Hybrid Models, and Strategies for Retaining Gen Z Talent in the Age of AI

Preet Kanwal
https://orcid.org/0009-0006-5114-8381
Lovely Professional University, India

Pranav Malik
https://orcid.org/0009-0003-9126-3219
Lovely Professional University, India

Jasleen Purty
https://orcid.org/0009-0001-3374-2380
Lovely Professional University, India

Neesha Rawat
https://orcid.org/0009-0005-3214-2905
Lovely Professional University, India

Sandeep Kaur Randhawa
https://orcid.org/0009-0001-7436-7943
Conestoga College Institute of Technology and Advanced Learning, Canada

Kulpreet Kaur
https://orcid.org/0000-0001-8028-7889
O.P. Jindal Global University, India

ABSTRACT

The emergence of Artificial Intelligence in the workplace is changing management techniques, engagement, and employment patterns. To retain such talent, organizations need to be extremely aligned with Gen-Z's demands. Nowadays, hybrid work is common; Gen Z workers value independence. Talent is drawn to remote employment, but there are drawbacks as well, such as communication breakdowns and cultural disintegration. Digital tools must be embraced by companies for effective collaboration. AI-driven change increases productivity, but companies need to have a stand between automation and the human touch. Gen-Z expects workplaces to foster Diversity, Equity and Inclusion more than just being an organization with policies. Hybrid models enable flexibility and collaboration, but robust strategies enable thriving. The businesses that embrace the ideals of community, purpose, and flexibility held by Gen - Z will succeed. The future workplace will focus more on establishing an inclusive, sustainable, and fulfilling work environment for everyone by adjusting to new technologies.

DOI: 10.4018/979-8-3373-1270-5.ch018

INTRODUCTION

Fate parted in a hundred ways, and AI poses serious difficulties to businesses all over the world. As businesses adopt AI technologies, there will be widespread change in organizational strategy, the conditions in which we work, and human resource practices. What was once considered a phenomenon of the distant future is today an indispensable part of workplaces across sectors, as artificial intelligence (AI) has revolutionized the way tasks are performed and the work itself. The sudden need for its use forced companies to innovate and rethink conventional ways of approaching business, leading to adjustment in behavior within the fast-changing digital economy.

Due to extensive Kyml usage, business processes have transformed significantly, since applying AI offers massive benefits based on scalability, accuracy, and efficiency. Monotonous and mundane jobs such as scheduling, data entry, and customer support can all be performed by AI-powered programs, allowing human employees to concentrate on higher-level creative, strategic, and problem-solving tasks. For example, natural language processing (NLP)-powered chatbots for customer support may answer common questions 24/7, guaranteeing quicker response times and raising client satisfaction. Similarly, by spotting patterns, projecting results, and allocating resources as efficiently as possible, AI-driven predictive analytics help businesses make data-driven decisions.

The Rise of Remote Work

Remote work has been the most significant change in the modern workplace, radically changing how companies operate and how individuals engage with their work. Although remote work has become more popular in recent decades, the COVID-19 pandemic hastened the pace of change by forcing companies that had previously relied on face-to-face interactions to quickly adopt virtual and remote work practices. This rapid transition not only altered working techniques but also shifted company and employee expectations. This shift has opened up new opportunities for the majority of businesses, such as accessing a larger talent pool, increasing productivity, and giving workers the flexibility they so much want (Jetha et al., 2023).

Talent Pool Globalization

One of the most remarkable impacts of remote work has been the globalisation of the talent pool. With geographical boundaries broken, companies are now able to tap into a wealth of talent and expertise from all around the world. Remote work enables organizations to source skills from all over the world, driving creativity, innovation and problem-solving from different viewpoints (Collings et al., 2018; Haziazi, 2021). A Silicon Valley-based tech company can now easily collaborate with software engineers working in Bangalore, designers in Tokyo, and marketing professionals in London without having to physically relocate (Ye, 2023).

The global pool of talent affects companies in multiple ways. First, it enables them to employ specialists with specialized skills that do not be available in their vicinity (Saad & Mayouf, 2018). It also helps companies operate 24/7 collaborating with people across time zones., it allows them to fill skill gaps by exploring new markets (Vandy, 2023; Collings & Isichei, 2017).

However, this global talent pool comes with its downsides. Companies must tackle cultural gaps, which influence communication styles, decision-making, and working approaches. Two different time zones make scheduling meetings and collaborating in real time a challenge. For one, businesses must abide by local labor laws and tax regulations that vary from country to country (Haziazi, 2021). So, organizations must have robust tools and systems that can ease communication, collaboration, and cultural understanding among individuals to handle these challenges (Salamin & Hanappi, 2014). Training classes for working with different cultures or clear work rules are examples of the types of classes that can increase global team collaboration (Todorović & Ivanović, 2018).

Balance in Life and Work

Local had built up a commercial empire in a world where freedom had morphed into one of the most desirable perks of modern employment, completely reworking the landscape of how businesses interact with recruiting and retaining talent (Ayar et al., 2021; Begum, 2024). Employees happily embrace working from anywhere to suit their work-life needs. Flexibility has become especially helpful for people with multiple commitments: working parents, caregivers, or students attending graduate school (Yang et al., 2018; Liswandi & Muhammad, 2023; Gadzali, 2023).

For example, parents are now able to attend to family matters, such as helping kids with school assignments or participating in school events, without putting any major brake on their career (Begum, 2024; Zhang et al., 2024). A few hours of time saved within the week provide remote-working employees a little respite from the worry of whether commuting would wear them out before they reach the office (Yang et al., 2018). This time savings can do wonders for health and well-being, giving people enough physical and mental energy to finish their work wholeheartedly (Limanta et al., 2023; Krishnan et al., 2023).

Additionally, companies with remote arrangements tend to enjoy higher job satisfaction and employee retention. Workers report that remote employees are 22% happier than office-based counterparts, greatly underscoring flexibility within the modern workspace (Azeem & Akhtar, 2014; Ayar et al., 2021; Hsu et al., 2019). When workers are given the time and space to arrange their work-life, they typically feel that they are more trusted and valued by their employer. This, in turn, generates loyalty and performance on the part of workers (Yang et al., 2021; Bataineh, 2019).

Flexibility offered by working outside the company is not free, though. Most employees struggle to create boundaries between work and personal life, which causes their daily lives both inside and outside of the office to become unsustainable and eventually lead to burnout (Azeem & Akhtar, 2014; Gadzali, 2023). Organizations should therefore urge their members to establish work-life boundaries, such as set working hours, frequent scheduled breaks, and occasional digital withdrawal, in an effort to counteract this propensity. Businesses can also help employees cope with the particular stressors of working from home by implementing wellness programs and mental health perks (Hsu et al., 2019; Fathya et al., 2024).

Technology's Role in Remote Work

The massive shift to remote work would not have been feasible without technology. Over the past ten years, advancements in project management, communication, and collaboration technology have made it possible for geographically separated teams to collaborate productively. These days, companies rely on tools like Zoom, Slack, Microsoft Teams, and Asana for task management, file sharing, video conferencing, and instant messaging. These tools keep employees motivated, organized, and productive no matter where they work.

Remote work is changing due to AI-based technology. Real-time translation promotes inclusivity by removing language barriers. AI scheduling tools make meetings across time zones easier. By analyzing productivity, machine learning provides businesses with information to enhance workflows and eliminate bottlenecks. These developments improve teamwork, productivity, and the working environment in general.(Jetha et al., 2023).

Along with its advantages, technology has certain drawbacks in the context of remote work too. Extended dependence on digital devices leads to "digital fatigue" in affecting sensations of fatigue and reduction of productivity with excessing time behind a screen and constant connectivity. In addition, the collapse of physical separation between work and housing can blur boundaries so that workers will struggle to put work down.

To combat problems like these, businesses must seek thoughtful technologies and approaches. They can also use deferred communication tools, such as emails and videotaped updates, when interaction in real time is not inevitable. This mechanism alleviates some of the load of being "always online" and allows employees to regain control over when they perform their work tasks. Also to shape time limits on meetings and how often to avoid unwanted online meetings and reduce digital fatigue (Jetha et al., 2023).

Remote Work's Future

As remote working continues to develop, it becomes increasingly evident that this is not a fad but rather a fundamental change in business operations. Due to hybrid work cultures, which combine the advantages of office and remote work and are growing in popularity as companies want to provide flexibility while also encouraging community and connectivity, it now seems like business will never be the same. These methods enable companies to accommodate a variety of needs and preferences by letting workers split their time between virtual and real workspaces.

To thrive in this new age, companies need to focus on flexibility and innovation. They need to invest in technology that facilitates frictionless hybrid working arrangements, like virtual reality working platforms, hot-desking technologies, and cutting-edge cybersecurity tools. To ensure that all employees—whether full-time, part-time, or hybrid—are engaged and motivated, companies need to create a culture of trust, transparency, and inclusion (Sucipto, 2024).

Lastly, the increase in remote work highlights the need to reevaluate conventional management approaches. Leaders need to have a results-oriented mindset and prioritize production above hours. They should also make it a point to speak with team members frequently, not only to keep tabs on developments but also to discuss challenges and offer assistance. Businesses can fully benefit from remote employment while fostering a productive and enjoyable work environment by putting these methods into practice.

Digital Transformation and Integration of AI

Work is changing like never before due to the digital revolution being driven by artificial intelligence. AI is used by businesses to enhance decision-making, automate processes, and derive value from data. This change helps organizations remain competitive by increasing customer satisfaction, cutting expenses, and improving efficiency. Supply chain optimization, predictive marketing, and improved customer experiences are all made possible by AI, as demonstrated by AI-driven shopping recommendations. AI is used by sectors including banking and healthcare to identify fraud and assist in recovery. But integrating AI is not without its challenges. As AI becomes a crucial component of key systems, organizations must strike a balance between accelerating adoption and coordinating its strength and speed with moral principles and corporate objectives. (Katsaros, 2024).

The Evolution of AI in Workforce Dynamics

Workplace AI has also dramatically altered roles and responsibilities between individuals, significantly changing the relationships within the workforce. AI now serves as an efficient agent for repetitive and mundane jobs like data entry, scheduling and customer service (Nalwade, 2024). For example, natural language processing (NLP)-based chatbots are able to respond to customer inquiries around the clock, reducing the burden on human employees and enabling them to focus on higher value work (Kim & Kim, 2024). Robotic process automation (RPA), likewise, is automating workflows in areas such as invoice processing and compliance reporting, increasing the accuracy and speed of this work and allowing staff to focus on making strategic choices. While AI is automating these functions, it is also creating new opportunities for human labor (Liu, 2024). Jobs in data science, machine learning and AI ethics and algorithm auditing are coming up with salaries that become very lucrative for individuals with the right skill sets. Moreover, AI is creating demand for cross-disciplinary expertise, with professionals in social science fields like psychology, sociology, and law, joining forces with students of computer science and engineering to navigate AI's broader ramifications. But that change brings challenges too — especially for employees in occupations vulnerable to automation (Tabbassum et al., 2024). Organizations must now invest in reskilling and upskilling programs to combat this. Corporate training, for example, may include educating workers on how to collaborate well with AI so they can transition to jobs that require critical thinking, creativity and emotional intelligence — areas that fall yet in the realm of humans (Mossavar-Rahmani & Zohuri, 2024). In an AI-enabled economy, when organizations are restructured on the basis of machine learning and automation, a culture in which continuous learning becomes normal can equip employees to pivot to evolving needs, while their organizations stay competitive too (Hamarat et al., 2024).

Implications for Ethics

The ethical issues raised by AI must be addressed by businesses, especially the prejudice in algorithms that may encourage discrimination in hiring, resource distribution, and law enforcement. If AI hiring tools are educated on biased data, they may favor particular groups, so sustaining systemic injustices. Similar to this, AI in law enforcement has come under fire for unfairly singling out underprivileged groups, which has raised questions about transparency. Since AI gathers a lot of personal data, data privacy is also essential. Businesses need to put cybersecurity safeguards in place and abide by laws like GDPR. Fairness, accountability, and trust in the workplace depend on the ethical deployment of AI since failure to do so could result in legal repercussions and harm to one's reputation (Chand et al., 2024).

Furthermore, automation's capacity to threaten jobs has sparked disputes around the social obligations of businesses. While AI can improve efficiency, it can also lead towards a decrease in staff, creating economic and behavioral problems. To mitigate these risks, businesses should prioritize transparency in AI strategy and actively engage a broad cross-section of stakeholders—workers, regulators, and public representatives—within the decision-making process.

Ethics in Sustainability Whereas the clear guidelines and standards associated with sustainable development hinge on trust and long-term viability; ethical guidelines regulating the application of AI and servitization are unquestionably necessary. Practices such as regular auditing of AI systems, precise accountability regarding decision-making, and establishing collaboration between technical and non-technical teams can be embedded into an organization. Through the infusion of ethical considerations into their AI plans, companies can mitigate risks and, more importantly, realize the promise of AI in a responsible and equitable manner.

AI for Improving Experience of Employee

AI's impact on creativity and productivity is only one dimension; it can fundamentally enhance people's entire work lives. AI enhances workplace satisfaction and productivity by taking over repetitive admin tasks, allowing all employees to focus their time and energy on creative, strategic, and problem-solving work. AI systems, for example, do things like appointment scheduling, email sorting and report making, leaving employees able to focus on more meaningful parts of their jobs.AI is also transforming professional development through the personalization of learning experiences. AI-enabled learning systems can evaluate an individual's skill sets, find discrepancies, and suggest training classes according to their career objectives. For instance, an employee who is looking to transition to a managerial role can be offered AI-recommended courses in leadership, conflict management and team management. This tailored learning experience accelerates skill acquisition and also empowers employees to take ownership of their career growth (Islam & Zhou, 2024).

For example, AI can play a significant role in encouraging inclusivity in the workplace: AI programs featuring real-time language translation capabilities allow seamless communication within organizations with multi-linguistic workforce, leading to the removal of language barriers and the improvement of cultural collaboration. Similarly, AI-based accessibility tools such as speech-to-text converters and screen readers can help disabled employees to participate in workplace activities fully.However, introducing AI into the worker experience is not without challenges. AI Tools Cause Digital Fatigue In WorkplacesRe-mote and hybrid workplaces have given rise to more digital communications between colleagues — and with that comes over-reliance on AI tools which can lead to digital fatigue. To solve this, businesses can manufacture routes to be able to possess a healthy balance of technology utilization vs human connection. For example, encouraging habitual in-person team-building meetings and restricting AI technologies to work-related tasks will reduce digital fatigue without sacrificing productivity.By enhancing the employee experience through AI, organizations can create a more resilient, engaged, and connected workforce. Ultimately, this leads to improved performance, increased retention, and a corporate culture centred on creativity and the well-being of workers (Kaur, 2024).

The Significance of Diversity and Inclusion

Diversity and inclusion (D&I) have become top priorities in today's workplace, a reflection of a greater appreciation for their role in organizational success. With the rise of remote and hybrid work environments, creating inclusive environments has become more critical to the recruitment, retention, and enablement of diverse talent (Mitchell et al., 2015). Diversity is no longer a matter of compliance or social obligation; it is a central driver of innovation, collaboration, and business performance (Jaiswal & Dyaram, 2019).

Businesses with a culture that embraces diversity and inclusion are better positioned to thrive in an increasingly interconnected and globalized world. Businesses may foster a sense of belonging that fosters creativity and resilience by recognizing and valuing the unique perspectives of workers from a range of backgrounds, abilities, genders, and ethnicities. Additionally, D&I is a strategic need that benefits an organization at all levels and is not just a moral requirement (Le et al., 2018).

Benefits of a Diverse Workforce

Multicultural teams combine multiple perspectives, backgrounds, and approaches to solving problems, thus acting as an accelerator for innovation and creativity. When people of different backgrounds come together, they challenge the normal way of thinking and provide unique insights, resulting in more complete and successful solutions. For example, a multicultural marketing team is more likely to develop campaigns that will appeal to a global public (Bodla et al., 2016).

Research consistently demonstrates the tangible benefits of workplace diversity. Businesses in the top quartile for ethnic and cultural diversity had a 35% higher chance of outperforming their rivals financially, according to a McKinsey analysis. Similarly, companies with more diverse genders are 21 percent more likely to be profitable than average. These numbers demonstrate the clear connection between diverse teams and improved company outcomes, such as more devoted clients, improved decision-making, and increased staff engagement (Mathuki & Zhang, 2022).

Beyond powering innovation and financial success, a diverse workforce also enables businesses to understand and respond to the needs of a growing, increasingly diverse customer base. Businesses that match their products or services with the tastes of diverse segments are best able to win market share and establish long-term relationships with customers. For instance, a consumer products firm with a multicultural product development team can create products that suit diverse tastes and preferences, thus increasing its reach and sales (Maj, 2023).

Furthermore, diversity enhances a company's reputation as a top employer. Employers who prioritize diversity and inclusion are likely to attract top talent, particularly from younger generations who are concerned with social responsibility and inclusivity. According to the Deloitte Global Millennial Survey, 74% of millennials believe that an inclusive culture fosters innovation in their organizations, bolstering the idea that diversity and inclusion are essential to long-term success (Leroy et al., 2021).

Creating an Inclusive Work Environment

Inclusion is about creating an environment where everyone may feel appreciated, respected, and empowered to contribute, whereas diversity is about representation. In order to create an inclusive workplace, deliberate efforts must be made to remove structural obstacles and promote equity at all organizational levels (Jerónimo et al., 2021).

Policies and Practices for Inclusion

It all starts with leadership buy-in in order for an inclusive work environment to flourish. A diverse leadership teams signals the company's commitment to fairness and representation." Getting there requires them to adopt policies that promote diverse leadership pipelines — including targeted recruitment, sponsorship, and succession planning.

A third, critical step toward building inclusion is closing pay gaps. Transparent compensation frameworks, regular salary audits and promotion processes based on merit go a long way in eliminating biases in the organizations and ensuring all employees are paid equally for the value they bring. Mentorship and sponsorship programs are a key to inclusion as a whole as well, particularly for diverse populations! By pairing staff with mentors who provide guidance and support, organizations can help close gaps in opportunity and enable professional advancement (Triana et al., 2010).

Using Technology to Foster Inclusion

Technology can be a great diversity and inclusion enabler, providing solutions and tools to neutralize biases and improve accessibility. For instance, artificial intelligence (AI) can be employed to minimize bias in the hiring process. AI-powered recruitment platforms can anonymize CVs so that hiring is made based on qualification and skills and not on unconscious biases based on names, gender, or ethnicity. Moreover, analytics enabled by AI can monitor diversity metrics, offering organizations actionable information to enhance their D&I efforts (Kaur, 2024).

Digital accessibility is another field where technology can foster inclusivity. Organizations need to make their tools and platforms accessible to people with disabilities. This involves functionalities like screen readers, closed captions, and keyboard navigation. By making accessibility a priority, companies can have a work environment where every worker can excel despite physical or cognitive capabilities.

Remote work, now the norm in the post-pandemic world, also presents special opportunities for promoting inclusion. Flexible work options allow organizations to draw on a larger pool of talent, including people who might have difficulty in a traditional office setting. Parents who are caregiving, for instance, people with mobility issues, and employees in remote locations are all examples of people who can gain from the flexibility of remote work (Rožman & Tominc, 2024).

Cultivating a Culture of Belonging

It is easier said than done, as inclusion is not just practice and policy — it has to be a culture shift that makes every employee feel that there is a place for them in the system. That is creating spaces where people feel comfortable bringing their ideas to the table, sharing their stories, and challenging the status quo with no fear of being judged or discriminated against."

Then, they can begin to foster this culture, actively celebrating diversity (including employee resource groups (ERGs), cultural awareness activities and inclusive communications). For example, ERGs corresponding to particular identity groups — such as LGBTQ+ employees or women in leadership positions — can create a sense of advocacy and belonging at work. Likewise, acknowledging and celebrating cultural holidays, achievements, and anniversaries add value to diversity-based solutions (Wolfgruber et al., 2021; Anggoro & Anjarini, 2024).

Equipping employees and managers with training on unconscious bias, cultural competency, and inclusive leadership is another facet of awareness and accountability. On these training courses, pupils learn to overcome prejudices, develop empathy and hold inclusive conversations (Ullrich et al., 2024).

Understanding Hybrid Work Models

Over the last few years, as remote work has ceased to be just a passing phase, the modern workplace has evolved dramatically, giving rise to hybrid work models as the most coveted answer for organizations eager to find the right balance between remote work and traditional work. For organizations Hybrid work models allow employees the flexibility to work in a style and way that best complements their lifestyle and needs whilst still providing organizations with the "community", "collaborative" and "aligned with business goals" aspect (Santillan et al., 2023). Hybrid work arrangements influence not just how work is completed but also foreshadow a tectonic shift in organizational culture and employee expectations. In principle, a hybrid work pattern is a blend of remote and on-location work and provides employees the finest of both worlds. Thus, organizations can meet diverse needs of employees, enhance work-life balance and ultimately productivity. Hybrid work patterns also enable these firms to optimize resources, cut down costs on office space, and cast their talent nets wide by factoring in applicants from all geographical locations inclusivity (Rožman & Tominc, 2024).

Types of Hybrid Work Models

Hybrid work patterns take many different forms, each responding to distinct organizational needs and employee tastes. The model to use is usually determined by the type of work, the corporate culture, as well as the level of flexibility desired by the employees. Some of the most frequent types of hybrid work arrangements are listed below:

- **Flexible Hybrid Model**

Using an agile hybrid model empowers staff to decide when they want to collaborate in-person, versus when they want to work from home. Flexible working: This is the most flexible option, allowing employees to create a schedule according to personal and professional needs. An employee, for example, could do intense workdays at home and come into the office for meetings and team building.This model has become popular among workers, especially those who value work-life balance and freedom over their working conditions. Studies show that independent work leads to higher job satisfaction, greater motivation, and more production. However, for companies, an all-about hybrid model necessitates robust communication tools, a clear policy and a culture of trust to ensure seamless coordination between teams (Pei et al., 2024).

- **Hybrid Office-First Model**

Under the office-first hybrid model, employees can work from home on a restricted number of days, but the office remains the primary location for work. For example, a company might assign workers to work four days a week at the office and allow them to work from home on the fifth day.

This strategy maintains a strong degree of community among team members and places a high priority on in-person cooperation. It works best for businesses or occupations that need physical presence, such as manufacturing, healthcare, or creative teams that gain from in-person interactions and brainstorming sessions. For workers who choose to work remotely or who find it difficult to go to the office, the office-first paradigm may be constraining. Businesses using this strategy must strike a balance between ensuring that workers feel valued (Tong et al., 2021).

- **Remote-First Hybrid Model**

As the name indicates, the remote-first hybrid model emphasizes remote working as the default setup. The employees spend most of their time working at home or other remote sites and meet up in person intermittently for meetings, events, or team-building exercises. This type of model became much more popular amid the COVID-19 pandemic and remains popular with companies that prioritize flexibility and cost-effectiveness.

Organizations can save money on office space, promote a better work-life balance, and access a global talent pool by implementing the remote-first strategy. It gives employees the flexibility to work remotely while still taking advantage of infrequent in-person meetings that foster camaraderie and teamwork. To get around potential problems, including remote workers feeling disconnected or isolated, companies must invest in technology solutions, staff engagement initiatives, and effective communication procedures (Nyathani, 2023).

Advantages of Hybrid Work Models

Hybrid work arrangements have transformed the contemporary workplace by meeting the varied needs of workers while promoting organizational effectiveness. The models, which integrate the best practices of both in-office and remote work, provide a wide range of advantages beyond mere operational flexibility. Below, we discuss in depth how hybrid work arrangements enhance worker satisfaction, better work-life balance, and promote productivity and ultimately organizational success (Niebuhr et al., 2022).

Improved Employee Satisfaction

Employee happiness is greatly increased by hybrid employment since it provides flexibility and autonomy. Trust between companies and employees is fostered as a result of employees feeling empowered to organize their schedules. Because of their independence, employees can choose their workspace; those who require concentration can work from home, while those who would like collaborate can work in an office setting. By honoring personal preferences, this kind of customisation increases loyalty. Furthermore, by doing away with strict office hours, hybrid models lessen stress and help avoid burnout. According to a FlexJobs poll, flexible employment made 80% of workers feel more dedicated. Because of these advantages, hybrid employment benefits firms by increasing retention rates and lowering turnover costs. (Aprilina & Martdianty, 2023).

Better Work-Life Balance

By enabling workers to successfully balance their personal and professional obligations, hybrid work models improve work-life balance. Caregivers and lifelong learners may easily accommodate their demands, and working parents can attend family gatherings without jeopardizing their professional development. Another significant advantage is shorter commutes, which provide workers more time for family, leisure, and self-care and increase job satisfaction. Employees are more attentive and efficient when they are not as exhausted from traveling. As more people look for positions that offer flexibility and a better balance between work and life, companies that prioritize work-life balance through hybrid models have a competitive edge in attracting and retaining talent. (Yang et al., 2021).

Increased Productivity

Hybrid work models are best suited to improve productivity by enabling workers to work in settings that best meet their individual requirements. By providing people with the option of where and how they can work more effectively, organizations can release greater levels of engagement and effectiveness.

Remote work provides a distraction-free atmosphere that allows employees to work intently and think deeply, allowing them to perform at their best. The hybrid model, on the other hand, is well-suited to strike a balance between individual and collaborative productivity since face-to-face working fosters creativity, problem-solving, and teamwork.

Research has confirmed the link between increased productivity and flexible work arrangements. According to a study by Owl Labs, 90% of employees who worked remotely or in a hybrid setting said they were just as productive—if not more so—than those who worked in regular office settings. This demonstrates how the hybrid model can both meet various work requirements and capitalize on personnel capabilities (Katsande et al., 2022).

Furthermore, hybrid work models lower presenteeism—a condition where employees are present but not actively engaged as a result of stress or fatigue. By allowing employees to work their schedules in alignment with their energy levels and priorities, hybrid models ensure optimal employee performance (Katsande et al., 2022).

Greater Access to Talent

Organizations may hire people from all around the world because to hybrid work models, which increase talent pools by eliminating regional restrictions. In areas where local expertise is scarce, this fills skill gaps and introduces new ideas and varied viewpoints. For instance, a New York-based business may hire a designer in Buenos Aires or a software developer in Mumbai. Having access to a wide range of skills encourages creativity and innovation. By incorporating those with disabilities and those who live in remote regions, hybrid employment also promotes diversity and makes workplaces more welcoming. Organizations increase workforce diversity and flexibility by meeting the requirements of various employees, fostering a more creative and dynamic work environment (Beňo, 2021).

Cost Savings for Employees and Organizations

Employers and employees can both save money with hybrid work schedules. The economic benefits for employees include reduced transit expenses, lower costs for business attire, and lower daily costs for daycare or eating out.

Hybrid models save businesses a significant amount of money on maintenance, utilities, and office space. To accommodate the fluctuating number of on-site employees, businesses can either build co-working spaces or decrease their physical presence. These savings can then be put back into technology, staff development, or other strategic goals (Beňo, 2021).

Challenges of Hybrid Work Models

Hybrid work models, as much as they provide several advantages, come with a distinctive set of challenges. These challenges mainly stem from the requirement of balancing the in-office and remote team dynamics and ensuring productivity, collaboration, and inclusivity. The following is an in-depth discussion of the major challenges that organizations encounter while adopting hybrid work models, including practical strategies for overcoming them (Katsande et al., 2022).

Communication Barriers

Keeping geographically dispersed teams' communication open is one of the biggest problems with hybrid work arrangements. There is a risk of creating an information gap when employees are split between home and workplace locations. Important talks that take place informally at work, such as during coffee breaks or conversations in the corridor, may be excluded from remote workers.

As a result, inconsistent communication causes miscommunications, delays in decision-making, and a decline in team trust. Furthermore, distant workers typically struggle to participate effectively in hybrid meetings when bad meeting behavior or technical difficulties arise (Buła et al., 2024).

To cross such barriers, organizations need to

Implement next-generation communication tools: Tools such as Slack, Zoom, and Microsoft Teams have the potential to bridge the remote-in-office gap. These should be incorporated into regular workflows to promote inclusivity.

Establish strict hybrid meeting guidelines: Invite hosts to adopt practices such as virtual-first agendas, equitable speaking time, and chat functions to promote inclusive participation.

Promote transparency: Develop avenues for constant updates and recording to make available to all the same information accessible to all staff, irrespective of their location (Katsande et al., 2022).

Sustaining Organizational Culture

Another hybrid work model challenge is sustaining a unified organizational culture. In the conventional office setup, culture is developed through shared experiences, face-to-face interactions, and spontaneous collaboration. But in a hybrid environment, these opportunities are lost, resulting in a disjointed workplace culture.

Remote workers may experience loneliness or exclusion as a result of feeling cut off from their coworkers in the workplace. Both team morale and corporate ideals may be impacted (Jindain & Gilitwala, 2023).

In order to maintain a productive corporate culture, businesses should

Make team-building activities a priority: Plan regular events, such as virtual happy hours, business vacations, or video games, that bring together both in-office and remote employees.

Indicate success in a comprehensive way: Recognize success in methods that involve all employees, for as through firm-wide announcements or virtual town hall meetings.

Communicate and uphold shared values: To make sure that every employee is aligned with the company's vision, communicate the mission and values frequently through internal communications (Buła et al., 2024).

Employee Isolation and Loneliness

Emotional isolation and loneliness are prevalent among remote workers, especially in blended work arrangements where some team members work together in-person while others work remotely. The absence of casual conversations and social bonding can adversely affect mental well-being and productivity.

To mitigate these issues, organizations must

- **Foster casual interactions:** Provide avenues for casual conversations via virtual coffee breaks or social forums in workplace communication platforms.
- **Offer mental health support:** Provide access to counseling sessions, employee assistance programs, or mindfulness resources to enhance employee well-being.
- **Facilitate mentorship opportunities**: Match remote employees with mentors or buddies to increase their sense of belonging to the team.
- **Inequity in Opportunities:**Unintentionally, hybrid work models may lead to differences between employees who work remotely and those who work in offices. Employees that work in offices are frequently more visible to managers, which can result in more chances for recognition, project assignments, and promotions. Conversely, remote workers could feel underappreciated or ignored (Jindain & Gilitwala, 2023).
- **In order to guarantee equity, businesses must:**Put performance-based assessments into practice . Pay more attention to results and contributions than to location or hours worked.
- **Standardize possibilities for development:** Give remote workers equitable access to leadership development courses, training courses, and high-profile initiatives.
- **Give fair feedback:** To find out what's wrong and to give equitable opportunities, hold frequent one-on-one sessions with both in-person and remote staff.

Challenges with Work-Life Boundaries

Hybrid work arrangements blur the boundaries between work and personal life, particularly for remote workers. The lack of a distinct separation between professional and personal environments can result in overwork, burnout, and inability to "switch off."(Aprilina & Martdianty, 2023).

To assist employees in achieving work-life balance, organizations must

- **Establish clear boundaries:** Ask employees to set specific work hours and share them with their teams.
- **Encourage the right to disconnect:** Deter late-night emails and make sure workers are not ashamed to take a break.
- **Offer ergonomic assistance:** Provide stipends or resources for remote workers to create dedicated workspaces that eliminate distractions.

Technological Dependence

Hybrid work is dependent greatly on technology, which at times results in overdependence. Digital exhaustion, caused by too much screen time and consecutive virtual meetings, is a current issue in hybrid environments. Further, technical problems like slow internet connectivity or older versions of software can deter productivity (Katsande et al., 2022).

To counter these issues, organizations must

- **Invest in quality technology:** Give employees the equipment, including laptops, software, and fast internet, that they need to carry out their tasks efficiently.
- **Maximize meeting procedures:** Reduce the frequency of virtual meetings and promote asynchronous communication methods, such as recorded briefings or documents shared.Provide IT support: Provide employees with access to technical support to address issues quickly.

Handling Accountability and Performance

Managers may find it challenging to monitor performance and uphold accountability when employees follow hybrid work patterns. Aside from physical presence, some managers may find it difficult to trust workers who work from home, which can result in micromanagement or skewed assessments of output.

In order to overcome the obstacle, managers must: Pay attention to results: Instead of keeping track of hours, start measuring deliverables and results.

Make use of project management software. Asana, Trello, and Monday.com are a few examples of tools that may be used to monitor progress and keep teams accountable.

Managers of trains: Give leaders the skills they need to lead hybrid teams, including cooperation and trust-building strategies (Beňo, 2021).

- **Security and Compliance Risks:** Hybrid work patterns bring new security issues, e.g., data leaks and unauthorized access to confidential data. Remote workers using unsecured networks or machines can potentially expose the company to danger.

- **To counteract these risks, companies ought to:** Maintain strong cybersecurity practices: Utilize VPNs, firewalls, and endpoint security tools to safeguard firm data.
- **Offer cybersecurity training:** Educate employees on best practices, including identifying phishing efforts and locking personal devices.
- **Implement compliance-friendly tools:** Make sure all digital tools are industry-regulation and data-protection-compliant (Katsande et al., 2022).

Understanding Generation Z

Generation Z (Gen Z), generally defined as those born between the mid-1990s and early 2010s, is the first demographic generation to have grown up entirely in a digitally interconnected world. As digital natives, they have never known a world without smartphones, social media, and instant access to information, which has significantly shaped their worldview, values, and expectations—especially in the workplace. Gen Z views the boundaries between physical and digital spaces as fluid and expects the same flexibility in their professional environments. They prioritize adaptability, meaningful work, and social responsibility, making these key considerations for companies looking to attract and retain top talent from this generation. At the core of Gen Z's professional identity lies a strong commitment to work-life integration, mental health, and continuous personal and professional growth. Having witnessed the stress and burnout experienced by millennials, they actively seek work environments that prioritize mental well-being and foster a culture where employees can thrive. Gen Z workers are also deeply values-driven, gravitating toward companies that uphold ethical business practices and contribute to causes such as environmental sustainability, diversity and inclusion, and corporate social responsibility. Organizations that wish to engage and retain this socially conscious generation must adapt their policies to align with these expectations (Fredberg & Schwarz, 2024)

Gen Z workers look for work that reflects their values and emphasizes both purpose and profit. They like companies that are dedicated to social impact, such diversity in employment and sustainable operations, because they grew up in an era of political unrest, social inequality, and climate change. Businesses that don't embody these principles run the danger of losing Gen Z's support. In contrast to earlier generations, Gen Z openly talks well-being and expects companies to do the same. Mental health is as vital. In order to avoid burnout, they place a high importance on work-life balance policies, counseling services, and mental health initiatives. Maintaining their well-being requires flexible work arrangements, such as remote and hybrid models. Employers are more likely to retain Gen Z talent and ensure long-term engagement and commitment when they create an inclusive, stigma-free workplace where staff members feel supported.

As digital natives, Gen Z anticipates light, innovative technology integration in the workplace and shows swig ability in utilizing digital tools aimed at boosting efficiency and collaboration. Companies that employ outdated or no technology may have to deal with a more disengaged generation. They like tools such as AI-powered workflow platforms such as Slack and Microsoft Teams and general software that optimizes productivity. Inclusivity also plays a major role; artificial intelligence tools for hiring that mitigate bias and virtual collaboration platforms for hybrid work are appealing to them. Still, the technology must not only exist but make the work easier. Gen Z are also evaluating, shaped by online interactions with prospective employers, and prefer organizations with transparent corporate value and culture. Social responsibility is a big deal to them: a focus on diversity, inclusion, and sustainability in employers who actively champion this. Companies must undertake real efforts towards addressing inequality, encouraging diverse leadership, and fostering an inclusive workplace. Transparency and authenticity matter as Gen Z has a low tolerance for performative activism. Prioritizing equity and inclusivity, therefore, gives businesses the means to attract and retain this socially aware labor force. (Morandini et al., 2023).

Retention Strategies for Gen Z Talent

They are already accustomed to living in a digital world with technology that is intuitive to them and embedded throughout their everyday lives, so organizations looking to attract and retain this top tier of talent can benefit by leveraging technology to improve the workplace experience. They want technology to automate work processes and enable better collaboration and communication. This encourages organizations to focus on getting platforms that are easy to use and digital tools that empower collaboration, work more efficiently and ensure that work is more enjoyable. Key instruments include project management software, artificial intelligence task planners, and real-time communication platforms —creating an environment well-suited for Gen Z's digital proclivities. Moreover, confirming efficient use of technology in workflows sends a message to Gen Z employees that innovation matters to the organization and that it is committed to staying ahead of the curve in a fast-digitalizing world. Another critical aspect in retaining Gen Z employees is providing access to online learning and development resources that demonstrate a company's commitment to their career growth. Gen Z workers are driven by the desire for continuous growth and want to acquire new skills to remain relevant in a more dynamic job market. Training modules, online workshops, and certifications offered by organizations to help the employees grow professionally and personally. By doing so, companies could offer their Gen Z employees much-needed guidance and sense of purpose in their professional lives, by setting them on clear growth trajectories that have straightforward goals and measurable indicators of performance. Mentorship programs for employees that permanently assign junior employees to senior executives is another way in which employees can foster a culture of learning and provide guidance; employees also have the opportunity to establish goals that point towards their own personal development as they work toward greater value for the company (Flathmann et al., 2024). Investing in their growth and development leads to improved retention rates and creates a skilled and engaged workforce driving the organization's long-term success. Another key retention tactic among Gen Z employees is workplace flexibility — as a generation that places immense value on work-life balance, Gen Z workers want jobs that help them juggle work and home life effectively. Companies must adopt work arrangements that accommodate these needs like telecommuting, hybrid work arrangements and customized scheduling. When organizations give workers the choice of where, when, and how they work, this leads to an environment that aligns choice with autonomy, and allows people to perform at their peak. For example, allowing employees to work from home a few days a week prevents them from having to endure long commutes, gives them access to spend more time with loved ones and engage in activities that directly impact their well-being. By splitting their time between office and remote work, hybrid approaches offer the best balance of teamwork and autonomy, ensuring that all Gen Z employees feel connected to their organization while being masters of their own schedule. This flexibility is no longer just a perk; it must become an expectation to cultivate loyalty and satisfaction in Gen Z workers, who will be less hesitant to leave behind inflexible, antiquated workspaces for those that cater to their need for agility. While they may be digital workers – Gen Z wants rich relationships and a high degree of belonging among their organizations, so in-work sense of community is just as important for keep Gen Z talent engaged. The organization can create this sense of community through various community-building programs, including team-building programs, social activities, and mentorship programs. To bring local and remote employees closer together and make them both feel valued, virtual team-building exercises can be highly effective. Virtual and in-person social events allow workers to connect with their colleagues on a personal level and develop lasting relationships. Mentorship programs can not only propel employees in their careers; they can help to also deepen their connection to the organization, as that's how an ally system is formed. Developing a healthy and good corporate culture positively affects staff comfort, satisfaction, and retention rates. In addition to these strategies, business leaders can take the initiative to recognize and reward the contributions of their Gen Z employees to keep them inspired and involved. Formal rewards could include recognition, promotions, and other accolades, while informal rewards might include shout-outs in team meetings or thank you notes. By recognizing employees for their efforts and accomplishments, you make your employees feel valued, and create a culture of appreciation that will drive them to stay in the organization. Gen Z employees can also be encouraged to work at their peak through incentives tied to performance, such as bonuses or additional days off. Furthermore, giving employees exposure to new technologies and opportunities to share their skills and work on exciting projects can help create a sense of pride in their work and loyalty to the firm. One more essential aperture is aligning an organization's values and those of its GenZ employees who care deeply about social and environmental issues. This generation, however, does care, and they are drawn to firms that demonstrate genuine engagement in positively affecting society. Companies have a queer way of expecting this by conducting business in planet-friendly way, towards communities and also promote diversity and inclusion in their workplaces. For instance, Gen Z workers who are environmentally conscious will appreciate green efforts to reduce emissions, conserve resources, or finance sustainable energy projects. Likewise, while establishing an open and diverse workplace where all employees are treated with dignity and respect can increase the company's appeal to Gen Z talent and improve the overall employee experience. Those businesses that can demonstrate improvements in these areas are much more likely to attract Gen Z talent — and retain it as a sense of pride and dedication to the company's mission forms. Finally, open communication and transparency are important in establishing trust and loyalty with Gen Z workers. This generation values honesty and they want employers to provide transparency with clear and genuine communication about corporate goals, attitudes, and performance expectations. Organisations need to hold regular check-ins and town hall meetings, along with open-door policies to cultivate a culture where employees feel heard and valued. It empowers and engages employees to offer a channel for expressing their opinions, giving feedback, and generating ideas. Open decision-making also builds trust and cultivates the feeling that employees are part of the organization's journey (Katsaros, 2024). Applying these techniques can help organizations build a work culture that attracts and retains Gen Z talent over time. While this generation deserves a targeted, considered response that understands its distinctive likes and needs, the pay-off — engaged, inspired and highly skilled employees — is well worth it. Employers that successfully respond to the needs of Gen Z employees will be the front-runners in a labour market that is increasingly competitive, ensuring that they are the employer of choice for the next generation of talent (Katsaros, 2024).

CONCLUSION

Attitudes toward work are being radically altered, with the kinetic energies for these metamorphoses driven primarily by changing labor practices, workforce management, and employee engagement. Understanding the individualistic perspectives of Gen Z regarding talent retention will become critical as organizations field their manpower toward reinventing themselves in light of these tectonic shifts in work. Hybrid work-combining remote and in-office work-is observed as a strategy to elicit efficiency and satisfaction. Remote work was hastened by the COVID-19 pandemic that made it more a necessity than a luxury for the younger, flexible cohorts of workers, such as Gen Z. While flexible work arrangements enable companies to attract top personnel, this shift also has its share of issues, primarily communication gaps and an erosion of corporate culture. Organizations must invest in gear for the digital cooperation that creates an advanced and connected working environment.

The change taking place in the workplace dominate the ways work ought to be done, enhancing productivity, accuracy, and innovation. Growing up in a hyper-connected world, Gen Z believes in tech enablement to enhance productivity and do away with the mundane. Organizations must now balance tech enablement with a people-the-most-importance sort of approach, so employees feel valued and engaged, as opposed to being replaced. Rather than redundant tasks, technology, in this case, should execute human capabilities and allow employees to concentrate on critical thinking and high-level decision-making. This balance creates a modern, very human workplace.

Diversity and inclusion are fundamental to Generation Z. Generation Z seeks decisive action in the face of systemic inequalities, placing a pivotal importance on diversity, equity, and inclusion initiatives when it comes to attracting and retaining millennial talent. DEN fails to prioritize DEI issues are at risk of the possible absence of workers valuing representation and equality. Companies that effectively embed these principles will profit from a nimble, collaborative workforce that's also more innovative. Diversity stimulates creativity by allowing varied groups to coalesce at the table.

REFERENCES

Aprilina, R. and Martdianty, F. (2023). The role of hybrid-working in improving employees' satisfaction, perceived productivity, and organizations' capabilities. Jurnal Manajemen Teori Dan Terapan | Journal of Theory and Applied Management, 16(2), 206-222. DOI: 10.20473/jmtt.v16i2.45632

Ayar, D., Karaman, M., & Karaman, R. (2021). Work-life balance and mental health needs of health professionals during covid-19 pandemic in turkey. *International Journal of Mental Health and Addiction*, *20*(1), 639–655. DOI: 10.1007/s11469-021-00717-6 PMID: 34849106

Azeem, S., & Akhtar, N. (2014). The influence of work life balance and job satisfaction on organizational commitment of healthcare employees. *International Journal of Human Resource Studies*, *4*(2), 18. DOI: 10.5296/ijhrs.v4i2.5667

Bataineh, K. (2019). Impact of work-life balance, happiness at work, on employee performance. *International Business Research*, *12*(2), 99. DOI: 10.5539/ibr.v12n2p99

Begum, G. (2024). Achieving sustainable development goals for mental health and gender equality through work-life balance and emotional intelligence. *Gender in Management*, *40*(1), 134–150. DOI: 10.1108/GM-04-2023-0149

Beňo, M. (2021). On-site and hybrid workplace culture of positivity and effectiveness: Case study from austria. *Academic Journal of Interdisciplinary Studies*, *10*(5), 331. DOI: 10.36941/ajis-2021-0142

Bodla, A., Tang, N., Jiang, W., & Tian, L. (2016). Diversity and creativity in cross-national teams: The role of team knowledge sharing and inclusive climate. *Journal of Management & Organization*, *24*(5), 711–729. DOI: 10.1017/jmo.2016.34

Buła, P., Thompson, A., & Żak, A. (2024). Nurturing teamwork and team dynamics in a hybrid work model. *Central European Management Journal*, *32*(3), 475–489. DOI: 10.1108/CEMJ-12-2022-0277

Chand, H., Kumar, K., Sikanda, S., Sabharwal, S., & Kumar, S. (2024). A study on the impact of artificial intelligence on talent sourcing. Iaes International Journal of Artificial Intelligence (Ij-Ai), 13(1), 1. DOI: 10.11591/ijai.v13.i1.pp1-8

Collings, D., & Isichei, M. (2017). The shifting boundaries of global staffing: Integrating global talent management, alternative forms of international assignments and non-employees into the discussion. *International Journal of Human Resource Management*, *29*(1), 165–187. DOI: 10.1080/09585192.2017.1380064

Collings, D., Mellahi, K., & Cascio, W. (2018). Global talent management and performance in multinational enterprises: A multilevel perspective. *Journal of Management*, *45*(2), 540–566. DOI: 10.1177/0149206318757018

Fathya, D., Salsabilla, F., Sugiarto, M., & Taryana, A. (2024). Unlocking productivity and well-being: Exploring the four-day workweek and design thinking for its implementation. *Jurnal Syntax Admiration*, *5*(5), 1830–1841. DOI: 10.46799/jsa.v5i5.1168

Flathmann, C., Schelble, B., & Galeano, A. (2024). Empirical impacts of independent and collaborative training on task performance and improvement in human-ai teams. *Proceedings of the Human Factors and Ergonomics Society Annual Meeting*, *68*(1), 1447–1453. DOI: 10.1177/10711813241274425

Fredberg, T., & Schwarz, G. (2024). What ai knows: Shaping work and pushing ideas on changing organizations. *The Journal of Applied Behavioral Science*, *60*(4), 581–588. DOI: 10.1177/00218863241285218

Gadzali, S. (2023). Application of work-life balance in banking: A study of its impact on employee well-being. *Return Study of Management Economic and Bussines*, *2*(8), 814–820. DOI: 10.57096/return.v2i8.138

Hamarat, H., Şahin, H., & Apuhan, A. (2024). The dark side of artificial intelligence: Threats to tourism workers. *Worldwide Hospitality and Tourism Themes*, *16*(2), 127–137. DOI: 10.1108/WHATT-03-2024-0061

Haziazi, M. (2021). Development of framework for talent management in the global context. *Open Journal of Business and Management*, *09*(04), 1771–1781. DOI: 10.4236/ojbm.2021.94096

Hsu, Y., Bai, C., Yang, C., Huang, Y., Lin, T., & Lin, C. (2019). Long hours' effects on work-life balance and satisfaction. *BioMed Research International*, *2019*, 1–8. DOI: 10.1155/2019/5046934 PMID: 31341900

Islam, T. and Zhou, E. (2024). Unpacking the reasons shaping employee acceptance and attitudes towards ai assistant services in the hotel industry: a behavioral reasoning perspective., 109-141. DOI: 10.47260/amae/1457

Jaiswal, A., & Dyaram, L. (2019). Perceived diversity and employee well-being: Mediating role of inclusion. *Personnel Review*, *49*(5), 1121–1139. DOI: 10.1108/PR-12-2018-0511

Jerónimo, H., Henriques, P., & Carvalho, S. (2021). Being inclusive boosts impact of diversity practices on employee engagement. *Management Research the Journal of the Iberoamerican Academy of Management*, *20*(2), 129–147. DOI: 10.1108/MRJIAM-05-2021-1175

Jetha, A., Bakhtari, H., Rosella, L., Gignac, M., Biswas, A., Shahidi, F., Smith, B. T., Smith, M. J., Mustard, C., Khan, N., Arrandale, V. H., Loewen, P. J., Zuberi, D., Dennerlein, J. T., Bonaccio, S., Wu, N., Irvin, E., & Smith, P. (2023). Artificial intelligence and the work–health interface: A research agenda for a technologically transforming world of work. *American Journal of Industrial Medicine*, *66*(10), 815–830. DOI: 10.1002/ajim.23517 PMID: 37525007

Jindain, C., & Gilitwala, B. (2023). The factors impacting the intermediating variable of employee engagement toward employee performance in a hybrid working model. *Rajagiri Management Journal*, *18*(2), 167–179. DOI: 10.1108/RAMJ-08-2023-0237

Katsande, R., Farhana, N., & Devi, A. (2022). Hybrid models for remote work practices in the post pandemic era: Prospects and challenges. *International Journal of Academic Research in Business & Social Sciences*, *12*(11). Advance online publication. DOI: 10.6007/IJARBSS/v12-i11/15582

Katsaros, K. (2024). Gen z employee adaptive performance: The role of inclusive leadership and workplace happiness. *Administrative Sciences*, *14*(8), 163. DOI: 10.3390/admsci14080163

Kaur, A. (2024). Untitled. *International Journal of Applied Research, 10*(4). Advance online publication. DOI: 10.22271/allresearch.2024.v10.i4.a

Kim, J., & Kim, Y. (2024). Acceptance of artificial intelligence technology and optimism regarding its impact on the job market among high school students. *Journal of Higher Education Theory and Practice, 24*(10). Advance online publication. DOI: 10.33423/jhetp.v24i10.7373

Krishnan, C., Singh, S., & Baba, M. (2023). Effect of work from home and employee mental health through mediating role of workaholism and work-family balance. *The International Journal of Social Psychiatry, 70*(1), 144–156. DOI: 10.1177/00207640231196741 PMID: 37712681

Le, H., Jiang, Z., Fujimoto, Y., & Nielsen, I. (2018). Inclusion and affective well-being: Roles of justice perceptions. *Personnel Review, 47*(4), 805–820. DOI: 10.1108/PR-03-2017-0078

Leroy, H., Buengeler, C., Veestraeten, M., Shemla, M., & Hoever, I. (2021). Fostering team creativity through team-focused inclusion: The role of leader harvesting the benefits of diversity and cultivating value-in-diversity beliefs. *Group & Organization Management, 47*(4), 798–839. DOI: 10.1177/10596011211009683

Limanta, A., Prihanto, Y., & Situmorang, R. (2023). Analysis of the influence of work-life balance, work stress, and job satisfaction when working from home on the implementation of permanent telework culture in legal business. Journal of Business Management Review, 4(1), 001-016. DOI: 10.47153/jbmr41.5922023

Liswandi, L., & Muhammad, R. (2023). *The association between work-life balance and employee mental health: a systemic review*. Asia Pacific Journal of Health Management., DOI: 10.24083/apjhm.v18i3.2565

Liu, J. (2024). The impact of the development of artificial intelligence on unemployment rates. *Advances in Economics Management and Political Sciences, 121*(1), 154–163. DOI: 10.54254/2754-1169/121/20242410

Maj, J. (2023). Influence of inclusive work environment and perceived diversity on job satisfaction: Evidence from poland. *Central European Business Review, 12*(4), 105–122. DOI: 10.18267/j.cebr.334

Mathuki, E., & Zhang, J. (2022). Cognitive diversity, creativity and team effectiveness: The mediations of inclusion and knowledge sharing. *VINE Journal of Information and Knowledge Management Systems, 54*(6), 1379–1403. DOI: 10.1108/VJIKMS-06-2022-0190

Mitchell, R., Boyle, B., Parker, V., Giles, M., Chiang, C., & Joyce, P. (2015). Managing inclusiveness and diversity in teams: How leader inclusiveness affects performance through status and team identity. *Human Resource Management, 54*(2), 217–239. DOI: 10.1002/hrm.21658

Morandini, S., Fraboni, F., Angelis, M., Puzzo, G., Giusino, D., & Pietrantoni, L. (2023). The impact of artificial intelligence on workers' skills: upskilling and reskilling in organisations. Informing Science the International Journal of an Emerging Transdiscipline, 26, 039-068. DOI: 10.28945/5078

Mossavar-Rahmani, F., & Zohuri, B. (2024). Artificial intelligence at work: Transforming industries and redefining the workforce landscape. *Journal of Economics & Management Research, 1-4*, 1–4. Advance online publication. DOI: 10.47363/JESMR/2024(5)213

Nalwade, P. (2024). Adapting to tomorrow's workforce: Navigating the impacts of artificial intelligence on employment. *Interantional Journal of Scientific Research in Engineering and Management, 08*(04), 1–5. DOI: 10.55041/IJSREM30664

Niebuhr, F., Borle, P., Börner-Zobel, F., & Voelter-Mahlknecht, S. (2022). Healthy and happy working from home? effects of working from home on employee health and job satisfaction. *International Journal of Environmental Research and Public Health, 19*(3), 1122. DOI: 10.3390/ijerph19031122 PMID: 35162145

Nyathani, R. (2023). Ai in performance management: Redefining performance appraisals in the digital age. *Design of Single Chip Microcomputer Control System for Stepping Motor, 1-5*, 1–5. Advance online publication. DOI: 10.47363/JAICC/2023(2)134

Pei, J., Wang, H., Peng, Q., & Liu, S. (2024). Saving face: Leveraging artificial intelligence-based negative feedback to enhance employee job performance. *Human Resource Management, 63*(5), 775–790. Advance online publication. DOI: 10.1002/hrm.22226

Rožman, M., & Tominc, P. (2024). Navigating gender nuances: Assessing the impact of ai on employee engagement in slovenian entrepreneurship. *Systems, 12*(5), 145. DOI: 10.3390/systems12050145

Saad, H., & Mayouf, M. (2018). Talent management strategies and practices in five star hotels: An exploratory study. *International Journal of Heritage Tourism and Hospitality, 12*(2), 32–49. DOI: 10.21608/ijhth.2019.31649

Salamin, X., & Hanappi, D. (2014). Women and international assignments. *Journal of Global Mobility, 2*(3), 343–374. DOI: 10.1108/JGM-09-2013-0058

Santillan, E., Santillan, E., Doringo, J., Pigao, K., & Mesina, V. (2023). Assessing the impact of a hybrid work model on job execution, work-life balance, and employee satisfaction in a technology company. *Journal of Business and Management Studies, 5*(6), 13–38. DOI: 10.32996/jbms.2023.5.6.2

Sucipto, H. (2024). The impact of artificial intelligence (ai) on human resource management practices. *PRODUCTIVITY, 1*(1), 138–145. DOI: 10.62207/xey9mx18

Tabbassum, A., Chintale, P., Praveen, G., & Najana, M. (2024). The impact of ai on future employment patterns.. DOI: 10.21428/e90189c8.e99f270c

Todorović, M. and Ivanović, T. (2018). Employee training in international luxury hotel chains: evidence from serbia., 667-685. DOI: 10.31410/tmt.2018.667

Triana, M., García, M., & Colella, A. (2010). Managing diversity: How organizational efforts to support diversity moderate the effects of perceived racial discrimination on affective commitment. *Personnel Psychology, 63*(4), 817–843. DOI: 10.1111/j.1744-6570.2010.01189.x

Ullrich, L., Ogawa, J., & Jones-London, M. (2024). A retrospective analysis of career outcomes in neuroscience. Eneuro, 11(5), ENEURO.0054-24.2024. DOI: 10.1523/ENEURO.0054-24.2024

Vandy, E. (2023). Future of work - opportunities, challenges and implications for international, comparative and cross-national hrm. *International Journal on Recent and Innovation Trends in Computing and Communication, 11*(9), 4300–4306. DOI: 10.17762/ijritcc.v11i9.9887

Wolfgruber, D., Stürmer, L., & Einwiller, S. (2021). Talking inclusion into being: Communication as a facilitator and obstructor of an inclusive work environment. *Personnel Review*, *51*(7), 1841–1860. DOI: 10.1108/PR-01-2021-0013

Yang, E., Kim, Y., & Hong, S. (2021). Does working from home work? experience of working from home and the value of hybrid workplace post-covid-19. *Journal of Corporate Real Estate*, *25*(1), 50–76. DOI: 10.1108/JCRE-04-2021-0015

Yang, J., Suh, C., Lee, C., & Son, B. (2018). The work–life balance and psychosocial well-being of south korean workers. *Annals of Occupational and Environmental Medicine*, *30*(1), 38. Advance online publication. DOI: 10.1186/s40557-018-0250-z PMID: 29928507

Yang, Y., Wang, T., & Leon, J. (2021). Study on the effect of work-life balance on the intention to leave of grassroots employees in the service industry. *Academic Journal of Business & Management*, *3*(8). Advance online publication. DOI: 10.25236/AJBM.2021.030801

Ye, C. (2023). Generation zs willingness to accept international assignments after covid-19—A quantitative study among british, chinese and indian students. *Advances in Economics Management and Political Sciences*, *53*(1), 229–241. DOI: 10.54254/2754-1169/53/20230841

Zhang, J., Rehman, S., Addas, A., & Ahmad, J. (2024). Influence of work-life balance on mental health among nurses: The mediating role of psychological capital and job satisfaction. *Psychology Research and Behavior Management*, *17*, 4249–4262. DOI: 10.2147/PRBM.S497305 PMID: 39679316

Chapter 19

Transforming Traditional Outsourcing Models:
The Disruptive Impact of AI

Gunjan Mohan Sharma
https://orcid.org/0000-0003-2272-7385
O.P. Jindal Global University, India

Azadeh Amoozegar
INTI International University, Malaysia

Ali Najeeb
https://orcid.org/0000-0003-4663-9347
Qasim Ibrahim School of Business, Villa College, Maldives

ABSTRACT

This chapter explores the transformative impact of Artificial Intelligence (AI) on traditional outsourcing models, highlighting both the disruption and opportunities AI presents for the outsourcing industry. As AI technologies automate routine tasks and enable data-driven decision-making, outsourcing providers are evolving from cost-centric service providers to strategic partners in digital transformation. The chapter examines how AI-driven models, such as automation, predictive analytics, and machine learning, are reshaping outsourcing functions, offering businesses greater efficiency, innovation, and customization. However, the shift to AI-powered outsourcing also introduces challenges related to workforce displacement, ethical concerns, and the need for new governance frameworks. The future of outsourcing will depend on the ability of providers to adapt to AI technologies, upskill their workforce, and address the social and regulatory implications of AI adoption.

1. INTRODUCTION

The global outsourcing industry, once characterized by the offshoring of labor-intensive tasks to low-cost regions, has undergone a significant transformation in recent years. Traditionally, outsourcing was a strategic decision aimed at reducing operational costs, accessing specialized skills, and improving business flexibility (Doh, 2005). Companies in manufacturing, customer service industries, and

DOI: 10.4018/979-8-3373-1270-5.ch019

technology-related businesses take advantage of the low-cost labor sources through outsourcing models common in emerging economies (Kotabe & Mol, 2009). The old model of outsourcing strictly relied on human resources and its very productivity rested upon low-paid workers performing monotonous work.

The challenges and changes in these models have significantly been driven by new technology - artificial intelligence. AI technologies, including machine learning and natural language processing (NLP), as well as robotic process automation (RPA), fundamentally alter the outsourcing landscape (Brynjolfsson & McAfee, 2014). New technological innovations can displace or supplement human labor with faster, more accurate, and less expensive automated systems in performing tasks (Chui et al., 2016). Its ability to process huge amounts of data, learn by patterns, and perform complex cognitive functions made it a very fast adopter in most sectors or industries such as finance, health, and customer service. This has forced organizations to adapt the ways in which they structure their outsourced strategies, because the rise of automation displaces labor-intensive tasks (West, 2018).

Artificial intelligence will transform outsourcing models, moving them away from technological disruption and to a perspective about labor markets, ethics, and the future of work. With AI-driven automation, company-specific workforce displacement issues are related to various data privacy concerns while upskilling the employee workforce to collaborate with intelligent systems (Susskind & Susskind, 2015). This chapter discusses how AI is transforming traditional outsourcing models and explores both the opportunities and challenges of this transformation. It also takes a closer look at the changing role of outsourcing providers in this AI-centric era and forecasts the future course of the industry as it moves to adapt to this new technological paradigm.

By the end of this discussion, readers will gain a deeper understanding of how AI is not just augmenting but fundamentally reshaping the outsourcing landscape, paving the way for more efficient, scalable, and sophisticated outsourcing practices.

2. UNDERSTANDING TRADITIONAL OUTSOURCING MODELS

Traditional outsourcing is the leasing of specific functions or processes outside to service providers, usually for cost-cutting purposes, specialization, or productivity enhancement (Gable et al., 2008). The concept originated decades ago wherein companies from distinct industries, majorly manufacturing and IT, also customer service engaged in finding relatively cheaper ways about focusing on specific competencies where they are actually good at with outsourcing the lesser ones. The model that finally emerged in the late 20th century was as often based on a labor arbitrage strategy: in order to save on wages, companies outsourced customer support, data entry, or back-office operations to locations like India, the Philippines, and Eastern Europe (Doh, 2005).

Cost savings was one of the major reasons driving traditional outsourcing. Companies could reduce operational costs by transferring labor-intensive and repetitive tasks to regions with lower labor costs. This way, businesses could reallocate resources to more strategic areas, such as research and development, marketing, or innovation (Kotabe & Mol, 2009). Moreover, outsourcing provided access to specialized expertise in certain fields, particularly in technology and customer support, where external providers possessed advanced skills and knowledge that organizations might not have in-house.

At its core, traditional outsourcing models focused on efficiency through scale and cost advantages. Service providers typically managed operations remotely, ensuring that business processes such as call centers, IT infrastructure, and finance-related tasks were handled by teams of workers. The reliance on human labor as the primary driver of outsourcing meant that businesses optimized cost savings primarily through labor reduction and task specialization (Gable et al., 2008). These outsourcing models also introduced a rigid division of labor: companies would specify processes and deliverables in contracts, while the outsourcing provider was responsible for execution, often with limited collaboration or integration into the client's organization (Lacity & Willcocks, 2001).

However, the traditional outsourcing models did not come without their challenges. Such models have been criticized to cause job displacement in developed economies and also problems related to communication barriers, quality control, and management of geographically dispersed teams. Further, the complexity of legal and regulatory environments to be dealt with by businesses further complicated these arrangements. As businesses looked for more flexibility and agility, many started questioning the long-term sustainability of relying on labor-intensive, low-cost outsourcing as their primary strategy for reducing costs and driving growth (Bunyaratavej et al., 2007).

As the outsourcing industry grew, the importance of conventional models that focus strictly on cost saving and operational efficiency were not satisfactory for the growth experienced in such a fast-paced technology-oriented global economy. In that respect, with AI, began challenging the foundational thinking of outsourcing based on how traditional outsourcing practice operated by making it possible to apply new modes for process automation as well as the improvement of decisions without sole dependence on low-priced labor.

3. ARTIFICIAL INTELLIGENCE

An Introduction Artificial Intelligence is defined as the imitation of human intelligence in machines which are programmed to think, learn, reason, and perform other functions that have a human element. These functions may include but not be limited to problem-solving, speech recognition, and decision-making. The field of AI traces its roots back to the mid-20th century, but the recent improvements in computational power, data availability, and algorithmic techniques have led to rapid growth and practical application across a broad range of industries (Russell & Norvig, 2016). AI is now broadly classified into narrow or weak AI, designed for specific tasks, and general or strong AI, which would be able to perform any intellectual task that a human can do (Boden, 2016). General AI is still a far-off dream, but narrow AI is already transforming industries such as healthcare, finance, and retail, often in the form of specialized systems that can automate complex processes and make data-driven decisions.

One of the most significant breakthroughs in AI in recent years has been the development of machine learning (ML), a subset of AI that enables systems to improve from experience without being explicitly programmed. By using large amounts of data, machine learning algorithms can discover patterns and insights that humans cannot, usually with a much higher degree of accuracy. Deep learning is a specific type of more advanced machine learning that uses artificial neural networks, simulating human brain processes. This enables the AI to work on tasks like image and speech recognition with outstanding precision (LeCun et al., 2015). These technologies are increasingly used to automate a wide range of tasks, from simple customer service interactions through chatbots and virtual assistants to sophisticated data analysis and predictive modeling in sectors such as finance, marketing, and logistics (Müller & Bostrom, 2016).

NLP is the other main branch of AI: it is enabling machines to process, understand, interpret, and generate human language. NLP is crucial for applications like chatbots, voice assistants, and sentiment analysis, where understanding context, tone, and nuance in communication is essential. Tools like OpenAI's GPT (Generative Pre-trained Transformer) models have shown impressive capabilities in generating coherent, contextually relevant text based on vast amounts of data, thereby enhancing customer service, content creation, and even creative writing (Vaswani et al., 2017). AI has significant implications in processing and understanding language for the industry traditionally based on human interactions such as legal services, customer support, and media.

The impact of AI on business and technology is significant in both its optimization and automation potential but even more in changing entire business models. In the context of outsourcing, AI enables the automation of a wide array of functions that were traditionally outsourced to human workers. For example, robotic process automation (RPA) is a fast-growing AI application that automates repetitive and rules-based tasks, such as data entry, invoice processing, and customer support. Thus, the rise in the use of AI-driven tools has led to a shift from traditional labor-intensive outsourcing models that relied on human workforces, located in low-cost regions, for simple routine tasks to more technology-driven modes in which most of these responsibilities can be handled by AI-powered systems and with more efficiency (Avasarala et al., 2020).

However, widespread adoption of AI brings up many concerns related to job displacement, ethical issues, and management of AI systems. As machines assume more roles that are traditionally performed by humans, the pressure on the workforce to adapt and develop new skills that complement AI technologies is mounting. However, it is undeniable that AI is reshaping the landscape of business operations, and the integration of AI into outsourcing models is likely to continue disrupting the industry in profound ways in the years ahead.

4. AI-INDUCED DISRUPTION OF TRADITIONAL OUTSOURCING

AI is disrupting the old outsourcing models quickly by bringing more efficient, automated solutions that have less human intervention and open new avenues for the improvement of business operations. The traditional outsourcing approach was based primarily on cost reduction through offshoring labor-intensive tasks to low-wage countries by relying on human workers to do repetitive, rule-based activities like data entry, customer service, and assembly line work (Doh, 2005). However, technologies such as machine learning, RPA, and NLP are fundamentally changing this model because of the automation of many of these tasks and the elimination of such dependence on low-cost labor and the embracing of technology-driven efficiencies instead (Brynjolfsson & McAfee, 2014).

The ability of AI to automate the repetitive as well as clerical process has caused a displacement of many jobs that were hitherto outsourced. For example, AI chatbots and virtual assistants can take customer service calls today and respond rapidly and personally to customers at any time of the day without human assistance (West, 2018). In finance, AI algorithms can process huge amounts of data and make decisions for large-scale business operations, which reduces the requirement for outsourced human labor for data processing and report generation (Chui et al., 2016). All these technologies decrease operational expenses but increase speed and accuracy, thus reducing human errors, making outsourcing models that do not rely on technology less competitive.

Among the biggest impacts AI brings to the world of outsourcing is business process automation through RPA. This technique makes use of AI to automate any type of back-office work-from-invoicing to payroll and compliance checks. These tasks, which were traditionally outsourced to remote service providers, are now handled by intelligent software robots that can operate at scale and speed, with minimal human oversight (Avasarala et al., 2020). The use of AI-powered systems also enables organizations to implement more complex automation solutions, such as predictive analytics and intelligent decision-making, which were not possible under traditional outsourcing models reliant on human workers.

Nevertheless, AI also allows for a transition from low-cost labor outsourcing toward a high-skill, tech-based model of outsourcing. Currently, AI is capable of tasks that are more complicated than routine and repetitive functions, thus no longer confining outsourcing to such things. For instance, companies are increasingly outsourcing tasks that necessarily involve specific knowledge and complex technological know-how, including data analysis, AI model development, and software engineering (Susskind & Susskind, 2015). The skill sets demanded in the outsourcing industry are now changing with the ever-increasing need for technology savvy providers. This will require outsourcing service providers to keep investing in newer capabilities, like AI infrastructure and advanced data analytics, to maintain their competitive edge within this rapidly shifting landscape.

With the clear-cut advantages come numerous challenges in the form of AI-driven disruption of traditional outsourcing models. The risk of job displacement is a fundamental concern associated with the automation of low-skilled jobs, especially for those regions where outsourcing has been a key economic driver (Frey & Osborne, 2017). Finally, the integration of AI into outsourcing agreements involves major investments in technology, skilled talent, and infrastructure. Service providers might be challenged to manage the shift from human-dependent to AI-based systems, especially in industries where human competence and judgment are highly valued (Bunyaratavej et al., 2007). In addition, concerns about data privacy and security and ethical issues related to making decisions with AI must be managed stringently in such a way that the benefits from outsourcing to AI-based services do not undermine trust and accountability.

In summary, AI is not only complementing the traditional outsourcing practice but is also changing it by automating processes, shifting outsourcing models toward more specialized services, and challenging the reliance on cheap labor. As companies embrace AI technologies, they will need to reassess their outsourcing strategies to take advantage of new opportunities while addressing the challenges that come with the integration of AI into their operations.

5. AI-DRIVEN MODELS IN OUTSOURCING

The integration of Artificial Intelligence (AI) into outsourcing models is not a simple enhancement of traditional practices, but it has actively driven the creation of new business models that benefit from the power of technology for faster, more efficient, and scalable services. These AI-based models are fundamentally altering how companies do outsourcing by making complex processes simpler, optimizing workflow, and adding advanced analytics that were not accessible before. Instead of relying on humans to execute the routine labor-intensive tasks, AI-driven outsourcing models use intelligent systems which are capable of learning and adapting themselves, making them more dynamic and cost-efficient alternatives.

The most prominent AI-driven model in outsourcing is Robotic Process Automation (RPA). RPA uses AI and machine learning algorithms to automate repetitive, rules-based tasks such as data entry, invoicing, and transaction processing. These tasks, which were earlier outsourced to offshore workers, are now performed by software robots that can execute them with greater speed, consistency, and accuracy (Avasarala et al., 2020). RPA has especially become prevalent in industries such as finance, healthcare, and insurance, where compliance and operational efficiency are crucial. The mass adoption of RPA allows outsourcing service providers to process high volumes of work without adding headcount, thereby reducing costs significantly while maintaining high service levels.

Besides RPA, AI-based customer service solutions are revolutionizing the way outsourcing companies interact with their clients. Intelligent virtual assistants and chatbots, powered by NLP, are increasingly replacing human agents in managing customer inquiries, technical support, and even complex troubleshooting tasks. These AI-based solutions can understand customer queries in real time and answer them, which means 24/7 service and learning through past interactions for continuous improvement. For example, in the telecommunications and retail industries, AI-based virtual assistants can undertake a range of customer service operations, from taking orders to handling complaints, entirely without human interaction (West, 2018). These systems, in addition to improving customer satisfaction through quicker response, free human agents to do more complex and value-added tasks.

The other core aspect of AI-based outsourcing models is the application of machine learning and predictive analytics for decision-making purposes. In supply chain management, for example, AI algorithms are used to analyze vast amounts of historical and real-time data to predict trends, optimize inventory management, and improve demand forecasting. Companies can be sure that they are not only cutting costs but also making smarter, data-driven decisions that improve business outcomes by including machine learning in outsourcing models. This phenomenon can be clearly identified especially in industries such as logistics and e-commerce: AI-based models are applied to achieve predictive delivery times, the optimization of routes, and personalized marketing efforts-cases in which flexibility and customization can be significantly offered in an outsourcing procedure (Chui et al., 2016).

Hybrid models of outsourcing are also being made possible by AI, combining human expertize with the speed and efficiencies of intelligent systems. In these models, AI handles routine tasks while human workers oversee complex decision-making and provide oversight for AI systems. For instance, in the healthcare industry, AI-driven diagnostic tools can analyze medical images and detect anomalies, but it is human doctors who make the final diagnosis and treatment recommendations. This hybrid approach thus allows companies to take the best from both worlds; the scalability and precision of AI with the nuances and creativity of human decision-making. As AI grows, these hybrid models are more likely to mushroom, thus marking a more complementary relationship between humans and intelligent systems in the workplace (Susskind & Susskind, 2015).

AI-driven models of outsourcing will also be able to scale far better and respond more flexibly than traditional outsourcing models. The more upward and downward fluctuation there is in service demand, the more AI systems can scale up and down in operation without hiring additional staff or investing in new infrastructure. Such adaptability is especially useful for businesses operating during seasonal peaks or in fast-paced industries that require agility. Providers that apply AI in their outsourcing business models can give the client real-time adjustment of service levels, reducing inefficiencies and responsiveness (Müller & Bostrom, 2016).

In summary, AI-driven outsourcing models revolutionize the industry as they automate mundane tasks, improve decisions, and bring more personalized, scalable solutions. Companies are, therefore, in a position to reduce costs through the replacement or supplementation of human labor with AI systems, increasing operational efficiency, and quality in services. The increasing use of AI-based models in outsourcing presents a shift away from labor-based methods to technology-driven ones, with the potential for businesses to adopt more agile and innovative ways of getting their needs fulfilled while driving value for their customers.

6. OPPORTUNITIES AND ADVANTAGES OF AI IN OUTSOURCING

The role of Artificial Intelligence in outsourcing models has opened avenues and benefits to reshape the business world. AI technologies offer the outsourcing firm and its clients opportunities for streamlining operations, cost cutting, service improvement, and, indeed, breakthroughs in new sources of innovation. One of the most obvious and significant gains is the dramatically lower operational cost. Companies can also reduce their reliance on human workers by automating routine and labor-intensive tasks, which saves wages, benefits, and other overheads associated with traditional outsourcing (Chui et al., 2016). The high-volume, repetitive tasks such as data entry, invoice processing, and customer queries can be performed by AI-driven systems, such as RPA, in a more efficient, faster, and accurate manner, thereby avoiding the use of expensive human labor in these areas.

Besides cost savings, AI presents the possibility of greatly improving the speed and scalability of outsourcing services. In traditional outsourcing models, it takes a long lead time to recruit, train, and deploy human workers in new locations or for new tasks. In contrast, AI systems can be scaled up or down quickly depending on demand. This is particularly advantageous for businesses that face fluctuating demands or seasonal spikes in workload. For example, e-commerce companies can adjust their customer service and logistics support levels during high-demand periods like Black Friday or holiday shopping seasons without the complexities of hiring and training additional human workers (Müller & Bostrom, 2016). This enables outsourcing firms to respond to client needs with unmatched agility, ensuring that businesses can scale operations as required. AI also improves the quality and accuracy of outsourced services. One of the key advantages of AI systems is their ability to process and analyze vast amounts of data with unparalleled speed and precision. For example, customer service chatbots powered by AI can address numerous inquiries at once without losing quality and making errors. Continuous improvement in the long run by the learning nature of AI means the service is always improving, getting better and more efficient over time. Further, AI systems can recognize patterns, trends, and anomalies that would otherwise not be observable to the human worker. Therefore, such systems provide insight into better decision-making and enhanced service delivery (West, 2018). For instance, in the financial services industry, AI algorithms can identify real-time fraudulent transactions from a large dataset of transactional data, something too complex for human workers to execute efficiently.

Beyond cost reduction and efficiency gains, AI in outsourcing provides an opportunity for businesses to innovate and differentiate themselves in the marketplace. Machine learning and predictive analytics are some of the AI technologies that enable outsourcing firms to offer more sophisticated services beyond the execution of basic tasks. By leveraging AI to analyze customer behavior, predict market trends, or optimize supply chains, companies can deliver more value-added services to clients, enabling them to gain a competitive edge in their respective industries (Susskind & Susskind, 2015). For example,

AI-driven customer insights can enable businesses to offer hyper-personalized marketing campaigns, targeted promotions, and customized product recommendations, all of which drive customer engagement and loyalty. The potential to deliver such transformational services puts outsourcing service providers as part of business change instead of purely a cost-out source.

Furthermore, AI brings in more flexibility and agility to outsourcing since it elevates the capacities of service providers in having much more proactive and astute kinds of outsourcing relationship. The fixed-contract forms of outsourcing as well as inflexible SLAs used to prevail. With AI, outsourcing agreements can evolve into more agile, results-driven models that emphasize continuous improvement and innovation. For example, AI-powered predictive models can anticipate clients' needs before they arise, ensuring that service providers are always one step ahead in delivering services. This means that AI-driven, adaptive outsourcing models will create value in the long run for both the clients and providers by having a more collaborative and strategic relationship rather than a transactional one (Chui et al., 2016).

Last but not least, AI will also make the human aspects of outsourcing even better. While automation reduces the need for low-skilled workers, it creates an opportunity for outsourcing firms to redeploy human talent into higher-value, more strategic roles that require creativity, problem-solving, and emotional intelligence. For example, customer service agents can focus on more complex issues that require human empathy, judgment, or negotiation, while AI handles routine inquiries. This symbiotic relationship between human workers and AI systems will lead to more rewarding work environments and better job satisfaction, freeing employees from the drudgery of monotonous tasks and instead allowing them to engage in meaningful, impactful work (Susskind & Susskind, 2015).

The benefits and opportunities offered by AI in outsourcing are diverse, ranging from cost savings and improved service quality to scalability, innovation, and changes in workforce dynamics. This transformation by businesses toward the adoption of AI technologies does not only transform the outsourcing models but also positions the ground for more efficient, dynamic, and value-driven global service delivery. In that context, being able to utilize AI for better streamlining operations, smarter decisions, and innovative services places an outsourcing firm at a better competitive edge and places them at an edge to achieve long-term success in the world dominated by AI.

7. CHALLENGES AND RISKS IN THE AI-DRIVEN OUTSOURCING ERA

The integration of Artificial Intelligence (AI) into outsourcing models offers a wide range of opportunities, but it also brings with it a variety of challenges and risks that organizations must navigate carefully. One of the most pressing concerns is the displacement of jobs. The jobs most at risk due to automation of tasks traditionally done by humans are in areas like customer service, data processing, and even higher-skilled roles like legal analysis. In low-cost outsourcing destinations, there is a great likelihood of job loss. The social and economic implications for the workers whose jobs become redundant because of automation are an important concern. In countries that heavily rely on outsourcing for employment, such as India and the Philippines, large-scale job displacement could lead to unemployment, economic instability, and increased social inequality (Frey & Osborne, 2017). While AI offers the potential for job creation in tech-focused roles, the transition may be difficult for workers without the necessary skills or access to reskilling opportunities.

One of the biggest challenges of the AI-driven outsourcing era is the complexity involved in implementing and managing AI technologies. AI systems, including machine learning algorithms and RPA, often require significant investment in infrastructure, talent, and time to integrate into business processes effectively. Many organizations find it challenging to select the right AI tools, customize them according to specific business needs, and ensure seamless integration with existing systems. AI solutions also require highly skilled professionals, such as data scientists, AI engineers, and machine learning specialists. The supply of these professionals is in short supply, and their salaries are relatively high. Therefore, the investment for the outsourcing firms not only lies in AI infrastructure but also in ensuring that the workforce has been adequately prepared to work with such advanced technologies (Chui et al., 2016). If the investment isn't made into these things, then those companies will lose and not compete for outsourcing. This, in particular is because the problem of data security and privacy worsens when all outsourcing companies employ AI in such a wide amount of their works, in huge volumes, often involving very personal data. The primary concerns associated with the use of AI systems are their vulnerability to potential data breaches and cyberattacks since they are employed for analyzing customer information, financial records, and proprietary business data. As such, with an increasing number of sophisticated cyber threats, organizations have to ensure that their AI-driven outsourcing models align with strict data security standards and regulatory frameworks in place, including the General Data Protection Regulation in the European Union or similar privacy laws in other regions. A breach of sensitive data can lead to financial losses on the one hand, while on the other hand, erode customer trust, damage the reputation of a company, and even invite legal liabilities. Thus, outsourcing firms need to invest in robust cybersecurity measures so that AI systems do not become a vulnerable point in the supply chain.

Moreover, reliance on AI in outsourcing raises ethical considerations, especially in decision-making, accountability, and transparency. AI systems are often designed to make decisions based on data and algorithms, but these systems can be opaque, making it difficult to understand how decisions are made or why certain outcomes are chosen over others. The "black-box" nature of AI has brought with it certain risks to be posed by these applications in sectors like finance, healthcare, and legal services where decisions must be both transparent and explainable. Some algorithms could inherit biases from data used in their training process. For instance, an AI used in the process of hiring or granting loans can be said to propagate gender and racial bias, especially when such an AI has been trained with uncared-for data. These biases lead to unfair practices and legal issues, which further undermine the legitimacy of AI-driven outsourcing models (O'Neil, 2016). Ethical AI practices that include fairness, transparency, and accountability are thus essential for companies that intend to integrate AI in their outsourcing models.

The relationship between AI systems and human workers is another issue to be managed. Although AI can automate routine tasks, many outsourcing models still require human oversight and collaboration to manage more complex, nuanced activities. The tension between automation and human expertise may lead to resistance from employees, particularly if they feel their jobs are at risk or if they are unprepared for the shift toward more technologically advanced roles. To be successfully implemented through outsourcing, there needs to be a balance to ensure that humans are augmented in their work by the AI rather than being completely substituted. This also calls for on-going engagement, reskilling programs, and an organizational cultural shift that motivates collaboration with human workers and AI systems in place (Susskind & Susskind, 2015). Companies also need to address the psychological and emotional effects on employees who may feel anxious or fearful about their job security as automation rises.

Lastly, the speed of AI development itself is a challenge. As AI technologies advance, outsourcing firms must constantly adapt and stay ahead of the curve to stay competitive. This encompasses not only the adoption of the latest AI tools but also ensuring that they can integrate new innovations seamlessly into their existing outsourcing operations. However, the speed of technological change can be overwhelming for many organizations, particularly those with limited resources or expertise. Firms need to invest in research and development, innovation, and strategic partnerships to avoid being left behind in the increasingly AI-driven outsourcing landscape (Brynjolfsson & McAfee, 2014). Failure to keep up with AI advancements will leave a firm losing its market relevance and competitiveness.

In conclusion, while AI-driven outsourcing models offer many benefits, including cost savings, scalability, and improved service quality, they also introduce significant challenges and risks. These include potential job displacement, high implementation costs, data privacy and security concerns, ethical dilemmas, workforce resistance, and the need for constant technological adaptation. To successfully manage such risks, the organizations should become proactive and strategic and ensure AI deployment in such a manner that ensures efficiency coupled with ethical consideration and workforce development. In so doing, by countering such risks, the outsourcing firms would realize the real power of AI with minimal risks to make sustainable value-based solutions for the clients.

8. THE ROLE OF OUTSOURCING PROVIDERS IS EVOLVING

This has led to the use of artificial intelligence in a way that is changing how outsourcing providers are now supposed to work. They have less to do with the traditional "execution"-oriented service delivery model and more with their becoming dynamic and strategic partners to businesses in transformation. Traditionally, outsourcing providers were considered mere cost-reduction solutions, focusing on repetitive tasks and standardized services for reduced costs. However, changes have been observed, especially as AI technologies rapidly advance. Today, outsourcing firms are expected not only to manage operational tasks efficiently but also to offer innovative, value-added services that enhance their clients' competitiveness and drive business growth.

One of the most important changes in the role of outsourcing providers is from a task-focused service delivery model to a more consultative and strategic role. While automation eliminates routine and simple tasks from an organization's to-do list, the requirement from outsourcing vendors grows exponentially on the incorporation of more complex skills and technology at the negotiation table. The latest examples have become finance and health care; they now include outsourced firms with whom clients have integrated AI capabilities toward improving their outcomes, be it predictive analytics-based risk management, or self-autonomous medical diagnoses (West, 2018). The service providers need to utilize their technical expertise to include AI technologies within the business operations of their clients, thereby achieving measurable improvements in efficiency, quality of service, and customer experience.

Outsourcing providers are increasingly being perceived as a necessary enabler for digital transformation. Companies are not only using AI technologies to automate tasks but are also using these technologies to reimagine their business models and operations. Outsourcing firms, especially those that specialize in IT services, are playing an essential role in guiding clients through this transformation journey. They provide the expertise necessary to design, implement, and manage AI-driven solutions, ensuring that these technologies are seamlessly integrated with the client's legacy systems and organizational workflows. The role of the outsourcing providers, therefore, is now changing into a strategic partner in digital transformation that helps the clients navigate through the complexities of AI adoption while maximizing the return on their investments (Chui et al., 2016).

The shift in the role of outsourcing providers also means shifting the composition of their workforce. Outsourcing providers used to depend much on the availability of large numbers of low-cost labor in offshore locations for the performance of repetitive tasks. In an effort to keep pace with the clients, today's outsourcing companies are more heavily recruiting experts; these are high skills professionals in this case AI Specialists, data scientists and machine learning engineers. It also includes working close to clients not only building maintaining AI systems and developing bespoke customized AI solutions at the direction of clients solving well-defined business needs. This shift in the workforce requires outsourcing firms to invest heavily in recruitment, training, and employee development programs, ensuring that their talent pool is equipped to handle the growing complexity of AI technologies (Müller & Bostrom, 2016).

Additionally, outsourcing providers must evolve their business models to incorporate AI as a core offering, moving beyond the traditional service level agreements (SLAs) and fixed-price contracts that defined past outsourcing relationships. The shift towards AI-driven solutions requires a more agile, results-based pricing structure, with providers compensated based on the results delivered and the value added, rather than by volume of work performed. Such an arrangement encourages collaboration and shared responsibility between clients and outsourcing providers, for both cooperate to drive AI system success and perpetual optimization. Further, it has a more individualized service, given that outsourcers may deliver AI-powered solution tailored for unique needs and specific goals for different clients (Susskind & Susskind, 2015).

On the other hand, AI will change how an outsourcing company serves its customers. The automaton and analytical potential of AI are what enables a firm providing outsource services to provide the clarity of delivery through real-time statistics on the levels of service as well as operational and business-related performance indicators. This change towards data-driven engagement is equipping clients with more informed decision-making and continuous monitoring of the effectiveness of AI solutions. For instance, outsourced service providers can now utilize AI analytics to track the performance of outsourced services and predict issues before they become problems so that the client gets proactive support and continuous improvement (Avasarala et al., 2020). This new role allows the provision of real-time visibility into performance, which creates stronger, trust-based relationships between outsourcing providers and clients: outsourcing as a more collaborative, results-oriented activity.

However, with this responsibility comes a greater accountability for the outsourcing provider. With increased strategic responsibilities come the need to ensure that the AI solutions implemented are ethical, transparent, and in line with the standards of the industry. This will be to ensure issues with data privacy, security, and probable biases in AI algorithms are addressed. Outsourcing providers should work vigilantly towards implementing safeguards and adopting ethical practices concerning AI, to make sure that the technologies they deploy are regulatory compliant and not facilitators of discriminatory or unfair patterns (O'Neil, 2016). The increasing complexity and ethical considerations of AI-driven solutions mean that outsourcing providers need to maintain strong governance frameworks to mitigate risks and ensure that their solutions are fair and accountable.

In conclusion, the role of outsourcing providers is undergoing a profound transformation as AI reshapes the outsourcing landscape. Providers are transforming from cost-centric service delivery agents to strategic partners in digital transformation, offering highly specialized AI-driven solutions that drive business performance and innovation. This transformation mandates that outsourcing firms invest in talent, adopt new business models, and build deeper, more collaborative relationships with clients. As demand for AI-powered outsourcing services grows, outsourcing providers need to embrace their new role and strike a balance between technological innovation and ethical considerations in order to stay competitive and continue delivering value to their clients.

9. THE FUTURE OF OUTSOURCING IN THE AGE OF AI

The future of outsourcing in the age of Artificial Intelligence (AI) promises to be a time of great transformation, with AI technologies defining the scope, structure, and expectations of outsourcing engagements. As businesses increasingly adopt AI to drive efficiency, scalability, and innovation, outsourcing providers will need to evolve their strategies to stay relevant in this rapidly changing landscape. In this case, AI outsourcing will be far more than mere automation and cost reduction. Its scope would reach into offering high-value solutions with specific characteristics of customized and addressing complex and dynamic business needs. Probably, one of the major shifts is away from traditional outsourcing models, where the primary goal has been labor arbitrage towards a much more sophisticated and knowledge-intensive model by leveraging AI and automation (Brynjolfsson & McAfee, 2014). This evolution will see outsourcing providers move from being providers of commoditized services to strategic partners in clients' digital transformation journeys.

Another significant aspect of the future of outsourcing is ever more reliance on AI to undertake sophisticated and judgmental tasks that have traditionally required human expertise for centuries. In finance, healthcare, and customer service, AI systems will automate not only routine but also intelligent insights, making predictive analytics available to help businesses make well-informed decisions. It will empower the outsourcing provider to offer more sophisticated services, which would include personal recommendations, fraud detection, and predictive maintenance critical to enhanced customer satisfaction and business performance. For example, AI systems can process consumer data in real-time and customize marketing strategies and product offers for better customer engagement and loyalty. The future of outsourcing will thus be more sophisticated and value-added services with measurable business outcomes rather than cost reduction (West, 2018).

As a result, outsourcing providers will have to adopt more flexible, outcome-based pricing models that offer more value-added services. Indeed, traditional outsourcing contracts, driven by fixed costs and SLAs, will make way for more dynamic, results-oriented arrangements. An AI-driven outsourcing ecosystem is likely to work in the following manner: value-based remuneration, measured in terms of better operational efficiency, customer experience, or revenue growth. This model encourages a more collaborative approach to outsourcing, where both the client and provider share in the responsibility for achieving business goals and success. This shift in pricing structure will also push outsourcing firms to continuously innovate and optimize their AI-driven solutions to ensure they remain competitive and deliver maximum value to clients (Chui et al., 2016).

Furthermore, the future of outsourcing will see a closer alignment between AI-driven outsourcing and the concept of "smart" outsourcing, where technology enables not just cost savings but the creation of more agile and adaptive business processes. Outsourcing providers will leverage AI not only to automate tasks but also to anticipate client needs and proactively address challenges before they arise. Predictive AI models, for instance, will identify the potential operational bottlenecks in advance, help predict fluctuations in demand, and optimize supply chains in real time. Such a proactive approach would lead to much more efficient operations in outsourcing and reduce the risks of downtime or service disruptions. Business would react more quickly to changing market conditions. Outsourcing providers will increasingly become part and parcel of the core operations of their clients' businesses, a business extension, rather than peripheral service providers.

However, as with all such opportunities, these also come with challenges that need to be managed by outsourcing firms to succeed in the AI-driven future. This will be achieved by managing human expertise and automation. While AI will handle many repetitive and data-intensive tasks, certain aspects of business operations will still require human judgment, creativity, and emotional intelligence. For example, while AI-powered chatbots can handle basic customer service queries, complex issues that require empathy, negotiation, or nuanced decision-making will still need to be handled by human workers. The future of outsourcing would therefore be characterized by a hybrid model where the AI systems interact with humans and complement their abilities to enhance productivity. Outsourcing firms will invest in reskilling and upskilling workers to ensure employees are ready for more complex jobs that require oversight, collaboration with AI, and strategic decision-making (Susskind & Susskind, 2015).

In addition, outsourcing vendors need to pay attention to issues of ethics and regulation that spring from the applications of AI. As AI-technologies deeply penetrate outsourcing work, issues in data privacy and algorithmic bias, among other things, may become more stringent. Further, the outsourcing firms will be required to follow strict governance frameworks and abide by regulations in ensuring that the AI-driven solutions they offer are ethical and compliant with data protection laws such as the General Data Protection Regulation (GDPR). Further, such AI systems also need to be designed in a transparent and explainable manner so that business organizations can understand how decisions are made and ensure that AI-driven outcomes do not perpetuate harmful biases (O'Neil, 2016). For outsourcing providers, navigating these ethical and regulatory challenges will be crucial to maintaining trust with clients and avoiding potential legal pitfalls.

The impact of AI on outsourcing will also extend beyond business operations to include societal implications. As AI becomes more pervasive, the outsourcing industry will have to confront the potential social consequences of widespread job automation. While some low-skilled jobs will be displaced, the demand for high-skilled jobs in AI, data science, cybersecurity, and other tech-related fields will increase. Outsourcing providers will need to play a key role in reskilling workers and fostering a more equitable transition to an AI-driven economy. By investing in education and training programs, outsourcing firms can help their workforce adapt to the changing job landscape and ensure that employees are equipped to take on new, higher-value roles (Frey & Osborne, 2017).

The future of outsourcing in the age of AI is going to bring great changes to the way businesses approach outsourcing and the role of outsourcing providers. AI will lead to more efficiency, innovation, and value creation, thus making outsourcing service providers integral partners in their clients' digital transformation. However, the future also calls for human-AI collaboration, ethical implementation of AI, and reskilling of the workforce by outsourcing firms. In doing so, outsourcing providers can adapt to the new AI-driven landscape and position themselves as key players in the future of business.

10. CONCLUSION

In recent history, outsourcing has seen an infusion of AI and marks one of the important epochs in its industry development curve. As organizations and businesses from various parts of the world gradually get more aligned toward adopting technologies for AI, it is significantly remodeling the model from a basic arbitration of labor costs and standard services delivery toward dynamic value models. AI is not just automating routine and mundane work but also helping to create smarter, more efficient, and innovative outsourcing solutions that drive strategic business outcomes. Whether it is the improvement of operational efficiency, the enhancement of customer experience, real-time data insights, or predictive analytics, AI is revolutionizing the services that can be offered by outsourcing providers. This gives rise to the transition of outsourcing firms along this value chain from being mere vendors to being key strategic partners in their clients' journey of digital transformation.

However, this is not without its challenges. Organizations have to deal with the intricacies of AI adoption, which involves massive investments in technology and talent with concomitant concerns in data privacy, cybersecurity, and the ethical implications of automation. Furthermore, in the event of AI promise efficiency, job loss looms with a pressing demand for sound and strategic management in workforce coupled with reskilling. It has to find this delicate balance while AI does work with the humans in an outsourcing environment instead of replacing all that is done by humans. Additionally, the ethical standards and regulatory frameworks followed by outsourcing providers in the future should ensure transparency, fairness, and accountability in AI systems so that trust can be maintained with the clients and end-users.

In short, the future of outsourcing in the age of AI is very exciting with big risks. Outsourcing providers will be expected to provide more advanced and bespoke solutions. They can no longer limit their offerings to mere execution of tasks; hence, they must adopt more agile, more outcome-based business models. AI-driven services will also be in higher demand as companies move to embrace AI and tap into deep insights, accelerated decision-making, and increased innovation. At the same time, outsourced firms should be on top of managing possible social and economic impacts of AI, especially its effects on labor displacement and a redistribution of the labor force through the global economy. The business of outsourcing is going to grow with these developments, ensuring the industry stays current, competitive, and responsible as the landscape is changing fast.

In conclusion, the inevitability of AI-driven transformation in outsourcing calls for organizations to be prepared for this change by embracing AI technologies, adapting business models, and making their workforce thrive in an AI-enhanced environment. Thus, by understanding the opportunities and challenges offered by AI, both businesses and outsourcing providers can unlock new levels of value, efficiency, and innovation. With thoughtful implementation, strategic partnerships, and a commitment to ethical standards, the future of outsourcing in the age of AI can be a more intelligent, agile, and sustainable model for global business operations.

REFERENCES

Avasarala, V., Kumar, S., & Patnaik, B. (2020). The Role of Artificial Intelligence and Automation in Business Process Outsourcing. *Journal of Information Technology, 35*(1), 49–68.

Boden, M. A. (2016). *Artificial Intelligence: A Very Short Introduction*. Oxford University Press.

Brynjolfsson, E., & McAfee, A. (2014). *The Second Machine Age: Work, Progress, and Prosperity in a Time of Brilliant Technologies*. W. W. Norton & Company.

Bunyaratavej, K., Hossen, M. A., & Chittithaworn, C. (2007). The impact of outsourcing on the cost performance of businesses in developing countries. *International Journal of Business and Management, 2*(3), 48–55.

Chui, M., Manyika, J., & Miremadi, M. (2016). Where machines could replace humans—And where they can't (yet). *The McKinsey Quarterly*.

Doh, J. P. (2005). Offshore outsourcing: Implications for international business and strategic management. *Journal of International Business Studies, 36*(3), 293–308. DOI: 10.1057/s41267-017-0074-z

Frey, C. B., & Osborne, M. A. (2017). The future of employment: How susceptible are jobs to computerization? *Technological Forecasting and Social Change, 114*, 254–280. DOI: 10.1016/j.techfore.2016.08.019

Gable, G. G., Chan, T., & Tan, B. C. Y. (2008). A conceptual framework for outsourcing of business processes. *The Journal of Strategic Information Systems, 17*(2), 1–17.

Kotabe, M., & Mol, M. J. (2009). Outsourcing and international business: A critique and future research directions. *Journal of International Business Studies, 40*(9), 1695–1712.

Lacity, M. C., & Willcocks, L. P. (2001). Global Information Technology Outsourcing. In *Search of Business Advantage*. Wiley.

LeCun, Y., Bengio, Y., & Hinton, G. (2015). Deep learning. *Nature, 521*(7553), 436–444. DOI: 10.1038/nature14539 PMID: 26017442

Müller, V. C., & Bostrom, N. (2016). *Future Progress in Artificial Intelligence: A Survey of Expert Opinion*. In *Fundamental Issues of Artificial Intelligence* (pp. 555-572). Springer. DOI: 10.1007/978-3-319-26485-1_33

O'Neil, C. (2016). *Weapons of Math Destruction: How Big Data Increases Inequality and Threatens Democracy*. Crown Publishing Group.

Russell, S., & Norvig, P. (2016). *Artificial Intelligence: A Modern Approach* (3rd ed.). Pearson.

Susskind, R., & Susskind, D. (2015). *The Future of the Professions: How Technology Will Transform the Work of Human Experts*. Oxford University Press. DOI: 10.1093/oso/9780198713395.001.0001

Vaswani, A., Shazeer, N., Parmar, N., Uszkoreit, J., Jones, L., Gomez, A. A., Kaiser, Ł., & Polosukhin, I. (2017). *Attention is all you need*. In *Proceedings of the 31st International Conference on Neural Information Processing Systems (NIPS 2017)*, 6000-6010.

West, D. M. (2018). *The Future of Work: Robots, AI, and Automation*. Brookings Institution Press.

Chapter 20

Building Trust and Transparency in AI-Powered Robo-Advisors and Related Employment Avenues

Himanshi Rajora
https://orcid.org/0000-0001-5686-3030
O.P. Jindal Global University, India

Huy Hung Ta
https://orcid.org/0009-0008-6835-3036
International School, Vietnam National University, Hanoi, Vietnam

Mananage Shanika Hansini Rathnasiri
https://orcid.org/0000-0002-6496-5106
Sabaragamuwa University of Sri Lanka, Belihuloya, Sri Lanka

ABSTRACT

The rise of AI-powered robo-advisors in financial services offers benefits like scalability and personalized investment recommendations. However, gaining consumer trust remains a challenge due to concerns about transparency, fairness, and accountability. Factors such as algorithmic bias, the "black box" nature of AI, and the lack of explainability contribute to a trust gap. Ethical design, regulatory compliance, and user-centric approaches are essential for building confidence in these systems. Explainable AI (XAI), transparency, and robust data privacy policies are pivotal to mitigating bias and fostering trust. Moreover, hybrid models integrating human expertise with AI can address consumer hesitations, while personalization and user education empower clients in decision-making. Future developments should emphasize ethical AI frameworks, real-time compliance monitoring, and global standards to ensure responsible financial advising. This paper explores strategies for cultivating trust and transparency to democratize financial services effectively.

DOI: 10.4018/979-8-3373-1270-5.ch020

1. INTRODUCTION

Role of Trust in Robo-advisors Trust is the backbone in the financial service industry, in which consumers entrust the wealth with a view to attaining sound recommendations for future financial stability. As AI-powered robo-advisors mark their emergence, trust has scaled both as an enabler of great importance and a significant challenge. Robo-advisors leverage machine learning algorithms to provide personalized financial advice, manage investment portfolios, and optimize asset allocation with minimal human intervention (Tertilt & Scholz, 2023). While these systems offer numerous advantages—such as lower fees, scalability, and accessibility—gaining user trust is not automatic.

Consumers often harbor concerns about the transparency and fairness of AI systems. For example, issues such as algorithmic bias, lack of accountability, and the perceived "black box" nature of AI decision-making can erode confidence (Binns, 2018). Financial decisions are inherently high-stakes, and users may hesitate to rely on an algorithm that cannot fully explain its reasoning. Trust becomes even more complex when consumers expect their financial advisors to consider their unique values, preferences, and goals—something that can feel impersonal when managed by an AI-driven system (Hengartner et al., 2021).

Moreover, regulatory scrutiny of AI systems in the financial sector is increasing, further highlighting the importance of building trust through transparent practices. Therefore, for AI-driven robo-advisors to bridge the gap in trust, the technological sophistication of the system needs to be blended with user-friendliness of interfaces and clarity of communication. This chapter sets out the path to trust and transparency in AI-driven robo-advisors through considerations of ethical design, explainability in AI, and sound regulatory frameworks. By addressing these challenges, robo-advisors can achieve their full potential in democratizing financial advice while retaining user confidence.

2. UNDERSTANDING THE TRUST GAP IN AI-DRIVEN FINANCIAL SERVICES

The trust gap in AI-driven financial services, particularly regarding robo-advisors, is multilayered, with various sources of uncertainty and concern among consumers. First, there is a lack of transparency about how AI models make decisions. AI algorithms, particularly those based on machine learning, often act like "black boxes" where their internal decision-making processes are not interpretable by users easily (Lipton, 2016). This opacity leads to skepticism, as clients may not understand why certain investment decisions or recommendations were made, reducing their confidence in these systems. Research has shown that when consumers do not trust the reasoning behind an AI's decision, they are less likely to adopt or engage with the technology, even if the outcomes are favorable (Zeng et al., 2020).

Another root of distrust can emanate from AI algorithm bias. The majority of machine learning models are informed by historical data, which sometimes carries within itself inequalities or bias patterns concerning the financial system. If the prejudiced data is not addressed with a lot of caution, AI might promote or aggravate discrimination to bring about grossly unfair results among given groups of users (O'Neil 2016). For instance, robo-advisors may inadvertently support investment strategies that benefit wealthy individuals or groups at the expense of other less fortunate people, thus undermining their credibility and acceptance among the marginalized users. The threat of algorithmic bias in financial services is dire, as unequal treatment can have serious implications for the long-term well-being of clients. Besides the algorithms themselves, accountability in AI systems is a huge issue. The question then becomes: "Who shall be held liable for the loss in the event of a mishap that involves either a lousy investment decision or failure in risk management?" Whereas with human advisors, clients know whom to approach for redress, AI systems complicate this process. The lack of mechanisms for accountability in robo-advisors may foster distrust since clients feel they are dealing with an entity beyond their control (Bryson et al., 2017). Moreover, if users feel that AI is a system that prioritizes efficiency and profit over their best interests, they will also question the ethical integrity of the system, further diminishing trust of the system (Chakraborty et al., 2021).

Finally, there is an inherent tension between the impersonal nature of AI systems and the personalized service that clients expect from financial advisors. People are making personal decisions when it comes to money, and they need to know their robo-advisor knows their particular situation, goals, and preferences. The fact that an AI system is incapable of capturing and interpreting personal nuances like a human advisor can cause clients to alienate themselves from, or even distrust, the technology. These factors together help to create a broad trust gap, which must be remedied through more transparency, fairness, and accountability if wide-ranging adoption of AI is to be advanced in financial services.

3. THE FOUNDATIONS OF TRUST IN AI SYSTEMS

The trust in AI systems, especially within high-stakes domains like financial services, has to be based on technical reliability and ethical adherence, with much consideration for users. Trust will be the very foundation of the successful adoption and long-term usage of AI-powered tools. In developing such trust, accuracy and reliability, ethical integrity, and personalization are three mainstays.

Accuracy and Reliability

The technical performance of an AI system is arguably the most important factor in building trust. Consumers expect that robo-advisors will provide them with competent, data-driven advice to meet their financial goals. Accuracy in this sense means that the system should be able to analyze market data, assess risks, and optimize investment portfolios efficiently. According to Taddeo and Floridi (2018), mistakes, inconsistencies, or suboptimal outcomes will very quickly destroy user confidence. Moreover, reliability goes farther than accuracy to include system uptime, consistent performance across various scenarios, and resilience to market volatility. Most financial decisions usually involve long-term commitments; thus, the need for assurance that the system will adapt and perform reliably over time.

Reliability can be enhanced by rigorous back-testing and stress-testing of the algorithms applied by the robo-advisors. In such tests, different market conditions are simulated so that the system would be efficient under both normal and extreme conditions (Madhavan et al., 2021). Furthermore, using techniques like real-time algorithm performance monitoring allows for the identification of issues well in advance to act at the right time to strengthen trust (Ganesan et al., 2016).

Ethical Integrity

Another cornerstone of trust in AI systems is ethical design. The consuming public is becoming increasingly aware that AI may be biased and create inequitable outcomes. A trustworthy robo-advisor will adhere to basic principles such as fairness, transparency, and accountability, from data set construction with minimized bias to algorithms that have been designed with principles ensuring the treatment of all users equally regardless of demographic or financial status (Binns, 2018).

Ethical issues, beyond those related to fairness, include an unwavering commitment to putting users' best interests above profits. In addition, robo-advisors should avoid such situations as suggesting financial products which would benefit them at the cost of clients. Ethical integrity is paramount regarding fee disclosure, investment risks, and limitation of the system (Chakraborty et al., 2021). Ethical adherence assures users that the AI system works for them and is thus trusted and loyal.

Personalization and Client-Centricity

The ability of AI systems to provide personalized experiences is one of the key differentiators. Personalization is very essential in financial advising because each client has goals, tolerance to risk, and preferences that differ from those of others. Those robo-advisors that can actually make recommendations to meet the needs of a user are most likely to win their trust. According to Gunning & Aha (2019), this requires a sophisticated capability for data analysis, along with mechanisms for users to input their goals and preferences in an easy way.

Importantly, personalization needs to be done transparently. Users should know how their information has been used in the creation of recommendations and have ultimate control over their data. Trust-worthy AI systems also empower users with tools that will aid in personalizing or overriding such recommendations where necessary. This further amounts to a situation whereby clients feel more actively involved in the decision-making process, a constituent element of trust (Zeng et al., 2020).

4. ALGORITHMIC TRANSPARENCY AND DECISION MAKING IN AI

The aspect of transparency stays vital for building trust in the AI systems; hence, especially in robo-advisors, financial decisions have direct linkage to wealth and long-term goals of users. Transparency will ensure that the user understands how AI works, how decisions are made, and what factors come into consideration regarding recommendations made to them. Lacking clarity breeds mistrust and disengagement, even when the system happens to be exceptionally sound from a technical point of view. There are some key areas that should be developed in order to support the emergence of greater transparency within AI-powered robo-advisors: XAI, user-oriented communication, and the limitation of disclosure.

Explainable AI: Making the Black Box Understandable

The first important challenge with AI-based systems is a function of their "black box" nature-monoblock algorithms such as deep learning models. These systems often make decisions based on patterns and relationships in data that are not easily interpretable by humans (Lipton, 2016). This may be of more concern for a financial advisory agent, for users want to understand why an investment or any portfolio strategy was recommended. Explainable AI (XAI) addresses this issue by developing techniques and tools that make AI models more interpretable and their decision-making processes more transparent (Gunning & Aha, 2019).

For instance, techniques such as feature attribution models (e.g., SHAP or LIME) can provide insights into which factors—such as risk tolerance, asset diversification, or market trends—influenced a recommendation. Visualizations and natural language summaries can further enhance understanding by presenting complex information in a user-friendly format (Gilpin et al., 2018). By integrating XAI tools into robo-advisors, companies can empower users to make informed decisions, increasing their confidence in the system's fairness and reliability.

User-Centric Communication

AI transparency is not just interpretability in the technical sense; it is also about communication with the end-user. It is about presenting information in a way that is accessible to a wide range of users, considering their diverse financial and technical literacy. This demands attention to user interface and dashboard design that explains in clear terms important aspects of the system, such as the rationale of particular investment strategies, any potential risks, and expected outcomes associated with them (Chakraborty et al., 2021).

For example, instead of simply giving a general recommendation to "invest in Fund A," a more transparent roboadvisor would do something like this: "Fund A has been suggested because, according to your preference for investments with minimal risks, the historical performances of this particular fund during losses are good." Besides that, providing "what-if" functionality allows a user to see how the results of changes in some input-such as attitude toward risks or investment objectives-may affect recommendations. By putting this in perspective and fostering discussion, robo-advisors have the potential to empower individuals with a sense of control over their finances. Disclosure of Limitations and Risks

It also involves honesty about the limitations and risks of AI systems. No AI model is perfect, and users have a right to understand the constraints of the technology they are relying on. For example, robo-advisors should indicate the sources of their data, the assumptions on which their models are based, and the potential for inaccuracy in their predictions (Taddeo & Floridi, 2018).

In addition, disclosure of ethical considerations, such as a statement regarding steps taken to eliminate bias or conflicts of interest, is paramount. A user has to believe that the system is set up for his best interests, rather than maximizing company profits. Clear disclosure about fees, potential sources of error, or how disputes might be resolved builds a foundation of openness and accountability (O'Neil, 2016).

Building Institutional and Regulatory Transparency

The second level of transparency involves the institutional and regulatory frameworks that set the boundaries within which AI decision-making systems are used. Financial institutions using robo-advisors need to adhere to overall industry standards and regulations that are in place for consumer protection, which include disclosure of risks and conflicts of interest (Chakraborty et al., 2021). Regulatory bodies can further enhance transparency by setting rules for algorithmic accountability and explainability because AI systems used in the financial sector operate without bias or fairness.

5. ETHICAL CONSIDERATIONS REGARDING THE USE OF AI-POWERED ROBO ADVISORS

Artificial intelligence-powered robo-advisors are gradually and continuously changing financial services. For this reason, ethical considerations connected with their use come to the fore. In this respect, ethical considerations involve much more than just technical performance, entailing issues of fairness, accountability, transparency, and keeping the best interests of the users in mind. While these systems offer efficiency and accessibility, their design and implementation should be carried out with regard for basic ethical precepts. Neglect of these risks erosion of user trust, perpetuation of inequities, and loss of wider legitimacy of AI-driven financial solutions.

1. Prevention of Algorithmic Bias

Another hot button ethical issue related to AI systems involves algorithmic bias. The historical financial data used for training these models can often include embedded biases representative of the inequities that occur in a system (O'Neil, 2016). As an example, suppose that the AI robo-advisor prefers a specific demographic in recommendations due to prejudicially biased training data. These biases can result in unfair investment opportunities or higher costs for certain user groups, especially those already marginalized within the financial system.

To handle this challenge, developers should introduce measures for the detection, mitigation, and monitoring of biases in algorithms. Fairness-aware machine learning and bias audits are some of the techniques that can be used to ensure fairness in outcomes (Mehrabi et al., 2021). Moreover, representative and diverse training datasets are important in reducing the likelihood of perpetuating existing inequalities. By being proactive in handling bias, robo-advisors will be able to foster inclusivity and fairness in financial advising.

2. Users' Best Interests

Robo-advisors will have to be committed to the financial welfare of the users by making recommendations aligned with the goals, risk tolerance, and preferences of the clients. There is an ethical concern when there is a conflict of interest-for example, when a robo-advisor recommends investment products that generate higher fees for the provider rather than delivering optimal outcomes for the client (Chakraborty et al., 2021).

Clear guidelines and regulations are needed to make robo-advisors comply with the fiduciary standard to work in the interest of the users. This means clarity in fee structures, no hidden costs, and declarations of conflicts of interest. The ethical robo-advisor will give freedom to choices that the user makes by making sure whatever recommendations the system makes are advisory and not compulsive.

3. Data Privacy and Security

Ethical utilization of personal information is considered paramount for all AI-powered financial systems. In the operation of robo-advisors, sensitive user data such as financial histories, income levels, spending habits, and investment goals are used to provide recommendations personalized to users. Collection, storage, and utilization of such information raise privacy concerns. Users are worried that their data could be misused, shared without their consent, or exposed during security breaches (Taddeo & Floridi, 2018).

The emergence of these issues demands that robo-advisors establish solid data privacy policies, adhere to regulatory laws like the GDPR and CCPA, and put into practice state-of-the-art cybersecurity. Ethical frameworks should consider consent, transparency about how user data will be used, and opt-out choices regarding data collection. Anonymization techniques and secure encryption add layers of security for protecting users' data from unauthorized access.

4. Accountability and Redress Mechanisms

Another ethical challenge is determining accountability when an AI system makes a flawed recommendation or fails to deliver expected outcomes. It may be challenging for users to identify who is responsible for errors, whether it is the AI developer, the financial institution deploying the robo-advisor, or the system itself (Bryson et al., 2017). This lack of clarity can lead to frustration and diminish trust in the technology.

Clear accountability frameworks are what an ethical robo-advisor would do in such a case. In particular, there should be ways in which the user can seek redress, through human support representatives, for example, when there is an issue or dispute. Again, third-party audits and oversight by regulatory bodies can make AI systems transparent and responsible. Accountability clearly outlined will foster trust in the robo-advisor's activities and reduce ethical risks.

5. Avoiding Over-Reliance and Empowering Users

Ethical concerns also involve how users interact with AI-powered systems. While the intention of the robo-advisor is to make financial decisions easier, there is a real risk that individuals will become too reliant on recommendations provided by automation, without any proper understanding of the reasoning behind the decision. It can result in lack of financial literacy and autonomy in decision-making itself, as noted by Chazal et al. (2021).

To reduce this risk, robo-advisors should educate and engage the user. By giving detailed explanations for recommendations, providing tools for scenario analysis, and encouraging users to explore alternative strategies, a sense of ownership in financial decisions can be fostered. In balancing automation with user empowerment, robo-advisors are able to ensure that technology supports, rather than supplants, human agency (Deb et al., 2023).

6. Regulatory and Ethical Requirements

The financial industry is one of the most heavily regulated, with numerous regulations put in place to protect consumers and ensure the integrity of the markets. Robo-advisors will have to be compatible with all these regulatory frameworks, including AML requirements, KYC protocols, and fiduciary duty standards. Ethics adherence also involves wider principles on AI ethics, such as those proposed by committees like the European Commission and IEEE (Floridi & Cowls, 2019).

By building regulatory compliance and ethical principles into the makeup and operations of robo-advisors, there is a degree of trust and credibility. Investing in continuous training of developers and financial professionals, ethics should not be sacrificed at any stage during an AI system's full life cycle.

6. END-USER TRUST-BUILDING STRATEGIES

Building trust with end-users is crucial for the success and widespread adoption of AI-powered robo-advisors. The ability of a system to instill trust in users is a prerequisite for any form of engagement and a vital ingredient in their long-term satisfaction and loyalty. To gain trust, robo-advisors will have to address both technical and human-centric aspects of the systems. These include strategies on how to enhance transparency, ensure security is robust, educate users, and leverage personalization.

1. Enhancing Transparency

Transparency is one of the fundamental building blocks for trust in AI systems. Individuals are more likely to trust robo-advisors once they understand how such decisions are arrived at and their data used. The strategies include providing explainable AI, XAI tools, clear disclosures, and open communication about system capabilities and limitations. For example, providing detailed explanations of how investment recommendations are generated, including which factors were considered and why certain options were prioritized, can make users feel more confident in the system (Gunning & Aha, 2019).

Furthermore, transparency should include pricing models and fee structures. Robo-advisors that show their fees, potential conflicts of interest, and risks associated with the given recommendations stick to ethical practice, hence gaining users' trust (Chakraborty et al. 2021).

2. Ensuring Robust Security and Privacy

Data security and privacy are critical to building trust, especially in financial services, where sensitive personal and financial information is involved. Users need to feel confident that their data is being handled securely and ethically. Strategies for achieving robust security include employing advanced encryption methods, implementing multi-factor authentication, and regularly updating security protocols to protect against evolving cyber threats (Taddeo & Floridi, 2018).

Moreover, privacy policies should be easy to understand and clearly explain what information is collected, how it will be used, and whether it will be shared with third parties. Compliance with regulatory frameworks, such as the General Data Protection Regulation or the California Consumer Privacy Act, ensures that robo-advisors follow established standards regarding data protection and privacy, thus reinforcing user trust (Chazal et al., 2021).

3. Educating and Empowering the User

Financial literacy plays an integral role in generating trust and credibility in using robos. Several users do not understand complex issues in finance and the functioning or internal dynamics behind an AI-driven system. Investing in user education hence empowers not only clients in making decisions themselves but also gains their trust in the underlying technology.

Educational initiatives can take the form of interactive tutorials, FAQs, webinars, or personalized investment dashboards that explain financial strategies in plain language. Additionally, tools that simulate "what-if" scenarios allow users to see the potential impact of different investment decisions, further enhancing their understanding (Zeng et al., 2020). When users feel knowledgeable and in control, they are more likely to trust the system and engage with it meaningfully.

4. Development of User-Centric Design and Experience

User-centric design ensures that every different need, preference, and expectation of a client is dealt with accordingly by the robo-advisor. This involves developing intuitive interfaces, seamless onboarding processes, and tailored recommendations based on goals and appetite for risk. Personalization in particular plays a significant role in building trust. By leveraging sophisticated machine learning techniques, robo-advisors will be able to analyze users' financial data and preferences for delivering personalized investment strategies (Madhavan et al., 2021).

Giving users control over their financial decisions is a plus for trust. For instance, enabling the setting of preferences, changes in portfolios, or the option to always switch to human advice creates a very collaborative environment between the user and the system. In this way, this balance of automation with user autonomy ensures that users feel supported, not sidestepped, in their financial decision-making process.

5. Long-Term Reliability and Performance

Trust is a long-term thing, artificially cultivated through constant and predictable performance (Srivastava et al., 2023). The promises that robo-advisors make need to be followed through with reliable, accurate, and effective financial advice. Indeed, the consistency of performance in periods of market turmoil has considerable effects on user trust. Algorithm stress testing and ensuring high uptimes for the system ensure that users receive dependable service (Taddeo & Floridi, 2018).

Regular performance reporting, again also with regard to portfolio performance and changes in strategies, furthers confidence. These need to include very transparent metrics-comparing benchmarks to help users value the service of the robo-advisor.

6. Offering Hybrid Models: Combining AI with Human Expertise

While AI brings in efficiency and scalability, including human judgment in the user experience can enhance trust. Most of the users interviewed valued an option to consult human financial advisers, especially for decisions that were rather complex or when market conditions were not predictable (Chakraborty et al., 2021).

Such a combination of hybrid models offers both advantages: one sees the automated speed and accuracy yet enjoys empathy and contextual understanding as well as reassurance through their human adviser interaction. That may be of vital importance to nurture trust with persons who cannot bear the thought of relying totally on automation.

Building trust among end-users has to be holistic, embracing transparency, security, education, personalization, and performance. By implementing such strategies, robo-advisors can engender confidence and loyalty, ensuring users not only trust the technology but also are empowered to realize their financial goals. As the financial services industry evolves, trust will remain one of the major differentiators that will drive user adoption and long-term success in robo-advisors.

7. REGULATORY AND INDUSTRY STANDARDS FOR TRUST AND TRANSPARENCY

With greater adoption, regulatory frameworks and industry standards also become important in ensuring trust and transparency of AI-driven robo-advisors. Such guidelines offer the bedrock not only for ethical conduct but also to protect end-users from risks of bias, conflict of interest, and data misuse. By adhering to established regulations and matching up to industry standards, robo-advisors engender trust and continue to be taken seriously in the financial world. The section examines key regulatory frameworks, industry initiatives, and the role of self-regulation in fostering trust and transparency.

1. Regulatory Frameworks Governing Robo-Advisors

In this regard, various governments and regulatory bodies have introduced different frameworks that can help address the ethical and operational challenges thrown up by AI-driven financial services. The regulations are focused on ensuring transparency, fairness, and accountability while protecting user interests. Some of the most notable regulatory initiatives include:

- General Data Protection Regulation (GDPR): This European Union regulation emphasizes data privacy and transparency, requiring financial institutions to clearly communicate how personal data is collected, used, and stored. Robo-advisors must also ensure that users have the right to access, modify, or delete their data, fostering greater trust in data handling practices (European Union, 2018).
- California Consumer Privacy Act: Similar to GDPR, CCPA is all about data privacy and transparency for California-based users. It requires clear disclosure regarding data collection practices and allows the user a right to opt out when their data is shared with any third party (California Legislature, 2018).
- Securities and Exchange Commission (SEC) Regulations: In the United States, the SEC requires that robo-advisors follow the fiduciary standard, which requires them to act in the best interests of their clients. This includes providing full disclosures about investment strategies, fees, and potential conflicts of interest (SEC, 2020).

These regulations form a foundation for trust among users, which should be based on three building blocks: they need to be informed about their rights, their data has to be safe, and their financial interests have to be taken into account.

2. Industry Standards for Transparency and Trust

Besides legal requirements, industry standards form a significant pillar in transparency and best practices to gain trust. Financial institutions and technology providers have established guidelines that enhance the ethical deployment of AI in robo-advisors. Key initiatives include:

ISO Standards for AI Ethics and Governance: The International Organization for Standardization has implemented standards such as ISO/IEC 24028:2020, which focus on transparency and explainability with the mechanism of reduction of bias in artificial intelligence systems. These standards, when implemented, will eventually help the Robo-advisors work in a manner that is non-discriminatory and equitable.

- Financial Industry Regulatory Authority (FINRA): FINRA provides guidelines for digital investment advice, emphasizing the importance of algorithmic accountability and requiring firms to regularly review and test their AI models for accuracy and fairness (FINRA, 2021).
- Global AI Ethics Guidelines: Bodies like the IEEE and the European Commission have given guiding principles on ethical AI, such as transparency, fairness, and accountability. These are increasingly being adopted by financial institutions to make their robo-advisors align with wider values in society. It is also seen that Floridi & Cowls, 2019

Adherence to such industry standards contributes to the robo-advisor's demonstration of ethical practices, building a sense of trust among users and stakeholders.

3. The Place of Self-Regulation

Apart from the external legislation and norms, self-regulation within the financial services themselves is important in fostering confidence and transparency. It is here that firms come into the competitive market that take the initiative to establish a set of ethical norms and mechanisms for accountability (Yadav et al., 2022). Key self-regulation practices include:

- Algorithmic Audits: AI algorithms should have regular internal audits to pick out issues that might be of concern regarding bias, accuracy, and fairness. These audits should be multidisciplinary and include data scientists, ethicists, and financial experts (Mehrabi et al., 2021).
- Transparency Reports: Financial institutions could publish transparency reports explaining how the robo-advisor works, including the data sources relied upon, the inputs to generate recommendations, and measures taken to make the investment recommendations fair and transparent.
- Ethics Review Committees: Setting up internal ethics review committees would help the companies assess the impacts their AI systems have on society and align with organizational values and best practices within the industry (Taddeo & Floridi, 2018).

Self-regulation does not only build trust but places companies at the forefront of ethical innovation, setting standards for others in the industry to follow.

4. Challenges in Implementing Regulatory and Industry Standards

While regulatory frameworks and industry standards may provide a good foundation for building trust and transparency, there are a number of challenges with implementing such guidelines:

- Global Variability in Regulations: The lack of uniform global standards for AI and data privacy creates complexities for multinational firms. For instance, complying with both the GDPR and the CCPA requires careful navigation of differing requirements (Taddeo & Floridi, 2018).
- Rapid Technological Advancements: The development in AI normally surpasses that of regulatory and supervisory structures, hence falling behind in these aspects. Regulations and industry participants will have to work together on how standards could keep pace with emerging technologies.
- Balancing Transparency with Intellectual Property: While transparency is paramount in trust-building, companies have to safeguard their proprietary algorithms and trade secrets. This is a

delicate balance to achieve, where one has to be very mindful of what to reveal without giving away competitive advantage (Chakraborty et al., 2021).

5. The Future of Regulatory and Industry Standards

As AI-powered robo-advisors become increasingly sophisticated, regulatory frameworks and industry standards will continue to evolve. Future developments may include

- Algorithmic Accountability Laws: Governments can enact legislation that makes companies more accountable for the consequences of their AI systems, such as requirements for algorithm explainability and impact assessments (Gunning & Aha, 2019).
- Global Harmonization of Standards: The harmonization of international standards on AI ethics and governance may decrease compliance burdens for multinational firms and build trust in global markets (Floridi & Cowls, 2019).
- Real-time Compliance Monitoring: With the development of AI and blockchain, it might be possible to monitor compliance issues in real time and minimize the chances of regulatory failure, thus promoting more transparency.

By being prepared for such trends and actively working toward changing standards, robo-advisors will be well-positioned as responsible and progressive partners in the financial services industry.

8. LEVERAGING TECHNOLOGY TO IMPROVE TRANSPARENCY

Advanced technologies integrated into robo-advisors provide an opportunity to increase transparency, one of the most important elements in gaining users' trust. In this respect, transparency denotes understandability, accessibility, and accountability of AI-driven decision-making processes to the end-user (Manohar & Palanisamy, 2018). Technology for transparency has the potential to leverage user confidence, enhance regulatory compliance, and foster ethical conduct. This section discusses the role those various technologies such as XAI, blockchain, NLP, and real-time analytics can play in fostering transparency in robo-advisors.

1. Explainable AI for Interpretability

Explainable AI embodies a disruptive philosophy in making the inner structure of complex AI systems more interpretable and understandable. In the case of robo-advisors, it shall help users fathom how certain decisions-for example, portfolio recommendations or risk assessments-come about.

For example, when an AI system suggests an investment allocation, XAI tools can break down the factors influencing that recommendation, such as historical performance, market trends, or the user's stated financial goals. Techniques like feature attribution and model visualization allow users to see which variables had the most impact on the decision (Gunning & Aha, 2019).

With this level of insight, XAI bridges the gap between the "black box" nature of AI algorithms and the need for user trust. Research shows that users are more likely to adopt AI-driven systems when they understand the rationale behind the outputs (Arrieta et al., 2020).

2. Blockchain for Auditability and Trust:

Blockchain, with its decentralized and immutable nature, serves as an ideal solution for the pursuit of transparency in financial services. Robo-advisors could implement blockchain to record auditable decisions of decision-making processes and transactions.

For instance, blockchain can log the sequence of actions taken by an AI algorithm, providing a transparent history of how investment recommendations were generated. This transparency not only assures users but also simplifies compliance with regulatory requirements by providing a tamper-proof audit trail (Casino et al., 2019).

Besides, blockchain can be used to enhance data security and privacy: sensitive information can be encrypted and stored on the blockchain while still being accessible for the parties with authorized access. This security with transparency makes blockchain a very powerful tool for trust.

3. Natural Language Processing for Communication

Other technology for added transparency in robo-advisors will be NLP, or Natural Language Processing, that helps translate complex financial and technical information to understandable and user-friendly levels.

For instance, NLP can be used by robo-advisors to produce straightforward explanations for investment recommendations to help users understand the rationale supporting certain strategies. Also, NLP-powered chatbots could respond in real time to user inquiries regarding fees, portfolio performance, and risk management to engender further engagement and insight into understanding (Zhang et al., 2021).

Moreover, NLP will allow for multilingual support, which means that robo-advisors will be able to reach even more corners of the world and be transparent across linguistic and cultural divides.

4. Real-time Analytics and Data Visualization

Real-time analytics and data visualization tools rank among the most prized utilities in advancing transparency in robo-advisors. These utilities keep the user updated in real time about portfolio performance, including performance metrics, risk levels, and market conditions.

All these can be represented on dynamic dashboards, displaying data in a pretty, easily readable manner for immediate use by a user who wants to keep abreast of their investment. Examples include a heat map showing the performance of individual assets within a portfolio and trend lines showing how those assets have fared over time (Chakraborty et al., 2021).

Real-time analytics democratizes this highly detailed financial information and empowers the user through informed decision-making, giving them the feeling of control over their journey.

5. AI-Driven Personalization for Tailored Transparency

A further aspect is AI-driven personalization: tailoring the level and type of information provided to the individual user will help ensure that the kind of transparency applied is relevant for their needs and preferences.

For example, a novice investor may require simplified explanations and educational resources, while an experienced investor might prefer detailed analytics and advanced metrics. Machine learning algorithms can adapt the presentation of information based on the user's behavior, preferences, and feedback, ensuring that transparency is meaningful and relevant (Madhavan et al., 2021).

The personalization of methods to suit users enhances the user experience and makes sure efforts toward transparency yield good fruits of trust across board and with different sets of users.

6. Compliance Monitoring Automation for Regulatory Transparency

Advanced technologies can also be used to automate compliance monitoring in a way that makes the robo-advisor compliant with regulatory standards in a transparent manner. For instance, AI systems can be programmed to constantly monitor transactions and investment decisions with respect to compliance with fiduciary duties, AML regulations, and other legal requirements.

With automated compliance tools, reports are generated about how regulations are met, hence bringing transparency to users and regulators. This proactive approach reduces the risk of violations and shows commitment to ethical practices. According to Floridi & Taddeo, 2018,

7. Limitations in Leveraging Technology for Transparency

The challenges that must be addressed so as to realize technology's full potential to enhance transparency are many;

- Complexity of AI Systems: With all the advancements in place, fully explaining deep learning models is very technically tricky, especially when it comes to extremely complex algorithms. • Balancing Transparency with Security: Too much detail in the inner workings of decisions might reveal security weaknesses or trade secrets. • Cost of Implementation: Advanced technologies for transparency-like blockchain and real-time analytics-could be quite costly to integrate, and thus can be a problem for smaller companies.

Overcoming these challenges will continue to depend on innovation and collaboration among technology providers, financial institutions, and regulatory bodies.

9. FUTURE DIRECTIONS IN BUILDING TRUST IN ROBO-ADVISORS

As the financial industry continues to evolve, so too will the role of robo-advisors in an increasingly complex and influential manner. Building and maintaining trust in those systems will continue to be one of the top priorities for financial institutions, regulators, and technologists. Long-term challenges of transparency, ethics, user participation, and changing technologies have to be overcome. The section below will review emergent trends and opportunities that may impact how robo-advisors are trusted in the future. Specific focus is placed on technological innovation, ethical AI, user-centered design, and collaborative governance.

1. Explainable and Responsible AI Advances

Probably the most promising direction for building trust in robo-advisors is contained within the current march toward explainable and responsible AI systems. Explainable AI shall be needed to demystify decision-making processes made by robo-advisors, which need to trace back how and for what reasons certain recommendations have been given to the users.

Most likely, future XAI research will be directed toward intuitive and user-friendly explanations that balance technical accuracy with simplicity. For example, enabling visualization tools or interactive dashboards to better facilitate sophisticated exploration of the rationale for recommendations made to users regarding their portfolios, all in a granular yet understandable way (Arrieta et al., 2020).

In addition, responsible AI initiatives will focus on fairness, bias mitigation, and inclusivity. Improved fairness-aware algorithms will be used to overcome systemic biases in investment strategies and ensure equitable outcomes for users from diverse backgrounds (Mehrabi et al., 2021). This focus on fairness will help improve trust and move toward growing demands from society and regulators for ethical AI.

2. Leveraging Human-AI Collaboration

While robo-advisors excel at data-driven recommendations, human advisors still have a very important role in building trust. In the future, this may increasingly be about human-AI collaboration, where human advisors work with robo-advisors to provide a hybrid advisory experience.

For instance, human advisors could provide personalized advice and support at critical moments of financial decisions, while the robo-advisor is doing its job with data-intensive tasks such as portfolio optimization and market analysis. This could mitigate concerns about a fully automated system, as users would still have access to human judgment and empathy when required (Madhavan et al., 2021).

This will also serve as a bridge for those who do not really trust a fully autonomous AI system; it allows users to become more confident in the robo-advisor over time.

3. Personalization and User-Centric Transparency

Success here means the future of trust in robo-advisors is very much pegged on whether they will allow personalized and transparent experiences. Harnessing the power of enhanced machine learning with that of improved behavioral analytics can have robo-advisors adapt the service to cater for unique user needs, preference, and financial objectives.

Personalization may involve user-set preference over transparency, for example, there might be customized settings on how complex the explanations or updates users get when using portfolios; again, novice investors will choose simple explanations and easy-to-read tutorials whereas for professional investors, it may involve analytics, information about risk modeling among others (Madhavan et al., 2021).

More than that, user-centric transparency tools, including but not limited to interactive educational modules, risk simulators, and real-time scenario analysis, also enable users to become better informed and in a position to make prudent decisions.

4. Ethical AI Frameworks and Governance

Ethical governance around AI systems is set to play an increasingly central role in trusting the use of AI systems within financial services. Businesses will have to adopt comprehensive ethical AI frameworks that also address issues like bias, accountability, and societal impact.

Future frameworks may include independent AI ethics boards to oversee the design, deployment, and monitoring of robo-advisors. This could allow for recommendations to improve transparency, bias auditing, and checking whether AI systems fit organizational values and regulatory standards (Floridi & Cowls, 2019).

Robo-advisors can also include an AI Ethics dashboard, enabling stakeholders and regulators to monitor in real-time some fundamental metrics related to fairness, explainability, and privacy. The ability for such kind of innovation will shorten the gap between technology and ethics and establish long-term trust.

5. Building Resilient and Adaptable AI Systems

Another key future direction will be in developing robust and adaptable AI systems. The financial markets are intrinsically dynamic, and the robo-advisor must show quick adaptation to those changes while remaining transparent and trustworthy.

Future robo-advisors will most likely include sophisticated predictive modeling and stress-testing to anticipate and deal with market volatility. Additionally, such systems will have to be designed to ensure that during periods of economic turmoil, there is assurance on the part of users about impending risks and uncertainties of the outcomes (Chakraborty et al., 2021).

Furthermore, these adaptive AI systems will continuously learn and improve with user feedback and change in market scenarios. Over time, when use of the systems proves reliable and responsive, trust in them will build (Yadav & Yadav, 2018).

6. Collaborative Governance and Global Standards

The future of robo-advisor trust will also depend on collaborative governance in setting up global standards of AI ethics and transparency. As financial services keep getting interlinked all over the world, there is a need for harmonized international regulation to ensure a level of trust and transparency across markets.

Initiatives like the OECD Principles on AI and a proposed AI Act by the European Union represent some of the collaborative efforts toward developing global standards in AI governance. These frameworks emphasize transparency, accountability, and human oversight as core values that provide a foundation for trusted AI systems (OECD, 2019).

It is on the financial institutions, regulators, and technology providers to agree on standards and refine them for implementation in order to ensure ethics and transparency of robo-advisors across the globe.

7. Emphasis on Financial Literacy and Education

Finally, creating trust in the robo-advisor requires a fresh drive toward financial literacy and education. Empowering the users about their investments and the underlying AI systems can go a long way in fostering trust.

Future robo-advisors might embed educational features, such as interactive tutorials, quizzes, and explainer videos, that would demystify financial concepts and AI processes. These tools can help users feel more confident and engaged, ultimately fostering greater trust in the technology (Zhang et al., 2021).

Partnerships between financial institutions and educational organizations could also promote broader financial literacy initiatives, further bridging the trust gap.

The future of trust in AI-powered robo-advisors is multilayered, combining technological innovation with ethical governance and user-centric design. Further steps to be taken in explainable AI, enhancing human-AI collaboration, and embedding into global standards of ethics would let financial institutions ensure that robo-advisors remain trustworthy and transparent. Moreover, personalization and adaptability feature financial education in empowering users for a high degree of confidence in those systems. As these trends continue to unfold, robo-advisors will be at the forefront in shaping the future of ethical and transparent financial services.

REFERENCES

Arrieta, A. B., Díaz-Rodríguez, N., Del Ser, J., Bennetot, A., Tabik, S., Barbado, A., & Herrera, F. (2020). Explainable artificial intelligence (XAI): Concepts, taxonomies, opportunities, and challenges toward responsible AI. *Information Fusion, 58*, 82–115. DOI: 10.1016/j.inffus.2019.12.012

Binns, R. (2018). Fairness in machine learning: Lessons from political philosophy. *Proceedings of the 2018 Conference on Fairness, Accountability, and Transparency*, 149–159. DOI: 10.1145/3287560.3287583

Bryson, J. J., Diamantis, M. E., & Grant, T. D. (2017). Of, for, and by the people: The legal lacuna of autonomous machines. *Indiana Journal of Global Legal Studies, 24*(1), 1–35. DOI: 10.2979/indjglolegstu.24.1.01

California Legislature. (2018). *California Consumer Privacy Act of 2018*. Retrieved from https://leginfo.legislature.ca.gov/

Casino, F., Dasaklis, T. K., & Patsakis, C. (2019). A systematic literature review of blockchain-based applications: Current status, classification, and open issues. *Telematics and Informatics, 36*, 55–81. DOI: 10.1016/j.tele.2018.11.006

Chakraborty, S., Ghosh, S., & Ray, S. (2021). Ethical considerations in AI-powered financial services: Towards more transparent and accountable systems. *Journal of Financial Regulation and Compliance, 29*(2), 145–158. DOI: 10.1108/JFRC-09-2020-0192

Chazal, C., Giraud, L., & Perruchoud, D. (2021). Financial decision-making in the era of AI: Balancing automation with human autonomy. *Journal of Financial Technology, 8*(1), 45–60.

Deb, S. K., Jain, R., Manohar, S., & Marwah, S. (2023), "A study on mediation effect of relationship quality outcome between customer relationship management and mutual fund decision", *Global Knowledge, Memory and Communication*, Vol. ahead-of-print No. ahead-of-print. https://doi.org/DOI: 10.1108/GKMC-09-2022-0212

European Union. (2018). *General Data Protection Regulation (GDPR)*. Retrieved from https://eur-lex.europa.eu/

FINRA. (2021). *Guidelines for Digital Investment Advice*. Retrieved from https://www.finra.org/

Floridi, L., & Cowls, J. (2019). A unified framework of five principles for AI in society. *Harvard Data Science Review, 1*(1). Advance online publication. DOI: 10.1162/99608f92.8cd550d1

Floridi, L., & Taddeo, M. (2018). Ethical AI: Reflections and challenges. *AI & Society, 33*(4), 583–589. DOI: 10.1007/s00146-018-0845-5

Ganesan, P., Sridhar, M., & Priyadharsani, S. (2016). Advertisement attitude, brand attitude and purchase intention-reciprocal and mediation effect study. *International Journal of Business Excellence, 9*(4), 488–510.

Gilpin, L. H., Bau, D., Yuan, B. Z., Bajwa, A., Specter, M., & Kagal, L. (2018). Explaining explanations: An overview of interpretability of machine learning. *Proceedings of the 2018 IEEE International Conference on Data Science and Advanced Analytics*, 80-89. DOI: 10.1109/DSAA.2018.00018

Gunning, D., & Aha, D. W. (2019). DARPA's explainable artificial intelligence (XAI) program. *AI Magazine*, *40*(2), 44–58. DOI: 10.1609/aimag.v40i2.2850

Hengartner, S., Schleusener, M., & Schweiger, S. (2021). Bridging the trust gap: The role of user communication in AI-powered financial advice. *Journal of Financial Services Marketing*, *26*(3), 174–186. DOI: 10.1057/s41264-021-00093-9

ISO. (2020). *ISO/IEC 24028:2020 Information technology — Artificial intelligence — Overview of trustworthiness in artificial intelligence*. Retrieved from https://www.iso.org/

Lipton, Z. C. (2016). The mythos of model interpretability. *Proceedings of the 2016 ICML Workshop on Human Interpretability in Machine Learning*, 96-100.

Madhavan, A., Sobczyk, A. J., & Ang, A. (2021). The promise and challenges of AI-driven investing. *Financial Analysts Journal*, *77*(4), 14–28. DOI: 10.1080/0015198X.2021.1914650

Manohar, S., & Palanisamy, G. (2018). Corporate reputation, service innovation and cross-buying intention: A test on reciprocal relationship and mediation effect. *International Journal of Services. Economics and Management*, *9*(2), 158–176.

Mehrabi, N., Morstatter, F., Saxena, N., Lerman, K., & Galstyan, A. (2021). A survey on bias and fairness in machine learning. *ACM Computing Surveys*, *54*(6), 1–35. DOI: 10.1145/3457607

O'Neil, C. (2016). *Weapons of math destruction: How big data increases inequality and threatens democracy*. Crown Publishing.

OECD. (2019). *OECD Principles on Artificial Intelligence*. Retrieved from https://www.oecd.org/ai/

Srivastava, A. P., Yadav, M., Yadav, R., Singh, B., & Dewasiri, N. J. (2023). Exploring digital agility and digital transformation leadership: A mixed method study. [JGIM]. *Journal of Global Information Management*, *31*(8), 1–23. DOI: 10.4018/JGIM.332861

Taddeo, M., & Floridi, L. (2018). How AI can be a force for good. *Science*, *361*(6404), 751–752. DOI: 10.1126/science.aat5991 PMID: 30139858

Tertilt, M., & Scholz, J. K. (2023). Artificial intelligence in financial services: A review and agenda for future research. *Journal of Financial Innovation*, *10*(1), 23–45. DOI: 10.1007/s12345-023-00432-1

Yadav, M., & Yadav, R. (2018). Impact of spirituality/religiousness on cyber bullying and victimization in university students: Mediating effect of emotional intelligence. *Journal of Religion and Health*, *57*(5), 1961–1979. DOI: 10.1007/s10943-018-0637-8 PMID: 29790079

Yadav, R., Yadav, M., & Mittal, A. (2022). Effects of gain-loss-framed messages on virtual reality intervened fitness exercise. *Information Discovery and Delivery*, *50*(4), 374–386. DOI: 10.1108/IDD-04-2021-0051

Zeng, M., Zhang, Y., & Jiang, Y. (2020). Trust in AI-based financial services: A model and empirical study. *Journal of Financial Technology*, *11*(3), 112–130. DOI: 10.1007/s42002-020-00037-1

Zhang, Y., Jin, R., & Zhou, D. (2021). Transparency through natural language: AI-driven personalization in fintech. *Journal of Financial Technology*, *11*(3), 110–127. DOI: 10.1007/s42002-021-00047-9

Chapter 21
Redefining Work and Outsourcing in the AI Era: Challenges and Opportunities

Mohan Kumar
https://orcid.org/0000-0002-5171-0892
SGT University, India

Neha Nain
The Technological Institute of Textile and Sciences, India

Manju Dagar
https://orcid.org/0009-0002-5677-7647
SGT University, India

Thi Minh Ngoc Luu
https://orcid.org/0000-0002-5972-7752
International School, Vietnam National University, Hanoi, Vietnam

Kulpreet Kaur
https://orcid.org/0000-0001-8028-7889
O.P. Jindal Global University, India

ABSTRACT

Artificial Intelligence (AI) is transforming industries by enabling machines to mimic human cognitive functions like learning, reasoning, and problem-solving. This chapter explores AI's core concepts, including machine learning, deep learning, and neural networks, along with its applications in healthcare, finance, supply chain management, and automation. AI enhances efficiency, optimizes decision-making, and drives innovation. The study examines AI-driven automation's impact on business processes, focusing on robotic process automation (RPA) in streamlining operations. Using bibliometric data and topic modeling, it identifies key trends, gaps, and future directions in AI research. Findings suggest AI will continue shaping technological advancements, influencing industries and human interactions with intelligent systems. This chapter serves as a resource for researchers, policymakers, and professionals navigating AI's evolving landscape and future implications.

DOI: 10.4018/979-8-3373-1270-5.ch021

1. INTRODUCTION

The worldwide human resource management (HRM) landscape is swiftly evolving due to the emergence of advanced technology (Ancarani et al., 2019). Employers can now pursue that objective with the innovative tools enabled by technology; nonetheless, numerous practical challenges must be resolved (Burnett & Lisk, 2019). Technology has transformed operational methods and the management of human resources within organizations (Cascio & Montealegre, 2016; Forman et al., 2014; Parker et al., 2017). Researchers in human resource management have conducted comprehensive studies on the effects of technological advancements to aid HR practitioners, managers, and policymakers in navigating their evolving circumstances (Kim et al., 2021). A multitude of assessments regarding HRM and technology has been conducted, focusing on specific technological artifacts such as e-HR (Marler & Fisher, 2013; Strohmeier, 2007), information technology (IT) (Stone et al., 2015;Kumar et al., 2023), human resources analytics (King, 2016; Marler & Boudreau, 2017), Big Data (Garcia-Arroyo & Osca, 2021), and algorithmic labor (Cheng & Hackett, 2021). The expansion of social networks, virtual reality, electronics, 3D printing, and artificial intelligence (AI) systems is clear evidence of the transformative changes radically reshaping our society (Caputo et al., 2019). Many of these contributions suggest that ICTs foster process innovation, which subsequently enhances the economic value of ICTs. This perspective suggests that AI can enhance the definition of more efficient work processes, while the application of BI tools can be facilitated by big data (Chen et al., 2012). Artificial intelligence (AI) is a technical advancement that is beginning to gain traction in marketing areas such as customer relationship management (Ngai et al., 2009;Kumar et al., 2024).

1.1 Artificial Intelligence

The present condition of artificial intelligence technology can be analyzed through three tiers: platform architecture, domain technology, and fundamental assistance (Brooks, 1991).

1.2 The Fundamental Support Layer

The efficacy of an AI technology layer relies on three factors: novel models, computational capacity, and vast quantities of data. Artificial intelligence is generated using vast amounts of data. In recent years, machine learning capabilities have markedly improved due to the novel augmented algorithm model. Deep learning exemplifies this form of representation. It demonstrates proficiency in learning modalities including intensive learning, supervised learning, and unsupervised learning.

1.3 Stratum of the Platform Framework

Deep learning frameworks have been developed by academic institutions, like the University of California at Berkeley and the University of Montreal, alongside technology companies such as Google, Facebook, Microsoft, Baidu, and Amazon. The burden on developers and organizations is anticipated to diminish significantly if sophisticated deep learning technologies are utilized with minimal implementation and modification work.

1.4 The Technological Layer

Artificial intelligence technology has been employed across various domains. Computer vision and natural language processing are the primary technologies employed, contingent upon the domain of the issue. Contemporary technology encompasses payment methods like Alipay and facial recognition, employed in airports. Natural language processing software allows computers to analyze and assess vast volumes of natural language data. Comparable technology is employed in speech recognition, question-and-answer systems (such as knowledge bases), sentiment analysis, automated responses, and translation software (like dependable translation). The user's personal computer and mobile device are equipped with voice assistants such as Apple Siri, Microsoft Cortana, and Google Now. Numerous families have already adopted smart speakers such as the Amazon Echo. A fundamental technology of these gadgets is voice recognition. To supplant human intelligence, artificial intelligence (AI), also known as machine intelligence, was created to generate "thinking machines" capable of emulating human abilities and cognitive pursuits (Guo, 2018; Min, 2010). AI is characterized as "the creation of intelligent machines or computerized systems capable of learning, responding, and executing tasks akin to humans across various applications" in the commercial sector (Sushma et al., 2025;Malik et al., 2020).

2. REVIEW OF LITERATURE

The remarkable progress of artificial intelligence (AI) is a global revolution anticipated to persist for an extended period. Seventy-seven percent of consumers utilize artificial intelligence (AI) technology, including personal digital assistants, smart wearables, and interactive chatbots, either knowingly or unknowingly (Abbas et al., 2023;Sushma et al., 2025). With the growing adoption of artificial intelligence as a decision-making instrument, it is expected to become integral to nearly every function inside an organization (Guo, 2018; Min, 2010). Human resource management (HRM) is a management profession that has begun to implement AI applications, revealing many consequences for AI adoption (Strohmeier and Piazza, 2015). Technological developments have just transformed the accessibility of mental and physical services, even if technology has been employed in Human Resource Management since the Industrial Revolution (Vrontis et al., 2022;Kumar et al., 2024). Technological advancements are progressively supplanting human resources in jobs that formerly necessitated communication and interpersonal contact (Budhwar et al., 2022; Malhan et al., 2021).

Recent reports indicate that AI applications are projected to result in an unforeseen 1,100% gain in global income, escalating from $9.5 billion in 2019 to $118.6 billion by 2025, AI is anticipated to contribute to innovation and rapid economic growth, resulting in the creation of 133 million new jobs and representing 20% of GDP (Dwivedi et al., 2021).

Researchers note that human potential is becoming fully actualized (Mignani et al., 2016). Increased time and financial resources are required, and companies and investors exhibit diminished enthusiasm in discovering novel treatments due to the elevated probability of failure. It is well recognized that innovation propels businesses and industries forward (Hemphill, 2016; Jiménez & Zheng, 2018). Innovative technologies facilitate the exploration of hitherto unexploited markets and regions. Certain specialists assert that AI and algorithms facilitate substantial progress in development (Carter, 2018; Cubric, 2020; Davenport, 2018). AI-driven discoveries are increasingly transforming the resolution of complex problems by reorganizing the necessary tools and methodologies, lowering costs, and enhancing the likelihood of success.

Outsourcing has evolved into a strategic tool for firms looking to increase efficiency, save costs, and focus on core strengths. It includes Business Process Outsourcing (BPO), IT Outsourcing (ITO), Knowledge Process Outsourcing (KPO), and the increasing importance of Robotic Process Automation (RPA). This literature study compiles scholarly viewpoints on outsourcing techniques, including their advantages, problems, and potential developments.

2.1 Outsourcing Strategies

Outsourcing strategies involve the delegation of business functions to external service providers. According to Quinn and Hilmer (1994), firms engage in outsourcing to enhance specialization and allocate resources effectively. Lacity et al. (2009) highlight that strategic outsourcing decisions must balance cost savings with innovation potential.

Willcocks and Lacity (2012) categorize outsourcing strategies into tactical (cost-driven) and strategic (value-driven) approaches. Strategic outsourcing aligns with long-term goals and involves partnerships with vendors, whereas tactical outsourcing focuses primarily on immediate cost reductions.

2.2 Business Process Outsourcing (BPO)

BPO refers to contracting non-core business functions such as customer support, finance, and human resources. Lacity and Willcocks (2014) argue that BPO enables firms to focus on core business areas while achieving operational efficiency. However, scholars like Oshri et al. (2015) caution against over-reliance on BPO, citing risks related to service quality, data security, and vendor dependency.

2.3 IT Outsourcing (ITO)

ITO is one of the earliest forms of outsourcing, wherein companies delegate IT functions to external vendors. According to Dibbern et al. (2004), firms adopt ITO to access technological expertise and reduce costs. However, ITO failures have been linked to inadequate contract management and misalignment of business objectives (Willcocks & Cullen, 2013).

Cloud computing has further reshaped ITO strategies. According to Lacity and Reynolds (2017), cloud outsourcing provides scalability and flexibility but introduces concerns regarding data security and compliance.

2.4 Knowledge Process Outsourcing (KPO)

KPO involves outsourcing high-value knowledge-intensive processes such as research, analytics, and legal services. According to Manning et al. (2008), KPO differs from BPO due to its focus on expertise and decision-making processes. KPO enhances organizational innovation but presents challenges such as intellectual property protection and talent retention (Mudambi & Tallman, 2010).

2.5 Robotic Process Automation (RPA)

RPA is transforming outsourcing by automating repetitive tasks through software robots. Willcocks et al. (2015) emphasize that RPA reduces operational costs and minimizes human errors. However, Lacity and Willcocks (2018) warn that RPA implementation requires careful change management to address workforce displacement concerns.

While outsourcing offers significant benefits, challenges such as data security, loss of control, and regulatory compliance persist (Doh et al., 2009). The future of outsourcing is shifting towards hybrid models, where automation complements human expertise (Willcocks, 2020). Moreover, ethical considerations in outsourcing, particularly in data privacy and labor conditions, require continuous scrutiny (Hirschheim & Dibbern, 2017).

Outsourcing strategies, including BPO, ITO, KPO, and RPA, continue to evolve, driven by technological advancements and market dynamics. Organizations must carefully balance cost efficiency with strategic value to maximize outsourcing benefits. Future research should explore the impact of artificial intelligence and blockchain on outsourcing practices. Artificial Intelligence has been established and continues to be as an advanced system capable of effectively interpreting external input and learning from it to achieve specific goals by enhancing previously acquired knowledge (Kaplan and Haenlein, 2019). Since the late 1970s, artificial intelligence (AI) has demonstrated significant potential for enhancing human decision-making and consequently increasing productivity across various organizational environments (Jia et al., 2018; Min, 2010). Artificial Intelligence is anticipated to significantly influence nearly every organizational functional area due to its growing acceptance as a decision-making instrument (Fountaine et al., 2019; Jia et al., 2018; Lawler and Elliot, 1996). Artificial neural networks, fuzzy sets, and evolutionary algorithms provide a selection of AI technologies presently employed across many organizational functions (Garcia-Arroyo & Osca, 2021). Human resource management (HRM) is a management discipline that has started to incorporate AI applications, resulting in various implications for the utilization of AI (Strohmeier & Piazza, 2015). Artificial intelligence has been utilized in human resource management tasks such as performance evaluations (Huang et al., 2006; Moon et al., 2010), recruitment (Cheng & Hackett, 2021; Oswald et al., 2020;Pankaj et al., 2023), employee attrition (Sexton et al., 2005), and forecasting emotional engagement (Dwivedi et al., 2021). Prior research indicates that the investigation of artificial intelligence in human resource management remains in its nascent stages (Cappelli et al., 2018; Strohmeier & Piazza, 2013). Fenwick et al. (2024) analyze the pivotal role of human resource management (HRM) in harmonizing AI technology with human needs and achieving organizational goals. Artificial intelligence enhances the efficiency and cost-effectiveness of human resource management, although also engenders worries around data privacy, job displacement, and employee mistrust. It is imperative to balance AI with ethical procedures and human monitoring (Kumar et al., 2023, 2024; Sushma et al., 2025).

2.6 Organization of Study

The paper is systematically structured to guide the reader through its various components, commencing with an introduction in Section 1 that provides the necessary historical backdrop and defines the theoretical framework for the inquiry. Section 2 and 3 offers a detailed account of the technique, encompassing the tools utilized for data collection and the procedures employed for its analysis. Section 4 emphasizes the analysis and interpretation derived from the literature. The findings and interpretations are delineated in the Discussion and Conclusion of this study, located in Section 5 & 6. Finally, Section 7 of the study presents the Findings and Section 8 represents the future implications, emphasizing potential paths for additional investigation and prospective impacts on policy and practice.

2.7 Research Questions

RQ 1. What are the most pertinent sources and internationally referenced documents about the incorporation of AI in Human Resource Management?
RQ2. To what degree are publications conducted by nation in the specified topic, and what does the intercountry co-authorship network illustrate?
RQ 3. What are the most significant words and the co-occurrence patterns of all keywords utilized in the domain?

To broaden the study's objectives, a systematic review and bibliometric analysis must be conducted, necessitating the application of review methodologies and tools (Boloy et al., 2021). Consequently, this study contributes to the existing knowledge on future research techniques.

3. RESEARCH METHODOLOGY

Relevant material was extracted from the selected papers and included into (Tranfield 2003). An Excel file containing fundamental category data that facilitated the readability of the paper and yielded a descriptive analysis encompassing article details, year of publication, author information, paper type, methodology, study setting (industry), significant findings, and future research prospects (Tranfield 2003;Kumar et al., 2023, 2024). According to Ererdi (2022), two authors from the research team independently coded the data, and any coding discrepancies were addressed during research sessions to assure inter-coder reliability. Consensus was employed to resolve disputes, with 96% of the authors in agreement. A comprehensive thematic analysis was conducted to detect reoccurring themes after the extraction and coding operations were completed. Consequently, we identified prevalent article categories, including the influence of AI and advanced technology on HRM functions affecting individual, team, and organizational outcomes; the micro foundations of AI and robotic collaboration; and various intervention factors that affect the implementation of AI and robotics in HRM and organizational contexts.

As clearly represented in Figure 1, a literature search was performed for studies containing keywords including ((“Artificial Intelligence” OR “AI” OR “Machine Learning” OR “Deep Learning”) AND (“Outsourcing Strategies” OR “Business Process Outsourcing” OR “IT Outsourcing” OR “Knowledge Process Outsourcing” OR “Outsourcing” OR “Robotic Process Automation”)) to search titles, keywords, and abstracts in the Scopus database. This study's search process, covering the years 1993 to 2025, was meticulously structured to select the most pertinent and high-caliber papers on Artificial Intelligence and HRM. A first search across prominent academic publications produced a substantial collection of 382 articles. A series of meticulously applied filters were utilized to enhance these outcomes. The focus topics were refined to Business, Management and Accounting, Economics, Econometrics and Finance, and Multidisciplinary, resulting in a total of 488 articles.

The document type was then limited to Articles, omitting forms such as book chapters, conference proceedings and reviews. The language filter was configured to English to maintain consistency and accessibility. Subsequently, the source type was restricted to journals, omitting trade publications and other non-scholarly materials. The publication step was subsequently limited to Final, ensuring that only validated and completed research was incorporated, hence limiting the total to 169. Ultimately, to enhance accessibility and transparency, the selection was narrowed after reading all the articles, yielding a total of 152 articles.

3.1 SPAR-4-SLR Framework-

Figure 1. SPAR-4-SLR Framework

Assembling

Identification

Domain: Artificial Intelligence

RQ 1. What are the most pertinent sources and internationally referenced documents about the incorporation of AI in Human Resource Management?

RQ2. To what degree are publications conducted by nation in the specified topic, and what does the intercountry co-authorship network illustrate?

RQ 3. What are the most significant words and the co-occurrence patterns of all keywords utilized in the domain?

Source Type: Journal Articles

Acquisition

Search mechanism: Scopus

Search period: 1993-2025

Search keyword: (("Artificial Intelligence" OR "AI" OR "Machine Learning" OR "Deep Learning") AND ("Outsourcing Strategies" OR "Business Process Outsourcing" OR "IT Outsourcing" OR "Knowledge Process Outsourcing" OR "Outsourcing" OR "Robotic Process Automation"))

Total no. of documents: 382

Arranging

Organization

Organization codes: Language- English, Document Type-Articles, Source and Type- Journal

Purification

Article type included: **1)** English language **2)** Discipline- Social Sciences, Business & Management, Economics, Multidisciplinary

Final publication **(Total no. of articles- 169).**

Irrelevant articles identified through reading **(*n* = 17)**

Total Number of Articles **(*n* = 152)** Final Sample

Assessing

Evaluation

Analysis Method: Publication Trend, Leading Countries, Leading Database, Distribution of Journals, LDA

Reporting

Reporting conventions: Combination of discussion and summaries (tables and figures)

Source: Author's own development

4. DATA ANALYSIS

4.1 Number of Document Per Topic

Figure 2. Number of Document Per Topic

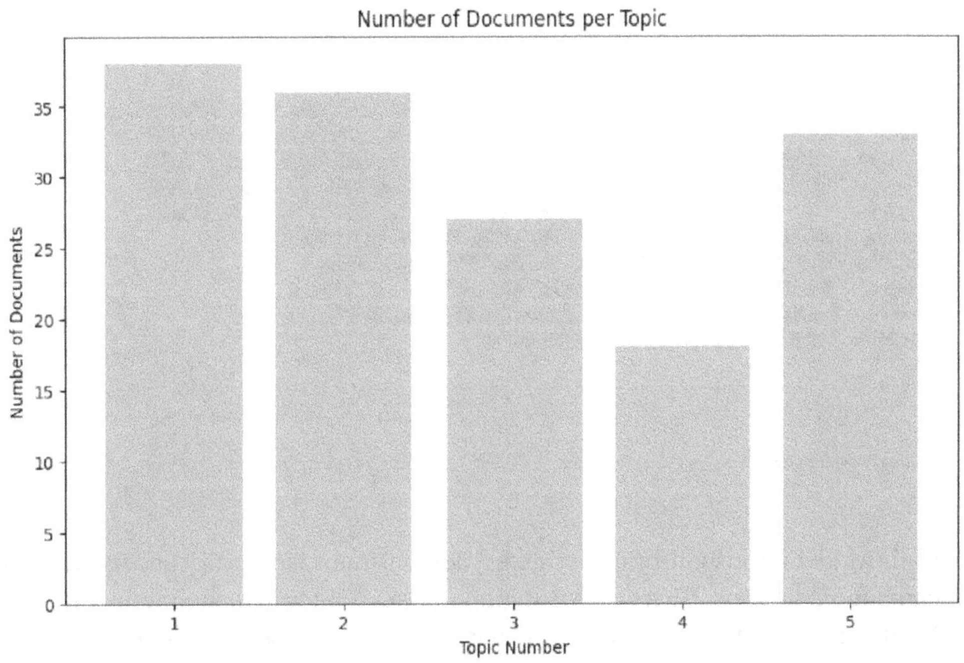

Source: Author's own development

The bar chart in the figure 2 depicts the allocation of papers among several research areas. The x-axis denotes subject numbers, whilst the y-axis signifies the quantity of papers linked to each topic. The disparity in bar heights indicates that certain areas have garnered greater academic focus than others. The graphic reveals that Topic 1 and Topic 2 possess the greatest quantity of documents, signifying that these research domains are the most extensively investigated within the dataset. Topics 3 and 5 possess a significant quantity of documents, albeit slightly fewer. Topic 4 contains the fewest documents, indicating it is a less-explored domain in the literature. This analysis offers insight into the research focus and deficiencies within the field. Subjects with a greater volume of documents indicate popular and well-studied fields, whereas those with fewer documents may signify nascent or inadequately investigated research avenues. These findings can inform future research by pinpointing deficiencies in the literature and potential avenues for further exploration.

4.2 LDA Topic Modeling Visualization

Figure 3. LDA Topic Modeling Visualization

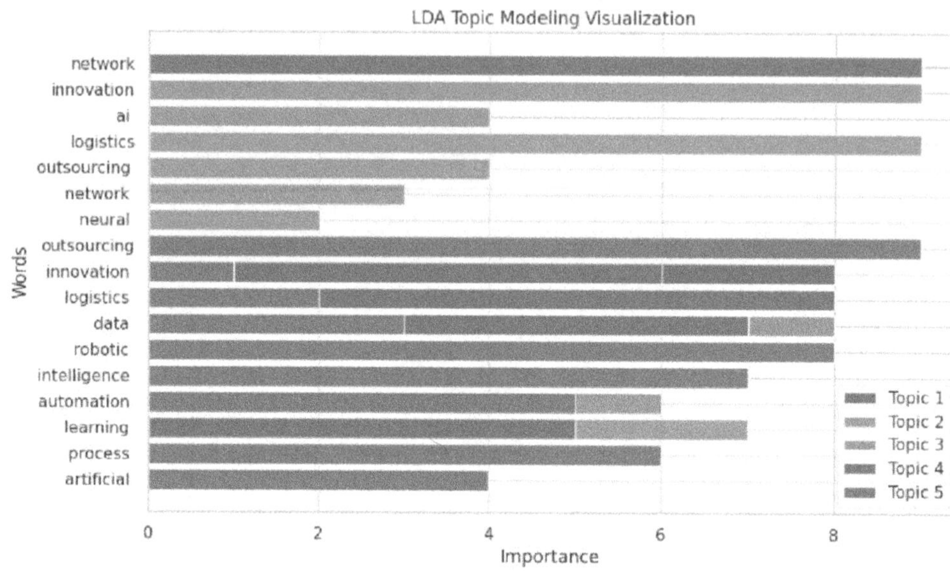

Source: Author's own development

The LDA Topic Modeling Visualization in figure 3 demonstrates the significance of key terms related to various research topics. Latent Dirichlet Allocation (LDA) is a topic modeling method employed to reveal concealed thematic frameworks within a corpus of materials. The x-axis denotes the significance of words, whilst the y-axis enumerates the key terms identified in the investigation. Various colors denote specific subjects, as illustrated in the legend.

The graphic indicates that the terms "artificial," "process," "automation," "intelligence," and "robotic" are highly pertinent to Topic 5, implying a significant emphasis on AI-driven automation. Topic 2 is defined by phrases like "outsourcing" and "logistics," signifying a study focus on company operations and supply chain management. Topic 3, encompassing phrases such as "AI" and "innovation," indicates an emphasis on technical progress. Topic 4 encompasses "learning" and "data," corresponding with machine learning and data-centric research. Topic 1 encompasses phrases like "innovation" and "logistics," signifying a convergence of commercial tactics and nascent technologies. This analysis offers significant insights into the principal themes and research trajectories within the discipline. The allocation of terminology among subjects underscores the interdisciplinary character of AI, automation, and business processes. The results can assist researchers in pinpointing prevailing fields of study and identifying potential deficiencies in the literature, hence directing future research initiatives.

4.3 Year wise Distribution of LDA Topics

Figure 4. Year wise Distribution of LDA Topics

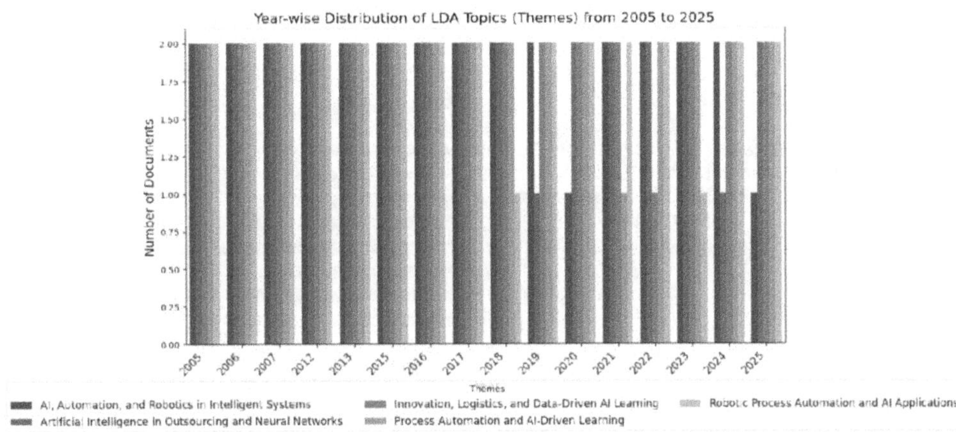

Source: Author's own development

The bar chart (Figure 4) depicts the annual distribution of Latent Dirichlet Allocation (LDA) topics from 2005 to 2025, highlighting subject trends in AI and automation research. Each bar denotes the quantity of documents linked to particular themes for a specified year, with five distinct themes identified: (1) AI, Automation, and Robotics in Intelligent Systems, (2) Artificial Intelligence in Outsourcing and Neural Networks, (3) Innovation, Logistics, and Data-Driven AI Learning, (4) Process Automation and AI-Driven Learning, and (5) Robotic Process Automation and AI Applications. The bars are color-coded to distinguish between these themes, emphasizing their relative significance across time. The data indicates a uniform publishing frequency across the years, with each theme equally represented, reflecting persistent academic and industrial interest in AI and automation. This bibliometric analysis provides insights into research trajectories, illustrating the evolution of AI-related studies while preserving equilibrium among various subfields. It also emphasizes the multidisciplinary character of AI applications in fields such as logistics, robotics, neural networks, and intelligent systems.

4.4 Most Relevant Sources

Figure 5. Most Relevant Sources

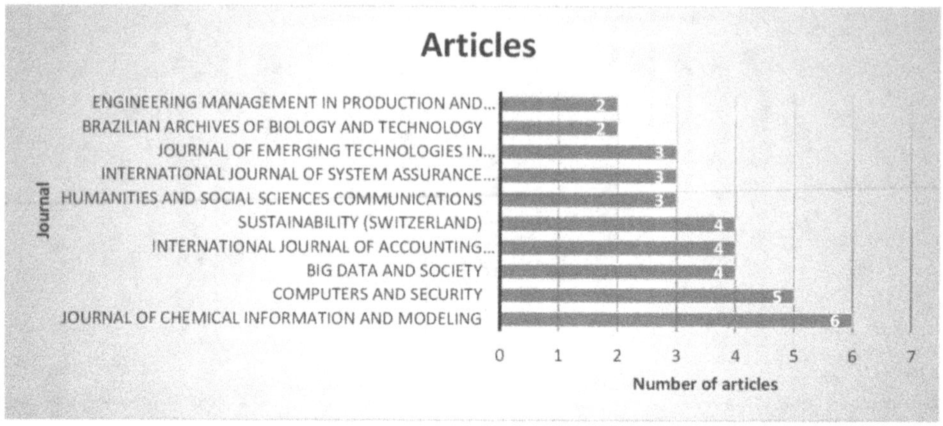

Source: Author's own development

The bar graph (Figure 5) illustrates the allocation of papers among different academic journals, emphasizing the publishing frequency in each. The Journal of Chemical Information and Modeling has the greatest article count with six, followed by Computers and Security with five articles. Big Data and Society, International Journal of Accounting Information Systems, and Sustainability (Switzerland) each published four articles, whereas Humanities and Social Sciences Communications, International Journal of System Assurance, and Journal of Emerging Technologies in Accounting each published three articles. The Brazilian Archives of Biology and Technology and Engineering Management in Production and Services both have the lowest count, with merely 2 articles. This bibliometric analysis elucidates the distribution of research across many fields, highlighting the significance of studies linked to AI, cybersecurity, sustainability, and accounting in recent academic publications. The disparity in publication counts indicates the varying degrees of interest and significance of certain subjects within the purview of each magazine.

4.5 Country Scientific Production

Figure 6. Country Scientific Production

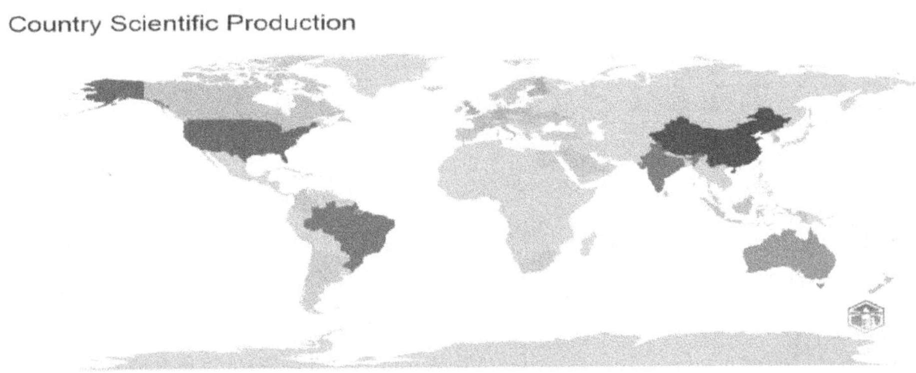

Source: Author's own development

The world map in the above Figure 6 is "Country Scientific Production" illustrates the international research production, emphasizing the geographical distribution of scientific contributions. The map employs a color gradient to illustrate fluctuations in publication volume, with darker hues indicating greater scientific output. Countries like China, the United States, and India are significant providers, but African regions and smaller nations demonstrate diminished research output. This graphic is essential for comprehending worldwide inequalities in knowledge creation and recognizing nascent research centers. Bibliometric data for these maps is frequently sourced from Scopus, which monitors publication counts, citation impact, and collaborative research patterns. Through the analysis of these patterns, researchers and governments may evaluate the growth trajectories of scientific disciplines, allocate funds judiciously, and promote international research cooperation. This analysis highlights the changing dynamics of global scientific influence, illustrating the contributions of various countries to AI, automation, and other technical progressions. Incorporating these insights with thematic trends in AI research, exemplified by Latent Dirichlet Allocation (LDA) topic modeling, can augment our comprehension of the temporal evolution of scientific focus areas while preserving interdisciplinary significance across domains such as automation, neural networks, and intelligent systems.

4.6 Word Cloud

Figure 7. Word Cloud

Source: Author's own development

The word cloud (Figure 7) underscores the principal topics and trends within the domains of Artificial Intelligence (AI), automation, and business process management. The key phrases, including "Artificial Intelligence," "process automation," "Machine Learning," "Robotic Process Automation (RPA)," and "outsourcing," suggest that a substantial segment of the research concentrates on AI-driven automation and its applications in business operations. The inclusion of terminology such as "financial performance," "accounting," "management," "supply chain," and "logistics" indicates a robust multidisciplinary framework, wherein AI and automation are being assimilated across diverse sectors, including finance, logistics, and corporate management. Furthermore, terms like "Blockchain," "Cloud computing," "big data," "neural network," and "deep learning" signify the technical progress facilitating enhanced decision-making and operational efficiencies. The presence of phrases like as "audit," "tax," "privacy," and "education" indicates an increasing focus on the regulatory, compliance, and scholarly dimensions of AI implementation. The word cloud offers a thorough summary of the principal research domains, nascent technologies, and commercial ramifications of AI and automation, rendering it an essential instrument for comprehending contemporary trends and prospective trajectories in this sector.

5. DISCUSSION

Artificial Intelligence (AI) has become a disruptive force in various industries, transforming processes, improving efficiency, and facilitating automation to unprecedented degrees. The study emphasizes AI's significant influence on industries including healthcare, banking, manufacturing, and education, where its incorporation has resulted in enhanced productivity, less errors, and superior decision-making. Nonetheless, despite these benefits, substantial hurdles remain, especially concerning ethical issues, data privacy, and bias in AI models. The ethical implications of AI are a persistent focus in the paper, highlighting how biased algorithms might result in inequitable decision-making, particularly in crucial domains such as employment, finance, and law enforcement. Confronting these difficulties necessitates proactive governance, ethical AI design, and transparent algorithmic methodologies. A significant topic of discourse is the swift progression of AI technologies, especially in machine learning and deep learning. These advancements have facilitated the creation of advanced models proficient in executing intricate cognitive tasks, like natural language processing and computer vision, with exceptional accuracy. As AI capabilities advance, worries about responsibility, security, and regulatory supervision intensify. Autonomous technologies, like self-driving vehicles and AI-driven robotics, present significant hazards, requiring rigorous testing and safety protocols. Moreover, the expanding use of AI in corporate functions, including robotic process automation (RPA) and supply chain management, illustrates its capacity to optimize workflows and diminish operational expenses. Nonetheless, the displacement of human labor caused by automation is a significant societal issue, necessitating adaptable workforce policies and skill development initiatives to alleviate economic disruptions.

The discourse also examines the ramifications of AI in data management and analytics. The capacity of AI to process and analyze extensive data sets has proven essential in facilitating data-driven decision-making within organizations. This dependence on data engenders significant privacy issues, especially concerning user consent, data security, and the possible exploitation of personal information. The research highlights the imperative of formulating stringent data protection regulations and ethical standards to guarantee responsible AI implementation. The interdisciplinary character of AI research underscores the necessity for collaboration among technical specialists, policymakers, and social scientists to design AI systems that conform to human values and societal requirements.

6. CONCLUSION

The research indicates that AI is a transformative technology with significant potential to redefine industries, enhance operations, and elevate human existence. Nevertheless, despite its transformational advantages, the deployment of AI necessitates careful consideration of the ethical, legal, and social concerns it poses. Although AI markedly improves automation and efficiency, its use requires regulation to mitigate biases, protect privacy, and guarantee equitable decision-making. The study underscores the significance of ethical AI governance, emphasizing openness, accountability, and fairness to cultivate confidence in AI systems. Furthermore, the finding underscores the imperative for ongoing progress in AI education and workforce adjustment. As AI becomes more integrated into diverse businesses, people must possess the requisite abilities to manage the changing technological landscape. Investing in AI literacy programs, reskilling initiatives, and interdisciplinary research collaborations is essential for optimizing AI's advantages and minimizing its potential hazards. Moreover, regulatory frameworks must progress alongside AI innovations to guarantee safe utilization and alleviate unforeseen repercussions. Moreover, the study emphasizes the significance of human supervision in AI-facilitated decision-making. Although AI models can process data with remarkable speed and precision, they must be subjected to human assessment to mitigate biases and guarantee ethical adherence. The study emphasizes that a balanced strategy—utilizing AI's capabilities while ensuring human-centered supervision—will be crucial in maximizing the potential of AI technology.

7. FINDINGS

The research reveals multiple significant discoveries concerning the effects and obstacles of AI. A key discovery is that AI markedly improves productivity across sectors by automating repetitive work, minimizing human error, and refining decision-making processes. AI-driven solutions have proven effective in enhancing accuracy and optimizing operations across various domains, including healthcare diagnostics and financial risk assessment. Nonetheless, the study highlights issues pertaining to ethical challenges and algorithmic biases, especially in the contexts of hiring practices, criminal justice systems, and financial services. A crucial discovery is that AI's dependence on extensive datasets generates substantial data privacy issues. The report emphasizes that AI systems frequently necessitate substantial personal and organizational data to operate well, rendering them vulnerable to security breaches and privacy infringements. Consequently, there is an increasing requirement for legal frameworks to safeguard user data and establish ethical norms for AI utilization. The research indicates that the swift progress of AI is transforming the employment market, resulting in both job displacement and the emergence of new opportunities. Although automation poses a risk to some conventional positions, it simultaneously creates new opportunities in AI development, data science, and digital transformation. Thus, the study underscores the necessity for educational and vocational training initiatives to facilitate persons' transfer into AI-driven sectors. Furthermore, the results indicate that AI is integral to autonomous systems, encompassing robotics, self-driving vehicles, and intelligent infrastructure. Although these advances offer potential benefits in efficiency and safety, they also introduce considerable regulatory and safety issues. The research advocates for more stringent testing processes and legislative frameworks to guarantee the secure incorporation of AI-driven autonomous systems into society.

8. FUTURE IMPLICATIONS

As artificial intelligence advances, several future ramifications must be contemplated to guarantee its responsible and effective use. The establishment of more robust ethical and regulatory frameworks is paramount. Governments and organizations must collaborate to establish policies that foster ethical AI practices, guaranteeing justice, transparency, and accountability in AI-driven decision-making. In the absence of sufficient rules, AI may perpetuate biases, violate privacy, and result in unintended societal repercussions. A further notable impact is the growing necessity for investment in AI education and workforce development. The demand for AI knowledge will persist, requiring the integration of AI-related curricula in educational institutions and vocational training programs. Policymakers and corporate leaders must endorse efforts that provide individuals with the essential skills to succeed in an AI-driven economy. Furthermore, organizations ought to emphasize staff reskilling initiatives to facilitate workers' move into positions that enhance AI technologies rather than contend with them. The research underscores the necessity for improvements in AI security and privacy protocols. As AI systems increasingly integrate into vital sectors, establishing effective cybersecurity measures will be crucial to avert data breaches and harmful use. Subsequent research ought to concentrate on creating AI models that emphasize user privacy while preserving superior performance capabilities. Moreover, the amalgamation of AI with nascent technologies, including blockchain and quantum computing, has the potential to augment security measures and bolster data integrity.

A significant implication is the function of AI in sustainability and environmental effects. Artificial intelligence possesses the capacity to enhance sustainable development through the optimization of energy usage, the augmentation of supply chain efficiency, and the promotion of smart city projects. Future research and funding should investigate how AI might be utilized to tackle global concerns, such as climate change, resource management, and waste reduction. As AI progresses, cultivating public trust and acceptance will be essential. Transparency in AI decision-making, user education, and ethical AI design will be crucial in positioning AI as an instrument for beneficial society change rather than a disruptive entity. Cooperative initiatives of governments, corporate leaders, and research institutions will be crucial in determining the future of AI to ensure it serves humanity while minimizing its threats.

In summary, AI possesses significant potential to enhance creativity and efficiency in multiple fields; but its deployment must be governed by ethical principles, regulatory supervision, and a dedication to human welfare. The trajectory of AI will be dictated by society's ability to confront its challenges while capitalizing on its opportunities. With responsible development and proactive control, AI can operate as a significant catalyst for advancement, creating a future that is technologically sophisticated and ethically robust.

REFERENCES

Abbas, S. M., Liu, Z., & Khushnood, M. (2023). When Human Meets Technology: Unlocking Hybrid Intelligence Role in Breakthrough Innovation Engagement via Self-Extension and Social Intelligence. *Journal of Computer Information Systems*, *63*(5), 1183–1200. DOI: 10.1080/08874417.2022.2139781

Ancarani, A., Di Mauro, C., & Mascali, F. (2019). Backshoring strategy and the adoption of Industry 4.0: Evidence from Europe. *Journal of World Business*, *54*(4), 360–371. DOI: 10.1016/j.jwb.2019.04.003

Boloy, R. A. M., da Cunha Reis, A., Rios, E. M., de Araújo Santos Martins, J., Soares, L. O., de Sá Machado, V. A., & de Moraes, D. R. (2021). Waste-to-Energy Technologies Towards Circular Economy: A Systematic Literature Review and Bibliometric Analysis. *Water, Air, and Soil Pollution*, *232*(7), 1–25. DOI: 10.1007/s11270-021-05224-x

Brooks, R. A. (1991). Intelligence without representation. In Artificial Intelligence (Vol. 47). DOI: 10.1016/0004-3702(91)90053-M

Budhwar, P., Malik, A., De Silva, M. T. T., & Thevisuthan, P. (2022). Artificial intelligence–challenges and opportunities for international HRM: a review and research agenda. In International Journal of Human Resource Management (Vol. 33, Issue 6, pp. 1065–1097). Routledge. https://doi.org/DOI: 10.1080/09585192.2022.2035161

Burnett, J. R., & Lisk, T. C. (2019). The Future of Employee Engagement: Real-Time Monitoring and Digital Tools for Engaging a Workforce. *International Studies of Management & Organization*, *49*(1), 108–119. DOI: 10.1080/00208825.2019.1565097

Cappelli, P., Tambe, P., & Yakubovich, V. (2018). Artificial Intelligence in Human Resources Management: Challenges and a Path Forward. SSRN Electronic Journal. https://doi.org/DOI: 10.2139/ssrn.3263878

Caputo, F., Cillo, V., Candelo, E., & Liu, Y. (2019). Innovating through digital revolution: The role of soft skills and Big Data in increasing firm performance. *Management Decision*, *57*(8), 2032–2051. DOI: 10.1108/MD-07-2018-0833

Carter, D. (2018). How real is the impact of artificial intelligence? The business information survey 2018. *Business Information Review*, *35*(3), 99–115. DOI: 10.1177/0266382118790150

Cascio, W. F., & Montealegre, R. (2016). How Technology Is Changing Work and Organizations. In Annual Review of Organizational Psychology and Organizational Behavior (Vol. 3, pp. 349–375). Annual Reviews Inc. https://doi.org/DOI: 10.1146/annurev-orgpsych-041015-062352

Chen, H., Chiang, R. H. L., Storey, V. C., Lindner, C. H., & Robinson, J. M. (2012). Business Intelligence and Analytics: From Big Data to Big Impact Quarterly-Business Intelligence and Analytics: From Big Data to Big Impact. In Source. *Management Information Systems Quarterly*, *36*(4), 1165. DOI: 10.2307/41703503

Cheng, M. M., & Hackett, R. D. (2021). A critical review of algorithms in HRM: Definition, theory, and practice. *Human Resource Management Review*, *31*(1), 100698. Advance online publication. DOI: 10.1016/j.hrmr.2019.100698

Cubric, M. (2020). Drivers, barriers and social considerations for AI adoption in business and management: A tertiary study. *Technology in Society*, *62*, 101257. Advance online publication. DOI: 10.1016/j.techsoc.2020.101257

Davenport, T. H. (2018). From analytics to artificial intelligence. *Journal of Business Analytics*, *1*(2), 73–80. DOI: 10.1080/2573234X.2018.1543535

Dibbern, J., Goles, T., Hirschheim, R., & Jayatilaka, B. (2004). Information systems outsourcing: A survey and analysis of the literature. *ACM Computing Surveys*, *35*(4), 321–350.

Doh, J. P., Bunyaratavej, K., & Hahn, E. D. (2009). Separable but not equal: The location determinants of discrete services offshoring activities. *Journal of International Business Studies*, *40*(6), 926–943. DOI: 10.1057/jibs.2008.89

Dwivedi, Y. K., Hughes, L., Ismagilova, E., Aarts, G., Coombs, C., Crick, T., Duan, Y., Dwivedi, R., Edwards, J., Eirug, A., Galanos, V., Ilavarasan, P. V., Janssen, M., Jones, P., Kar, A. K., Kizgin, H., Kronemann, B., Lal, B., Lucini, B., & Williams, M. D. (2021). Artificial Intelligence (AI): Multidisciplinary perspectives on emerging challenges, opportunities, and agenda for research, practice and policy. *International Journal of Information Management*, *57*, 101994. Advance online publication. DOI: 10.1016/j.ijinfomgt.2019.08.002

Ererdi, C., Nurgabdeshov, A., Kozhakhmet, S., Rofcanin, Y., & Demirbag, M. (2022). International HRM in the context of uncertainty and crisis: A systematic review of literature (2000–2018). *International Journal of Human Resource Management*, *33*(12), 2503–2540. DOI: 10.1080/09585192.2020.1863247

Fenwick, A., Molnar, G., & Frangos, P. (2024). The critical role of HRM in AI-driven digital transformation: A paradigm shift to enable firms to move from AI implementation to human-centric adoption. *Discover Artificial Intelligence*, *4*(1), 34. DOI: 10.1007/s44163-024-00125-4

Forman, C., King, J. L., & Lyytinen, K. (2014). Special section introduction-Information, technology, and the changing nature of work. *Information Systems Research*, *25*(4), 789–795. DOI: 10.1287/isre.2014.0551

Garcia-Arroyo, J., & Osca, A. (2021). Big data contributions to human resource management: A systematic review. *International Journal of Human Resource Management*, *32*(20), 4337–4362. DOI: 10.1080/09585192.2019.1674357

Guo, Y. (2018). A conceptual artificial intelligence application framework in human resource management. In ICEB.

Hemphill, T. A. (2016). Responsible innovation in industry: A cautionary note on corporate social responsibility. *Journal of Responsible Innovation*, *3*(1), 81–87. DOI: 10.1080/23299460.2016.1178896

Hirschheim, R., & Dibbern, J. (2017). *Information systems outsourcing: Towards sustainable business value*. Springer.

Huang, M. J., Tsou, Y. L., & Lee, S. C. (2006). Integrating fuzzy data mining and fuzzy artificial neural networks for discovering implicit knowledge. *Knowledge-Based Systems*, *19*(6), 396–403. DOI: 10.1016/j.knosys.2006.04.003

Jia, Q., Guo, Y., Li, R., Li, Y., & Chen, Y. (2018). Association for Information Systems AIS Electronic Library (AISeL) A Conceptual Artificial Intelligence Application Framework in Human Resource Management Recommended Citation "A Conceptual Artificial Intelligence Application Framework in Human Resource Management." https://aisel.aisnet.org/iceb2018/91

Jiménez, A., & Zheng, Y. (2018). Tech hubs, innovation and development. *Information Technology for Development*, *24*(1), 95–118. DOI: 10.1080/02681102.2017.1335282

Kim, S., Wang, Y., & Boon, C. (2021). Sixty years of research on technology and human resource management: Looking back and looking forward. *Human Resource Management*, *60*(1), 229–247. DOI: 10.1002/hrm.22049

King, K. G. (2016). Data Analytics in Human Resources: A Case Study and Critical Review. *Human Resource Development Review*, *15*(4), 487–495. DOI: 10.1177/1534484316675818

Kulkov, I. (2021). The role of artificial intelligence in business transformation: A case of pharmaceutical companies. *Technology in Society*, *66*, 101629. Advance online publication. DOI: 10.1016/j.techsoc.2021.101629

Kumar, M., Jain, A., Mittal, A., Gera, R., Biswal, S. K., Yadav, M., Hung, T. H., & Priya Srivastava, A. (2024). Inclusion of Neural Networks in Higher Education: A Systematic Review and Bibliometric Analysis. *2024 4th International Conference on Innovative Practices in Technology and Management (ICIPTM)*, 1–6. https://doi.org/DOI: 10.1109/ICIPTM59628.2024.10563852

Kumar, M., Yadav, R., Suresh, A. S., Singh, R., Yadav, M., Balodi, A., Vihari, N. S., & Srivastava, A. P. (2023). Mapping AI-Driven Marketing: Review of Field and Directions for Future Research. *2023 2nd International Conference on Futuristic Technologies (INCOFT)*, 1–5. https://doi.org/DOI: 10.1109/INCOFT60753.2023.10425169

Lacity, M. C., Khan, S. A., & Willcocks, L. P. (2009). A review of the IT outsourcing literature: Insights for practice. *The Journal of Strategic Information Systems*, *18*(3), 130–146. DOI: 10.1016/j.jsis.2009.06.002

Lacity, M. C., & Reynolds, P. (2017). Cloud outsourcing: Balancing risks and rewards. *MIS Quarterly Executive*, *16*(3), 153–167.

Lacity, M. C., & Willcocks, L. P. (2014). Business process outsourcing and dynamic innovation. *MIS Quarterly Executive*, *13*(1), 21–33.

Lacity, M. C., & Willcocks, L. P. (2018). Robotic process automation: The next transformation lever for shared services. *Journal of Information Technology*, *33*(3), 201–211.

Luo, X., Tong, S., Fang, Z., & Qu, Z. (2019). Frontiers: Machines vs. humans: The impact of artificial intelligence chatbot disclosure on customer purchases. *Marketing Science*, *38*(6), 937–947. DOI: 10.1287/mksc.2019.1192

Malhan, D. (2021). Probing Anterior of Entrepreneurial Intentions of Youngsters in India, an Analytical Approach. *Academy of Strategic Management Journal*, *20*, 1–10.

Malik, A., Budhwar, P., & Srikanth, N. R. (2020). Gig Economy, 4IR and Artificial Intelligence: Rethinking Strategic HRM. In Human and Technological Resource Management (HTRM): New Insights into Revolution 4.0 (pp. 75–88). Emerald Group Publishing Ltd. https://doi.org/DOI: 10.1108/978-1-83867-223-220201005

Manning, S., Massini, S., & Lewin, A. Y. (2008). A dynamic perspective on next-generation offshoring: The global sourcing of science and engineering talent. *The Academy of Management Perspectives*, *22*(3), 35–54. DOI: 10.5465/amp.2008.34587994

Marler, J. H., & Boudreau, J. W. (2017). An evidence-based review of HR Analytics. *International Journal of Human Resource Management*, *28*(1), 3–26. DOI: 10.1080/09585192.2016.1244699

Marler, J. H., & Fisher, S. L. (2013). An evidence-based review of e-HRM and strategic human resource management. In Human Resource Management Review (Vol. 23, Issue 1, pp. 18–36). https://doi.org/DOI: 10.1016/j.hrmr.2012.06.002

Mignani, S., Huber, S., Tomás, H., Rodrigues, J., & Majoral, J. P. (2016). Why and how have drug discovery strategies in pharma changed? What are the new mindsets? In Drug Discovery Today (Vol. 21, Issue 2, pp. 239–249). Elsevier Ltd. https://doi.org/DOI: 10.1016/j.drudis.2015.09.007

Min, H. (2010). Artificial intelligence in supply chain management: Theory and applications. *International Journal of Logistics*, *13*(1), 13–39. DOI: 10.1080/13675560902736537

Moher, D., Liberati, A., Tetzlaff, J., & Altman, D. G.PRISMA Group. (2009). Preferred reporting items for systematic reviews and meta-analyses: The PRISMA statement. *BMJ (Clinical Research Ed.)*, *339*(jul21 1), b2535. DOI: 10.1136/bmj.b2535 PMID: 19622551

Moon, C., Lee, J., & Lim, S. (2010). A performance appraisal and promotion ranking system based on fuzzy logic: An implementation case in military organizations. *Applied Soft Computing*, *10*(2), 512–519. DOI: 10.1016/j.asoc.2009.08.035

Mudambi, R., & Tallman, S. (2010). Make, buy, or ally? Theoretical perspectives on knowledge process outsourcing through alliances. *Journal of Management Studies*, *47*(8), 1434–1456. DOI: 10.1111/j.1467-6486.2010.00944.x

Ngai, E. W. T., Xiu, L., & Chau, D. C. K. (2009). Application of data mining techniques in customer relationship management: A literature review and classification. In Expert Systems with Applications (Vol. 36, Issue 2 PART 2, pp. 2592–2602). Elsevier Ltd. https://doi.org/DOI: 10.1016/j.eswa.2008.02.021

Oshri, I., Kotlarsky, J., & Willcocks, L. (2015). *The handbook of global outsourcing and offshoring*. Palgrave Macmillan. DOI: 10.1057/9781137437440

Oswald, F. L., Behrend, T. S., Putka, D. J., & Sinar, E. (2020). Big data in industrial-organizational psychology and human resource management: Forward progress for organizational research and practice. *Annual Review of Organizational Psychology and Organizational Behavior*, *7*(1), 505–533.

Parker, S. K., Van Den Broeck, A., & Holman, D. (2017). Work design influences: A synthesis of multilevel factors that affect the design of jobs. In Academy of Management Annals (Vol. 11, Issue 1, pp. 267–308). Routledge. https://doi.org/DOI: 10.5465/annals.2014.0054

Quinn, J. B., & Hilmer, F. G. (1994). Strategic outsourcing. *Sloan Management Review*, *35*(4), 43–55.

Sexton, R. S., McMurtrey, S., Michalopoulos, J. O., & Smith, A. M. (2005). Employee turnover: A neural network solution. *Computers & Operations Research*, *32*(10), 2635–2651. DOI: 10.1016/j.cor.2004.06.022

Stone, D. L., Deadrick, D. L., Lukaszewski, K. M., & Johnson, R. (2015). The influence of technology on the future of human resource management. *Human Resource Management Review*, *25*(2), 216–231. DOI: 10.1016/j.hrmr.2015.01.002

Strohmeier, S. (2007). Research in e-HRM: Review and implications. *Human Resource Management Review*, *17*(1), 19–37. DOI: 10.1016/j.hrmr.2006.11.002

Strohmeier, S., & Piazza, F. (2013). Domain driven data mining in human resource management: A review of current research. *Expert Systems with Applications*, *40*(7), 2410–2420. DOI: 10.1016/j.eswa.2012.10.059

Strohmeier, S., & Piazza, F. (2015). Artificial intelligence techniques in human resource management—A conceptual exploration. *Intelligent Systems Reference Library*, *87*, 149–172. DOI: 10.1007/978-3-319-17906-3_7

Sushma, M. (2025). Exploring Workplace Dynamics: A Systematic Review and Bibliometric Analysis of Work Stress, Gender Diversity, and Job Satisfaction in Higher Education Institutions. *Journal of Information Systems Engineering & Management*, *10*(5(s)), 786–803. DOI: 10.52783/jisem.v10i5s.772

Tranfield, D., Denyer, D., & Smart, P. (2003). Towards a Methodology for Developing Evidence-Informed Management Knowledge by Means of Systematic Review.

Vrontis, D., Christofi, M., Pereira, V., Tarba, S., Makrides, A., & Trichina, E. (2022). Artificial intelligence, robotics, advanced technologies and human resource management: A systematic review. *International Journal of Human Resource Management*, *33*(6), 1237–1266. DOI: 10.1080/09585192.2020.1871398

Willcocks, L. P. (2020). Future outsourcing trends: Automation, AI, and digital transformation. *Journal of Information Technology*, *35*(4), 276–289.

Willcocks, L. P., & Cullen, S. (2013). *The outsourcing enterprise: From cost management to collaborative innovation*. Palgrave Macmillan.

Willcocks, L. P., & Lacity, M. C. (2012). *The new IT outsourcing landscape: From innovation to cloud computing*. Palgrave Macmillan. DOI: 10.1057/9781137012296

Willcocks, L. P., Lacity, M. C., & Craig, A. (2015). The impact of robotic process automation on outsourcing. *The Journal of Strategic Information Systems*, *24*(3), 209–222.

Yadav, R., Naim, I., Kumar, M., Misra, S., Dewasiri, N. J., Rathnasiri, M. S. H., ... & Vihari, N. S. (2023, December). An exploratory study to identify effects of Blockchain technology on organizational change and practices. In 2023 IEEE Technology & Engineering Management Conference-Asia Pacific (TEMSCON-ASPAC) (pp. 1-8). IEEE.

Chapter 22
Transformational HR for Generation Z:
Gig Economy Efficiency and Adaptability

Shivani Dhand
https://orcid.org/0000-0002-4809-1365
Lovely Professional University, India

Rimpa Kar
https://orcid.org/0009-0004-1184-5276
Lovely Professional University, India

Avtar Singh
https://orcid.org/0000-0002-9592-9319
Lovely Professional University, India

Ujjwal Kumar Pathak
https://orcid.org/0000-0003-3865-044X
Amity University, Gwalior, India

Aayushi Pandey
https://orcid.org/0000-0001-7584-0520
Lovely Professional University, India

Jeayaram Subramanian
O.P. Jindal Global University, India

Sandeep Kaur Randhawa
https://orcid.org/0009-0001-7436-7943
Conestoga College Intitute of Technology and Advanced Learning, Canada

ABSTRACT

The contemporary workforce is being radically transformed by the emergence of Generation Z and the explosive growth of the gig economy. Gen Z differs from other generations in valuing flexibility, autonomy, and purposeful work more than the long-term employment model. Their technological literacy has redefined work standards, with freelancing, temporary contracts, and remote work becoming the new norm. While this trend is beneficial in the sense that it provides work-life balance and diversified sources of income, it has challenges in employment security, mental well-being, and career advancement. HR practitioners need to shift by embracing innovation, technology, and flexibility. The old model of employment does not suit Gen Z's needs anymore, calling for dynamic practices such as on-demand learning, customized benefits, and AI-enabled talent management. Yet, aligning digital evolution with a people-centric strategy continues to be the key.

DOI: 10.4018/979-8-3373-1270-5.ch022

INTRODUCTION

The workplace is also experiencing a seismic shift, fuelled by rapid technology changes, evolving social realities, and changed workforce expectations. Spearheading this revolution is Generation Z (Gen Z), a generation redefining career aspirations and work-life balance in unprecedented forms. Unlike their predecessors, Gen Z employees are free from conventional linear career tracks focusing on long-term security and hierarchical advancement. Instead, they are embracing the gig economy—a platform based on flexibility, task-based work, and online connectivity. This shift is not a trend but a profound metamorphosis in how work is structured and valued. For Human Resource (HR) practitioners, this means rewriting traditional frameworks and building resilient plans that address the requirements of this evolving workforce. Born during the mid-1990s and early 2010s, Gen Z grew up under a world of digital innovation, financial insecurity, and growing emphasis on social responsibility. Gen Z is a generation of digital natives who have seamlessly integrated technology into every sphere of life, be it communication, learning, or even working. With all information at their fingertips, this generation values efficacy, transparency, and self-governance. They are less content with rigid corporate structures and more attracted to work that is meaningful to their values, permits them to innovate, and offers continuous learning. As a result, traditional 9-to-5 employment with secure jobs and long-term contracts is becoming less attractive to them, resulting in an exponential rise in gig work, freelancing, and remote working.

The gig economy, once considered a non-conventional form of employment, is now a mainstream workforce trend. The likes of Fiverr, Upwork, and Toptal have provided an easier opportunity than ever for a professional to engage in temporary work, selling their services to various employers instead of one firm. Companies too are finding the benefits of employing gig workers—they gain access to specialized skills, reduce overhead costs, and have flexibility in staff. But with this change come new challenges that must be addressed by HR professionals. How do companies recruit, retain, and motivate best Gen Z talent with declining job loyalty? What is the role of HR in offering gig workers fair compensation, career development opportunities, and access to mental wellbeing resources? All these are some of the core questions at the center of HR's evolving role in the digital technology era.

Gen Z appreciates autonomy and work-life blending, with a preference for work that fits into their lifestyle instead of compartmentalizing work and personal life. They prefer experiences over material comfort, with work that enables travel, career exploration, and ongoing learning. HR leaders need to create policies that enable flexibility, telecommuting, and non-linear career progression. Organizations that fail to accommodate these preferences will lose best talent to more flexible and innovative rivals.

Gen Z's approach to work is also driven by purpose-based work. This generation is highly conscious of problems in the world such as climate change, social justice, and ethics in business. They are not just looking for a pay check; they want to work for companies that share their own values and contribute positively. HR professionals therefore must go beyond the conventional recruitment processes and create employer brands that promote corporate social responsibility (CSR), sustainability, and ethical leadership. It has been documented that emotionally intelligent leadership correlates with improved outcomes in various organizational metrics, including employee satisfaction, engagement, and productivity (Feather, 2009;, Koutsioumpa, 2023). Companies that can integrate these elements into the work culture will be able to attract and retain Gen Z employees searching for purpose as much as profit.

Technology, such as AI, machine learning, and data analytics, is essential to the future of HR in the gig economy. Gen Z expects digital experiences, from AI-driven hiring to virtual communication tools. HR needs to balance automation and personalization so that technology amplifies, and does not displace, the human touch in workforce management.

Upskilling and ongoing learning are also the required components of HR's new role within the gig economy. The technology's fast-forward character renders expertise outdated within years, or even months. Gen Z employees are highly aware of this fact and deliberately seek out lifelong learning experiences. They are not attracted to the typical corporate training sessions, but to micro-learning modules, digital certifications, and peer-to-peer mentorship programs that are actionable and flexible. HR leaders therefore have to invest in upskilling initiatives that meet this demand so that gig workers can have access to the tools they need to stay relevant in an increasingly changing job market.

Though the gig economy offers great opportunities, it also presents significant challenges with regard to job security, financial security, and mental health. In contrast to traditional employees, gig workers don't receive traditional benefits such as health insurance, paid leave, or retirement plans. Moreover, algorithmic management commonly employed by gig platforms exacerbates these challenges. This approach can lead to vague operational parameters, where workers find it difficult to understand how their performance is evaluated and compensated, leading to feelings of instability and stress (Shanshan & Liu, 2024). To enable Gen Z in the gig economy, HR needs to provide personalized benefits, create psychological safety, and enable mental wellness. Old ways of measuring performance are obsolete; HR needs to prioritize impact, innovation, and adaptability. Professional development must be fluid, with opportunities in leadership and skills. The next-generation workforce will be hybrid, comprising gig workers and full-timers. HR needs to develop inclusive cultures, open policies, and collaboration by embracing digital transformation, well-being, and lifelong learning in order to attract top talent and enable innovation.

THE GIG ECONOMY AS THE CURRENT NORM

The Transition from Conventional Employment to Gig Work

The character of work has dramatically changed over the last ten years, with the gig economy becoming the new standard instead of a substitute employment paradigm. The conventional idea of long-term employment, where workers would commit decades to one firm in return for job security, regular income, and benefits, has become less appealing, particularly to Generation Z and Millennials. Conversely, the gig economy provides flexibility, independence, and diversification of income, which is an attractive option for those who value work-life balance and self-development over corporate security. The gig economy represents a significant shift from traditional employment structures, where work is typically characterized by long-term, stable contracts. Instead, it fosters an environment where individuals engage in short-term, task-based roles enabled by digital platforms. This transformation requires HRM to continuously evolve to address the unique challenges posed, including legal compliance, talent acquisition, and performance management specific to gig workers (Jayakarthika et al., 2024; Joshi et al., 2024).

This transformation is not taking place in a vacuum. It is a reaction to technological changes, economic instability, and changing expectations of the workforce. The emergence of online platforms such as Uber, Upwork, Fiverr, and TaskRabbit has transformed the manner in which individuals access work, with gig opportunities now more accessible than ever before. With a smartphone and internet connection, employees can now access projects from anywhere in the globe, eliminating conventional employment barriers. The fragmented nature of gig work makes it challenging for workers to connect and advocate for their rights collectively. The lack of a cohesive community further compounds the difficulties workers face in addressing grievances or advocating for better working conditions (Bunders & Akkerman, 2022). Businesses are recruiting gig workers to lower their expenses, streamline processes, and keep pace with changing markets without permanent job offers. Though the gig economy provides the benefit of flexibility, it has some problems such as insecurity in employment, no benefits, economic instability, and extreme competition. Gig workers are deprived of health coverage provided by their employers, pension, and legal protections and thus remain at the mercy of changes in the economy. In spite of these disadvantages, the gig economy keeps expanding, with most believing its advantages are greater than the disadvantages. It is crucial for workers, businesses, and policymakers to navigate this change, as it will determine the future of work.

The Rise of Independent Work: Why People Are Turning to Gigs Over Jobs

The increasing demand for gig employment is not just a fad—it is an adaptation to the new economic, technological, and societal environment. Perhaps one of the most fundamental explanations for this trend is the need for greater flexibility. In contrast to the typical job, gig employment provides workers with the ability to create their own schedules, pick their own projects, and work from anywhere. This freedom is especially attractive to individuals who desire to work at several different things, provide for their families, or explore the world while still making a living. Liu and Renzy underscore this issue by highlighting how immigrant workers in the gig economy experience even lower job quality and reduced benefits, reflecting a double disadvantage that intensifies job insecurity and financial instability (Liu & Renzy, 2025).

The gig economy provides employees with financial autonomy through diversification of earnings from various projects, minimizing dependency on one employer. It appeals to entrepreneurial personalities who can develop businesses, control their own fees, and market themselves. The internet, artificial intelligence, and automation further give gig workers an upper hand through global networking and continuous upskilling. Businesses gain by lowering overheads, tapping global talent, and expanding operations without long-term obligations. Startups and big businesses alike depend on gig workers for specialized skills and to handle peak workloads effectively.

The Disadvantages of Gig Work: Challenges and Reality of the New Workforce Model

Although gig work has numerous advantages, it is not without major challenges, mostly financial instability. Unlike permanent employees with fixed salaries, gig workers have irregular earnings, which makes it hard to plan financially. Work is irregular, and payment depends on the completion of a project, leading to uncertain cash flow. Most gig workers are subjected to delayed or non-payments and do not have a financial cushion, and they are compelled to keep looking for new assignments to survive. The gig economy is transforming the old model of employment, but it also generates insecure working conditions for most workers. One primary disadvantage of gig work is the lack of job security and the absence of traditional employment benefits such as health insurance and paid leave. This lack of safety nets leaves workers vulnerable to economic instability, especially in times of crisis. According to Reynolds and Kincaid, gig platforms often create conditions that manipulate the market to exert control over workers, obscuring the necessity of gig work to supplement low wages or insufficient employment in the mainstream labour market (Reynolds et al., 2024).

There is no security of employment, and no benefits are another major disadvantage of working on a gig basis. Traditional full-time workers usually get healthcare insurance, paid time off, retirement schemes, and other benefits, whereas the gig workers need to pay for these themselves. This can especially be problematic during medical emergencies, economic recessions, or personal crises, where gig workers lack employer-provided support. Moreover, there is no legal provision for job security for gig workers, so they can get denied work opportunities at any moment without notification or severance pay. Social isolation is another major drawback faced by gig workers, who often perform tasks in isolation without the support networks found in traditional workplaces. This condition can foster feelings of loneliness and disconnection, negatively impacting mental health and work satisfaction (Johan et al., 2022). The regulatory landscape surrounding gig work adds another layer of disadvantage. As noted by Au-Yeung et al., weak government regulation leaves gig workers without essential employment protections, such as unemployment benefits and proper compensation for injuries incurred during work (Au-Yeung et al., 2024).

The Gig Economy and the Role of Businesses and HR in Supporting It

As gig work gains prominence, HR professionals need to evolve by bringing gig workers into workforce planning. This involves reframing recruitment, compensation, engagement, and planning to be fair and business-savvy. Organizations can provide fair compensation, clear payment terms, and competitive pay, as well as financial planning tools, insurance, and wellness programs to help gig workers achieve financial stability. Creating a culture of inclusion that respects gig workers is important. Including them in team meetings, recognizing their contributions, and providing professional growth opportunities can establish belonging. Hiring based on skills, rather than education, can also be done by HR. Many companies hire gig workers based on skills rather than education. Offering continuous learning and mentorship can assist gig workers in growing professionally.

The Gig Economy is Here to Stay

The gig economy is not a passing trend anymore—it has become a fundamental change in work patterns. With both opportunities and challenges, what is certain is that flexibility, autonomy, and digitalization have made gigging the preferred choice for many workers. But, to make the gig economy sustain itself in the long term, companies, HR professionals, and policymakers need to fill the vacuum of job security, equitable payment, and career advancement. By adopting modern workforce approaches, responsible labour practices, and fair policies, firms can design a platform in which gig workers excel alongside full-time employees. Work is future-friendly, globalized, and driven by expertise, and firms embracing this phenomenon are the ones who will excel in the dynamic jobs landscape.

Addressing the Gen z's work mentality

With the changing world of work, Generation Z (born 1997-2012) is entering the workplace with a fundamentally new mindset compared to earlier generations. In contrast to their predecessors, who emphasized job security, hierarchical advancement, and long-term employment, Gen Z focuses on meaningful work, adaptability, mental health, and skill variety. They have grown up in a world characterized by digital innovation, economic uncertainty, social transformation, and remote interconnectivity, which has informed their expectations regarding work and achievement.

Employers, HR executives, and companies are now confronted with an unprecedented challenge and opportunity—comprehending what motivates this generation and how to balance workplace design with their expectations. This chapter examines the fundamental drivers, preferences, and challenges of Gen Z, providing insights into how companies can change to recruit, retain, and engage this workforce successfully.

A Digital-Native Generation: Redefining Work Through Technology

In contrast to any previous generation, Gen Z is the first digitally native workforce. Raised with smartphones, social media, and immediate access to information, they have formed a distinctive learning style, way of communicating, and method of problem-solving. They anticipate workplaces to natively embed technology, from AI-facilitated automation to real-time collaboration software.

Speed and efficiency are not negotiable for Gen Z. They resent bureaucracy, unnecessary paperwork, and old corporate ways that hamper productivity. They want companies that use technology to make quick decisions, offer remote work, and open communication. Companies that continue to use strict 9-to-5 arrangements, too many meetings, and slow hierarchical decision-making might find it difficult to keep them.

In addition, Gen Z is very focused on self-learning and upskilling. In contrast to earlier generations that were dependent on conventional college degrees, Gen Z is convinced of ongoing learning via online channels, certifications, and micro-credentials. They resort to sites such as LinkedIn Learning, Coursera, and YouTube tutorials to learn new skills on demand, and they expect employers to offer on-the-job learning and professional development opportunities instead of old-school training.

Flexibility is the New Money: Unbundling from 9-to-5 Models

If there's one characterizing feature in Gen Z's work ethic, it is their insistence on flexibility. Having witnessed their parents and older millennials work hard on work-life balance, they will not buy into traditional productivity models that value hours worked rather than quality output. In contrast to older generations who related hard work to physical presence in the workplace, Gen Z measures success in terms of output, not hours logged at a desk. This change has compelled companies to rethink their models of work. Several companies have launched hybrid and fully remote jobs, flexible timings, and project-based work to attract Gen Z workers. They appreciate being able to work whenever they're most productive, early morning or late evening, over adhering to conventional schedules.

But flexibility is not only about working remotely; it also applies to career paths and job functions. Gen Z employees do not care about linear career paths. Rather than ascending a corporate ladder in one company, they want a portfolio career—a combination of freelancing, side hustles, passion projects, and regular employment. They want job rotations, cross-functional jobs, and the ability to test different industries instead of being stuck in one job for decades.

Purpose Over Paycheck: The Emergence of Mission-Based Careers

Gen Z is values-driven and looks for employers who share their values, such as climate change, diversity, mental health, and corporate social responsibility. A Deloitte survey discovered more than 60% of Gen Z workers would not work for employers who don't share their values. In order to appeal to this generation, companies need to put purpose ahead of profit, with a focus on sustainability, employee health, and fair labour practices. Gen Z is calling for transparency and will not stand behind brands that perform activism without actual follow-through.

Mental Health and Work-Life Balance: A Non-Negotiable Priority

Gen Z is more outspoken about mental health than any generation before them. Having been raised in a time when anxiety, depression, and burnout are freely talked about, they put mental health at the forefront of their work choices. In contrast to older generations who saw stress as just part of the job, Gen Z is convinced that boundaries need to be set and self-care prioritized over work demands. They look for employers that provide mental health support, wellness benefits, and a culture of psychological safety. Employers that ignore burnout, celebrate overwork, or shame mental health conversations are not able to hold onto Gen Z talent. Firms are now spending on employee assistance programs (EAPs), mental health days, therapy assistance, and wellness programs to address this demand.

Additionally, toxic workplaces are a deal-breaker for Gen Z. They do not hesitate to quit jobs that are not inclusive, fair, and emotionally supportive. Unlike past generations who may tolerate toxic leadership or strict corporate hierarchies, Gen Z is not afraid to speak out against bad practices and demand workplaces where they are respected, valued, and psychologically safe.

Instant Feedback Culture: The Need for Continuous Recognition

Gen Z wants immediate feedback rather than the conventional annual performance reviews, having been brought up in a rapid, digital world. They want continuous communication, constructive feedback, and mentorship instead of waiting for official reviews. Companies with peer reward systems, real-time performance tracking, and mentorship initiatives have experienced greater engagement from Gen Z employees. Gen Z also wants quick career progression, such as well-defined career advancement plans and opportunities for skill development. If such opportunities are not available, they leave work immediately.

Diversity, Inclusion, and Equity: Non-Negotiable Expectations

Gen Z is the most diverse generation to date, and they want their workplaces to be similarly diverse. Previous generations considered diversity a corporate agenda, but Gen Z expects inclusion, equity, and representation as minimums. They are very concerned about gender equity, racial diversity, LGBTQ rights, and just pay practices. Organizations that neglect inclusive recruitment tactics, diverse top leadership, and merit-based advancement frameworks are at a loss for attracting Gen Z workers. In addition, they expect equal possibilities for every single worker, visible pay scales, and accountability with regard to employee policies. A diverse workforce is no longer simply a compliance necessity—for Gen Z, it's a dealbreaker. They enthusiastically endorse businesses that actually do the work toward inclusivity and not those that merely practice tokenism or performative diversity.

The Future of Work is Gen Z-Driven

The old corporate playbook no longer holds for Gen Z. They've rewritten the meaning of work—emphasizing flexibility, purpose, mental wellness, belonging, and skill development over traditional job arrangements. Companies that don't shift with this trend will face high turnover, disengagement, and inability to attract best-in-class talent. To successfully incorporate Gen Z into the working population, businesses need to embrace transformation, revamp work policies, and establish a culture that suits Gen Z's expectations. Work in the future is being shaped by innovation, purpose, and well-being, and companies that understand and adopt these values will succeed in the changing job market.

HR's Role in Enabling Efficiency and Flexibility

Human Resources (HR) has long been considered a key department that takes care of the fundamentals—recruitment, managing benefits, compliance, and employee relations. Yet, in the fast-paced business world of today, HR is not merely an administrative role. It has become a strategic ally that plays a vital role in determining organizational success. As organizations evolve to more flexible, agile work settings, HR is central to creating efficiency and encouraging flexibility, allowing organizations to thrive in a faster-changing, increasingly competitive world.

The adoption of innovative HR strategies that cater to these preferences can enhance organizational appeal and retention rates among Gen Z employees, as they seek environments that promote both career success and personal well-being (Basid & Atmaja, 2022; Jin & Liu-Lastres, 2024). The swift shift towards remote working, digitalization, and people-centric cultures necessitates a profound shift in how HR operates. HR is charged with making the workforce productive, engaged, and resilient to such change. Flexibility in work timing, work place, and team structure, coupled with the requirement for organizational effectiveness, has become the foundation on which contemporary enterprises are established. HR is at the center of executing measures that enable organizations to become more effective, responsive, and able to accommodate various work styles while enhancing overall performance.

Defining Efficiency and Flexibility

In the contemporary workplace, flexibility and efficiency are not catchphrases—they are essential pillars for organizations seeking to stay competitive. Let's take a closer examination of what each of these words means in the context of HR and the workplace:

Efficiency in the workplace is all about maximizing productivity by ensuring that processes, resources, and human capital are utilized in the best manner. HR's intervention in enhancing efficiency is to identify inefficiencies, streamline operations, and ensure that teams are supported and resourced to produce optimal results. Flexibility, however, refers to the freedom to allow workers to control their work schedule, location, and workload. Flexibility enables employees to balance their work and life effectively, diminishing burnout and enhancing job satisfaction. From the provision of working from home arrangements to flexible time arrangements and job sharing, the HR function can play an important role in having a flexible working environment. Additionally, issues related to work schedules and platform dependence can further entrench economic vulnerabilities for gig workers. Many rely on gig platforms for their primary source of income, leading to dissatisfaction when unable to control their work schedules (Reynolds & Kincaid, 2024). Both efficiency and flexibility are dependent on each other and essential to the success of an organization. An efficient workforce can produce the maximum output without undue strain, and a flexible workforce can quickly switch and adjust to change, a major plus in today's world of work.

The Evolving Role of HR in Contemporary Organizations

Historically, HR was mostly focused on transactional activities such as payroll, compliance, and grievance handling. Now, HR has evolved into a strategic force behind organizational success, affecting everything from culture to innovation, productivity, and retention of talent. One of the most significant functions of HR is to ensure that employees can work effectively while having a nimble attitude toward the evolving requirements of their job and life.

HR as a Strategic Partner

HR is no longer merely the "people management" department; it is now a strategic business partner in facilitating business success. This change has transformed HR's role from mere filling of positions and maintaining discipline to a more integrated approach that includes:

Aligning HR practices with business goals to ensure that people are not only filling positions but working towards long-term objectives. Embedding technology to enhance processes, enhance staff engagement, and enable flexibility in how work is performed. Creating and reinforcing a robust organizational culture based on common values, openness, and flexibility while enhancing operational efficiency. HR is also an agent of change in organizations, facilitating employees in adjusting to emerging technologies, work processes, and job functions. Jayakarthika et al. underscore that effective HRM strategies must integrate artificial intelligence and data analytics to improve performance outcomes in such fluid work environments (Jayakarthika et al., 2024). Through driving a culture of ongoing learning and responsiveness, HR can future-proof the workforce.

Facilitating Efficiency Through HR Practices

One of the primary functions of HR is to facilitate efficiency in all facets of the workplace. Efficiency is not about cutting costs; it's about designing systems and processes that enable workers to maximize their time doing high-impact work. The following are some ways HR can facilitate more efficiency:

Talent Acquisition and Optimization

Effective HR starts with the right talent being hired in the right job. Talent acquisition has evolved into a very strategic activity, fuelled by technology and data. HR not only needs to spot the skills gaps but also make sure that the applicants are aligning with the company's value, objective, and culture. The role of HR in fostering a culture of continuous digital transformation is paramount. As organizations strive for agility in the face of rapid technological advancements, they must ensure that their workforce is adept and capable of leveraging new technologies effectively. Studies demonstrate that digital transformation in HR practices pushes for enhanced recruitment processes, expanded training programs focused on digital skills, and innovative employee engagement strategies that resonate with a digitally-savvy workforce (James et al., 2023; Bahiroh & Imron, 2024; Asfahani, 2024). Automated recruitment software and AI-based recruitment platforms simplify the recruitment process, enabling HR teams to rapidly screen high numbers of applications. This saves time-to-hire and allows only the best candidates to be shortlisted. HR also provides employees with the training and development they need to develop their skills, resulting in greater efficiency in daily operations. Moreover, HR's involvement in employee training and development is crucial for responding to the demands instigated by both digital transformation and gig economy dynamics. Continuous learning and reskilling initiatives are essential to equip workers with the competencies needed for success in increasingly digital workplaces (Barišić et al., 2021; Iskandar, 2023).

Simplifying Processes and Eliminating Redundancy

HR can make a big difference in organizational effectiveness by streamlining unnecessary administrative functions and minimizing redundancy. For instance, automating HR functions like payroll, benefits administration, and time tracking enables HR professionals to concentrate on more strategic projects.

Technology like Human Resource Management Systems (HRMS) and Applicant Tracking Systems (ATS) allow HR departments to process large volumes of data and reduce administrative burden. This decreases errors, increases precision, and leads to overall smoother operations in the long run. HR functions also make it easy to automate performance management through the use of continuous feedback and rapid performance reviews so that teams are able to clearly define objectives and track progress more often.

Streamlining Communication and Collaboration

HR is also responsible for facilitating internal communication and ensuring effective teamwork. Communication platforms such as Slack, Microsoft Teams, and project management tools such as Asana or Trello have transformed the way employees communicate, exchange ideas, and monitor progress. HR's responsibility is to make these tools not just accessible but also completely embedded in the processes of teams within the organization. HR must ensure that policies facilitate collaboration and sharing of information, dismantle silos, and facilitate cross-departmental collaborations to ensure efficiency.

Maintaining Work-Life Balance

Ensuring that employees have a healthy work-life balance is another critical component of efficiency. Productivity can be impacted when employees are burned out or overworked. HR can prevent burnout by developing policies that enhance well-being. This dependency can negatively impact worker satisfaction and perpetuate a cycle of instability, where gig workers struggle to secure consistent income or maintain a balanced work-life dynamic (Hwang, 2024).

Critical to both the gig economy and the management of Generation Z employees is the concept of work-life integration. This approach recognizes the fluid boundaries between work and personal life and actively supports the need for balance, which is particularly valued by younger workers (Basid & Atmaja, 2022). Flexible work options, including work at home, job sharing, or flexible schedules, assist employees in balancing personal needs and work. HR is also responsible for tracking employee well-being and health, providing interventions as necessary, and making sure that employees have the tools they need to cope with stress. Importantly, Basid and Atmaja note that the unique characteristics of Generation Z can significantly boost the efficiency of the gig economy, particularly when organizations successfully implement work-life integration strategies (Basid & Atmaja, 2022).

Flexibility as a Solution to Employee Satisfaction and Retention

As companies work to become more efficient, HR also needs to design a work environment that is conducive to employee flexibility. Furthermore, ongoing research by Ayanponle et al. discusses how HR functions are tasked with evolving from administrative roles to strategic partnerships that influence organizational decision-making in accordance with these flexible employment models (Ayanponle et al., 2023). The workforce of today, especially millennials and Gen Z, wants work-life balance and the freedom to work from home or on flexible hours. Flexibility is not just a perk for employees; it is one of the major drivers of attracting and retaining top talent.

Remote and Hybrid Work Models

The mass acceptance of remote and hybrid work, fueled by COVID-19, has increased the demand for flexibility. As companies go back to the office, HR is instrumental in defining remote work policies that are flexible and productive. The major responsibilities include providing access to tools required, establishing clear communication expectations, and creating hybrid work policies that enable employees to switch between home and office depending on their requirements.

Flexible Work Hours and Schedules

Flexible working time is now an important aspect of flexible work. Flexible schedules can be offered by HR to help workers work during the hour's most conducive to their life. This can include compressing workweeks, staggered scheduling, or even giving workers flexibility to work out their schedules around their needs. HR should also aim at instituting policies that enable employees to control their schedule without undermining their productivity. This can include:

Providing asynchronous work arrangements, where workers can perform projects and assignments at their own leisure, without having to be online simultaneously with others. Job-sharing arrangements, where two or more workers may share duties of a full-time position, enabling a more balanced life and higher job satisfaction.

Assisting Employee Well-being

Flexibility is not just about time or place but also about supporting the well-being of employees. HR's involvement in championing health and wellness programs is central to the creation of a flexible work environment. Mental well-being is especially critical, and HR must ensure that resources are available so that employees feel cared for. Providing access to mental health services, including counselling, wellness programs, and stress management training, illustrates HR's commitment to the well-being of employees.

Instituting mental health days and providing liberal sick leave policies gives employees the autonomy to take time off when they need it, ensuring a balanced and productive workforce.

HR as an Organizational Change Agent

HR's function in facilitating efficiency and adaptability goes beyond tactical roles. HR is also an organizational change agent in bringing about transformation. As companies implement new technologies, transform to respond to new customer needs, and react to changing markets, HR has to drive and oversee the changes that form the workforce.

HR can facilitate transformation by:

- **Enabling organizational flexibility** Fostering an adaptive mindset throughout the organization to ensure that employees and teams are able to adapt to new challenges.
- **Creating talent management plans** that will meet future needs, enabling the workforce to shift to new jobs, technologies, and expectations.
- **Embracing analytics:** Applying employee data to make informed performance, engagement, and satisfaction decisions, and using this data to drive additional enhancements in workplace flexibility and efficiency.

The Collaborative Work Model of the Future

Overall, HR plays a critical function in allowing organizations to work effectively while offering flexibility to their employees. Combining technology, culture, and organizational policies is necessary in developing a balanced, effective work environment. The successful integration of these initiatives leads to improved employee performance and fosters a resilient workforce that can adapt to ongoing changes and uncertainties in the work environment (Kristanti & Hariyanti, 2024; Winarni et al., 2024). By emphasizing talent management, process optimization, and employee well-being, HR can assist organizations in achieving long-term success. As companies evolve further, HR needs to keep playing the role of a strategic partner, navigating the organization through transformation while developing an environment of efficiency and flexibility. The workplace of the future will be determined by how effectively HR empowers workers, facilitates well-being, and accommodates emerging technologies and work styles to make organizations both agile and efficient, and in a position to succeed in an ever-changing environment.

Upskilling, Perpetual Learning, and Career Development

In the high-speed, fast-changing working world of the times, career relevancy no longer means coasting on achievements. Upskilling and constant learning have now been at the center of professional realty, revolutionizing the mindset both of workers and employers toward career growth. With industries changing continuously because of technological advancements, globalization, and changing workforce patterns, the employees need to proactively manage their career development by learning and adapting on a continuous basis. This shift in paradigm highlights the significance of skill development and improvement.

The Need for Upskilling in the Modern Workplace

The contemporary workforce is characterized by fast-paced technological innovation, changing business models, and shifting employee needs. To stay ahead of the game, one has to be proactive in developing their skills. Indeed, upskilling—or the acquisition of new skills or enhancement of existing ones—has become a necessary weapon for not just staying relevant in the workplace but also for future-proofing one's career. Businesses have also seen that promoting a culture of upskilling is good for the company and its people. Upskilling enables workers to move up in their positions while making companies maintain trends in the market and resist skill obsolescence. Upskilling increases career progression, confidence, and job satisfaction. With fast technological advancement in AI, data science, and cybersecurity, acquiring new technical skills is essential for remaining competitive.

Perpetual Learning as a Mindset

Perpetual learning is ongoing knowledge and skill acquisition throughout one's working life, as opposed to conventional learning that has a clear beginning and conclusion. Lifelong learning promotes resilience and development by challenging workers to acquire new knowledge through training, certification, and self-improvement. Such an attitude makes professionals more adaptable, keeping them relevant in the face of changing industries. By adopting lifelong learning, one not only responds to existing job requirements but also anticipates future careers in a rapidly changing working environment. Employees also need to be encouraged with a culture of continuous learning by their employers. This might include having continuous training, granting employees learning access, or establishing a learning environment at work. When the company makes an investment in employee skill development, they reap rewards in terms of improved employee engagement, greater innovation, and increased business competitiveness. Businesses such as Google, Amazon, and Microsoft have long advocated a culture of ongoing learning by allowing employees to learn new skills even beyond their actual job descriptions.

The Role of Career Development

Career development is an integrated process that facilitates employees' advancement from junior to leadership positions. It extends beyond learning new skills and involves mentoring, career advancement opportunities, and linking personal objectives with corporate goals. Organizations that invest in career development experience increased employee retention, satisfaction, morale, and productivity. Career advancement today is frequently non-linear, with employees acquiring varied skills through job changes and cross-functional experiences. Such adaptability, along with ongoing learning, keeps workers motivated and at their best, and it profits both the person and the company.

The Contribution of Technology to Upskilling and Career Advancement

Technology is now a primary driver of upskilling and career growth. Learning Management Systems (LMS), online courses, and webinars provide simple access to training. AI-based tools tailor learning by assessing skill gaps and career aspirations, making upskilling more efficient. Technology allows companies to monitor employee progress, making data-driven career growth possible. Also, virtual reality (VR) and augmented reality (AR) are augmenting learning experiences, offering hands-on training in simulated environments, particularly useful for industries such as healthcare and manufacturing, where workers can hone skills in a safe environment before implementing them in actual settings.

Bridging the Skills Gap

The shortage of skills continues to be a problem for most industries, especially in technical and complex positions. To solve this, organizations can emphasize upskilling existing employees through training programs, mentorship, and cross-training, which also increases employee morale and retention. Firms are increasingly collaborating with schools, community organizations, and professional networks to build learning pipelines, which provide new employees and existing employees with the appropriate skills for the job. For instance, technology firms partner with universities for mentorship or internship schemes, and provide sponsorships or scholarships to pursue higher studies, bridging the skills gap.

Learning from Failures and Developing Resilience

One of the important aspects of constant learning and career growth is resilience building. It is impossible to avoid failures, setbacks, and challenges in today's dynamic world. Nonetheless, accepting failure as a lesson opportunity instead of a setback is instrumental in both professional and personal advancement.

HR departments and managers need to develop cultures where failure is recognized as a learning experience. Workers need to be allowed to experiment, take risks, and create new solutions for problems without fear of failure. A culture that is psychologically safe, where workers can take risks and learn from failure, will innovate and learn continuously. Training sessions must also cover growth mindset, which is the perception that one's abilities and intelligence can be developed through effort, persistence, and learning. Employees with a growth mindset are more likely to welcome challenges and perceive failures as opportunities to learn, eventually creating an environment where continuous learning is part of the company culture.

The Future of Upskilling and Career Development

The future of career development and upskilling is inextricably tied to the evolution of technology and shifting workforce expectations. As businesses are increasingly being disrupted by technology, the need for workers to possess a broad and flexible skill set will continue to grow. Companies will have to focus on ongoing learning to remain competitive and attract the right people. A future where upskilling is naturally embedded in the workday and career development is a routine part of an employee's day is imminent. Organizations will more readily adopt agile learning frameworks, enabling employees to learn and evolve in real-time. Collaborative learning tools, gamified learning tools, and real-time feedback processes will enhance the learning process.

Upskilling, continuous learning, and career development are intertwined. As businesses change, so must workers. By encouraging a culture of ongoing learning and development, companies not only bridge the skills gap but also keep their workers engaged, resilient, and future-ready. It is not just the employee's responsibility but also of organizations that need to develop the resources, opportunities, and settings to enable lifelong learning. As we progress, career development and upskilling will no longer be a choice—they will be a requirement for success in the contemporary workforce.

Emotional Intelligence (EI) & Mental wellness

In a world of fast-paced workplace, technological evolution, and universal challenges, Emotional Intelligence (EI) and emotional well-being have become essential factors of individual success and organizational efficacy. The increasingly recognized role of EI in leadership, decision-making, and co-operation highlights its essence in creating a healthy, effective, and congenial workplace. Concurrently, mental well-being also has a very important role to play in the overall health of individuals, allowing them to deal with the intricacies of life with resilience, compassion, and equilibrium. Thus, leadership training that incorporates emotional intelligence development is crucial for organizations aiming to achieve both high performance and employee well-being (Jackman-Ryan et al., 2022;, Prado et al., 2022;, Tang et al., 2010).

Moving into a time of high performance, flexibility, and emotional resilience, which are decisive factors for achieving success, we must incorporate Emotional Intelligence with strategies for mental well-being. Herein, the chapter discusses EI and mental well-being, how they overlap and impact individuals and organizations, as well as the means by which they lead towards a healthier and more productive employee base.

Understanding Emotional Intelligence (EI)

Emotional Intelligence (EI) is the capacity to be aware of, comprehend, and control both our own feelings and others' emotions. It plays a crucial role in how people relate, make choices, and solve issues. Five primary elements of EI, as explained by Daniel Goleman, are self-awareness, where one identifies one's emotions and how they influence thoughts and actions; self-regulation, controlling negative emotions and channelling them positively; motivation, where an individual stays on track with goals even in the face of failure; empathy, understanding and sharing others' emotions and viewpoints; and social skills, which allow for effective collaboration and communication. Though IQ and technical expertise are valuable, EI is usually a better indicator of success, particularly in leadership. High EI leaders are able to motivate teams, build collaboration, and navigate intricate social dynamics, establishing a culture of trust, empathy, and respect.

The Relationship between Emotional Intelligence and Mental Health

There is a strong correlation between Emotional Intelligence and mental well-being. People with high emotional intelligence are likely to be in good mental health since they can better handle stress, establish stronger relationships with people, and make more balanced choices. Practicing the regulation of one's own emotions, being aware of triggers, and empathizing with others directly results in a feeling of psychological well-being.

For example, self-awareness, a primary element of EI, allows individuals to identify early warning signs of emotional or mental distress. Increased self-awareness can serve as an early warning system, warning people of the necessity for mental wellness interventions. Self-aware people are more likely to notice negative thinking patterns, acknowledge when they're feeling overwhelmed, and take action to resolve their mental health before burnout or exhaustion occurs.

Empathy, yet another essential EI component, has a key function in building empathetic relationships. In both daily life and at the workplace, individuals with a high degree of empathy create situations where others are heard and felt, promoting total mental well-being. Empathy enables one to deeply connect with others, become aware of their emotional requirements, and provide care during stressful periods, creating an atmosphere of togetherness and emotional safety.

Psychological Health in the Workplace

With the hectic and stressful work environment, mental health has become increasingly relevant. The pressure of meeting tight deadlines, high stress, and shifting business demands can wear out employees' mental resources. Stress, anxiety, or burnout is an all-too-familiar feeling among employees as they balance individual and work-related needs. The pressure to comply with opaque rules can contribute to overworking among gig workers, resulting in adverse health effects like sleep deprivation and exhaustion (Li et al., 2022).

Organizations are now more aware of the value of investing in employees' mental health. Good mental health translates into a more productive, committed, creative, and resilient workforce. Mental well-being programs, including employee assistance programs (EAPs), stress management training, mindfulness initiatives, and flexible work arrangements, are key. Promoting breaks, work-life balance, and psychological safety culture enables employees to feel supported and decreases stress. Firms that focus on mental health enhance job satisfaction, decrease turnover, and increase productivity.

Building Emotional Intelligence for Better Mental Health

Building Emotional Intelligence (EI) is central to enhancing mental well-being and relationships. Self-awareness is the starting point—paying attention to one's emotions and responses in order to control them better. Self-reflection allows one to know where they need to get better, like stress management or communication. Self-regulation, an important EI aspect, controls stress, anxiety, and anger, enabling people to react coolly to difficulties. Mindfulness, meditation, and breathing exercises facilitate self-regulation. Moreover, cultivating empathy enhances interpersonal relationships, generating supportive communities that promote individual and collective well-being by making other people feel understood and valued.

Mental Wellness Strategies for Maximizing EI

Emotional Intelligence (EI) is an important aspect of mental well-being, but stress and emotional management strategies such as mindfulness and emotional regulation are needed to manage emotions and stress. Mindfulness allows one to remain present, manage negative emotions, and develop self-awareness, while emotional regulation promotes a healthy mental attitude. Therapeutic treatments, including Cognitive Behavioral Therapy (CBT), also improve EI by enabling the individual to see the connection between thoughts, emotions, and behavior, resulting in healthier choices and emotional strength. Second, having a robust support structure of family, friends, and colleagues is also a source of emotional support, which acts as a buffer to stress and for improved mental well-being.

The Role of Leadership in Fostering EI and Mental Well-being

Furthermore, the cultivation of emotional intelligence within leadership development programs has been shown to yield substantial benefits (Filice & Weese, 2024; Duygulu et al., 2011). Leaders are responsible for the cultivation of Emotional Intelligence and mental health in the workplace. Leadership plays a pivotal role in fostering emotional intelligence (EI) and mental well-being among team members within organizations. Emotional intelligence encompasses the ability to recognize, understand, and manage one's own emotions as well as the emotions of others, and it is increasingly recognized as an essential skill for effective leadership (Jackman-Ryan et al., 2022; Filice & Weese, 2024;, Koutsioumpa, 2023). Several studies highlight the significant relationship between leadership practices, emotional intelligence, and the overall well-being of employees.

Leaders who exhibit high EI—particularly self-awareness, empathy, and emotional control—establish the tone for the entire organization. The compassionate approach of such leaders not only elevates employee morale but also facilitates stress management and conflict resolution, thereby promoting mental health within teams (Koon et al., 2023;, Plessis et al., 2015). They establish settings where employees are safe, respected, and nurtured. Further, when leaders discuss mental health openly and give wellness programs priority, it establishes a culture in which employees feel encouraged to ask for help when they need it. Research indicates that emotionally intelligent leaders significantly contribute to positive workplace climates, enhance team cohesion, and foster psychological safety—all critical components of mental well-being (Mintz & Stoller, 2014;, Feather, 2009;, Slaski & Cartwright, 2002). By prioritizing mental wellness, leaders not only improve the quality of life for their workers but also the overall performance and success of the organization.

CONCLUSION

The Future of Work: Focusing on People, Flexibility, and Ongoing Upskilling

The work of the future is centered on humans, not productivity or technology. As AI expands, organizations need to put human connections, flexibility, and well-being at the center. The COVID-19 pandemic hastened this change, emphasizing emotional intelligence and flexibility. Organizations that weigh employee well-being against productivity, such as Microsoft, Spotify, and Dropbox, will flourish.Upskilling is a necessity for career longevity. Due to the speed of technological shifts, 50% of employees will require reskilling by 2025. Amazon, IBM, and Google are among the companies investing in training to remain ahead of disruptions. Lifelong learning is necessary to remain relevant in the changing job market.

Emotional Intelligence & Mental wellbeing

leaders who practice transformational leadership—characterized by inspiration and motivation—often exhibit high levels of emotional intelligence, thereby creating supportive environments for their subordinates (Koutsioumpa, 2023;, Dabke, 2016). As remote work and digital communication gain popularity, emotional intelligence (EI) has never been more essential. Managers who are empathetic, listen actively, and are flexible build more cohesive and resilient teams. Leaders with developed emotional intelligence are better equipped to understand and meet the emotional needs of their followers, which is crucial for guiding teams through challenges like those posed by crises, including the COVID-19 pandemic Jackman-Ryan et al. (2022). Future leaders will no longer be merely decision-makers and strategists but visionaries, mentors, and coaches who create psychologically safe spaces.

Workplace mental health is a matter that organizations can no longer afford to overlook. Burnout, stress, and toxicity result in decreased productivity and increased turnover. Goldman Sachs, for instance, was criticized in 2023 for having junior analysts work 100-hour weeks, which led to a reconsideration of its culture and the implementation of wellness initiatives. Deloitte and Unilever are at the forefront with mental health days, therapy services, and mindfulness training. The take-away: Not only is employee mental health an HR concern, but it is a business imperative. Investing in well-being ensures stronger engagement, retention, and long-term success.

Forecasts for the Future of Work

The following decade will usher in a drastic change in work, with skill-based recruitment, AI integration, and mission-focused workplaces taking the center stage. Skills will trump degrees, leading to the entrance of a wider talent pool into the corporate sector. Mental wellbeing will become the central business model, with prevention of burnout and improved productivity through wellness programs. AI will augment human ingenuity and problem-solving skills and not replace employees. Companies will prioritize socially responsible, mission-oriented objectives, drawing in workers who want meaning from their jobs. Those that fail to comply will lose market share to more forward-thinking rivals.

A Call for Human-Centric Leadership

The changing workforce requires people-oriented, emotionally intelligent leadership that focuses on inclusion, flexibility, and engagement. Leaders of tomorrow will have to reconcile business requirements with employees' well-being, encourage continuous learning, and motivate both productivity and satisfaction. Leadership that focuses on emotional bonds and social abilities enhances team performance and endorses the mental wellbeing of employees. Specifically, authentic leadership, which emphasizes transparency and ethical practices, has been linked to increased well-being among employees, further underscoring the importance of EI in leadership roles (Koon et al., 2023;, YUE, 2024). The ability of these leaders to build trust and facilitate open communication is paramount to creating a healthy workplace where psychological needs are met (Bethari, 2024).

Emotional intelligence will also emerge as a mandatory leadership trait under which employees are placing more premium than ever before on empathy, transparency, and ethics. Success in a firm will no longer be measured in terms of income but in its capacity to enable and nurture its workers.

The Human Side of Progress

The future of work is inherently human. Even as AI and automation advance, creativity, emotional intelligence, and agility will characterize top-performing organizations. Organizations that value employees as assets, not resources, will have engaged, motivated teams. The greatest workplaces will focus on mental well-being, ongoing learning, and meaningful work, establishing cultures where workers feel valued and fulfilled. Apart from profitability and efficiency, the future of work is in fostering innovation while at the same time making sure that this reaches both companies and those that are fueling it. A human-centered approach will make organizations succeed while making their employees powerful.

REFERENCES

Asfahani, A. (2024). Fusing talent horizons: The transformative role of data integration in modern talent management. *Discover Sustainability*, *5*(1), 25. Advance online publication. DOI: 10.1007/s43621-024-00212-7

Au-Yeung, T., Chan, C., Ming, C., & Tsui, W. (2024). The gig economy, platform work, and social policy: Food delivery workers' occupational welfare dilemma in hong kong. *Journal of Social Policy*, •••, 1–19. DOI: 10.1017/S0047279423000673

Ayanponle, L., Elufioye, O., Asuzu, O., Ndubuisi, N., Awonuga, K., & Daraojimba, R. (2023). The future of work and human resources: A review of emerging trends and hr's evolving role. *International Journal of Science and Research Archive*, *11*(2), 113–124. DOI: 10.30574/ijsra.2024.11.2.0151

Bahiroh, E., & Imron, A. (2024). Innovative human resource management strategies in the era of digital transformation. *PRODUCTIVITY*, *1*(2), 154–162. DOI: 10.62207/6wnrgj39

Barišić, A., Barišić, J., & Miloloža, I. (2021). Digital transformation: challenges for human resources management. Entrenova - Enterprise Research Innovation, 7(1), 365-375. DOI: 10.54820/GTFN9743

Basid, R. and Atmaja, J. (2022). The effect of generation z workforce characteristics on the gig economy with work life integration as a mediator. DOI: 10.4108/eai.31-3-2022.2320670

Bethari, A. (2024). Role of emotional intelligence and social skills in effective leadership and teamwork in indonesia. *Journal of Human Resource and Leadership*, *9*(2), 13–23. DOI: 10.47604/jhrl.2340

Bunders, D., & Akkerman, A. (2022). Commitment issues? analysing the effect of preference deviation and social embeddedness on member commitment to worker cooperatives in the gig economy. *Economic and Industrial Democracy*, *44*(4), 1007–1026. DOI: 10.1177/0143831X221101425

Dabke, D. (2016). Impact of leader's emotional intelligence and transformational behavior on perceived leadership effectiveness: A multiple source view. *Business Perspectives and Research*, *4*(1), 27–40. DOI: 10.1177/2278533715605433

Duygulu, S., Hİçdurmaz, D., & Akyar, İ. (2011). Nursing students' leadership and emotional intelligence in turkey. *The Journal of Nursing Education*, *50*(5), 281–285. DOI: 10.3928/01484834-20110130-07 PMID: 21323258

Feather, R. (2009). Emotional intelligence in relation to nursing leadership: Does it matter? *Journal of Nursing Management*, *17*(3), 376–382. DOI: 10.1111/j.1365-2834.2008.00931.x PMID: 21456323

Filice, L., & Weese, W. (2024). Developing emotional intelligence. *Encyclopedia*, *4*(1), 583–599. DOI: 10.3390/encyclopedia4010037

Hwang, J. (2024). The gig economy and its effects on the labor market. *International Journal of Science and Research Archive*, *13*(1), 3394–3404. DOI: 10.30574/ijsra.2024.13.1.1231

Iskandar, Y. (2023). Digital transformation model and the role of hr in indonesian msmes. *International Journal of Business Law and Education*, *4*(2), 1427–1453. DOI: 10.56442/ijble.v4i2.334

Jackman-Ryan, S., Bass, L., Jackson, M., Hoeflaken, K., & Picart, J. (2022). School leadership during covid-19: emotionally intelligent crisis management.. DOI: 10.36315/2022v2end101

James, O., Udeh, C., Daraojimba, C., Ogedengbe, D., Elufioye, O., & Samod, B. (2023). A review of the impact of digital transformation on hr practices and strategies in the nigerian renewable energy sector. j.trd.wrld.econ, 1(1), 36-46. DOI: 10.26480/jhcdc.01.2023.36.46

Jayakarthika, K., Aravind, J., Ilakkiya, N., Karthiga, G., Farha, A., & Varun, C. (2024). Unlocking the potential: Hrm integration of ai in the gig economy for enhanced erp performance. *Int Res J Adv Engg Hub*, *2*(06), 1683–1687. DOI: 10.47392/IRJAEH.2024.0232

Jin, D., & Liu-Lastres, B. (2024). Critical reflection on the impact of the gig economy on the hospitality workforce. *International Journal of Contemporary Hospitality Management*, *37*(1), 18–35. DOI: 10.1108/IJCHM-08-2023-1297

Johan, Z., Yusoff, R., Daud, A., & Sulaiman, S. (2022). The aspects of job quality and work precarity of on-demand gig workers: A systematic literature review. *Journal of Advanced Research in Business and Management Studies*, *27*(1), 10–15. DOI: 10.37934/arbms.27.1.1015

Joshi, A., Jain, S., & Gupta, P. (2024). Challenges and impact of the gig economy. *Sustain. Econ.*, *2*(2), 96. DOI: 10.62617/se.v2i2.96

Koon, S., Ciftci, T., & Jufri, Y. (2023). Impact of authentic leadership on employee well-being and work-life balance in suntory beverage & food limited, japan. *Journal of Human Resource &Leadership*, *7*(6), 11–20. DOI: 10.53819/81018102t5276

Koutsioumpa, E. (2023). Contribution of emotional intelligence to efficient leadership. a narrative review. *Technium Social Sciences Journal*, *48*, 204–216. DOI: 10.47577/tssj.v48i1.9529

Kristanti, D., & Hariyanti, S. (2024). Employee competency development strategy in the digital transformation era: Approach from an hr development perspective. *Jurnal Manajemen Bisnis Akuntansi Dan Keuangan*, *3*(1), 13–20. DOI: 10.55927/jambak.v3i1.8765

Li, C., Lin, C., & Chin, T. (2022). How does the paradoxical leadership of cross-border e-commerce (cbec) gig workers influence chinese company performance: The role of psychological well-being. *Sustainability (Basel)*, *14*(19), 12307. DOI: 10.3390/su141912307

Liu, C., & Renzy, R. (2025). Good jobs or bad jobs? immigrant workers in the gig economy. *The International Migration Review*, 01979183241309585. Advance online publication. DOI: 10.1177/01979183241309585

Mintz, L., & Stoller, J. (2014). A systematic review of physician leadership and emotional intelligence. *Journal of Graduate Medical Education*, *6*(1), 21–31. DOI: 10.4300/JGME-D-13-00012.1 PMID: 24701306

Plessis, M., Wakelin, Z., & Nel, P. (2015). The influence of emotional intelligence and trust on servant leadership. *SA Journal of Industrial Psychology*, *41*(1). Advance online publication. DOI: 10.4102/sajip.v41i1.1133

Prado, J., Torres, R., Tafur-Mendoza, A., Ospina, R., & Sarmiento, C. (2022). Impact of leadership practices on manager's pathways to goal attainment: The mediating effect of emotional intelligence. *The International Journal of Organizational Analysis*, *31*(7), 2889–2902. DOI: 10.1108/IJOA-01-2022-3110

Reynolds, J., & Kincaid, R. (2024). It depends: platform dependence, schedule control, and satisfaction among gig workers on amazon's mechanical turk platform. Sociological Forum. DOI: 10.1111/socf.13029

Reynolds, J., Quintero, D., Aguilar, J., & Kincaid, R. (2024). Work schedules, finances, and freedom: Work schedule fit and platform dependence among gig workers on amazon's mechanical turk platform. *Socius: Sociological Research for a Dynamic World*, *10*, 23780231241286933. Advance online publication. DOI: 10.1177/23780231241286933

Shanshan, Z., & Liu, Y. (2024). Job demands-resources on digital gig platforms and counterproductive work behavior. *Frontiers in Psychology*, *15*, 1378247. Advance online publication. DOI: 10.3389/fpsyg.2024.1378247 PMID: 39355288

Slaski, M., & Cartwright, S. (2002). Health, performance and emotional intelligence: An exploratory study of retail managers. *Stress and Health*, *18*(2), 63–68. DOI: 10.1002/smi.926

Tang, H., Yin, M., & Nelson, D. (2010). The relationship between emotional intelligence and leadership practices. *Journal of Managerial Psychology*, *25*(8), 899–926. DOI: 10.1108/02683941011089143

Winarni, E., Mujannah, S., Halik, A., & Pardosi, P. (2024). Reskilling and upskilling: Hr adaptation strategies to digital transformation in the traditional sector. *Ekoma Jurnal Ekonomi Manajemen Akuntansi*, *4*(1), 2747–2756. DOI: 10.56799/ekoma.v4i1.6237

Yue, Z. (2024). Leadership styles of school leaders and the mental health of teachers in a university in beijing, china. *Pacific International Journal*, *6*(4), 98–102. DOI: 10.55014/pij.v6i4.483

Chapter 23
Ethical Implications of AI-Driven Outsourcing:
Ensuring Bias Mitigation, Fairness, and Accountability

Gunjan Mohan Sharma
https://orcid.org/0000-0003-2272-7385
O.P. Jindal Global University, India

Xuan-Hoa Nghiem
https://orcid.org/0000-0003-2292-0257
Vietnam National University, Hanoi, Vietnam

Priya Gaur
GLA University, India

Damith Gangodawilage
https://orcid.org/0000-0001-7968-6284
Qasim Ibrahim School of Business, Villa College, Maldives

ABSTRACT

This chapter explores the ethical considerations surrounding AI-powered outsourcing, focusing on key issues such as bias, fairness, accountability, and transparency. As AI technologies are increasingly used to automate tasks traditionally performed by human workers, ethical challenges arise, particularly concerning the impact on global labor markets and workers' rights. The chapter examines the sources and impact of AI bias, the importance of ensuring fairness in decision-making, and the need for robust accountability mechanisms in AI systems. It also highlights the role of transparency and explainability in AI models, which are essential for building trust and ensuring ethical outcomes. Addressing inequalities and discrimination in AI systems is crucial to prevent further exacerbating societal divisions. Finally, the chapter proposes frameworks for responsible AI deployment in outsourcing and emphasizes the importance of continuous improvement, collaboration, and human-centered approaches for a sustainable and equitable future in AI-powered outsourcing

DOI: 10.4018/979-8-3373-1270-5.ch023

1. AI-POWERED OUTSOURCING: THE NEW FRONTIER

AI-powered outsourcing has become a massive trend in the global business world, changing how companies manage their operations, cut costs, and scale services. This section examines the rise of artificial intelligence (AI) in outsourcing, its benefits, challenges it poses, and the importance of ethical considerations in this ever-changing landscape.

The Role of AI in Outsourcing

Artificial intelligence is increasingly being applied in outsourcing operations, where activities that were performed by humans are now automated through machine learning, NLP, and RPA. AI's capability to analyze huge datasets, predict outcomes, automate repetitive processes, and provide real-time insights makes it a great tool for companies outsourcing customer support, data analysis, software development, and even complex decision-making tasks (Dastin, 2018).

AI-powered outsourcing is not limited to simple tasks; it is also revolutionizing high-skill industries such as finance, healthcare, and legal services. For example, AI is being employed to automate claim processing in insurance, assist in diagnosing diseases through medical imaging, and even aid legal firms in reviewing contracts (Brynjolfsson & McAfee, 2017). By leveraging AI, organizations can access specialized expertise and 24/7 availability, enhancing efficiency while reducing labor costs (Davenport et al., 2020).

Technological advancements in AI adoption

Several technological advancements have led to the growth of AI-powered outsourcing. Improvements in machine learning algorithms, greater availability of data, and cloud computing have empowered organizations to leverage powerful AI systems without having to build extensive infrastructure in-house (Chui et al., 2018). Machine learning models can now analyze and process huge amounts of unstructured data such as text, images, and speech, thereby making AI applications more accurate and context-aware.

In particular, deep learning has pushed forward tremendous breakthroughs in those areas namely NLP where AI systems can be enabled to respond to customer service conversations, manage supply chains, and predict market trends. The capability to build AI models that understand and generate human-like responses further advanced the possibility of outsourcing tasks to AI systems (Silver et al., 2016).

Importance of Ethical Considerations in AI Outsourcing

Even as AI promises such tremendous benefits for businesses in cost saving, scalability, and efficiency, deployment of AI into outsourcing also throws up critical questions in ethics. Probably the first concern is fair accountability and transparency in decision making. As the use of AI in decisions influencing human life expands—hiring, customer services, and legal judgments, to name a few—a need for these systems to be developed and implemented responsibly is seen to build confidence in AI technology (O'Neil, 2016).

For example, algorithmic bias, where the system has favored or disadvantaged certain people, has occurred through AI-driven outsourcing. It may be based on biased training data or design flaws. Unless addressed, these biases can exacerbate social imbalances, with minorities facing discriminatory practices in hiring, loan applications, or treatment at hospitals (Angwin et al., 2016). Furthermore, the opaqueness of some AI systems, especially in deep learning areas, poses a challenge to accountability. In such situations where AI systems make decisions that have far-reaching consequences, there is a need to know how and why those decisions were made, especially when things go wrong (Raji & Buolamwini, 2019).

With such questions of accountability, the concerns raised against ethical AI-powered outsourcing are compounded. Who is held accountable when a deployed AI for outsourcing makes some unethical decision or causes harm? Is it the developer, or the business in question that utilises the technology, or indeed the AI? These questions thus require careful considerations to ensure the alignment of such AI systems towards ethical values, and proper mechanisms in place regarding potential harm.

Therefore, AI in outsourcing must be approached with a serious consideration of its ethical implications so that it can be aligned with human rights, fairness, and corporate social responsibility. This chapter explores these concerns by delving into the various ethical challenges posed by AI-powered outsourcing, focusing on the issues of bias, fairness, and accountability.

2. UNDERSTANDING AI BIAS: SOURCES AND IMPACT

While AI systems provide the greatest promise to improve the operational efficiency of tasks, they inevitably reflect and reproduce biases existing in the data from which they learn. The next section explores sources of AI bias, its types, and significant implications on AI-powered outsourcing and how this problem raises critical ethical concerns.

What is AI Bias?

AI bias refers to systematic and unfair discrimination in the outputs of an AI system. This bias often comes from the data that feeds into machine learning models or the design of the algorithms themselves. Bias in AI can take a variety of forms, from unfair treatment of certain groups to skewed predictions or decisions that continue existing inequalities. Since AI systems are perceived as neutral and objective, the recognition and mitigation of bias are critical to ensure that these systems do not harm vulnerable populations or contribute to societal disparities (O'Neil, 2016).

The problem of AI bias can be more severe within the context of outsourcing. Automated decision-making systems, designed to take important decisions in hiring, credit scoring, fraud detection, customer service, and even judicial decisions, tend to heighten social and economic inequalities. Historical stereotypes may be perpetuated, or disadvantages are put on vulnerable groups due to such AI systems unless such systems are audited about their fairness (Dastin, 2018).

Sources of AI Bias

1. The bias of AI lies typically in the information or data for which it's being trained by an AI system. Patterns or learning occurs using historical data to determine decisions that an AI is supposed to present, so there's a direct relationship with being biased as shown by historical biases. This is particularly wor-

risome in outsourcing applications where AI systems are trained on data derived from human practices, such as hiring data, criminal justice data, or customer service interactions (Angwin et al., 2016).

Historical Bias: Data collected in the past might reflect societal prejudices, such as gender, racial, or age-based discrimination. For example, if an AI hiring tool is trained on data from a company where most employees are male, it may learn to favor male candidates over equally qualified female candidates (Dastin, 2018).

Sampling Bias: If the data that is used to train an AI system is not representative of the population or situation it is supposed to serve, it might lead to biased results. For instance, an AI model that is trained on data from a single geographic region might not generalize well to other regions, leading to incorrect or unfair outcomes (Binns, 2018).

2. Algorithmic Bias: Besides biased data, the algorithms used to process this data also introduce bias in case they do not account for fairness in the design. This is because any choice made while designing an algorithm can influence its outcome, like the features that are selected and the model parameters and decision thresholds. This kind of bias is sometimes less observable since it may not be immediately apparent in the training data but becomes apparent only during real-world deployment scenarios (Barocas et al., 2019).

3. Human Bias: AI systems often find their way out into the real world via human teams, and biases from the developers or decision-makers can inadvertently influence AI outcomes. If the developers do not take into account diversity or ignore potential biases in their training data or algorithms, they can create systems that inadvertently disadvantage certain groups. Human bias can also be introduced in the feedback loop, where developers rely on biased AI decisions to improve the model, thereby reinforcing existing biases (Kleinberg et al., 2018).

Types of AI Bias

AI bias can take various forms, each impacting the fairness and reliability of outsourcing decisions differently:

1. Discrimination Bias: Discrimination bias involves an AI system leading to adverse treatment of particular groups based on protected characteristics, such as race, gender, or age. For instance, AI-based hiring systems were discovered to favor male applicants for tech positions over females who had the same qualification profile (Dastin, 2018). In outsourcing, the inequality in job distribution, customer service delivery, or being qualified for financial services will result from such discrimination by the bias in AI systems.

    2.Representation Bias: Representation bias occurs when certain groups are underrepresented or misrepresented in the data used to train AI systems. In outsourcing, this would present as an inaccurate or ineffective AI model for customer service, product recommendations, or market analysis when the data failed to depict the type of diversity found amongst the customer or clients (Chouldechova, 2017). For example, if an AI system is trained on data from a specific demographic group, it may fail to adequately serve others, leading to suboptimal experiences for marginalized customers.

    3.Measurement Bias: Measurement bias occurs when the metrics or criteria applied by AI systems in decision-making are inadequate or incorrect. In outsourcing scenarios, this might result in AI models being optimized to achieve efficiency or profitability while fairness is sacrificed. For instance, in financial outsourcing, credit-scoring algorithms might be biased towards past repayment of debts, thereby disproportionately impacting the lower-income sections, and so the cycle of exclusion continues (Barocas et al., 2019).

Impact of AI Bias on Outsourcing

The impact of AI bias in outsourcing can be so extensive and negative to both businesses and society.

1. Strengthening Social Inequality: AI systems will perpetuate or worsen societal inequalities if trained on biased data. For instance, biased recruitment AI algorithms continue to favor men for leadership positions while female and minority candidates remain underrepresented in decision-making positions. Therefore, businesses risk reinforcing the gender and racial disparities existing in the workforce (Binns, 2018).
2. Legal and Reputational Risks: Companies deploying AI systems in outsourcing can face legal and reputational consequences if their AI tools are found to be discriminatory. If AI-driven hiring practices, customer service models, or loan approval systems result in biased outcomes, companies may be subject to lawsuits or government intervention. Reputational damage can also occur when consumers or employees learn that AI systems have unfairly treated certain groups (O'Neil, 2016).
3. Lack of Trust and Credibility: In the case where outsourcing AI systems appear to have bias, there may be an erosion of trust within the organization and, therefore, with the technology as a whole. The customers or clients might start mistrusting the entire process as driven by AI. Consequently, the satisfaction of the customer as well as their loyalty might drop due to distrust (Raji & Buolamwini, 2019). A loss of trust could be damaging not only to a company's reputation but also to its long-term success.

4.Inefficiency and Performance Loss: Inadequate AI-based systems that ignore fairness and inclusion may lead to inefficiencies. For instance, biased recommendation engines or customer service bots that lack the reflection of diverse customer needs may result in poor service provision or give bad recommendations, all of which deteriorate business performance. This especially applies in outsourcing globally, in which the customers' needs would vary by regions, hence, more inclusive AI systems must adapt to such varied needs (Davenport et al., 2020).

Addressing AI Bias: Ethical Implications

Addressing AI bias requires more than technical solutions; it demands an ethical commitment to fairness, transparency, and inclusivity. Developers and businesses must ensure that AI models are built on diverse and representative datasets, implement fairness-aware algorithms, and establish accountability mechanisms to monitor and mitigate bias over time (Barocas et al., 2019). Critical also is that as AI increasingly participates in the outsourced decisionmaking process, such organizations need to ensure that in the development and deployment of evaluation of AI, ethical principles permeate all elements to safeguard human and societal value.

3. FAIRNESS OF AI: SYMBIOSIS WITH INTERESTS

Of course, with the use of AI, its fairness will require balancing of individual and collective interest. As AI systems become more and more relied on to make decisions in hiring, loan approvals, performance evaluations, and customer service, it becomes more important to address fairness to better handle the inherent bias and asymmetric effects that may impact all stakeholders. In this section, the concept of fairness in AI is discussed, including types of fairness metrics and frameworks, and the challenges in balancing fairness with other business objectives such as efficiency and profitability.

Define fairness in AI

In the context of AI, fairness generally refers to the idea that AI systems should treat all individuals or groups in an equitable manner. However, fairness is not a one-size-fits-all concept—what constitutes fair treatment can vary based on the values, goals, and context of the application. While humans may have an intuitive sense of fairness, defining and operationalizing fairness in AI is complex due to the multiplicity of stakeholders, decision-making contexts, and potential consequences.

Fairness can come in different forms in AI:

1. Individual Fairness: The principle states that similar individuals ought to be treated similarly. This means that for AI systems, two people having the same qualification or needs are supposed to be treated similarly; however, regardless of other characteristics such as gender, race, or age, they should have similar outcomes. For instance, in an AI hiring system, if two applicants with similar qualifications apply for a similar position, the system ought to treat them similarly, with no undue preference to one person based on irrelevant characteristics (Dastin, 2018).
2. Group Fairness: Group fairness cares about the fact that various groups, defined by some attributes such as race, gender, or socioeconomic status, should be fairly treated. In AI systems applied to outsourcing, this would mean that the decision -- loan approval or hiring selection -- should not unfairly disadvantage a certain demographic group. For instance, a fairness approach could focus on making sure that the job opportunities that AI systems offer are fairly distributed across groups and not discriminative against the historically marginalized population (Angwin et al., 2016).
3. Fairness through Unawareness: Unawareness aims to achieve the goal of fair decision-making when sensitive attributes are ignored in any decision-making task. This aspect seems to appear simple, however, it brings about several complex issues, among which is it may lead unintentionally to discrimination on grounds of past and systemic discrimination that these variables represent. Therefore, if hiring algorithm ignores the gender, there is a huge possibility that men will be promoted more than the women because data used for its training is discriminatory (Binns, 2018).
4. Fairness as Calibration: In some cases, fairness can be determined based on how accurately an AI system's predictions align with the real outcome. For instance, a recidivism prediction system that is used in the criminal justice system can be checked for fairness by ensuring that the prediction of the likelihood of re-offending for an individual is equally accurate across racial groups (Chouldechova, 2017). This approach is often linked to the idea of calibration—ensuring that the system's outcomes are consistent and reliable across different groups.

Fairness Metrics and Frameworks

To implement fairness in AI systems, various fairness metrics and frameworks have been proposed. These tools help assess whether AI systems are operating in a fair manner and identify areas where adjustments may be necessary. Some of the most common fairness metrics include:

1. Demographic Parity: Demographic parity means that the rate of positive outcomes (such as hiring or loan approvals) should be the same for all groups defined by a sensitive attribute (such as race or gender). For instance, if 50% of male applicants are hired, demographic parity would require that 50% of female applicants be hired, regardless of their qualifications. Although demographic parity encourages fairness, it sometimes works against individual merit and can cause inefficiency in outcomes (Zemel et al., 2013).
2. Equalized Odds: Equalized odds aims at the error rates of the AI system being approximately the same for the different demographic groups. In outsourcing, an AI system should have equal false positives and false negatives across groups. For instance, in credit scoring equalized odds implies that loan applications by different races or ethnic backgrounds may have a similar rejection rate when they have a similar financial background (Hardt et al., 2016).
3. Predictive Parity: This predictive parity form seeks to ensure that the positive predictive value (chance that a person predicted to succeed will actually succeed) is the same for all groups. This would be the metric that would ensure the predictions of the AI system were accurate for all groups, for instance, races or genders, of candidates (Chouldechova, 2017). It ensures no group is systematically disadvantaged in terms of predicted success but does not address disparities in the underlying data.
4. Fairness through Accountability: Some fairness approaches focus on holding AI systems accountable for their decisions. In outsourcing contexts, this could involve clear documentation and justification of the decision-making process, particularly when AI systems make important or high-stakes decisions. Transparency in how AI systems operate allows for accountability and helps mitigate unfair practices (Dastin, 2018).

Challenges in Balancing Fairness with Business Objectives

Balancing fairness with other business interests—such as efficiency, profitability, and scalability—presents a great deal of challenge. Although fairness is very important ethically, in practice, sometimes its implementation does not go in tandem with the other operational objectives. Some of the major challenges include:

1. Fairness vs. Efficiency: In many outsourcing operations, the prime motive is efficiency—automating tasks, reducing costs, and maximizing throughput. Fairness, especially group fairness, could be at loggerheads with the efficiency goals. For instance, ensuring an AI hiring tool is fair to all demographic groups requires additional training data, algorithmic adjustments, and human oversight. These measures are important for fairness but increase the operational costs of the hiring process and decrease the efficiency of that process (Binns, 2018).

In addition, some fairness metrics, such as demographic parity, might result in suboptimal outcomes if the group distributions are not aligned with the actual needs of the business or industry. For example, compelling an AI system to attain demographic parity in hiring may mean hiring less qualified candidates just to satisfy quotas, which would eventually hurt the long-term performance of the organization.

2. Fairness vs. Profitability: Businesses using AI for outsourcing are forced to balance between fairness and profitability. For instance, in marketing or customer services, AI algorithms may target only high-value customers, thus leading to discrimination of certain groups. Companies can easily justify this since they would have to make a higher return on investment (ROI) or have to meet certain profitability goals. But in so doing, the practice could reinforce inequality and fuel undesirable societal effects like exclusion or prejudice against disadvantaged sections of society (O'Neil, 2016).

3.Complexity in Defining Fairness Across Stakeholders: Achieving fairness in AI is also complicated by differing stakeholder perspectives. Different stakeholders—such as customers, employees, regulators, and AI developers—may have varying definitions of what constitutes fairness. For instance, in outsourcing operations, customers may prioritize personalized, efficient service, which might not always align with fairness objectives aimed at ensuring equal treatment across diverse groups. Balancing these competing interests demands great negotiation and awareness of the ethical dimensions of each choice that must be done (Dastin, 2018).

4. Dynamics of Fairness: Fairness is dynamic. What may appear to be fair today may not be considered fair tomorrow, or vice versa, given the dynamism of social values. So AI must always and continually be reviewed and updated to mirror the considered acceptable standards of fairness. For example, gender equality might be defined in various ways within different cultures, and achieving equity in international outsourcing activities requires an approach to fairness that is flexible and sensitive to the context (Brynjolfsson & McAfee, 2017).

Achieving a Fair AI Future

To overcome the challenges of balancing fairness with business goals, companies must adopt strategies that integrate fairness into the AI development process. These include:

- Regular Audits and Assessments: Third-party audits or internal reviews to regularly check AI systems for bias and fairness.
- Inclusive Design and Diverse Teams: Ensuring that AI systems are designed by diverse teams that represent a broad range of perspectives.
- Transparency and Stakeholder Engagement: Engaging stakeholders, including affected communities, in conversations about fairness and AI deployment to ensure that decisions reflect a wide array of concerns and interests.
- Long-Term Investment in Fairness: Fairness is not treated as an afterthought but as a core component of AI strategy that drives trust, customer loyalty, and long-term business success.

4. ACCOUNTABILITY IN AI SYSTEMS

Accountability is one of the most critical components of ethical AI deployment, especially in AI-powered outsourcing, where decision-making processes are automated and can have a huge impact on individuals and society. Ensuring accountability in AI systems means that organizations are responsible for the outcomes produced by their AI tools, including the identification and correction of mistakes, mitigating harm, and ensuring transparency in decision-making. As AI becomes increasingly integrated into business operations, the need for clear accountability structures grows, as AI systems can operate at scale, making decisions that affect a wide array of stakeholders, including customers, employees, and broader society.

One of the most important aspects of AI accountability is transparency. For there to be accountability within AI, it would require stakeholders-mostly the user, consumer, or even regulation bodies-to understand how decisions and choices are being made. This relates to both the technical details regarding the AI system but also the underlying processes, assumptions, and biases affecting its outcomes. Transparency de-mystifies AI, creates trust, and opens avenues for external audit, which is very important because AI is increasingly being used for sensitive tasks, such as hiring, loan approval, or even criminal sentencing (Raji & Buolamwini, 2019). For instance, if a machine learning algorithm rejects a loan or job application, there needs to be a clear explanation for such decisions based on objective criteria, such as credit history, or subjective judgments possibly based on biased data.

Another dimension of AI accountability is the assignment of responsibility. As AI systems operate autonomously, it is often difficult to decide who is responsible for the actions or consequences of these systems. When an AI system makes an erroneous decision, such as unfairly rejecting a job applicant or erroneously flagging a customer's credit as poor, it is essential to pinpoint who is accountable: the developers who created the system, the data scientists who trained it, or the companies that deployed it. In the case of harm or discrimination, there should be an explicit structure of accountability in which those who are responsible will correct themselves accordingly (Crawford, 2016). For instance, rectifying mistakes within AI systems should include avoiding perpetuation of biased data leading to unfair outcomes and ensuring that a system stays compliant with ethical standards and regulatory guidelines.

Auditability is another key element in AI accountability. Regular auditing of AI systems is necessary to check whether they are working as expected and whether their decisions are fair, ethical, and aligned with organizational values. Audits help identify issues such as algorithmic bias or unintentional harm caused by AI systems. For instance, if AI is being used in the recruitment process, audits can detect whether the system is inadvertently showing favoritism to one demographic or another, and thus corrective actions will be taken in case of a disparity (Binns, 2018). Third-party independent audits also offer an objective view of the fairness and accountability of the AI system, especially in building public trust and maintaining legitimacy.

A strong system of accountability includes governance frameworks in the design, deployment, and monitoring of AI systems. These will help set both ethical guidelines and legal requirements for how AI should be used responsibly while protecting stakeholders from potential harm. The governments, industry bodies, and organizations are gradually implementing guidelines and regulations around ethical use of AI. For example, the European Union's General Data Protection Regulation has provisions for AI, including the right to explanation, where it is stated that an individual should be allowed to request an explanation if he or she is affected by automated decision-making. Similar efforts, for example, OECD's principles on AI, require that AI systems are transparent, fair, and accountable. This sets a clear guideline for organizations regarding the rules of their AI deployment (OECD, 2019).

Redress mechanisms have to be developed to ensure that people who suffer harm from decisions taken by AI systems have an easy route to contest and obtain redress for those decisions. For example, if an AI system wrongly denies a loan or job to a person, there must be a mechanism to review and correct the decision. This includes the creation of appeal mechanisms for decisions made by AI systems, which are transparent, accessible, and fair. The right to redress is not only a significant aspect of individual rights but also a crucial feature of an accountable AI system, as it ensures that organizations are responsive to concerns and proactive in addressing errors (Sweeney, 2013).

Accountability in AI systems requires a multi-dimensional approach involving transparency, responsibility, auditability, governance, and redress mechanisms. These components all ensure that AI is deployed responsibly and that its outputs answer the values of society. With AI systems increasingly being integrated into outsourcing operations and shaping areas of life crucial to the human, it is critical that businesses, governments, and other stakeholders focus on accountability to protect against damage and ensure fairness and equity in AI decision-making.

5. EFFECTS OF AI ON WORKERS AND LABOR RIGHTS

The advent of AI-powered outsourcing has profound implications for workers and labor rights, as it fundamentally reshapes the landscape of employment, job security, and working conditions. While automation and AI systems promise efficiency and cost savings for businesses, they also pose significant challenges for workers, particularly in industries that rely heavily on manual labor or repetitive tasks. There are many ways in which workers are impacted by the implementation of AI-driven outsourcing, ranging from job displacement, changes in required skills at the workplace, increased surveillance of workers, and exploitation of labor through outsourced operations.

Job Displacement and Economic Inequality

The immediate effect of AI-based outsourcing will be job displacement, particularly among low-skilled, labor-intensive jobs. With the development of AI systems, several tasks that used to be humanly performed would not be necessary to be manned anymore. For instance, in the area of customer service, there is the automation of a huge number of queries using chatbots and AI-driven call centers that are replacing human agents. Similarly, in the manufacturing sector, the role of assembly lines is being increasingly taken over by robots and automated systems. Such a trend has sparked fears about massive job losses, especially for workers in developing economies who depend on outsourced labor for their livelihoods (Brynjolfsson & McAfee, 2017).

The shift toward AI-driven outsourcing is likely to increase existing economic inequalities because it impacts workers with less education or those whose skills are not easily transferable to the digital economy. For instance, workers in the retail, hospitality, and transportation sectors will have a hard time moving into other jobs without major retraining. This puts these workers at risk of economic marginalization, as they may not have alternative employment opportunities. Additionally, the wealth created by AI and automation tends to accrue to large corporations and shareholders rather than the displaced workers, thereby exacerbating income inequality and social cleavages (Arntz, Gregory, & Zierahn, 2016).

Changing Skill Requirements and the Need for Reskilling

AI-driven outsourcing shifts labor demand from routine, manual work to complex, cognitive work that involves problem-solving, creativity, and emotional intelligence. Thus, although this would mean new jobs developed, it may put a tremendous burden on workers to learn new skills. When routine tasks are automated, workers in low-wage, low-skill jobs are either upskilled or reskilled to survive in the labor market. Given this increasing reliance on AI, one can assume familiarity with digital tools, data analysis, and machine learning may become very important for even the most basic or non-technical jobs (Chui, Manyika, & Miremadi, 2016).

However, this is not possible through reskilling alone since many workers belonging to marginalized communities or regions will not have ready access to necessary educational resources. The gap between the skills demanded by AI-powered jobs and those possessed by the existing workforce could create a divide between those who are able to adapt to the new digital economy and those who are left behind. Moreover, the pace at which AI technologies change means that reskilling programs may become outdated very fast, and workers are left in a cycle of training without guaranteed long-term job security (World Economic Forum, 2020). This is a continuous challenge that requires public and private sector collaboration to create robust reskilling and upskilling programs that ensure workers are prepared for the future of work.

Surveillance and Worker Privacy

AI-powered outsourcing can also have important implications for worker privacy and autonomy. Many businesses use AI and machine learning to monitor and assess employee performance, often through automated systems that track productivity, time on task, and even employee behavior. In some cases, AI-driven tools can provide real-time feedback to workers, while in others, they might monitor workers' actions to detect inefficiencies or potential violations of company policies. Improving efficiency, these systems might lead to a surveillance-heavy work environment, resulting in major concerns over worker privacy and autonomy.

Take call center or delivery services as an example. AI systems can track every movement or interaction an employee makes, giving workers a feeling of being constantly watched and evaluated. Such surveillance can be the root of increased stress levels, reduction of job satisfaction, and burnout. Furthermore, AI-based performance metrics are not transparent, and often, workers will not know the ways in which their actions are being monitored or what criteria are being used to judge their performance. This lack of transparency can create feelings of powerlessness and alienation among workers (Zuboff, 2019). The ethical implications are significant because these surveillance practices might violate workers' rights to privacy and undermine dignity at work.

Exploitation and the Gig Economy

AI-powered outsourcing has also fueled the growth of the gig economy, which is often characterized by short-term, contract-based work rather than stable, full-time employment. Although the gig economy provides flexibility for workers, it often comes at the cost of job security, benefits, and protections typically associated with traditional employment. Many workers in the gig economy, such as drivers for ride-sharing services or freelance workers in tech, are considered independent contractors rather than employees, meaning they do not receive benefits like healthcare, paid leave, or retirement savings.

In an AI-driven outsourcing context, gig workers are often subjected to algorithmic management, where AI systems determine their schedules, tasks, and pay based on performance data. This can create a situation where workers are forced to meet arbitrary targets set by algorithms, with little room for negotiation or human intervention. In addition, algorithmic management systems can be opaque and difficult for workers to understand, making it challenging for them to contest unfair decisions or to gain clarity on how their wages are determined (Huws, 2014). Lack of labor rights for gig workers and the uneven power dynamic under algorithmic control have brought significant concerns regarding worker exploitation and deterioration of labor rights.

Labor Rights in the Digital Age of Outsourcing by Artificial Intelligence

Increasing AI-based outsourcing calls for much stronger labor protection and revised and updated frameworks in labor rights. Labor laws, as applicable nowadays, were largely crafted within an altogether different economic context - a context, that is, where work was much more stable, predictable, and localized. In today's digital and globalized economy, many workers are dispersed across borders, and the very work may be decentralized or hidden behind layers of outsourcing and other mechanisms that obscure the work. AI and automation exacerbate these challenges by enabling businesses to engage in practices that undermine workers' bargaining power and reduce the demand for traditional labor protections.

To address these concerns, governments, labor unions, and international organizations need to develop and implement new policies that protect workers in an AI-powered economy. This may include legislation that ensures fair wages for gig workers, clearly defines AI surveillance and performance monitoring, and provides resources for reskilling workers displaced by automation. Collaboration between employers, employees, and policymakers is also essential in creating a more inclusive labor market where workers' rights are upheld and the benefits of AI technologies are shared equitably.

In conclusion, though outsourcing with the power of AI does have many positive implications for the business, there are severe consequences for the worker, mainly about job displacement, changing skills in the workplace, surveillance in the workplace, and the eroding of labor rights. In any case, where AI will transform the world of work, rights and welfare should be protected by the transparent policy and fair practices for reskilling opportunities. Such a transition would need a collective effort from all the stakeholders to make it just, inclusive, and equitable for all workers.

6. TRANSPARENCY AND EXPLAINABILITY IN AI DECISION-MAKING

Translating into the context of AI-powered outsourcing, transparency and explainability represent very important ethical considerations that discuss how AI systems make decisions, communicate those decisions to stakeholders, and how organizations can ensure AI works in a way that is understandable, fair, and accountable. As AI algorithms increasingly assume tasks that have hitherto been reserved for human performance, including hiring decisions to financial forecasting, the growing concern relates to lack of clarity in AI decision-making processes and risks that come with these "black box" systems. Transparency in explainability becomes more urgent in contexts wherein AI decisions directly affect individuals' lives, such as recruitment, credit scoring, healthcare, or law enforcement. These principles form the basis of the fact that AI systems should not only be effective but also responsible so that users and those impacted by AI systems can know and understand what and how decisions are being made.

Transparency in AI Systems

Transparency means that the level at which people, who use or whose life is impacted, can understand and read the operation of the AI system and its ability to make decisions. A transparent AI system offers clear insight into its design, data inputs, and operational processes, so that stakeholders can understand how and why decisions are being made. This is particularly important in outsourced AI applications where decisions may be made at scale and can affect individuals' opportunities and well-being. The stakeholders-including customers, employees, or regulators-do not have access to information regarding what may cause variations in the output from an AI-based process, hence causing distrust and high risks of abuse without transparency.

Many of these complex systems involve many factors of an AI-based model that has resulted in most challenges associated with obtaining transparency. Machine learning algorithms can learn from massive datasets and alter their behavior in response to the patterns of data. While this is what makes AI systems highly effective at doing specific tasks, it also means that the decision-making process can be extremely intricate and impossible to trace. At times, the developers who designed the algorithm are not even fully aware of how a model arrived at a specific conclusion (Lipton, 2016). This lack of insight is often termed as the "black box" problem, and this can sometimes be a barrier for organizations in justifying decisions made by AI to the stakeholders or even in detecting potential errors or biases within the system.

For instance, with AI-powered hiring platforms, it is critical to have transparency in order to ensure that the candidates are treated equitably and justly. If an AI system rejects a job applicant based on factors such as educational background, work experience, or demographic characteristics, the candidate and the organization need to be able to understand the rationale behind the decision. Without transparency, a candidate may have no way of knowing why they were rejected, which can lead to frustration, confusion, and even legal challenges related to discrimination.

Efforts to enhance transparency in AI decision-making include disclosing the algorithms used, making datasets available for scrutiny, and providing clear documentation about how the system operates. Engaging with external auditors or stakeholders to ensure that the system is aligned with ethical standards and regulations can reduce the risks of harm or discrimination in transparent AI practices (Diakopoulos, 2016).

Explainability in AI Decision-Making

Explainability is the ability to express and communicate how an AI system has arrived at a particular decision in a manner that is understandable to humans. Transparency, on the other hand, deals with giving access to the inner workings of an AI system, while explainability deals with making those inner workings intelligible to a broader audience, including users, regulatory bodies, and affected individuals. Revealing the structure of the model or its training data is not enough for AI to be ethically responsible and trustworthy. Decision-makers must be able to explain how AI systems reach conclusions in a manner that is accessible and comprehensible to non-experts.

Explainability is especially crucial in AI-powered outsourcing scenarios, where the outcomes of AI decisions can have significant consequences for individuals and organizations. For example, when an AI system is used to screen loan applications or determine eligibility for government benefits, it must be able to explain its decisions in a way that is understandable to the individual whose application is rejected or who is offered unfavorable terms. If the algorithm cannot explain its decision, the affected individual may feel treated unfairly or not have the information needed to contest the decision.

Various strategies can be considered for the explainability of AI systems. Development of interpretability methods, as techniques to explain the predictions or behaviors of complex AI models, is one approach. For example, in machine learning, methods like LIME (Local Interpretable Model-Agnostic Explanations) and SHAP (Shapley Additive Explanations) attempt to break down complex models and provide simpler, human-readable explanations for individual predictions (Ribeiro et al., 2016). These methods allow organizations to generate insights into how a specific input (such as a customer's financial history) results in a particular output (such as a loan rejection), making the decision-making process more transparent.

In some cases, explainable AI models have to be built from scratch. These models are designed specifically to be interpretable and provide clear explanations for their decisions, even when dealing with large and complex datasets. For instance, decision trees or linear regression models are used in scenarios where explainability is paramount because their decision-making processes can be easily understood by humans. However, explainable models may come at the cost of reduced predictive accuracy, which means organizations must weigh the trade-offs between explainability and performance when selecting AI tools (Gilpin et al., 2018).

The Ethical Significance of Explainability and Transparency

The ethical implications of transparency and explainability are profound. Without explainability, AI systems can undermine principles of fairness, justice, and accountability. For example, if an AI system refuses a job application based on certain data patterns, but the reasoning is not clear, it becomes difficult to determine whether the decision is fair or biased. Lack of transparency can also lead to the perpetuation of discriminatory practices, especially if the underlying data used by the AI model is biased. Without an understanding of the decision-making process, it becomes almost impossible to identify and rectify these issues.

Transparency and explainability are crucial to preserve individual autonomy. Individuals affected by AI decisions should have the right to know how and why decisions are being made about them. This is particularly critical in contexts such as credit scoring, insurance pricing, or hiring, where AI systems can determine life-altering outcomes. When AI decisions are explainable, individuals can challenge them if they feel that the decision is unjust or incorrect, thus promoting a sense of empowerment and fairness.

In addition, transparency and explainability generate trust in AI systems. Given the increasing reliance of industries on AI, especially in healthcare, finance, and law enforcement, it is of paramount importance that the public and stakeholders trust the systems that are shaping their lives. Transparency enables the organizations to prove that the AI systems work as expected. Explainability brings the clarity which is required for verification of fairness and ethics behind the decisions being made. With trusted AI, stakeholders are likely to accept AI, which is important for its successful integration into society.

Regulatory and Legal Considerations

Governments and regulatory bodies are now starting to realize the need for transparency and explainability in AI systems, and many are enacting policies that require AI systems to be more interpretable. For instance, the General Data Protection Regulation of the European Union includes provisions that allow individuals to contest decisions made by automated systems and to seek an explanation of how those decisions were reached (European Commission, 2018). As stated previously, the Algorithmic Accountability Act introduced in the U.S. legislature in 2019 demands high transparency in such algorithmic mechanisms, such as forcing companies into AI impact assessments whereby their AI doesn't harm single individuals or other groups (U.S. Congress, 2019).

But as outsourcing and other areas where AI will play a greater role evolve, there is an increasing necessity for strong regulations that enforce transparency and explainability. Policymakers will have to convene and engage with AI developers, ethicists, and other relevant stakeholders to develop clear, overarching frameworks that ensure AI systems are understandable, transparent, and accountable to all whom they affect.

7. COMBATING INEQUITY AND BIAS IN AI-POWERED OUTSOURCING

AI-powered outsourcing has the potential to increase efficiency, reduce costs, and improve decision-making processes across various industries. However, the deployment of AI technologies also raises significant concerns about the potential for perpetuating or even exacerbating existing inequalities and discrimination. The design, implementation, and outcomes of AI systems are inherently influenced by the data they are trained on, the algorithms that power them, and the biases of the individuals who create them. In the absence of careful attention to fairness and inclusivity, AI may inadvertently reinforce societal biases in practices that have seriously negative implications for a different group: marginalized or vulnerable people. Addressing inequality and discrimination in AI, therefore, becomes critical to the contribution of these technologies toward an equitable future instead of perpetuating existing power imbalances.

Role of Data in Perpetuating Bias

The quality of data used in the training of AI systems will determine how good the system will be. Where the data has historical patterns of inequality or discrimination, such biases can be learned and replicated by the AI model. In outsourcing scenarios, AI systems rely extensively on vast datasets aggregating historical information about hiring practices, customer behaviors, or financial transactions. When these datasets are biased by historical prejudices or structural inequalities, AI models inadvertently reproduce and amplify them in decision-making.

This way, for example, an AI that is used as a recruitment system might be taught based on history data about recruitment that indicates whites and males in comparison to other races and sexes are preferred during recruitment. From this biased historical data, such AI could end up reflecting the same disparities in future recruiting processes, continuing the gender and racial imbalances in the workplaces. On the other hand, an AI loan-approval system might discriminate against loan applicants from certain neighborhoods or backgrounds, even though such factors are unrelated to applicants' creditworthiness.

These kinds of biases can result in discrimination in various AI systems, influencing people on grounds of race, gender, age, disability status, or other protected characteristics.

A major challenge in mitigating discrimination through AI is that of finding and eliminating such biases inherent in the data. The first step in the development of fair AI systems is to ensure that the data used for training is representative of diverse populations and free from discriminatory patterns. Techniques such as data augmentation (increasing the diversity of data used for training), data anonymization (removing sensitive demographic information), and bias correction algorithms can help reduce the impact of biased data on AI decision-making (Mehrabi et al., 2019). However, even these techniques are not foolproof, and biases may still emerge due to systemic inequalities embedded in society and reflected in the data.

Algorithmic Bias and its Impact on Discrimination

Biases in AI can also arise from the algorithms themselves. While the data used for training AI systems plays a significant role in shaping outcomes, the algorithms that process this data can also introduce biases. Algorithmic bias occurs when the design, parameters, or assumptions underlying an algorithm result in decisions that disproportionately disadvantage certain groups. This is a significant problem where algorithms are deployed in hiring, lending, healthcare, and criminal justice, leading to unequal opportunities and outcomes.

For instance, facial recognition technology has been demonstrated to be less accurate for individuals with darker skin tones, women, and older adults (Buolamwini & Gebru, 2018). If an AI-powered facial recognition system is used in the hiring process, it may be biased against candidates from underrepresented groups. Similarly, in the criminal justice sector, predictive algorithms used to forecast the likelihood of reoffending have been proven to flag disproportionate numbers of Black defendants as high-risk, despite having similar backgrounds to white defendants. These biases in AI models can result in racial discrimination, reinforcing existing inequalities in criminal sentencing, policing, and incarceration rates.

To address algorithmic bias, it is essential to adopt more inclusive and transparent algorithmic design practices. One promising approach is algorithmic fairness, which seeks to ensure that AI systems treat all individuals and groups equitably. There are different types of fairness criteria that could be applied to AI models, such as demographic parity, equalized odds, and individual fairness, that aim to balance the likelihood of a positive or negative outcome across different demographic groups (Dastin, 2018). Achieving fairness in AI models is however very challenging because sometimes conflict arises among different fairness criteria due to the trade-offs necessary among fairness, accuracy, and performance.

Inclusive design and diversity in AI development

To fight inequality and discrimination, inclusivity from the data-collection stage to final algorithm design, therefore, will be very central in fighting issues of inequality or discrimination. This must ensure that more diverse perspectives become involved in development and deployment efforts for AI. Inclusive design is the method of considering the experiences and needs of different demographic groups, especially among marginalized or less represented communities while creating AI.

Having a diverse AI development team involves engineers and designers who can recognize some of the problems that might arise and address such biases that no one else knows about. Those teams that aren't diverse sometimes fail to capture the unique challenges which women, minority groups, and those from differing socioeconomic backgrounds could face, ending up creating less-than-effective systems for these targeted groups. Research has shown that diverse teams are better at identifying and mitigating biases in both data and algorithms, which ultimately leads to more equitable and inclusive outcomes (West et al., 2019).

In addition to fostering diversity in AI development teams, organizations must also engage with stakeholders from the communities affected by AI decisions. This could include holding consultations or focus groups with underrepresented groups to understand their concerns and experiences, as well as working with advocacy organizations that represent marginalized communities. By prioritizing the inclusion of diverse voices in the development process, organizations can ensure that AI systems are designed to serve the needs of all people, not just the majority.

Regulation and Accountability in AI Systems

Addressing inequality and discrimination in AI-powered outsourcing requires proper regulatory frameworks and accountability mechanisms. Governments and regulatory bodies are coming to realize that policies that could mitigate the risk of discrimination must be put in place to ensure the responsible use of AI technologies. For instance, the General Data Protection Regulation of the EU has stipulations for a complainant to appeal against an automated decision, and have an explanation of the rationale behind such automated decision-making (European Commission, 2018). This legislation in the United States also establishes the Algorithmic Accountability Act of 2019, which obliges more accountability and transparency concerning algorithmic decisions with the necessity to conduct impact assessments to ensure whether AI systems pose discriminatory impacts on people (U.S. Congress, 2019).

These regulations form an important step toward AI systems being used in ways that respect human rights and promote fairness. Additional legal frameworks can be complemented by businesses embracing ethical AI principles that guide the design, deployment, and monitoring of AI systems. These principles could include commitments to fairness, accountability, and transparency, as well as mechanisms for auditing AI systems to ensure they are operating as intended and not perpetuating harmful biases.

Ensuring Equity in AI-Powered Outsourcing

In the context of AI-powered outsourcing, addressing inequality and discrimination is essential to preventing the exploitation of workers and customers in the global economy. AI systems that are used to manage outsourcing processes—whether for recruitment, contract management, or customer service—must be designed to ensure that they do not disproportionately disadvantage workers from marginalized communities. This includes ensuring that outsourcing decisions, such as the allocation of tasks or the determination of wages, are made based on fair and unbiased criteria rather than discriminatory factors such as race, gender, or geographic location.

Additionally, companies should have a keen watch on the extent to which their outsourced operations through AI systems may affect workers and customers. They should implement recurrent audits to detect whether AI makes a fair decision in its judgments, and whether some unintended discriminatory outcomes would happen. This promotes accountability and betterment of the AI systems with the aim that organizations are promoting a fair and just global labor force.

8. ETHICAL FRAMEWORKS FOR RESPONSIBLE AI OUTSOURCING

As AI-based outsourcing continues to grow, the need for setting up ethical frameworks that guide responsible development, deployment, and management of AI systems is imperative. These frameworks would help organizations in navigating the complex landscape of ethical concerns regarding bias, fairness, accountability, transparency, and human rights. Ethical frameworks for AI outsourcing guarantee that AI systems are not only efficient and cost-effective but also consistent with social, legal, and moral requirements, especially when such systems touch vulnerable groups or sensitive sectors of society. By using such frameworks, companies can avoid doing harm, ensure fairness, and gain trust in their AI practice.

1. The demand for ethical frameworks in AI outsourcing

AI outsourcing involves the delegation of decision-making to systems that are designed to optimize tasks traditionally carried out by human workers. This has profound implications, as AI can both improve operational efficiency and introduce risks related to bias, discrimination, and lack of transparency. Without a strong ethical framework, organizations risk perpetuating harmful biases, violating individuals' privacy rights, or failing to provide adequate explanations for AI decisions. Ethical frameworks provide guidelines for organizations to mitigate these risks while ensuring that AI systems benefit all stakeholders equitably, rather than disproportionately benefiting certain groups over others.

Outsourcing decisions made by AI, especially in recruitment, hiring, resource allocation, and contract management, must be scrutinized under ethical standards to ensure that the technology is deployed responsibly. This is particularly crucial in industries with a history of discrimination or exploitation, where AI may inadvertently continue such practices. For example, an AI system assessing job applicants might unfairly favor applicants from certain demographic groups or geographic locations over others unless proper ethical frameworks are in place to mitigate such biases.

2. Key Ethical Principles for AI Outsourcing

Therefore, some key ethical principles have to guide responsible AI outsourcing with enough weight that AI systems can be both fairly and effective in the deployment. These include:

- Fairness: AI systems must be constructed in such a way that they can make decisions without causing unjust discrimination against any one group. Fairness in AI is concerned with treating individuals and groups equally; thus the system should not continue historical injustices. Fairness can be achieved by careful data management, inclusive design practices, and regular auditing for biased outcomes. Procedural fairness in AI also includes encouraging fairness in decision-making processes in a manner that is transparent, consistent, and justifiable.
- Accountability: Accountability mechanisms need to be established for decisions made by AI-powered outsourcing. This includes clearly defining responsibility for the actions of AI systems, particularly when those actions cause harm or lead to unjust outcomes. Organizations must be held accountable for their AI systems' behavior, and there must be systems in place to rectify errors or unjust decisions. Accountability can be facilitated through transparent documentation of how AI systems operate, as well as external audits and impact assessments.

- Transparency: A transparent AI ensures that the decision-making processes are understandable to its users and people affected by decisions. The operations of AI systems should be opened up for inspection, and firms should be able to share information about the data and algorithms used in them and how a decision is actually made. A transparent approach does not only facilitate trust but enables stakeholders to check any unfair and biased decisions that may be caused by an algorithm.
- Privacy: AI systems applied in outsourcing should respect the privacy rights of individuals. Personal data should be collected, processed, and stored in a manner that complies with data protection laws and ethical standards. Privacy-preserving techniques, such as anonymization and encryption, can be applied to minimize the risks of data breaches or misuse.
- Human Dignity: Ethical deployment of AI in outsourcing would ensure respect for human dignity. AI systems should support humans rather than replacing them. The use of AI to augment decisions should enhance human well-being and autonomy. In outsourcing, AI should empower the workers and make sure that the workers have an opportunity to meaningfully participate in decisions that impact their lives.
- Justice: AI should be used to advance social justice, helping to create more equitable outcomes for all stakeholders, particularly those from disadvantaged backgrounds. It is essential to ensure that AI technologies do not reinforce existing power imbalances or perpetuate inequality. In outsourcing contexts, justice also involves ensuring that workers are treated fairly, that their rights are protected, and that AI systems do not exploit or dehumanize them.

3. Ethical Design in AI Outsourcing

An ethical AI framework would not be complete without integrating ethical design at every stage of an AI system's lifecycle. From data collection to model development and deployment, ethical considerations have to be sewn into each phase of AI development. The following are the essential strategies for including ethical design in AI outsourcing:

- Inclusive Data Collection: Ethical AI begins with ethical data collection. Organisations should be sure that the data they employ to train their AI systems are diverse, representative, and free of historical biases. Data should reflect all groups of people affected by the AI system, especially the marginalised or vulnerable ones. Techniques for bias mitigation should be applied at the data collection and pre-processing stages to limit the risk of perpetuating hurtful stereotypes.
- Bias Detection and Mitigation: Ethical AI design involves developing robust methods to detect and mitigate bias throughout the lifecycle of the AI system. Techniques include algorithmic fairness checks, regular audits, and diverse testing groups to ensure that AI systems are not producing biased outcomes. Bias detection algorithms identify problematic trends in predictions or outcomes, while mitigation strategies adjust for biases before they impact real-world decisions (Barocas et al., 2019).
- Stakeholder Engagement: Stakeholder engagement is a way of ethical outsourcing when diversified stakeholders participate in the design and deployment of an AI system. Organizations should seek consultation with people and communities that may be impacted by their AI decision. This engagement ranges from workers, customers, to advocacy groups. Participatory design helps in the identification of potential ethical issues before they pose a problem and ensures that AI can serve diverse stakeholders' needs.

- Ethical Auditing: Conducting regular ethical audits is an important step toward ensuring that deployed AI systems do not deviate from ethical guidelines. Audits would review how well the AI systems are performing to achieve fairness, accountability, and transparency, and evaluate whether the system behavior remains in agreement with societal expectations. Independent audits from third-party experts may add additional layers of objectivity and credibility to the process of ethical oversight.
- Human-in-the-Loop (HITL) Approaches: Human oversight in AI decision-making is important to mitigate the risks associated with fully automated systems. A human-in-the-loop (HITL) approach keeps humans involved in critical decision-making processes, allowing them to intervene when necessary. In outsourcing, HITL approaches ensure that AI does not have unchecked authority over decisions, particularly when these decisions affect people's lives or livelihoods.

4. Clear Governance and Accountability Structures

The ethical deployment of AI in outsourcing also requires strong governance and accountability frameworks. Companies should establish clear lines of responsibility for AI decision-making, ensuring that all stakeholders know who is responsible for the outcomes of AI systems. This would involve establishing ethics officers or responsible AI teams that monitor AI development, deployment, and performance so that ethical standards are met from the beginning of the process to the end. These roles could also include routine audits, assessments, and reporting and resolution procedures for ethical concerns.

External oversight mechanisms such as independent audits or reviews should also be included in governance structures that align with national and international ethical guidelines and regulatory frameworks. For instance, an AI system would have to adhere to the General Data Protection Regulation of Europe or other country-specific data privacy regulations to ensure privacy and data rights are respected (European Commission, 2018). In addition, adherence to guidelines such as the OECD AI Principles can also give further confidence that AI systems are operating in an ethical manner and in public interest (OECD, 2019).

5. Legal and Ethical Compliance

Legal frameworks form an important basis through which AI-powered outsourcing will observe the laws enacted in individual nations and internationally, which protects individuals and guarantees that it is fair in the AI system. The applicable laws for discrimination, privacy, and labor rights can be aligned with the ethical AI frameworks. Legal compliance reduces litigation risks and reputational damage, but more importantly, it requires AI technologies to exert their forces in ways that adequately protect fundamental human rights and promote social good.

For instance, any hiring AI-based outsourcing system needs to adhere to the anti-discrimination law, for example, in the United States, the EEO guidelines; or in the UK, the Equality Act. It prohibits the discrimination of an individual in their employment based on their race, gender, disability, or any other protected characteristics. Similarly, financial services AI systems must comply with the Fair Lending Act and other regulations so that AI-driven lending decisions are not discriminatory to certain groups in terms of race or socioeconomic status.

Ethical frameworks for responsible AI outsourcing provide the necessary guidance to organizations seeking to deploy AI technologies in ways that respect human rights, promote fairness, and minimize harm. These frameworks focus on the importance of fairness, accountability, transparency, and human dignity in AI decision-making and promote the ethical design, development, and deployment of AI systems. Ethical frameworks help organizations reduce the risk of discrimination and bias, ensure that AI systems are transparent and understandable, and foster trust with their stakeholders. Responsible AI outsourcing is not only about better business outcomes but also about a future where AI technologies contribute to a more just and equitable society.

9. FUTURE OUTLOOK: ETHICAL AI IN OUTSOURCING

The future of ethical AI in outsourcing holds vast potential to shape not only how businesses operate but also how technology interacts with global labor markets, workers, and society as a whole. As AI continues to advance, it is likely to impact quite a significant number of sectors, starting from hiring and human resource management to customer services, designing a supply chain logistics network, and many more. But the future in store will be challenging; the more complex and powerful an AI system becomes, the greater the need to critique and address the ethical considerations of AI outsourcing to prevent harm, ensure fairness, and protect human rights. This will determine how business, government, and society, working together, addresses equity, accountability, transparency, and regulation in relation to the path AI will take with outsourcing.

1. Growing Involvement of AI in Outsourcing

Increasingly, AI technologies are seen as more deeply implicated in the process of outsourcing due to routine task automation, improvements in the operational efficiency, and lower cost structures. Over the next decade, businesses may leverage AI to handle even more complex outsourcing tasks, such as customer service, recruitment, and contract negotiations. As AI systems become more sophisticated, they will not only replace manual labor but also augment human decision-making, making operations smarter and more efficient. For example, AI tools can help identify the most suitable candidates for outsourcing contracts, track performance metrics, and ensure that tasks are completed in the most optimal manner possible.

However, as AI systems become more embedded in outsourcing practices, the risk of unethical outcomes—such as bias, discrimination, and job displacement—also increases. This implies that AI may significantly transform labor markets, making ethical use of AI in outsourcing contingent on robust frameworks to protect human dignity and rights. Unchecked AI will entrench inequality in outsourcing by automatically putting developing economy workers on the sharp end of the automation process, with minimal protection or chances of upskilling.

2. Advancements in AI Ethics and Governance

As AI technologies emerge, the ethics of AI likewise progress. The future of ethical AI in outsourcing will very much depend on the creation of better ethical frameworks, tools, and governance structures that propel organizations forward with the responsible use of AI. It is this realization of the potential harms created by the poor design or misuse of AI systems that has spurred concerted global efforts to create guidelines, principles, and regulatory frameworks.

Industry and the government will thus work together, in the upcoming years, for clearer and better standardized approaches concerning ethical AI during outsourcing. Future expectations would mean the establishment of global frameworks, compliance standards geared toward ensuring these AI systems could be designed in a manner supporting fairness, being transparent, and very accountable. International agreements, such as the OECD AI Principles and the UN Guiding Principles on Business and Human Rights, are already laying the groundwork for ethical AI governance. In the future, these frameworks could evolve into binding agreements or regulations, setting the standard for AI-powered outsourcing worldwide.

Secondly, companies can take up third-party audits and ethical impact assessment reports and a transparency report to showcase their AI adhering to set guidelines. An ethical AI program might also provide organizations with avenues for proving a commitment to fairness, bias minimization, and accountability.

3. Addressing work-force impacts; Reskilling and Human-Centric AI

Arguably, a great ethical question regarding AI outsource is one related to employee displacement. The automation of routine and even complex tasks raises fears of job loss, particularly in the bottom-wage or outsourced sectors. In the future, to mitigate the side effects of AI on labor, reskilling workers will be crucial so that they can transition to new jobs that AI technologies have generated. One of the key ethical concerns in the deployment of AI is to ensure that the AI system is not used as a substitute for human labor that would lead to the suffering or exploitation of an individual or a group.

Human-centric AI will most likely become the central development. Human-centric AI focuses on the collaboration of human workers and AI systems, instead of fully substituting human labor. Organizations that deploy AI in outsourcing are expected to be reskilled in the future. This reskilling will equip the workers with tools and knowledge in adapting to changes in the job market. For instance, there could be training in data analysis, AI management, and other technical skills complementary to AI technology.

Moreover, AI-augmented work—where AI complements human capabilities rather than replacing them—may become the future of ethical AI deployment. This will ensure that human workers are empowered to make decisions and contribute meaningfully while benefiting from AI's efficiencies. Outsourcing companies may increasingly adopt hybrid work models, where AI handles repetitive tasks, but human workers remain central to the decision-making process.

4. Fairness and Reduction of Bias in AI Systems

Core problems of ethical AI in outsourcing will be the neutralization of bias and the guarantee of fairness. As AI models expand into all fields, their possible perpetuation of existing biases, thereby amplifying them, creates a significant threat. AI systems may inadvertently retain discriminatory patterns they have learned if historical data represents systemically unequal treatments, such as gender or race discrimination in hiring or credit scores.

The future of ethical AI will therefore be very much bias detection and mitigation technique. Currently, the results of machine learning research are already evolving toward more advanced bias identification and correction methods for AI systems. However, even at this stage, current techniques for bias mitigation are promising, but they still have limitations-particularly in dealing with complex and realistic applications. Future developments in explainable AI and fairness-aware machine learning algorithms will likely help address these issues more effectively, providing businesses with tools to ensure that their AI systems do not unfairly disadvantage any group.

Algorithmic transparency will remain another key area where ethical AI continues to focus its attention. In the future, stakeholders will expect more transparency concerning the decision-making processes of an AI system. We can certainly expect an upsurge of explainable AI—systems capable of providing clear and justifiable explanations for the decisions they made. This would be critical for outsourcing contexts: hiring, promotion, and allocation of contracts, among others.

5. Legal and Regulatory Frameworks

The future of ethical AI in outsourcing will also be influenced by increasingly evolving legal and regulatory frameworks. As more people become integrated into the AI world, governments will increasingly feel pressured to regulate how their citizens utilize the technologies available in this new world. The European Union's AI Act, for instance, is one of the first moves towards comprehensive regulation of AI systems, and the approach will set standards for countries across the globe. It organizes AI applications by risk profile and offers instructions for how the more dangerous ones—like hiring tools or those that have to do with criminal justice—should function with high integrity.

In the near future, we will likely have global AI regulations that lay out minimal standards for ethics in AI in outsourcing and other industries. Some of these may address data privacy, algorithm accountability, and fairness issues and also carry penalties for non-compliance. Stricter labor protection laws would be implemented to prevent the exploitation of workers with the help of AI algorithms for outsourcing.

Moreover, the regulations may force organisations to incorporate impact assessments into their AI system's design and rollout, assessing impacts that AI systems would bring about regarding the workers and the consumers themselves as well as on society as a whole. In the increasingly AI-based world of outsourcing, businesses will need to ensure compliance of their AI system and prove them as not bad for workers, which do not allow inequality between two groups or groups of any two different classifications.

6. The Role of Public and Private Sector Collaboration

A possible future for the ethical AI approach in outsourcing rests on the need for collaboration from both the private and public sectors. Governments, therefore, would have to produce policies that entice the building of ethical AI technologies while remaining strict on enforcement on businesses in terms of policies. Public-private partnership can help enable the sharing of best practices as well as provide the development and implementation of ethics standards for AI and educational training programs for its workers.

In addition, industry collaboration will be essential for creating shared ethical guidelines and standards that address the challenges of AI-powered outsourcing. This collaboration could take the form of industry alliances, working groups, or consortia focused on responsible AI practices. By sharing knowledge and resources, companies can collectively address the ethical challenges posed by AI outsourcing and create a more just and sustainable future for all.

The future of ethical AI in outsourcing is both challenging and full of opportunities. Businesses will have to emphasize ethical considerations when AI transforms the industries of the world. Ensuring that AI systems are used responsibly and having positive impacts on workers, consumers, and society will be at the forefront of ethical considerations. It is likely that more robust ethical frameworks will be developed, advanced techniques for mitigating bias will emerge, greater transparency and accountability in AI decision-making will be pursued, and regulatory oversight will become stronger.

Ultimately, the success of ethical AI in outsourcing depends on collaboration between governments, businesses, and civil society to create policies, frameworks, and technologies that promote fairness, transparency, and respect for human rights. Navigating the future of AI with ethical foresight will ensure that AI-driven outsourcing contributes to a more equitable, inclusive, and sustainable global economy.

10. CONCLUSION: PUSHING FOR ETHICAL AI-POWERED OUTSOURCING

With the evolution of AI and its impact on reshaping industries and global labor markets, one cannot ignore the ethical implications of AI-based outsourcing. With great potential in operational efficiency and cost-cutting benefits, it helps streamline business processes, while creating numerous challenges relating to bias, fairness, accountability, transparency, and its impact on workers. In order to grasp the full benefits of AI outsourcing while minimizing the risks presented, organizations need to take proactive steps in insulating ethics into every stage of AI deployment from design and development to implementation and monitoring.

The core of ethical AI in outsourcing lies in ensuring that these technologies are not only efficient but also just and equitable. Companies must prioritize creating AI systems that promote fairness, transparency, and accountability, especially in decision-making processes that have far-reaching consequences on workers' lives, societal dynamics, and the overall economy. In particular, AI applications in hiring, workforce management, and performance evaluations must be scrutinized to avoid perpetuating existing biases or reinforcing historical inequalities.

1. Stakeholder's Role for Ethical Outsourcing with the Help of Artificial Intelligence

Now, it isn't the concern of companies or any single institution alone. It includes all stakeholders within it, involving businesses, lawmakers, labor institutions, consumers and even the whole technology sector by themselves. A shared responsibility plays its role while ensuring that everyone promotes a level playing field whereby AI is integrated responsibly and impartially.

- Business Leaders: Corporate leaders need to hold themselves accountable to the ethical connotations of the AI systems within their businesses. This extends beyond the promotion of fairness, accountability, and transparency in developing AI but further requires investment into ongoing monitoring, auditing, and detection of bias of AI systems to sustain their ethical deployment over time. Furthermore, businesses must commit to reskilling workers and creating pathways for those displaced by AI automation, ensuring that technological progress does not come at the expense of labor rights or human dignity.
- Policymakers and Regulators: Governments play a crucial role in regulating AI and setting standards that protect workers and society from the potential harms of AI-powered outsourcing. Through the creation of clear regulations and ethical frameworks, policymakers can ensure that AI technologies are deployed responsibly. For instance, laws around data privacy, anti-discrimination, and labor protection must evolve to account for the unique challenges posed by AI systems,

guaranteeing that workers' rights are safeguarded, and that vulnerable populations are not unfairly impacted.

- Labour Unions and Advocacy Organizations: Labour unions and advocacy organisations have to further press for working rights, guarantee that AI-serviced subcontracting does not foster exploitative operations or the cheapening of labour jobs. Advocate further for mechanisms intended to cushion weak workers; as well engage efforts to enjoin workers within conversations on how to implement as well as enact policies on the usage of Artificial Intelligence. Engagement in dialogue around AI's impact on the workforce is key to ensuring that technological adoption benefits workers rather than marginalizing them.
- Consumers and Society: As the end-user of AI-powered outsourcing, the consumer has a right to ensure that corporations implement AI responsibly. Public campaigns, consumer force, and consumer pressure on firms will motivate these firms to engage in more responsible conduct. An educated society can make the firms go more responsive to societal concerns by adapting more socially conscious AI solutions to serve the common good.

2. Continuous Improvement and Adaptation

Ethical AI is not a one-time achievement but rather an ongoing commitment to continuous improvement. Just as AI systems change and grow, so too should the ethical standards guiding their deployment. The technological landscape is constantly shifting, with new challenges arising all the time, from unexpected biases in new datasets to changing concerns over data privacy. This commitment, to revisit often AI systems already created, revisit often the appropriate updating of such frameworks, and develop better-decision making processes among participants, translates to ethical audit/bias-mitigation methods being integrated during continued development as well as operational activities in running these AI models. AI cannot be a "set it and forget" model-the continued monitoring necessary should ensure an algorithm that fulfills the better good of serving its public function. Organizations must develop loops of feedback mechanisms that allow AI models to iterate and refine on a continuous basis in order to keep up with the changing circumstances of society, market conditions, and consumer expectation. In doing so, organizations will have to foster a culture of ethical innovation while challenging teams to think critically about the social and moral implications of AI technologies they produce, even as they advance technical capability.

3. Human-Centred Approach towards AI

At the heart of ethical AI is the recognition that AI should augment human capabilities, not replace them. This human-centered approach ensures that AI technologies are designed with empathy and respect for human dignity, ensuring that workers are treated as valuable assets, not just data points to be optimized. With AI-driven outsourcing, companies should concentrate on solutions that improve the value of human workers through human-in-the-loop models, rather than replacing them entirely. This will ensure that humans remain central to decision-making, oversight, and strategic thinking.

AI-powered outsourcing should finally aim at elevating human potential by giving new opportunities to the workers to grow and upskill. Rather than replacing human labor, AI can empower people to do more complex, creative, and fulfilling work by automating low-skilled and repetitive activities. Organizations need to take responsibility to ensure that AI augments human labor by giving proper resources for worker retraining and career development.

It means that if there is going to be widespread deployment of AI in the market, organizations should take care of technology implementation while exercising empathy with it, where users, be they customers or workers, have friendly engagements with the AI systems. In essence, an organization should try its best in producing ethical user-friendly interfaces when interacting with an AI system respecting their privacy needs as well as one that fulfills the numerous different needs but doesn't help sustain harm.

4. Developing Worldwide Consensus Regarding the Ethics of AI

While ethical concerns involving AI in outsourced operations affect more than a country or specific business sector but indeed, transcend worldwide. Increasing usage of the technology across most geographies gives way to needful international dialogue regarding globalized norms and best practices related to its application. United Nations, Organization for Economic Co-operation and Development have already made steps to share some consensus. In the future, border collaboration must move forward to secure human values in terms of equity, fairness, and justice realized through AI technology.

Efforts to address AI's ethical challenges must be inclusive, ensuring that stakeholders from diverse regions, cultures, and socioeconomic backgrounds are involved in shaping global standards. This inclusivity will help ensure that AI technologies are applied in ways that benefit all members of society, not just a select few, and that no group is left behind in the AI revolution.

5. Final Thoughts: A Commitment to Ethical Progress

The ethical implications of AI powered outsourcing arc profound but not insurmountable. In the future, there will not be one answer that fits all in terms of AI challenges but there is a path forward through collective responsibility, continuous adaptation, and a focus on human well-being. The ethical deployment of AI in outsourcing will depend on a deep commitment to values like fairness, accountability, and transparency along with a forward-looking approach to technology design and governance.

Focusing on embedding ethical principles into all aspects of the development of AI and outsourcing, businesses can build trust, mitigate risks, and maximize the positive impact of AI on society. With AI's endless evolution and the endless expansion of its applications, we must stay alert so that the AI system works toward humanity's best interest-by changing lives, providing opportunities for people, and building a more equitably efficient global economy. Pursuing ethical AI-powered outsourcing is not just a moral imperative but a key to one day living a world where technology serves all of us, rather than a select few.

REFERENCES

Angwin, J., Larson, J., Mattu, S., & Kirchner, L. (2016). *Machine Bias*. ProPublica. Retrieved from https://www.propublica.org/article/machine-bias-risk-assessments-in-criminal-sentencing

Arntz, M., Gregory, T., & Zierahn, U. (2016). *The Risk of Automation for Jobs in OECD Countries: A Comparative Analysis*. OECD Social, Employment and Migration Working Papers No. 189. OECD Publishing.

Barocas, S., Hardt, M., & Narayanan, A. (2019). *Fairness and Machine Learning*. Cambridge University Press.

Binns, R. (2018). *Fairness in Machine Learning: Lessons from Political Philosophy*. In *Proceedings of the 2018 CHI Conference on Human Factors in Computing Systems* (pp. 1-12). ACM.

Binns, R. (2018). On the Importance of Transparency in AI Systems: Ethical Implications for Society. *ACM Computing Surveys*.

Brynjolfsson, E., & McAfee, A. (2017). *The Second Machine Age: Work, Progress, and Prosperity in a Time of Brilliant Technologies*. W. W. Norton & Company.

Buolamwini, J., & Gebru, T. (2018). *Gender Shades: Intersectional Accuracy Disparities in Commercial Gender Classification*. In *Proceedings of the 1st Conference on Fairness, Accountability, and Transparency* (pp. 77–91). ACM.

Chouldechova, A. (2017). Fair Prediction with Disparate Impact: A Study of Bias in Recidivism Prediction Algorithms. *Proceedings of the 2017 ACM Conference on Computer and Communications Security*, 903–922.

Chui, M., Manyika, J., & Miremadi, M. (2016). *Where Machines Could Replace Humans—and Where They Can't (Yet)*. McKinsey & Company.

Chui, M., Manyika, J., & Miremadi, M. (2018). *Artificial Intelligence: The Next Digital Frontier?* McKinsey & Company. Retrieved from https://www.mckinsey.com/business-functions/mckinsey-digital/our-insights/artificial-intelligence-the-next-digital-frontier

Crawford, K. (2016). *Artificial Intelligence's White Guy Problem*. The New York Times. Retrieved from https://www.nytimes.com/2016/06/26/opinion/artificial-intelligences-white-guy-problem.html

Dastin, J. (2018). *Amazon Scraps Secret AI Recruiting Tool That Showed Bias Against Women*. Reuters. Retrieved from https://www.reuters.com/article/us-amazon-com-jobs-automation-insight-idUSKCN1MK08G

Davenport, T. H., Guha, A., Grewal, D., & Bressgott, T. (2020). How Artificial Intelligence Will Change the Future of Marketing. *Journal of the Academy of Marketing Science*, *48*(1), 24–42. DOI: 10.1007/s11747-019-00696-0

Diakopoulos, N. (2016). *Algorithmic Accountability: A Primer*. Data & Society Research Institute.

European Commission. (2018). *General Data Protection Regulation (GDPR).* Official Journal of the European Union.

European Commission. (2021). *Proposal for a Regulation on Artificial Intelligence.* AI Act.

Gilpin, L. H., Caruana, R., DiSalvo, D., & Wallach, H. (2018). *Explaining Explanations: An Overview of Interpretability of Machine Learning.* In *Proceedings of the 2018 CHI Conference on Human Factors in Computing Systems* (pp. 1–11). ACM. DOI: 10.1109/DSAA.2018.00018

Hardt, M., Price, E., & Srebro, N. (2016). Equality of Opportunity in Supervised Learning. *Proceedings of the 30th International Conference on Neural Information Processing Systems*, 3315–3323.

Huws, U. (2014). *Labor in the Global Digital Economy: The Cybertariat Comes of Age.* Monthly Review Press.

Kleinberg, J., Lakkaraju, H., Leskovec, J., Ludwig, J., & Ribas, V. (2018). Human Decisions and Machine Predictions. *Nature, 572*(7767), 653–657. DOI: 10.1038/s41586-019-1361-1 PMID: 29755141

Lipton, Z. C. (2016). *The Mythos of Model Interpretability.* In *Proceedings of the 2016 ICML Workshop on Human Interpretability in Machine Learning* (pp. 96-100).

Mehrabi, N., Morstatter, F., Saxena, N., Lerman, K., & Galstyan, A. (2019). A Survey on Bias and Fairness in Machine Learning. *ACM Computing Surveys, 54*(6), 1–35. DOI: 10.1145/3457607

O'Neil, C. (2016). *Weapons of Math Destruction: How Big Data Increases Inequality and Threatens Democracy.* Crown Publishing Group.

OECD. (2019). *OECD Principles on Artificial Intelligence.* Organisation for Economic Co-operation and Development. Retrieved from https://www.oecd.org/going-digital/ai/principles/

Raji, I. D., & Buolamwini, J. (2019). *Actionable Auditing: Investigating the Impact of Publicly Naming Biased Performance Results of Commercial AI Products.* In *Proceedings of the 2019 CHI Conference on Human Factors in Computing Systems* (pp. 1–15). ACM. DOI: 10.1145/3306618.3314244

Ribeiro, M. T., Singh, S., & Guestrin, C. (2016). *Why Should I Trust You? Explaining the Predictions of Any Classifier.* In *Proceedings of the 22nd ACM SIGKDD International Conference on Knowledge Discovery and Data Mining* (pp. 1135-1144). DOI: 10.18653/v1/N16-3020

Silver, D., Hubert, T., & Schrittwieser, J.. (2016). Mastering Chess and Shogi by Self-Play with a General Reinforcement Learning Algorithm. *Nature, 550*(7676), 350–354. DOI: 10.1038/nature24270 PMID: 29052630

Sweeney, L. (2013). *Discrimination in Online Ad Delivery.* ACM Digital Library., DOI: 10.1145/2460276.2460278

UNESCO. (2021). *Recommendation on the Ethics of Artificial Intelligence.* United Nations Educational, Scientific and Cultural Organization.

U.S. Congress. (2019). *Algorithmic Accountability Act of 2019.*

West, S. M., Whittaker, M., & Crawford, K. (2019). *Discriminating Systems: Gender, Race, and Power in AI*. AI Now Institute.

World Economic Forum. (2020). *The Future of Jobs Report 2020*. World Economic Forum.

Zemel, R. S., Wu, Y., Swersky, K., Pitassi, T., & Dwork, C. (2013). *Learning Fair Representations*. In *Proceedings of the 30th International Conference on Machine Learning* (Vol. 28).

Zohar, D., & Arad, A. (2018). Transparency in Algorithmic Decisions: A Roadmap for Implementation. *AI and Ethics*.

Zuboff, S. (2019). *The Age of Surveillance Capitalism: The Fight for a Human Future at the New Frontier of Power*. PublicAffairs.

Chapter 24
Navigating the AI Outsourcing Wave:
Threats to Employment and the Imperative for Upskilling

Gayathri Sethuraman
Institute of Business Management, GLA University, Mathura, India

Sucheta Agarwal
https://orcid.org/0000-0001-6525-3007
Institute of Business Management, GLA University, Mathura, India

ABSTRACT

The rise of artificial intelligence (AI) outsourcing practices presents significant challenges to existing employees and the broader labour market. This chapter examines how the integration of AI in outsourced tasks threatens job security by automating roles traditionally held by human workers, particularly in industries such as IT, customer service, and data management. The ripple effects of these changes on the labour market are explored, including increased competition and displacement of low-skilled jobs. Recognizing the critical need for adaptability, this study emphasizes the importance of upskilling in AI-related technologies to remain competitive. It also proposes actionable strategies for mitigating the threats posed by AI outsourcing, including fostering education in AI, implementing supportive labour policies, and encouraging ethical outsourcing practices. By addressing these issues, the chapter aims to equip organizations, policymakers, and workers with tools to navigate the evolving landscape of AI-driven outsourcing.

INTRODUCTION

The rapid progress of artificial intelligence (AI) technologies has brought major changes to the global workforce (Jaiswal et al., 2023; Karthikeyan and Singh, 2025). Among its most profound impacts is the growing trend of outsourcing tasks to AI systems, a practice reshaping an industry traditionally reliant on human labour. From IT and customer service to data management, AI-driven outsourcing offers businesses the promise of increased efficiency, cost savings, and scalability. However, these advantages

DOI: 10.4018/979-8-3373-1270-5.ch024

come with substantial challenges, particularly for employees and the broader labour market. The concerns include job displacement, labour market competition, wage suppression, work force stability, skill gaps, socio-economic disparities, lack of ethical oversight, pressure on policy makers, resistance to change and uncertain long-term impact.

This chapter explores the dual-edged nature of AI outsourcing, focusing on how automation combined together with outsourcing disrupts traditional job roles, intensifies labour market competition, and disproportionately displaces low-skilled workers. As organizations adopt AI solutions to perform tasks previously handled by humans, the resulting economic ripple effects demand urgent attention. Without proactive measures, these changes risk exacerbating inequalities and leaving many workers ill-prepared to navigate the shifting employment landscape. Recognizing the critical need for adaptability, this study calls attention making it necessary of providing the workforce with right skills appropriate to an AI-driven changing demands. By nurturing education in AI technologies, implementing supportive labour policies, and encouraging ethical outsourcing practices, stakeholders can mitigate these challenges and harness AI's transformative potential responsibly. This chapter aims to provide actionable insights and strategies to help organizations, policymakers, and workers navigate this evolving paradigm.

Objectives:

1. Analyse the Impact of AI Outsourcing - Examine how AI-driven outsourcing affects job security, workforce stability, and socio-economic disparities, with a focus on industries such as IT, customer service, and data management.
2. Highlight Labor Market Challenges - Identify the ripple effects of AI outsourcing, including job displacement, wage suppression, and increased competition, particularly for low-skilled workers.
3. Promote Workforce Adaptability - Advocate for upskilling and reskilling initiatives to equip workers with AI-related competencies and ensure their competitiveness in an evolving job market.
4. Propose Ethical and Supportive Practices - Develop strategies for ethical AI outsourcing, including fair labour policies, transparent practices, and equitable distribution of AI's economic benefits.
5. Empower Key Stakeholders - Provide actionable recommendations to organizations, policymakers, and workers for mitigating risks and leveraging the opportunities presented by AI outsourcing.
6. Encourage Long-Term Sustainability - Foster a balanced approach to AI integration that supports innovation while safeguarding employment opportunities and promoting inclusive economic growth.

Conceptual Background

Outsourcing has long been a source of insecurity for employees, often perceived as a threat to job stability. This has created a persistent pressure to develop the right skills to safeguard one's position. While outsourcing and offshoring have traditionally been appealing to companies, the advent of AI is set to accelerate this trend. Workers will increasingly contend with global competition, as technology enables greater automation and efficiency, making overseas counterparts more formidable competitors. The pandemic forced the companies to experiment with remote-work as a feasible option, proved to companies that having all employees in a central location is not a prerequisite for maintaining productivity. This shift in perspective has led many organizations to reconsider their operational models. As Scott Vincent, CEO of Digital Futures, notes, "More organizations are looking at lower-cost locations to tap into workers." Vincent described this trend as 'a real acceleration' [Business Insider, 2024] describing the surge of offshoring across several businesses since the pandemic. Vincent further emphasized, "It is an exponential trend in terms of the pace at which it's moving," highlighting how rapidly the offshoring landscape is evolving.

With remote work proving viable, companies are increasingly inclined to offshore roles to regions where labour costs are lower, without sacrificing output or efficiency. This realization has opened the door to exploring a broader, more cost-effective talent pool worldwide. This trend is expected to continue as businesses seek to balance cost savings with the need for skilled labour, further fuelling the growth of a global, distributed workforce.

Vincent [Business Insider, 2024] pointed out the challenges this trend poses, stating, "*It poses a significant threat to the labour market*." The offshore threat not only extends beyond workers in high-cost regions like the UK or the US being weakened by parallel employees in emerging markets but also making it more problematic for companies to train their own employees who are capable of growth and advancing within the organization. As more roles are outsourced, opportunities for local employees to gain the necessary experience for leadership positions diminish, potentially impacting long-term talent development and organizational stability.

Beyond the immediate productivity gains, Vincent sees a more consequential effect: an "*outflow of human capital*" driven by AI's expanding capabilities. (Business Insider, 2024) As AI evolves to perform increasingly complex tasks, the potential for job displacement grows, leading to a significant migration of skilled roles to regions or systems where AI can be most effectively utilized. This shift could fundamentally reshape the global labour market, with profound implications for both workers and companies.

Threats to Employment

Job displacement is a significant consequence of outsourcing and technological advancement. Because of number of tasks that AI is capable of, Cesario (Business Insider, 2024) expects there will be an extensive job displacement both within the country and across the world. AI-powered offshoring could threaten workforces in major economies by making low-cost employees more efficient and capable of handling high-skilled jobs. AI, with its advanced capabilities, low-cost labour, and its ability to perform tasks more efficiently, is set to displace many conventional jobs. This shift will predominantly affect roles involving routine, repetitive tasks, as these are the most susceptible to automation. It could replace jobs like data entry, accounting, and customer support. It could also take on more complex tasks such as creating AI prompts, high-tech customer service, and marketing. This shift, as experts told Business Insider (Business Insider, 2024), highlights the growing power of AI on the employment. Industries such as manufacturing, customer service, and data processing are already experiencing these transitions. As AI continues to advance, even more complex jobs in sectors like healthcare, finance, and legal services may also face the risk of automation. Digital technology is bound to replace some of the tasks that humans once used to do. Studies show a complex and nuanced connection between artificial intelligence (AI), automation, and low-skilled jobs (Giwa et al., 2024). Although there is an unanimity that automation poses a substantial threat to some less-skilled jobs, its impact varies across industries and regions.

The Routine-Biased Technological Change (RBTC) theory (Autor et al., 2003) explains that automation tends to target routine tasks, which can be either cognitive or manual. Routine tasks follow clear, explicit rules, making them easier to automate with machines or AI. Common examples include data entry, factory assembly work, and certain administrative roles. As automation progresses, these tasks are increasingly performed by technology, reducing demand for workers in routine-heavy, low-skill occupations. The RBTC theory also highlights that this displacement contributes to labour market polarization, as middle-skill jobs decline, making the gap between high-skill and low-skill roles wider (Mondolo, 2022).

Labour market competition

The increasing reliance on AI intensifies competition for the remaining jobs, particularly disadvantaging low-skilled workers who often struggle to find alternative employment. AI and automation often work together in outsourced environments to increase productivity, reduce costs, and minimize the need for human labour. AI-powered outsourcing essentially combines the benefits of outsourcing with the advancements of AI and automation.

In a way, 'Automation' can even be 'redefined' as 'Outsourcing-powered by AI' or the term 'Outsourcing' can be also be redefined as 'the tasks delegated to machines' powered by AI. There is a relationship between automation, low-skilled employment, and outsourcing. Both automation and outsourcing are strategies used by companies to reduce costs. Automation replaces human labour with machines or AI, while outsourcing delegates work to external providers in regions with cheaper labour. Both primarily impact routine tasks. Automation uses technology to handle repetitive tasks, while outsourcing often shifts these same tasks (such as data entry, customer service, or manufacturing) to lower-cost regions. Companies sometimes face a choice between automating a task or outsourcing it. For instance, a company might choose to automate an assembly line with robots rather than outsourcing manufacturing to a low-wage country. Similarly, AI chatbots might replace outsourced customer service.

As automation technology becomes cheaper and more effective, companies may increasingly favour automation over outsourcing. Automation addresses certain challenges of outsourcing, such as time zone differences, communication barriers, and quality control issues. Moreover, automation and outsourcing can complement each other. Outsourced tasks can themselves be automated by the outsourcing provider: for example, a company that outsources payroll processing might rely on an outsourcing provider who uses automated systems to perform these tasks more efficiently.

So, automation can be outsourced in some cases. Companies may choose to outsource the setup and implementation of automation systems (like robotic process automation or AI solutions) to specialized firms. In some cases, outsourcing providers may also use automation themselves to perform tasks more efficiently. After automating processes, companies can also outsource the ongoing maintenance and optimization of automation systems to external vendors who specialize in managing automated technologies. while automation itself involves using technology to replace human labour, the entire process of automating certain tasks or managing automation can be outsourced to specialized providers. This allows companies to benefit from advanced technology without needing to invest heavily in the infrastructure or expertise themselves. In all these scenarios there is job displacement affecting low-skilled workers.

Certain low-skill professions remain particularly vulnerable to AI-driven automation. Jobs involving repetitive physical tasks—such as those in manufacturing, retail, and logistics—are at higher risk. Even middle-skill professions within these industries face increasing threats from advancing AI technologies (Badiuzzaman and Rafiquzzaman, 2020). Smith and Anderson (2014) emphasized that robots are increasingly capable of performing standardized tasks across various industries, creating new efficiencies but posing challenges to workers in occupations reliant on routine or standardized labour.

According to a new study, robots are taking over low-skilled jobs making it difficult for the workers to grow, earn more or change jobs (Basiouny, 2024). The numbers are weighty: Between 2004 and 2008, for every 1000 workers, one robot assigned, reduced the average income in local market by $3900, and by $2,480 between 2008 and 2016. This is equivalent to 1.7% and 1.1% drop of the average career values compared to the year 2000. In the areas where more robots are used, the career earnings declined even further. The low-skilled workers were hit hard after the automation took over their jobs. They struggled to find better similar or better paying jobs. The major reason of the income decline was due to fewer chances of moving up in their careers (Maria, Schubert, Bledi, Pinar, 2024). It means that low-skilled workers experienced a greater drop in career value compared to others, largely because they found it harder to advance or improve their job prospects after automation displaced them. Low-skilled workers felt a bigger negative impact on their career earnings or career opportunities from outsourcing. These workers struggled more to move up in their careers or get better jobs. Many of them could not find new opportunities that paid as much as their previous jobs or offered better prospects for growth. Low-skilled workers whose jobs are displaced by automation and robots struggle more to find better jobs than high-skilled employees (Angie Basiouny, Knowledge at Wharton, 2024).

Essentially, the integration of automation and outsourcing affected low-skilled workers not just by taking away their current jobs, but also by making it tougher for them to move into higher-paying or to be in more stable positions in the future.

The integration of AI outsourcing can drive down wages as automation reduces the demand for human labour, particularly in repetitive or low-value tasks. Industries affected are Manufacturing, Technology and Services, Healthcare and Education. Outsourcing often benefits corporate profits and shareholders while suppressing wages for workers. Jobs that provided stable incomes in sectors like manufacturing and services are replaced with lower-paying or precarious positions. It can also exploit workers in those regions by offering them low wages and poor working conditions. Workers in digital sweatshops (Wikipedia, 2022) often referred to as data workers, play a crucial role in training AI systems by categorizing and labelling data. These sweatshops are typically internet cafes, small office spaces, or homes filled with workers performing repetitive tasks. In the Philippines alone, over 2 million people engage in this type of work to support AI systems. Remotasks, a platform owned by Scale AI, employs at least 10,000 Filipino workers. However, these workers are paid extremely low wages, often below the country's minimum wage, and face delayed or withheld payments with limited avenues for recourse.

As automation and outsourcing become more intertwined, it ultimately leads to wage stagnation and displacement of workers. Some jobs, like software design, computer programming, and content creation (especially animation), may face growing wage stagnation because of outsourcing. For example, countries like South Korea and Canada create a lot of animation work for U.S. companies at lower costs. This outsourcing can lead to lower wages in the U.S. for junior animators, storyboard artists, or graphic designers as the cost of labour in places like South Korea is much lower. The increasing use of AI tools in animation like background generation could lead to fewer entry-level opportunities for animators, potentially suppressing wages in the industry. When tasks are outsourced or replaced by AI tools, the need for human labour in those roles diminishes, resulting in lower wages or job displacement. Some content creators and animators, particularly in places like California, have fought for better wages and working conditions, but the global competition for labour keeps the pressure on companies to outsource work to cheaper regions.

A significant amount of programming and software design work is outsourced to countries with lower labour costs, such as India, Eastern Europe, and Southeast Asia. This allows companies to cut expenses, but it can lead to wage stagnation in countries where wages were once higher. The competition with outsourced labour in places like India or the Philippines has led to stagnant wages for entry-level developers in the U.S. Despite the increasing demand for tech talent, wages have remained relatively flat in certain areas as companies look to outsource specific tasks like coding, debugging, or quality assurance. As more tasks become automated through AI and machine learning, even more jobs within software development are at risk of being offshored, adding another layer to the potential wage suppression.

As tasks are offshored to regions with lower costs of living and labour, workers in high-cost countries often experience wage stagnation. Even though the overall demand for tech and creative jobs may increase, outsourcing can create a two-tier wage system, where a segment of workers experience reduced wages or job insecurity. The entry of workers from lower-wage countries can lead to an oversupply of talent in the global market, which further suppresses wages. Companies can afford to hire at lower rates or demand higher levels of expertise for the same pay. Outsourcing tends to impact lower- and middle-skill jobs more than high-skill, specialized ones. However, as AI becomes a greater part of the picture, even some higher-skill positions might be at risk, which could create a wider income difference between high-skilled and low-skilled workers.

Tasks like code generation, bug fixing, and even user interface design are increasingly being automated through AI-powered tools. These tasks, once handled by software engineers, are now being substituted by algorithms that can do the same work at a little cost. AI tools like deep learning and neural networks can generate animations, design graphics, or even write content. As a result, jobs in animation studios, once performed by junior animators or designers, can now be partially or fully automated, reducing the need for human labour. This further suppresses wages in creative industries. As AI systems replace jobs traditionally outsourced to cheaper labour regions, the competitive pressure on human workers increases, contributing to wage stagnation even in high-wage regions. AI tools being used in regions that already have lower labour costs, workers face wage suppression even in these "offshored" markets. For instance, companies might reduce the number of human workers and instead invest in AI-powered solutions that eliminate the need for manual labour entirely. In sectors like customer service, software support, or animation, AI chatbots and generative AI can replace the roles of entire teams in lower-cost regions. The displaced workers in these countries now face even more difficulty finding work at their previous wage levels, which adds another layer of wage suppression in already low-wage markets. The introduction of AI tools that make it easier to work remotely or to offload tasks to cheaper regions leads to a more globalized labour market. Workers in high-wage countries face increased competition from individuals in lower-wage regions who may be using AI to do the same tasks at a lower cost. AI-powered outsourcing tends to favour higher-skill jobs (like AI developers or data scientists) while pushing lower-skill jobs (like manual labour or data entry) into more vulnerable, lower-wage markets. The lower-skilled jobs in software development, animation, and other creative fields are at risk of being fully automated or outsourced, which leads to wage stagnation and a widening wage gap. Workers in high-wage countries face increased competition from individuals in lower-wage regions who may be using AI to do the same tasks at a lower cost. AI-powered outsourcing tends to favour higher-skill jobs (like AI developers or data scientists) while pushing lower-skill jobs (like manual labour or data entry) into more vulnerable, lower-wage markets. The lower-skilled jobs in software development, animation, and other creative fields are at risk of being fully automated or outsourced, which leads to wage stagnation and a widening wage gap. Even as AI and automation increase productivity, companies may still choose to outsource jobs to AI-driven platforms or lower-cost labour markets, putting downward pressure on wages for local workers. For example, even though the demand for software engineers may be high, AI tools allow companies to reduce the number of developers needed, limiting the upward pressure on wages. Roles that are repetitive and labour-intensive, such as customer service, animation in some cases, or even programming in certain subfields, are at risk of being automated or sent to AI-powered outsourcing solutions. As a result, workers in these fields may find their wages stagnating as employers can rely on cheaper or more efficient solutions.

Wage suppression

Wage suppression due to AI-powered outsourcing is closely tied to the trends as it introduces additional layers of complexity and speed in how outsourcing impacts wages. AI-powered outsourcing amplifies the effect by automating tasks that were once manually handled by low-wage workers, making it easier and more cost-effective for companies to outsource even more jobs to regions with cheaper labour.

RBTC theory speculates that technological progress impacts different types of tasks and jobs to varying degrees, leading to changes in employment and wage disparities (Autor et al., 2003). Workers with high skills in non-routine occupations or unique occupations are in greater demand and paid more due to their balance with advancing technology or their usage of technology. In contrast, low-skilled workers performing routine tasks often face loss of jobs and wage stagnation or decline as machines replace their roles. This rising difference worsens income inequality, as the wages of high-skilled AI workers increase at a much faster rate than those of low-skilled workers. The shifting demand for labour caused by advancing technology significantly impacts wage dynamics. As demand for low-skilled labour declines, these workers may face stagnant or decreasing wages. Meanwhile, high-skilled workers, particularly those who are knowledgeable in AI-related fields, are likely to experience wage growth due to increased demand for their specialized skills (Autor et al., 2003). Businesses might start moving jobs or tasks (outsourcing) to countries where labour costs are much lower compared to wealthier nations. Countries like India, Bangladesh, and the Philippines have a large workforce willing to work for significantly lower wages due to economic conditions. This creates an opportunity for companies to reduce expenses by outsourcing work to these countries, especially for tasks that do not require a physical presence in a specific location or can be done remotely. AI enables companies to manage global teams and use distributed workflows, intensifying competition for routine and even semi-routine tasks. The reliance on AI tools increases the premium on skills needed to leverage these technologies, pushing workers into either low-wage, low-skill jobs or highly skilled, high-paying ones. This is a highlight concerning about how global wage inequalities might drive offshoring trends, potentially affecting local jobs in higher-wage countries.

In local labour markets with higher automation exposure, employment shares and wages decline in a multitude of industries, including those that are not directly facing automation themselves. The findings show that lower employment or a wage decline for industries such as retail, wholesale trade, healthcare, construction, and professional and technical services. The negative labour market outcomes observed in these industries could be because workers whose own industries are impacted by automation may have to or want to migrate to other industries, increasing competition, particularly among less-than-college-educated workers. Increased supply of workers may reduce their negotiation power for wages and lead to a decline in wages if the demand for workers in non-manufacturing industries cannot accommodate these workers (Petrova, Gregor, Bledi, Yildirim, 2024). The rapid adoption of AI technologies disrupts workforce stability, creating uncertainty and anxiety among employees about their job security. The adoption of AI technologies can indeed create significant disruptions in the workforce, leading to concerns about job security. Automation and AI have the potential to take over routine and repetitive tasks, which can lead to job displacement in certain industries. On the flip side, new opportunities may emerge in fields related to AI development, data science, and machine learning, but the shift may not always be smooth for all workers. This can cause uncertainty, especially for employees in sectors where automation is most likely to take hold. AI-driven outsourcing contributes to job instability. With AI tools taking over more tasks, companies can hire freelance workers or gig economy workers to perform jobs, but at much lower wages than full-time employees would receive. This is especially true for tasks in programming, animation, and design where automation reduces demand for traditional full-time roles. Workers in AI-enhanced outsourcing industries may find themselves lacking the benefits and job security that come with traditional regular employment, contributing to long-term wage stagnation. The production of AI-powered platforms means that more workers are forced into the gig economy, where wages are often lower and work is more unwarranted highlights a significant challenge tied to workforce stability and the adoption of AI technologies: the erosion of bargaining power for lower-skilled workers. As automation and AI outsourcing displace certain jobs, these workers may face limited options for transitioning into new industries, especially if they lack the skills needed for higher-demand roles. This dynamic can lead to fewer opportunities and increased competition for the remaining jobs, workers may feel compelled to accept lower wages, even in other industries. As mobility decreases, workers may find it difficult to advance their careers or shift to more stable roles. This could result in long-term income inequality and reduced economic resilience for affected populations. Higher-skilled individuals may benefit from opportunities created by AI and automation, while lower-skilled individuals face reduced prospects, deepening economic divides (Yildirim, 2024).

Work force Stability

Layoffs and workforce reductions continue in 2025, following two years of significant job cuts across industries such as technology, media, finance, manufacturing, retail, and energy. While the reasons for these staff reductions vary among companies, many of the cost-cutting measures are taking place against the backdrop of rapid technological advancements and transformation (Business Insider, 2025). This is also creating uncertainty and anxiety among employees about their job security.

When the workers are displaced in one industry, they often spill into other sectors, creating a "crowding effect" in the labour market (Petrova et al., 2024). Industries already impacted by automation can see displaced workers moving into adjacent roles, such as warehouse operations or service jobs, further saturating the market. This increased competition, particularly among workers without a college degree, can drive wages down and make jobs harder to secure for everyone in those industries. Often a fallback for displaced workers, but with more people competing for the same pool of jobs, wages, and job security decline.

Socio-economic disparity

The economic benefits of AI outsourcing are often concentrated among a few stakeholders, exacerbating existing inequalities and leaving vulnerable groups at greater risk. AI outsourcing can amplify economic inequalities if not managed carefully. While it can drive efficiency and reduce costs for businesses, the wealth generated often flows to a small group—typically major corporations, investors, and tech professionals—while those in lower-income or outsourced roles may see limited benefits. Additionally, workers in vulnerable groups may face job displacement as automation replaces tasks they traditionally perform. Without proper policies like retraining programs, equitable wealth distribution, and regulations to ensure fair wages in outsourced AI-related jobs, the disparities could deepen further.

Moreover, low-skilled workers' career prospects were affected the most. This decline in opportunities made people change their long-term decisions, such as housing and education, voting, and political decisions. It is important to consider the impacts of automation from a broader perspective- focusing not only on industries affected and occupation of workers but beyond. Automation and robotization affect both workers' wages and occupational mobility, and expectations regarding future wages and mobility may influence individuals' long-term investments, perceptions, and political behaviours today (Petrova, Gregor, Bledi, Yildirim, 2024). When low-skilled workers face diminished career prospects due to automation or AI outsourcing, it can trigger ripple effects throughout their lives. Automation or outsourcing reduces wages in one industry and has a 'spillover effect' (Angie Basiouny, Knowledge at Wharton, 2024) on other industries, in part because workers earn less and have less money to spend. The buying power of the workers is reduced. Job insecurity and reduced opportunities often push individuals to make more cautious or even limiting choices in critical areas like housing, education, and family planning. People might opt for less stable or lower-quality housing to cut costs, which can affect their long-term financial security and quality of life. Families may deprioritize higher education for their children due to financial constraints or a belief that certain career paths are no longer viable. Declining opportunities in certain regions can lead to depopulation, as people migrate to areas with more promising job markets, further weakening the local economy.

Policymakers face challenges

Policymakers face challenges in balancing to support innovation with the protection of workers' rights and job security in the face of rapid technological change. They often walk a tightrope between fostering innovation and ensuring workers' rights and job security, particularly in an era marked by rapid advancements in technology. It is challenging in several ways. Many new jobs in the tech-driven economy (e.g., gig work) often lack traditional protections like benefits, job security, and union representation. Crafting policies to extend these protections to non-traditional workers is essential. A critical issue that highlights the tension between technological progress and worker rights, particularly when it comes to the acceptance of AI, automation, or outsourcing. Labor unions like the American Federation of Labor and Congress of Industrial Organizations (AFL-CIO) (Peopleresults,2025) are rightly concerned about the lack of transparency and collaboration in implementing these technologies. U.S. labour unions are increasingly alarmed by the rapid adoption of advanced technologies and their integration into production processes. Union leaders are particularly concerned that business owners are implementing these changes to hire, monitor, evaluate, discipline, and even terminate employees without consulting their workforces.

Policymakers must balance incentivizing businesses to adopt these technologies while creating safety nets for affected workers. The displacement of salaried employees and the rise of offshore outsourcing in the service sector have sparked commotion among economists, business consultants, academics, politicians, and the media. In response to growing criticism toward offshore outsourcing in the U.S., local, state, and federal governments have felt compelled to act. By the end of 2006, lawmakers in more than 40 states had issued proposals aimed at restricting the offshore outsourcing of government contracts (Youxu Cai Tjader, Jennifer S. Shang, Luis G. Vargas, 2010).

Meanwhile, the advocates of free trade, led by mainstream economists, have strongly criticized these actions, labelling them as a reviving the old policies that protect local industries by taxing imports and cautioning them of potential negative consequences. This clash between supporters and opponents of outsourcing has drawn significant attention from the public and lawmakers alike.

As pressure mounts on governments at all levels to address the issue, offshore outsourcing has become a critical policy challenge. Should policymakers intervene in the offshoring practices of U.S. businesses, or should they allow the free market to operate unhindered? The decisions made will have far-reaching implications for the well-being of U.S. citizens, as well as for businesses and individuals around the world (Youxu Cai Tjader, Jennifer S. Shang, Luis G. Vargas, 2010).

Resistance to change

The most challenging phase of Outsourcing is the Transition phase. Workers and organizations may resist adopting new technologies or training programs due to fear of change or lack of resources, further hindering adaptation. Resistance to change, whether from workers or organizations, can be a significant barrier to adopting new technologies or training programs. This resistance often stems from several key factors. Workers may worry that new technologies will automate their roles, making them redundant. The need to learn new skills can feel overwhelming, especially for employees with limited prior experience in similar tools or systems. Organizations might struggle to allocate sufficient resources—financial or otherwise—for training programs or technology investments. Long-standing organizational norms or fear of disrupting established workflows can discourage change. Leadership might fail to communicate the benefits or long-term necessity of adopting new solutions effectively. Within an organisational structure people may resist change due to loss of control, loss of their assigned tasks, loss of comfort (Dent, E.B., Galloway Goldberg, 1999), or fear of the unknown (A. Plugge and J. Brook, 2012). Losing control and losing comfort are likely to be the key factors for influencing the perceived degree of resistance. The co-ordination of labour is strongly dependent on the complexity of the providers' sourcing delivery model. To be specific, the more a provider applies a blended approach of its sourcing delivery model (e.g. onsite, onshore, offshore), the more the co-ordination of labour increases (A. Plugge and J. Brook, 2012). From worker's perspective, employees may feel they have less autonomy or input in their roles when new technologies or processes are introduced. For example, automated systems might shift decision-making away from individuals, leading to feelings of disempowerment. From organization's perspective, departments or subunits might resist changes if they perceive that adopting new technologies could centralize control, diminishing their influence or decision-making power. Changes often require individuals to step outside their comfort zones, which can create anxiety and fear of failure. This is particularly true if the new system or training program is perceived as too complex or unfamiliar. Subunits that have optimized their workflows over time may view changes as disruptions that add uncertainty and unpredictability. Fear of the unknown is another crucial factor influencing resistance to change. This fear arises when individuals or subunits feel uncertain about how new technologies, systems, or training programs will impact their roles or the organization. It ties closely with psychological discomfort and apprehension about unforeseen consequences. Employees may question whether the new technology or training will benefit them or if it could lead to challenges, like skill mismatches or performance scrutiny. Subunits might worry about how the change will impact overall workflows or interdepartmental relationships. When details about changes are vague or not effectively communicated, it fuels doubt and speculation, increasing anxiety. This often results in worst-case scenario thinking, where individuals assume the change could have negative consequences. People naturally gravitate toward routines and familiar processes because they feel predictable and safe. Uncharted territory can seem threatening, even if the long-term outcome could be positive.

THE IMPERATIVE FOR UPSKILLING

Andrew Yeung (Business Insider, 2024) predicts we will see "an army of offshore talent equipped with AI tools." It is a fascinating trend in the global workforce. The idea suggests a significant shift in how businesses leverage human and technological resources. This could mean that companies will increasingly tap into global talent pools, empowering offshore workers with cutting-edge AI tools to enhance productivity, reduce costs, and scale operations more efficiently. With this it also raises interesting questions about the dynamics of remote work, talent competition, and upskilling (Jaiswal et al., 2023; Karthikeyan and Singh, 2025). One of the most common threats is 'AI will not take your job, but someone who knows how to use it will' (Andrew Yeung, 2024). It is very likely that someone who is based abroad and skilled in AI will take your job. It is a powerful statement that captures the essence of the AI revolution. The idea is that the tools themselves are not inherently job-stealers, but rather enablers for those who embrace and master them. It is a wake-up call for individuals and organizations to adapt and evolve their skill sets. The phrase emphasizes the importance of adaptability and lifelong learning. By embracing AI and understanding how to use it effectively, individuals can future-proof their careers and stay relevant in a rapidly changing job market. Jeff Maggioncalda of Coursera emphasizes that this threat simply comes from 'someone who matches you but costs less' (Jeff Maggioncalda, 2024). It also means that the person overseas does not certainly have to be better (Business Insider, 2024). This is interesting in context of globalization, cost effectiveness, global talent competition and the future of work. Andrew (Andrew Yeung, X, 2024) also predicts that the combination of offshore talent and AI is rapidly shifting the landscape of white-collar work. If founders and executives can leverage AI-assisted offshore workers who are good enough at engineering, design, marketing, and admin tasks, the traditional high-cost workforce could be in trouble.

It is not even about whether offshore workers are better—just that they are cheaper and can now use AI to close the skill gap. It is both an opportunity and a threat, depending on how individuals and industries adapt. AI and offshore talent are democratizing access to skills, which is great for startups and companies looking to scale quickly and cost-effectively. But for professionals in high-cost regions, it is a wake-up call. It is no longer enough to rely on traditional skills—one must learn how to work alongside AI, specialize in areas where human insight or creativity still outshines machines, or focus on roles that require deep interpersonal or cultural knowledge. The real question is: What happens to professionals in high-cost regions? Do they need to become AI-enhanced specialists, or will certain jobs just disappear? It is both an opportunity and a threat, depending on how individuals and industries adapt. AI and offshore talent are democratizing access to skills, which is great for startups and companies looking to scale quickly and cost-effectively. AI can also make everyone more productive. Instead of seeing offshore talent equipped with AI as competition, some might see them as collaborators—offloading routine tasks so local professionals can focus on higher-value work. The challenge lies in keeping up with this rapid pace of change and avoiding complacency. Offshore workers who collaborate with AI might initially benefit from increased efficiency and access to global opportunities, but as AI systems become more advanced and autonomous, their roles could eventually become redundant. The big question is whether people in these roles will have time and resources to reskill or pivot into higher-value areas before it is too late.

The AI implementation impact on employment requires re-skilling and up-skilling programs for low-skilled employees to learn and improve their abilities so that they can be competent with the changing demands of the job market (Fiyinfoluwa Giwa, Nicholas Ngepah, 2024). Offshore workers who use AI tools to perform tasks (e.g., coding, design, content creation, or data analysis) are essentially helping to refine and improve those tools. As AI becomes more capable, the need for human intervention decreases. A designer using AI tools to create graphics may eventually be replaced by an AI that can generate designs autonomously. A programmer using AI coding assistants may train the AI to write code independently, reducing the need for human programmers. This phenomenon is not limited to offshore workers. Many roles across industries involve tasks that AI can do on its own or improved by AI, and workers in these roles may inadvertently contribute to their own obsolescence.

Sagar Khatri, co-founder and CEO of Multiplier, supports Andrew Yeung's thesis. Companies will feel an immense burden to offshore and outsource—not only for cost-cutting but also for accessing skilled talent (Business Insider, 2024). With many businesses automating payroll and labour law compliance, employers can now hire workers from anywhere, making geographic barriers less relevant in the hiring process. This aligns with the broader trend of companies shifting from cost-driven outsourcing to talent-driven outsourcing. As automation simplifies administrative hurdles like payroll and compliance, businesses are no longer constrained by geographic hiring limitations. Instead of just seeking cheaper labour, they are now searching for the best available talent worldwide, accelerating the demand for offshore professionals with specialized skills. Many industries are facing a shortage of skilled workers, particularly in tech, healthcare, and engineering. This shortage is pushing companies to look beyond their local talent pools. Offshore and remote hiring allows companies to tap into a global talent pool, where skilled workers may be more abundant. Tools like Multiplier (Sagar Khatri's company), Deel, and Remote simplify cross-border payroll, taxes, and benefits administration. This removes a significant barrier to hiring internationally. AI-driven platforms can navigate the complexities of local labour laws, ensuring that companies remain compliant when hiring workers in different countries. The rise of collaboration tools (e.g., Slack, Zoom, Microsoft Teams) and cloud-based platforms makes it easier for distributed teams to work together seamlessly. Certain skills may be scarce in one region but readily available in another. For example, a company in the U.S. might hire AI specialists from Eastern Europe or software developers from India. While cost is not the primary driver, it remains a factor. Skilled workers in lower-cost regions often command lower salaries than their counterparts in high-cost areas. Offshore hiring allows companies to scale their teams quickly without being limited by local talent availability.

AI can boost the efficiency of foreign workers and enable them with higher-skill roles. Based on the benefits of AI, a company in New York might find it easier to hire from developing countries like the Philippines, Mexico, Indonesia, India, Pakistan, Brazil, Vietnam, and Egypt. Workers in high-cost regions may face stiffer competition from highly skilled, lower-cost workers abroad. killed professionals in emerging markets will have more opportunities to work for global companies, often at competitive salaries by local standards. Traditional job markets may become more globalized, with companies prioritizing skills and experience over geographic location. Sagar Khatri's insight underscores a fundamental shift in the global workforce: the democratization of opportunity. As technology breaks down barriers, skilled workers from anywhere in the world can compete for top jobs, and companies can build diverse, high-performing teams without being constrained by geography. However, this also means that workers must be proactive in adapting to this new reality.

This shift also reinforces the idea that AI and automation do not just replace jobs—they also reshape labour markets by making global talent more accessible. While this creates new opportunities for skilled professionals in emerging markets, it also intensifies competition for workers in developed economies. AI is not just enabling offshore hiring; it is also transforming how work gets done. AI-powered recruitment platforms can identify and vet candidates from around the world. Automation tools can handle monotonous tasks, permitting workers in other countries to focus on important and complex tasks instead of routine work. This means that geographic location will matter less as companies prioritize skills and expertise over proximity. AI is making it affordable to people not only to teach AI and other topics in English but also in different languages. Everybody can learn this as language is not an obstacle anymore. Professionals will increasingly compete (and collaborate) with peers from around the world. To remain competitive, workers will need to continuously update their skills and adapt to new technologies. The key takeaway is that adaptability is survival. Workers—whether offshore or onshore—must embrace lifelong learning and stay ahead of technological trends to remain relevant in the workforce.

Jeff Maggioncalda, CEO of Coursera said that in abroad online learning is providing greater access to acquiring skills, especially for young professionals (Business Insider, 2024). In many developing countries, labour markets are more flexible, making it easier for companies to hire, fire, and relocate workers as needed. This flexibility is particularly appealing for startups and businesses in fast-changing industries. Severance packages and legal risks associated with layoffs are often lower in developing countries, reducing the financial burden on companies. Additionally, a large portion of the workforce consists of young professionals who are highly motivated and eager to acquire new skills and advance their careers. When equipped with AI tools, these workers often experience a significant boost in productivity, sometimes surpassing more experienced professionals in efficiency. This is because younger workers are typically more adaptable to new technologies, quicker to learn emerging tools, and less constrained by traditional workflows. AI enhances their capabilities, allowing them to automate repetitive tasks, analyse data more effectively, and optimize decision-making, making them highly valuable in a globally competitive job market.

This is a crucial point and highlights why developing countries are becoming increasingly attractive to employers looking to build agile, cost-effective, and highly productive teams. This dynamic is so impactful as this is an amiable situation for companies and workers. From companies per se, it is access to a highly motivated, cost-effective workforce, the ability to scale operations quickly and efficiently, and increased productivity and innovation driven by AI-enabled workers. New technology is gradually being used to handle tasks and roles in outsourcing and offshoring businesses. This will affect Global employment and the impact will vary between emerging and developed countries. The emerging countries will experience a 40% impact due to automation, up-skilling, and job shift and a 60% impact in developed economies due to higher automation, re-skilling, AI integration, and Global job competition (IMF- Mauro, Florence, Longji, Giovanni, Augustus, Carlo, Emma, Marina, 2024).

From workers per se there are opportunities to work with global companies and gain valuable experience, exposure to cutting-edge tools and technologies that enhance their skill sets, and higher earning potential compared to local job markets. When young, tech-savvy workers in developing countries are given access to AI tools, the productivity gains can be significant, example: a marketer using AI for content generation and campaign optimization can achieve results comparable to a high-end agency, a software developer using AI coding assistants can produce high-quality code faster than a more experienced developer working without AI.

AI tools often come with built-in tutorials and intuitive interfaces, enabling workers to quickly learn and apply new skills. The technology can help workers in developing countries to learn faster and compete with higher-salaried workers in developed countries. As workers in developing countries gain access to better-paying jobs and skill-building opportunities, they contribute to the growth of a global middle class. This trend is helping to redistribute economic opportunities to developing countries, potentially reducing global inequality over time. To remain competitive, businesses in developed economies will need to focus on innovation, creativity, and high-value tasks that are harder to automate or outsource.

Rather than viewing this trend as a threat, workers and companies in developed countries can explore ways to collaborate with global talent, creating win-win partnerships. The key to success in helping the business grow is the ability of many workers to quickly learn new skills and execute them to add value. The combination of a young, ambitious workforce in developing countries and the power of AI tools is reshaping the global labour market. Although it is challenging, it also creates huge opportunities for both businesses and workers. The key for companies is to harness this potential responsibly, and for workers—whether in developing or developed countries—is to continuously adapt and upskill.

So basically, it means that the era of AI-driven work is here, and integrating AI skills into your resume is no longer optional—it is essential. Having AI expertise makes you noticeable in an increasingly competitive job market if you have to automate tasks, boost productivity, or make an informed decision. (Business Insider, 2024). Employers are looking for candidates who can leverage AI tools effectively, not just to replace manual work but to innovate and optimize workflows. So, now is the time to embrace AI, upskill, and future-proof your career (Jaiswal et al., 2023; Karthikeyan and Singh, 2025). Whether you are just starting or looking to pivot in your career, adding AI skills to your toolkit can open doors to new opportunities and help you stay ahead of the curve. Companies are increasingly looking for candidates who can leverage AI tools to drive efficiency, innovation, and growth. As AI continues to transform industries, having AI skills ensures you remain relevant and adaptable. AI tools can enable you to work efficiently, not harder, by automating irrelevant tasks and offering valuable insights.

According to a World Economic Forum report, new job roles will require expertise in blockchain technology, analytics, cloud operations, data science, and automation. As outsourcing evolves, acquiring these new skills makes the workers capable of future jobs. Maintaining the salaries of offshore professionals like data scientists and engineers is more cost-effective than onshore teams. In the coming years, businesses and organizations in major outsourcing countries will consider AI-prepared outsourcing companies while making decisions. With the development of AI, and its other new advanced data technologies, the outsourcing or offshoring industry will transform permanently making it inevitable for remote employees to be updated in advanced AI technological skill sets.

Layoffs and workforce reductions have persisted into 2025, following two years of significant job cuts across industries including tech, media, finance, manufacturing, retail, and energy. Companies cite various reasons for downsizing, many cost-cutting measures are occurring against the backdrop of rapid technological change. According to a recent World Economic Forum survey (Global Risks Report, 2024), approximately 41% of companies worldwide anticipate reducing their workforces over the next five years due to the increasing adoption of artificial intelligence. Major corporations such as Dropbox, Google, and IBM have already announced job cuts linked to AI-driven efficiencies. Businesses are increasingly relying on AI to stay competitive in a rapidly evolving technological landscape. This shift underscores the need for workers to adapt by acquiring new skills that are in demand in the AI-driven economy.

A recent finding suggests that ChatGPT is unlikely to take away jobs in the years to come. However, a Gen Zer expert in AI technology is likely to substitute. As per the predictions of experts, Gen Zers are well-positioned to take advantage of the AI revolution (Business Insider, 2023). Before the launch of ChatGPT in late 2022, younger generations—such as Millennials and Gen Z—were generally more comfortable with and receptive to AI developments compared to older generations. Younger people tend to be more adaptable to new technologies and are often early adopters. They are more likely to experiment with and embrace AI tools, whether for productivity, creativity, or entertainment. This contrasts with older generations, who may be more hesitant or skeptical about adopting new technologies. As AI continues to evolve, bridging the generational gap in comfort and understanding will be crucial. Efforts to educate and train older generations on AI tools, as well as addressing concerns about job security and ethical use, will ensure that AI perks are accessible to everyone, regardless of age. Employers and employees when surveyed, more than 90% said generative AI has helped them with time-saving, creativity-enhancing, and getting better business outcomes. Flexing your AI skills helps you get that pay rise; a recent study suggests.

STATISTICS – WHY AI IS NO LONGER A 'NICE TO HAVE SKILL' BUT 'IT IS A MUST-HAVE SKILL'

Pew Research poll, conducted in March, out of 10,701 in the US, young adults (18 - 29)- 18% use ChatGPT at work compared to middle-aged adults (30-49) - 13% use ChatGPT at work, and among older adults (50-64), only 8% use ChatGPT at work. In April, a Resume Builder survey of nearly 1,200 business leaders found that 90% were actively looking to hire employees with ChatGPT experience (CU Today, 2024). A study analyzed over 1.3 million job posts on a major freelancing platform from July 2021 to July 2023 to see how Gen AI tools affected job demand. The impact of ChatGPT after it was introduced, jobs that could be automated saw 21% fewer postings per week. Writing jobs had the biggest decline (30.37% fewer postings). Software, app, and web development jobs dropped by 20.62%. Engineering jobs saw a smaller decline (10.42%) (Harvard Business Review, 2024). Freelance jobs in graphic design and 3D modeling dropped by 17.01% within a year. The gen AI tools formed a great impact. The drop in demand happened as more people learned about Gen AI tools and wanted to use them. The study also considered other factors, like how complex the jobs were and how much employers were willing to pay. The number of skills needed for each job measured the job complexity. After ChatGPT, complexity increased by 2.18% for jobs that could be automated, compared to manual jobs. For automation-prone jobs, employers increased the pay by 5.71%. This means that while some jobs became more complex, employers were also willing to pay more for them. Since the launch of ChatGPT, 903 job postings were identified that mentioned ChatGPT in their skill requirements. Over 88% of these roles fall into categories likely to be affected by automation. The majority (82%) are linked to software, app, and web development. The demand for ChatGPT skills has steadily increased, with an average rise of 0.68 job postings per week since its release. This trend highlights ChatGPT's growing relevance in the job market, particularly in fields prone to automation, emphasizing its role in shaping future employment opportunities (Harvard Business Review, 2024).

These results show that using AI tools at work is becoming more important. Workers are likely learning new skills to include Gen AI in their jobs to stay competitive considering it as a highly valued skill. This trend shows that reskilling is already happening and is becoming essential as the job market changes due to progress in generative AI. As businesses and industries adapt to these technological shifts, the demand for workers proficient in AI tools like ChatGPT is likely to grow, emphasizing the need for continuous learning and upskilling to remain competitive in an AI-driven economy. (Harvard Business Review, 2024).

ACTIONABLE STRATEGIES AND HOW YOU CAN USE TECHNOLOGY

It is suggested that education departments should work on improving and updating training and learning programs while fostering deeper collaboration between industry, academia, and research institutions. (Yang Shen and Xiuwu Zhang, 2024).

As a policy recommendation, this study suggests introducing targeted training programs to help workers develop the skills needed for the changing job market shaped by technology. It also highlights the need to track AI adoption and create proactive policies to reduce potential job market disruptions, ensuring a smooth transition for everyone involved. (Fiyinfoluwa Giwa, Nicholas Ngepah, 2024).

Overall, the interplay between automation and outsourcing underscores the need for targeted interventions to address their combined effects. Updating education and training systems to equip workers with skills for emerging roles, strengthening social safety nets, and implementing policies to support displaced workers are critical to mitigating job displacement and reducing economic disparities.

Vincent, CEO of digital Futures, said governments and businesses in developed countries must collaborate to report the impending changes in the job market. Companies that offshore due to a lack of skilled labour should see improvements in education systems to better prepare the workforce. Governments could introduce regulations limiting the number of employees a company can hire overseas. This means setting a cap on how many jobs a company can outsource to other countries, ensuring that a certain percentage of jobs remain within the domestic labour market. The goal of such regulation would likely be to protect local employment opportunities and reduce the potential negative impacts of outsourcing on the domestic workforce (Business Insider, 2024).

Jeff Maggioncalda of Coursera suggests that imposing tariffs or similar protections could help balance the cost of labour between countries. Just as tariffs on imported goods increase their price to reflect the domestic cost, regulating or taxing offshore labour could make it less financially advantageous for companies to outsource. This could help level the playing field by making domestic labour more competitive with lower-cost overseas labour, thereby reducing the pressure on local wages and job security (Business Insider, 2024).

The way companies communicate is important. Being open with employees about how AI could change jobs helps build trust. While some jobs may be affected, clear and honest discussions can reduce uncertainty and help workers prepare for future changes. (Ozge, Jonas and Xinrong zhu, 2024). Companies in industries at high risk of automation should act quickly. They should clearly explain how AI will be used and why, while also reassuring employees that their work is always valued.

While there is a worry about job losses, AI can also help improve jobs and boost productivity. The study shows that jobs needing AI skills, like using ChatGPT, are increasing. As AI becomes part of more roles, companies should train workers with a mix of skills to adapt and work alongside these new technologies.

To stay competitive, workers need to keep learning and improving their skills. AI is changing jobs by taking over routine tasks, allowing people to focus more on judgment and decision-making. Research points out that AI integration boosts productivity across various skill levels to a greater extent, with the greatest benefits seen among low-wage workers. Investing in AI training is a smart strategy for closing skill gaps and improving productivity. To make the most of these advancements, managers should focus on providing AI tools to lower-wage workers and developing practical training programs that support their growth and adaptability. (Ajay, Joshua, and Avi, 2019).

The new findings reveal a clear gender gap in ChatGPT usage at work, with women less likely to adopt the technology as compared to men. This demands a need for specialized training programs to bridge this gap and ensure everyone has equal access to the benefit of generative AI (Anders, Emilie, 2024).

It is not enough to simply provide AI access to employees- companies need to consciously invest in focused, job-specific targeted training programs to ensure employees can effectively use these tools and improve their work (Emma Wiles and her coauthors, 2024).

Working with industry experts and educational institutions and partnering with them can help managers create training programs that keep up with changing skill demands. For ex., Microsoft and IBM. These companies are known for their strong AI training initiatives, and setting standards to stay ahead in AI adoption in businesses (Ozge, Jonas and Xinrong zhu, 2024).

Managers will also need to develop new competencies, particularly in AI task delegation. Managers need to guide their teams in deciding which tasks should be handled by AI and which should stay with human employees. As AI takes on move routine work, leveraging the strengths of both humans and technology is a key factor in improving efficiency and preserving creativity and control (Ozge, Jonas and Xinrong zhu, 2024).

Organizations must capitalize in training their workforce to integrates AI in everyday tasks, to stay ahead. The emphasis should be on enhancing human skills and not on replacing them. Managers who implement this forward-thinking approach within their organization will help their teams to adapt to new technologies, drive long-term growth and flexibility, innovation, and long term success.

CONCLUSION

It is assuming that the companies will spend much more on hiring workers overseas (Business Insider, 2024). A study by Digital Futures found that the UK's 100 largest companies spend about £750 million ($951 million) per year on offices abroad. The UK could be missing out on 1.2 million jobs. This could also mean a loss of £16 billion in tax revenue. This shows how much outsourcing might be impacting the UK economy. Companies need to find a better balance between saving money by hiring overseas and supporting jobs and the economy at home. there is an ongoing struggle between improving efficiency (getting work done faster and cheaper) and keeping people employed, when companies replace human workers with machines or outsource. (Yang Shen & Xiuwu Zhang, 2024, Liu 2018; Morgan 2019). There is ongoing debate about where technology is leading us, how AI will change the way humans work, and whether increased productivity could lead to large-scale job losses. (Yang Shen & Xiuwu Zhang, 2024, Liu 2018; Morgan 2019). In this rapidly evolving landscape, both employees and employers must address the challenges of job displacement by promoting continuous learning, adopting technological innovations, and creating new opportunities for value creation that cannot be solely achieved through technology.

The uncertainty around the timeline of AI-driven transformation makes adaptability crucial. The focus on collaboration with AI rather than outright replacement suggests that workers who proactively reskill and embrace AI as a tool will likely have a competitive edge (Akansha et al., 2021). Since 2016, demand for AI skills has grown quickly, especially in IT, finance, and professional services. This shows how AI is changing industries and the job market. (Alexander et al., 2024). Instead of directly measuring how much AI technology is being used in companies, researchers look at how many job postings require AI skills (Grennan and Michaely, 2020; Acemoglu et al., 2022). If a company is hiring more workers with AI skills, it is likely investing in AI and integrating it into its operations. Researchers use job demand for AI-skilled workers as a signal that AI is being implemented. AI deployment may lead to shifts in job roles, skill requirements, and wage structures. Potential effects include job displacement in routine tasks and increased demand for high-skilled workers. Upskilling involves learning new abilities to better understand and use AI systems. Hence, gaining AI-related skills is essential for employees to stay employable in the future. (Akansha, Joe Arun, Arup, 2021). Around 30–40% of employees will need to improve their skills significantly within the next 10 years. Big companies like Walmart, IBM, Infosys, and Amazon are working on AI-powered products and services. These companies are also investing in training their employees with the right technical and soft skills. This shows that as AI grows, both companies and workers need to adapt (Hancock et al.,2020). Modern companies don't see AI as a replacement for humans. Instead, they believe AI and humans can work together, using their strengths to complement each other. Coursera's Jeff Maggioncalda (Business Insider, 2024) emphasized that workers must focus on how they can "add real value in a world where more and more pieces of their job get automated or outsourced." This means letting go of repetitive tasks and focusing more on work that requires thinking, creativity, problem-solving, and smart decision-making. Instead of competing with AI, workers should use it as a tool to work faster and better. The key is to develop uniquely human skills—like emotional intelligence, leadership, and complex problem-solving—that AI cannot easily replicate. By doing so, workers can remain indispensable in an increasingly automated world. He also emphasizes the urgency of embracing AI. Workers should find ways to use technology to automate parts of their jobs. If they do not, someone else—possibly in another country—will do it instead. In other words, learn to work with AI and automation, or risk being left behind.

In a long run, companies that focus on training employees for new skills will be better prepared to succeed as AI continues to grow. Businesses can stay competitive by training employees to handle complex tasks and encouraging continuous learning. This helps improve innovation, increase productivity, and keep up with fast-changing technology. (Ozge eta l., 2024).

To empower organizations, policymakers, and employees with actionable strategies for navigating the transformative impact of AI-driven outsourcing, fostering adaptability, promoting equitable labour practices, and ensuring a sustainable and inclusive future of work. Gen AI will keep transforming the job market by automating many tasks and changing the skills needed to succeed.

ACKNOWLEDGMENT

The authors would like to acknowledge the use of AI for enhancing language and correcting grammatical errors in the present study.

REFERENCES

Agrawal, A., Gans, J., & Goldfarb, A. (2019). *Prediction machines*. Harvard Business Review Press.

Autor, D. (2019). *Work of the past, work of the future* (Working Paper No. 25588). National Bureau of Economic Research. http://www.nber.org/papers/w25588

Autor, D. H. (2003). The skill content of recent technological change: An empirical exploration. *The Quarterly Journal of Economics*, *118*(4), 1279–1333.

Badiuzzaman, M., & Rafiquzzaman, M. (2020). Automation and robotics: A review of potential threat on unskilled and lower skilled labour unemployment in highly populated countries. *International Business Management*, *14*(1), 16–24.

Basiouny, A. (2024, November 5). Robots are taking over low-skilled jobs—and changing votes. *Knowledge at Wharton.* https://knowledge.wharton.upenn.edu/article/robots-are-taking-over-low-skilled-jobs-and-changing-votes/

Demirci, O., Hannane, J., & Zhu, X. (2024). Research: How Gen AI is already impacting the labor market. *Harvard Business Review.* https://hbr.org/2024/11/research-how-gen-ai-is-already-impacting-the-labor-market

Giwa, F., & Ngepah, N. (2024). The relationship between artificial intelligence and low-skilled employment in South Africa. *Heliyon*, *10*(23), e40640.

Grennan, J., & Michaely, R. (2020). Artificial intelligence and high-skilled work: Evidence from analysts. *Swiss Finance Institute Research Paper No. 20-84.* https://ssrn.com/abstract=3681574

Jaiswal, A., Arun, C. J., & Varma, A. (2023). Rebooting employees: Upskilling for artificial intelligence in multinational corporations. In *Artificial intelligence and international HRM* (pp. 114–143). Routledge.

Karthikeyan, C., & Singh, S. (2025). Skill development challenges in the era of artificial intelligence (AI). In *Integrating technology in problem-solving educational practices* (pp. 189–218). IGI Global.

Liu, L. (2018). Occupational therapy in the fourth industrial revolution. *Canadian Journal of Occupational Therapy*, *85*(4), 272–283.

Liu, Y., & Peng, J. (2023). The impact of "AI unemployment" on contemporary youth and its countermeasures. *Youth Exploration*, *241*(1), 43–51. https://doi.org/10.13583/j.cnki.issn1004-3780.2023.01.004

McKinsey & Company. (2017a). *Jobs lost, jobs gained: Workforce transitions in a time of automation.* https://www.mckinsey.com/~/media/BAB489A30B724BECB5DEDC41E9BB9FAC.ashx

McKinsey & Company. (2017b). *A future that works: Automation, employment and productivity*. https://www.mckinsey.com/~/media/mckinsey/featured%20insights/Digital%20Disruption/Harnessing%20automation%20for%20a%20future%20that%20works/MGI-A-future-that-works-Executive-summary.ashx

Mondolo, J. (2022). The composite link between technological change and employment: A survey of the literature. *Journal of Economic Surveys*, *36*(4), 1027–1068.

Morgan, J. (2019). Will we work in twenty-first century capitalism? A critique of the fourth industrial revolution literature. *Economy and Society*, *48*(3), 371–398. https://doi.org/10.1080/03085147.2019.1620027

Nedelkoska, L., & Quintini, G. (n.d.). *Automation, skills use and training* (OECD Social, Employment and Migration Working Papers No. 202). https://dx.doi.org/10.1787/2e2f4eea-en

Paradis, T. (2024, June 16). The impact of artificial intelligence on employment: The role of virtual agglomeration. *Business Insider.* https://www.businessinsider.com/ai-supercharge-offshoring-making-foreign-workers-more-efficient-stronger-cheaper-2024-6

Petrova, M., Schubert, G., Taska, B., & Yildirim, P. (n.d.). *Automation, career values, and political preferences* (Working Paper No. 32655).

Reuter, D., Stewart, A., Goel, S., Jackson, S., & Syme, P. (2025, January 16). The list of major companies laying off staff in the new year. *Business Insider.* https://www.businessinsider.com/recent-company-layoffs-laying-off-workers-2025

Shen, Y., & Zhang, X. (2024). Article. *Humanities & Social Sciences Communications*, *11*, 122. https://www.nature.com/articles/s41599-024-02647-9

Today, C. U. (2024). New Pew Research survey shows Americans increasingly using ChatGPT. *CU Today.* https://www.cutoday.info/Fresh-Today/New-Pew-Research-Survey-Shows-Americans-Increasingly-Using-ChatGPT

Wiles, E., Krayer, L., Abbadi, M., Awasthi, U., Kennedy, R., Mishkin, P., Sack, D., & Candelon, F. (2024). GenAI as an exoskeleton: Experimental evidence on knowledge workers using GenAI on new skills. *SSRN.* https://ssrn.com/abstract=4944588

World Economic Forum. (2023, April 30). *The future of jobs report 2023.* https://www.weforum.org/publications/the-future-of-jobs-report-2023/

World Economic Forum. (2025, January). *Future of jobs report 2025.* https://reports.weforum.org/docs/WEF_Future_of_Jobs_Report_2025.pdf

Chapter 25
Reskilling for the AI Age: Project Management Approaches and Organisational Strategies for Workforce Readiness

Geshwaree Huzooree
https://orcid.org/0000-0001-8076-6636
Edinburgh Napier University, UK

Jeayaram Subramanian
O.P. Jindal Global University, India

Narayanage Jayantha Dewasiri
https://orcid.org/0000-0002-5908-8890
Sabaragamuwa University of Sri Lanka, Sri Lanka & Qasim Ibrahim School of Business, Villa College, Maldives

ABSTRACT

The rapid advancement of artificial intelligence (AI) is transforming industries and job roles, driving a shift in the skills required for success. As automation and data-driven decision-making become central to operations, traditional competencies are becoming obsolete. To remain competitive, organisations must align their workforce with AI-driven demands through reskilling and upskilling initiatives. This chapter explores organisational strategies for workforce readiness, focusing on project management approaches and theoretical frameworks that support skill development. Key models are reviewed to create a framework for developing essential competencies, including interpersonal, intrapersonal, and digital literacy skills. Practical methods such as training programs, partnerships, and continuous feedback are examined. Challenges such as resistance to change, resource constraints, and unequal access to skills development are addressed. By integrating project management with workforce development strategies, organisations can prepare their workforce for evolving demands.

DOI: 10.4018/979-8-3373-1270-5.ch025

1 INTRODUCTION

The rapid advancement of technology, particularly Artificial Intelligence (AI), is profoundly transforming the global economy, business landscapes, and societal structures. AI, described as "a system's ability to interpret external data accurately, learn from it, and apply that knowledge to achieve specific objectives through adaptive decision-making" (Kaplan & Haenlein, 2019), is revolutionizing industries by augmenting or, in some cases, replacing human-driven tasks. For organizations, the challenge lies not only in adopting AI technologies but also in managing the human capital and structural changes necessary for these innovations to thrive (Vrontis et al., 2023; Xu el al., 2023). In this context, project management emerges as a critical discipline, guiding organizations through AI integration while ensuring that the workforce remains agile, skilled, and adaptable to new technologies (Taboada et al., 2023). The application of project management methodologies such as Agile, Lean, and Change Management becomes central to successfully navigating the complexities of AI adoption, workforce reskilling, and organizational transformation (Savio & Ali., 2023; Shoushtari et al., 2024).

At the core of modern AI advancements lies Machine Learning (ML), a subset of AI that enables systems to identify patterns and derive insights from vast datasets without explicit programming (Rane et al., 2024). For organizations, effectively managing the deployment of ML and other AI technologies requires structured project management frameworks that align both technological objectives and workforce readiness (Niederman., 2021; Uren & Edwards., 2023). Project management plays a central role in ensuring that AI projects are executed on time, within budget, and with the right skillsets embedded within the workforce (Project Management Institute, 2021). These methodologies enable the delivery of AI solutions that are not only technically robust but also supported by the requisite human capital, ensuring that employees are prepared through targeted upskilling and reskilling programs. As AI-driven automation redefines job roles, project management techniques like risk management, resource allocation, and stakeholder engagement ensure that these transitions are managed effectively and that workers are equipped to take on new responsibilities (Akeiber, 2025; Savio & Ali, 2023).

The integration of AI has significant implications for both knowledge workers and blue-collar laborers, as it holds the potential to automate a wide range of tasks traditionally carried out by humans (Chan, 2025; Snell & Gekara, 2023). For project managers, this transformation involves not only overseeing the technical deployment of AI systems but also managing the human side of change, ensuring that the workforce is prepared for new roles through effective reskilling and upskilling initiatives. Based upon McKinsey Global Institute's research, it is expected that by 2030, approximately 375 million people, or 14% of the global workforce, may need to transition to new roles due to AI-driven advancements (Manyika et al., 2017). Project management methodologies such as change management are critical during these transitions, helping organizations plan, implement, and communicate the changes necessary for workforce evolution (Chan., 2025; Lokesh et al., 2024). The role of project managers extends beyond the technical implementation of AI to managing the emotional and psychological impacts on workers, ensuring they feel supported and confident as they navigate new opportunities created by AI (Jariwala, 2024; Niederman, 2021).

As AI continues to evolve, the influence on human skills will vary depending on the specific tasks and competencies being automated (Akeiber, 2025; Kaplan & Haenlein, 2019). Certain tasks, such as routine manual labor, are highly susceptible to automation, whereas others, such as critical thinking and problem-solving, will become even more valuable. For project managers, this means developing adaptive strategies to ensure that employees are continuously equipped with the necessary skills. Managing the reskilling and upskilling of employees requires project managers to apply Agile and Lean frameworks, which enable organizations to respond quickly and iteratively to changes in skill requirements (Barach, 2025; Gowrishankkar et al., 2025). These frameworks allow for the continuous adaptation of training programs to meet the needs of both the organization and its employees, ensuring that workforce readiness remains aligned with the rapidly changing landscape of AI technology. Project managers, as the leaders of these efforts, must act as catalysts for change, ensuring that reskilling initiatives are integrated seamlessly into AI adoption strategies (Lokesh et al., 2024; Martins, 2023).

This chapter focuses on how AI is reshaping professional skills and the critical role of project management in overseeing the successful reskilling of the workforce. The project management approach is indispensable when designing and delivering upskilling programs, as it ensures that these initiatives are aligned with the organization's AI integration plans and broader strategic goals. Previous studies have underscored the need for organizations to create training programs or change management programs that are responsive to the evolving demands of AI (Ademola, 2024; Ononiwu et al., 2024). Project management methodologies such as Agile, which fosters flexibility and rapid response to changes in technology is invaluable in this context. These approaches ensure that workforce development efforts are not only efficient but also impactful, helping employees stay ahead of technological advancements (Jariwala, 2024; Taboada et al., 2023; Varshney, 2000).

This chapter examines the impact of AI advancements on workforce skills and provides strategies for project managers to support organizations in reskilling and upskilling their employees. By analyzing frameworks that explain AI's influence on human skills and exploring project management methodologies that facilitate workforce development, this study highlights how organizations can integrate AI adoption with targeted training initiatives. It also emphasizes the importance of an interdisciplinary perspective, combining insights from project management, psychology, and related fields to address both the technical and human aspects of AI integration. Additionally, the study introduces a comprehensive framework outlining the key skills needed in the AI era, offering organizations a structured approach to workforce development. Finally, the chapter identifies areas for future research, particularly on how project management strategies can evolve to meet the challenges of workforce readiness in an AI-driven world.

2 ADVANCEMENTS IN AI AND THEIR IMPACT ON WORKFORCE SKILLS

Recent advancements in AI have significantly reshaped industrial operations and workplace dynamics, introducing both challenges and opportunities for organizations. Historically, AI technologies were leveraged to automate administrative and operational tasks, ranging from data processing and document organization to customer support and financial management. These early applications were primarily focused on streamlining repetitive tasks, improving efficiency, and reducing human error (Niederman, 2021; Rane et al., 2024). From a project management perspective, managing AI adoption during this phase required the implementation of structured processes to ensure smooth integration, minimize disruption, and maintain operational continuity. This is where traditional project management tools such as risk management, scope control, and resource allocation were critical to the success of AI-driven automation projects (Project Management Institute, 2021).

One of the most transformative advancements in AI is the rise of generative AI, which goes beyond traditional AI applications by creating entirely new content rather than simply analyzing existing data. Generative AI models, such as those used in text, image, and even drug development, learn from vast datasets to generate outputs that mimic the characteristics of their inputs (Gangwal et al., 2024). For project managers, this shift introduces a new layer of complexity in planning and executing AI adoption strategies. The need to identify skilled resources who can manage the integration of such innovative technologies is paramount. These technologies not only require robust technical management but also necessitate strategic workforce planning. As generative AI continues to evolve, project managers must anticipate the upskilling and reskilling needs of employees to manage the adoption of new AI systems, ensuring workforce adaptability and readiness.

For instance, the deployment of generative AI models requires significant project management expertise in coordinating teams across various departments, research, development, training, and deployment, ensuring clear communication and effective cross-functional collaboration (Barcaui & Monat., 2023). Managers must use frameworks like Agile to drive iterative, flexible planning, enabling rapid responses to emerging challenges and ensuring that AI solutions align with evolving business objectives (Huzooree, 2024). Such an approach enhances the likelihood of a smooth integration while fostering continuous learning and improvement in AI deployment.

From a project management perspective, implementing AI-driven solutions that enhance employee skills requires careful planning to align technological advancements with organizational needs. This involves assessing the current skill gaps and developing targeted training programs. Project managers must ensure that employees possess the required technical and soft skills, and that reskilling efforts are executed systematically to maximize both individual growth and sustainable organizational resilience (Huzooree & Yadav, 2025). Methods such as stakeholder engagement, impact assessments, and regular progress reviews can be used to monitor and evaluate the effectiveness of these training initiatives.

Beyond communication, AI advancements are reshaping human-like reasoning, problem-solving, and creativity. Notable examples include conversational AI systems like ChatGPT to simulate dynamic and intelligent human-like exchanges (Jaiswal et al., 2023). Managing the implementation of such advanced systems requires a strategic project management approach, ensuring that AI adoption is aligned with broader organizational goals and that the necessary infrastructure, training, and support are in place. Projects focusing on integrating these AI systems into organizational workflows must consider the project lifecycle in its entirety, from initial planning, through execution, to final assessment to ensure long-term success.

Generative models like DALL-E 2, which generate images from text, offer additional challenges for project management (Alhabeeb & Al-Shargabi, 2024; Kanabar, 2023). The development, deployment, and refinement of these systems require iterative project cycles that include feedback loops, performance evaluation, and scaling strategies. Project managers overseeing AI-based creative projects need to incorporate tools for managing scope creep, mitigating risks, and ensuring that resources are effectively allocated. Additionally, because AI models like DALL-E 2 continuously learn from prior outputs, it is critical to ensure that the team stays updated with evolving technologies, best practices, and user feedback. Effective project management also ensures that these technologies are integrated into business operations in ways that maximize their impact on organizational creativity and productivity.

Another significant development is Edge AI, which refers to performing computations locally rather than relying on centralized cloud processing (Deng et al., 2020). Edge AI is valuable in real-time applications such as autonomous vehicles, industrial automation, and monitoring systems (Biswas, 2023). From a project management perspective, the integration of Edge AI into business operations requires careful risk analysis, resource management, and coordination across technical teams (Kanabar, 2023; Kerzner, 2025). The deployment of Edge AI solutions calls for planning that incorporates both the technological challenges (e.g., real-time data processing, hardware limitations) and the workforce implications (e.g., skill development for technicians and engineers) (Sharma et al., 2024). Additionally, project managers must ensure that the real-time data generated by Edge AI systems is integrated into decision-making processes, improving operational efficiency and productivity.

As organizations embrace AI technologies like Edge AI, they are moving towards Industry 5.0, which represents the convergence of automation, AI, and human-machine collaboration (Sharma et al., 2025; Vrontis et al., 2023; Xu et al., 2023). Industry 5.0 promises to significantly impact workforce skills, offering new opportunities for productivity, job stability, and skill development. However, from a project management perspective, navigating this transition requires a comprehensive understanding of the challenges and opportunities that AI presents in the workforce. These challenges include ensuring that employees are equipped with the skills necessary to collaborate effectively with AI systems while also managing the organizational change associated with the adoption of AI technologies. As Sheikh et al (2024) notes, Industry 5.0 requires a delicate balance between human and technological capital to ensure that the benefits of AI, such as enhanced productivity and efficiency, do not come at the cost of employee well-being. Project managers play a pivotal role in facilitating this balance, guiding organizations through the adoption process, and ensuring that workers are not only able to leverage AI-driven efficiencies but also receive fair treatment and access to career growth opportunities.

The development of Artificial General Intelligence (AGI), which represents an advanced form of AI capable of performing a wide range of intellectual tasks, is another area where project management expertise will be crucial (Dou et al., 2023). The potential of AGI to automate tasks traditionally requiring human intelligence poses significant implications for workforce development. As AGI systems are deployed, project managers must assess the impact on organizational processes and workforce skills, ensuring that employees are reskilled to work alongside these advanced systems. The challenge will be to design project plans that support both the integration of AGI technologies and the development of new skills among the workforce, while managing the associated risks and opportunities. As AGI systems are likely to automate high-level cognitive tasks, project management efforts must focus on aligning the workforce development strategy with the strategic objectives of the organization, ensuring that employees have the tools and skills needed to thrive in an AI-augmented workplace.

3 THEORETICAL FRAMEWORKS AND STRATEGIC APPROACHES

Various theories and frameworks aim to explain the impact of AI on human skills in organizations. These frameworks guide how AI affects workforce skills, shapes employee roles, and influences project planning, execution, and delivery.

3.1 Cognitive Load Theory

Cognitive Load Theory (Sweller, 2011) emphasizes that learning is most effective when cognitive resources are efficiently managed—a key consideration in project management when integrating AI systems. AI can enhance productivity by reducing cognitive overload, automating repetitive tasks, and enabling employees to focus on complex problem-solving and decision-making. For project managers, it is essential to ensure that AI systems streamline workflows rather than introduce unnecessary complexity. Poorly designed AI tools may unintentionally increase cognitive load, hindering productivity.

Additionally, project managers should develop structured training programs that equip employees with the skills needed to navigate AI technologies effectively. Evaluating cognitive load should be incorporated into performance metrics to assess how AI impacts both individual and team efficiency over time. By thoughtfully integrating AI, project managers can optimize cognitive resources, ensuring that employees can engage in more strategic, high-value work.

3.2 Creative Destruction Theory

Creative Destruction Theory (Mathews, 2018) explains how technological advancements like AI can displace existing jobs while creating new opportunities in AI-driven industries. For project managers, this theory underscores the need to anticipate both job losses and emerging roles when planning AI adoption. Managing workforce transitions is a critical responsibility, requiring reskilling and upskilling programs to equip employees for evolving roles that involve human-AI collaboration. Strategic workforce planning and risk management must be integrated into the project lifecycle to prepare for shifts in job functions. Additionally, project managers should engage stakeholders in open discussions about potential job displacement and implement support mechanisms such as retraining programs, career counseling, and role redesign initiatives. By proactively addressing these changes, organizations can help employees adapt and remain competitive in an AI-driven workplace.

3.3 Task-Based Model of Automation

The Task-Based Model of Automation (Raisch & Krakowski, 2021) suggests that AI will not replace entire jobs but will automate specific tasks, particularly those that are routine and rule-based. For project managers, this highlights AI's potential to streamline administrative duties like data entry and scheduling, allowing employees to focus on more complex tasks requiring creativity, judgment, and emotional intelligence. As AI evolves, it is increasingly capable of handling cognitively complex tasks such as data analysis and decision-making. While automation may diminish some roles, it will also create new opportunities that require collaboration between humans and AI, especially in sectors like healthcare, finance, and management. Project managers must lead this transition by implementing reskilling initiatives that prepare employees for AI-enhanced roles. Rather than replacing jobs entirely, AI will reshape work by altering the nature of tasks. Organizations must invest in strategic workforce development to help employees adapt, ensuring they remain competitive in a rapidly changing technological environment. Project managers will play a crucial role in facilitating this shift, guiding employees through the process of integrating AI into their work.

3.4 Adaptive Expertise Theory

The Adaptive Expertise Theory (Hatano & Inagaki, 1986) highlights the need for both technical proficiency and the flexibility to navigate evolving technological landscapes. In project management, this theory underscores the importance of balancing efficiency in routine tasks with the ability to adapt to AI-driven changes. As AI reshapes workflows, project managers must foster a culture of continuous learning, ensuring employees not only acquire technical skills but also develop adaptive problem-solving abilities. This includes equipping workers to integrate AI into processes, adjust to new tools, and apply their expertise in shifting contexts. To support AI adoption, organizations must create environments that encourage both technical training and cross-functional collaboration. Project managers play a key role in facilitating skill development programs that promote innovation and agility, helping teams stay competitive in an AI-driven market. Given AI's rapid evolution, long-term workforce development is essential. By embedding continuous learning into organizational culture, project managers can ensure employees remain relevant and capable of leveraging AI effectively, supporting both individual career growth and overall business success.

3.5 Skill Decay and Retention Theory

Understanding the impact of AI on skill retention and decay is crucial for organizations, particularly in project management. Skill decay, the decline of expertise due to reduced practice (Arthur et al., 2025), can occur as AI automates tasks and limits opportunities for skill development. Project managers must proactively address skill decay through continuous training initiatives. In industries like transportation, where AI-driven systems replace human roles, workers need reskilling programs to transition into new positions. Similarly, in education, AI automates administrative and assessment tasks, requiring project managers to implement professional development initiatives that keep educators engaged with evolving teaching methods. In the legal sector, AI streamlines research and contract review, reducing opportunities for lawyers to refine traditional skills. Project managers must foster learning ecosystems that help legal professionals develop new expertise and collaborate effectively with AI. Likewise, in healthcare, AI's role in diagnostics risks diminishing clinicians' hands-on experience. To counter this, project managers should promote adaptive expertise through continuous learning, ensuring healthcare professionals maintain proficiency in an AI-integrated environment. By prioritizing ongoing skill development, project managers can mitigate skill decay and ensure workers remain adaptable, fostering a workforce that thrives alongside AI rather than becoming obsolete.

3.6 Knowledge Management Theory

Knowledge Management Theory (Tzortzaki & Mihiotis, 2014) provides essential strategies for organizations navigating AI adoption by emphasizing the acquisition, distribution, and application of knowledge. Effective knowledge management ensures employees are equipped with the skills and information necessary to adapt to AI-driven transformations. Project managers play a crucial role in balancing explicit knowledge (e.g., documented procedures) and tacit knowledge (e.g., personal expertise) to facilitate AI integration. They must establish systems that enable seamless knowledge sharing, ensuring employees can effectively collaborate and adapt to evolving technologies. While AI-powered knowledge management tools can streamline these processes, their success depends on fostering a culture of openness, collaboration, and continuous learning. Key components of Knowledge Management Theory, knowledge creation, sharing, and integration into decision-making, are particularly relevant to AI adoption. Organizations must develop new approaches to AI implementation, promote cross-team collaboration, and ensure that insights are shared effectively. Project managers should design learning environments that encourage the exchange of expertise, allowing employees to optimize AI tools and workflows. Additionally, organizational culture plays a critical role in knowledge management success. A workplace that encourages openness and proactive knowledge sharing enhances AI adoption and maximizes its benefits. Project managers must remove barriers to collaboration and ensure employees feel empowered to engage with new technologies. Finally, structured knowledge management systems are essential for capturing and disseminating AI-related insights. By ensuring that employees have continuous access to relevant knowledge, project managers can facilitate workforce adaptability, support ongoing skill development, and ensure the long-term success of AI integration efforts.

4 PROPOSED FRAMEWORK FOR KEY SKILLS FOR THE AGE OF AI

The integration of AI technologies into organizational operations has underscored the increasing need for the development of transferable skills, often referred to as soft skills, that are applicable across multiple roles and industries (Hart et al., 2021). These skills, such as critical thinking, problem-solving, communication, and collaboration, are essential for effectively interacting with AI systems and adapting to the evolving workplace (Huzooree et al., 2024). From a project management perspective, these skills are crucial for fostering cross-functional collaboration, ensuring that AI tools are integrated efficiently into ongoing projects, and managing the change process. As AI automates routine tasks, project managers and teams are freed to focus on higher-order activities requiring complex decision-making, innovation, and creativity, ultimately driving productivity, improving project outcomes, and transforming workflows (Dhand et al., 2025; Huzooree & Soupramanien, 2024).

While transferable skills are not a new concept, their significance in today's rapidly evolving work environment has increased, particularly with the growing influence of AI. Huzooree et al. (2024) proposed a framework emphasizing the importance of transferable skills across work, learning, and life contexts. These competencies include interpersonal skills (e.g., communication, collaboration, leadership) and intrapersonal skills (e.g., self-awareness, active learning, creativity), which are integral to the project management processes of planning, execution, monitoring, and closing (Huzooree, 2024). These skills foster teamwork, help resolve conflicts, and enable agile responses to changing project requirements, making them indispensable in AI-driven project environments. By embedding these skills into organizational structures, project managers can ensure their teams are adaptable to the challenges posed by AI advancements while cultivating a culture of continuous learning and innovation.

As organizations increasingly adopt AI and other digital technologies, the necessity for digital literacy skills has become paramount, especially in the context of managing complex projects. Digital communication, as defined by Lapidoth (2017), involves engaging and interacting using various digital tools and platforms, such as email, social media, and video conferencing. For project managers, effective digital communication is essential for stakeholder engagement, aligning team goals, and ensuring that project timelines are met. Scholars emphasize that digital communication goes beyond technical proficiency and involves adapting messages for diverse audiences, conveying ideas concisely, and fostering engagement across various platforms (Ononiwu et al., 2024). AI-powered communication tools, such as chatbots and virtual assistants, can enhance communication by automating scheduling, coordinating team activities, and managing information flows across digital channels (Savio & Ali, 2023; Sharma et al., 2024; Sheikh et al., 2024). For project managers, these tools can significantly improve responsiveness and ensure timely, effective communication, which is critical for keeping projects on track.

Technology proficiency, articulated by Christensen and Knezek (2017), reflects an individual's ability to effectively navigate digital tools and adapt to new technologies. In the project management context, this proficiency extends beyond basic usage to include a deeper understanding of how emerging technologies can be leveraged to optimize project planning, resource allocation, and risk management. With AI becoming more embedded in organizational processes, project managers must be able to understand, utilize, and integrate these systems into their project workflows. Vaid and Sharma (2022) note that leveraging AI technologies effectively can streamline decision-making, reduce costs, and optimize resource management. For project managers, technology proficiency is not just a technical requirement but also a strategic asset that drives project success in an increasingly digital and automated environment.

In tandem, information literacy has emerged as a critical skill for project management in the digital age. According to Saranto and Hovenga (2004), information literacy involves the ability to not only find and access information but also critically assess and apply it. In AI-powered project environments, the volume of data generated can overwhelm teams, making the ability to filter and analyze data essential. For project managers, effective information literacy enables informed decision-making, risk mitigation, and accurate forecasting. With AI-driven analytics tools, project teams can leverage real-time data to make more accurate predictions, adjust timelines, and anticipate potential risks before they impact project delivery.

Finally, digital citizenship encompasses the ethical, responsible, and respectful use of technology, as discussed by Mossberger et al (2007). In the context of project management, digital citizenship ensures that all project stakeholders, including team members, clients, and external partners, engage with digital tools and platforms responsibly. This includes protecting privacy, respecting intellectual property, and ensuring that AI systems are used ethically within projects. As Mossberger et al (2007) highlights, digital citizenship involves understanding not only the rules governing online behavior but also fostering a culture of accountability, transparency, and positive engagement in digital spaces. For project managers, embracing digital citizenship within teams ensures that the use of AI tools aligns with organizational values, regulatory requirements, and industry best practices, ultimately safeguarding the project's reputation and ensuring compliance.

Building on Huzooree et al.'s (2024) foundational framework, this research expands the original model by introducing a third dimension: digital literacy. Recognizing the increasing importance of technology in project management and organizational success, this added dimension reflects the growing necessity for competencies such as digital communication, technology proficiency, information literacy, and digital citizenship. From a project management standpoint, these skills are essential for navigating the complexities of AI adoption, managing cross-functional teams, and ensuring the ethical and effective integration of AI into projects. By incorporating these elements, this research provides a more comprehensive understanding of the skills required to effectively engage with AI technologies, ensuring that project teams are equipped to navigate the challenges of a digitally-driven, AI-enhanced environment (as shown in Figure 1).

Figure 1. Proposed Framework for Key Skills required in the age of AI (adapted from Huzooree et al., 2024)

Table 1 outlines the essential soft skills required for the modern workforce and their alignment with key skills needed in the AI era, with a focus on how AI technologies can enhance project management practices. It emphasizes how AI-driven tools, such as project management platforms, communication assistants, sentiment analysis, and predictive analytics, can streamline tasks, foster collaboration, improve decision-making, and optimize resource allocation. The integration of AI into project management not only automates routine processes but also helps enhance leadership, innovation, and emotional intelligence, ensuring that project teams can effectively navigate complex, AI-driven environments while maintaining ethical standards and promoting continuous learning.

Table 1. Key skills needed in AI era and potential of AI potentials in enhancing skills

Key Soft Skills for Modern Workforce	Key Skills Needed in the AI Era	How AI Can Enhance Skills in Project Management
Interpersonal Skills		
Collaboration and Teamwork	- Effective collaboration in diverse and cross-functional teams. - Ability to work in virtual and remote teams. - Building trust and fostering positive relationships. - Conflict resolution and negotiation skills.	- AI-powered project management platforms (e.g., Asana, Trello, Microsoft Teams) facilitate seamless collaboration and communication. - AI-driven sentiment analysis tools can assess team dynamics and suggest improvements to foster stronger collaboration. - AI chatbots and virtual assistants can help coordinate tasks and automate workflows, enhancing team efficiency.
Communication Skills	- Clear and concise verbal communication across digital platforms. - Proficient written communication for project documentation and reporting. - Active listening and feedback mechanisms. - Adaptability in communication styles based on project stakeholders.	- AI-powered language processing tools (e.g., Grammarly, natural language processing in emails) can enhance clarity in project communication. - AI-driven meeting transcription and summarization tools (e.g., Otter.ai, Fireflies.ai) improve documentation and ensure project alignment. - AI chatbots can assist in stakeholder engagement by automating responses and providing quick project updates.
Leadership and Social Influence	- Visionary leadership for driving AI-integrated project innovation. - Influencing stakeholders toward shared project goals, and motivating project teams. - Strategic delegation and empowerment of team members. - Ethical decision-making in AI-driven projects.	- AI-driven data analytics can provide leaders with insights into project performance, risk areas, and predictive trends, aiding informed decision-making. - AI-based sentiment analysis can help leaders gauge team morale and engagement, allowing for targeted motivational strategies. - AI-driven automation reduces administrative burden, enabling leaders to focus on strategic project management.
Organizational and Managerial Skills	- Efficient time management and prioritization of project tasks. - Project management methodologies (Agile, Scrum, Waterfall, etc.). - Budgeting and resource allocation. - Risk management and crisis handling.	- AI-based project management software (e.g., Monday.com, ClickUp, Jira) automates scheduling, task assignments, and resource tracking, optimizing project execution. - AI-driven predictive analytics help anticipate project risks and suggest mitigation strategies. - AI-powered budgeting tools analyze financial trends to optimize cost management.
Intrapersonal Skills		
Active Learning and Resilience Skills	- Adaptability to evolving AI-driven project environments. - Resilience in overcoming project setbacks. - Openness to feedback and continuous learning. - Comfort with uncertainty and ambiguity in project execution.	- AI-powered learning management systems (LMS) offer personalized training, ensuring project managers and team members stay updated on AI-driven innovations. - AI-driven real-time feedback tools assist in skill refinement and adaptive learning. - AI-powered scenario simulations prepare professionals for project risks and decision-making under uncertainty.
Critical Thinking and Problem-solving Skills	- Analytical thinking for project-based problem-solving. - Data-driven decision-making. - Identifying patterns and forecasting project trends.	- AI-powered data analysis tools (e.g., Power BI, Tableau) provide real-time insights into project trends, facilitating proactive decision-making. - AI-enhanced risk assessment tools predict potential bottlenecks and suggest preventive measures. - AI-powered brainstorming tools generate alternative solutions for complex project challenges.

continued on following page

Table 1. Continued

Key Soft Skills for Modern Workforce	Key Skills Needed in the AI Era	How AI Can Enhance Skills in Project Management
Emotional Intelligence and Self-awareness	- Self-awareness to enhance project leadership. - Emotional intelligence for managing diverse teams. - Stress management and resilience in project delivery.	- AI-driven emotional intelligence coaching tools help project managers improve team relations and stakeholder engagement. - AI-powered wellness platforms monitor stress levels and suggest personalized stress management techniques.
Creativity and Innovation	- Thinking creatively to generate novel solutions. - Encouraging innovation in AI-integrated project processes. - Adaptability to new project management technologies.	- AI-driven ideation platforms (e.g., IBM Watson, ChatGPT) assist in brainstorming and innovation. - AI-generated market insights help drive creative solutions and competitive project strategies.
Digital Literacy Skills		
Digital Communication	- Proficiency in managing digital interactions across AI-powered platforms. - Ability to tailor communication styles for AI-integrated environments.	- AI-powered communication assistants (e.g., ChatGPT, Slack AI) enhance digital messaging and knowledge-sharing in projects. - AI-driven collaboration platforms facilitate real-time engagement across teams and stakeholders.
Technology Proficiency	- Understanding and leveraging AI tools in project workflows. - Ability to integrate emerging technologies into project execution.	- AI-powered training modules help professionals upskill in AI-driven project management tools. - No-code AI platforms allow project managers to automate workflows without deep technical expertise.
Information Literacy	- Ability to evaluate and utilize AI-generated insights for decision-making. - Critical assessment of AI-driven data sources.	- AI-powered research tools streamline data collection and analysis for project decisions. - AI can filter and summarize vast amounts of project-related information, ensuring accurate reporting and data-driven strategies.
Digital Citizenship	- Ethical and responsible AI usage in projects. - Awareness of legal and compliance requirements for AI-driven projects.	- AI-powered compliance and governance tools ensure adherence to data privacy laws and ethical AI practices. - AI-driven security monitoring systems safeguard project data from cyber threats.

5 THE TWO-FOLD IMPACT OF AI ON PROFESSIONAL COMPETENCIES

The integration of AI into project management environments brings a dual impact on professional competencies, enhancing certain skills while presenting challenges that may hinder skill development if not managed effectively. On the positive side, AI can significantly boost efficiency by automating repetitive tasks. Project managers and teams can leverage AI-driven tools to streamline scheduling, task allocation, and resource management, freeing up time for higher-level cognitive activities such as strategic planning, risk management, and innovation. Additionally, AI can support continuous development through personalized training programs, adaptive learning platforms, and real-time performance feedback, helping professionals at all levels acquire new skills that align with the evolving demands of AI-enhanced roles.

However, AI's presence also raises concerns if not properly implemented. One issue is the risk of deskilling, especially in tasks that were previously handled manually. Professionals may become overly reliant on automated project management systems or AI-driven decision-making tools, losing an understanding of the underlying processes and diminishing their ability to make autonomous decisions. In project management, this could result in a reduced capacity to adapt when AI systems encounter limitations or errors. Furthermore, AI-driven project tools may foster a sense of detachment among team members who depend heavily on automation for tasks like scheduling, status updates, or progress tracking, without understanding the reasons behind certain project decisions.

The impact of AI on skill development will vary depending on the complexity of the project and the existing skill level of the professionals involved. For high-skilled project management roles, AI can enhance analytical thinking, data-driven decision-making, and productivity by processing complex project data and identifying trends or risks. However, it may also diminish the autonomy of project managers, as AI might take over some decision-making processes. For middle-skilled professionals, AI can improve efficiency and workflow management but may increase pressure due to the constant interaction with AI systems or the need to manage complex AI-driven processes. For lower-skilled professionals, AI may accelerate the pace of work but offer fewer opportunities for learning and development as tasks become increasingly automated.

Ethical and psychological considerations are also critical when integrating AI into project management. AI systems can perpetuate biases, such as algorithmic discrimination based on gender, race, or experience, potentially leading to unequal distribution of tasks, promotions, or opportunities. If AI-driven performance monitoring systems are implemented, the resulting surveillance can cause stress, anxiety, and job insecurity, diminishing overall team morale and engagement. In project management, where teamwork and collaboration are essential, these effects can create an environment where professionals feel undervalued or replaceable, reducing their commitment to the project's success.

To mitigate these challenges, project managers must adopt a balanced approach to AI integration. AI should complement human capabilities rather than fully automate tasks that require critical thinking and human judgment. Promoting human-AI collaboration ensures that AI tools are used to augment decision-making rather than replace it. Additionally, transparency in AI decision-making, through explainable AI, helps professionals understand how and why AI makes specific recommendations or decisions, building trust in the system. Ethical frameworks must be established to minimize bias and ensure fairness in AI systems. Reskilling and upskilling programs should be prioritized to equip professionals with both technical and transferable skills, enabling them to leverage AI tools while maintaining autonomy in decision-making.

6 STRATEGIES FOR EFFECTIVE UPSKILLING AND RESKILLING

As AI continues to reshape industries, project management professionals must embrace continuous upskilling and reskilling to stay competitive and agile. To successfully integrate AI and remain adaptable, organizations must adopt multi-faceted workforce training strategies. These strategies should focus not only on transferring knowledge but also on fostering ongoing learning, using cutting-edge technologies, and ensuring that project managers and teams are engaged in their professional development. This creates a workforce equipped to drive both personal growth and organizational success, especially in an AI-driven project management landscape.

6.1 Structured Training Programs and Learning Frameworks

Central to any upskilling and reskilling strategy is the development of structured training programs that align with the evolving demands of AI-enhanced project management. Microlearning is an effective method, breaking down complex AI-related concepts into manageable units, ensuring that learning is efficient and adaptable to the fast pace of the project management environment. This bite-sized learning format allows project professionals to acquire new skills just-in-time, helping them to quickly apply knowledge in real-world projects.

Integrating AI-powered learning paths into microlearning programs further enhances personalization, catering to each individual's specific development needs and progress. This dynamic approach ensures that project managers not only gain essential skills but also remain agile in the face of AI-driven changes in their industry. Additionally, using data-driven decision-making to assess employee progress, training effectiveness, and areas for improvement optimizes engagement and skill retention. AI analytics can track progress, fine-tuning learning pathways to enhance the overall development experience.

6.2 Training for Skillful Human-AI Interaction

Project management professionals must be prepared not only to use AI tools but also to interact effectively with AI systems to drive innovation and productivity. As AI increasingly becomes integrated into decision-making, scheduling, and risk management in project management, it's essential for project managers to understand AI outputs and how to collaborate with AI systems to make informed decisions.

Training programs should focus on AI literacy, enabling project managers to interpret AI-driven recommendations, troubleshoot when necessary, and refine AI algorithms. This ensures that AI becomes a powerful ally in managing project complexities, rather than a "black-box" tool. Developing data analytics skills within project teams is crucial as they work alongside AI in areas such as performance tracking, predictive risk management, and resource allocation. By combining human expertise with AI capabilities, project managers can ensure that both work synergistically to enhance project outcomes and workforce readiness.

6.3 Industry Partnerships and Experiential Learning

Organizations should collaborate with academic institutions, professional associations, and industry leaders to co-create training programs that reflect the latest trends and practices in AI-enhanced project management. This allows professionals to gain access to up-to-date skills and knowledge relevant to their specific industry. For example, certification programs, industry-sponsored workshops, and co-designed curricula offer practical, industry-specific insights that bridge the gap between theory and practice.

Additionally, organizations should emphasize experiential learning opportunities that allow professionals to apply new skills in real-world project settings. Mentorship programs and job rotation schemes are vital for accelerating skill development by allowing less experienced professionals to learn from seasoned project managers. These programs help foster cross-functional understanding, promote workforce readiness and increase adaptability within diverse project teams.

6.4 Hackathons and Innovation-Driven Learning

Hackathons are a dynamic strategy for fostering collaborative learning and driving innovation in AI-powered project environments. These intense, time-limited events encourage teams to solve technology-driven challenges in AI, coding, and data analytics. By engaging in these real-world scenarios, project managers can develop technical skills, problem-solving abilities, and teamwork strategies. Hackathons also foster a culture of innovation, pushing participants to experiment with novel ideas that can be applied to enhance project management processes, leading to more efficient and creative solutions.

In addition to developing technical expertise, hackathons promote cross-functional collaboration, helping teams break out of silos and think outside the box. They also serve as a platform for discovering emerging talent and generating innovative solutions that can propel project teams forward in AI-driven projects.

6.5 Continuous Evaluation, Feedback, and Adaptation

For upskilling and reskilling programs to remain effective in an AI-driven world, continuous evaluation and feedback mechanisms must be established. Regular assessments ensure that employees are progressing and mastering the necessary skills for successful project management in the AI era. Real-time feedback helps learners adjust their approaches, keeping the training dynamic and responsive to changing needs.

Incorporating learning analytics into these evaluations helps organizations make data-driven decisions about training effectiveness. By tracking performance metrics and progress, organizations can pinpoint skill gaps, refine learning paths, and tailor future development initiatives. This not only enhances the efficiency of training but also ensures that the workforce's skills remain aligned with the company's strategic goals and the evolving demands of AI-driven project management.

7 CHALLENGES AND BARRIERS TO UPSKILLING AND RESKILLING

The integration of AI into organizational workflows is a significant change that requires project management professionals to continually adapt. As AI and automation technologies evolve, there is an increasing need for upskilling and reskilling to keep up with these developments. However, organizations face several challenges as they work to integrate AI into their project management processes. Understanding and addressing these challenges is key to ensuring that organizations can develop a skilled, future-ready project management team.

7.1 Resistance to Change and Organizational Culture

One of the primary barriers organizations face in upskilling and reskilling initiatives is resistance to change. Project teams, particularly those with established processes, may be wary of new technologies or learning methods, especially when AI tools are perceived as threats to traditional roles. Senior project managers, who have been in the field for years, might view AI integration as an encroachment on their expertise, making them reluctant to embrace training programs. Furthermore, in organizations where the culture does not prioritize continuous learning, there may be limited motivation to engage with skill development initiatives.

Organizations must therefore prioritize the creation of a learning culture, one that encourages a mindset of lifelong learning. This can be achieved through leadership that actively supports and models learning behaviors, along with an organizational commitment to upskilling as a strategic priority. In addition, incorporating personalized and AI-powered training tools that cater to individual learning styles and career paths can help alleviate resistance and demonstrate the tangible value of continuous skill development.

7.2 Resource Constraints and Budgetary Challenges

Another key challenge is the issue of budget constraints. Upskilling and reskilling programs often require significant investment in terms of time, resources, and finances. For many organizations, particularly small and medium-sized enterprises, securing the necessary funding to implement comprehensive training initiatives is a substantial hurdle. The costs of developing, delivering, and maintaining training programs, especially those that incorporate emerging technologies such as AI, can be prohibitive.

To overcome this barrier, organizations can explore strategic partnerships with academic institutions, industry bodies, or technology providers that can help share the financial burden. Governments and private organizations may also offer subsidies or grants that support training initiatives. Additionally, organizations can implement cost-effective training solutions such as microlearning, which minimizes time and resource investment by delivering learning content in small, targeted modules that employees can complete at their own pace.

7.3 Skill Assessment and Curriculum Alignment

A major challenge in upskilling and reskilling is the accurate assessment of skill gaps. Organizations often struggle to understand exactly what skills their employees have and which skills they need to develop. This issue becomes more complicated when technological advances, such as AI, quickly change the skills required for project management roles. Training programs that are designed today may be outdated by the time they are delivered, which makes it hard to keep up with the latest developments in AI.

Organizations should use data-driven tools to assess and track skill development in real time. AI-powered assessment tools can help organizations monitor progress and adjust training programs as needed. Collaborating with industry experts and academic institutions can also help ensure that training programs remain aligned with the latest trends in AI and project management, ensuring that employees are learning relevant and up-to-date skills.

7.4 Inequalities in Access and Inclusion

Up-skilling and reskilling efforts can also be hindered by social and demographic inequalities. In many countries, particularly in developing regions, access to quality education and training is limited, making it difficult for workers to acquire the skills necessary for emerging job roles. Vulnerable groups, such as women, older workers, and those in lower socioeconomic brackets, often face additional barriers to accessing technology and educational resources.

A gender-sensitive approach to upskilling is essential to ensure equal opportunities for all workers. The gender-related digital divide remains a significant issue, with women often having less access to the internet, digital devices, and technical education. As AI technologies become more pervasive, this divide can exacerbate existing inequalities in the workforce, limiting women's participation in high-growth sectors such as AI, STEM, and digital innovation.

To address this, organizations must ensure that training programs are inclusive and provide equal access to resources for all employees, regardless of gender, age, or background. For instance, ensuring that training platforms are accessible on multiple devices and that content is available in different languages or formats can bridge accessibility gaps. Additionally, public policies promoting gender equality in tech education and greater participation in the digital economy are critical for ensuring that underrepresented groups are not left behind.

7.5 The Age-Related Digital Divide

The age-related digital divide also poses a significant barrier to upskilling and reskilling initiatives. Older employees may find it more challenging to adapt to new technologies, particularly AI-driven tools, due to lack of exposure or limited digital literacy. This divide can result in age discrimination, with older workers potentially being marginalized in workplaces increasingly reliant on digital skills.

Organizations must take proactive steps to support older workers by offering tailored training programs that cater to varying levels of technological proficiency. Mentorship and job rotation schemes can also encourage intergenerational learning, allowing younger employees to share their digital expertise while learning from the experience and insights of their more seasoned colleagues. A culture of inclusivity, where continuous learning is valued across all age groups, can significantly mitigate the age-related digital divide and enhance the contributions of older workers to organizational innovation.

7.6 Global Disparities in Skills Development

Global disparities in access to education and skills development further complicate efforts to close skill gaps. While advanced economies invest heavily in upskilling and reskilling programs, developing nations often face structural challenges in providing accessible and effective training. These challenges may include limited infrastructure, insufficient government support for education, and the informal nature of many local economies.

International organizations, governments, and the private sector must work together to establish global frameworks for skills development. Initiatives such as public-private partnerships, international knowledge exchange programs, and cross-border collaborations can help bridge these gaps by providing resources, expertise, and opportunities for workers in underserved regions.

8 CONCLUSIONS

The integration of AI into the workforce represents a transformative shift in how organizations operate, posing both opportunities and challenges. As this chapter has explored, the rapid advancements in AI technologies are reshaping job roles and skill demands, pushing the boundaries of what is possible in the workplace. However, the successful adoption of AI requires more than just technological upgrades, it necessitates a deep investment in human capital through upskilling and reskilling efforts. As AI systems increasingly perform tasks traditionally carried out by humans, organizations must address the evolving needs of their workforce to ensure a seamless transition into the future of work.

Central to this transformation is the need to foster a learning culture within organizations. While AI has the potential to augment human capabilities, it also poses significant challenges, including resistance to change, skill gaps, and the need for constant curriculum adaptation. This chapter has outlined the importance of not only investing in technical training but also in developing soft skills, such as critical thinking, creativity, and emotional intelligence, that AI cannot replicate. Addressing these gaps through structured training programs, mentorship, job rotation, and AI-powered learning tools will enable workers to thrive in an increasingly AI-driven environment.

Central to this transformation is the need for organizations to develop a structured approach to learning and development, aligning training efforts with strategic objectives. A project management mindset, defined by clear goals, timelines, and resource allocation, can ensure that upskilling and reskilling initiatives are well-executed and sustainable. Moreover, as AI systems increasingly perform tasks once managed by humans, organizations must focus on mitigating skill gaps through carefully managed projects that prioritize timely and cost-effective training solutions. The project management discipline provides the tools for organizations to manage the complexities of workforce development, balancing technical training with the cultivation of soft skills such as critical thinking, creativity, and emotional intelligence, skills that AI cannot replicate.

The success of AI adoption within an organization also hinges on overcoming the challenges of resistance to change and organizational culture, which can impede the smooth execution of upskilling initiatives. Resistance to new technologies and approaches is a common barrier, and in this context, effective change management strategies, a cornerstone of project management, become critical. Change management frameworks can support leadership in creating a culture that embraces continuous learning and skill enhancement.

As organizations adopt AI, it is vital that they consider inclusivity and diversity in their upskilling efforts. Project managers, tasked with overseeing the design and implementation of training programs, must ensure that all training initiatives are equitable. This includes addressing the specific barriers faced by underrepresented groups such as women, older workers, and employees in developing regions. An inclusive project management approach can help ensure that resources and learning tools are accessible to a diverse workforce, ensuring that no group is excluded from the opportunities AI affords. This can be achieved by ensuring accessibility in training platforms and content, thus enabling organizations to develop a truly inclusive learning culture.

Furthermore, the pace of technological change requires organizations to adopt flexible, iterative project management methods. The need for continuous curriculum updates and real-time adaptation of training materials can be effectively managed using Agile or Lean principles, which emphasize continuous improvement and responsiveness to feedback. By incorporating these agile methodologies, organizations can ensure that their upskilling and reskilling efforts remain dynamic and aligned with evolving technological trends, ensuring that employees can keep pace with rapid advancements in AI.

Lastly, the evidence gathered suggests that the successful integration of AI into the workforce requires a collaborative approach, one that crosses disciplinary and organizational boundaries. Drawing on insights from various fields, technology, sociology, economics, and education, project managers must coordinate cross-functional teams to address both the technical and human aspects of AI implementation. A systems thinking approach, combined with project management methodologies, allows organizations to align their AI adoption strategies with long-term goals while managing the inherent complexities of such a wide-reaching change. Collaboration with industry experts, educators, and policymakers will be key to ensuring that project initiatives are comprehensive, sustainable, and beneficial to the broader workforce.

In a nutshell, the future of work in an AI-driven environment relies on the strategic efforts of organizations, workers, and policymakers. By adopting project management methodologies, organizations can implement upskilling and reskilling programs that are aligned with both the technical demands of AI and the broader organizational goals. The application of Agile, Lean, or traditional project management frameworks will ensure that the adoption of AI is efficient, scalable, and inclusive. Through these approaches, organizations can unlock the full potential of AI, enhance human capabilities, and ensure that all workers are equipped to succeed in the evolving digital economy.

REFERENCES

Ademola, O. E. (2024). Change Management Trends in the AI Modern World: Adapting to the Future of Work. *Journal of Behavioral Informatics*.

Akeiber, H. J. (2025). Artificial Intelligence in Engineering Management: Revolutionizing Decision-Making and Automation. *Al-Rafidain Journal of Engineering Sciences*, 317-349.

Alhabeeb, S. K., & Al-Shargabi, A. A. (2024). Text-to-image synthesis with generative models: Methods, datasets, performance metrics, challenges, and future direction. *IEEE Access : Practical Innovations, Open Solutions*, *12*, 24412–24427. DOI: 10.1109/ACCESS.2024.3365043

Arthur, W.Jr, Naber, A. M., Muñoz, G. J., Keiser, N. L., Atoba, O. A., Cho, I., & Bennett, W.Jr. (2025). A Comparison of Individual and Team Skill Acquisition, Retention (Decay), and Reacquisition Using a Synthetic Task Environment. *Human Performance*, *38*(1), 43–60. DOI: 10.1080/08959285.2024.2436171

Barach, J. (2025). Integrating AI and HR Strategies in IT Engineering Projects: A Blueprint for Agile Success. *Emerging Engineering and Mathematics*, 1-13.

Barcaui, A., & Monat, A. (2023). Who is better in project planning? Generative artificial intelligence or project managers? *Project Leadership and Society*, *4*, 100101. DOI: 10.1016/j.plas.2023.100101

Biswas, A., & Wang, H. C. (2023). Autonomous vehicles enabled by the integration of IoT, edge intelligence, 5G, and blockchain. *Sensors (Basel)*, *23*(4), 1963. DOI: 10.3390/s23041963 PMID: 36850560

Chan, C., Tan, J., Billett, S., & Chong, W. H. (2025). Blue-Collar Workers Adaptation to Digitalization: A Career Construction Theory Analysis.

Christensen, R., & Knezek, G. (2017). Validating the technology proficiency self-assessment questionnaire for 21st century learning (TPSA C-21). *Journal of Digital Learning in Teacher Education*, *33*(1), 20–31. DOI: 10.1080/21532974.2016.1242391

Deng, S., Zhao, H., Fang, W., Yin, J., Dustdar, S., & Zomaya, A. Y. (2020). Edge intelligence: The confluence of edge computing and artificial intelligence. *IEEE Internet of Things Journal*, *7*(8), 7457–7469. DOI: 10.1109/JIOT.2020.2984887

Dhand, S., Singh, S. K., & Le, T. M. (2025). Automating routine tasks to improve entrepreneurial productivity. In *Improving Entrepreneurial Processes Through Advanced AI* (pp. 99–128). IGI Global.

Dou, F., Ye, J., Yuan, G., Lu, Q., Niu, W., Sun, H., . . . Song, W. (2023). Towards artificial general intelligence (agi) in the internet of things (iot): Opportunities and challenges. *arXiv preprint arXiv:2309.07438*.

Gangwal, A., Ansari, A., Ahmad, I., Azad, A. K., Kumarasamy, V., Subramaniyan, V., & Wong, L. S. (2024). Generative artificial intelligence in drug discovery: Basic framework, recent advances, challenges, and opportunities. *Frontiers in Pharmacology*, *15*, 1331062. DOI: 10.3389/fphar.2024.1331062 PMID: 38384298

Gowrishankkar, V., Shanmugam, V., Kapuria, M., Pavan, K. A., Vaishnavi, D., & Paneru, D. R. (2025). Agile HR Professionals in Industry 5.0: Navigating the Dynamic Evolution of Skills and Competencies. In *Expanding Operations Through Agile Principles and Sustainable Practices* (pp. 321-340). IGI Global Scientific Publishing.

Hart, J., Noack, M., Plaimauer, C., & Bjørnåvold, J. (2021). Towards a structured and consistent terminology on transversal skills and competences. *Brüssel: Europäische Kommission und Cedefop. Towards a structured and consistent terminology on transversal skills and competences| Esco (europa. eu), 1*, 645-670.

Hatano, G., & Inagaki, K. (1986). Two courses of expertise. *Child development and education in Japan, 17*, 262-272.

Huzooree, G. (2024). From Concept to Completion: Critical Success Factors in Agile Project Management for IT Projects. In *Practical Approaches to Agile Project Management* (pp. 9-31). IGI Global.

Huzooree, G., & Soupramanien, L. D. B. (2024). *Empowering Students for the 21st Century Through Digital Literacy*. IGI Global. DOI: 10.4018/979-8-3693-3856-8.ch005

Huzooree, G., Soupramanien, L. D. B., & Rughoobur-Seetah, S. (2024). *Fostering Critical Soft Skills of Graduates for Employability and Professional Growth*. IGI Global. DOI: 10.4018/979-8-3693-3856-8.ch003

Huzooree, G., & Yadav, M. (2025). Sustainable Project Management and Organizational Resilience. In *Enhancing Resilience in Business Continuity Management* (pp. 137–172). IGI Global Scientific Publishing. DOI: 10.4018/979-8-3693-8809-9.ch005

Jaiswal, A., Arun, C. J., & Varma, A. (2023). Rebooting employees: Upskilling for artificial intelligence in multinational corporations. In *Artificial Intelligence and International HRM* (pp. 114–143). Routledge. DOI: 10.4324/9781003377085-5

Jariwala, M. (2024). Integrating artificial intelligence to enhance sustainability in project management practices. *International Journal of Computer Applications, 186*(20), 35–42. DOI: 10.5120/ijca2024923627

Kanabar, V. (2023). *The AI Revolution in Project Management: Elevating Productivity with Generative AI*. Sams Publishing.

Kaplan, A., & Haenlein, M. (2019). Siri, Siri, in my hand: Who's the fairest in the land? On the interpretations, illustrations, and implications of artificial intelligence. *Business Horizons, 62*(1), 15–25. DOI: 10.1016/j.bushor.2018.08.004

Kerzner, H. (2025). *Project management: a systems approach to planning, scheduling, and controlling*. John Wiley & Sons.

Lapidoth, A. (2017). *A foundation in digital communication*. Cambridge University Press. DOI: 10.1017/9781316822708

Lokesh, G. R., Harish, K. S., Sangu, V. S., Prabakar, S., Kumar, V. S., & Vallabhaneni, M. (2024). AI and the Future of Work: Preparing the Workforce for Technological Shifts and Skill Evolution. In *2024 International Conference on Knowledge Engineering and Communication Systems (ICKECS)* (Vol. 1, pp. 1-6). IEEE. DOI: 10.1109/ICKECS61492.2024.10616486

Manyika, J., Lund, S., Chui, M., Bughin, J., Woetzel, J., Batra, P., & Sanghvi, S. (2017) Jobs Lost, Jobs Gained: What the Future of Work Will Mean for Jobs, Skills, and Wages, McKinsey Global Institute. Available online: https://www.mckinsey.com/featured-insights/future-ofwork/jobs-lost-jobs-gained-what-the-future-of-work-will-mean-for-jobs-skills-and-wages (accessed March, 2025).

Martins, M. R. (2023). Adapting change management strategies for the AI Era: Lessons from large-scale IT integrations. *World Journal of Advanced Research and Reviews*, *19*(3), 1604–1629. DOI: 10.30574/wjarr.2023.19.3.1556

Mathews, J. (2018). Schumpeter in the twenty-first century: Creative destruction and the global green shift. In *Schumpeter's Capitalism, Socialism and Democracy* (pp. 233-254). Routledge.

Mossberger, K., Tolbert, C. J., & McNeal, R. S. (2007). *Digital citizenship: The Internet, society, and participation*. MIt Press.

Niederman, F. (2021). Project management: Openings for disruption from AI and advanced analytics. *Information Technology & People*, *34*(6), 1570–1599. DOI: 10.1108/ITP-09-2020-0639

Ononiwu, M. I., Onwuzulike, O. C., & Shitu, K. (2024). The role of digital business transformation in enhancing organizational agility. *World Journal of Advanced Research and Reviews*, *23*(3), 285–308. DOI: 10.30574/wjarr.2024.23.3.2670

Project Management Institute. (2021). A Guide to the Project Management Body of Knowledge (PMBOK® Guide)–Seventh Edition and The Standard for Project Management. Project Management Institute.

Raisch, S., & Krakowski, S. (2021). Artificial intelligence and management: The automation–augmentation paradox. *Academy of Management Review*, *46*(1), 192–210. DOI: 10.5465/amr.2018.0072

Rane, N. L., Paramesha, M., Choudhary, S. P., & Rane, J. (2024). Artificial intelligence, machine learning, and deep learning for advanced business strategies: A review. *SSRN*, *2*(3), 147–171. DOI: 10.2139/ssrn.4835661

Saranto, K., & Hovenga, E. J. (2004). Information literacy—what it is about?: Literature review of the concept and the context. *International Journal of Medical Informatics*, *73*(6), 503–513. DOI: 10.1016/j.ijmedinf.2004.03.002 PMID: 15171979

Savio, R. D., & Ali, J. M. (2023). Artificial intelligence in project management & its future. *Saudi Journal of Engineering and Technology*, *8*(10), 244–248. DOI: 10.36348/sjet.2023.v08i10.002

Sharma, M., Tomar, A., & Hazra, A. (2024). Edge computing for industry 5.0: Fundamental, applications and research challenges. *IEEE Internet of Things Journal*, *11*(11), 19070–19093. DOI: 10.1109/JIOT.2024.3359297

Sheikh, R. A., Ahmed, I., Faqihi, A. Y. A., & Shehawy, Y. M. (2024). Global Perspectives on Navigating Industry 5.0 Knowledge: Achieving Resilience, Sustainability, and Human-Centric Innovation in Manufacturing. *Journal of the Knowledge Economy*, •••, 1–36. DOI: 10.1007/s13132-024-02498-4

Shoushtari, F., Daghighi, A., & Ghafourian, E. (2024). Application of Artificial Intelligence in Project Management. *International journal of industrial engineering and operational research, 6*(2), 49-63.

Snell, D., & Gekara, V. (2023). Re-examining technology's destruction of blue-collar work. *New Technology, Work and Employment, 38*(3), 415–433. DOI: 10.1111/ntwe.12259

Sweller, J. (2011). Cognitive load theory. [). Academic Press.]. *Psychology of Learning and Motivation, 55*, 37–76. DOI: 10.1016/B978-0-12-387691-1.00002-8

Taboada, I., Daneshpajouh, A., Toledo, N., & De Vass, T. (2023). Artificial intelligence enabled project management: A systematic literature review. *Applied Sciences (Basel, Switzerland), 13*(8), 5014. DOI: 10.3390/app13085014

Tzortzaki, A. M., & Mihiotis, A. (2014). A review of knowledge management theory and future directions. *Knowledge and Process Management, 21*(1), 29–41. DOI: 10.1002/kpm.1429

Uren, V., & Edwards, J. S. (2023). Technology readiness and the organizational journey towards AI adoption: An empirical study. *International Journal of Information Management, 68*, 102588. DOI: 10.1016/j.ijinfomgt.2022.102588

Vaid, A., & Sharma, C. (2022). Leveraging SAP and artificial intelligence for optimized enterprise resource planning: Enhancing efficiency, automation, and decision-making. *DOI, 3*.DOI: <ALIGNMENT.qj></ALIGNMENT>10.30574/wjarr

Varshney, D. (2020). Digital transformation and creation of an agile workforce: Exploring company initiatives and employee attitudes. In *Contemporary global issues in human resource management* (pp. 89–105). Emerald Publishing Limited. DOI: 10.1108/978-1-80043-392-220201009

Vrontis, D., Christofi, M., Pereira, V., Tarba, S., Makrides, A., & Trichina, E. (2023). Artificial intelligence, robotics, advanced technologies and human resource management: a systematic review. *Artificial intelligence and international HRM*, 172-201.

Xu, W., Dainoff, M. J., Ge, L., & Gao, Z. (2023). Transitioning to human interaction with AI systems: New challenges and opportunities for HCI professionals to enable human-centered AI. *International Journal of Human-Computer Interaction, 39*(3), 494–518. DOI: 10.1080/10447318.2022.2041900

Chapter 26
Investor Perception and Transforming Decision-Making in the Age of AI-Driven Work Arrangements

Mansi Panwar
https://orcid.org/0009-0007-0470-8216
School of Commerce, Devi Ahilya Vishwavidyalaya, Indore, India

Mohit Verma
https://orcid.org/0009-0001-2447-9656
O.P. Jindal Global University, India

Bhumika Ray
O.P. Jindal Global University, India

Aishwarya Vashishtha
Rutgers University, USA

Shashank Mittal
https://orcid.org/0000-0002-8666-5323
O.P. Jindal Global University, India

Mananage Shanika Hansini Rathnasiri
https://orcid.org/0000-0002-6496-5106
Sabaragamuwa University of Sri Lanka, Belihuloya, Sri Lanka

ABSTRACT

As behavioral finance explores market imperfections and investor rationality in the absence of seamless access to market information, artificial intelligence emerges as a transformative force in financial decision-making. AI enhances market operations by offering a platform for real-time, accurate, and transparent access to information, thereby influencing investor perception. With its ability to conduct in-depth fundamental and technical analyses, AI plays a pivotal role in identifying stocks, assessing risks, managing funds, and optimizing portfolios. Additionally, AI-driven work arrangements are reshaping financial decision-making by enabling automated trading, algorithmic investment strategies, and data-driven market predictions. As AI fosters greater investor participation and efficiency, it addresses market inefficiencies while making investors more informed and rational participants in equity markets. This study examines the intersection of AI and investor perception in equity markets through a bibliometric and thematic analysis.

DOI: 10.4018/979-8-3373-1270-5.ch026

INTRODUCTION

Artificial intelligence (AI) has gained significant academic and practical attention for its transformative role in financial market operations. AI-driven advancements empower investors with sophisticated tools that enable real-time market analysis, automated trading platforms, and enhanced portfolio management strategies (Buchanan, 2019; Chen et al., 2019). These developments have not only reshaped investment strategies but also influenced investor perceptions, altering traditional financial decision-making patterns. With AI applications optimizing high-frequency trading, portfolio diversification, credit risk evaluation, and fraud detection, financial markets are experiencing an unprecedented shift toward efficiency and automation (Jiang et al., 2022; Kou et al., 2021). Simultaneously, AI-driven work arrangements have redefined financial decision-making processes by enabling algorithmic strategies, robo-advisory services, and sentiment-driven investment models, making AI an integral force in shaping modern financial landscapes.

Behavioral finance has long provided insights into market inefficiencies by explaining how cognitive biases, psychological factors, and emotional influences impact investor decision-making. Scholars such as Barberis and Thaler (2003) and Kahneman (2011) have demonstrated that heuristics, loss aversion, and overconfidence often lead to irrational investment behaviors. AI, however, mitigates these biases by processing vast datasets, identifying hidden patterns, and generating data-driven investment recommendations (Boussaidi, 2013; Zahera & Bansal, 2018). Statman (2019) highlights how AI systematically reduces irrational tendencies by offering structured financial insights. The integration of AI with behavioral finance provides a powerful solution to enhance investment strategies and market efficiency, bridging the gap between psychological decision-making and data-driven financial models (Alsabah et al., 2021).

The evolution of AI in finance has extended beyond algorithmic trading to include sentiment analysis, robo-advisory services, and risk management tools. AI-powered sentiment analysis platforms assess market activities and macroeconomic indicators, improving decision-making accuracy (Tsai et al., 2020; Mizgajski et al., 2020). AI-driven investment strategies enhance market predictability by leveraging machine learning techniques that embed behavioral finance principles into analytical models (Goodell et al., 2020). As AI increasingly influences investment decision-making, concerns surrounding investor trust, regulatory transparency, and ethical AI implementation continue to emerge, necessitating further research (Kumar & Palvia, 2022).

This study examines the impact of AI on investor perception in equity markets and its implications for financial decision-making in an era of AI-driven work arrangements. By utilizing VOSviewer and bibliometric analysis, this research explores author collaborations, document co-occurrences, and citation patterns in the literature. Additionally, qualitative content analysis is employed to identify dominant themes and research trends. The findings aim to synthesize existing knowledge while outlining future research avenues, offering a comprehensive understanding of how AI is reshaping investor behavior and transforming financial decision-making in the evolving landscape of AI-driven finance.

2. LITERATURE REVIEW

Behavioral Biases and AI Intervention

Behavioral finance establishes its core position to study investor behavioral patterns. Investors defy rationality based on Efficient Market Hypothesis (EMH) assumptions because of cognitive and emotional biases according to Markowitz (1952) and Barberis & Thaler (2003). Financial market inefficiencies occur because investors make wrong choices due to the behavioral biases of overconfidence and loss aversion and herding behavior (Zahera & Bansal, 2018; Kartini & Nahda, 2021).

The emergence of AI has produced an effective instrument that assists in reducing biases through objective datasets for generating recommendations. The integration of machine learning algorithms in AI decision support systems enables investigators to handle historical information and forecast market behaviors thus leading them to make logical decisions (Alsabah et al., 2021; Goodell et al., 2020). Sentiment analysis through AI technology and Natural Language Processing (NLP) allows investors to detect market attitudes through text interpretation of economic news alongside business reports and social media activities thus minimizing automatic assumption-driven prejudices and emotional impulses (Mizgajski et al., 2020; Tsai et al., 2020).

AI-Driven Tools and Technologies

AI systems introduced within equity markets utilize various tools and technologies which improve investor choices. AI offers to the equity market three main assets which are robo-advisors alongside algorithmic trading systems as well as sentiment analysis tools and predictive analytics. AI revolutionized financial operations through its capability to process large data volumes and detect patterns in the sector (Zhang et al., 2019).

The affordability of robo-advisors allows customers to obtain algorithm-based investment portfolio guidance since it costs less than traditional financial management (Syed 2024). Boreiko and Massarotti (2020) discussed how robo-advisors use individual risk preferences to match investment strategies which leads to optimal portfolio results. The platforms utilize machine learning algorithms to read market data and generate unique recommendations which combat human bias elements.

The speed and precision of trading operations experienced revolutionary changes through algorithmic trading which is an innovation driven by AI. Tsai et al. (2020) proved that AI system automation in trading delivers fast independent high-speed trading along with reduced transaction fees and improved market liquidity speed. Real-time market condition analysis through these systems provides investors the chance to seize fleeting market opportunities which manual analysis methods cannot detect.

Natural financial market operations have experienced transformation because of AI implementation within algorithmic trading systems. High-frequency trading (HFT) systems operated by AI trading models perform speedy trading activities because they utilize predictive analytics linked to real-time data processing (Ren, 2021; Jiang et al., 2022). The performance of artificial intelligence trading algorithms surpasses human trading approaches because they automatically adjust to market changes along with improving fluidity and minimizing transaction prices (Kou et al., 2021).

Market stability continues to face uncertainty in the face of present-day AI developments. The rapid trading through AI systems results in volatility according to Gomber et al. (2018) and Chartier et al. (2021) because these systems perform automated trades without human monitoring. Risk management protocols and regulatory frameworks are crucial elements which minimize possible market instability that occurs from algorithmic trading systems (Kumar & Palvia, 2022).

Investor Trust in AI-Based Financial Decisions

The acceptance of AI-powered investment strategies heavily depends on how confident investors are with artificial intelligence applications for their investments. Investors seem hesitant to depend entirely on automated systems for investing according to Boreiko and Massarotti (2020). The public shows reluctance regarding AI decision systems because they want better clarity in how these decisions work and details about ethical boundaries as well as complete system transparency.

XAI (explanation AI) frameworks serve to enhance AI recommendation transparency thus building trust in AI financial systems (Sun 2020, Ho et al 2017). Study results by Rehman et al. (2023) and Costello et al. (2020) demonstrate why emotional intelligence (EI) should be incorporated into AI-managed financial advisory service platforms. Users develop trust and increased engagement with AI-enabled behavioral funding principles leading to investment combinations between automated precision and human decision-making abilities.

Investor Decision-Making

Artificial intelligence affects investor decisions to great depths because it provides technology that addresses behavioral distortions and enhances rational thought processes. The decision-making accuracy of AI improves because it works objectively instead of being distorted by human emotional influences on judgment as described by Chartier et al. (2021). Through AI-powered digital instruments investors gain factual insights about stock performance and sectoral trends and economic data for facts-based investment decisions.

According to Ren (2021) artificial intelligence serves to boost the forecasting capabilities of financial information. AI-based market prediction depends on the evaluation of historical patterns and trends which enables accurate movement forecasts. Such analytical ability proves especially useful during periods of market uncertainty since standard evaluation techniques stop being effective. The combination of artificial intelligence technology allows investors to perform risk evaluation and optimize their portfolios through generated strategies that protect from losses while maximizing their earnings.

The practice of relying on AI systems causes doubts to emerge about how humans should remain involved in decision tasks. AI technology excels at quick data processing yet it remains incapable of comprehending human emotional traits which define behavior patterns (Marheni et al., 2024). The restricted ability emphasizes the requirement for maintaining equilibrium between AI processing strength and emotional human judgment for decision-making purposes.

3. RESEARCH METHODOLOGY

3.1 Phase 1: Data Retrieval and Search Strategy

For the systematic analysis, data were retrieved from the Scopus database, one of the leading global academic information sources that provide comprehensive access to peer-reviewed literature, abstracts, and citations, ensuring the thoroughness of the search and representativeness of the selected studies (de Moya-Anegon et al., 2007). A search was conducted using the terms (TITLE-ABS-KEY ("Artificial Intelligence" OR "AI" OR "Machine Learning" OR "Deep Learning" OR "Neural Networks" OR "Algorithmic Intelligence") AND ("Investor Perception" OR "Investor Psychology" OR "Investor Behavior" OR "Investor Sentiment" OR "Behavioral Finance" OR "Cognitive Bias" OR "Market Perception" OR "Investor Beliefs" OR "Investment Attitudes") AND ("Stock Market" OR "Equity Market" OR "Capital Markets" OR "Financial Markets" OR "Investment Decision" OR "Market Dynamics" OR "Trading Behavior")), which yielded 354 records.

3.2 Phase 2: Filtering and Selection Criteria

Further relevant filters were applied to ensure that the results are limited to specific subject areas, including (Economics, Econometrics and Finance), (Business, Management and Accounting), Decision Sciences (DECI), Sociology (SOCI), and Psychology (PSYC). The review exclusively uses literature available in the English language. The search parameters used filtering to extract academic and research materials from specified disciplines while disregarding unrelated subject areas and non-English publications until a total of 183 usable records remained.

3.3 Bibliometric Study:

Research publications regarding specific topics receive quantitative examination throughout predetermined timeframes by using the bibliometric analysis method (Almind & Ingwersen, 1997; Persson et al., 2009). As a powerful analytical technique it has become prominent during the last twenty years for science and research policy studies and multiple diverse subject areas.

Bibliometric methods serve three main objectives as part of widespread research practice: domain expansion and research group assessment and study impact measurement (Pilkington & Meredith, 2009). Bibliometric analysis functions as one of the rare interdisciplinatory research methods which gives understanding of multiple scientific fields through their research spaces (Glänzel, 2003).

This research method evaluates scientific study and technological development changes using citation analysis and content analysis tools to track progress from researchers to societal organizations (De Bellis, 2009; Okubo, 1997).

This research used VOSviewer software for bibliometric analysis due to its ability to visualize and analyze research networks as described in (van Eck & Waltman, 2010). The application permits users to generate understandable graphical patterns which aid in understanding intricate bibliometric interconnections (Laengle et al., 2018).

The objective of this study is to address the following key questions in the context of artificial intelligence and investor perception in equity markets:

RQ1: How has the publication trend in artificial intelligence and investor perception in equity markets evolved over time?
RQ2: Who are the most prolific authors contributing to research on artificial intelligence and investor perception in equity markets?
RQ3: Which countries contribute the most to research on artificial intelligence and investor perception in equity markets?
RQ4: Which institutions are leading contributors to research in artificial intelligence and investor perception in equity markets?
RQ5: Which academic journals publish the most research on artificial intelligence and investor perception in equity markets?
RQ6: What are the different types of documents published on artificial intelligence and investor perception in equity markets?
RQ7: What are the major subject areas covered in research on artificial intelligence and investor perception in equity markets?
RQ8: Which funding sponsors have contributed the most to research on artificial intelligence and investor perception in equity markets?

Co-Authorship Analysis:

RQ9: What are the key research trends in artificial intelligence and investor perception in equity markets based on co-authorship analysis, including prolific authors, leading organizations, and dominant contributing countries?

Co-Occurrence Analysis:

RQ10: What are the key research trends in artificial intelligence and investor perception in equity markets based on co-occurrence analysis of all keywords, author keywords, and index keywords?

Citation Analysis:

RQ11: What are the key research trends in artificial intelligence and investor perception in equity markets based on citation analysis of influential documents, sources, authors, organizations, and contributing countries?

RESULTS AND FINDINGS

Figure 1. Documents by Year on the Role of Artificial Intelligence in Shaping Investor Perception in Equity Markets (2004–2025), Showing Trends in Research Publications from Scopus.

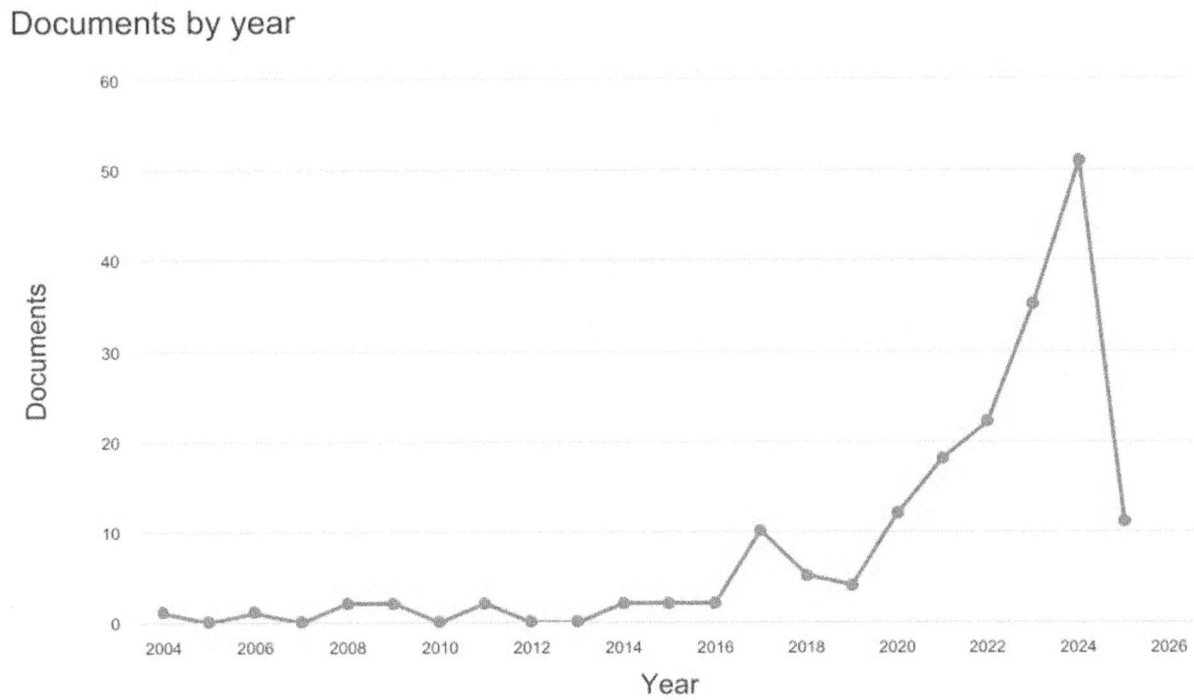

Research documents about AI and investor perception of equity markets showed substantial growth following 2020 according to the line graph presented. Academic interest rose incrementally from 2015 before experiencing a rapid growth from 2021 to 2024 which reached maximum levels during 2024. The analysis shows that academic circles currently understand AI to have a fundamental effect on how investors make decisions and how markets function. The considerable decrease in data for 2025 could have two potential reasons: first, there was limited research collection or second, researchers pivoted their focus in another direction. The increasing number of academic publications shows the necessity to examine AI-driven investment strategies regarding their behavioral consequences and ethical issues and prognostic abilities better.

Figure 2. Documents by Author on the Role of Artificial Intelligence in Shaping Investor Perception in Equity Markets, Highlighting the Top Contributors from Scopus.

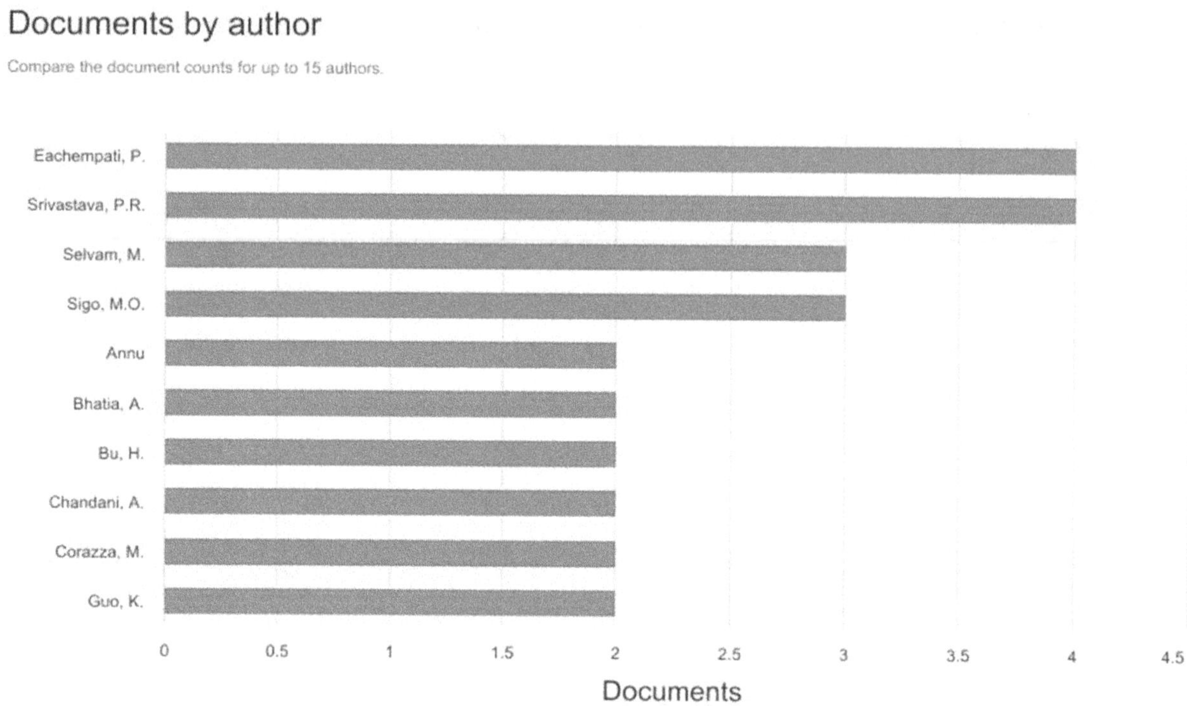

This research field shows two authors named Eachempati P. and Srivastava P.R. have the highest number of publications among all authors in their domain. The next most active contributors to this field stand as Selvam, M. and Sigo, M.O. This field of investigation sees additional contributions from authors including Annu, Bhatia A. and Bu H. The similar numbers of documents published by various researchers indicate increasing teamwork dedicated to understanding how AI influences equity market investor perception. The research reveals dominant authors in this field whose works establish guiding principles for additional research in this domain.

Figure 3. Documents by Country on the Role of Artificial Intelligence in Shaping Investor Perception in Equity Markets, Highlighting Leading Research-Contributing Nations from Scopus.

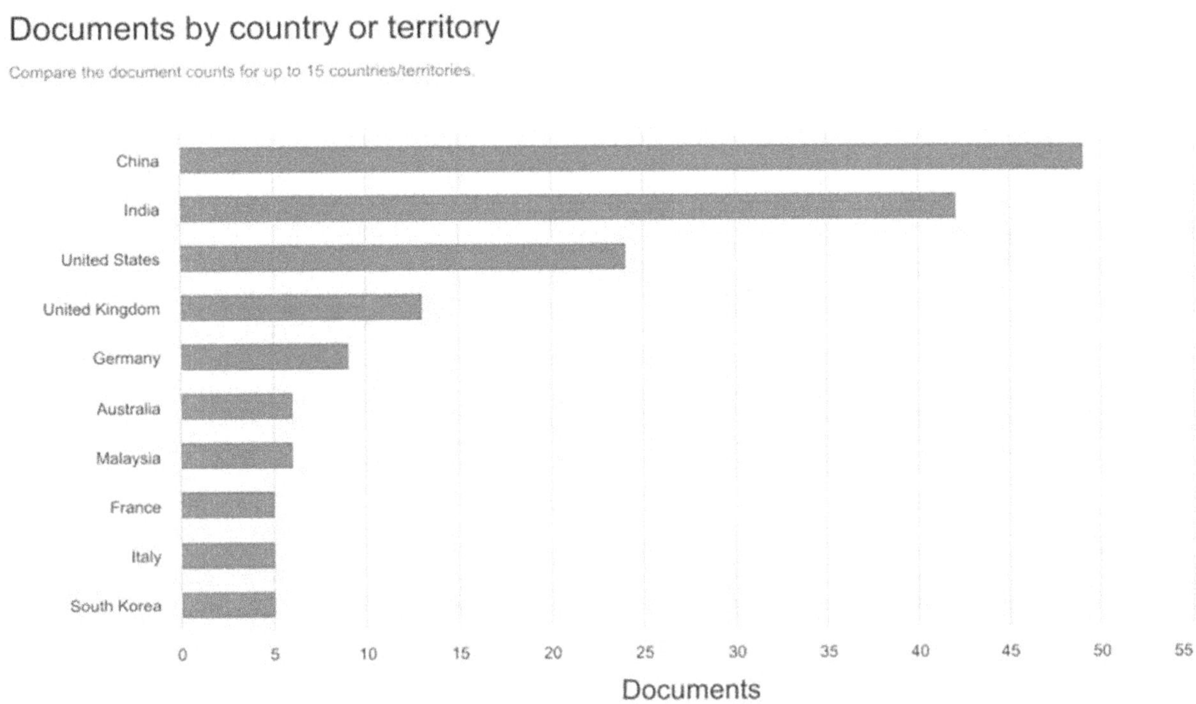

Research publications on AI's impact on equity market investor perception show China as the leading nation while India maintains a close second position and the United States follows after them. The academic and industrial interest in AI-driven financial decision-making stands most prominent in these three countries which control the research literature. Research activity in European markets is substantial based on the notable research contributions from both the United Kingdom and Germany. The field has gained rising international attention as emerging research emerges from countries including Australia and Malaysia as well as France and Italy and South Korea.

Figure 4. Documents by Affiliation on the Role of Artificial Intelligence in Shaping Investor Perception in Equity Markets, Highlighting Leading Academic Institutions from Scopus.

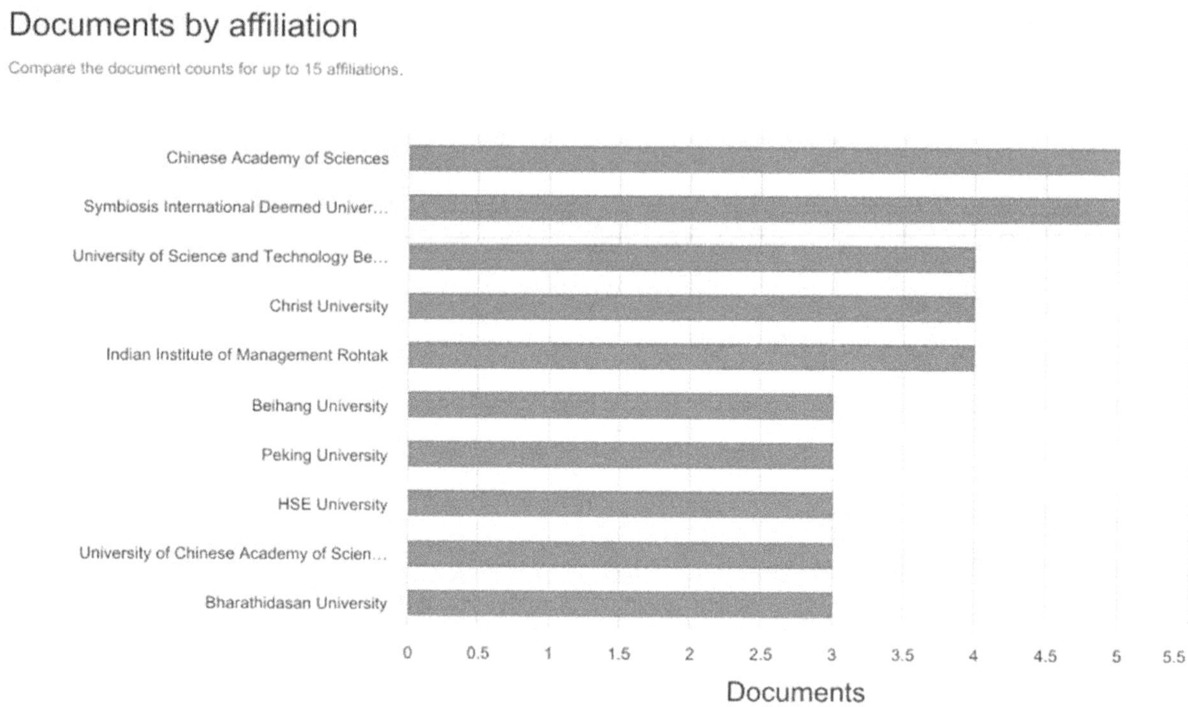

Chinese Academy of Sciences along with Symbiosis International Deemed University stand at the forefront of institutions which produce research about AI-based influence on equity market investor perception. Academic interest in the topic emerges from multiple Chinese and Indian institutions including University of Science and Technology Beijing and Christ University in addition to Indian Institute of Management Rohtak. The global reach in this field is visible through academic institutions such as Beihang University, Peking University and HSE University and University of Chinese Academy of Sciences along with Bharathidasan University. The rising dominance of Chinese and Indian institutions within AI and financial research is shown through the multiple universities listed while Russian and other international institutions contribute to expanding worldwide academic partnerships.

Figure 5. Documents by Year on the Role of Artificial Intelligence in Shaping Investor Perception in Equity Markets (2008-2025), Showing Trends in Research Publications from Scopus.

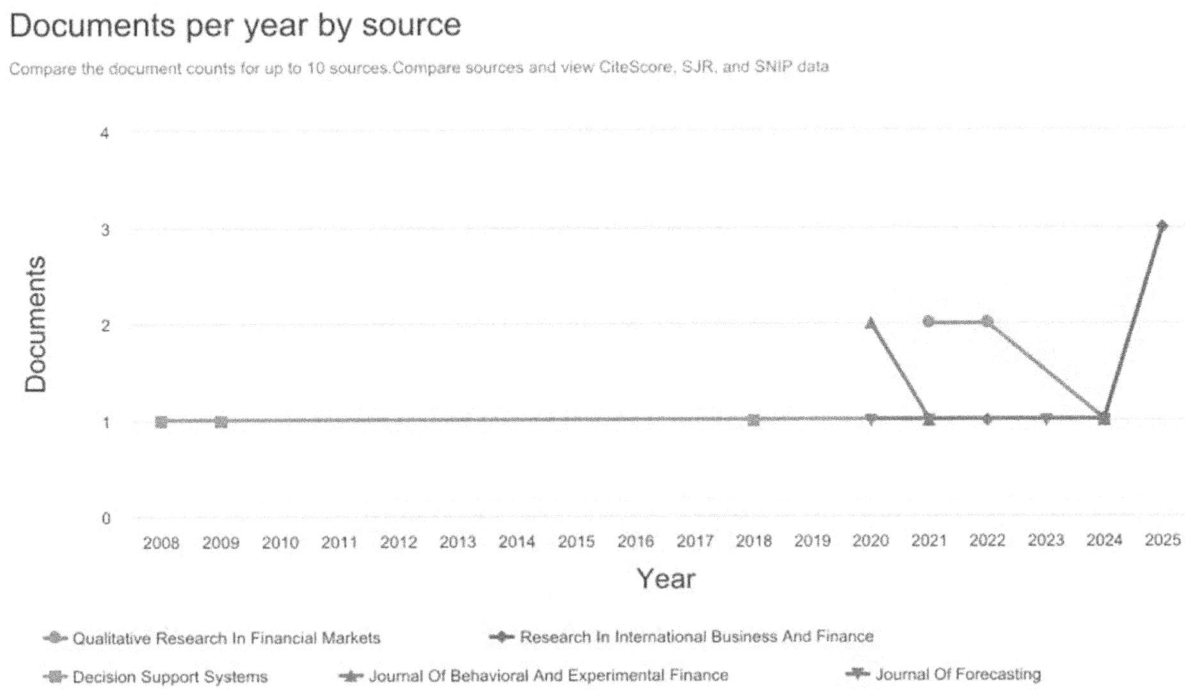

Decision Support Systems published research documents continuously throughout the research domain until 2018 while consistently maintaining its research presence each year. The financial research field demonstrates a significant change because Qualitative Research in Financial Markets and Journal of Behavioral and Experimental Finance have published an increased number of studies from 2020 to 2022. Their research activities show a reduction after this period. Research in International Business and Finance exhibits the most recent surge of publications since taking over first position in 2025. The research landscape seems to be evolving as newer journals start conducting AI-driven financial market studies because AI applications continue to gain significance in financial and investment decision-making domains.

Figure 6. Documents by Subject Area on the Role of Artificial Intelligence in Shaping Investor Perception in Equity Markets, Representing the Disciplinary Distribution of Research from Scopus

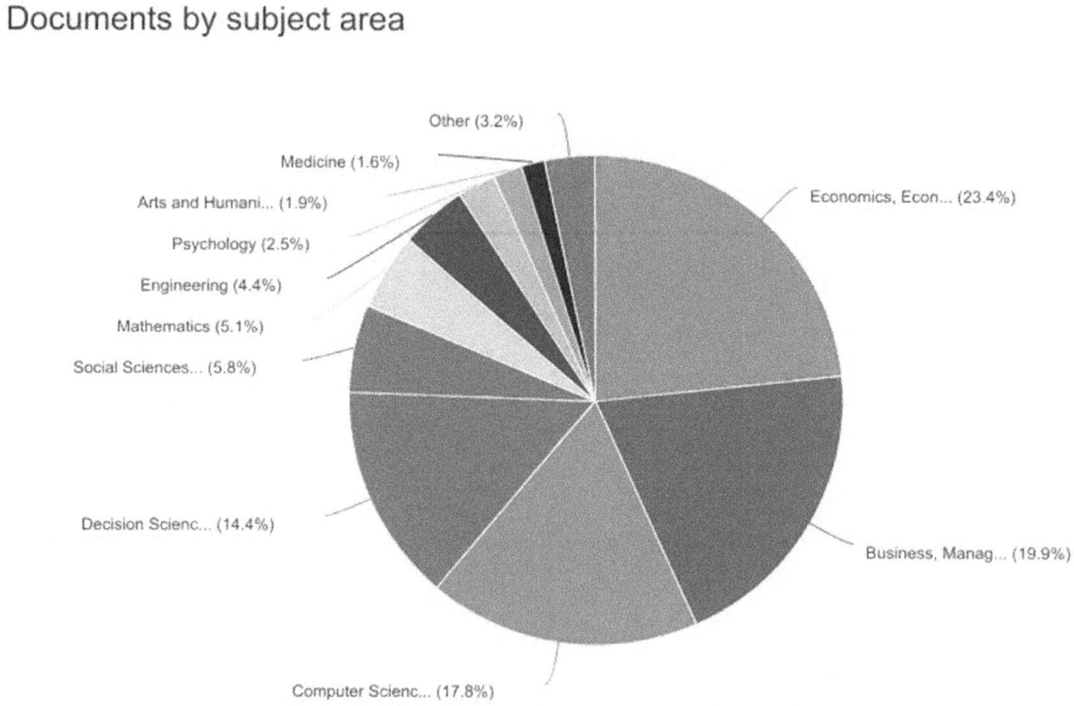

The research primarily concentrates on financial economic management subjects based on the subject area distribution where Economics (23.4%) and Business & Management (19.9%) represent the biggest categories. The fields of Computer Science and Decision Science (14.4%) together with Computer Science (17.8%) show substantial contributions which demonstrates research focuses on technological applications and analytical decision support. The research support comes from Social Sciences which makes up 5.8% of the distribution and from Mathematics with 5.1% while Engineering contributes 4.4% of the analytical landscape. The research share is split with Psychology holding 2.5% and Arts & Humanities along with Medicine securing 1.9% and 1.6% respectively while remaining divisions command a lower share. Research primarily focuses on economics business and technology-based fields according to these distribution results.

Figure 7. Documents by Funding Sponsor on the Role of Artificial Intelligence in Shaping Investor Perception in Equity Markets, Illustrating Research Support from Various Institutions.

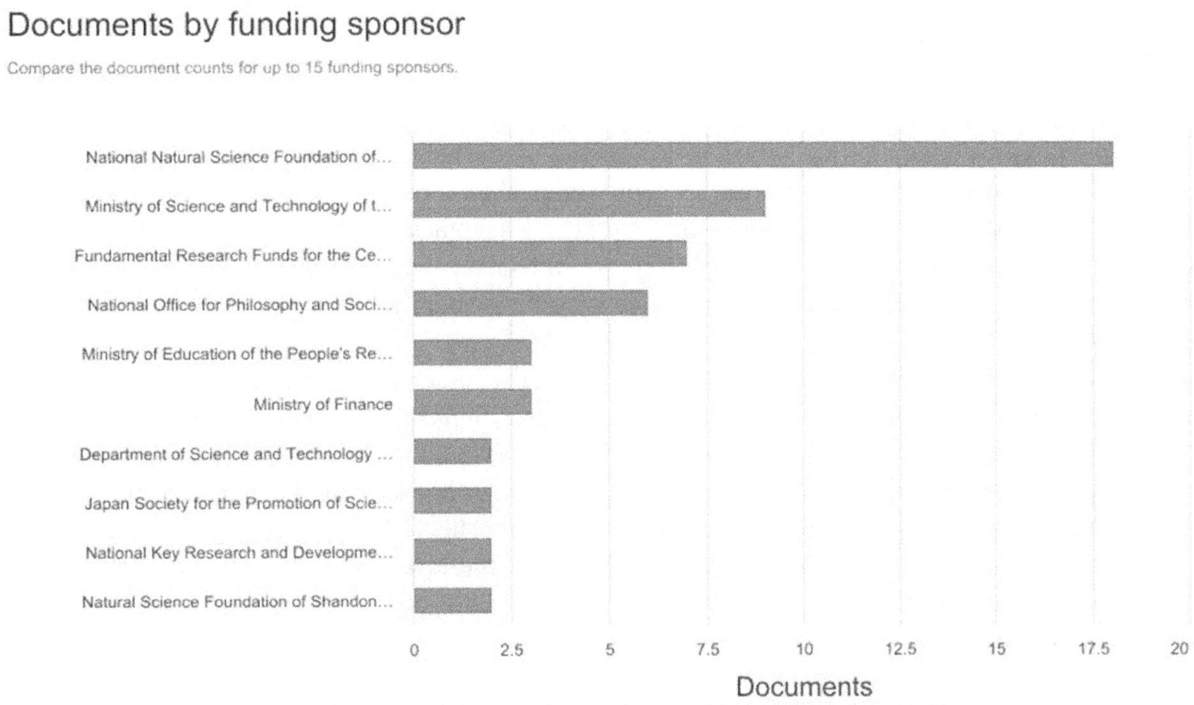

Different sponsorship organizations funded numerous documents according to the presented chart and the National Natural Science Foundation emerged as the leading sponsor. Research funding from the Ministry of Science and Technology follows the National Natural Science Foundation while receiving substantial support from the Fundamental Research Funds for the Central Universities. Beyond scientific and technical disciplines the National Office for Philosophy and Social Sciences demonstrates substantial financial backing according to the funding distribution. Additional funding sources for The Pollution Journal come from various organizations such as the Ministry of Education and Ministry of Finance as well as international groups like the Japan Society for the Promotion of Science. Research funding shows a clear state dominance through multiple government research programs which also receives additional support from specialized and international organizations.

CO-AUTHORSHIP ANALYSIS (AUTHORS, ORGANIZATIONS, COUNTRIES)

Types of analysis: Co-authorship

Unit of analysis: Author

The co-authorship statistics combined with author evaluations provide essential perspectives regarding the research community's cooperation regarding AI influence on equity markets perception. A total of 547 authors completed the study criteria by having at least one publication without any detected citations. Network analysis shows that research cohesiveness remains low because most authors in the field exist in independent domains with only 10 authors effectively collaborating. Future research should address the limited researcher collaboration by developing academic networks because interest in the field already exists widely.

A total of ten authors form two separate clusters within the co-authorship network. Cluster 1 includes authors Balasundram Maniam, Kannaiah Desti, Kathiravan Chinnadurai, Sigo Marxia Oli and Vadivel Thanikachalam together with Cluster 2 members Maniam Balasundram, Selvam Murugesan, Sigo Marxia Oli, Subramaniam Geetha and Venkateswar Sankaran. Sigo Marxia Oli and Balasundram Maniam connect the two separate clusters by appearing across them. The 31 links in the network demonstrate a combination of 36 total link strength which shows a middle-level connectedness between authors. The separated cluster structure indicates researchers need to work together more extensively across the whole research field.

Figure 8. Bibliometric co-authorship network map based on authors.

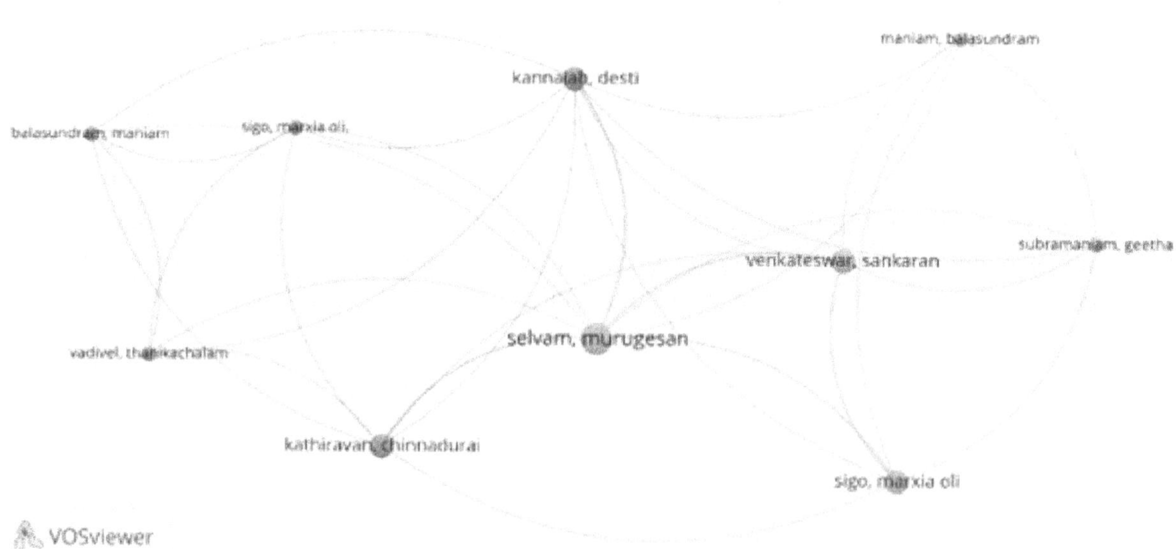

Source: Generated from VOSviewer.

The co-authorship network displays two reddish and greenish clusters whose levels of connection patterns differ. The co-authorship network shows the red Cluster 1 having its core members as Kannaiah Desti, Kathiravan Chinnadurai, Vadivel Thanikachalam, Balasundram Maniam and Sigo Marxia Oli. Cluster 2 (green) focuses on Selvam Murugesan, Venkateswar Sankaran, Subramaniam Geetha, Maniam Balasundram and Sigo Marxia Oli. Research indicates Sigo Marxia Oli and Balasundram Maniam function as main bridging figures between the two research groups through their collaborative activities. Research networks in AI and investor perception of equity markets require stronger interdisciplinary cooperation because of sparse connections between cluster groups.

Figure 9. Bibliometric co-authorship overlay map based on authors.

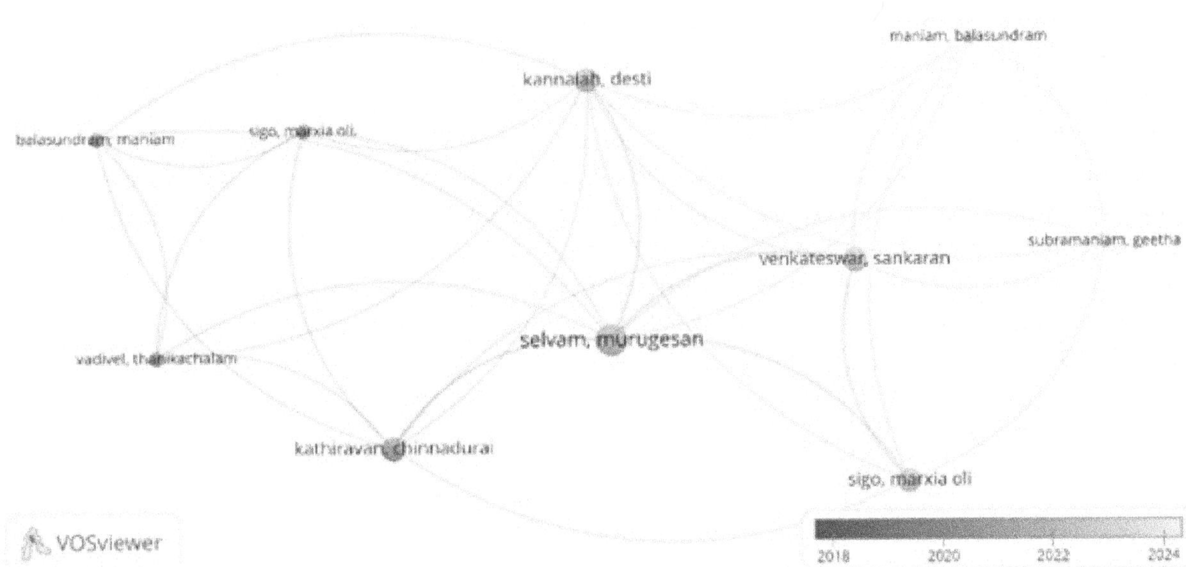

Source: Generated from VOSviewer.

Through the overlay visualization researchers can explore chronological changes in the dynamics of co-authorship relationships regarding AI investment-related studies in equity markets. The blue nodes represent earliest collaborative networks during 2018–2019 where Kathiravan Chinnadurai, Vadivel Thanikachalam, Balasundram Maniam, along with Sigo Marxia Oli formed the primary research group. During (2020-2021) the authors Kannaiah Desti and Selvam Murugesan joined the network as it expanded with increasing collaboration among researchers. Three researchers namely Maniam Balasundram, Subramaniam Geetha and Venkateswar Sankaran lead research efforts during the period from 2022 through 2024 according to the yellow nodes. Research activity exhibits progress as it evolves from individual research groups to connect more businesses and academics in the field demonstrating increased research enthusiasm.

Types of analysis: Co-authorship

Unit of analysis: Organisation

Multiple institutions lack collaborative publishing patterns when researching how AI influences investor perceptions in equity markets according to organizational co-authorship analysis. Among the 384 studied organizations all exceed the minimum criteria of publishing two papers with no citations but the network shows minimal inter-organizational ties. Six organizations form the largest interconnected research group while the rest demonstrate weak relationships throughout institutions. The wide number of contributing organizations in the field appear to operate without established partnerships between institutions. Mutual cooperation between organizations would increase the sharing of intellectual knowledge while fueling cross-disciplinary research which accelerates the pace of development within this dynamic field.

The organizational co-authorship analysis groups six institutions which form a single connected network that extends between the United Kingdom and Poland and South Africa. The educational institutions Aberdeen Business School (Robert Gordon University, UK) together with Newcastle Business School (Northumbria University, UK) and University of Łódź (Poland) and Kozminski University (Poland) as well as University of Cape Town (South Africa) and University of Pretoria (South Africa) operate as partners within a research network. This research network shows moderate institutional cooperation through its 15 reported connections because it investigates AI's impact on equity market investor perception. The single connecting group highlights a restricted scope of global institutional research alliances which demonstrates a potential opportunity to develop new partnerships for better international knowledge transfer.

Figure 10. Bibliometric co-authorship network map based on organizations.

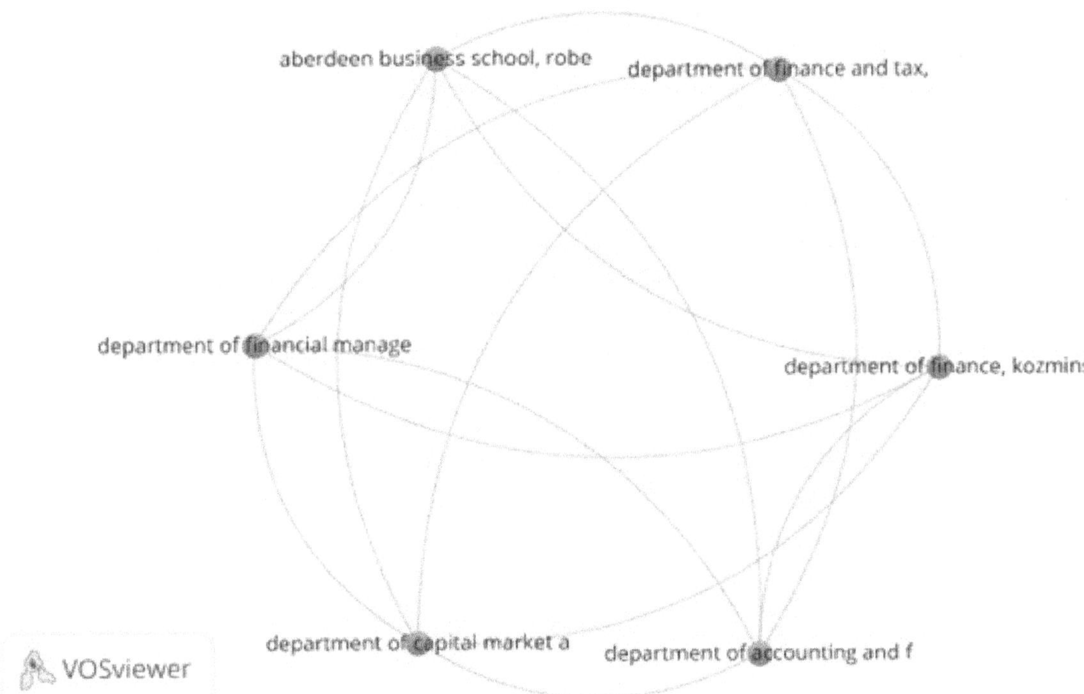

Source: Generated from VOSviewer

The network analysis shows that six institutions create a tightly connected research and collaborative group. The presented visualization shows robust connections between research institutions in the United Kingdom, Poland and South Africa which demonstrates their joint work regarding AI's effects on investor perception in equity markets. Collaboration within the institution network becomes more frequent because multiple links demonstrate regular joint research publishing among these institutions. Research within this domain shows concentrations within a limited network of institutions because additional clusters are absent so broader insights require additional global partnerships between institutions.

Types of analysis: Co-authorship

Unit of analysis: Countries

The country-level co-authorship study shows an extensive global research network which demonstrates limited network connections in AI research into equity market investor perception modifications. Among 53 countries every nation has at least published one paper while none received zero citations. A majority of 53 countries participate in co-authorship research but among these the largest collaborative network connects 42 nations. The occurrence of global research connections is strong but the research network remains fragmented because some countries operate independently. By promoting international partnership and transnational research collaboration the exchange of information will increase along with numerous research viewpoints that can investigate the changing dynamics of AI and equity markets.

Research investigating AI's impact on investor perception of equity markets displays a worldwide research network with multiple independent segments described at the country level. The 42 countries linked through research show regional or collaborative trends which group them into nine clusters. The research collaborations shown through Cluster 1 and 2 present notable regional strengths among Finland, Italy, New Zealand, Norway, Poland, South Africa, Switzerland, Czech Republic, Germany, Monaco, Romania, Spain, and Taiwan while smaller clusters featuring China, Macao, Thailand and Ireland, Malaysia, Singapore indicate local research partnerships. The network's international participation reaches a moderate level because it contains 84 links with a combined strength of 99 but still displays evidence of disjointed connections. The expansion of alliances between research clusters would develop an interconnected method to explore AI's contribution to equity markets and increase mutual understanding throughout multiple regional industries and technical domains.

Figure 11. Bibliometric co-authorship network map based on countries.

Source: Generated from VOSviewer.

Research on AI and investor perception demonstrates that countries in the co-authorship network exist in globally networked but segregated groups. The research network's central roles belong to India along with China and the United Kingdom because these three nations establish sustained research partnerships with multiple counties. The research patterns form separate clusters because Australia together with Tunisia and Bangladesh create their own research connection around India and Germany with Romania along with China create another collaborative hub. The research network features distinct clusters that show some nations exist on its outer edges because their research activities remain separated from the main interconnected areas. Exterior cluster collaboration development will improve worldwide knowledge sharing which establishes a more complete analysis of AI effects on equity market investor perceptions.

Figure 12. Bibliometric co-authorship overlay map based on countries.

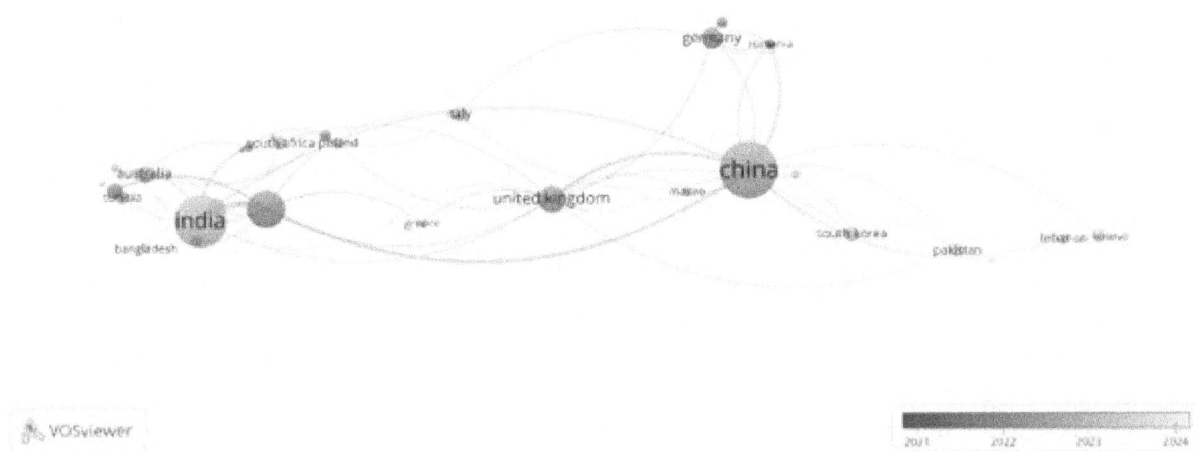

Source: Generated from VOSviewer

The visual representation of worldwide co-authorship between researchers demonstrates the historical development of international collaboration patterns during the analyzed periods. This research domain originated during 2021–2022 from countries which are represented by darker colors such as India, Australia and South Africa. Yellow-green shades in the visualization indicate how research collaborations involving Pakistan and Kosovo with Lebanon have become prominent since 2023-2024 because these nations demonstrate rising research interest in different world territories. The research hubs operated consistently by China and the United Kingdom maintained connectivity throughout different time periods. The global interest in AI-driven investor perception research continues to expand since new participants from different regions connect existing knowledge gaps through international collaborations.

CO-OCCURRENCE ANALYSIS (ALL KEYWORDS, AUTHOR KEYWORDS, INDEX KEYWORDS)

Types of analysis: Co-occurrence

Unit of analysis: All keywords

The keyword co-occurrence analysis identifies central patterns and mainstream topics regarding AI perception by investors in equity markets. The selected keywords total 1,044 and among these 99 reached the minimum occurrence criterion of three times during the analysis period. The wide research area contains a small set of dominant keywords which covers artificial intelligence applications together with behavioral finance and sentiment analysis and market prediction domains. The research process using identified keywords reveals current academic trends because it discovers both established fields and possible unaddressed areas that could become study topics.

The whole research domain shows strong network connections through six clusters which group a total of 99 key terms according to the co-occurrence analysis method. The analysis demonstrates powerful connections between different AI-driven investment subjects because it contains 1,501 links and a combined link strength of 3,295. The strong link strength between keywords indicates that different concepts frequently appear together in research which demonstrates an extensive academic approach to AI investor perception. The clustering reflects key focus areas such as machine learning, investor sentiment, stock market prediction, behavioral finance, and financial forecasting. Through its organized structure this network reveals major subjects and evolving trends about AI functions in equity markets.

Figure 13. Bibliometric co-occurrence network map based on All keywords.

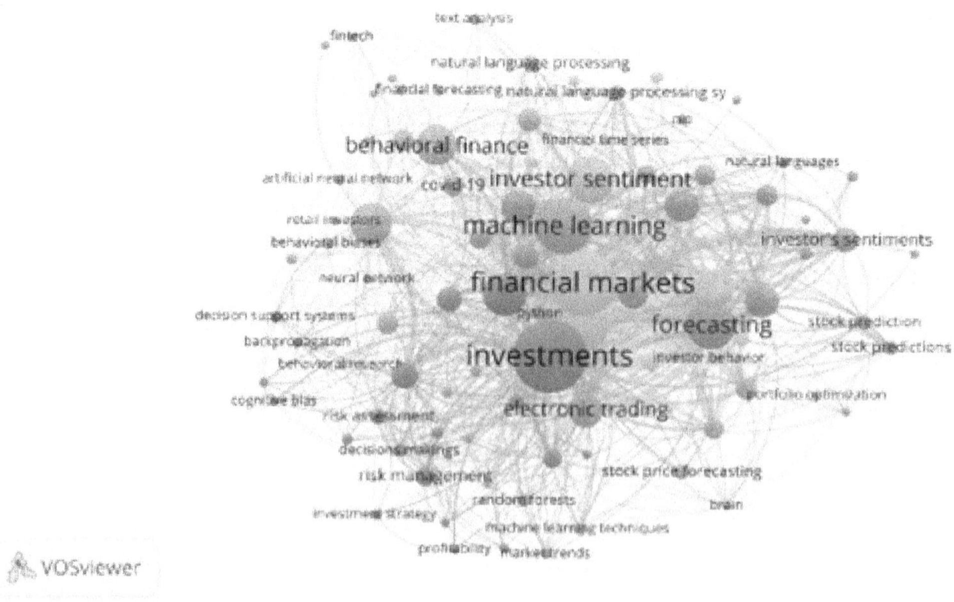

Source: Generated from VOSviewer.

The network illustration integrates main concepts from research about AI-driven investor perception studies. The vital concepts "financial markets" and "investments" and "machine learning" together with "investor sentiment" maintain close connectivity in their relationships which demonstrates that AI has a significant influence on decision-making processes. The research clusters show how AI drives predictions in equity markets through combined efforts of behavioral finance with forecasting and risk management and algorithmic trading along with NLP applications. The extensive array of connections demonstrates academic colleges merging financial and technological and psychological expertise to develop next-generation investment approaches.

Types of analysis: Co-occurrence

Unit of analysis: Author keywords

Author keyword co-occurrence patterns establish main concepts within research about investors' perception of AI. A total of 91 keywords met the research criteria after analysis of 572 keywords and 90 of them created a linked network structure. The analysis shows how the majority of research fields strongly attach to one another through persistent concepts such as machine learning and investor sentiment and risk management and financial forecasting. The presence of specific isolated keywords demonstrates researchers are establishing new domains that remain separate from the dominant research fields. The analysis delivers guidance for academic researchers to create connections and boost cooperative effects between diverse artificial intelligence applications within equity market systems.

A co-occurrence analysis for author keywords found 90 key terms divided into 11 clusters which represents the multiple topics explored in research about AI-driven investor perception. The network shows a strong conceptual connection through 384 links that sum up to 491 total link strength between machine learning with financial forecasting and investor sentiment and risk management. The domain contains numerous clusters which demonstrates a research field consisting of different specialized sub-areas. The large number of connections between research studies shows progress in the research domain since AI applications in equity markets now interact regularly to form new investment approaches and market analysis methodologies.

Figure 14. Bibliometric co-occurrence network map based on Author keywords.

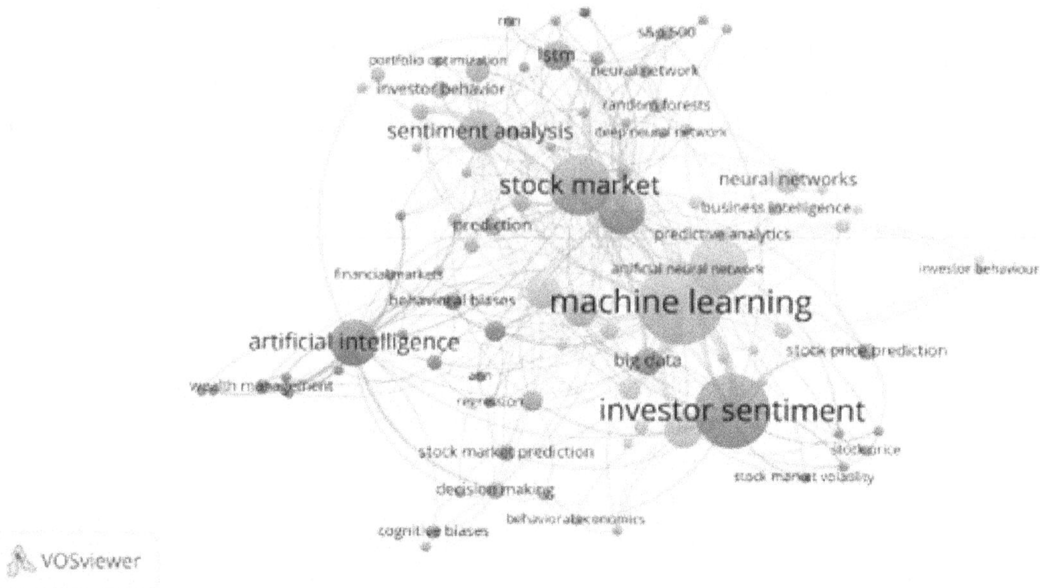

Source: Generated from VOSviewer.

The network visualization system provides clarity on fundamental topics regarding artificial intelligence applications affecting investor perception in equity markets. "Machine learning" functions as the dominant keyword which connects "investor sentiment" with "stock market" as well as "artificial intelligence" and "sentiment analysis" concepts. AI techniques maintain essential functions for financial decision-making based on their strong connections with related concepts. Research in this field explores four main areas which involve predictive analytics, behavioral finance, portfolio optimization and deep learning models in addition to having multiple separate research clusters. The high number of research connections demonstrates a strong integration among investigative areas because AI increasingly influences investment methods and market activity.

Types of analysis: Co-occurrence

Unit of analysis: Index keywords

Study of investor views about AI in equity markets shows preference to linked research areas which emerged from co-occurrence analysis and the study of index keywords. The 630-total keywords contain 143 research areas that received at least two appearances according to the minimum requirement. Since particular topics receive in-depth exploration more investigations many other crucial areas lack sufficient research. The consultant utilizes findings to demonstrate how unified conceptual understanding of emerging ideas leads to whole understanding about AI in present-day financial decision applications.

Analysis through co-occurrence along with index keyword methods generates important information about research patterns related to Artificial Intelligence's effect on equity market investors' perceptions. The research network establishes 8 clusters that encompass 143 keywords thus demonstrating multiple yet overlapping research fields. The field shows strong development because the analysis reveals 2098 linked relationships with a cumulative link strength reaching 3756 between its main topics. Multiple clusters within the research demonstrate its multidimensional nature yet different themes exist in deep interconnected relationships which makes necessary interdisciplinary team work to develop a comprehensive understanding of this domain.

Figure 15. Bibliometric co-occurrence network map based on Index keywords.

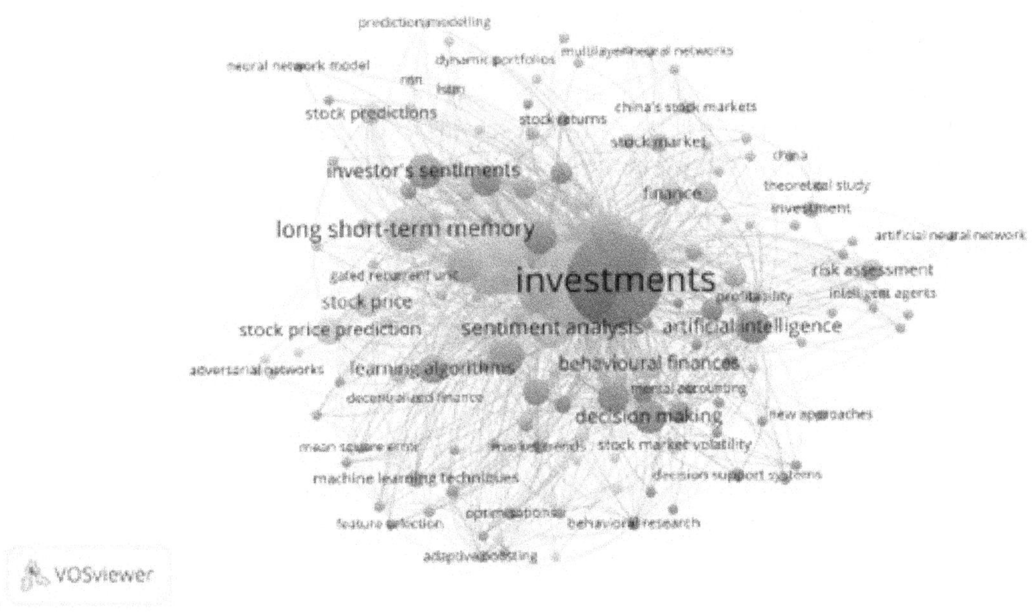

Source: Generated from VOSviewer.

The graph visualization using co-occurrence and index keyword examination shows the fundamental areas investigated about AI's role in transforming equity market investor precepts. The primary research areas consist of “investments” and “sentiment analysis” together with “artificial intelligence” and “decision making” which demonstrate their fundamental relationship inside the field. Research clusters display diversity because behavioral finance supports machine learning techniques to assess stock market volatility and decision making through sentiment analysis which build connected but distinct research branches. Research directions in AI-driven financial decision-making continue to evolve because new keywords emerge between established keywords that show a well-integrated body of knowledge.

CITATION ANALYSIS (DOCUMENT, SOURCE, AUTHORS, ORGANIZATIONS AND COUNTRIES)

Types of analysis: Citation

Unit of analysis: Document

This analysis both consults citations and examines documents so researchers can recognize key works that define discussions about AI's effects on equity market investor perception. Out of 182 documents, 95 meet the minimum citation threshold, indicating a strong base of relevant literature. Analyzing the network shows weak interdocument connections because only 10 works establish significant citation relationships among them. Studies in this field need to merge existing knowledge better so future research can utilize fundamental works to improve cross-document references while maximizing collaborative study effects.

A linked network consisting of six small clusters groups the 10 studied documents in a fragmented research field. Research about AI impact on investor perception in equity markets maintains its advancement in independent segments because the analysis shows only 10 interlinked studies. This lack of strong interconnections presents an opportunity for future studies to bridge gaps between different research streams, fostering a more cohesive and interdisciplinary understanding of the subject.

Figure 16. Bibliometric citation network map based on Documents.

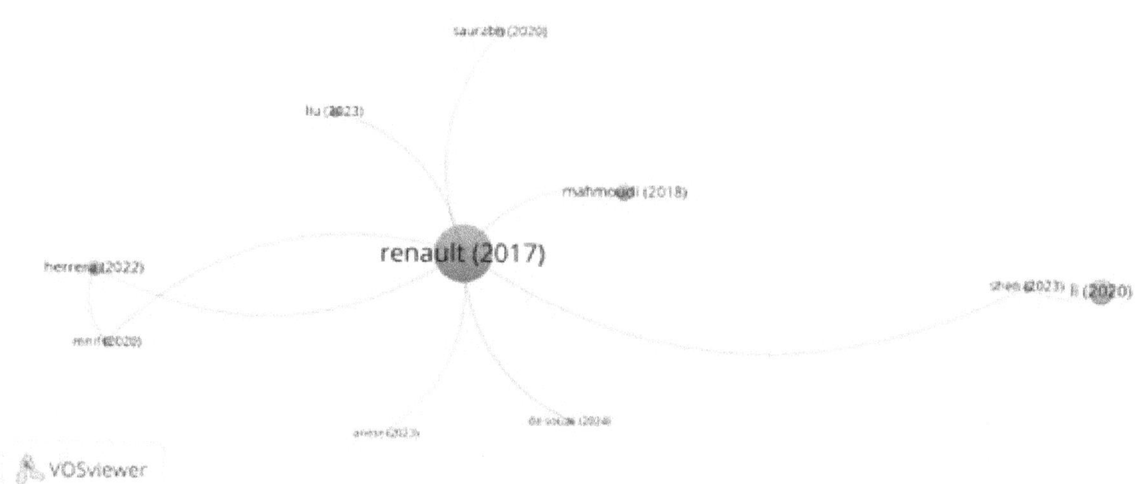

Source: Generated from VOSviewer.

The network map demonstrates that Renault (2017) stands as the key research that multiple studies reference. The foundational role of Renault's (2017) study is demonstrated through multiple citations from Liu (2023), Anese (2023) and De Souza (2024) and other authors. Shen (2023) and Li (2020) established their own distinct research stream based on their separate citation relationship. Elementary research connections exist in this framework since studies connect mostly through direct references to Renault (2017) while showing limited support for concurrent scholarly activities.

Types of analysis: Citation

Unit of analysis: Source

The citation and source analysis demonstrates how varied academic papers contribute to research about AI's impact on investor perceptions within equity markets. The 147 available research sources satisfy the minimum thresholds which indicates a vibrant and wide-ranging research field. The network analysis displays disconnectivity because it shows that 21 sources form a complete network structure while all other research stays individual and separated. Many academic journals add to the field although source interconnection seems scarce among them. Inter-source connection development would boost knowledge integration between sources and promote collaborative research and unified scientific base establishment.

Research on AI's impact on equity market investor perceptions has multiple dispersed and varied approaches according to the citation and source analysis. The distribution of 21 sources across 8 clusters indicates low intercluster connectivity since it contains 22 links that produce a total link strength of 24. Few academic connections exist between multiple sources in the research field because cross-referencing and inter-journal collaboration remain minimal. Additional linkages between research sources would improve both knowledge integration and fundamental research cohesion in the ongoing evolutionary field.

Figure 17. Bibliometric citation network map based on Source.

Source: Generated from VOSviewer.

This network visualization shows that research on AI's influence on investor equity market perceptions exists within an untightly connected academic field. This graphic reveals separate clusters of research publications which demonstrate minimal reference exchanges between them thus indicating fragmented research distribution across different scientific journals. According to the network visualization Decision Support Systems and Qualitative Research in Finance act as so-called central sources whereas many other sources stay individually disconnected or demonstrate weak associations. The research field benefits from improved academic journal integration since this would create a stronger and more connected research network.

Types of analysis: Citation

Unit of analysis: Authors

Analysis shows extensive research fragmentation because only 47 authors out of the 547 author threshold created a connected network. It shows that existing scholarly investigations examining AI's investor perception manipulation stand widely published but authors fail to collaborate frequently. The finding of numerous disconnected authors suggests that research activities play out independently of each other which prevents interdisciplinary learning opportunities. Academic alliances coupled with co-authored research initiatives have the potential to raise the impact of studies and promote innovation while setting a better research structure for examinations in this field.

The research network demonstrates extensive fragmentation because 47 authors split into 17 clusters through 100 connecting ties. The extensive cluster distribution demonstrates that studies on AI and equity market investor perception research show diversity yet weak connections between academic scholars. Research groups show minimal cooperative behavior through network analysis despite the fact that some authors achieve substantial influence. Academic collaborations and interdisciplinary partnerships between researchers will improve both knowledge unification and research results in the developing field.

Figure 18. Bibliometric citation network map based on Authors.

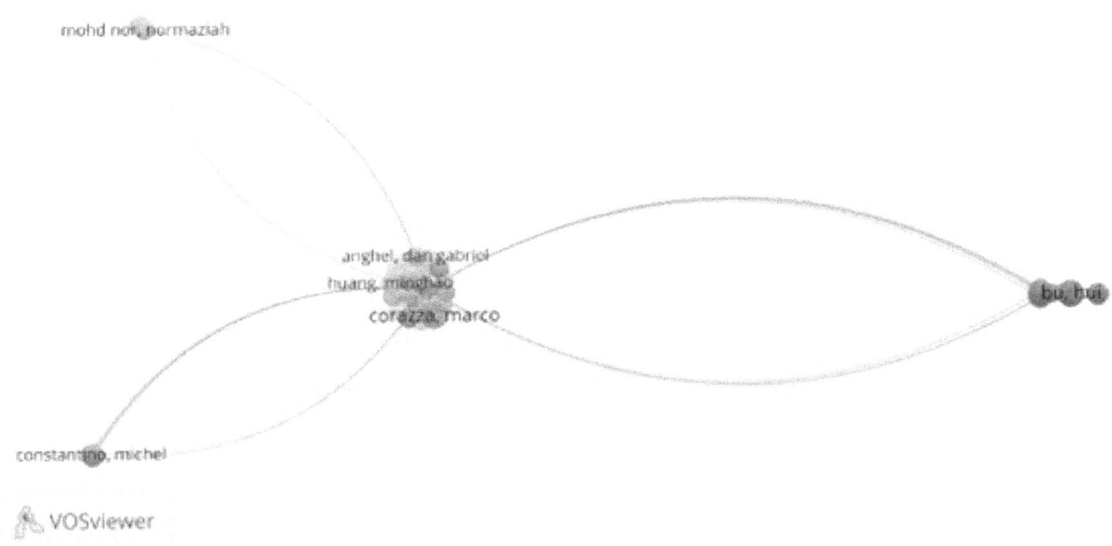

Source: Generated from VOSviewer.

The visual representation of citation analyses based on authors as nodes shows a dispersed structure of research entities with specific academic groups investigating investor perception of AI. Multiple academic researchers including Corazza Marco Anghel Dan Gabriel and Huang Minghao form the core of a network system which supports knowledge exchange between researchers. Multiple independent research groups work separately from each other due to the limited scholar collaboration between the isolated clusters. Strengthened field performance can result from developing better collaboration between researchers across different disciplines which will generate unified understanding of academic content.

Types of analysis: Citation

Unit of analysis: Organization

Research institutions at large maintain substantial interest in analyzing how artificial intelligence affects investor perception of equity markets. All 384 research institutions match the minimum thresholds but the connected research structure includes only 39 organizations throughout the network. Many different institutions participate in the study but show minimal joint cooperation along the research path. Unified institutional alliances and international research partnerships will improve knowledge exchanges and bring unified interdisciplinary understanding that boosts the effectiveness of artificial intelligence-based financial studies.

Research conducted at the organizational level shows scattered evolution within the research field. Among 39 total organizations which belong to 13 clusters researchers have established 100 citation links showing that institutions maintain active involvement yet their joint efforts mainly occur between small clusters. The distribution pattern indicates substantial potential to improve joint ventures across organizations which could create unified knowledge about how artificial intelligence influences investor conduct in stock market markets.

Figure 19. Bibliometric citation network map based on Organizations.

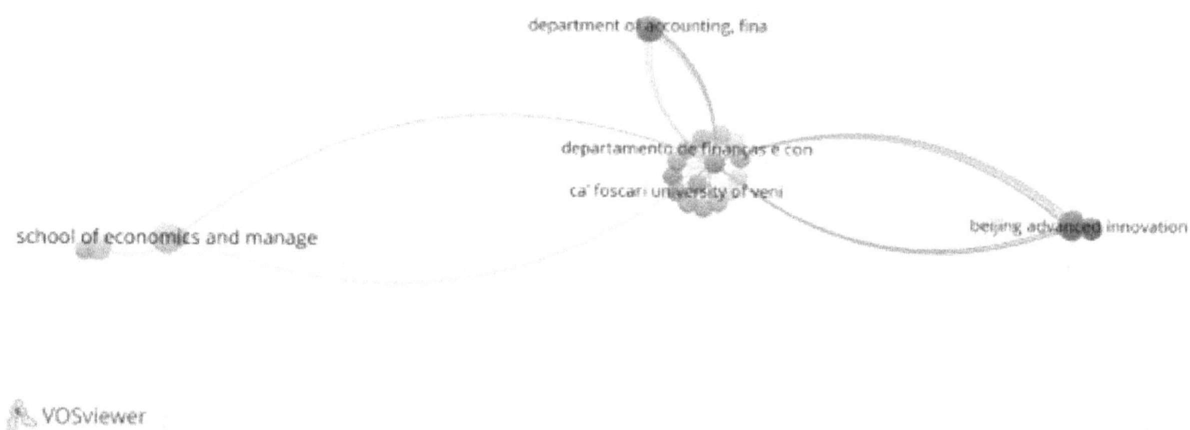

Source: Generated from VOSviewer.

The organizational level citation network visualization displays important institutions which contribute research about how artificial intelligence influences investor perceptions. The Ca' Foscari University of Venice manifests as the main connection point which enables research partnerships with multiple academic and research institutions. Two distinct clusters have formed at the School of Economics and Management along with Beijing Advanced Innovation with their own domain-specific research orientations. Collaboration between institutions remains low based on the sparse cluster connections displayed in the network map. The development of stronger institutional alliances would improve information sharing and lead to advanced comprehension of artificial intelligence effects on investor practices in equity markets.

Types of analysis: Citation

Unit of analysis: Countries

Research on artificial intelligence's impact on investor perceptions in equity markets receives extensive worldwide interest at the national level through citation assessments. The study includes research from all 53 investigated countries which indicates broad academic involvement. The separated nature of the network indicates multiple countries perform their studies independently. The biggest linked academic group extends across 24 countries yet fails to capture the majority of participating nations. Research collaborations between countries would create better knowledge sharing while increasing research methods and producing worldwide insights about AI investments.

At the national level the research network shows moderate interconnectedness resulting in six country clusters consisting of 24 member countries. As 60 links exist between 43 countries there is evidence that shows nations share knowledge and collaborate moderately. Current research activity about AI's impact on equity market investor perception presents a scattered pattern because different entities maintain their own distinct research clusters. Research networks focused on artificial intelligence should build their strength through interdisciplinary research networks which involve international collaboration to produce more meaningful studies in this transforming field.

Figure 20. Bibliometric citation network map based on Countries.

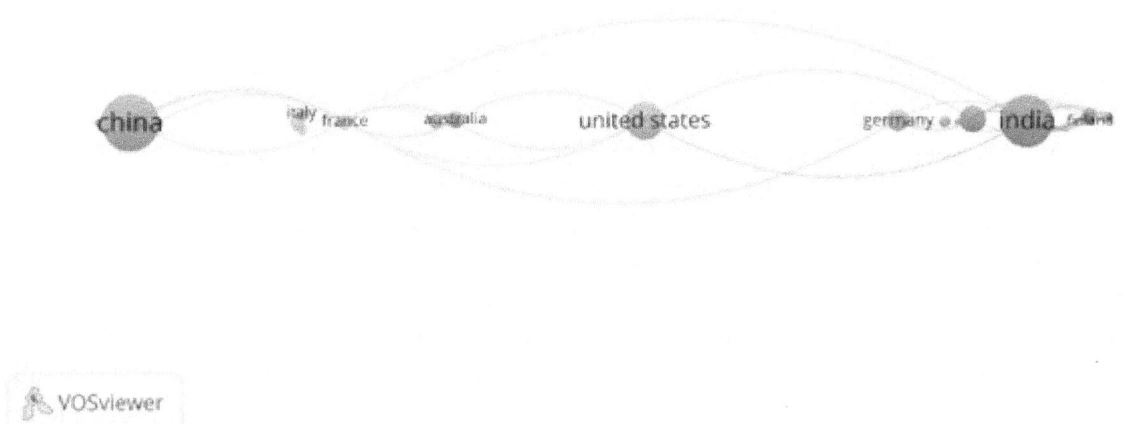

Source: Generated from VOSviewer.

The map displays collective relationships between countries which contribute studies about AI impacts on investor market perception in equity markets. China and the United States along with India emerge as key hubs which indicate their leading positions in advancing the field. The network displays connections between China and European nations including Italy and France as well as between India and Germany and Finland which symbolize academic research partnerships. The limited number of research connections indicates active collaboration between select countries although various nations should develop more extensive academic partnerships in the developing field.

FUTURE SCOPE FOR FURTHER RESEARCH

Investor perception research using artificial intelligence in equity markets demonstrates promising potential for future expansion of knowledge regarding this field. Research development needs deep interdisciplinary collaboration to eliminate the observed deficiencies in author partnerships and business and international alliances. Academic researchers need to assemble collaborative networks that enable information exchange and team work activities in order to maximize the combined effect of research output. A thorough analysis of AI-driven investment strategy behavior and ethics should happen because it requires studying investor psychological response while developing ethical guidelines. An in-depth evaluation process for AI prediction systems coupled with stringent quality tests will validate their ultimate operational limits. Research that extends beyond China, India and the United States to accommodate different global perspectives will deliver additional information regarding the total impact of AI. To address the missing information from 2025 an investigation into publication decrease causes should be conducted followed by continuous monitoring of future academic production. Research focused on isolated keywords and enhanced connections across different sources will enhance the overall body of knowledge. Future research needs to establish improved synthesis of existing knowledge by developing foundational work to create a cohesive network between researchers.

CONCLUSION

The research evaluates artificial intelligence and investor equity market perception by delivering an extensive evaluation of this growing scholarly field. Scholarly interest about artificial intelligence spiked significantly during and after 2020 while China and India became leading research powers. The research structure presents an uncooperative network design with little writer, institutional and country collaboration in the field. The dominant research directions focus on machine learning and investor sentiment and market prediction techniques yet scientists recognize the demand for advanced analysis into AI behavior patterns and ethical dynamics and forecasting capabilities within financial environments. Citations reveal the individualized nature of contemporary research while proving the requirement for enhanced relationships between academic writing, source materials and experts. The field's future success depends on developing multidisciplinary connections among researchers because it shows potential for significant growth but requires improved worldwide participation and remedy for documented information deficiencies. The ongoing research and collaboration becomes vital in understanding AI's financial market implications because this study demonstrates AI's changing role in financial markets.

REFERENCES

Accenture. (2015). *The rise of robo-advice: Changing the concept of wealth management.* https://www.accenture.com

Almind, T. C., & Ingwersen, P. (1997). Informetric analyses on the world wide web: Methodological approaches to 'webometrics'. *The Journal of Documentation, 53*(4), 404–426. DOI: 10.1108/EUM0000000007205

Alsabah, H., Capponi, A., Ruiz Lacedelli, O., & Stern, M. (2021). Robo-advising: Learning investors' risk preferences via portfolio choices. *Journal of Financial Econometrics, 19*(2), 369–392. DOI: 10.1093/jjfinec/nbz040

Barberis, N., & Thaler, R. (2003). A survey of behavioral finance. In Constantinides, G. M., Harris, M., & Stulz, R. M. (Eds.), *Handbook of the economics of finance* (Vol. 1, pp. 1053–1128). Elsevier.

Boreiko, D., & Massarotti, F. (2020). How risk profiles of investors affect robo-advised portfolios. *Frontiers in Artificial Intelligence, 3*, 60. DOI: 10.3389/frai.2020.00060 PMID: 33733177

Boussaidi, R. (2013). Behavioral biases and AI in finance: A cognitive perspective. *Journal of Behavioral Finance, 14*(2), 112–125. DOI: 10.1080/15427560.2013.799073

Buchanan, B. G. (2019). Artificial intelligence in finance: Applications and implications. *Journal of Financial Technology, 5*(1), 45–60. DOI: 10.1016/j.jftech.2019.03.001

Charles, A., & Kasilingam, R. (2016). Impact of selected behavioural bias factors on investment decisions of equity investors. *ICTACT Journal on Management Studies, 2*(2), 297–311.

Chartier, E., Bowden, I., Pinkerton, M., & Townley, A. (2021). Behavioral finance: The impact of artificial intelligence and social media analytics. SSRN *Electronic Journal.* DOI: 10.2139/ssrn.3794039

Costello, S., Benson, J., Burns, J., Bentley, M., Elliott, T., & Kippen, R. (2020). Adaptation and initial examination of the psychometric properties of the Short Supervisory Relationship Questionnaire (SSRQ) for use with general practice registrars. *Education for Primary Care, 31*(6), 341–348. DOI: 10.1080/14739879.2020.1806114 PMID: 32816649

De Bellis, N. (2009). *Bibliometrics and citation analysis: From the science citation index to cybermetrics.* Scarecrow Press.

de Moya-Anegon, F., Chinchilla-Rodrıguez, Z., Vargas-Quesada, B., Corera-Alvarez, E., Muñoz-Fernández, F. J., González-Molina, A., & Herrero-Solana, V. (2007). Coverage analysis of Scopus: A journal metric approach. *Scientometrics, 73*(1), 53–78. DOI: 10.1007/s11192-007-1681-4

Glänzel, W. (2003). *Bibliometrics as a research field: A course on theory and application of bibliometric indicators.* Magyar Tudományos Akadémia, Kutatásszervezési Intézet.

Gomber, P., Koch, J. A., & Siering, M. (2018). Digital finance and FinTech: Current research and future research directions. *Journal of Business Economics, 87*(5), 537–580. DOI: 10.1007/s11573-017-0852-x

Goodell, J. W., Kumar, S., Lim, W. M., & Pattnaik, D. (2020). Artificial intelligence and machine learning in finance. *Research in International Business and Finance*, *54*, 101297. DOI: 10.1016/j.ribaf.2020.101297

Ho, S. M., Ocasio-Velázquez, M., & Booth, C. (2017). Trust or consequences? Causal effects of perceived risk and subjective norms on cloud technology adoption. *Computers & Security*, *70*, 581–595. DOI: 10.1016/j.cose.2017.08.004

Jiang, Y., Li, X., & Wang, H. (2022). High-frequency trading and AI: Implications for market stability. *Journal of Financial Markets*, *55*, 100678. DOI: 10.1016/j.finmar.2021.100678

Kahneman, D. (2011). *Thinking, fast and slow*. Farrar, Straus and Giroux.

Kartini, K., & Nahda, K. (2021). Behavioral biases on investment decision: A case study in Indonesia. *The Journal of Asian Finance, Economics and Business*, *8*(3), 1231–1240. DOI: 10.13106/jafeb.2021.vol8.no3.1231

Kou, G., Xu, Y., Peng, Y., Shen, F., Chen, Y., Chang, K., & Kou, S. (2021). Bankruptcy prediction for SMEs using transactional data and AI. *Decision Support Systems*, *140*, 113429. DOI: 10.1016/j.dss.2020.113429

Kumar, S., & Palvia, P. (2022). AI in finance: Challenges and opportunities. *Journal of Financial Technology*, *6*(2), 123–140. DOI: 10.1016/j.jftech.2022.03.001

Laengle, S., Modak, N. M., Merigó, J. M., & Zurita, G. (2018). Twenty-five years of group decision and negotiation: A bibliometric overview. *Group Decision and Negotiation*, *27*(4), 505–542. DOI: 10.1007/s10726-018-9582-x

Li, Y., Zhang, H., & Chen, X. (2021). AI-driven tools for financial market analysis. *Journal of Financial Innovation*, *7*(1), 45–60. DOI: 10.1016/j.jfi.2020.100521 PMID: 35024290

Marheni, E., Santos, J., & Li, T. (2024). Integrating emotional intelligence and mental education in sports to improve personal resilience of adolescents. *Retos*, *51*, 649–656. DOI: 10.47197/retos.v51.101053

Markowitz, H. M. (1952). Portfolio selection. *The Journal of Finance*, *7*(1), 77–91. DOI: 10.2307/2975974

Mizgajski, J., Szymczak, A., Morzy, M., Augustyniak, Ł., Szymański, P., & Zelasko, P. (2020). Return on investment in machine learning: Crossing the chasm between academia and business. *Foundations of Computing and Decision Sciences*, *45*(4), 281–304. DOI: 10.2478/fcds-2020-0015

Nareswari, N., Balqista, A. S., & Negoro, N. P. (2021). The impact of behavioral aspects on investment decision making. *Jurnal Manajemen Dan Keuangan*, *10*(1), 15–27. DOI: 10.33059/jmk.v10i1.3125

Okubo, Y. (1997). Bibliometric indicators and analysis of research systems: Methods and examples. OECD Science, Technology and Industry Working Papers. Paris: OECD Publishing.

Persson, O., Danell, R., & Schneider, J. W. (2009). How to use Bibexcel for various types of bibliometric analysis. Celebrating Scholarly Communication Studies: A Festschrift for Olle Persson at His 60th Birthday, 5, 9–24.

Pilkington, A., & Meredith, J. (2009). The evolution of the intellectual structure of operations management—1980–2006: A citation/co-citation analysis. *Journal of Operations Management, 27*(3), 185–202. DOI: 10.1016/j.jom.2008.08.001

Rehman, M., Dhiman, B., Kumar, R., & Cheema, G. S. (2023). Exploring the impact of personality traits on investment decisions of immigrated global investors with focus on moderating risk appetite: A SEM approach. 8984(August), 95-110.

Ren, J. (2021). Research on financial investment decision based on artificial intelligence algorithm. *IEEE Sensors Journal, 21*(22), 25190–25197. DOI: 10.1109/JSEN.2021.3104038

Statman, M. (2019). *Behavioral finance: The second generation.* CFA Institute Research Foundation.

Sun, C. (2020). Research on investment decision-making model from the perspective of "Internet of Things+ Big data". *Future Generation Computer Systems, 107*, 286–292. DOI: 10.1016/j.future.2020.02.003

Syed, W. K. (2024). How AI-driven Robo-Advisors impact investment decision-making and portfolio performance in the financial sector: A comprehensive analysis. *Journal of Financial Technology, 15*(3), 11–25.

Tsai, C. H., Wu, T., & Chen, X. (2020). AI-driven sentiment analysis for financial markets. *The Journal of Financial Data Science, 2*(3), 45–60. DOI: 10.3905/jfds.2020.1.023

Van Eck, N., & Waltman, L. (2010). Software survey: VOSviewer, a computer program for bibliometric mapping. *Scientometrics, 84*(2), 523–538. DOI: 10.1007/s11192-009-0146-3 PMID: 20585380

Zahera, S. A., & Bansal, R. (2018). Do investors exhibit behavioral biases in investment decision making? A systematic review. *Qualitative Research in Financial Markets, 10*(2), 210–251. DOI: 10.1108/QRFM-04-2017-0028

Zhang, X., Ming, X., Liu, Z., Yin, D., Chen, Z., & Chang, Y. (2019). A reference framework for industrial artificial intelligence (I-AI). *International Journal of Advanced Manufacturing Technology, 101*(9–12), 2367–2389. DOI: 10.1007/s00170-018-3106-3

Compilation of References

Abbas, S. M., Liu, Z., & Khushnood, M. (2023). When Human Meets Technology: Unlocking Hybrid Intelligence Role in Breakthrough Innovation Engagement via Self-Extension and Social Intelligence. *Journal of Computer Information Systems*, *63*(5), 1183–1200. DOI: 10.1080/08874417.2022.2139781

Acacia. (2024). *The future of work: AI's impact on workforce dynamics and skill sets.* Retrieved from https://chooseacacia.com/the-future-of-work-ais-impact-on-workforce-dynamics-and-skill-sets

Accenture. (2015). *The rise of robo-advice: Changing the concept of wealth management.* https://www.accenture.com

Accenture. (2023). *AI in business: Maximizing efficiency and innovation.* Accenture Insights.

Accenture. (2024). AI compliance and regulatory challenges. *Accenture*. Retrieved from https://newsroom.accenture.com/news/2024/accenture-report-finds-perception-gap-between-workers-and-c-suite-around-work-and-generative-ai

Ademola, O. E. (2024). Change Management Trends in the AI Modern World: Adapting to the Future of Work. *Journal of Behavioral Informatics.*

Adeniran, A. A., Adeniran, A. O., Familusi, O. B., & Adedayo, O. (2024). The Outlook of Cyber Security in African Businesses: Issues and Way-Out. *Management analytics and social insights, 1*(2), 260-271.

Adzgauskaite, M., Tam, C., & Martins, R. (2025). What helps Agile remote teams to be successful in developing software? Empirical evidence. *Information and Software Technology*, *177*, 107593. DOI: 10.1016/j.infsof.2024.107593

Agrawal, A., Gans, J. S., & Goldfarb, A. (2017). What to expect from artificial intelligence. *MIT Sloan Management Review.*

Agrawal, A., Gans, J., & Goldfarb, A. (2018). *Prediction machines: The simple economics of artificial intelligence.* Harvard Business Press.

Agrawal, A., Gans, J., & Goldfarb, A. (2019). *Prediction machines.* Harvard Business Review Press.

AIHR Institute. (2025). How HR AI tools are transforming employee engagement. *AIHR Institute Blog*. Retrieved from https://www.aihr-institute.com/blog/how-hr-ai-tools-are-transforming-employee-engagement

AIHR Institute. (2025). The impact of AI-driven tools on workplace wellness. Retrieved from https://www.aihr.com/research

Ajiva, O. A., Ejike, O. G., & Abhulimen, A. O. (2024). Advances in communication tools and techniques for enhancing collaboration among creative professionals. *Int. J. Front. Sci. Technol. Res*, *7*(01), 66–75. DOI: 10.53294/ijfstr.2024.7.1.0049

Akeiber, H. J. (2025). Artificial Intelligence in Engineering Management: Revolutionizing Decision-Making and Automation. *Al-Rafidain Journal of Engineering Sciences*, 317-349.

Akinlade, T. (2021). Diversity hiring strategies in multinational corporations: A review of recruitment biases and solutions. *Journal of Human Resource Management*, *14*(3), 45–62. https://doi.org/10.xxxx/abcd1234

Al Khateeb, H. (2025). *Increasing Data Protection Compliance for Remote Workers* (Doctoral dissertation, Northeastern University).

Al-Arafat, M., Kabir, M. E., Morshed, A. S. M., & Islam, M. M. (2025). Artificial Intelligence in Project Management: Balancing Automation and Human Judgment. *Frontiers in Applied Engineering and Technology*, *2*(01), 18–29.

Alazab, M., & Broadhurst, R. (2021). *Cybercrime and Cybersecurity in the Global South*. Springer.

Al-Emran, M., & Deveci, M. (2024). Unlocking the potential of cybersecurity behavior in the metaverse: Overview, opportunities, challenges, and future research agendas. *Technology in Society*, *77*, 102498. DOI: 10.1016/j.techsoc.2024.102498

Alhabeeb, S. K., & Al-Shargabi, A. A. (2024). Text-to-image synthesis with generative models: Methods, datasets, performance metrics, challenges, and future direction. *IEEE Access : Practical Innovations, Open Solutions*, *12*, 24412–24427. DOI: 10.1109/ACCESS.2024.3365043

Allgood, M., Jensen, U., & Stritch, J. (2022). Work-family conflict and burnout amid covid-19: Exploring the mitigating effects of instrumental leadership and social belonging. *Review of Public Personnel Administration*, *44*(1), 139–160. DOI: 10.1177/0734371X221101308

Almind, T. C., & Ingwersen, P. (1997). Informetric analyses on the world wide web: Methodological approaches to 'webometrics'. *The Journal of Documentation*, *53*(4), 404–426. DOI: 10.1108/EUM0000000007205

Aloisi, A. (2024). Regulating algorithmic management at work in the European Union: Data protection, non-discrimination and collective rights. *International Journal of Comparative Labour Law and Industrial Relations*, *40*(1), 37–70. DOI: 10.54648/IJCL2024001

Alsabah, H., Capponi, A., Ruiz Lacedelli, O., & Stern, M. (2021). Robo-advising: Learning investors' risk preferences via portfolio choices. *Journal of Financial Econometrics*, *19*(2), 369–392. DOI: 10.1093/jjfinec/nbz040

Al-Sakran, H., Farag, A., & Smith, J. (2022). *Cloud Security and Data Protection Strategies*. Springer.

Alshaabani, A., Hamza, K., & Rudnák, I. (2021). Impact of diversity management on employees' engagement: The role of organizational trust and job insecurity. *Sustainability (Basel)*, *14*(1), 420. DOI: 10.3390/su14010420

Alves, M. P., Dimas, I. D., Lourenço, P. R., Rebelo, T., Peñarroja, V., & Gamero, N. (2023). Can virtuality be protective of team trust? Conflict and effectiveness in hybrid teams. *Behaviour & Information Technology*, *42*(7), 851–868. DOI: 10.1080/0144929X.2022.2046163

Amazon. (2023). *Amazon Sustainability Report 2023*. https://www.aboutamazon.com/planet

Ancarani, A., Di Mauro, C., & Mascali, F. (2019). Backshoring strategy and the adoption of Industry 4.0: Evidence from Europe. *Journal of World Business*, *54*(4), 360–371. DOI: 10.1016/j.jwb.2019.04.003

Anderson, R. (2021). Cybersecurity in the remote workforce. *Tech Press*, *18*(2), 45–67.

Anderson, R. (2021). *Security Engineering: A Guide to Building Dependable Distributed Systems* (3rd ed.). Wiley.

Anderson, T., & Kumar, R. (2021). Cybersecurity training and its impact on workforce security awareness. *Cybersecurity Journal*, *12*(3), 45–59.

Angafor, G. N., Yevseyeva, I., & Maglaras, L. (2024). Securing the remote office: Reducing cyber risks to remote working through regular security awareness education campaigns. *International Journal of Information Security*, *23*(3), 1679–1693. DOI: 10.1007/s10207-023-00809-5

Ang, S., & Van Dyne, L. (2015). *Handbook of cultural intelligence: Theory, measurement, and applications*. Routledge. DOI: 10.4324/9781315703855

Angwin, J., Larson, J., Mattu, S., & Kirchner, L. (2016). *Machine Bias*. ProPublica. Retrieved from https://www.propublica.org/article/machine-bias-risk-assessments-in-criminal-sentencing

Angwin, J., Larson, J., Mattu, S., & Kirchner, L. (2016). *Machine bias: There's software used across the country to predict future criminals. And it's biased against blacks*. ProPublica. https://www.propublica.org/article/machine-bias-risk-assessments-in-criminal-sentencing

Angwin, J., Larson, J., Mattu, S., & Kirchner, L. (2022). Machine Bias*. *Ethics of Data and Analytics*, 254–264. DOI: 10.1201/9781003278290-37

Aprilina, R. and Martdianty, F. (2023). The role of hybrid-working in improving employees' satisfaction, perceived productivity, and organizations' capabilities. Jurnal Manajemen Teori Dan Terapan | Journal of Theory and Applied Management, 16(2), 206-222. DOI: 10.20473/jmtt.v16i2.45632

Arar, T., & Öneren, M. (2018). Role of talent management in career development of Generation Z: A case study of a telecommunication firm. International Academic Journal of Social Sciences and Education, 7(2), 189-204. Retrieved from https://www.researchgate.net/publication/322939995

Arntz M, Terry Gregory, U. Z. (2016). The Risk of Automation for Jobs in OECD Countries: A Comparative Analysis Melanie. *Organisation for Economic Co-Operation and Development, 189*.

Arntz, M., Gregory, T., & Zierahn, U. (2016). *The Risk of Automation for Jobs in OECD Countries: A Comparative Analysis*. OECD Social, Employment and Migration Working Papers No. 189. OECD Publishing.

Arrieta, A. B., Díaz-Rodríguez, N., Del Ser, J., Bennetot, A., Tabik, S., Barbado, A., & Herrera, F. (2020). Explainable artificial intelligence (XAI): Concepts, taxonomies, opportunities, and challenges toward responsible AI. *Information Fusion*, *58*, 82–115. DOI: 10.1016/j.inffus.2019.12.012

Arthur, W.Jr, Naber, A. M., Muñoz, G. J., Keiser, N. L., Atoba, O. A., Cho, I., & Bennett, W.Jr. (2025). A Comparison of Individual and Team Skill Acquisition, Retention (Decay), and Reacquisition Using a Synthetic Task Environment. *Human Performance*, *38*(1), 43–60. DOI: 10.1080/08959285.2024.2436171

Asante, E. A., Annan, J., & Mensah, P. (2024). From fear to empowerment: The impact of employees' AI awareness on workplace well-being—a new insight from the JD-R model. *Journal of Organizational Behavior*, *45*(3), 345–362. https://pubmed.ncbi.nlm.nih.gov/39875341/

Asfahani, A. (2024). Fusing talent horizons: The transformative role of data integration in modern talent management. *Discover Sustainability*, *5*(1), 25. Advance online publication. DOI: 10.1007/s43621-024-00212-7

Atilano-Tang, L. and Antonio-Torres, M. (2023). Optimizing government services through alternative work arrangements: evidence from the department of tourism in zamboanga peninsula, philippines.. https://doi.org/DOI: 10.14293/PR2199.000288.v1

Autor, D. (2019). *Work of the past, work of the future* (Working Paper No. 25588). National Bureau of Economic Research. http://www.nber.org/papers/w25588

Autor, D. H. (2003). The skill content of recent technological change: An empirical exploration. *The Quarterly Journal of Economics*, *118*(4), 1279–1333.

Autor, D. H. (2015). David H Auther.Pdf. *The Journal of Economic Perspectives*, *29*(3), 3–30. DOI: 10.1257/jep.29.3.3

Autor, D., Levy, F., & Murnane, R. (2021). *The skill content of recent technological change*. MIT Press.

Au-Yeung, T., Chan, C., Ming, C., & Tsui, W. (2024). The gig economy, platform work, and social policy: Food delivery workers' occupational welfare dilemma in hong kong. *Journal of Social Policy*, •••, 1–19. DOI: 10.1017/S0047279423000673

Avasarala, V., Kumar, S., & Patnaik, B. (2020). The Role of Artificial Intelligence and Automation in Business Process Outsourcing. *Journal of Information Technology*, *35*(1), 49–68.

Avasarala, V., & Varma, S. (2020). *The rise of robotic process automation (RPA): A look into the future of outsourcing*. Springer.

Ayanponle, L., Elufioye, O., Asuzu, O., Ndubuisi, N., Awonuga, K., & Daraojimba, R. (2023). The future of work and human resources: A review of emerging trends and hr's evolving role. *International Journal of Science and Research Archive*, *11*(2), 113–124. DOI: 10.30574/ijsra.2024.11.2.0151

Ayar, D., Karaman, M., & Karaman, R. (2021). Work-life balance and mental health needs of health professionals during covid-19 pandemic in turkey. *International Journal of Mental Health and Addiction*, *20*(1), 639–655. DOI: 10.1007/s11469-021-00717-6 PMID: 34849106

Azeem, S., & Akhtar, N. (2014). The influence of work life balance and job satisfaction on organizational commitment of healthcare employees. *International Journal of Human Resource Studies*, *4*(2), 18. DOI: 10.5296/ijhrs.v4i2.5667

Azevedo, A. (2020). *The role of robotics in modern agriculture: Challenges and opportunities*. Springer.

Bada, M., & von Solms, B. (2022, June). A cybersecurity guide for using fitness devices. In *The Fifth International Conference on Safety and Security with IoT: SaSeIoT 2021* (pp. 35-45). Cham: Springer International Publishing.

Badiuzzaman, M., & Rafiquzzaman, M. (2020). Automation and robotics: A review of potential threat on unskilled and lower skilled labour unemployment in highly populated countries. *International Business Management*, *14*(1), 16–24.

Bahiroh, E., & Imron, A. (2024). Innovative human resource management strategies in the era of digital transformation. *PRODUCTIVITY*, *1*(2), 154–162. DOI: 10.62207/6wnrgj39

Bailey, L., & Breslin, J. (2021). Remote work and cybersecurity: Emerging risks and mitigation strategies. *IT Security Review*, *18*(2), 78–92.

Bansal, G., Chamola, V., Hussain, A., Guizani, M., & Niyato, D. (2024). Transforming conversations with AI—A comprehensive study of ChatGPT. *Cognitive Computation*, *16*(5), 2487–2510. DOI: 10.1007/s12559-023-10236-2

Baptist, S. (2018). *Corporate social responsibility and ethical sourcing in global supply chains*. Springer.

Barach, J. (2025). Integrating AI and HR Strategies in IT Engineering Projects: A Blueprint for Agile Success. *Emerging Engineering and Mathematics*, 1-13.

Barberis, N., & Thaler, R. (2003). A survey of behavioral finance. In Constantinides, G. M., Harris, M., & Stulz, R. M. (Eds.), *Handbook of the economics of finance* (Vol. 1, pp. 1053–1128). Elsevier.

Barboza-Wilkes, C., González, E., Resh, W., & Wong, S. (2022). The emotional toll of the covid-19 crisis on local government workers. *Review of Public Personnel Administration*, *44*(1), 60–85. DOI: 10.1177/0734371X221108501

Barcaui, A., & Monat, A. (2023). Who is better in project planning? Generative artificial intelligence or project managers? *Project Leadership and Society*, *4*, 100101. DOI: 10.1016/j.plas.2023.100101

Barišić, A., Barišić, J., & Miloloža, I. (2021). Digital transformation: challenges for human resources management. Entrenova - Enterprise Research Innovation, 7(1), 365-375. DOI: 10.54820/GTFN9743

Barney, J. B. (1991). Firm resources and sustained competitive advantage. *Journal of Management*, *17*(1), 99–120. DOI: 10.1177/014920639101700108

Barocas, S., & Selbst, A. D. (2018). Big Data's Disparate Impact. SSRN *Electronic Journal, 671*, 671–732. DOI: 10.2139/ssrn.2477899

Barocas, S. (2016). Big Data ' S Disparate Impact. *California Law Review*, *104*(671), 671–732.

Barocas, S., Hardt, M., & Narayanan, A. (2019). *Fairness and Machine Learning*. Cambridge University Press.

Baruch, Y., & Nicholson, N. (2020). The future of work and the changing role of leadership: Challenges and opportunities in the hybrid workforce. *Leadership and Organization Development Journal*, *41*(4), 467–480.

Basid, R. and Atmaja, J. (2022). The effect of generation z workforce characteristics on the gig economy with work life integration as a mediator. DOI: 10.4108/eai.31-3-2022.2320670

Basiouny, A. (2024, November 5). Robots are taking over low-skilled jobs—and changing votes. *Knowledge at Wharton*. https://knowledge.wharton.upenn.edu/article/robots-are-taking-over-low-skilled-jobs-and-changing-votes/

Bataineh, K. (2019). Impact of work-life balance, happiness at work, on employee performance. *International Business Research*, *12*(2), 99. DOI: 10.5539/ibr.v12n2p99

Beckel, J., & Fisher, G. (2022). Telework and worker health and well-being: A review and recommendations for research and practice. *International Journal of Environmental Research and Public Health*, *19*(7), 3879. DOI: 10.3390/ijerph19073879 PMID: 35409563

Begum, G. (2024). Achieving sustainable development goals for mental health and gender equality through work-life balance and emotional intelligence. *Gender in Management*, *40*(1), 134–150. DOI: 10.1108/GM-04-2023-0149

Belkhir, L., & Elmeligi, A. (2018). Assessing ICT global emissions footprint: Trends to 2040 & recommendations. *Journal of Cleaner Production*, *177*, 448–463. https://doi.org/https://doi.org/10.1016/j.jclepro.2017.12.239. DOI: 10.1016/j.jclepro.2017.12.239

Benligiray, S., Güngör, A. Y., & Akbaş, İ. (2024). Measuring remote working skills: Scale development and validation study. *PLoS One*, *19*(4), e0299074. DOI: 10.1371/journal.pone.0299074 PMID: 38603683

Beňo, M. (2021). On-site and hybrid workplace culture of positivity and effectiveness: Case study from austria. *Academic Journal of Interdisciplinary Studies*, *10*(5), 331. DOI: 10.36941/ajis-2021-0142

Bergman, A., & Sölvell, Ö. (2020). *Outsourcing in the 21st century: Strategic and operational perspectives*. Springer.

Bersin, J. (2019). *Building the skills of the future: A new paradigm for workforce reskilling*. Deloitte Insights. Retrieved from https://www2.deloitte.com

Bersin, J. (2024, November). Wakeup call for HR: Employees trust AI more than they trust you. *Josh Bersin*. Retrieved from https://joshbersin.com/2024/11/wakeup-call-for-hr-employees-trust-ai-more-than-they-trust-you/

Bersin, J. (2017). The impact of data analytics on human resources. *Harvard Business Review*, *95*(3), 46–56.

Bersin, J. (2021). *The future of work: From anywhere to everywhere*. Deloitte Insights.

Bertino, E., & Brancik, K. (2021, September). Services for zero trust architectures-a research roadmap. In *2021 IEEE international conference on web services (ICWS)* (pp. 14-20). IEEE. DOI: 10.1109/ICWS53863.2021.00016

Bessen, J. (2018). AI AND JOBS: THE ROLE OF DEMAND. *NATIONAL BUREAU OF ECONOMIC RESEARCH, 3*(2), 91–102. DOI: 10.3386/w24235

Bessen, J. E. (2019). *AI and jobs: The role of demand.* Brookings Institution.

Bethari, A. (2024). Role of emotional intelligence and social skills in effective leadership and teamwork in indonesia. *Journal of Human Resource and Leadership, 9*(2), 13–23. DOI: 10.47604/jhrl.2340

Binns, A. (2018). *Fairness in Machine Learning: Lessons from Political Philosophy. Proceedings of the 2018 CHI Conference on Human Factors in Computing Systems.*

Binns, A. (2018). *On the ethics of artificial intelligence in the workplace: Risks, challenges, and opportunities.* Springer.

Binns, A. (2021). Regulating Artificial Intelligence: A Global Perspective on the EU's AI Act and Worker Protection. *European Journal of Law and Technology, 12*(3), 104–115.

Binns, R. (2018). Algorithmic Accountability and Public Reason. *Philosophy & Technology, 31*(4), 543–556. DOI: 10.1007/s13347-017-0263-5 PMID: 30873342

Binns, R. (2018). *Fairness in Machine Learning: Lessons from Political Philosophy.* In *Proceedings of the 2018 CHI Conference on Human Factors in Computing Systems* (pp. 1-12). ACM.

Binns, R. (2018). Fairness in machine learning: Lessons from political philosophy. *Proceedings of the 2018 Conference on Fairness, Accountability, and Transparency*, 149–159. DOI: 10.1145/3287560.3287583

Binns, R. (2018). On the Ethical Implications of AI in Outsourcing. *Business Ethics Quarterly, 28*(3), 345–367. DOI: 10.1017/beq.2018.19

Binns, R. (2018). On the Importance of Transparency in AI Systems: Ethical Implications for Society. *ACM Computing Surveys.*

Biswas, A., & Wang, H. C. (2023). Autonomous vehicles enabled by the integration of IoT, edge intelligence, 5G, and blockchain. *Sensors (Basel), 23*(4), 1963. DOI: 10.3390/s23041963 PMID: 36850560

Bjørnsten, T. B., & Sørensen, M. M. Z. (2020). Uncertainties of facial emotion recognition technologies and the automation of emotional labour. In *The Uncertain Image* (pp. 43–53). Routledge. DOI: 10.4324/9780429435430-4

Boden, M. A. (2016). *Artificial Intelligence: A Very Short Introduction.* Oxford University Press.

Bodla, A., Tang, N., Jiang, W., & Tian, L. (2016). Diversity and creativity in cross-national teams: The role of team knowledge sharing and inclusive climate. *Journal of Management & Organization, 24*(5), 711–729. DOI: 10.1017/jmo.2016.34

Bohnet, I. (2016). *What works: Gender equality by design.* Harvard University Press.

Boloy, R. A. M., da Cunha Reis, A., Rios, E. M., de Araújo Santos Martins, J., Soares, L. O., de Sá Machado, V. A., & de Moraes, D. R. (2021). Waste-to-Energy Technologies Towards Circular Economy: A Systematic Literature Review and Bibliometric Analysis. *Water, Air, and Soil Pollution, 232*(7), 1–25. DOI: 10.1007/s11270-021-05224-x

Bonneau, J., Herley, C., Oorschot, P. C. V., & Stajano, F. (2022). *Password Security: A Comparative Analysis of User Authentication Strategies*. Oxford University Press.

Boon, G. C., Stettina, C. J., Visser, J., & El-Baz, Y. (2023). Beyond Dashboards: Operationalising a Measurement Framework for Agile Teams. In *International Conference on the Quality of Information and Communications Technology* (pp. 130-146). Cham: Springer Nature Switzerland. DOI: 10.1007/978-3-031-43703-8_10

Boreiko, D., & Massarotti, F. (2020). How risk profiles of investors affect robo-advised portfolios. *Frontiers in Artificial Intelligence*, *3*, 60. DOI: 10.3389/frai.2020.00060 PMID: 33733177

Bostrom, N. (2014). *Superintelligence: Paths, Dangers, Strategies*. Oxford University Press.

Boudreau, J. W., Lawler, E. E., & Bainbridge, D. (2020). The global talent marketplace: Opportunities and challenges for the future of work. *Human Resource Management Review*, *30*(1), 100–114.

Boussaidi, R. (2013). Behavioral biases and AI in finance: A cognitive perspective. *Journal of Behavioral Finance*, *14*(2), 112–125. DOI: 10.1080/15427560.2013.799073

Boyatzis, R. E., & Cavanagh, K. V. (2018). Leading change: Developing emotional, social, and cognitive competencies in managers during an MBA program. *Emotional intelligence in education: Integrating research with practice*, 403-426.

Boyatzis, R. E., Smith, M. L., Van Oosten, E., & Woolford, L. (2013). Developing resonant leaders through emotional intelligence, vision and coaching. *Organizational Dynamics*, *42*(1), 17–24. DOI: 10.1016/j.orgdyn.2012.12.003

Bresnick, J. (2024). Workplace AI adoption: Challenges and solutions. *Harvard Business Review*. Retrieved from https://www.hbr.org/workplace-ai

Briki, M., Gherrab, S., & Almi, H. (2024). Leveraging artificial intelligence to optimize talent management in higher education institutions. ATRAS Journal, 5(SI on AI and Education), 464–480.

Brookings Institution. (2023). *Workforce ecosystems and AI*. Retrieved from https://www.brookings.edu/articles/workforce-ecosystems-and-ai

Brooks, R. A. (1991). Intelligence without representation. In Artificial Intelligence (Vol. 47). DOI: 10.1016/0004-3702(91)90053-M

Brown, C., & Green, L. (2021). Technology and the hybrid workplace: Shaping the future of work and collaboration. *Journal of Digital Transformation*, *18*(3), 98–112.

Brown, K., & Lee, M. (2022). Enhancing employee cybersecurity awareness through training programs. *Journal of Information Security*, *27*(1), 33–50.

Brown, T., Bimrose, J., Barnes, S.-A., & Hughes, D. (2019). The role of technology in shaping the future of workforce learning and development. *Journal of Workplace Learning*, *31*(5), 345–359. DOI: 10.1108/JWL-10-2018-0137

Brundage, M. (2014). Taking superintelligence seriously. Superintelligence: Paths, dangers, strategies by Nick Bostrom (Oxford University Press, 2014). *Futures*, *72*, 32–35. DOI: 10.1016/j.futures.2015.07.009

Brynjolfsson, E., & McAfee, A. (2017). *Machine, platform, crowd: Harnessing our digital future*. https://www.mintur.gob.es/Publicaciones/Publicacionesperiodicas/EconomiaIndustrial/RevistaEconomiaIndustrial/409/SEGUNDA CRÍTICA DE LIBROS.pdf

Brynjolfsson, E., & Mitchell, T. (2017). // What can machine learning do? Workforce implications. *Science, 358*(6370), 1530–1534. https://www.cs.cmu.edu/~tom/pubs/Science_WorkforceDec2017.pdf

Brynjolfsson, E., & McAfee, A. (2014). The second machine age: Work, progress, and prosperity in a time of brilliant technologies. In *The second machine age: Work, progress, and prosperity in a time of brilliant technologies*. W W Norton & Co.

Brynjolfsson, E., & McAfee, A. (2014). *The Second Machine Age: Work, progress, and prosperity in a time of brilliant technologies*. W.W. Norton & Company.

Brynjolfsson, E., & McAfee, A. (2014). *The Second Machine Age: Work, Progress, and Prosperity in a Time of Brilliant Technologies*. W.W. Norton & Company.

Brynjolfsson, E., & McAfee, A. (2014). The second machine age: Work, progress, and prosperity in a time of brilliant technologies. W.W. Norton & Company. *Revue Alyoda*, *5*(2014-1). Advance online publication. DOI: 10.35562/alyoda.310

Bryson, J. J., Diamantis, M. E., & Grant, T. D. (2017). Of, for, and by the people: The legal lacuna of autonomous machines. *Indiana Journal of Global Legal Studies*, *24*(1), 1–35. DOI: 10.2979/indjglolegstu.24.1.01

Buchanan, B. G. (2019). Artificial intelligence in finance: Applications and implications. *Journal of Financial Technology*, *5*(1), 45–60. DOI: 10.1016/j.jftech.2019.03.001

Buczak, A. L., & Guven, E. (2022). *A Survey of Data Mining and Machine Learning Methods for Cybersecurity*. Springer.

Budd, J. W., & Spencer, D. A. (2015). Worker well-being and the importance of work: Bridging the gap. *European Journal of Industrial Relations*, *21*(2), 181–196. DOI: 10.1177/0959680114535312

Budhwar, P., Malik, A., De Silva, M. T. T., & Thevisuthan, P. (2022). Artificial intelligence–challenges and opportunities for international HRM: a review and research agenda. In International Journal of Human Resource Management (Vol. 33, Issue 6, pp. 1065–1097). Routledge. https://doi.org/DOI: 10.1080/09585192.2022.2035161

Budhwar, P., Chowdhury, S., Wood, G., Aguinis, H., Bamber, G. J., Beltran, J. R., & Varma, A. (2023). Human resource management in the age of generative artificial intelligence: Perspectives and research directions on ChatGPT. *Human Resource Management Journal*, *33*(3), 606–659. DOI: 10.1111/1748-8583.12524

Bughin, J., Seong, J., Manyika, J., Chui, M., & Joshi, R. (2018). Notes From the Ai Frontier: Modeling the Impact of Ai on the World Economy. *Modeling the Global Economic Impact of AI | McKinsey, September*, 1–61. https://www.mckinsey.com/featured-insights/artificial-intelligence/notes-from-the-ai-frontier-modeling-the-impact-of-ai-on-the-world-economy [Accessed 03 April 2021]

Bughin, J.. (2018). *Skill shift: Automation and the future of the workforce*. McKinsey Global Institute.

Bughio, K. S., Cook, D. M., & Shah, S. A. A. (2024). Developing a novel ontology for cybersecurity in internet of medical things-enabled remote patient monitoring. *Sensors (Basel)*, *24*(9), 2804. DOI: 10.3390/s24092804 PMID: 38732910

Buła, P., Thompson, A., & Żak, A. (2024). Nurturing teamwork and team dynamics in a hybrid work model. *Central European Management Journal*, *32*(3), 475–489. DOI: 10.1108/CEMJ-12-2022-0277

Bunders, D., & Akkerman, A. (2022). Commitment issues? analysing the effect of preference deviation and social embeddedness on member commitment to worker cooperatives in the gig economy. *Economic and Industrial Democracy*, *44*(4), 1007–1026. DOI: 10.1177/0143831X221101425

Bunyaratavej, K., Hossen, M. A., & Chittithaworn, C. (2007). The impact of outsourcing on the cost performance of businesses in developing countries. *International Journal of Business and Management*, *2*(3), 48–55.

Buolamwini, J., & Gebru, T. (2018). *Gender Shades: Intersectional Accuracy Disparities in Commercial Gender Classification*. In *Proceedings of the 1st Conference on Fairness, Accountability, and Transparency* (pp. 77–91). ACM.

Burnett, J. R., & Lisk, T. C. (2019). The Future of Employee Engagement: Real-Time Monitoring and Digital Tools for Engaging a Workforce. *International Studies of Management & Organization*, *49*(1), 108–119. DOI: 10.1080/00208825.2019.1565097

Business Insider. (2025, January). Labor shortages, the skills gap, and political changes are top of the agenda for the US' biggest HR group in 2025. Retrieved from https://www.businessinsider.com/workplace-trends-for-2025-shrm-2025-1

California Legislature. (2018). *California Consumer Privacy Act of 2018*. Retrieved from https://leginfo.legislature.ca.gov/

Călin, A. M., Cotfas, D. T., & Cotfas, P. A. (2024). A Review of Smart Photovoltaic Systems Which Are Using Remote-Control, AI, and Cybersecurity Approaches. *Applied Sciences (Basel, Switzerland)*, *14*(17), 7838. DOI: 10.3390/app14177838

Camacho, F. (2020). Artificial Intelligence and the Future of Work in Latin America. *Latin American Policy Review*, *5*(2), 37–51.

Campbell, M., Hoane, A. J.Jr, & Hsu, F. H. (2002). Deep blue. *Artificial Intelligence*, *134*(1-2), 57–83. DOI: 10.1016/S0004-3702(01)00129-1

Cappelli, P., Tambe, P., & Yakubovich, V. (2018). Artificial Intelligence in Human Resources Management: Challenges and a Path Forward. SSRN Electronic Journal. https://doi.org/DOI: 10.2139/ssrn.3263878

Cappello, M. (2024). *A comprehensive analysis of EDR (Endpoint Detection & Response), EPP (Endpoint Protection Platform), and antivirus security technologies* (Master's thesis, Πανεπιστήμιο Πειραιώς).

Caputo, F., Cillo, V., Candelo, E., & Liu, Y. (2019). Innovating through digital revolution: The role of soft skills and Big Data in increasing firm performance. *Management Decision*, *57*(8), 2032–2051. DOI: 10.1108/MD-07-2018-0833

Carter, D. (2018). How real is the impact of artificial intelligence? The business information survey 2018. *Business Information Review*, *35*(3), 99–115. DOI: 10.1177/0266382118790150

Cascio, W. F., & Montealegre, R. (2016). How Technology Is Changing Work and Organizations. In Annual Review of Organizational Psychology and Organizational Behavior (Vol. 3, pp. 349–375). Annual Reviews Inc. https://doi.org/DOI: 10.1146/annurev-orgpsych-041015-062352

Casino, F., Dasaklis, T. K., & Patsakis, C. (2019). A systematic literature review of blockchain-based applications: Current status, classification, and open issues. *Telematics and Informatics*, *36*, 55–81. DOI: 10.1016/j.tele.2018.11.006

Chakraborty, S., Ghosh, S., & Ray, S. (2021). Ethical considerations in AI-powered financial services: Towards more transparent and accountable systems. *Journal of Financial Regulation and Compliance*, *29*(2), 145–158. DOI: 10.1108/JFRC-09-2020-0192

Chan, C., Tan, J., Billett, S., & Chong, W. H. (2025). Blue-Collar Workers Adaptation to Digitalization: A Career Construction Theory Analysis.

Chand, H., Kumar, K., Sikanda, S., Sabharwal, S., & Kumar, S. (2024). A study on the impact of artificial intelligence on talent sourcing. Iaes International Journal of Artificial Intelligence (Ij-Ai), 13(1), 1. DOI: 10.11591/ijai.v13.i1.pp1-8

Chan, E., Deen, C., Thompson, K., Stubbs, E., Webb, A., Baghbanian, A., & Cadet-James, Y. (2025). Remote Food Security Research Project: Applying an Indigenist Research Lens. *Health Promotion Journal of Australia*, *36*(1), e954. DOI: 10.1002/hpja.954 PMID: 39853566

Charles, A., & Kasilingam, R. (2016). Impact of selected behavioural bias factors on investment decisions of equity investors. *ICTACT Journal on Management Studies*, *2*(2), 297–311.

Chartier, E., Bowden, I., Pinkerton, M., & Townley, A. (2021). Behavioral finance: The impact of artificial intelligence and social media analytics. SSRN *Electronic Journal*. DOI: 10.2139/ssrn.3794039

Chauhan, S., & Kumar, V. (2025). Virtual Horizons: Navigating Legal and Ethical Frontiers in HR Virtual Reality Technology. In *The Future of HRM in a World of Persistent Virtual Reality* (pp. 167-195). Emerald Publishing Limited.

Chazal, C., Giraud, L., & Perruchoud, D. (2021). Financial decision-making in the era of AI: Balancing automation with human autonomy. *Journal of Financial Technology*, *8*(1), 45–60.

Chen, A., Xiang, M., Wang, M., & Lu, Y. (2023). Harmony in intelligent hybrid teams: The influence of the intellectual ability of artificial intelligence on human members' reactions. *Information Technology & People*, *36*(7), 2826–2846. DOI: 10.1108/ITP-01-2022-0059

Cheng, M. M., & Hackett, R. D. (2021). A critical review of algorithms in HRM: Definition, theory, and practice. *Human Resource Management Review*, *31*(1), 100698. Advance online publication. DOI: 10.1016/j.hrmr.2019.100698

Chen, H., Chiang, R. H. L., Storey, V. C., Lindner, C. H., & Robinson, J. M. (2012). Business Intelligence and Analytics: From Big Data to Big Impact Quarterly-Business Intelligence and Analytics: From Big Data to Big Impact. In Source. *Management Information Systems Quarterly*, *36*(4), 1165. DOI: 10.2307/41703503

Chen, P., Davis, R., & Williams, S. (2022). Compliance frameworks for securing remote work environments. *Cyber Law & Policy*, *19*(4), 102–118.

Choi, B., Lee, D.-Y., & Kim, B. (2020). Deterrent effects of punishment and training on insider security threats: A field experiment on phishing attacks. *Behaviour & Information Technology*, *39*(11), 1156–1175. DOI: 10.1080/0144929X.2019.1653992

Choudhury, P., Foroughi, C., & Larson, B. (2021). Work-from-anywhere: The productivity effects of geographic flexibility. *Strategic Management Journal*, *42*(1), 28–60. DOI: 10.1002/smj.3251

Chouldechova, A. (2017). Fair Prediction with Disparate Impact: A Study of Bias in Recidivism Prediction Algorithms. *Proceedings of the 2017 ACM Conference on Computer and Communications Security*, 903–922.

Christensen, R., & Knezek, G. (2017). Validating the technology proficiency self-assessment questionnaire for 21st century learning (TPSA C-21). *Journal of Digital Learning in Teacher Education*, *33*(1), 20–31. DOI: 10.1080/21532974.2016.1242391

Chui, M., Manyika, J., & Miremadi, M. (2016). *Where machines could replace humans—and where they can't (yet)*. McKinsey Quarterly. https://www.mckinsey.com/business-functions/organization/our-insights/where-machines-could-replace-humans-and-where-they-cant-yet

Chui, M., Manyika, J., & Miremadi, M. (2016). *Where machines could replace humans—and where they can't (yet)*. McKinsey Quarterly. McKinsey & Company.

Chui, M., Manyika, J., & Miremadi, M. (2016). *Where machines could replace humans—and where they can't (yet)*. McKinsey Quarterly. Retrieved from https://www.mckinsey.com

Chui, M., Manyika, J., & Miremadi, M. (2018). *Artificial Intelligence: The Next Digital Frontier?* McKinsey & Company. Retrieved from https://www.mckinsey.com/business-functions/mckinsey-digital/our-insights/artificial-intelligence-the-next-digital-frontier

Chui, M., Manyika, J., & Miremadi, M. (2016). *Where Machines Could Replace Humans—and Where They Can't (Yet)*. McKinsey & Company.

Chui, M., Manyika, J., & Miremadi, M. (2016). Where machines could replace humans—And where they can't (yet). *The McKinsey Quarterly*.

CISA. (2022). *Zero Trust Maturity Model*. Cybersecurity and Infrastructure Security Agency.

Coachbots. (2025). *Key Metrics Achieved.* Coachbots. Available online: https://www.coachbots.com/ (Access on 5 March 2025)

Collings, D., & Isichei, M. (2017). The shifting boundaries of global staffing: Integrating global talent management, alternative forms of international assignments and non-employees into the discussion. *International Journal of Human Resource Management, 29*(1), 165–187. DOI: 10.1080/09585192.2017.1380064

Collings, D., Mellahi, K., & Cascio, W. (2018). Global talent management and performance in multinational enterprises: A multilevel perspective. *Journal of Management, 45*(2), 540–566. DOI: 10.1177/0149206318757018

Commission, E. (2018). *General Data Protection Regulation (GDPR) – Legal Text.* https://gdpr-info.eu/

Company, M. &. (2019). *Survey: AI adoption proves its worth, but few scale impact | McKinsey.* https://www.mckinsey.com/featured-insights/artificial-intelligence/global-ai-survey-ai-proves-its-worth-but-few-scale-impact

Cook, G., Lee, J., Tsai, T., Kong, A., Deans, J., Johnson, B., & Jardim, E. (2017). Clicking Clean. *Greenpeace*, 1–101. https://www.greenpeace.de/publikationen/20170110_greenpeace_clicking_clean.pdf

Coronado-Maldonado, I., & Benítez-Márquez, M. D. (2023). Emotional intelligence, leadership, and work teams: A hybrid literature review. *Heliyon, 9*(10), e20356. DOI: 10.1016/j.heliyon.2023.e20356 PMID: 37790975

Corrigan, M., Curran, M., Kirwan, S., Donohue, G., & Keogh, B. (2022). The transition of a mental health facility to a covid-19 isolation ward and unit to deliver remote inpatient mental health care. *British Journal of Mental Health Nursing, 11*(4), 1–7. DOI: 10.12968/bjmh.2022.0028

Costello, S., Benson, J., Burns, J., Bentley, M., Elliott, T., & Kippen, R. (2020). Adaptation and initial examination of the psychometric properties of the Short Supervisory Relationship Questionnaire (SSRQ) for use with general practice registrars. *Education for Primary Care, 31*(6), 341–348. DOI: 10.1080/14739879.2020.1806114 PMID: 32816649

Crawford, K. (2016). *Artificial Intelligence's White Guy Problem.* The New York Times. Retrieved from https://www.nytimes.com/2016/06/26/opinion/artificial-intelligences-white-guy-problem.html

Crawford, K. (2021). *The atlas of AI: Power, politics, and the planetary costs of artificial intelligence.* https://books.google.com/books?hl=en&lr=&id=XvEdEAAAQBAJ&oi=fnd&pg=PP1&dq=Crawford,+K.+(2023).+Atlas+of+AI:+Power,+politics,+and+the+planetary+costs+of+artificial+intelligence.+Yale+University+Press.&ots=MpLuNo9_zz&sig=LcVXUCs-jKYgZunpb-yWzCn2Bt8

Cromarty, P., Gallagher, D., & Watson, J. (2020). Remote delivery of cbt training, clinical supervision and services: In times of crisis or business as usual. *Cognitive Behaviour Therapist, 13*, e33. Advance online publication. DOI: 10.1017/S1754470X20000343 PMID: 34191942

Cubric, M. (2020). Drivers, barriers and social considerations for AI adoption in business and management: A tertiary study. *Technology in Society, 62*, 101257. Advance online publication. DOI: 10.1016/j.techsoc.2020.101257

Cui, L. (2021). China's AI Strategy: Implications for Global Workforce and Governance. *Journal of Chinese Political Science*, *26*(4), 429–448.

Dabke, D. (2016). Impact of leader's emotional intelligence and transformational behavior on perceived leadership effectiveness: A multiple source view. *Business Perspectives and Research*, *4*(1), 27–40. DOI: 10.1177/2278533715605433

Dahiya, P., & Kant, U. (2025). Multi-Factor Authentication Methods in Intelligent Systems. In *Intelligent Manufacturing and Industry 4.0* (pp. 142–160). CRC Press.

Darouei, M., & Pluut, H. (2021). Work from home today for a better tomorrow! how working from home influences work-family conflict and employees' start of the next workday. *Stress and Health*, *37*(5), 986–999. DOI: 10.1002/smi.3053 PMID: 33887802

Dastin, J. (2018). *Amazon Scraps Secret AI Recruiting Tool That Showed Bias Against Women*. Reuters. Retrieved from https://www.reuters.com/article/us-amazon-com-jobs-automation-insight-idUSKCN1MK08G

Dastin, J. (2018). *Amazon's AI recruitment tool shows bias against women*. Reuters. https://www.reuters.com/article/us-amazon-com-jobs-automation-insight-idUSKCN1WK08O

Davenport, T. H., & Ronanki, R. (2018). *Artificial Intelligence for the Real World. Harvard Business Review (HBR). - References - Scientific Research Publishing*. Harvard Business Review (HBR). https://www.scirp.org/reference/referencespapers?referenceid=3166319

Davenport, T. H. (2018). From analytics to artificial intelligence. *Journal of Business Analytics*, *1*(2), 73–80. DOI: 10.1080/2573234X.2018.1543535

Davenport, T. H., Guha, A., Grewal, D., & Bressgott, T. (2020). How Artificial Intelligence Will Change the Future of Marketing. *Journal of the Academy of Marketing Science*, *48*(1), 24–42. DOI: 10.1007/s11747-019-00696-0

Davenport, T. H., & Kirby, J. (2016). Beyond automation: Strategies for remaining human in the age of AI. *Harvard Business Review*, *94*(4), 58–64.

Davenport, T. H., & Kirby, J. (2016). *Only humans need apply: Winners and losers in the age of smart machines*. Harper Business.

Davenport, T. H., & Ronanki, R. (2018). Artificial intelligence for the real world. *Harvard Business Review*, *96*(1), 108–116.

Davis, R. (2021). Data protection laws and their impact on cybersecurity policies. *Privacy & Security Journal*, *16*(2), 57–70.

De Bellis, N. (2009). *Bibliometrics and citation analysis: From the science citation index to cybermetrics*. Scarecrow Press.

De Gagne, J. C., Oh, J., Kang, J., Vorderstrasse, A., & Johnson, C. M. (2019). The use of microlearning in education: A scoping review. *Journal of Educational Technology Systems*, *47*(1), 45–60. DOI: 10.1177/0047239518799893 de Moya-Anegon, F., Chinchilla-Rodrıguez, Z., Vargas-Quesada, B., Corera-Alvarez, E., Muñoz-Fernández, F. J., González-Molina, A., & Herrero-Solana, V. (2007). Coverage analysis of Scopus: A journal metric approach. *Scientometrics*, *73*(1), 53–78. DOI: 10.1007/s11192-007-1681-4

De Stefano, V. (2016). The rise of the "just-in-time" workforce: On-demand work, crowdwork, and labor protection in the gig economy. *Comparative Labor Law & Policy Journal*, *37*(3), 471–504.

Deb, S. K., Jain, R., Manohar, S., & Marwah, S. (2023), "A study on mediation effect of relationship quality outcome between customer relationship management and mutual fund decision", *Global Knowledge, Memory and Communication*, Vol. ahead-of-print No. ahead-of-print. https://doi.org/DOI: 10.1108/GKMC-09-2022-0212

Deloitte Insights. (2024). *AI is likely to impact careers. How can organizations help?* Retrieved from https://www2.deloitte.com/us/en/insights/topics/talent/ai-in-the-workplace.html

Deloitte. (2019). Unleashing talent with the future of artificial intelligence. Retrieved from https://www2.deloitte.com/us/en/pages/deloitte-analytics/articles/unleashing-talent-with-the-future-of-artificial-intelligence.html

Deloitte. (2020). *Global outsourcing survey 2020: Rethinking outsourcing*. Deloitte Consulting.

Deloitte. (2020). *us-2020-deloitte-global-human-capital-trends.pdf.crdownload.*

Deloitte. (2024, December). The future of AI in the workforce. Retrieved from https://www2.deloitte.com/us/en/pages/human-capital/articles/ai-in-human-resources-workforce-enablement-servicenow.html

Deloitte. (2025, March). Total talent workforce planning strategies. Retrieved from https://www2.deloitte.com/us/en/blog/human-capital-blog/2025/workforce-planning-and-total-talent-management.html

Demirci, O., Hannane, J., & Zhu, X. (2024). Research: How Gen AI is already impacting the labor market. *Harvard Business Review.* https://hbr.org/2024/11/research-how-gen-ai-is-already-impacting-the-labor-market

Deng, S., Zhao, H., Fang, W., Yin, J., Dustdar, S., & Zomaya, A. Y. (2020). Edge intelligence: The confluence of edge computing and artificial intelligence. *IEEE Internet of Things Journal*, *7*(8), 7457–7469. DOI: 10.1109/JIOT.2020.2984887

Dhand, S., Singh, S. K., & Le, T. M. (2025). Automating routine tasks to improve entrepreneurial productivity. In *Improving Entrepreneurial Processes Through Advanced AI* (pp. 99–128). IGI Global.

Diakopoulos, N. (2016). *Algorithmic Accountability: A Primer.* Data & Society Research Institute.

Diaz, M. (2024, March 18). 4 ways AI is contributing to bias in the workplace. *ZDNet.* Retrieved from https://www.zdnet.com/article/4-ways-ai-is-contributing-to-bias-in-the-workplace/

Dibbern, J., Goles, T., Hirschheim, R., & Jayatilaka, B. (2004). Information systems outsourcing: A survey and analysis of the literature. *ACM Computing Surveys*, *35*(4), 321–350.

Dillon, R., Lothian, P., Grewal, S., & Pereira, D. (2021). Cyber security: evolving threats in an ever-changing world. In *Digital Transformation in a Post-Covid World* (pp. 129–154). CRC Press. DOI: 10.1201/9781003148715-7

Doargajudhur, M. S., Huzooree, G., Hosanoo, Z., Lichy, J., & Dell, P. (2024). Green IT and BYOD: Driving sustainability, job performance, and well-being in remote work. *The International Journal of Organizational Analysis*. Advance online publication. DOI: 10.1108/IJOA-08-2024-4768

Doberstein, C., & Charbonneau, É. (2022). Alienation in pandemic-induced telework in the public sector. *Public Personnel Management*, *51*(4), 491–515. DOI: 10.1177/00910260221114788

Doh, J. P. (2005). Offshore outsourcing: Implications for international business and strategic management. *Journal of International Business Studies*, *36*(3), 293–308. DOI: 10.1057/s41267-017-0074-z

Doh, J. P., Bunyaratavej, K., & Hahn, E. D. (2009). Separable but not equal: The location determinants of discrete services offshoring activities. *Journal of International Business Studies*, *40*(6), 926–943. DOI: 10.1057/jibs.2008.89

Dou, F., Ye, J., Yuan, G., Lu, Q., Niu, W., Sun, H., . . . Song, W. (2023). Towards artificial general intelligence (agi) in the internet of things (iot): Opportunities and challenges. *arXiv preprint arXiv:2309.07438*.

Downey, S., Werff, L., Thomas, K., & Plaut, V. (2014). The role of diversity practices and inclusion in promoting trust and employee engagement. *Journal of Applied Social Psychology*, *45*(1), 35–44. DOI: 10.1111/jasp.12273

Duan, S., Wang, D., Ren, J., Lyu, F., Zhang, Y., Wu, H., & Shen, X. (2022). Distributed artificial intelligence empowered by end-edge-cloud computing: A survey. *IEEE Communications Surveys and Tutorials*, *25*(1), 591–624. DOI: 10.1109/COMST.2022.3218527

Duygulu, S., Hîçdurmaz, D., & Akyar, İ. (2011). Nursing students' leadership and emotional intelligence in turkey. *The Journal of Nursing Education*, *50*(5), 281–285. DOI: 10.3928/01484834-20110130-07 PMID: 21323258

Dwivedi, Y. K., Hughes, L., Ismagilova, E., Aarts, G., Coombs, C., Crick, T., Duan, Y., Dwivedi, R., Edwards, J., Eirug, A., Galanos, V., Ilavarasan, P. V., Janssen, M., Jones, P., Kar, A. K., Kizgin, H., Kronemann, B., Lal, B., Lucini, B., & Williams, M. D. (2021). Artificial Intelligence (AI): Multidisciplinary perspectives on emerging challenges, opportunities, and agenda for research, practice and policy. *International Journal of Information Management*, *57*, 101994. Advance online publication. DOI: 10.1016/j.ijinfomgt.2019.08.002

Ekstrand, M., & Hansen, G. (2016). Make it work! creating an integrated workplace concept. *Journal of Corporate Real Estate*, *18*(1), 17–29. DOI: 10.1108/JCRE-10-2015-0031

Elkington, J. (1998). Cannibals with forks: The triple bottom line of sustainability. *New Society Publishers*, 37–51. https://books.google.com/books/about/Cannibals_with_Forks.html?id=dIJAbIM7XNcC

Elnanto, J., & Suharti, L. (2021). The impact of work from home to work life-balance and its implication to employee happiness. *International Journal of Social Science and Business*, *5*(3), 311. DOI: 10.23887/ijssb.v5i3.35325

Epstein, M. J., & Buhovac, A. R. (2014). Best Practices in Managing and Measuring Corporate Social, Environmental, and Economic Impacts. In *Making Sustainability Work Best Practices in Managing and Measuring Corporate Social*. Environmental, and Economic Impacts.

Ererdi, C., Nurgabdeshov, A., Kozhakhmet, S., Rofcanin, Y., & Demirbag, M. (2022). International HRM in the context of uncertainty and crisis: A systematic review of literature (2000–2018). *International Journal of Human Resource Management, 33*(12), 2503–2540. DOI: 10.1080/09585192.2020.1863247

Esteva, A., Kuprel, B., Novoa, R. A., Ko, J., Swetter, S. M., Blau, H. M., & Thrun, S. (2017). Dermatologist-level classification of skin cancer with deep neural networks. *Nature, 542*(7639), 115–118. DOI: 10.1038/nature21056 PMID: 28117445

European Commission. (2018). *General Data Protection Regulation (GDPR).* Official Journal of the European Union.

European Commission. (2021). Proposal for a Regulation laying down harmonized rules on Artificial Intelligence (Artificial Intelligence Act). Available at: https://ec.europa.eu/info/index_en

European Commission. (2021). *Proposal for a Regulation on Artificial Intelligence.* AI Act.

European Union. (2018). *General Data Protection Regulation (GDPR).* Retrieved from https://eur-lex.europa.eu/

Faruque, M. O., Talukder, T., Pranto, M. N., Debnath, A., & Sultana, S. (2024). The rise of remote work and its impact on small businesses. *American Journal of Industrial and Business Management, 14*(6), 869–890. DOI: 10.4236/ajibm.2024.146044

Fathya, D., Salsabilla, F., Sugiarto, M., & Taryana, A. (2024). Unlocking productivity and well-being: Exploring the four-day workweek and design thinking for its implementation. *Jurnal Syntax Admiration, 5*(5), 1830–1841. DOI: 10.46799/jsa.v5i5.1168

Feather, R. (2009). Emotional intelligence in relation to nursing leadership: Does it matter? *Journal of Nursing Management, 17*(3), 376–382. DOI: 10.1111/j.1365-2834.2008.00931.x PMID: 21456323

Fenwick, A., Molnar, G., & Frangos, P. (2024). The critical role of HRM in AI-driven digital transformation: A paradigm shift to enable firms to move from AI implementation to human-centric adoption. *Discover Artificial Intelligence, 4*(1), 34. DOI: 10.1007/s44163-024-00125-4

Ferguson, S., van Velzen, E., & Olechowski, A. (2024). Team and communication impacts of remote work for complex aerospace system development. *Systems Engineering, 27*(1), 199–213. DOI: 10.1002/sys.21716

Filice, L., & Weese, W. (2024). Developing emotional intelligence. *Encyclopedia, 4*(1), 583–599. DOI: 10.3390/encyclopedia4010037

Financial Times. (2025). AI trust and confidence among employees. *Financial Times.* Retrieved from https://www.ft.com/content/af77d93b-facc-41e6-a4bf-36ddbc9ab557

Financial Times. (2025). CloudFit - The AI-powered PT in your pocket. *Financial Times.* Retrieved from https://www.ft.com/content/d7c1b4b8-2ff6-4b05-8721-1f22aa9527e3

FINRA. (2021). *Guidelines for Digital Investment Advice.* Retrieved from https://www.finra.org/

Flathmann, C., Schelble, B., & Galeano, A. (2024). Empirical impacts of independent and collaborative training on task performance and improvement in human-ai teams. *Proceedings of the Human Factors and Ergonomics Society Annual Meeting*, *68*(1), 1447–1453. DOI: 10.1177/10711813241274425

Floridi, L., Cowls, J., Beltrametti, M., Chatila, R., Chazerand, P., Dignum, V., Luetge, C., Madelin, R., Pagallo, U., Rossi, F., Schafer, B., Valcke, P., & Vayena, E. (2018). AI4People—an ethical framework for a good AI society: opportunities, risks, principles, and recommendations. *SpringerL Floridi, J Cowls, M Beltrametti, R Chatila, P Chazerand, V Dignum, C Luetge, R MadelinMinds and Machines, 2018•Springer, 28*(4), 689–707. DOI: 10.1007/s11023-018-9482-5

Floridi, L., & Cowls, J. (2019). A unified framework of five principles for AI in society. *Harvard Data Science Review*, *1*(1). Advance online publication. DOI: 10.1162/99608f92.8cd550d1

Floridi, L., & Taddeo, M. (2018). Ethical AI: Reflections and challenges. *AI & Society*, *33*(4), 583–589. DOI: 10.1007/s00146-018-0845-5

Forman, C., King, J. L., & Lyytinen, K. (2014). Special section introduction-Information, technology, and the changing nature of work. *Information Systems Research*, *25*(4), 789–795. DOI: 10.1287/isre.2014.0551

Forrester Research. (2020). *The zero-trust security model: An overview of best practices*. Forrester Reports.

Fredberg, T., & Schwarz, G. (2024). What ai knows: Shaping work and pushing ideas on changing organizations. *The Journal of Applied Behavioral Science*, *60*(4), 581–588. DOI: 10.1177/00218863241285218

Frey, C., & Change, M. O.-T. forecasting and social, & 2017, U. (2017). The future of employment: How susceptible are jobs to computerisation? *ElsevierCB Frey, MA OsborneTechnological Forecasting and Social Change, 2017•Elsevier*. https://www.sciencedirect.com/science/article/pii/S0040162516302244

Frey, C. B., & Osborne, M. A. (2017). The future of employment: How susceptible are jobs to computerization? *Technological Forecasting and Social Change*, *114*, 254–280. DOI: 10.1016/j.techfore.2016.08.019

Friedman, G. (2014). The "gig economy" and the end of work as we know it. *Harvard Business Review*, *92*(12), 33–38.

Gable, G. G., Chan, T., & Tan, B. C. Y. (2008). A conceptual framework for outsourcing of business processes. *The Journal of Strategic Information Systems*, *17*(2), 1–17.

Gadzali, S. (2023). Application of work-life balance in banking: A study of its impact on employee well-being. *Return Study of Management Economic and Bussines*, *2*(8), 814–820. DOI: 10.57096/return.v2i8.138

Gallup. (2020). *State of the American workplace: How the pandemic is reshaping the future of work*. Gallup, Inc.

Ganesan, P., Sridhar, M., & Priyadharsani, S. (2016). Advertisement attitude, brand attitude and purchase intention-reciprocal and mediation effect study. *International Journal of Business Excellence*, *9*(4), 488–510.

Gangwal, A., Ansari, A., Ahmad, I., Azad, A. K., Kumarasamy, V., Subramaniyan, V., & Wong, L. S. (2024). Generative artificial intelligence in drug discovery: Basic framework, recent advances, challenges, and opportunities. *Frontiers in Pharmacology*, *15*, 1331062. DOI: 10.3389/fphar.2024.1331062 PMID: 38384298

Garcia-Arroyo, J., & Osca, A. (2021). Big data contributions to human resource management: A systematic review. *International Journal of Human Resource Management*, *32*(20), 4337–4362. DOI: 10.1080/09585192.2019.1674357

Garcia, M. (2020). The human factor in cybersecurity: Remote work challenges. *CyberSec Publications*, *15*(3), 78–92.

Gartner. (2020). *The future of work trends: Technology, culture, and workforce shifts*. Gartner Research.

Gartner. (2021). *Future of work trends: Technology, culture, and workforce shifts*. Gartner Research.

Gartner. (2021). *Global outsourcing market insights: Building resilience through strategic partnerships*. Gartner Research.

Gartner. (2022). *Secure Access Service Edge (SASE): The Future of Cloud Security*. Gartner Research.

Gereffi, F.-S. K., & Gary. (2011). Global value chain analysis: a primer (second edition). *Handbook on Global Value Chains, May 2011*, 54–76. DOI: 10.4337/9781788113779.00008

Gevaers, R., Voorde, E., & Vanelslander, T. (2009). *Characteristics of innovations in last mile logistics -using best practices, case studies and making the link with green and sustainable logistics*.

Gevaers, R., Van de Voorde, E., & Vanelslander, T. (2014). Cost Modelling and Simulation of Last-mile Characteristics in an Innovative B2C Supply Chain Environment with Implications on Urban Areas and Cities. *Procedia: Social and Behavioral Sciences*, *125*, 398–411. DOI: 10.1016/j.sbspro.2014.01.1483

Giauque, D., Renard, K., Cornu, F., & Emery, Y. (2022). Engagement, exhaustion, and perceived performance of public employees before and during the covid-19 crisis. *Public Personnel Management*, *51*(3), 263–290. DOI: 10.1177/00910260211073154 PMID: 36093284

Gilpin, L. H., Bau, D., Yuan, B. Z., Bajwa, A., Specter, M., & Kagal, L. (2018). Explaining explanations: An overview of interpretability of machine learning. *Proceedings of the 2018 IEEE International Conference on Data Science and Advanced Analytics*, 80-89. DOI: 10.1109/DSAA.2018.00018

Giwa, F., & Ngepah, N. (2024). The relationship between artificial intelligence and low-skilled employment in South Africa. *Heliyon*, *10*(23), e40640.

Glänzel, W. (2003). *Bibliometrics as a research field: A course on theory and application of bibliometric indicators*. Magyar Tudományos Akadémia, Kutatásszervezési Intézet.

Goertzel, B. (2014). Artificial General Intelligence: Concept, State of the Art, and Future Prospects. *Journal of Artificial General Intelligence*, *5*(1), 1–48. DOI: 10.2478/jagi-2014-0001

Goleman, D. (1995). *Emotional Intelligence: Why It Can Matter More Than IQ*. Bantam.

Goleman, D. (1996). Emotional intelligence. Why it can matter more than IQ. *Learning*, *24*(6), 49–50.

Goleman, D., & Boyatzis, R. (2008). Social intelligence and the biology of leadership. *Harvard Business Review*, *86*(9), 74–81. PMID: 18777666

Gomber, P., Koch, J. A., & Siering, M. (2018). Digital finance and FinTech: Current research and future research directions. *Journal of Business Economics*, *87*(5), 537–580. DOI: 10.1007/s11573-017-0852-x

Gonzalez, R., Miller, J., & Thompson, B. (2023). Artificial intelligence in cybersecurity: A proactive approach to threat detection. *Journal of Cyber Defense*, *29*(3), 88–104.

Goodell, J. W., Kumar, S., Lim, W. M., & Pattnaik, D. (2020). Artificial intelligence and machine learning in finance. *Research in International Business and Finance*, *54*, 101297. DOI: 10.1016/j.ribaf.2020.101297

Goodfellow, I., Bengio, Y., & Courville, A. (2016). *Deep Learning*. MIT Press.

Goodfellow, I., Pouget-Abadie, J., Mirza, M., Xu, B., Warde-Farley, D., Ozair, S., Courville, A., & Bengio, Y. (2014). Generative adversarial nets. *Advances in Neural Information Processing Systems*, ●●●, 27.

Gough, C., Mann, C., Ficke, C., Namukasa, M., & Carroll, M., & OConnor, T. J. (2024, March). Remote Controlled Cyber: Toward Engaging and Educating a Diverse Cybersecurity Workforce. In *Proceedings of the 55th ACM Technical Symposium on Computer Science Education* V. 1 (pp. 394-400). DOI: 10.1145/3626252.3630917

Gowrishankkar, V., Shanmugam, V., Kapuria, M., Pavan, K. A., Vaishnavi, D., & Paneru, D. R. (2025). Agile HR Professionals in Industry 5.0: Navigating the Dynamic Evolution of Skills and Competencies. In *Expanding Operations Through Agile Principles and Sustainable Practices* (pp. 321-340). IGI Global Scientific Publishing.

Greenpeace. (2020). *GREENPEACE INTERNATIONAL.*

Grennan, J., & Michaely, R. (2020). Artificial intelligence and high-skilled work: Evidence from analysts. *Swiss Finance Institute Research Paper No. 20-84.* https://ssrn.com/abstract=3681574

Gunning, D., & Aha, D. W. (2019). DARPA's explainable artificial intelligence (XAI) program. *AI Magazine*, *40*(2), 44–58. DOI: 10.1609/aimag.v40i2.2850

Guo, Y. (2018). A conceptual artificial intelligence application framework in human resource management. In ICEB.

Gupta, A., & Lee, J. (2021). Leading hybrid teams: Best practices for inclusivity and engagement. *Journal of Business Leadership*, *29*(2), 144–156.

Gurulakshmi, S., & Gayathri, R. (2025). The Human-AI Partnership: Elevating Leadership With Emotional Intelligence. In *Emotionally Intelligent Methods for Meaningful Leadership* (pp. 255-284). IGI Global Scientific Publishing.

Gutiérrez-Crocco, F., Martin-Caballero, A., & Godoy, A. (2024). The impact of remote work on managerial compliance: Changes in the control regime over line managers. *Work, Employment and Society*, *38*(2), 527–548. DOI: 10.1177/09500170221142713

Haenlein, M., & Kaplan, A. (2019). A brief history of artificial intelligence: On the past, present, and future of artificial intelligence. *California Management Review*, *61*(4), 5–14. DOI: 10.1177/0008125619864925

Hakim, M. (2023). Work-life balance, take home pay and workplace environment: Which one has the most influence toward employee performance on gen z? [Jurnal Sosial Humaniora Dan Pendidikan]. *JSHP*, *8*(1), 86–102. DOI: 10.32487/jshp.v8i1.1810

Hamarat, H., Şahin, H., & Apuhan, A. (2024). The dark side of artificial intelligence: Threats to tourism workers. *Worldwide Hospitality and Tourism Themes*, *16*(2), 127–137. DOI: 10.1108/WHATT-03-2024-0061

Hamari, J., Koivisto, J., & Sarsa, H. (2016). Does gamification work? A literature review of empirical studies on gamification. *Proceedings of the 47th Hawaii International Conference on System Sciences (HICSS)*. DOI: 10.1109/HICSS.2014.377

Hamer, A. (2021). The future of flexible work: Adapting to employee needs in the post-pandemic world. *Journal of Workforce Strategies*, *9*(4), 210–225.

Hardt, M., Price, E., & Srebro, N. (2016). Equality of Opportunity in Supervised Learning. *Proceedings of the 30th International Conference on Neural Information Processing Systems*, 3315–3323.

Harris, J., & Williams, M. (2021). The evolution of outsourcing: Understanding the new dynamics. *Global Outsourcing Journal*, *25*(3), 12–25.

Hart, J., Noack, M., Plaimauer, C., & Bjørnåvold, J. (2021). Towards a structured and consistent terminology on transversal skills and competences. *Brüssel: Europäische Kommission und Cedefop. Towards a structured and consistent terminology on transversal skills and competences| Esco (europa. eu), 1*, 645-670.

Hart, S. L., & Dowell, G. (2011). A natural-resource-based view of the firm: Fifteen years after. *Journal of Management*, *37*(5), 1464–1479. DOI: 10.1177/0149206310390219

Harvard Business Review. (2022, October). Where AI can—and can't—help talent management. Retrieved from https://hbr.org/2022/10/where-ai-can-and-cant-help-talent-management

Harvard Business Review. (2023, December). Talent management in the age of AI. Retrieved from https://hbr.org/2023/12/talent-management-in-the-age-of-ai

Harvard Business Review. (2023, September). Reskilling in the age of AI. Retrieved from https://hbr.org/2023/09/reskilling-in-the-age-of-ai

Hastie, T., Tibshirani, R., & Friedman, J. (2009). *The elements of statistical learning: Data mining, inference, and prediction* (2nd ed.). Springer. DOI: 10.1007/978-0-387-84858-7

Hatano, G., & Inagaki, K. (1986). Two courses of expertise. *Child development and education in Japan, 17*, 262-272.

Haziazi, M. (2021). Development of framework for talent management in the global context. *Open Journal of Business and Management*, *09*(04), 1771–1781. DOI: 10.4236/ojbm.2021.94096

Heeks, R. (2017). Decent work and the digital gig economy: a developing country perspective on employment impacts and standards in online outsourcing, crowdwork, etc. Development Informatics Working Paper, (71).

Heeks, R. (2022). Digital inequality beyond the digital divide: Conceptualizing adverse digital incorporation in the global South. *Information Technology for Development*, *28*(4), 688–704. DOI: 10.1080/02681102.2022.2068492

Hemphill, T. A. (2016). Responsible innovation in industry: A cautionary note on corporate social responsibility. *Journal of Responsible Innovation*, *3*(1), 81–87. DOI: 10.1080/23299460.2016.1178896

Hengartner, S., Schleusener, M., & Schweiger, S. (2021). Bridging the trust gap: The role of user communication in AI-powered financial advice. *Journal of Financial Services Marketing*, *26*(3), 174–186. DOI: 10.1057/s41264-021-00093-9

Hernández, Y., Parente, F., Faghy, M., Roscoe, C., & Maratos, F. (2021). Influence of the covid-19 lockdown on remote workers' physical and psychosocial wellbeing and work productivity. https://doi.org/DOI: 10.31234/osf.io/dnuk3

Hersch, E., Cohen, K., Saklecha, A., Williams, K., Tan, Y., & Lattie, E. (2022). Remote-delivered services during covid-19: A mixed-methods survey of college counseling center clinicians. *Journal of American College Health*, *72*(2), 423–431. DOI: 10.1080/07448481.2022.2038178 PMID: 35259062

Hirschheim, R., & Dibbern, J. (2017). *Information systems outsourcing: Towards sustainable business value*. Springer.

Hobsbawm, J. (2022). *The nowhere office: Reinventing work and the workplace of the future*. Hachette UK.

Hofstede, G. (2020). *Culture's consequences: Comparing values, behaviors, institutions, and organizations across nations* (3rd ed.). Sage Publications.

Holuša, V., Vaněk, M., Beneš, F., Švub, J., & Staša, P. (2023). Virtual reality as a tool for sustainable training and education of employees in industrial enterprises. *Sustainability (Basel)*, *15*(1), 310. DOI: 10.3390/su151712886

Hornung, S., Rousseau, D., & Glaser, J. (2009). Why supervisors make idiosyncratic deals: Antecedents and outcomes of i-deals from a managerial perspective. *Journal of Managerial Psychology*, *24*(8), 738–764. DOI: 10.1108/02683940910996770

Ho, S. M., Ocasio-Velázquez, M., & Booth, C. (2017). Trust or consequences? Causal effects of perceived risk and subjective norms on cloud technology adoption. *Computers & Security*, *70*, 581–595. DOI: 10.1016/j.cose.2017.08.004

Hsu, Y., Bai, C., Yang, C., Huang, Y., Lin, T., & Lin, C. (2019). Long hours' effects on work-life balance and satisfaction. *BioMed Research International*, *2019*, 1–8. DOI: 10.1155/2019/5046934 PMID: 31341900

Huang, M. H., & Rust, R. T. (2018). Artificial intelligence in service. *Journal of Service Research*, *21*(2), 155–172. DOI: 10.1177/1094670517752459

Huang, M. J., Tsou, Y. L., & Lee, S. C. (2006). Integrating fuzzy data mining and fuzzy artificial neural networks for discovering implicit knowledge. *Knowledge-Based Systems*, *19*(6), 396–403. DOI: 10.1016/j.knosys.2006.04.003

Huang, M.-H., & Rust, R. T. (2021). Artificial Intelligence in Service. *Journal of Service Research, 24*(1), 3–22. DOI: 10.1177/1094670521990564

Hughes, L. (2017). Blockchain for business and the workplace: Opportunities for security and transparency. *Journal of Business & Technology, 3*(2), 42–58.

Hutson, M. (2018). How researchers are teaching AI to learn like a child. *Science, 10*, 35–42. DOI: 10.1126/science.aau2576

Huws, U. (2014). *Labor in the Global Digital Economy: The Cybertariat Comes of Age*. Monthly Review Press.

Huzooree, G. (2024). From Concept to Completion: Critical Success Factors in Agile Project Management for IT Projects. In *Practical Approaches to Agile Project Management* (pp. 9-31). IGI Global.

Huzooree, G., & Soupramanien, L. D. B. (2024). *Empowering Students for the 21st Century Through Digital Literacy*. IGI Global. DOI: 10.4018/979-8-3693-3856-8.ch005

Huzooree, G., Soupramanien, L. D. B., & Rughoobur-Seetah, S. (2024). *Fostering Critical Soft Skills of Graduates for Employability and Professional Growth*. IGI Global. DOI: 10.4018/979-8-3693-3856-8.ch003

Huzooree, G., & Yadav, M. (2025). Sustainable Project Management and Organizational Resilience. In *Enhancing Resilience in Business Continuity Management* (pp. 137–172). IGI Global Scientific Publishing. DOI: 10.4018/979-8-3693-8809-9.ch005

Hwang, J. (2024). The gig economy and its effects on the labor market. *International Journal of Science and Research Archive, 13*(1), 3394–3404. DOI: 10.30574/ijsra.2024.13.1.1231

Iheduru-Anderson, K., & Wahi, M. (2018). Experiences of nigerian internationally educated nurses transitioning to united states health care settings. *Journal of Transcultural Nursing, 29*(6), 603–610. DOI: 10.1177/1043659618766225 PMID: 29618275

Infosys. (2023). *ESG is an opportunity- Mapping with UN SDGs*. 1–65.

Iqbal, M., & Moein, A. (2024). Work from home arrangements may boost employee happiness. *International Journal of Research and Review, 11*(2), 431–445. DOI: 10.52403/ijrr.20240246

Iskandar, Y. (2023). Digital transformation model and the role of hr in indonesian msmes. *International Journal of Business Law and Education, 4*(2), 1427–1453. DOI: 10.56442/ijble.v4i2.334

Islam, T. and Zhou, E. (2024). Unpacking the reasons shaping employee acceptance and attitudes towards ai assistant services in the hotel industry: a behavioral reasoning perspective., 109-141. DOI: 10.47260/amae/1457

ISO. (2020). *ISO/IEC 24028:2020 Information technology — Artificial intelligence — Overview of trustworthiness in artificial intelligence*. Retrieved from https://www.iso.org/

Ivan, S. C., Győrödi, R. Ş., & Győrödi, C. A. (2024). Sentiment Analysis Using Amazon Web Services and Microsoft Azure. *Big Data and Cognitive Computing, 8*(12), 166. DOI: 10.3390/bdcc8120166

Jackman-Ryan, S., Bass, L., Jackson, M., Hoeflaken, K., & Picart, J. (2022). School leadership during covid-19: emotionally intelligent crisis management.. DOI: 10.36315/2022v2end101

Jain, A. K., Ross, A., & Nandakumar, K. (2023). *Introduction to Biometrics: Security and Privacy Considerations*. Springer.

Jaiswal, A., Arun, C. J., & Varma, A. (2023). Rebooting employees: Upskilling for artificial intelligence in multinational corporations. In *Artificial intelligence and international HRM* (pp. 114–143). Routledge.

Jaiswal, A., Arun, C. J., & Varma, A. (2023). Rebooting employees: Upskilling for artificial intelligence in multinational corporations. In *Artificial Intelligence and International HRM* (pp. 114–143). Routledge. DOI: 10.4324/9781003377085-5

Jaiswal, A., & Dyaram, L. (2019). Perceived diversity and employee well-being: Mediating role of inclusion. *Personnel Review*, *49*(5), 1121–1139. DOI: 10.1108/PR-12-2018-0511

James, O., Udeh, C., Daraojimba, C., Ogedengbe, D., Elufioye, O., & Samod, B. (2023). A review of the impact of digital transformation on hr practices and strategies in the nigerian renewable energy sector. j.trd.wrld.econ, 1(1), 36-46. DOI: 10.26480/jhcdc.01.2023.36.46

Jangid, A. (2020). AI and employee wellbeing: How artificial intelligence can monitor and improve mental health in the workplace. *International Journal of Advanced Research*, Retrieved from https://www.journalijar.com/article/50677/ai-and-employee-wellbeing-how-artificial-intelligence-can-monitor-and-improve-mental-health-in-the-workplace/

Jariwala, M. (2024). Integrating artificial intelligence to enhance sustainability in project management practices. *International Journal of Computer Applications*, *186*(20), 35–42. DOI: 10.5120/ijca2024923627

Javed, U., Rohilla, A., Adnan, G., & Taj, N. (2025). Exploring how AI can be used to Promote Collaboration in group Project reduce Conflict in Team Dynamics and Enhance Cooperative Learning Experiences. *Review of Applied Management and Social Sciences*, *8*(1), 129–141. DOI: 10.47067/ramss.v8i1.441

Jayakarthika, K., Aravind, J., Ilakkiya, N., Karthiga, G., Farha, A., & Varun, C. (2024). Unlocking the potential: Hrm integration of ai in the gig economy for enhanced erp performance. *Int Res J Adv Engg Hub*, *2*(06), 1683–1687. DOI: 10.47392/IRJAEH.2024.0232

Jayarao, G. B., Ray, S., & Panigrahi, P. K. (2024). Information security threats and organizational readiness in nWFH scenarios. *Computers & Security*, *140*, 103745. DOI: 10.1016/j.cose.2024.103745

Jerónimo, H., Henriques, P., & Carvalho, S. (2021). Being inclusive boosts impact of diversity practices on employee engagement. *Management Research the Journal of the Iberoamerican Academy of Management*, *20*(2), 129–147. DOI: 10.1108/MRJIAM-05-2021-1175

Jetha, A., Bakhtari, H., Rosella, L., Gignac, M., Biswas, A., Shahidi, F., Smith, B. T., Smith, M. J., Mustard, C., Khan, N., Arrandale, V. H., Loewen, P. J., Zuberi, D., Dennerlein, J. T., Bonaccio, S., Wu, N., Irvin, E., & Smith, P. (2023). Artificial intelligence and the work–health interface: A research agenda for a technologically transforming world of work. *American Journal of Industrial Medicine*, *66*(10), 815–830. DOI: 10.1002/ajim.23517 PMID: 37525007

Jetullahu, I. (2020). Corporate social responsibility—Introducing a new model for improving the financial performance of large enterprises: The case of Kosovo. Rochester Institute of Technology. Retrieved from https://repository.rit.edu/theses/10501/

Jia, Q., Guo, Y., Li, R., Li, Y., & Chen, Y. (2018). Association for Information Systems AIS Electronic Library (AISeL) A Conceptual Artificial Intelligence Application Framework in Human Resource Management Recommended Citation "A Conceptual Artificial Intelligence Application Framework in Human Resource Management." https://aisel.aisnet.org/iceb2018/91

Jiang, F., Jiang, Y., Zhi, H., Dong, Y., Li, H., Ma, S., & Wang, Y. (2017). Artificial intelligence in healthcare: Past, present and future. *Seminars in Cancer Biology*, *38*, 23–31. DOI: 10.1016/j.semcancer.2017.07.003 PMID: 29507784

Jiang, Y., Li, X., & Wang, H. (2022). High-frequency trading and AI: Implications for market stability. *Journal of Financial Markets*, *55*, 100678. DOI: 10.1016/j.finmar.2021.100678

Jiménez, A., & Zheng, Y. (2018). Tech hubs, innovation and development. *Information Technology for Development*, *24*(1), 95–118. DOI: 10.1080/02681102.2017.1335282

Jin, D., & Liu-Lastres, B. (2024). Critical reflection on the impact of the gig economy on the hospitality workforce. *International Journal of Contemporary Hospitality Management*, *37*(1), 18–35. DOI: 10.1108/IJCHM-08-2023-1297

Jindain, C., & Gilitwala, B. (2023). The factors impacting the intermediating variable of employee engagement toward employee performance in a hybrid working model. *Rajagiri Management Journal*, *18*(2), 167–179. DOI: 10.1108/RAMJ-08-2023-0237

Jobin, A., Ienca, M., & Vayena, E. (2019). The global landscape of AI ethics guidelines. *Nature Machine Intelligence*, *1*(9), 389–399. DOI: 10.1038/s42256-019-0088-2

Johan, Z., Yusoff, R., Daud, A., & Sulaiman, S. (2022). The aspects of job quality and work precarity of on-demand gig workers: A systematic literature review. *Journal of Advanced Research in Business and Management Studies*, *27*(1), 10–15. DOI: 10.37934/arbms.27.1.1015

Johnson. (2023). *Johnson Controls wins 2023 Microsoft Global Independent Software Vendor Partner of the Year*. https://www.prnewswire.com/news-releases/johnson-controls-wins-2023-microsoft-global-independent-software-vendor-partner-of-the-year-301864598.html

Johnson, M., & Patel, S. (2021). The impact of remote work on cybersecurity threats. *Information Security Review*, *15*(1), 67–81.

Johnson, R. E., & Gueutal, H. G. (2022). Talent management in the context of AI adoption. *SSRN*. DOI: 10.2139/ssrn.5145205

Johnson, T. (2020). BYOD and security risks: Analyzing remote work threats. *InfoSec Journal*, *12*(4), 89–102.

Jones, N. (2018). How to stop data centres from gobbling up the world's electricity. *Nature*, *561*(7722), 163–166. DOI: 10.1038/d41586-018-06610-y PMID: 30209383

Jordan, M. I., & Mitchell, T. M. (2015). Machine learning: Trends, perspectives, and prospects. *Science*, *349*(6245), 255–260. DOI: 10.1126/science.aaa8415 PMID: 26185243

Joshi, A., Jain, S., & Gupta, P. (2024). Challenges and impact of the gig economy. *Sustain. Econ.*, *2*(2), 96. DOI: 10.62617/se.v2i2.96

Joshi, H. (2024). Artificial intelligence in project management: A study of the role of ai-powered chatbots in project stakeholder engagement. [IJSEPM]. *Indian Journal of Software Engineering and Project Management*, *4*(1), 20–25. DOI: 10.54105/ijsepm.B9022.04010124

Journal, H. I. P. A. A. (2024, October 10). When AI technology and HIPAA collide. *HIPAA Journal*. Retrieved from https://www.hipaajournal.com/when-ai-technology-and-hipaa-collide/

Jurafsky, D., & Martin, J. H. (2021). *Speech and Language Processing* (3rd ed.). Pearson.

Kahneman, D. (2011). *Thinking, fast and slow*. Farrar, Straus and Giroux.

Kalev, A., Dobbin, F., & Kelly, E. (2006). Best practices or best guesses? Assessing the efficacy of corporate affirmative action and diversity policies. *American Sociological Review*, *71*(4), 589–617. DOI: 10.1177/000312240607100404

Kamaruddin, N. H. C., & Zolkipli, M. F. (2024). The Role of Multi-Factor Authentication in Mitigating Cyber Threats. *Borneo International Journal eISSN 2636-9826, 7*(4), 35-42.

Kamble, R. R., & Misal, A. N. (2025). Indian Labor Laws and IT Industry: HR Compliance Challenges. *IUP Law Review, 15*(1).

Kanabar, V. (2023). *The AI Revolution in Project Management: Elevating Productivity with Generative AI*. Sams Publishing.

Kaplan, A., & Haenlein, M. (2019). Siri, Siri, in my hand: Who's the fairest in the land? On the interpretations, illustrations, and implications of artificial intelligence. *Business Horizons*, *62*(1), 15–25. DOI: 10.1016/j.bushor.2018.08.004

Karayel, T., Aktaş, B., & Akbıyık, A. (2025). Human factors in remote work: Examining cyber hygiene practices. *Information and Computer Security*, *33*(1), 96–116. DOI: 10.1108/ICS-11-2023-0215

Karras, T., Laine, S., & Aila, T. (2019). A style-based generator architecture for generative adversarial networks. *Proceedings of the IEEE Conference on Computer Vision and Pattern Recognition*, 4401-4410. DOI: 10.1109/CVPR.2019.00453

Karthikeyan, C., & Singh, S. (2025). Skill development challenges in the era of artificial intelligence (AI). In *Integrating technology in problem-solving educational practices* (pp. 189–218). IGI Global.

Kartini, K., & Nahda, K. (2021). Behavioral biases on investment decision: A case study in Indonesia. *The Journal of Asian Finance, Economics and Business*, *8*(3), 1231–1240. DOI: 10.13106/jafeb.2021.vol8.no3.1231

Katirai, A. (2024). Ethical considerations in emotion recognition technologies: A review of the literature. *AI and Ethics*, *4*(4), 927–948. DOI: 10.1007/s43681-023-00307-3

Katsande, R., Farhana, N., & Devi, A. (2022). Hybrid models for remote work practices in the post pandemic era: Prospects and challenges. *International Journal of Academic Research in Business & Social Sciences, 12*(11). Advance online publication. DOI: 10.6007/IJARBSS/v12-i11/15582

Katsaros, K. (2024). Gen z employee adaptive performance: The role of inclusive leadership and workplace happiness. *Administrative Sciences, 14*(8), 163. DOI: 10.3390/admsci14080163

Katz, L. F., & Krueger, A. B. (2019). *The rise of the gig economy: Fact or fiction?* Brookings Institution.

Kaufman, C. (2022). *Security in the Cloud: Managing Data Protection in Modern IT Environments*. Pearson.

Kaur, A. (2024). Untitled. *International Journal of Applied Research, 10*(4). Advance online publication. DOI: 10.22271/allresearch.2024.v10.i4.a

Kelly Services. (2024). *The rise of AI and its impact on your workforce.* Retrieved from https://set.kellyservices.us/resource-center/the-rise-of-ai-and-its-impact-on-your-workforce

Kerschbaum, F. (2023). *Secure Cloud Computing: Strategies for Data Privacy and Protection*. CRC Press.

Kerzner, H. (2025). *Project management: a systems approach to planning, scheduling, and controlling*. John Wiley & Sons.

Khalil, M. (2020). Digital nomads: How the world is becoming their office. *Forbes*.

Khan, A., & Turowski, K. (2016). A Perspective on Industry 4.0: From Challenges to Opportunities in Production Systems. *IoTBD 2016 - Proceedings of the International Conference on Internet of Things and Big Data, 2*, 441–448. DOI: 10.5220/0005929704410448

Khan, A. A., Laghari, A. A., Alroobaea, R., Baqasah, A. M., Alsafyani, M., Bacarra, R., & Alsayaydeh, J. A. J. (2024). Secure remote sensing data with blockchain distributed ledger technology: A solution for smart cities. *IEEE Access : Practical Innovations, Open Solutions, 12*, 69383–69396. DOI: 10.1109/ACCESS.2024.3401591

Khatib, M., Matrooshi, O., Salami, M., & Khadim, A. (2024). Technology as a source of risk in remote work. *International Journal of Theory of Organization and Practice (Ijtop), 3*(2), 119–136. DOI: 10.54489/ijtop.v3i2.310

Kim, B., & Lee, J. (2024). The mental health implications of artificial intelligence adoption: The crucial role of self-efficacy. *Humanities & Social Sciences Communications, 11*(1), 1–15. https://www.nature.com/articles/s41599-024-04018-w. DOI: 10.1057/s41599-024-04018-w

Kim, J., & Jung, H. (2022). The effect of employee competency and organizational culture on employees' perceived stress for a better workplace. *International Journal of Environmental Research and Public Health, 19*(8), 4428. DOI: 10.3390/ijerph19084428 PMID: 35457296

Kim, J., & Kim, Y. (2024). Acceptance of artificial intelligence technology and optimism regarding its impact on the job market among high school students. *Journal of Higher Education Theory and Practice, 24*(10). Advance online publication. DOI: 10.33423/jhetp.v24i10.7373

Kim, K., & Ko, E. J. (2021). The influence of emotional intelligence on team cohesion and the mediating effects of self-efficacy and trust: Time-lagged approach. *Team Performance Management, 27*(7/8), 540–552. DOI: 10.1108/TPM-12-2020-0102

Kim, S., Wang, Y., & Boon, C. (2021). Sixty years of research on technology and human resource management: Looking back and looking forward. *Human Resource Management, 60*(1), 229–247. DOI: 10.1002/hrm.22049

Kindervag, J. (2021). *Zero Trust Security: Building a Resilient Cyber Defense Strategy*. Wiley.

King, K. G. (2016). Data Analytics in Human Resources: A Case Study and Critical Review. *Human Resource Development Review, 15*(4), 487–495. DOI: 10.1177/1534484316675818

Kirkman, B. L., Rosen, B., Tesluk, P. E., & Gibson, C. B. (2004). The impact of team empowerment on virtual team performance: The moderating role of face-to-face interaction. *Academy of Management Journal, 47*(2), 175–192. DOI: 10.2307/20159571

Kleinberg, J., Lakkaraju, H., Leskovec, J., Ludwig, J., & Ribas, V. (2018). Human Decisions and Machine Predictions. *Nature, 572*(7767), 653–657. DOI: 10.1038/s41586-019-1361-1 PMID: 29755141

Koch, A. J., D'Mello, S. D., & Sackett, P. R. (2015). A meta-analysis of gender stereotypes and bias in hiring. *The Journal of Applied Psychology, 100*(1), 128–161. DOI: 10.1037/a0036734 PMID: 24865576

Kongsen, J., Chantaradsuwan, D., Koad, P., Thu, M., & Jandaeng, C. (2024). A secure blockchain-enabled remote healthcare monitoring system for home isolation. *Journal of Sensor and Actuator Networks, 13*(1), 13. DOI: 10.3390/jsan13010013

Koon, S., Ciftci, T., & Jufri, Y. (2023). Impact of authentic leadership on employee well-being and work-life balance in suntory beverage & food limited, japan. *Journal of Human Resource &Leadership, 7*(6), 11–20. DOI: 10.53819/81018102t5276

Koshy, B. A., Muthulakshmi, R., Rameena, K. A., & Sinija, A. S. (2023). Sustainable reporting for a resilient, responsible and reliable future: case of infosys.

Koshy, P., Koshy, D., & McDaniel, P. (2023). *Blockchain and Identity Security: Innovations in Authentication*. Springer.

Kotabe, M., & Mol, M. J. (2009). Outsourcing and international business: A critique and future research directions. *Journal of International Business Studies, 40*(9), 1695–1712.

Koubova, V., & Buchko, A. A. (2013). Life-work balance: Emotional intelligence as a crucial component of achieving both personal life and work performance. *Management Research Review, 36*(7), 700–719. DOI: 10.1108/MRR-05-2012-0115

Kou, G., Xu, Y., Peng, Y., Shen, F., Chen, Y., Chang, K., & Kou, S. (2021). Bankruptcy prediction for SMEs using transactional data and AI. *Decision Support Systems, 140*, 113429. DOI: 10.1016/j.dss.2020.113429

Koutsioumpa, E. (2023). Contribution of emotional intelligence to efficient leadership. a narrative review. *Technium Social Sciences Journal, 48*, 204–216. DOI: 10.47577/tssj.v48i1.9529

KPMG. (2020). *Global outsourcing report: Emerging markets and the new wave of outsourcing*. KPMG International.

Kraus, S., Paluch, S., & Jäger, J. (2020). *Digital Transformation in the Small and Medium-sized Enterprise (SME) Sector: Opportunities, Challenges, and Trends*. Springer Nature.

Krishnan, C., Singh, S., & Baba, M. (2023). Effect of work from home and employee mental health through mediating role of workaholism and work-family balance. *The International Journal of Social Psychiatry*, *70*(1), 144–156. DOI: 10.1177/00207640231196741 PMID: 37712681

Kristanti, D., & Hariyanti, S. (2024). Employee competency development strategy in the digital transformation era: Approach from an hr development perspective. *Jurnal Manajemen Bisnis Akuntansi Dan Keuangan*, *3*(1), 13–20. DOI: 10.55927/jambak.v3i1.8765

Krizhevsky, A., Sutskever, I., & Hinton, G. E. (2012). Imagenet classification with deep convolutional neural networks. *Advances in Neural Information Processing Systems*, *25*, 1097–1105.

Kshetri, N. (2023). *Cybersecurity Management in the Remote Work Era: Compliance and Policy Considerations*. Springer.

Kuhn, P., & Maleki, A. (2017). *The Gig Economy: The Future of Work and How to Navigate It*. Oxford University Press.

Kulkov, I. (2021). The role of artificial intelligence in business transformation: A case of pharmaceutical companies. *Technology in Society*, *66*, 101629. Advance online publication. DOI: 10.1016/j.techsoc.2021.101629

Kumar, M., Jain, A., Mittal, A., Gera, R., Biswal, S. K., Yadav, M., Hung, T. H., & Priya Srivastava, A. (2024). Inclusion of Neural Networks in Higher Education: A Systematic Review and Bibliometric Analysis. 2024 4th International Conference on Innovative Practices in Technology and Management (ICIPTM), 1–6. DOI: 10.1109/ICIPTM59628.2024.10563852

Kumar, M., Yadav, R., Suresh, A. S., Singh, R., Yadav, M., Balodi, A., Vihari, N. S., & Srivastava, A. P. (2023). Mapping AI-Driven Marketing: Review of Field and Directions for Future Research. 2023 2nd International Conference on Futuristic Technologies (INCOFT), 1–5. DOI: 10.1109/INCOFT60753.2023.10425169

Kumar, P.. (2023). AI-driven outsourcing models: Challenges and opportunities. *Global Business Review*.

Kumar, R., Gupta, B. B., & Choudhury, T. (2021). *Phishing Detection and Prevention: A Machine Learning Approach*. CRC Press.

Kumar, S., & Palvia, P. (2022). AI in finance: Challenges and opportunities. *Journal of Financial Technology*, *6*(2), 123–140. DOI: 10.1016/j.jftech.2022.03.001

Kurose, J. F., & Ross, K. W. (2022). *Computer Networking: A Top-Down Approach* (8th ed.). Pearson.

Lacity, M. C., Khan, S. A., & Willcocks, L. P. (2009). A review of the IT outsourcing literature: Insights for practice. *The Journal of Strategic Information Systems*, *18*(3), 130–146. DOI: 10.1016/j.jsis.2009.06.002

Lacity, M. C., & Reynolds, P. (2017). Cloud outsourcing: Balancing risks and rewards. *MIS Quarterly Executive*, *16*(3), 153–167.

Lacity, M. C., & Willcocks, L. P. (2001). Global Information Technology Outsourcing. In *Search of Business Advantage*. Wiley.

Lacity, M. C., & Willcocks, L. P. (2014). Business process outsourcing and dynamic innovation. *MIS Quarterly Executive*, *13*(1), 21–33.

Lacity, M. C., & Willcocks, L. P. (2018). Robotic Process Automation: The Next Transformation in Outsourcing. *Journal of Information Technology Teaching and Learning*, *22*(1), 1–16. DOI: 10.1080/02683966.2018.1497302

Lacity, M. C., & Willcocks, L. P. (2018). Robotic process automation: The next transformation lever for shared services. *Journal of Information Technology*, *33*(3), 201–211.

Lacity, M. C., & Willcocks, L. P. (2020). *Robotic Process Automation and the Future of Work: The New Age of Automation in Business*. Palgrave Macmillan.

Laengle, S., Modak, N. M., Merigó, J. M., & Zurita, G. (2018). Twenty-five years of group decision and negotiation: A bibliometric overview. *Group Decision and Negotiation*, *27*(4), 505–542. DOI: 10.1007/s10726-018-9582-x

Lapidoth, A. (2017). *A foundation in digital communication*. Cambridge University Press. DOI: 10.1017/9781316822708

LeCun, Y., Bengio, Y., & Hinton, G. (2015). Deep learning. *Nature*, *521*(7553), 436–444. DOI: 10.1038/nature14539 PMID: 26017442

Lee, I., & Lee, K. (2015). The Internet of Things (IoT): Applications, investments, and challenges for enterprises. *Business Horizons*, *58*(4), 431–440. https://doi.org/https://doi.org/10.1016/j.bushor.2015.03.008. DOI: 10.1016/j.bushor.2015.03.008

Lee, P., Kim, J., & Patel, R. (2021). Cloud security in the age of remote work. *Journal of Information Security*, *25*(3), 112–130.

Legg, S., & Hutter, M. (2007). A Collection of Definitions of Intelligence. *Frontiers in Artificial Intelligence and Applications*, *157*, 17–24.

Le, H., Jiang, Z., Fujimoto, Y., & Nielsen, I. (2018). Inclusion and affective well-being: Roles of justice perceptions. *Personnel Review*, *47*(4), 805–820. DOI: 10.1108/PR-03-2017-0078

Lekkala, S., & Gurijala, P. (2024). Endpoint and Mobile Security Imperatives. In *Security and Privacy for Modern Networks: Strategies and Insights for Safeguarding Digital Infrastructures* (pp. 155–165). Apress. DOI: 10.1007/979-8-8688-0823-4_15

Lemon, K. N., & Verhoef, P. C. (2016). Understanding customer experience throughout the customer journey. *Journal of Marketing*, *80*(6), 69–96. DOI: 10.1509/jm.15.0420

Leonardi, P. M., Parker, S. H., & Shen, R. (2024). How remote work changes the world of work. *Annual Review of Organizational Psychology and Organizational Behavior, 11*(1), 193–219. DOI: 10.1146/annurev-orgpsych-091922-015852

Leroy, H., Buengeler, C., Veestraeten, M., Shemla, M., & Hoever, I. (2021). Fostering team creativity through team-focused inclusion: The role of leader harvesting the benefits of diversity and cultivating value-in-diversity beliefs. *Group & Organization Management, 47*(4), 798–839. DOI: 10.1177/10596011211009683

Lescano, G., Lara, C., Collazos, C. A., & Costaguta, R. (2020). A technique for conflict detection in collaborative learning environment by using text sentiment. In *Advances in Computational Intelligence: 19th Mexican International Conference on Artificial Intelligence, MICAI 2020, Mexico City, Mexico, October 12–17, 2020* [Springer International Publishing.]. *Proceedings, 19*(Part II), 39–50.

Li, C., Lin, C., & Chin, T. (2022). How does the paradoxical leadership of cross-border e-commerce (cbec) gig workers influence chinese company performance: The role of psychological well-being. *Sustainability (Basel), 14*(19), 12307. DOI: 10.3390/su141912307

Limanta, A., Prihanto, Y., & Situmorang, R. (2023). Analysis of the influence of work-life balance, work stress, and job satisfaction when working from home on the implementation of permanent telework culture in legal business. Journal of Business Management Review, 4(1), 001-016. DOI: 10.47153/jbmr41.5922023

Lin, P. (2016). Why ethics matters for autonomous cars. In Lin, L. A. P., Abney, K., & Bekey, G. A. (Eds.), *Robot ethics: The ethical and social implications of robotics* (pp. 69–85). MIT Press.

Lipton, Z. C. (2016). *The Mythos of Model Interpretability*. In *Proceedings of the 2016 ICML Workshop on Human Interpretability in Machine Learning* (pp. 96-100).

Lipton, Z. C. (2016). The mythos of model interpretability. *Proceedings of the 2016 ICML Workshop on Human Interpretability in Machine Learning*, 96-100.

Liswandi, L., & Muhammad, R. (2023). *The association between work-life balance and employee mental health: a systemic review*. Asia Pacific Journal of Health Management., DOI: 10.24083/apjhm.v18i3.2565

Liu, Y., Smith, J., & Taylor, R. (2023). Automation in online labor markets: A generative AI perspective. Journal of Labor Studies.

Liu, C., & Renzy, R. (2025). Good jobs or bad jobs? immigrant workers in the gig economy. *The International Migration Review*, 01979183241309585. Advance online publication. DOI: 10.1177/01979183241309585

Liu, J. (2024). The impact of the development of artificial intelligence on unemployment rates. *Advances in Economics Management and Political Sciences, 121*(1), 154–163. DOI: 10.54254/2754-1169/121/20242410

Liu, J., Zhu, Y., & Wang, H. (2023). Managing the negative impact of workforce diversity: The important roles of inclusive hrm and employee learning-oriented behaviors. *Frontiers in Psychology, 14*, 1117690. Advance online publication. DOI: 10.3389/fpsyg.2023.1117690 PMID: 36844330

Liu, L. (2018). Occupational therapy in the fourth industrial revolution. *Canadian Journal of Occupational Therapy, 85*(4), 272–283.

Liu, W., Xu, Y., & Ma, D. (2021). Work-related mental health under covid-19 restrictions: A mini literature review. *Frontiers in Public Health*, *9*, 788370. Advance online publication. DOI: 10.3389/fpubh.2021.788370 PMID: 34900925

Liu, Y., & Peng, J. (2023). The impact of "AI unemployment" on contemporary youth and its countermeasures. *Youth Exploration*, *241*(1), 43–51. https://doi.org/10.13583/j.cnki.issn1004-3780.2023.01.004

Li, Y., Ochmann, S., & Laumer, S. (2021). Applying explainable AI to an AI-based system for candidate management: Reducing bias and enhancing diversity in hiring decisions. *Electronic Markets*, *32*(3), 707–721. DOI: 10.1007/s12525-022-00600-9

Li, Y., Zhang, H., & Chen, X. (2021). AI-driven tools for financial market analysis. *Journal of Financial Innovation*, *7*(1), 45–60. DOI: 10.1016/j.jfi.2020.100521 PMID: 35024290

Lokesh, G. R., Harish, K. S., Sangu, V. S., Prabakar, S., Kumar, V. S., & Vallabhaneni, M. (2024). AI and the Future of Work: Preparing the Workforce for Technological Shifts and Skill Evolution. In *2024 International Conference on Knowledge Engineering and Communication Systems (ICKECS)* (Vol. 1, pp. 1-6). IEEE. DOI: 10.1109/ICKECS61492.2024.10616486

Luo, L., Zhang, L., Zheng, X., & Wu, G. (2022). A hybrid approach for investigating impacts of leadership dynamics on project performance. *Engineering, Construction, and Architectural Management*, *29*(5), 1965–1990. DOI: 10.1108/ECAM-02-2020-0094

Luo, S., Luo, H., Cai, Q., & He, L. (2021). Using VR and AR for immersive training and education: A systematic review. *Educational Technology Research and Development*, *69*(1), 1–22. DOI: 10.1007/s11423-020-09921-4 PMID: 33551626

Luo, X., Tong, S., Fang, Z., & Qu, Z. (2019). Frontiers: Machines vs. humans: The impact of artificial intelligence chatbot disclosure on customer purchases. *Marketing Science*, *38*(6), 937–947. DOI: 10.1287/mksc.2019.1192

Madhavan, A., Sobczyk, A. J., & Ang, A. (2021). The promise and challenges of AI-driven investing. *Financial Analysts Journal*, *77*(4), 14–28. DOI: 10.1080/0015198X.2021.1914650

Maj, J. (2023). Influence of inclusive work environment and perceived diversity on job satisfaction: Evidence from poland. *Central European Business Review*, *12*(4), 105–122. DOI: 10.18267/j.cebr.334

Major, D., Verive, J., & Joice, W. (2008). Telework as a dependent care solution: Examining current practice to improve telework management strategies. *The Psychologist Manager Journal*, *11*(1), 65–91. DOI: 10.1080/10887150801967134

Malhan, D. (2021). Probing Anterior of Entrepreneurial Intentions of Youngsters in India, an Analytical Approach. *Academy of Strategic Management Journal*, *20*, 1–10.

Malik, A., Budhwar, P., & Srikanth, N. R. (2020). Gig Economy, 4IR and Artificial Intelligence: Rethinking Strategic HRM. In Human and Technological Resource Management (HTRM): New Insights into Revolution 4.0 (pp. 75–88). Emerald Group Publishing Ltd. https://doi.org/DOI: 10.1108/978-1-83867-223-220201005

Malik, A., Budhwar, P., & Patel, C. (2022). May the bots be with you! Delivering HR cost-effectiveness and individualized employee experiences in an MNE. *International Journal of Human Resource Management*, *33*(10), 2170–2194. DOI: 10.1080/09585192.2021.1892834

Maltoni, D., Maio, D., Jain, A. K., & Prabhakar, S. (2022). *Handbook of Fingerprint Recognition* (3rd ed.). Springer. DOI: 10.1007/978-3-030-83624-5

Manning, S., Massini, S., & Lewin, A. Y. (2008). A dynamic perspective on next-generation offshoring: The global sourcing of science and engineering talent. *The Academy of Management Perspectives*, *22*(3), 35–54. DOI: 10.5465/amp.2008.34587994

Manohar, S., & Palanisamy, G. (2018). Corporate reputation, service innovation and cross-buying intention: A test on reciprocal relationship and mediation effect. *International Journal of Services. Economics and Management*, *9*(2), 158–176.

Mansfield, A., Wayman, J. L., & Nixon, M. (2022). *Voice Biometrics and Speech Authentication: Security in the Digital Era*. CRC Press.

Manyika, J. (2017). A future that works: AI, automation, employment, and productivity. *Jbs.Cam.Ac.Uk*. https://www.jbs.cam.ac.uk/wp-content/uploads/2020/08/170622-slides-manyika.pdf

Manyika, J., Lund, S., Chui, M., Bughin, J., Woetzel, J., Batra, P., & Sanghvi, S. (2017) Jobs Lost, Jobs Gained: What the Future of Work Will Mean for Jobs, Skills, and Wages, McKinsey Global Institute. Available online: https://www.mckinsey.com/featured-insights/future-ofwork/jobs-lost-jobs-gained-what-the-future-of-work-will-mean-for-jobs-skills-and-wages (accessed March, 2025).

Manyika, J., Susan, L., Michael, C., Bughin, J., Jonathan, W., Batra, P., Ko, R., & Sanghvi, S. (2017). Workforce Transitions in a Time of Automation - Executive Summary. *Mckinsey Globar Institute, December*, 28. https://www.mckinsey.com/~/media/McKinsey/Featured Insights/Future of Organizations/What the future of work will mean for jobs skills and wages/MGI-Jobs-Lost-Jobs-Gained-Executive-summary-December-6-2017.ashx

Manyika, James, Susan Lund, Michael Chui, Jacques Bughin, Jonathan Woetzel, Parul Batra, Ryan Ko, and Saurabh Sanghvi. (2017). Jobs lost, jobs gained: What the future of work will mean for jobs, skills, and wages.

Manyika, J., Chui, M., Miremadi, M., Bughin, J., George, K., Willmott, P., & Dewhurst, M. (2017). *A future that works: Automation, employment, and productivity*. McKinsey Global Institute.

Marheni, E., Santos, J., & Li, T. (2024). Integrating emotional intelligence and mental education in sports to improve personal resilience of adolescents. *Retos*, *51*, 649–656. DOI: 10.47197/retos.v51.101053

Mariam, A., & Berrada, A. (2024). Human-Centric Enterprise Security: Advancing Access Control through AI-Driven Administration. *Authorea Preprints*.

Mariani, M., Cappa, F., & Saviolo, S. (2020). How AI Impacts the Digital Transformation of SMEs: Implications for Outsourcing Services. *International Journal of Information Management*, *50*, 24–33. DOI: 10.1016/j.ijinfomgt.2019.04.003

Marketing Engineers, A. I. (2024). *The impact of AI on workforce dynamics: Opportunities and challenges.* Retrieved from https://aimarketingengineers.com/the-impact-of-ai-on-workforce-dynamics-opportunities-and-challenges

Markowitz, H. M. (1952). Portfolio selection. *The Journal of Finance*, *7*(1), 77–91. DOI: 10.2307/2975974

Marler, J. H., & Fisher, S. L. (2013). An evidence-based review of e-HRM and strategic human resource management. In Human Resource Management Review (Vol. 23, Issue 1, pp. 18–36). https://doi.org/ DOI: 10.1016/j.hrmr.2012.06.002

Marler, J. H., & Boudreau, J. W. (2017). An evidence-based review of HR Analytics. *International Journal of Human Resource Management*, *28*(1), 3–26. DOI: 10.1080/09585192.2016.1244699

Martinez, D., & Robinson, L. (2023). The future of work and cybersecurity resilience. *TechTrends*, *30*(4), 112–127.

Martins, M. R. (2023). Adapting change management strategies for the AI Era: Lessons from large-scale IT integrations. *World Journal of Advanced Research and Reviews*, *19*(3), 1604–1629. DOI: 10.30574/wjarr.2023.19.3.1556

Mathews, J. (2018). Schumpeter in the twenty-first century: Creative destruction and the global green shift. In *Schumpeter's Capitalism, Socialism and Democracy* (pp. 233-254). Routledge.

Mathuki, E., & Zhang, J. (2022). Cognitive diversity, creativity and team effectiveness: The mediations of inclusion and knowledge sharing. *VINE Journal of Information and Knowledge Management Systems*, *54*(6), 1379–1403. DOI: 10.1108/VJIKMS-06-2022-0190

Matsuo, M., & Kusumi, T. (2020). Organizational learning and creativity: The mediating role of innovative work behavior. *Journal of Business Research*, *62*(1), 73–79. DOI: 10.1016/j.jbusres.2020.03.001

Mayer, J. D., & Salovey, P. (1990). Emotional intelligence: Imagination, cognition, and personality. *American Journal of Educational Research.*

McKinsey & Company. (2017a). *Jobs lost, jobs gained: Workforce transitions in a time of automation.* https://www.mckinsey.com/~/media/BAB489A30B724BECB5DEDC41E9BB9FAC.ashx

McKinsey & Company. (2017b). *A future that works: Automation, employment and productivity.* https://www.mckinsey.com/~/media/mckinsey/featured%20insights/Digital%20Disruption/Harnessing%20automation%20for%20a%20future%20that%20works/MGI-A-future-that-works-Executive-summary.ashx

McKinsey & Company. (2020). The future of work after [*Remote work and beyond.* McKinsey & Company.]. *COVID*, •••, 19.

McKinsey & Company. (2023a, June 5). Generative AI and the future of HR [Podcast]. Retrieved from https://www.mckinsey.com/capabilities/people-and-organizational-performance/our-insights/generative-ai-and-the-future-of-hr

McKinsey & Company. (2023b). Four ways to start using generative AI in HR. Retrieved from https://www.mckinsey.com/capabilities/people-and-organizational-performance/our-insights/the-organization-blog/four-ways-to-start-using-generative-ai-in-hr

McKinsey & Company. (2025). *The critical role of strategic workforce planning in the age of AI.* Retrieved from https://www.mckinsey.com/capabilities/people-and-organizational-performance/our-insights/the-critical-role-of-strategic-workforce-planning-in-the-age-of-ai

McKinsey & Company. (2025, March). The critical role of strategic workforce planning in the age of AI. Retrieved from https://www.mckinsey.com/capabilities/people-and-organizational-performance/our-insights/the-critical-role-of-strategic-workforce-planning-in-the-age-of-ai

Mehari, A., Birbirsa, Z., & Dinber, G. (2024). The effect of workforce diversity on organizational performance with the mediation role of workplace ethics: Empirical evidence from food and beverage industry. *PLoS One*, *19*(7), e0297765. DOI: 10.1371/journal.pone.0297765 PMID: 39024256

Mehrabian, A. (2017). Communication without words. In *Communication theory* (pp. 193–200). Routledge. DOI: 10.4324/9781315080918-15

Mehrabi, N., Morstatter, F., Saxena, N., Lerman, K., & Galstyan, A. (2021). A survey on bias and fairness in machine learning. *ACM Computing Surveys*, *54*(6), 1–35. DOI: 10.1145/3457607

Mensah, K. (2024). Impact of cultural intelligence on expatriate performance in multinational corporations in ghana. *International Journal of Business Strategies*, *10*(1), 1–12. DOI: 10.47672/ijbs.1820

Meyer, E. (2014). *The Culture Map: Breaking Through the Invisible Boundaries of Global Business.* PublicAffairs.

Microsoft. (2024). Microsoft. *Sustainability Report*, *2024*, •••. https://www.microsoft.com/en-in/sustainability

Mignani, S., Huber, S., Tomás, H., Rodrigues, J., & Majoral, J. P. (2016). Why and how have drug discovery strategies in pharma changed? What are the new mindsets? In Drug Discovery Today (Vol. 21, Issue 2, pp. 239–249). Elsevier Ltd. https://doi.org/DOI: 10.1016/j.drudis.2015.09.007

Miller, S., & Davis, L. (2021). VPN security and remote work: Challenges and solutions. *Network Security Review*, *19*(1), 34–50.

Miller, T., & Adams, P. (2022). Secure Access Service Edge (SASE) and its role in cloud security. *Cloud Security Today*, *22*(2), 55–73.

Min, H. (2010). Artificial intelligence in supply chain management: Theory and applications. *International Journal of Logistics*, *13*(1), 13–39. DOI: 10.1080/13675560902736537

Mintz, L., & Stoller, J. (2014). A systematic review of physician leadership and emotional intelligence. *Journal of Graduate Medical Education*, *6*(1), 21–31. DOI: 10.4300/JGME-D-13-00012.1 PMID: 24701306

Mishra, S., & Shukla, A. (2021). Collaboration and productivity in hybrid work environments: The role of digital tools. *International Journal of Hybrid Work*, *13*(1), 56–69.

Mitchell, R., Boyle, B., Parker, V., Giles, M., Chiang, C., & Joyce, P. (2015). Managing inclusiveness and diversity in teams: How leader inclusiveness affects performance through status and team identity. *Human Resource Management*, *54*(2), 217–239. DOI: 10.1002/hrm.21658

Mitchell, T. M. (1997). *Machine Learning*. McGraw-Hill.

Mittelstadt, B. D., Allo, P., Taddeo, M., Wachter, S., & Floridi, L. (2016). The ethics of algorithms: Mapping the debate. *Big Data & Society*, *3*(2), 2053951716679679. Advance online publication. DOI: 10.1177/2053951716679679

Mizgajski, J., Szymczak, A., Morzy, M., Augustyniak, Ł., Szymański, P., & Zelasko, P. (2020). Return on investment in machine learning: Crossing the chasm between academia and business. *Foundations of Computing and Decision Sciences*, *45*(4), 281–304. DOI: 10.2478/fcds-2020-0015

Moher, D., Liberati, A., Tetzlaff, J., & Altman, D. G.PRISMA Group. (2009). Preferred reporting items for systematic reviews and meta-analyses: The PRISMA statement. *BMJ (Clinical Research Ed.)*, *339*(jul21 1), b2535. DOI: 10.1136/bmj.b2535 PMID: 19622551

Mondo. (2024, July 15). The impact of AI on human resources: Opportunities and challenges. *Mondo*. Retrieved from https://mondo.com/insights/impact-of-ai-on-human-resources-opportunities-and-challenges/

Mondolo, J. (2022). The composite link between technological change and employment: A survey of the literature. *Journal of Economic Surveys*, *36*(4), 1027–1068.

Moon, C., Lee, J., & Lim, S. (2010). A performance appraisal and promotion ranking system based on fuzzy logic: An implementation case in military organizations. *Applied Soft Computing*, *10*(2), 512–519. DOI: 10.1016/j.asoc.2009.08.035

Morandini, S., Fraboni, F., Angelis, M., Puzzo, G., Giusino, D., & Pietrantoni, L. (2023). The impact of artificial intelligence on workers' skills: upskilling and reskilling in organisations. Informing Science the International Journal of an Emerging Transdiscipline, 26, 039-068. DOI: 10.28945/5078

Morgan, J. (2019). Will we work in twenty-first century capitalism? A critique of the fourth industrial revolution literature. *Economy and Society*, *48*(3), 371–398. https://doi.org/10.1080/03085147.2019.1620027

Mossavar-Rahmani, F., & Zohuri, B. (2024). Artificial intelligence at work: Transforming industries and redefining the workforce landscape. *Journal of Economics & Management Research*, *1-4*, 1–4. Advance online publication. DOI: 10.47363/JESMR/2024(5)213

Mossberger, K., Tolbert, C. J., & McNeal, R. S. (2007). *Digital citizenship: The Internet, society, and participation*. MIt Press.

Mudambi, R., & Tallman, S. (2010). Make, buy, or ally? Theoretical perspectives on knowledge process outsourcing through alliances. *Journal of Management Studies*, *47*(8), 1434–1456. DOI: 10.1111/j.1467-6486.2010.00944.x

Müller, V. C., & Bostrom, N. (2016). *Future Progress in Artificial Intelligence: A Survey of Expert Opinion*. In *Fundamental Issues of Artificial Intelligence* (pp. 555-572). Springer. DOI: 10.1007/978-3-319-26485-1_33

Murphy, W. (2018). Distinguishing diversity from inclusion in the workplace: Legal necessity or common sense conclusion. *Journal of Business Diversity*, *18*(4), 45–67. https://www.na-businesspress.com/JBD/JBD18-4/Murphy_18_4.pdf

Murray, S. C., Verhoef, A., Adak, A., Sen, D., Salzman, R., Jaiswal, P., & Naithani, S. (2025). Detecting novel plant pathogen threats to food system security by integrating the Plant Reactome and remote sensing. *Current Opinion in Plant Biology*, *83*, 102684. DOI: 10.1016/j.pbi.2024.102684 PMID: 39754892

Mushtaque, T., Jadoon, I., Idrees, R., Imran, A., & Rehman, Z. (2021). Workforce diversity and employee performance: a case of commercial banks in pakistan. Humanities & Social Sciences Reviews, 9(3), 09-15. DOI: 10.18510/hssr.2021.932

Nabahani, P., & Riyanto, S. (2020). Job satisfaction and work motivation in enhancing generation z's organizational commitment. *Journal of Social Sciences*, *1*(5), 234–240. DOI: 10.46799/jss.v1i5.39

Nair, N., & Vohra, N. (2015). Diversity and inclusion at the workplace: A review of research and perspectives. Academia.edu. https://www.academia.edu/download/106669970/8631467072015-03-34.pdf

Nakamoto, S. (2022). *Blockchain Security and Cryptographic Principles*. CRC Press.

Nalwade, P. (2024). Adapting to tomorrow's workforce: Navigating the impacts of artificial intelligence on employment. *Interantional Journal of Scientific Research in Engineering and Management*, *08*(04), 1–5. DOI: 10.55041/IJSREM30664

Nareswari, N., Balqista, A. S., & Negoro, N. P. (2021). The impact of behavioral aspects on investment decision making. *Jurnal Manajemen Dan Keuangan*, *10*(1), 15–27. DOI: 10.33059/jmk.v10i1.3125

Nawaz, S., Salman, W., Shahid, U., Khokhar, M. L., Iqbal, M. Z., & Hamid, A. (2024). A Survey on Latest Trends and Technologies of Computer Systems Network. *Spectrum of engineering sciences, 2*(4), 85-114.

Nazareno, L., & Schiff, D. S. (2021). The impact of automation and artificial intelligence on worker well-being. *Technology in Society*, *67*, 101679. DOI: 10.1016/j.techsoc.2021.101679

Nedelkoska, L., & Quintini, G. (n.d.). *Automation, skills use and training* (OECD Social, Employment and Migration Working Papers No. 202). https://dx.doi.org/10.1787/2e2f4eea-en

Nelson, B. (2021). Cybersecurity regulations and remote work compliance. *Legal & Tech Review*, *22*(2), 67–83.

Newman, S. A., & Ford, R. C. (2021). Five steps to leading your team in the virtual COVID-19 workplace. *Organizational Dynamics*, *50*(1), 100802. DOI: 10.1016/j.orgdyn.2020.100802 PMID: 36536689

Ngai, E. W. T., Xiu, L., & Chau, D. C. K. (2009). Application of data mining techniques in customer relationship management: A literature review and classification. In Expert Systems with Applications (Vol. 36, Issue 2 PART 2, pp. 2592–2602). Elsevier Ltd. https://doi.org/DOI: 10.1016/j.eswa.2008.02.021

Ng, E., & Sears, G. (2018). Walking the talk on diversity: Ceo beliefs, moral values, and the implementation of workplace diversity practices. *Journal of Business Ethics*, *164*(3), 437–450. DOI: 10.1007/s10551-018-4051-7

Nguyen, C. T. (2021). Bridging cultures and careers: The role of cultural intelligence in multinational corporations. *Journal of Organizational Behavior*, *42*(3), 421–437. https://doi.org/10.xxxx/abcd1234

Niebuhr, F., Borle, P., Börner-Zobel, F., & Voelter-Mahlknecht, S. (2022). Healthy and happy working from home? effects of working from home on employee health and job satisfaction. *International Journal of Environmental Research and Public Health, 19*(3), 1122. DOI: 10.3390/ijerph19031122 PMID: 35162145

Niederman, F. (2021). Project management: Openings for disruption from AI and advanced analytics. *Information Technology & People, 34*(6), 1570–1599. DOI: 10.1108/ITP-09-2020-0639

Nilsson, L., & Norström, W. (2024). Understanding Psychological Safety in Hybrid Work Teams: Experiences of Barriers and Facilitators.

NIST. (2021). *Guidelines for Cryptographic Protection of Sensitive Data (NIST Special Publication 800-175B)*. National Institute of Standards and Technology.

NIST. (2021). *Zero Trust Architecture (NIST Special Publication 800-207)*. National Institute of Standards and Technology.

NIST. (2023). *Cybersecurity Guidelines for Remote Work Security*. National Institute of Standards and Technology.

Nwankwo, E., Ogedengbe, D., Oladapo, J., Soyombo, O., & Okoye, C. (2024). Cross-cultural leadership styles in multinational corporations: A comparative literature review. *International Journal of Science and Research Archive, 11*(1), 2041–2047. DOI: 10.30574/ijsra.2024.11.1.0273

Nyathani, R. (2023). Ai in performance management: Redefining performance appraisals in the digital age. *Design of Single Chip Microcomputer Control System for Stepping Motor, 1-5*, 1–5. Advance online publication. DOI: 10.47363/JAICC/2023(2)134

O'Neil. (2022). *Weapons of math destruction:... - Google Scholar*. https://scholar.google.com/scholar?hl=en&as_sdt=0%2C5&q=O'Neil%2C+C.+%282022%29.+Weapons+of+math+destruction%3A+How+big+data+increases+inequality+and+threatens+democracy.+Crown+Publishing.&btnG=#d=gs_cit&t=1740380005537&u=%2Fscholar%3Fq%3Dinfo%3AyLJaG_yYh

O'Neil, C. (2016). *Weapons of Math Destruction: How Big Data Increases Inequality and Threatens Democracy*. Crown Publishing Group.

O'Neil, C. (2016). *Weapons of math destruction: How big data increases inequality and threatens democracy*. Crown Publishing.

Odugbesan, J. A., Aghazadeh, S., Al Qaralleh, R. E., & Sogeke, O. S. (2023). Green talent management and employees' innovative work behavior: The roles of artificial intelligence and transformational leadership. *Journal of Knowledge Management, 27*(3), 696–716. DOI: 10.1108/JKM-08-2021-0601

OECD. (2019). *OECD Principles on Artificial Intelligence*. Available at: https://www.oecd.org/going-digital/ai/

OECD. (2019). *OECD Principles on Artificial Intelligence*. Organisation for Economic Co-operation and Development. Retrieved from https://www.oecd.org/going-digital/ai/principles/

OECD. (2019). *OECD Principles on Artificial Intelligence*. Retrieved from https://www.oecd.org/ai/

OECD. (2020). Organisation for Economic Co-Operation and Development—OECD. *The Europa Directory of International Organizations*, *2020*, 691–701. DOI: 10.4324/9781003138587-53

OECD. (2023). *AI and work | OECD*. https://www.oecd.org/en/topics/sub-issues/ai-and-work.html

Ogbu, A. D., Ozowe, W., & Ikevuje, A. H. (2024). Remote work in the oil and gas sector: An organizational culture perspective. *GSC Advanced Research and Reviews*, *20*(1), 188–207. DOI: 10.30574/gscarr.2024.20.1.0261

Ogungbemi, O. S., Ezeugwa, F. A., Olaniyi, O. O., Akinola, O. I., & Oladoyinbo, O. B. (2024). Overcoming remote workforce cyber threats: A comprehensive ransomware and bot net defense strategy utilizing VPN networks. *Available atSSRN* 4911878.

Ogunleye, T., Adeyemi, B., & Chukwu, K. (2020). The role of mentorship and sponsorship in African Gen Z career advancement. *Journal of Leadership & Organizational Studies*, *27*(2), 140–157. https://doi.org/10.xxxx/qrst6789

Ohunakin, F., Adeniji, A., Ogunnaike, O., Igbadume, F., & Akintayo, D. (2019). The effects of diversity management and inclusion on organisational outcomes: A case of multinational corporation. *Business: Theory and Practice*, *20*, 93–102. DOI: 10.3846/btp.2019.09

Okoye, M. I. (2020). Managing remote work: Organizational best practices and strategies. *Journal of Business Research*, *117*, 444–451. DOI: 10.1016/j.jbusres.2019.10.038

Oksa, R., Kaakinen, M., Savela, N., Hakanen, J., & Oksanen, A. (2021). Professional social media usage and work engagement among professionals in finland before and during the covid-19 pandemic: Four-wave follow-up study. *Journal of Medical Internet Research*, *23*(6), e29036. DOI: 10.2196/29036 PMID: 34048356

Okubo, Y. (1997). Bibliometric indicators and analysis of research systems: Methods and examples. OECD Science, Technology and Industry Working Papers. Paris: OECD Publishing.

Ononiwu, M. I., Onwuzulike, O. C., & Shitu, K. (2024). The role of digital business transformation in enhancing organizational agility. *World Journal of Advanced Research and Reviews*, *23*(3), 285–308. DOI: 10.30574/wjarr.2024.23.3.2670

Oshri, I., Kotlarsky, J., & Willcocks, L. (2015). *The handbook of global outsourcing and offshoring*. Palgrave Macmillan. DOI: 10.1057/9781137437440

Oswald, F. L., Behrend, T. S., Putka, D. J., & Sinar, E. (2020). Big data in industrial-organizational psychology and human resource management: Forward progress for organizational research and practice. *Annual Review of Organizational Psychology and Organizational Behavior*, *7*(1), 505–533.

Outsourcing Center. (2023). *What is the impact of AI in outsourcing?* Retrieved from https://www.outsourcing-center.com/what-is-the-impact-of-ai-in-outsourcing

Page, S. E. (2007). *The difference: How the power of diversity creates better groups, firms, schools, and societies*. Princeton University Press.

Pak, R., Rovira, E., & McLaughlin, A. (2024). Polite AI mitigates user susceptibility to AI hallucinations. *Ergonomics*, ●●●, 1–11. DOI: 10.1080/00140139.2024.2434604 PMID: 39610202

Palmeter, K. (2022). Cyberattacks: An underlying condition exacerbated by the COVID-19 pandemic. *J. Bus. Entrepreneurship & L.*, *15*, 241.

Paradis, T. (2024, June 16). The impact of artificial intelligence on employment: The role of virtual agglomeration. *Business Insider.* https://www.businessinsider.com/ai-supercharge-offshoring-making-foreign-workers-more-efficient-stronger-cheaper-2024-6

Paramita, D., Okwir, S., & Nuur, C. (2024). Artificial intelligence in talent acquisition: Exploring organisational and operational dimensions. *The International Journal of Organizational Analysis*, *32*(11), 108–131. DOI: 10.1108/IJOA-09-2023-3992

Parasa, S. K. (2023). Impact of AI in employee wellness and well-being programs. *SSRN.* Retrieved from https://papers.ssrn.com/sol3/papers.cfm?abstract_id=5102825

Parker, S. K., Van Den Broeck, A., & Holman, D. (2017). Work design influences: A synthesis of multilevel factors that affect the design of jobs. In Academy of Management Annals (Vol. 11, Issue 1, pp. 267–308). Routledge. https://doi.org/DOI: 10.5465/annals.2014.0054

Park, S., Do, B., Yourell, J., Hermer, J., & Huberty, J. (2024). Digital methods for the spiritual and mental health of generation z: Scoping review. *Interactive Journal of Medical Research*, *13*, e48929. DOI: 10.2196/48929 PMID: 38261532

Patel, J. (2022). *Johnson, R.S. and Patel, P. (2022) Comparison of Different Chest Tube Sizes in Cardiac Surgery A Randomized Controlled Trial. European Journal of Cardio-Thoracic Surgery, 61, 178-185. - References - Scientific Research Publishing*. https://www.scirp.org/reference/referencespapers?referenceid=3859638

Patil, R. N., Rawandale, S. A., Yadav, G. B., & Kadam, P. (2025). Leveraging Machine Learning and Neural Networks for Enhanced Communication in Leadership. In *Leadership Paradigms and the Impact of Technology* (pp. 247–284). IGI Global Scientific Publishing. DOI: 10.4018/979-8-3693-7175-6.ch011

Pei, J., Wang, H., Peng, Q., & Liu, S. (2024). Saving face: Leveraging artificial intelligence-based negative feedback to enhance employee job performance. *Human Resource Management*, *63*(5), 775–790. Advance online publication. DOI: 10.1002/hrm.22226

People Management. (2024). AI integration challenges in HR. *People Management.* Retrieved from https://www.peoplemanagement.co.uk/article/1882806/navigating-ais-impact-employee-wellbeing

Persson, O., Danell, R., & Schneider, J. W. (2009). How to use Bibexcel for various types of bibliometric analysis. Celebrating Scholarly Communication Studies: A Festschrift for Olle Persson at His 60th Birthday, 5, 9–24.

Petrova, M., Schubert, G., Taska, B., & Yildirim, P. (n.d.). *Automation, career values, and political preferences* (Working Paper No. 32655).

Philips. (2024). *Philips Sustainability Report 2024.* https://www.philips.com/a-w/about/environmental-social-governance.html

Pilkington, A., & Meredith, J. (2009). The evolution of the intellectual structure of operations management—1980–2006: A citation/co-citation analysis. *Journal of Operations Management, 27*(3), 185–202. DOI: 10.1016/j.jom.2008.08.001

Pilkington, M. (2023). *Blockchain Technologies for Secure Digital Identity Management.* Wiley.

Pimentel, D., & McBride, A. (2020). Virtual reality and augmented reality in training: Changing the future of employee development. *Journal of Workplace Learning, 32*(1), 35–49.

Plessis, M., Wakelin, Z., & Nel, P. (2015). The influence of emotional intelligence and trust on servant leadership. *SA Journal of Industrial Psychology, 41*(1). Advance online publication. DOI: 10.4102/sajip.v41i1.1133

Porter, M. E., & Kramer, M. R. (2011). Creating shared value. *SSRN, 89*(1–2). Advance online publication. DOI: 10.2139/ssrn.3683975

Posada, J. (2020). The future of work is here: Toward a comprehensive approach to artificial intelligence and labor. Retrieved from https://arxiv.org/abs/2007.05843

Prado, J., Torres, R., Tafur-Mendoza, A., Ospina, R., & Sarmiento, C. (2022). Impact of leadership practices on manager's pathways to goal attainment: The mediating effect of emotional intelligence. *The International Journal of Organizational Analysis, 31*(7), 2889–2902. DOI: 10.1108/IJOA-01-2022-3110

Prodduturi, S. M. K. (2024). Investigating the challenges and opportunities of cybersecurity in the era of remote work. *European Journal of Advances in Engineering and Technology, 11*(10), 80–84.

Project Management Institute. (2021). A Guide to the Project Management Body of Knowledge (PMBOK® Guide)–Seventh Edition and The Standard for Project Management. Project Management Institute.

Prümmer, J., van Steen, T., & van den Berg, B. (2024). A systematic review of current cybersecurity training methods. *Computers & Security, 136*, 103585. DOI: 10.1016/j.cose.2023.103585

Qin, C., Zhang, L., Cheng, Y., Zha, R., Shen, D., Zhang, Q., Chen, X., Sun, Y., Zhu, C., Zhu, H., & Xiong, H. (2023). A comprehensive survey of artificial intelligence techniques for talent analytics. arXiv preprint arXiv:2307.03195.

Quinn, J. B., & Hilmer, F. G. (1994). Strategic outsourcing. *Sloan Management Review, 35*(4), 43–55.

Radford, A., Wu, J., Child, R., Luan, D., Amodei, D., & Sutskever, I. (2019). Language models are unsupervised multitask learners. OpenAI Blog, 1(8).

Rahaman, M. A., Rozony, F. Z., Mazumder, M. S. A., Haque, M. N., & Rauf, M. A. (2024). Big data-driven decision making in project management: A comparative analysis. *Academic Journal on Science, Technology, Engineering &. The Mathematics Educator, 4*(03), 44–62.

Raisch, S., & Krakowski, S. (2021). Artificial intelligence and management: The automation–augmentation paradox. *Academy of Management Review, 46*(1), 192–210. DOI: 10.5465/amr.2018.0072

Raji, I. D., Smart, A., White, R. N., Mitchell, M., Gebru, T., Hutchinson, B., Smith-Loud, J., Theron, D., & Barnes, P. (2020). Closing the AI accountability gap: Defining an end-to-end framework for internal algorithmic auditing. *FAT* 2020 - Proceedings of the 2020 Conference on Fairness, Accountability, and Transparency*, 33–44. DOI: 10.1145/3351095.3372873

Raji, I. D., & Buolamwini, J. (2019). *Actionable Auditing: Investigating the Impact of Publicly Naming Biased Performance Results of Commercial AI Products*. In *Proceedings of the 2019 CHI Conference on Human Factors in Computing Systems* (pp. 1–15). ACM. DOI: 10.1145/3306618.3314244

Rakha, N. (2023). Ensuring cyber-security in remote workforce: Legal implications and international best practices. *Irshad J. Law and Policy*, *1*(3). Advance online publication. DOI: 10.59022/ijlp.43

Rane, N. L., Paramesha, M., Choudhary, S. P., & Rane, J. (2024). Artificial intelligence, machine learning, and deep learning for advanced business strategies: A review. *SSRN*, *2*(3), 147–171. DOI: 10.2139/ssrn.4835661

Rehman, M., Dhiman, B., Kumar, R., & Cheema, G. S. (2023). Exploring the impact of personality traits on investment decisions of immigrated global investors with focus on moderating risk appetite: A SEM approach. 8984(August), 95-110.

Ren, J. (2021). Research on financial investment decision based on artificial intelligence algorithm. *IEEE Sensors Journal*, *21*(22), 25190–25197. DOI: 10.1109/JSEN.2021.3104038

Reuter, D., Stewart, A., Goel, S., Jackson, S., & Syme, P. (2025, January 16). The list of major companies laying off staff in the new year. *Business Insider*. https://www.businessinsider.com/recent-company-layoffs-laying-off-workers-2025

Reynolds, J., & Kincaid, R. (2024). It depends: platform dependence, schedule control, and satisfaction among gig workers on amazon's mechanical turk platform. Sociological Forum. DOI: 10.1111/socf.13029

Reynolds, J., Quintero, D., Aguilar, J., & Kincaid, R. (2024). Work schedules, finances, and freedom: Work schedule fit and platform dependence among gig workers on amazon's mechanical turk platform. *Socius: Sociological Research for a Dynamic World*, *10*, 23780231241286933. Advance online publication. DOI: 10.1177/23780231241286933

Rhee, H. (2008). Home-based telecommuting and commuting behavior. *Journal of Urban Economics*, *63*(1), 198–216. DOI: 10.1016/j.jue.2007.01.007

Ribeiro, M. T., Singh, S., & Guestrin, C. (2016). *Why Should I Trust You? Explaining the Predictions of Any Classifier*. In *Proceedings of the 22nd ACM SIGKDD International Conference on Knowledge Discovery and Data Mining* (pp. 1135-1144). DOI: 10.18653/v1/N16-3020

Rijal, R. (2023). The impact of workforce diversity management on organizational performance: A study in nepalese hospitality sector. *Quest Journal of Management and Social Sciences*, *5*(2), 148–164. DOI: 10.3126/qjmss.v5i2.60843

Robinson, B. (2023, September 2). Workers using AI technology taking mental health into their own hands. *Forbes*. Retrieved from https://www.forbes.com/sites/bryanrobinson/2023/09/02/workers-taking-wellness-into-their-own-hands-using-ai-backed-mental-health/

Rocco, B., Moschovas, M. C., Saikali, S., Gaia, G., Patel, V., & Sighinolfi, M. C. (2024). Insights from telesurgery expert conference on recent clinical experience and current status of remote surgery. *Journal of Robotic Surgery*, *18*(1), 240. DOI: 10.1007/s11701-024-01984-w PMID: 38833111

Rodriguez, C., & Carter, H. (2022). Insider threats in remote work environments. *Cybersecurity Insights*, *30*(1), 55–78.

Rosencrance, L. (2023). *Implementing Least Privilege and Access Control in Zero Trust Networks*. TechTarget.

Rožman, M., & Tominc, P. (2024). Navigating gender nuances: Assessing the impact of ai on employee engagement in slovenian entrepreneurship. *Systems*, *12*(5), 145. DOI: 10.3390/systems12050145

Ruslaini, R., Kusnanto, E., Santoso, S., Qalbiah, F., & Marhandrie, D. (2024). Diversity management strategies: Perspectives from multinational corporation. *Journal of Economics Finance and Management Studies*, *07*(03). Advance online publication. DOI: 10.47191/jefms/v7-i3-18

Russell, S., & Norvig, P. (2021). *Artificial Intelligence: A Modern Approach* (4th ed.). Pearson.

Rzemieniak, M., & Wawer, M. (2021). Employer branding in the context of the company's sustainable development strategy from the perspective of gender diversity of Generation Z. *Sustainability (Basel)*, *13*(2), 828. https://www.mdpi.com/2071-1050/13/2/828. DOI: 10.3390/su13020828

Saad, H., & Mayouf, M. (2018). Talent management strategies and practices in five star hotels: An exploratory study. *International Journal of Heritage Tourism and Hospitality*, *12*(2), 32–49. DOI: 10.21608/ijhth.2019.31649

Saks, A. M., & Burke, L. A. (2012). An investigation into the relationship between training evaluation and the transfer of training. *International Journal of Training and Development*, *16*(2), 118–127. DOI: 10.1111/j.1468-2419.2011.00397.x

Salamin, X., & Hanappi, D. (2014). Women and international assignments. *Journal of Global Mobility*, *2*(3), 343–374. DOI: 10.1108/JGM-09-2013-0058

Salesforce. (2025). *Salesforce to Coders: Thanks, But AI's Got This*. Salesforce Research. Available online: https://www.bitswithbrains.com/news/salesforce-to-coders%3A-thanks%2C-but-ai%E2%80%99s-got-this (Access on 5 March 2025)

Santillan, E., Santillan, E., Doringo, J., Pigao, K., & Mesina, V. (2023). Assessing the impact of a hybrid work model on job execution, work-life balance, and employee satisfaction in a technology company. *Journal of Business and Management Studies*, *5*(6), 13–38. DOI: 10.32996/jbms.2023.5.6.2

Saranto, K., & Hovenga, E. J. (2004). Information literacy—what it is about?: Literature review of the concept and the context. *International Journal of Medical Informatics*, *73*(6), 503–513. DOI: 10.1016/j.ijmedinf.2004.03.002 PMID: 15171979

Sarker, I. H., Janicke, H., Mohsin, A., Gill, A., & Maglaras, L. (2024). Explainable AI for cybersecurity automation, intelligence and trustworthiness in digital twin: Methods, taxonomy, challenges and prospects. *ICT Express*, *10*(4), 935–958. DOI: 10.1016/j.icte.2024.05.007

Satoh, K., Mitani, Y., Ishikane, M., & Kamada, S. (2023). A cross-sectional survey on generation z physicians: professional value, educational expectations, and work environment preferences. DOI: 10.21203/rs.3.rs-3766309/v1

Savio, R. D., & Ali, J. M. (2023). Artificial intelligence in project management & its future. *Saudi Journal of Engineering and Technology*, *8*(10), 244–248. DOI: 10.36348/sjet.2023.v08i10.002

Sayeduzzaman, M., Hasan, T., Nasser, A. A., & Negi, A. (2024). An internet of things-integrated home automation with smart security system. *Automated secure computing for next-generation systems*, 243-273.

Schmidt, F. L., & Hunter, J. E. (1998). The validity and utility of selection methods in personnel psychology: Practical and theoretical implications of 85 years of research findings. *Psychological Bulletin*, *124*(2), 262–274. DOI: 10.1037/0033-2909.124.2.262

Schneier, B. (2021). *Applied Cryptography: Protocols, Algorithms, and Source Code in C* (20th Anniversary ed.). Wiley.

Schneier, B. (2023). *Identity and Access Security in Remote Work Environments*. Wiley.

Schneier, B. (2023). *Regulatory Responses to Cybersecurity Threats: Trends and Implications*. Wiley.

Schwab, K., & Davis, N. (2024). *Shaping the future... - Google Scholar*. https://scholar.google.com/scholar?hl=en&as_sdt=0%2C5&q=Schwab%2C+K.%2C+%26+Davis%2C+N.+%282024%29.+Shaping+the+future+of+the+fourth+industrial+revolution.+World+Economic+Forum.&btnG=#d=gs_cit&t=1740379953232&u=%2Fscholar%3Fq%3Dinfo%3AD3nDk29euZYJ%3Aschol

Schwartz, E. (2025). The Role of Human-Centric Solutions in Tackling Challenges and Unlocking Opportunities in Industry 4.0. In *Artificial Intelligence Solutions for Cyber-Physical Systems* (pp. 365–375). Auerbach Publications.

SDG. (2023). — *SDG Indicators*. https://unstats.un.org/sdgs/report/2023/

Selesi-Aina, O., Obot, N. E., Olisa, A. O., Gbadebo, M. O., Olateju, O., & Olaniyi, O. O. (2024). The future of work: A human-centric approach to AI, robotics, and cloud computing. *Journal of Engineering Research and Reports*, *26*(11), 10–9734. DOI: 10.9734/jerr/2024/v26i111315

Seuring, S., & Müller, M. (2008). From a literature review to a conceptual framework for sustainable supply chain management. *Journal of Cleaner Production*, *16*(15), 1699–1710. https://doi.org/https://doi.org/10.1016/j.jclepro.2008.04.020. DOI: 10.1016/j.jclepro.2008.04.020

Sexton, R. S., McMurtrey, S., Michalopoulos, J. O., & Smith, A. M. (2005). Employee turnover: A neural network solution. *Computers & Operations Research*, *32*(10), 2635–2651. DOI: 10.1016/j.cor.2004.06.022

Seyfi, S., Vo-Thanh, T., & Zaman, M. (2024). Hospitality in the age of gen z: A critical reflection on evolving customer and workforce expectations. *International Journal of Contemporary Hospitality Management*, *36*(13), 118–134. DOI: 10.1108/IJCHM-01-2024-0035

Shad, R., & Potter, K. (2024). AI-powered chatbots and virtual assistants in enhancing business efficiency. *Artificial Intelligence*.

Shakilla, U., & Saputro, E. P. (2025). Revolutionizing Management: The Role of AI and Technology in Modern Leadership Practices. *Solo International Collaboration and Publication of Social Sciences and Humanities, 3*(01), 53–68. DOI: 10.61455/sicopus.v3i01.235

Shanshan, Z., & Liu, Y. (2024). Job demands-resources on digital gig platforms and counterproductive work behavior. *Frontiers in Psychology, 15*, 1378247. Advance online publication. DOI: 10.3389/fpsyg.2024.1378247 PMID: 39355288

Sharma, M., Tomar, A., & Hazra, A. (2024). Edge computing for industry 5.0: Fundamental, applications and research challenges. *IEEE Internet of Things Journal, 11*(11), 19070–19093. DOI: 10.1109/JIOT.2024.3359297

Sheikh, R. A., Ahmed, I., Faqihi, A. Y. A., & Shehawy, Y. M. (2024). Global Perspectives on Navigating Industry 5.0 Knowledge: Achieving Resilience, Sustainability, and Human-Centric Innovation in Manufacturing. *Journal of the Knowledge Economy*, •••, 1–36. DOI: 10.1007/s13132-024-02498-4

Shen, Y., & Zhang, X. (2024). Article. *Humanities & Social Sciences Communications, 11*, 122. https://www.nature.com/articles/s41599-024-02647-9

Shimura, A., Yokoi, K., Ishibashi, Y., Akatsuka, Y., & Inoue, T. (2021). Remote work decreases psychological and physical stress responses, but full-remote work increases presenteeism. *Frontiers in Psychology, 12*, 730969. Advance online publication. DOI: 10.3389/fpsyg.2021.730969 PMID: 34659039

Shoushtari, F., Daghighi, A., & Ghafourian, E. (2024). Application of Artificial Intelligence in Project Management. *International journal of industrial engineering and operational research, 6*(2), 49-63.

Silver, D., Huang, A., Maddison, C. J., Guez, A., Sifre, L., van den Driessche, G., Schrittwieser, J., Antonoglou, I., Panneershelvam, V., Lanctot, M., Dieleman, S., Grewe, D., Nham, J., Kalchbrenner, N., Sutskever, I., Lillicrap, T., Leach, M., Kavukcuoglu, K., Graepel, T., & Hassabis, D. (2016). Mastering the Game of Go with Deep Neural Networks and Tree Search. *Nature, 529*(7587), 484–489. DOI: 10.1038/nature16961 PMID: 26819042

Silver, D., Hubert, T., & Schrittwieser, J.. (2016). Mastering Chess and Shogi by Self-Play with a General Reinforcement Learning Algorithm. *Nature, 550*(7676), 350–354. DOI: 10.1038/nature24270 PMID: 29052630

Singh, E. (2025). *How artificial intelligence is transforming workforce patterns in banking BPO.* Retrieved from https://www.linkedin.com/pulse/how-artificial-intelligence-transforming-workforce-patterns-singh-ezwsc

Singh, L. (2022). Cyber crime, cyber resilience and security strategy in post pandemic world. *Supremo Amicus, 28*, 305.

Slaski, M., & Cartwright, S. (2002). Health, performance and emotional intelligence: An exploratory study of retail managers. *Stress and Health, 18*(2), 63–68. DOI: 10.1002/smi.926

Smith, E. (2025, February 15). Elise Smith defends DEI as good business. *Time.* Retrieved from https://time.com/7210609/elise-smith-ceo-dei-good-business/

Smith, A., & Taylor, B. (2022). *The hybrid workforce: Integration of AI and human talent. Journal of Organizational Studies. International Labour Organization (ILO). (2023). The impact of AI on employment: Trends and policy responses*. ILO Reports.

Smith, J., & Brown, K. (2022). Phishing in the remote work era: Strategies for mitigation. *IT Security Journal*, *27*(2), 98–115.

Smith, J., Taylor, L., & White, H. (2022). Cyber threats in the era of remote work. *Cybercrime Journal*, *20*(3), 89–105.

Smith, R., Cubino, M., & McKeon, E. (2024). *The AI Revolution in Customer Service and Support: A Practical Guide to Impactful Deployment of AI to Best Serve Your Customers*. Pearson Education.

Snell, D., & Gekara, V. (2023). Re-examining technology's destruction of blue-collar work. *New Technology, Work and Employment*, *38*(3), 415–433. DOI: 10.1111/ntwe.12259

Society for Human Resource Management (SHRM). (2024, May 10). HR adopts AI. *SHRM*. Retrieved from https://www.shrm.org/topics-tools/news/all-things-work/ai-hr-challenges-opportunities

Society for Human Resource Management. (2024, September). AI shapes the future of workplace tech. Retrieved from https://www.shrm.org/topics-tools/news/hr-quarterly/ai-shapes-the-future-of-workplace-tech

Society for Human Resource Management. (2025a, March). The future of work is personal: How AI is reshaping employee experiences. Retrieved from https://www.shrm.org/enterprise-solutions/insights/future-of-work-is-personal-how-ai-is-reshaping-employee

Society for Human Resource Management. (2025b). Artificial intelligence in the workplace playbook. Retrieved from https://www.shrm.org/topics-tools/topics/artificial-intelligence-in-the-workplace

Sofianti, T., Kurniawan, I., Pratama, A., & Florencia, J. (2023). Measuring worker perception on remote working adoption during covid-19 pandemic: An industrial engineering perspective. *Engineering Science Letter*, *2*(01), 1–8. DOI: 10.56741/esl.v2i01.239

Sommer, R., & Paxson, V. (2023). *Artificial Intelligence in Cybersecurity: Trends and Future Applications*. CRC Press.

Soulami, S., Benchekroun, T., & Galiulina, F. (2024). Exploring how AI adoption in the workplace affects employees: A bibliometric and systematic review. *Frontiers in Psychology*, *15*, 11602465. https://www.ncbi.nlm.nih.gov/pmc/articles/PMC11602465/ PMID: 39610851

Sposito, L., Scafuto, I. C., Serra, F. R., & Ferreira, M. P. (2024). Influence of the project managers' expertise and experience in the success of projects: The moderating effect of emotional intelligence. *International Journal of Managing Projects in Business*, *17*(1), 1–26. DOI: 10.1108/IJMPB-06-2023-0129

Srinivasan, R., & Li, W. (2021). The evolving landscape of outsourcing and offshoring in the digital age. *Journal of International Business Studies*, *52*(1), 37–56. DOI: 10.1057/s41267-020-00369-6

Srivastava, A. P., Yadav, M., Yadav, R., Singh, B., & Dewasiri, N. J. (2023). Exploring digital agility and digital transformation leadership: A mixed method study. [JGIM]. *Journal of Global Information Management, 31*(8), 1–23. DOI: 10.4018/JGIM.332861

Srivastava, S. K. (2007). Green supply-chain management: A state-of-the-art literature review. *International Journal of Management Reviews, 9*(1), 53–80. DOI: 10.1111/j.1468-2370.2007.00202.x

Stallings, W. (2022). *Cryptography and Network Security: Principles and Practice* (9th ed.). Pearson.

Statman, M. (2019). *Behavioral finance: The second generation.* CFA Institute Research Foundation.

Stella, L. (2023). Artificial intelligence and workers' well-being. *IZA Discussion Paper No. 16485.* Retrieved from https://docs.iza.org/dp16485.pdf

Stone, D. L., Deadrick, D. L., Lukaszewski, K. M., & Johnson, R. (2015). The influence of technology on the future of human resource management. *Human Resource Management Review, 25*(2), 216–231. DOI: 10.1016/j.hrmr.2015.01.002

Strohmeier, S. (2007). Research in e-HRM: Review and implications. *Human Resource Management Review, 17*(1), 19–37. DOI: 10.1016/j.hrmr.2006.11.002

Strohmeier, S., & Piazza, F. (2013). Domain driven data mining in human resource management: A review of current research. *Expert Systems with Applications, 40*(7), 2410–2420. DOI: 10.1016/j.eswa.2012.10.059

Strohmeier, S., & Piazza, F. (2015). Artificial intelligence techniques in human resource management—A conceptual exploration. *Intelligent Systems Reference Library, 87*, 149–172. DOI: 10.1007/978-3-319-17906-3_7

Strubell, E., Ganesh, A., & McCallum, A. (2020). Energy and policy considerations for modern deep learning research. *AAAI 2020 - 34th AAAI Conference on Artificial Intelligence*, 1393–13696. DOI: 10.1609/aaai.v34i09.7123

Sucipto, H. (2024). The impact of artificial intelligence (ai) on human resource management practices. *PRODUCTIVITY, 1*(1), 138–145. DOI: 10.62207/xey9mx18

Sun, C. (2020). Research on investment decision-making model from the perspective of "Internet of Things+ Big data". *Future Generation Computer Systems, 107*, 286–292. DOI: 10.1016/j.future.2020.02.003

Sushma, M. (2025). Exploring Workplace Dynamics: A Systematic Review and Bibliometric Analysis of Work Stress, Gender Diversity, and Job Satisfaction in Higher Education Institutions. *Journal of Information Systems Engineering & Management, 10*(5(s)), 786–803. DOI: 10.52783/jisem.v10i5s.772

Susskind, R. (2020). *A world without work: Technology, automation, and how we should respond.* Metropolitan Books.

Susskind, R. (2020). *Tomorrow's Lawyers: An Introduction to Your Future*. Oxford University Press.

Susskind, R., & Susskind, D. (2015). *The Future of the Professions: How Technology Will Transform the Work of Human Experts*. Oxford University Press., DOI: 10.1093/oso/9780198713395.001.0001

Sutarto, A., Wardaningsih, S., & Putri, W. (2021). Work from home: Indonesian employees' mental well-being and productivity during the covid-19 pandemic. *International Journal of Workplace Health Management, 14*(4), 386–408. DOI: 10.1108/IJWHM-08-2020-0152

Sweeney, L. (2013). *Discrimination in Online Ad Delivery*. ACM Digital Library., DOI: 10.1145/2460276.2460278

Sweller, J. (2011). Cognitive load theory. [). Academic Press.]. *Psychology of Learning and Motivation, 55*, 37–76. DOI: 10.1016/B978-0-12-387691-1.00002-8

Syahreen, M., Hafizah, N., Maarop, N., & Maslinan, M. (2024). A Systematic Review on Multi-Factor Authentication Framework. *International Journal of Advanced Computer Science and Applications, 15*(5). Advance online publication. DOI: 10.14569/IJACSA.2024.01505105

Syed, W. K. (2024). How AI-driven Robo-Advisors impact investment decision-making and portfolio performance in the financial sector: A comprehensive analysis. *Journal of Financial Technology, 15*(3), 11–25.

Tabak, R., Strickland, J., Stein, R., Dart, H., Colditz, G., Kirk, B., Dale, A. M., & Evanoff, B. (2018). Development of a scalable weight loss intervention for low-income workers through adaptation of interactive obesity treatment approach (iota). *BMC Public Health, 18*(1), 1265. Advance online publication. DOI: 10.1186/s12889-018-6176-0 PMID: 30445939

Tabbassum, A., Chintale, P., Praveen, G., & Najana, M. (2024). The impact of ai on future employment patterns.. DOI: 10.21428/e90189c8.e99f270c

Taboada, I., Daneshpajouh, A., Toledo, N., & De Vass, T. (2023). Artificial intelligence enabled project management: A systematic literature review. *Applied Sciences (Basel, Switzerland), 13*(8), 5014. DOI: 10.3390/app13085014

Taddeo, M., & Floridi, L. (2018). How AI can be a force for good. *Science, 361*(6404), 751–752. DOI: 10.1126/science.aat5991 PMID: 30139858

Taheri Khosroshahi, F. (2024). The Future of Project Management: Embracing artificial intelligence for enhanced efficiency, data-driven decision-making, and collaborative teamwork.

Tang, H., Yin, M., & Nelson, D. (2010). The relationship between emotional intelligence and leadership practices. *Journal of Managerial Psychology, 25*(8), 899–926. DOI: 10.1108/02683941011089143

Tapscott, D., & Tapscott, A. (2016). *Blockchain revolution: How the technology behind bitcoin is changing money, business, and the world*. Penguin.

Tebra. (2024, August 15). Healthcare AI and HIPAA privacy concerns: Everything you need to know. *Tebra*. Retrieved from https://www.tebra.com/theintake/practice-operations/legal-and-compliance/privacy-concerns-with-ai-in-healthcare

Tertilt, M., & Scholz, J. K. (2023). Artificial intelligence in financial services: A review and agenda for future research. *Journal of Financial Innovation, 10*(1), 23–45. DOI: 10.1007/s12345-023-00432-1

The Guardian. (2024). Less admin, more time with people: How an HR professional's job has been transformed by AI. *The Guardian*. Retrieved from https://www.theguardian.com/work-redefined/2024/dec/20/less-admin-more-time-with-people-how-an-hr-professionals-job-has-been-transformed-by-ai

The Guardian. (2025). AI's long-term impact on employee welfare. *The Guardian*. Retrieved from https://www.theguardian.com/business/2025/jan/27/ai-automation-jobs-could-increase-inequality-uk-report

The New Workforce. (2023). *How AI will impact outsourcing*. Retrieved from https://thenewworkforce.com/how-ai-will-impact-outsourcing

Thompson, E. (2024). AI and machine learning in cybersecurity: The future of remote work protection. *AI Security Studies*, *35*(4), 120–138.

Today, C. U. (2024). New Pew Research survey shows Americans increasingly using ChatGPT. *CU Today*. https://www.cutoday.info/Fresh-Today/New-Pew-Research-Survey-Shows-Americans-Increasingly-Using-ChatGPT

Todorović, M. and Ivanović, T. (2018). Employee training in international luxury hotel chains: evidence from serbia., 667-685. DOI: 10.31410/tmt.2018.667

Toscano, F., & Zappalà, S. (2020). Social isolation and stress as predictors of productivity perception and remote work satisfaction during the covid-19 pandemic: The role of concern about the virus in a moderated double mediation. *Sustainability (Basel)*, *12*(23), 9804. DOI: 10.3390/su12239804

Toxigon. (2025). AI in HR: Enhancing employee engagement. *Toxigon Blog*. Retrieved from https://toxigon.com/ai-in-hr-enhancing-employee-engagement

Tranfield, D., Denyer, D., & Smart, P. (2003). Towards a Methodology for Developing Evidence-Informed Management Knowledge by Means of Systematic Review.

Triana, M., García, M., & Colella, A. (2010). Managing diversity: How organizational efforts to support diversity moderate the effects of perceived racial discrimination on affective commitment. *Personnel Psychology*, *63*(4), 817–843. DOI: 10.1111/j.1744-6570.2010.01189.x

Tsai, C. H., Wu, T., & Chen, X. (2020). AI-driven sentiment analysis for financial markets. *The Journal of Financial Data Science*, *2*(3), 45–60. DOI: 10.3905/jfds.2020.1.023

Turing, A. (1950). Machinery and intelligence. Mind: A Quarterly Review of Psychology and Philosophy, 59(236), 433-460.

Tzortzaki, A. M., & Mihiotis, A. (2014). A review of knowledge management theory and future directions. *Knowledge and Process Management*, *21*(1), 29–41. DOI: 10.1002/kpm.1429

U.S. Congress. (2019). *Algorithmic Accountability Act of 2019*.

Ullrich, L., Ogawa, J., & Jones-London, M. (2024). A retrospective analysis of career outcomes in neuroscience. Eneuro, 11(5), ENEURO.0054-24.2024. DOI: 10.1523/ENEURO.0054-24.2024

UNEP. (2019). *EBA Action Plan. December*.

UNESCO. (2021). *Recommendation on the Ethics of Artificial Intelligence*. United Nations Educational, Scientific and Cultural Organization.

Unilever. (2023). *Unilever Sustainable Living Plan 2023*. https://www.unilever.com/sustainability/

Uren, V., & Edwards, J. S. (2023). Technology readiness and the organizational journey towards AI adoption: An empirical study. *International Journal of Information Management*, *68*, 102588. DOI: 10.1016/j.ijinfomgt.2022.102588

Vaghela, H., & Jadeja, M. (2023). Analyzing Sentiments of Global Workforce Towards Hybrid Work Culture in the New Normal. In International Conference on Smart Systems: Innovations in Computing (pp. 293-305). Singapore: Springer Nature Singapore.

Vaid, A., & Sharma, C. (2022). Leveraging SAP and artificial intelligence for optimized enterprise resource planning: Enhancing efficiency, automation, and decision-making. *DOI*, *3*.DOI: <ALIGNMENT.qj></ALIGNMENT>10.30574/wjarr

Van Eck, N., & Waltman, L. (2010). Software survey: VOSviewer, a computer program for bibliometric mapping. *Scientometrics*, *84*(2), 523–538. DOI: 10.1007/s11192-009-0146-3 PMID: 20585380

Vandy, E. (2023). Future of work - opportunities, challenges and implications for international, comparative and cross-national hrm. *International Journal on Recent and Innovation Trends in Computing and Communication*, *11*(9), 4300–4306. DOI: 10.17762/ijritcc.v11i9.9887

Vardakis, G., Hatzivasilis, G., Koutsaki, E., & Papadakis, N. (2024). Review of Smart-Home Security Using the Internet of Things. *Electronics (Basel)*, *13*(16), 3343. DOI: 10.3390/electronics13163343

Varshney, D. (2020). Digital transformation and creation of an agile workforce: Exploring company initiatives and employcc attitudes. In *Contemporary global issues in human resource management* (pp. 89–105). Emerald Publishing Limited. DOI: 10.1108/978-1-80043-392-220201009

Vasudevan, S. (2021). Leveraging AI for personalized learning in workforce development. *Journal of Artificial Intelligence in Education*, *31*(2), 213–229. DOI: 10.1007/s40593-021-00221-y

Vaswani, A., Shazeer, N., Parmar, N., Uszkoreit, J., Jones, L., Gomez, A. A., Kaiser, Ł., & Polosukhin, I. (2017). *Attention is all you need.* In *Proceedings of the 31st International Conference on Neural Information Processing Systems (NIPS 2017)*, 6000-6010.

Verma, A. (2024). Artificial Intelligence in Talent Management: Maximizing Human Resource Potential. In Futuristic Trends in Management (IIP Series, Vol. 3, Book 28, Part 8, pp. 135–150). India: Khalsa College of Engineering and Technology.

Villalobos, J., Chan, L., Chen, C., & Donaldson, S. (2020). Exploring adaptability and proactivity across cultural contexts. *International Journal of Cross Cultural Management*, *20*(3), 345–360. DOI: 10.1177/1470595820971011

Villarreal, S., & Carino, R. (2019). *The Philippines BPO industry: Building a competitive advantage*. Philippine Economic Zone Authority Report.

Vinayakumar, R., Alazab, M., & Soman, K. P. (2023). *Deep Learning Approaches for Cybersecurity Threat Detection and Prevention*. Wiley.

Vladi, B., Xhindi, T., & Dida, E. (2024). The role of sector and organizational size on employee's preference about teleworking (empirical evidences from albanian organizations). qas, 25(199). https://doi.org/DOI: 10.47750/QAS/25.199.33

Voigt, P., & von dem Bussche, A. (2017). *The EU General Data Protection Regulation (GDPR): A Practical Guide*. Springer. DOI: 10.1007/978-3-319-57959-7

Von Solms, R., & Van Niekerk, J. (2021). *Information Security: Fundamentals and Best Practices*. Springer.

Vries, H., Tummers, L., & Bekkers, V. (2018). The benefits of teleworking in the public sector: Reality or rhetoric? *Review of Public Personnel Administration*, *39*(4), 570–593. DOI: 10.1177/0734371X18760124

Vrontis, D., Christofi, M., Pereira, V., Tarba, S., Makrides, A., & Trichina, E. (2023). Artificial intelligence, robotics, advanced technologies and human resource management: a systematic review. *Artificial intelligence and international HRM*, 172-201.

Vrontis, D., Christofi, M., Pereira, V., Tarba, S., Makrides, A., & Trichina, E. (2022). Artificial intelligence, robotics, advanced technologies and human resource management: A systematic review. *International Journal of Human Resource Management*, *33*(6), 1237–1266. DOI: 10.1080/09585192.2020.1871398

Wadhwa, S., & Aggarwal, P. (2023). Impact of diversity and inclusion on workplace effectiveness. *Journal of Management and Public Policy*, *14*(2), 64–78. http://jmpp.in/wp-content/uploads/2023/07/JMPP-Vol-14-No.-2-June-2023.pdf#page=64

Wang, J., Zhang, Y., & Xu, Z. (2020). *Robotics in logistics: Automation, integration, and efficiency*. Springer.

Werbart, A., Jonsson, M., Jankowski, B., & Forsström, D. (2024). New skills for distance regulation: Therapists' experiences of remote psychotherapy following the COVID-19 pandemic. *Journal of Psychotherapy Integration*, *34*(1), 27–44. DOI: 10.1037/int0000310

West, D. M., & Allen, J. R. (2018). *How artificial intelligence is transforming the future of work*. Brookings Institution. Available at: https://www.brookings.edu/research/

West, D. M. (2018). *The ethics of artificial intelligence*. Brookings Institution Press.

West, D. M. (2018). *The Future of Work: Robots, AI, and Automation*. Brookings Institution Press.

Westerman, G., Bonnet, D., & McAfee, A. (2014). *Leading digital: Turning technology into business transformation*. https://books.google.com/books?hl=en&lr=&id=Fh9eBAAAQBAJ&oi=fnd&pg=PR4&dq=•%09Westerman,+G.,+Bonnet,+D.,+%26+McAfee,+A.+(2014).+Leading+Digital:+Turning+Technology+into+Business+Transformation.+Harvard+Business+Review+Press.&ots=oaPhAX3nvf&sig=A6rbmrmZHSfY_CH-jwJge2eD_zU

Westerman, G. (2020). *Digital transformation: Survive and thrive in an era of mass extinction*. Harvard Business Review Press.

West, J., & Bhattacharya, M. (2016). Intelligent financial fraud detection: A comprehensive review. *Computers & Security*, *57*, 47–66. DOI: 10.1016/j.cose.2015.09.005

West, S. M., Whittaker, M., & Crawford, K. (2019). *Discriminating Systems: Gender, Race, and Power in AI*. AI Now Institute.

White, M. (2021). Gearing up for gen z: an analysis of employers' recruitment marketing targeting the new, generation z, workforce. DOI: 10.32920/ryerson.14657964.v1

Wiles, E., Krayer, L., Abbadi, M., Awasthi, U., Kennedy, R., Mishkin, P., Sack, D., & Candelon, F. (2024). GenAI as an exoskeleton: Experimental evidence on knowledge workers using GenAI on new skills. *SSRN*. https://ssrn.com/abstract=4944588

Wiley Online Library. (2024, August 22). The effects of artificial intelligence on organizational culture in the workplace. *Wiley Online Library*. Retrieved from https://onlinelibrary.wiley.com/doi/10.1002/sres.3037

Willcocks, L., Hindle, J., & Lacity, M. (2018). KEYS TO RPA SUCCESS Part 4: Change Management & Capability Development - People, Process, & Technology: How Blue Prism Clients Gain Superior Long-Term Business Value. *Blueprint*, 1–16. www.knowledgecapitalpartners.com

Willcocks, L. P. (2020). Future outsourcing trends: Automation, AI, and digital transformation. *Journal of Information Technology*, *35*(4), 276–289.

Willcocks, L. P., & Cullen, S. (2013). *The outsourcing enterprise: From cost management to collaborative innovation*. Palgrave Macmillan.

Willcocks, L. P., & Lacity, M. C. (2012). *The new IT outsourcing landscape: From innovation to cloud computing*. Palgrave Macmillan. DOI: 10.1057/9781137012296

Willcocks, L. P., Lacity, M. C., & Craig, A. (2015). The impact of robotic process automation on outsourcing. *The Journal of Strategic Information Systems*, *24*(3), 209–222.

Willcocks, L., Lacity, M., & Craig, A. (2017). Robotic process automation: Strategic transformation lever for global business services? *Journal of Information Technology Teaching Cases*, *7*(1), 17–28. DOI: 10.1057/s41266-016-0016-9

Williams, D. (2023). Zero Trust Architecture: A secure approach to remote work. *TechSec Research*, *29*(3), 88–105.

Williamson, O. E. (1981). The economics of organization: The transaction cost approach. *American Journal of Sociology*, *87*(3), 548–577. DOI: 10.1086/227496

Williamson, S., Colley, L., & Hanna-Osborne, S. (2020). Will working from home become the 'new normal' in the public sector? *Australian Journal of Public Administration*, *79*(4), 601–607. DOI: 10.1111/1467-8500.12444

Williamson, S., Pearce, A., Connor, J., Weeratunga, V., & Dickinson, H. (2022). The future of working from home in the public sector: What does the evidence tell us? *Australian Journal of Public Administration*, *81*(4), 640–648. DOI: 10.1111/1467-8500.12556

Williams, R. (2023). Multi-factor authentication and endpoint security in remote work environments. *Information Technology & Security*, *25*(2), 40–59.

Winarni, E., Mujannah, S., Halik, A., & Pardosi, P. (2024). Reskilling and upskilling: Hr adaptation strategies to digital transformation in the traditional sector. *Ekoma Jurnal Ekonomi Manajemen Akuntansi*, *4*(1), 2747–2756. DOI: 10.56799/ekoma.v4i1.6237

Wolfgruber, D., Stürmer, L., & Einwiller, S. (2021). Talking inclusion into being: Communication as a facilitator and obstructor of an inclusive work environment. *Personnel Review*, *51*(7), 1841–1860. DOI: 10.1108/PR-01-2021-0013

Womick, B. (2024). Motivating employee acceptance of AI in the workplace. *FIU Business*. Retrieved from https://business.fiu.edu/academics/graduate/doctor-of-business-administration/docs/2024/benjamin-womick-etd.pdf

Woods, D. (2023). *Data Protection Laws and Cybersecurity Governance*. Oxford University Press.

Workforcestrategist. (2024). AI in employee wellness programs: Revolutionizing workplace well-being. *Workforcestrategist Blog*. Retrieved from https://workforcestrategist.com/index.php/2024/12/20/ai-in-employee-wellness-programs-revolutionizing-workplace-well-being/

World Economic Forum. (2020). The future of jobs report 2020 | world economic forum. *The Future of Jobs Report, October*, 1163. https://www.weforum.org/reports/the-future-of-jobs-report-2020/digest

World Economic Forum. (2020). *The Future of Jobs Report 2020*. Available at: https://www.weforum.org/reports/

World Economic Forum. (2020). *The future of jobs report 2020*. World Economic Forum.

World Economic Forum. (2020). *The Future of Jobs Report 2020*. World Economic Forum.

World Economic Forum. (2023). Future of jobs report 2023: Preparing for the AI-driven economy. World Economic Forum Publications.

World Economic Forum. (2023, April 30). *The future of jobs report 2023*. https://www.weforum.org/publications/the-future-of-jobs-report-2023/

World Economic Forum. (2024). *Reports | World Economic Forum*. https://www.weforum.org/publications/series/future-of-jobs/

World Economic Forum. (2025, January). *Future of jobs report 2025*. https://reports.weforum.org/docs/WEF_Future_of_Jobs_Report_2025.pdf

World Economic Forum. (2025a, January). AI is shifting the workplace skillset. But human skills still count. Retrieved from https://www.weforum.org/stories/2025/01/ai-workplace-skills

World Economic Forum. (2025b, April). Why workers must upskill as AI accelerates workplace changes. Retrieved from https://www.weforum.org/stories/2025/04/linkedin-strategic-upskilling-ai-workplace-changes

Xu, W., Dainoff, M. J., Ge, L., & Gao, Z. (2023). Transitioning to human interaction with AI systems: New challenges and opportunities for HCI professionals to enable human-centered AI. *International Journal of Human-Computer Interaction, 39*(3), 494–518. DOI: 10.1080/10447318.2022.2041900

Yadav, M., Mittal, S., Kumar, M., Sahoo, A., Jayarathne, P. G. S. A., Yadav, M., Mittal, S., Kumar, M., Sahoo, A., & Jayarathne, P. G. S. A. (2024). From Textbooks to Teamwork: The Importance of Collaboration Skills in Workforce Preparation. In *Revitalizing Student Skills for Workforce Preparation* (pp. 333–352). IGI Global Scientific Publishing. DOI: 10.4018/979-8-3693-3856-8.ch011

Yadav, R., Naim, I., Kumar, M., Misra, S., Dewasiri, N. J., Rathnasiri, M. S. H., ... & Vihari, N. S. (2023, December). An exploratory study to identify effects of Blockchain technology on organizational change and practices. In 2023 IEEE Technology & Engineering Management Conference-Asia Pacific (TEMSCON-ASPAC) (pp. 1-8). IEEE.

Yadav, M., & Yadav, R. (2018). Impact of spirituality/religiousness on cyber bullying and victimization in university students: Mediating effect of emotional intelligence. *Journal of Religion and Health, 57*(5), 1961–1979. DOI: 10.1007/s10943-018-0637-8 PMID: 29790079

Yadav, R., Yadav, M., & Mittal, A. (2022). Effects of gain-loss-framed messages on virtual reality intervened fitness exercise. *Information Discovery and Delivery, 50*(4), 374–386. DOI: 10.1108/IDD-04-2021-0051

Yang, E., Kim, Y., & Hong, S. (2021). Does working from home work? experience of working from home and the value of hybrid workplace post-covid-19. *Journal of Corporate Real Estate, 25*(1), 50–76. DOI: 10.1108/JCRE-04-2021-0015

Yang, J., Suh, C., Lee, C., & Son, B. (2018). The work–life balance and psychosocial well-being of south korean workers. *Annals of Occupational and Environmental Medicine, 30*(1), 38. Advance online publication. DOI: 10.1186/s40557-018-0250-z PMID: 29928507

Yang, Y., Wang, T., & Leon, J. (2021). Study on the effect of work-life balance on the intention to leave of grassroots employees in the service industry. *Academic Journal of Business & Management, 3*(8). Advance online publication. DOI: 10.25236/AJBM.2021.030801

Ye, C. (2023). Generation zs willingness to accept international assignments after covid-19—A quantitative study among british, chinese and indian students. *Advances in Economics Management and Political Sciences, 53*(1), 229–241. DOI: 10.54254/2754-1169/53/20230841

Yue, Z. (2024). Leadership styles of school leaders and the mental health of teachers in a university in beijing, china. *Pacific International Journal, 6*(4), 98–102. DOI: 10.55014/pij.v6i4.483

Zahari, A. I., Manan, D. I. A., Razali, F. M., Zolkaflil, S., & Said, J. (2024). Exploring the viability of remote work for SME. *Journal of Open Innovation, 10*(1), 100182. DOI: 10.1016/j.joitmc.2023.100182

Zahera, S. A., & Bansal, R. (2018). Do investors exhibit behavioral biases in investment decision making? A systematic review. *Qualitative Research in Financial Markets, 10*(2), 210–251. DOI: 10.1108/QRFM-04-2017-0028

Zavrazhnyi, K. Y., & Kulyk, A. K. (2024). Modern business cybersecurity challenges and the role of artificial intelligence in countering threats.

Zemel, R. S., Wu, Y., Swersky, K., Pitassi, T., & Dwork, C. (2013). *Learning Fair Representations*. In *Proceedings of the 30th International Conference on Machine Learning* (Vol. 28).

Zeng, D., Lu, W., & Zhao, Y. (2018). Privacy-preserving machine learning: Threats and solutions. *The Journal of Privacy and Confidentiality*, *8*(2), 1–19. DOI: 10.29012/jpc.v8i2.686

Zengler, T., & Finnegan, J. (2020). Navigating privacy regulations in the age of data breaches. *Journal of Data Privacy and Security*, *10*(2), 35–50.

Zeng, M., Zhang, Y., & Jiang, Y. (2020). Trust in AI-based financial services: A model and empirical study. *Journal of Financial Technology*, *11*(3), 112–130. DOI: 10.1007/s42002-020-00037-1

Zhang, C., Sun, G., Li, J., Wu, Q., Wang, J., Niyato, D., & Liu, Y. (2024). Multi-Objective Aerial Collaborative Secure Communication Optimization Via Generative Diffusion Model-Enabled Deep Reinforcement Learning. *IEEE Transactions on Mobile Computing*.

Zhang, J., Rehman, S., Addas, A., & Ahmad, J. (2024). Influence of work-life balance on mental health among nurses: The mediating role of psychological capital and job satisfaction. *Psychology Research and Behavior Management*, *17*, 4249–4262. DOI: 10.2147/PRBM.S497305 PMID: 39679316

Zhang, X., Ming, X., Liu, Z., Yin, D., Chen, Z., & Chang, Y. (2019). A reference framework for industrial artificial intelligence (I-AI). *International Journal of Advanced Manufacturing Technology*, *101*(9–12), 2367–2389. DOI: 10.1007/s00170-018-3106-3

Zhang, Y., Jin, R., & Zhou, D. (2021). Transparency through natural language: AI-driven personalization in fintech. *Journal of Financial Technology*, *11*(3), 110–127. DOI: 10.1007/s42002-021-00047-9

Zhao, W. (2020). Proximity bias and its impact on hybrid work: Creating an equitable workplace. *Journal of Management*, *46*(8), 1051–1070.

Zhao, W., Chellappa, R., & Phillips, P. J. (2023). *Face Recognition: Advances in Biometric Security and AI Integration*. Wiley.

Zhou, J., Shang, J., & Chen, T. (2024). Cybersecurity landscape on remote state estimation: A comprehensive review. *IEEE/CAA Journal of Automatica Sinica, 11*(4), 851-865.

Zhou, L., Song, Y., Ji, W., & Wei, H. (2022). Machine learning for combustion. *Energy and AI*, *7*, 100128. DOI: 10.1016/j.egyai.2021.100128

Zohar, D., & Arad, A. (2018). Transparency in Algorithmic Decisions: A Roadmap for Implementation. *AI and Ethics*.

Zuboff, S. (2019). *The Age of Surveillance Capitalism: The Fight for a Human Future at the New Frontier of Power*. PublicAffairs.

Zyskind, G., & Nathan, O. (2023). *Decentralized Identity: A Blockchain Approach to Authentication and Privacy*. MIT Press.

About The Contributors

Mohit Yadav is an Professor in Human Resource Management at Jindal Global Business School (JGBS). Prof. Mohit holds a Ph.D. from Department of Management Studies, Indian Institute of Technology Roorkee (IIT Roorkee) and has completed Master of Human Resource and Organizational Development (MHROD) from prestigious Delhi School of Economics, University of Delhi. He also holds a B.Com (Hons.) degree from University of Delhi and UGC-JRF scholarship. He has published various research papers and book chapters with reputed publishers like Springer, Sage, Emerald, Elsevier, Inderscience etc. and presented research papers in national and International conferences both in India and abroad. He has many best paper awards on his credit too. He is reviewer of various international journals like Computers in Human Behavior, Policing etc. His areas of interest are Organizational Behavior, HRM, Recruitment and Selection, Organizational Citizenship Behavior, Quality of work life and role.

Ashutosh Pandey earned his doctorate in marketing from ABV-Indian Institute of Information Technology and Management, Gwalior. He holds a UGC-NET Management qualification and has worked in industry and academics for over ten years. He has taught postgraduate and executive students about business research methods, advanced marketing research, services marketing, marketing management, consumer behavior, and structural equation modeling. His research has appeared in many prestigious journals, including Environment, Development, and Sustainability, Journal of Quality Assurance in Hospitality & Tourism, and International Journal of Tourism Cities. He has worked as a visiting professor at IMT Ghaziabad, the Indian Institute of Foreign Trade (IIFT) in New Delhi, and the Indian Institute of Travel and Tourism Management in Gwalior. Dr. Pandey has been a resource person for several qualitative and quantitative research workshops hosted at respected organisations such as NIT Allahabad, NIFTEM Sonipat and an invited speaker at the AICTE-sponsored Faculty Development Program.

Geshwaree Huzooree (The Business School, Edinburgh Napier University, Craiglockhart Campus, Edinburgh) Dr. Geshwaree Huzooree is a Lecturer in Strategy and Project Management for the MBA Programme at the Edinburgh Napier University. Prior to joining Edinburgh Napier University, she was a Senior IT lecturer at Curtin Mauritius for eight years. She also reckons seven years' IT industry experience in software application development and project management. She holds a PhD in Computer Science (2020), an MSc Software Engineering Projects and Management (2014) and a BSc Computer Science and Engineering (2007) from the University of Mauritius. Dr. Geshwaree has a close collaboration with various universities and institutions world-wide. Her main research interests include project management, health Informatics, social informatics, and mobile technologies. She is committed to carry out innovative applied research that tackles national challenges for a better future. She received the Best Oral Presenter Award in the National Research Week in the Higher Education Sector in the field of Science, Technology and Engineering on her innovative work on the "Recent Advances on Sensor Technologies for Monitoring Diabetes Patients" in 2018.

***

Sophia Abena Aboagye is an accomplished professional with expertise in administrative support, human resource management, and customer service. With over three years of experience, she has successfully streamlined operations, improved client satisfaction, and coordinated corporate events to enhance employee engagement. Her ability to handle complex tasks efficiently, combined with her strong analytical and communication skills, has made her a valuable asset in various organizations. Currently pursuing an MBA in Strategic Human Resource Management and E-Commerce at Lovely Professional University, India, she is dedicated to expanding her knowledge in business administration, leadership, and digital transformation. Her career spans roles in banking, corporate administration, and executive assistance, where she has demonstrated exceptional strategic planning and project coordination skills. As a Front Desk & Administrative Assistant at Intercontinental Group Ghana Limited, she optimized operational efficiency by reducing check-in times and ensuring seamless travel logistics for executives. Previously, at Fidelity Bank Ghana Limited, she played a pivotal role in customer service, increasing client satisfaction and transparency in financial transactions. Her experience as an Executive Assistant at the Association of Finance Houses further refined her organizational and leadership abilities, allowing her to manage high-level communications and executive meetings effectively. Beyond her professional achievements, Sophia is deeply committed to mentorship and community empowerment. As a Community Champion at ALX Africa, she has guided over 60 learners, helping them meet program requirements and develop essential skills. Her passion for data analytics, strategic planning, and women's empowerment reflects her dedication to making a meaningful impact in her field. Fluent in both English and Twi, she thrives in diverse environments and continuously seeks opportunities for growth and innovation.

Sucheta Agarwal, an Associate Professor at GLA University, Mathura, India, holds a PhD in Entrepreneurship from IIT Roorkee, India. With expertise in education, entrepreneurship, and HRM, she's published extensively in esteemed ABDC and Scopus journals. Honored with accolades such as the 'Young Research Scholarship Award', at AIT Bangkok by GRDS, she actively contributes to national and international conferences. Recognized for her outstanding contributions, she received the 'Outstanding Reviewer Award' from Elsevier. Dr. Agarwal supervises doctoral and master's students, nurturing the next generation of scholars.

Anjali Anand is a dedicated HR professional with a strong educational background and practical experience in talent acquisition, onboarding, and employee engagement. Her expertise spans HR, marketing, and general management, underpinned by internships at Max View Now, Forever Living Product International, and Aashman Foundation. She has contributed to developing detailed market trend analysis reports, implemented proactive recruitment strategies, and streamlined candidate onboarding processes. Her technical skills include proficiency in MS Excel, PowerPoint, Word, Power BI, and Zoho, which she leverages to create HR dashboards and manage data effectively. Her analytical skills are evident in projects like researching labor law impacts on worker productivity and conducting market surveys on psychometric testing. She holds certifications in Union and Collective Bargaining and is pursuing a Master of Industrial Organizational Psychology. Her academic achievements include a Master of

Business Administration from Lovely Professional University, where she has demonstrated leadership and time management skills. Her proactive approach and commitment to enhancing HR practices make her a valuable asset in organizational development.

Richa Banerjee is an Associate Professor at the Narsee Monjee Institute of Management Studies (NMIMS), specializing in Human Resource Management and Organizational Behavior. She holds a Ph.D. and an MBA, and has over 16 years of teaching and research experience. Dr. Banerjee has authored several publications, including books and research papers, focusing on areas such as sustainable finance, employee well-being, and knowledge management. Her work has been recognized for its contribution to both academic and practical aspects of management.

Badr-un-Nisa (Nisa) Chand, CPHR & SHRM-SCP, is an Assistant Professor at University Canada West, with over 12 years of experience in university-level teaching across Asia, the United Kingdom, and Canada. Dr. Chand holds a Ph.D. in Human Resource Management from Cardiff University, UK. Her research interest includes intersection of technology and HRM, particularly in relation to organizational performance and sustainability. She is the editor of International Human Resources (2023), published by TopHat, with the second edition releasing in 2025. Her recent scholarly contributions explore the role of artificial intelligence (AI) in facilitating sustainable HR practices and optimizing business operations.

Narendra Singh Chaudhary has more than 15 years of experience in the field of management education. His research interests lie in the domain of HRM and OB, including topics like whistleblowing intentions, higher education, and research in higher education and allied areas. He has published many articles in journals of repute listed in Scopus and ABDC, ESCI, etc., like the International Journal of Law and Management, Journal of Applied Research in Higher Education, Human Resource Management International Digest, International Journal of Learning and Change, International Journal of Business and Globalisation to name a few. He has published cases in Case Centre, articles in leading HR Magazines regularly, and book chapters with leading publishers like Taylor and Francis and IGI Global. He has edited books and is currently a guest editor for many journals in Scopus and ABDC. He is a reviewer of many reputed journals like Current Issues in Tourism and Gender in Management: An International Journal, to name a few. He is a Member of the Editorial Review Board of Society and Business Review-Journal, published by Emerald. He is a certified Publons Academy Peer Reviewer.

Manju Dagar, an esteemed Assistant Professor in the Department of Management Studies, boasts an impressive academic and professional profile. She completed her Ph.D. on the topic of "Attrition of women employees in the IT Industry". She has 13 years of academic experience and has also served as the head of the department. Dr. Dagar is a valued member of the University Placement Cell and HR association. Her areas of specialization include Human Resource Management and Marketing Management, showcasing well-rounded expertise that spans crucial aspects of organizational dynamics. In terms of research, Dr. Manju Dagar has made significant contributions, and her work has been published in various prestigious platforms. Her research papers have found a place in UGC CARE-recognized journals, international publications, and the esteemed Scopus database, reflecting high quality and global relevance to her scholarly output. Additionally, she has made innovative contributions to patents further highlighting her multifaceted approach to academic and intellectual pursuits. She has also successfully completed various Faculty Development Programs (FDPs) and workshops. Most recently, she completed a diploma in Coaching & Mentoring from Skills and Education Group based in United Kingdom organized by CEAPS SGT University.

Narayanage Jayantha Dewasiri, Ph.D., is a Chartered Manager at the Chartered Management Institute, UK. He conducts research at the Open University of Sri Lanka and the Sri Lanka Institute of Marketing. He is the founding Editor-in-Chief of the South Asian Journal of Marketing. His research interests are in corporate social responsibility, corporate governance, marketing and sales, management, and finance. He is working as the Head of Field Force at the HMD Global Inc., Sri Lanka. He also serves as a senior lecturer at University of Sabaragamuwa, Sri Lanka. He can be reached at dnjay@ou.ac.lk

Shivani Dhand is an Associate Professor (14+ years of experience),a Certified SHRM (Society for Human Resource Management)faculty in the department of Mittal School of Business of Lovely Professional University.She is NLP(Neuro Linguistics Programming) Practioner She is also a member of the Indian Society for Training and Development (ISTD) and the Indian Society of Labour Economics. She is also a core committee member and Mentor of an NGO(Shalini Fellowship) Shivani Dhand has worked in an IT company as an HR. She has published 15 research papers in various journals which include Scopus-indexed, UGC care and peer-reviewed journals. She is a certified POSH trainer. She has worked with CPSC (Columbo Plan Staff College) Manila Philippines, and trained the faculty and Principals of various Institutions in Bhutan (2015). In 2016, She worked on one of the projects," Austria as an Innovation leader in EU in Austria and was awarded as best presentation and Excellent paper. Her research is situated in the field of Startups, HR Practices Human Resource Management, Entrepreneurship, and social entrepreneurship with a special focus on academic entrepreneurship.

Damith Gangodawilage is a practicing scholar and professional with extensive experience in finance and accounting, business management, entrepreneurship, and innovation. Currently serving as the Deputy Dean at the Qasim Ibrahim School of Business (QISB) at Villa College, Maldives, he has consistently demonstrated leadership in fostering academic excellence and industry engagement. Damith is also the Director of the Centre for Innovation and Entrepreneurship Development (CIED), where he spearheads initiatives such as the VIgnite Business Incubator, driving innovation among youth in the Maldives. With a strong academic foundation, Damith has made significant contributions to teaching, research, and curriculum development. His expertise spans strategic areas such as design thinking, sustainable business practices, and digital transformation. An active researcher, he has authored numerous studies and presentations on topics like corporate sustainability and tax compliance behavior, establishing himself as a thought leader. Dr. Damith is a dedicated mentor and educator, passionately committed to equipping students with critical thinking and problem-solving skills.

S. Ida Evangeline, presently working as an Assistant Professor in the Department of Electrical and Electronics Engineering at the Government College of Engineering, Tirunelveli, Tamilnadu, India. She obtained her Bachelor's in Electrical and Electronics Engineering from Manonmaniam Sundaranar University in 2003, and Master's in Power Systems Engineering from Anna University, Chennai, Tamilnadu, India in 2005. She completed her PhD degree in 2023 at Anna University, Chennai, Tamilnadu, India. She has published six research papers in international journals. Her current research interests include optimal power flow, renewable energy, soft computing, machine learning, and deep learning.

J. Sudarvel working as an Assistant Professor of Management at Karpagam Academy of Higher Education. He produced five Ph.D. Scholars and four Ph.D. Scholars are under his guidance. Further, to his credit he published more than five articles in Scopus indexed journals and published more than 50 articles in international journals. He is acting as a Subject Experts in Board of studies of various autonomous colleges.

K. Jothi working as an Associate Professor and Head, Department of Commerce with E Commerce at KPR College of Arts, Science and Research, Coimbatore. She produced more than 10 Ph.D. Scholars and published more than 10 articles in Scopus Indexed Journals and more than 50 articles in International journals. She is also acting as a subject expert in Board of Studies at various colleges.

lPreet Kanwal completed her Post-Doctoral Fellowship at the ESG, University of Quebec in Montreal, Quebec, Canada, furthering research expertise in her field. During her Post Doctoral Fellowship, she worked on exploring demographic sensitivity and its impact on discrimination in HEIs while considering insights from Canada and India. Dr. Kanwal is an academician and researcher with over 22 years of experience in Human Resource Management. She holds a PhD in Human Resource Management from I.K. Gujral Punjab Technical University, Punjab, India, where she conducted an empirical study on the quality of work life in the textile industry of Punjab, India. She also has international experience teaching MBA students from Victoria University (Online), Australia, and Sunway University (Online), Malaysia. Dr. Kanwal's research interests revolve around the quality of work-life, work-life balance, industrial relations, labour laws, social security and labour welfare, organizational stress, and behaviour, particularly in the context of the textile industry. She has presented her research at numerous national and international conferences and published her work in Scopus-indexed and UGC-listed Journals. Additionally, she has authored more than 25 book chapters and research papers on related topics, underscoring her commitment to advancing knowledge in her field. Her contributions extend beyond teaching and research; she has been actively involved in organizing and leading training sessions, workshops, and conferences, both as a participant and as a session chair. Currently, she is working on a funded project titled, "Empowering Women Artisans for Vision Viksit Bharat@2047: Financial Inclusion, Market Access, and Skill Development in Selected States of India". She has organised an ICSSR-sponsored International Conference, "Empowering Women Artisans for Vision Viksit Bharat@ 2047: Financial Inclusion, Market Access, and Skill Development" at Mittal School of Business, Lovely Professional University.

Rimpa Kar is an MBA student specializing in Human Resource Management and Marketing, exploring the dynamic intersection of people strategy and brand management. With a background in Hotel Management, she possesses strong expertise in operations, guest relations, and event management. Passionate about organizational development, employee well-being, and market-driven strategies, her objective is to contribute valuable insights that enhance workplace efficiency, employee engagement, and business growth through innovative HR and marketing initiatives.

Gagandeep Kaur is working as an Professor at Global School of Finance & Accounting in Chandigarh University. She has nearly more than 14 years of work experience which includes both teaching and industry (HR and Administration).She has done her Doctorate Degree from Thapar University, Patiala. She has done her Masters in Management from Gian Jyoti Institute of Management, Mohali (PTU,

Jalandhar). She has also completed her Post Graduate Diploma in Human Resource Management from IGNOU. She has mainly performed HR activities and administration in industry (BelWoInc, Chandigarh and Core Logistics Pvt. Ltd, Chandigarh). She has also done online certification courses. She is UGC-NET qualified. Dr. Gagandeep Kaur has published national and international publications in journals. She has published papers also in Scopus & ABDC indexed journals. She has also presented papers in national and international conferences.

Mohan Kumar has a total of seven years of professional experience, both in the corporate sector and as an academician. Specifically, he has worked in the Public Sector Bank and State Government University, focusing on Marketing and Entrepreneurship Development. He has completed his PhD on the topic of "Motivational Factors and Challenges of Start-Ups in NCR" at the Institute of Management Studies and Research, Maharshi Dayanand University, located in Rohtak-124001, Haryana. He specializes in Marketing Management, Human Resource Management, Quantitative Analysis, and Entrepreneurship Development. He has published his research in various esteemed national and international journals. He has actively engaged in both national and international conferences, where he has showcased his research findings. In March 2022, he received the Best Research Paper Award at an international conference conducted by IITM, GGSIU, Delhi. He was awarded for his research paper titled: Psychological wellbeing before and During the COVID-19 Pandemic: A longitudinal sample study of creative writers and directors. He has successfully participated in various other workshops as well.

Thi Minh Ngoc Luu is currently the Head of the Department of Economics and Management at the International School, Vietnam National University, Hanoi. She has over 17 years of experience in teaching and researching human resource management, management control, corporate governance, individual and organizational behavior, leadership, and sustainable development.

Ishwarya M. is a dynamic Human resource enthusiastic with expertise in talent acquisition, onboarding, and employee engagement. With a strong foundation in HR, marketing, and general management, Ishwarya has gained valuable experience through internships at The Leading Solutions and SVS Foods. She has successfully developed HR dashboards in Excel, conducted compensation impact studies, and designed employee training programs focused on engagement and relations. Her proficiency in tools like Microsoft Excel, Tableau, and Canva, combined with leadership and time management skills, allows her to drive strategic HR initiatives effectively. She has also earned certifications in Microsoft Excel, recruitment, and HR strategy. Ishwarya has been recognized for her academic excellence and leadership, including being shortlisted for MBA interviews at BITS Pilani and receiving CAP calls from IIM Jammu and IIM Kashipur. Her passion for HR and business innovation positions her as a valuable asset in workforce management and organizational development.

Pranav Malik currently pursuing an MBA at Lovely Professional University. A graduate of Economics (Hons.) from SCD Government College, Ludhiana, under Punjab University, he possess a strong academic foundation. Beyond academics, he is a passionate classical dancer, having achieved consecutive wins at Youth Festival Zonals. This dedication extends beyond the arts, as demonstrated by participation in the National Integration Camp under the National Service Scheme (NSS).He is a focused and dedicated individual with a strong drive to succeed and actively participate in all endeavors.

Namita Mangla, Faculty at IBS, Gurgaon, in the area of Organizational Behavior and HR Analytics. With 7 years of diverse experience in both academia and industry, she has significant knowledge in analytical tools and has made significant contributions through research papers, case studies and book chapters published ABDC journals. Her research focus lies in cross-cultural management, and HR Analytics.

Garima Mathur is a Professor specializing in Human Resource Management and Organizational Behavior at thePrestige Institute of Management & Research, Gwalior. She holds a Ph.D. in Management from Jiwaji University, an MBA from Prestige Institute of Management, and a Master's in Psychology. Dr. Mathur is UGC-NET qualified and serves as the Head of the HR Department and Coordinator of the MBA Program. With over 20 years of academic and research experience, she has authored more than 90 national and international publications, including research papers and case studies in Scopus, Web of Science and ABDC databases. Dr. Mathur is an approved Ph.D. guide at Jiwaji University, with twelve scholars having completed their doctoral degrees under her supervision. She is actively involved in professional organizations such as the Indian Society for Training & Development (ISTD), where she serves as Secretary of the Gwalior Chapter, and is a member of the American Psychological Association (APA), Academy of International Business (AIB), Indian Accounting Association (IAA), and Gwalior Management Association (GMA). Additionally, Dr. Mathur is the editor of the 'Prestige International Journal of Management & IT - Sanchayan' and serves on the editorial and review boards of several reputed journals.

Shashank Mittal has done his FPM in Organizational behavior and Human Resource from Indian Institute of Management Raipur. He holds B. Tech from I.E.T. Lucknow. His post FPM work experience includes almost five years of industry and academics exposures in multiple roles. Prior to joining FPM, he has over two years of industrial experience and three years of teaching experience in various organizations. He has published multiple papers in ABDC ranked and SSCI indexed journals of international repute such as Journal of Knowledge Management, Journal of Behavioral and Experimental Finance, International Journal of Conflict Management, Journal of Management and Organization and Current Psychology. His current research interest includes Social identity, Knowledge exchanges, Status, Proactive helping, Employer branding, Organizational justice, and Humanitarian relief management. He enjoys badminton and cycling during leisure time.

Neha Nain is an Assistant Professor in The Technological Institute of Textile and Sciences, Bhiwani. Currently pursuing her Ph.D. from Maharshi Dayanand University's Institute of Management Studies and Research in Rohtak, India. She has a graduate and postgraduate degree from the Maharshi Dayanand University's Department of Commerce. Since 2022, she has been actively engaged in research, focusing on key areas such as women entrepreneurship, organizational behavior, e-commerce, and human resource management.

Ali Najeeb is an established academician with a strong publication record in top-tier journals and has presented his research at numerous international conferences. He currently serves as an Associate Professor at the Qasim Ibrahim School of Business, Villa College, Maldives, where he teaches Human Resource Management and Strategy at the postgraduate level. Dr. Najeeb's research primarily focuses on human resource management in the hospitality industry, particularly within the context of the Maldives. Through his extensive academic work, he has made significant contributions to understanding HR practices in this unique sector.

Nhat Tan Nguyen is currently a full-time lecturer at Faculty of Business Administration, Ho Chi Minh City University of Foreign Languages - Information Technology, Vietnam. He has completed his PhD in Business and Management, Nottingham University Business School, University of Nottingham. He holds a Bachelor Degree in External Economics from Foreign Trade University, Vietnam, and got a Master of International Business from Latrobe University, Melbourne, Australia. His main research interest is in business management, specifically looking into the linkages between leadership behaviours, employee attitudes and organisational outcomes within the context of public and private enterprises. He can be contacted at: tannn@huflit.edu.vn. https://orcid.org/ 0000-0002-4178-5110

Aayushi Pandey, am a dedicated and resourceful research scholar currently pursuing my PhD in Management at the Mittal School of Business, Lovely Professional University, Punjab, India. My research focuses on understanding the critical role of soft skills in enhancing employability and organizational success, with a particular emphasis on the BFSI sector. My academic interests include Human Resource Management, Organizational Behavior, innovation culture, employee engagement, and the integration of emerging technologies like AI and blockchain in HR practices. I have had the privilege of publishing research articles in esteemed journals, including The TQM Journal (Emerald) and UGC Care journals, and authoring several book chapters and research papers like with publishers like Emerald, IGI Global, and Bentham Science. My research work has also been presented at prestigious conferences, such as IIM Jammu and LPU International Conferences, showcasing my expertise in soft skills, technology integration, and employability strategies.In addition to my academic endeavors, I have secured top positions in national competitions like the International Mathematics Olympiad and Entrepreneurship Programs at Khaitan Public School and HRIT Group of Institutions. I have also earned certifications in SPSS, MAXQDA, and EBSCO Business Courses, further enhancing my research and data analysis skills. My professional experience includes internships in HR and digital marketing, where I developed a strong foundation in organizational behavior and innovative problem-solving.Passionate about academic excellence, I actively participate in workshops and FDPs to expand my knowledge and contribute to the academic community. I aim to bridge the gap between theory and practice by offering practical insights and evidence-based solutions to organizational challenge.

Mansi Panwar is a doctoral scholar, author, and researcher in the field of commerce. She is affiliated with the School of Commerce at Devi Ahilya Vishwavidyalaya, India. With a strong academic background, she has been actively involved in research and writing, contributing to various publications and academic discussions. Mansi holds a degree in commerce and has a keen interest in behavioral finance, financial accounting, finance, and financial management. As a Ph.D. scholar, her research focuses on analyzing emerging trends in these areas, bridging the gap between theoretical knowledge and practical applications. She has participated in multiple research projects and has presented papers at national and international conferences. Her work explores how financial behaviors impact decision-making and how financial management principles can be optimized for better economic outcomes. Currently, she continues to expand her research, collaborating with professionals and institutions to explore innovative solutions in the world of commerce and finance.

Monalisha Patel is an Assistant Professor, Mittal School of Business, Lovely Professional University,Phagwara,Punjab,India. She has completed her Ph.D in Human Resource Management domain from Sri Sri University. She has completed her PGDHA from MedVarsity, USA . She has been certified with Medical Tourism certification from same. She has completed her MBA (HR & Marketing) from Biju Pattanaik University of Technology affiliation.She has been certified with PGDCA from DOEACC Board . An active member of exam invigilator and evaluator under Biju Pattanaik University of Technology . She has successfully completed HR project titled " Training Need Analysis of Apollo Hospitals", Bhubaneswar. Prof. Patel has penned a book " Clean Energy and Rural Development, in Notion press bearing ISBN No. 9798887720401 ; July 2022 . She has published research papers indexed in the reputed ABDC/SCOPUS ranked journals. To her 12 plus years of rich experiences in to academics she has also contributed many articles in journals, magazines, patents. Prof. Patel has participated in a number of national and international conferences, seminars and workshops and also presented papers to her credit. She been resource person to corporate and has participated in various Symposia and keen to join in professional affiliation(s). She has successfully completed her Digital Marketing certification course from IIM Kozhikode.

Ujjwal Kumar Pathak has more than sixteen years of experience in teaching post gradutaes and under graduates students of management . Area of interest is labour laws, HRM and OB .Currently working in Amity Business School, Amity University,Madhya Pradesh as Assistant Professor . Previously worked in Lovely Professional University Punjab from December 2010 till May 2022 . From Hune 2022 till now working in Amity Business School, Amity University,Madhya Pradesh . Has got papers published is scopus indexed journal and ABDC journal

Jasleen Purty is an MBA Graduate from Lovely Professional University specializing in Human Resources and Marketing. She's a former BBA in Tourism and Travel Management from IITTM, Bhubaneshwar. The objective of her research is to contribute valuable insights that enhance organizational efficiency and employee experience and aims to contribute to the development of innovative solutions that enhance employee well-being, retention, and organizational success.

Majdi Anwar Quttainah earned his Ph.D. degree in Management from Rensselaer Polytechnic Institute, Lally School of Management & Technology (USA); MBA degree with merits from the Business School & Entrepreneurship at Newcastle University (UK), and bachelor's degree in International Business from the American International University in London (UK). Dr. Quttainah is an associate professor of management in the College of Business Administration at Kuwait University. His research and teaching interests are corporate governance and strategies, entrepreneurship & small businesses, and organizational development. In addition, as a recognition of his research, he was awarded the Best Young Researcher academic year 2016/2017 Kuwait University. He is an active scholar, presently working as senior editor of FIIB Business Review (Scopus Q1, WoS, Published by the Sage Publishing). His research won several recognition and awards including the Best Paper Award at the 76th Annual Meeting of the Academy of Management Anaheim, CA, the Best Paper Award at the AGBA's 12th Annual World Congress, Kuantan City (State of Pahang), Malaysia, and the Best Paper Award of the Gorontalo International Conference of Project Management (ICPM) - Gorontalo/Indonesia. Also, at the home country level the best paper award for the Kuwait Economic Researcher Award by the Central Bank of Kuwait; May 2019 and 2022.

R. Velmurugan presently working as an Associate Professor in Commerce, Karpagam Academy of Higher Education, Coimbatore. He started his career as a Project Fellow under UGC Sponsored Major Research Project at NGM College, Pollachi. He has 18 years of teaching experience has 15 years of research experience. To his credit he produced 22 Ph.D. Scholars and 5 M.Phil. Scholars. At present 1 scholar submitter his thesis, 6 Ph.D. Scholars are under his guidance. Moreover, to his credit he published 163 articles in various International Journals, of which 56 articles are published in Scopus Indexed Journals and 15 articles in Web of Science and 76 articles in edited volumes. He also participates and presented 27 papers in various International Seminar / Conference and 54 National Seminar / Conference. He acted as an external examiner for various M.Phil. and Ph.D. Viva voce examinations. He acted as a Vice Chancellor nominee for Doctoral Committee Expert at Bharathiar University, Coimbatore and Periyar University, Salem. He acted as a Chairperson at various National Level Conferences. He also acted as an Expert for Syllabus Scrutiny Committee, Question Paper Scrutiny Committee and Expert members for Board of Studies at various reputed Colleges. Considering his meritorious contribution, he received awards like Best Paper Presenter, Best Research Supervisor and Best Faculty Awards from various research foundations and councils. He too acted as a resource person for 27 Guest Lectures, 30 Workshops and 10 faculty development programmes.

Sandeep Randhawa, Dedicated university educator with more than nineteen years of classroom experience, committed to excellence in teaching. Passionate about enhancing the learning process by tailoring methods to meet individual student needs. Possesses exceptional interpersonal and communication skills, demonstrating a strong work ethic, continuous self- improvement, and the implementation of innovative educational approaches .Best Paper Presentation Award at the International Conference on Global Trends in Management, Economics, Commerce & Legal Studies, Dubai, 2019 and Sant Baba Malkit Singh Ji Memorial Excellence Award -2020 SBBSU Ambassador Award at the International Conference on Futuristic Strategies of ICT for Digital and Sustainable Development, February 2020.

Pooja Rani is a dedicated researcher currently pursuing her PhD in IMSAR at MDU, Rohtak. Her research focuses on the "Effect of Financial Incentives on the Adoption of Solar Photovoltaic Water Pumping System in Agriculture sector in Haryana," aiming to contribute to sustainable energy solutions and rural development. With a strong academic foundation and a passion for renewable energy technologies, Pooja is committed to exploring innovative strategies to promote the adoption of clean energy systems, particularly in agricultural and rural contexts. Her academic journey has equipped her with a solid understanding of quantitative analysis, policy frameworks, and the socio-economic factors influencing renewable energy adoption. As an emerging scholar, Pooja is actively engaged in academic research and aims to publish her findings in esteemed national and international journals. She is also keen on participating in conferences and workshops to present her research and collaborate with experts in the field of renewable energy and sustainability. Her work seeks to bridge the gap between policy interventions and on-ground implementation, with a focus on enhancing the accessibility and affordability of solar energy technologies for rural communities. Pooja aspires to contribute to the global transition toward clean energy by addressing critical challenges in renewable energy adoption and advocating for effective financial and policy mechanisms. Through her research, she aims to provide actionable insights for policymakers, stakeholders, and practitioners working toward a sustainable future.

Mananage Shanika Hansini Rathnasiri is a Lecturer attached to the Department of Marketing Management, Faculty of Management Studies (FMS), Sabaragamuwa University of Sri Lanka (SUSL). She serves as an Associate Editor cum Editorial Assistant of the South Asian Journal of Marketing, published by Emerald Publishing. She is also serving as an Editor of the book namely "Shaping Entrepreneurial Marketing: A South Asian Perspective," by Emerald Publishing. Furthermore, she contributes as an Editor of the Sri Lankan Marketer Magazine, published by the Sri Lanka Institute of Marketing, and Editor-in-Chief of the 'FMS Today' published by the FMS, SUSL.

Neesha Rawat is a dedicated professional with a background in Biotechnology from Kumaun University and an MBA in Human Resources from Lovely Professional University. Hailing from Uttarakhand, she developed resilience, adaptability, and leadership skills through her involvement in the NCC. Her professional journey includes roles in HR, project management, and social impact. As a Project Manager at Udarchis Social Federation, she led social welfare initiatives, while at Sems Welfare Foundation and Rablo, she gained expertise in recruitment, onboarding, and team communication. Passionate about HR and leadership, she aims to blend technical expertise with people management to contribute to growth-driven organizations.

Akhil S.A is a driven business development professional with expertise in marketing, sales strategy, and market research. Currently a *Business Development Executive at Metvy, he specializes in client acquisition and skill development programs. His experience spans **HR management at Learnx, **marketing at Epitome TRC, and **audit & certification processes in the calibration industry*. With a keen interest in *Web3 and blockchain, Akhil is actively expanding his expertise in emerging technologies. His background in **GST appeals, financial auditing, and e-commerce consumer behavior research* further strengthens his business acumen. Passionate about innovation and growth, he aims to bridge the gap between *technology, market trends, and strategic development* in the digital era.

Alka Sanjeev is an esteemed Assistant Professor at FCAM-SGT University, Gurugram, India, where she has been serving since June 2022. She has 19 years of academic and industry experience. She is committed to enhancing her teaching skills and research capabilities, aiming to publish high-quality research articles. She holds an MBA in International Business from the University Business School, Panjab University (second rank), and a BE in Civil Engineering from Punjab Engineering College, Panjab University. Her Ph.D. in management has been awarded by Aligarh Muslim University. Her teaching interests include international business, international trade, operations research, operations management and logistics and supply chain management. Her research interests span technology spillover, foreign direct investment, sustainability and supply chain management. She has published numerous research papers and presented at various international and national conferences. Ms. Sanjeev actively participates in faculty development programs and workshops, staying current with the latest advancements in her field. Ms. Alka Sanjeev has held significant roles and responsibilities at FCAM-SGT University, Jamia Hamdard, and other institutions. At FCAM-SGT University, she serves as the IIC (Institute's Innovation Council) Faculty Coordinator, a member of the Event Reports Website and Social Media Committee, and the Journal & International Conference Committee.

Kiran Sharma Pursuing an MBA in Human Resources and Marketing, dedicated to enhancing business growth by integrating effective talent management with strategic marketing solutions.

Avtar Singh is an accomplished Associate Professor of Marketing at the Mittal School of Business, Lovely Professional University. With a Ph.D. in Sports Marketing and a Master of Business Administration, Dr. Singh brings a wealth of academic and industry experience to his role. Dr. Singh's research expertise lies in the commercialization of academic research and global R&D. His 13+ years in the marketing industry have equipped him with a deep understanding of practical marketing strategies and challenges. A certified digital marketing professional, Dr. Singh is proficient in leveraging digital tools and analytics to drive business growth. His areas of specialization include social media marketing, sports marketing, and web-based marketing. Dr. Singh's passion for teaching and research is evident in his ability to engage students and contribute to the field of marketing. His expertise and insights make him a valuable asset to the academic community.

Sandeep Kumar Singh is a faculty in the area of Information Systems and Analytics at Jindal Global Business School, O.P. Jindal Global University, Sonipat. Prior to joining Jindal Global Business School, he worked as an Assistant Professor at JKLU Jaipur for two years. He has earned his Ph.D. in computational physics from Antwerpen University, Belgium. His PhD work focused on mathematical modeling and simulation of two-dimensional materials. Post to his PhD, he worked as a research scientist in Sweden for four years in energy storage systems, bioelectronics. He also did MTech in industrial mathematics and scientific computing from IIT Madras, Chennai. His current research interests are to apply complex mathematical modeling in the business and financial world.

Ravi Thirumalaisamy working as an Assistant Professor, Department of Business and Economics, Modern College of Business and Science. To his credit, he published more than 10 articles in Scopus indexed journals.

Shenki Tyagi is working as an assistant professor of marketing at IMS Ghaziabad, University Courses Campus, India. Her area of expertise is online marketing.

Mani Tyagi is an educationist and researcher; who has completed her doctorate in Management. She is a double post-graduate in MBA and PGDMM from Narsee Monjee University. She is a White Belt holder of Six Sigma from MSI, USA. She has 10 years of experience in industry and teaching. She has 12 copyrights registered under the Government of India.

Index

A

B

C

D

E

F

G

H

I

J

K

L

M

O

P

R

S

T

U

V

W

Z

www.ingramcontent.com/pod-product-compliance
Lightning Source LLC
LaVergne TN
LVHW080404011026
849161LV00009B/2342
9798337312705